SALLY M. PROMEY is professor of
American studies and professor of
religion and visual culture at Yale
University, where she is also founding
director of the Initiative for the Study
of Material and Visual Cultures of
Religion (mavcor.yale.edu) and deputy
director of the Yale Institute of Sacred
Music.

Sensational Religion

Sensational Religion

Sensory Cultures in Material Practice

EDITED BY

SALLY M. PROMEY

Yale UNIVERSITY PRESS

New Haven and London

This book is made possible through support from
the Henry Luce Foundation
and the Yale Institute of Sacred Music.

Yale University Press books may be purchased in quantity for educational, business, or promotional use. For
information, please e-mail sales.press@yale.edu (U.S. office) or sales@yaleup.co.uk (U.K. office).

Designed and set in Garamond Premier Pro with Seravee and Whitney display by
Princeton Editorial Associates Inc., Scottsdale, Arizona.

Printed in China through World Print Ltd.

Library of Congress Cataloging-in-Publication Data

Sensational religion : sensory cultures in material practice / edited by Sally M. Promey.
pages   cm
Includes bibliographical references and index.
ISBN 978-0-300-18735-9 (cloth : alk. paper)
1. Religion and culture.   2. Senses and sensation—Religious aspects.
3. Materialism—Religious aspects.   I. Promey, Sally M., 1953– editor of compilation.
BL65.C8S46   2014
200—dc23
2013034490

A catalogue record for this book is available from the British Library.

This paper meets the requirements of ANSI/NISO Z39.48-1992
(Permanence of Paper).

10 9 8 7 6 5 4 3 2 1

To Roger, for making sense of everything

We are astonished at thought, but sensation is equally wonderful.
Voltaire (1764), as quoted by Indian Springs Resort and Spa
in a 2010 advertisement

———————————

Subjectivity is physical. . . . Perception links the carnal subject with the world
in which the body is immersed like a fish in water. The sensible world,
from such a perspective, is animate, alive, active, an intercourse
between my body and the things that surround it.
Christopher Tilley, *The Materiality of Stone* (2004)

———————————

We think with the objects we love; we love the objects we think with. . . .
In every case, the object brings together intellect and emotion.
Sherry Turkle, *Evocative Objects* (2007)

———————————

Perhaps it is wishful smelling.
Tom Robbins, *Jitterbug Perfume* (1984)

CONTENTS

ACKNOWLEDGMENTS

This volume has grown from robust collaboration. From start to finish, many have generously and substantively contributed. I am especially grateful to Kathryn Lofton for careful reading, good conversation, and expert advice throughout. My intellectual debt to her far exceeds the bounds of this work and the capacity of mere words of acknowledgment.

Sensational Religion gained immeasurably from the wisdom, good counsel, and productive labors of Richard Meyer and Mia Mochizuki. From 2008 to 2012, Mochizuki and Meyer served as co-directors with me for the first project cycle of the Initiative for the Study of Material and Visual Cultures of Religion (MAVCOR), which I direct in its larger ongoing constellation (mavcor.yale.edu). As project cycle co-directors, Mochizuki and Meyer were also extraordinary editorial associates. Both together and with other Initiative Fellows we thought through possible arrangements and key subjects for this book and deliberated about the ideal shape of the volume.

In 2012–2013, two additional editorial associates, Kati Curts and Christopher Kramaric, played critical roles. Curts provided invaluable critiques of my own writing for the volume as well as useful commentary on other individual chapters. Kramaric's refined organizational skills and remarkable ability to attend simultaneously to the scholarly big picture and the smallest details have kept the book on track. Beyond those of any other individual collaborator, Kramaric's professional labors have secured the volume's timely completion and contributed to its final design.

Conversation among fellows in the first MAVCOR project cycle provided intellectual traction for innovation and enriched our mutual labors. Each fellow deserves individual mention here: Betty Livingston Adams, Kalman Bland, Shira Brisman, Meredith Gill, Perin Gurel, Paul Christopher Johnson, Dana Katz, Gregory Levine, Kathryn Lofton, Ashley Makar, Vasileios Marinis, Richard Meyer, Minoo Moallem,

Mia Mochizuki, Emerson Morgan, Barbara Mundy, Margaret Olin, Kathryn Reklis, Erinn Staley, Yui Suzuki, and David Walker.

Graduate associates who came a bit later to the project, including Curts, Emily Floyd, Olivia Hillmer, Kramaric, and Michelle Morgan, also invested in this scholarly enterprise, as did many other participants in the Sensory Cultures of Religion Research Group at Yale University. Among those faculty and graduate student members not yet otherwise named here, Anna Arabindan-Kesson, Megan Bernstein, Magdalene Breidenthal, Meredith Gamer, Marko Geslani, Phyllis Granoff, Molly Greene, Zareena Grewal, Ronald Grimes, Alexandra Kaloyanides, Drew Konow, Benjamin Lindquist, Richard Mammana, Joseph Plaster, Lindsay Riordan, Elizabeth Rodrick, Tamara Sears, Koichi Shinohara, Sara Shneiderman, Peter Sukonek, and Elaine Yau helped to further sharpen ideas that motivated this work.

Students in my graduate seminars on material sensations challenged and enlivened these subjects with energy and curiosity. The book, furthermore, owes a great deal to exchange fostered by Sensational Religion: Sense and Contention in Material Practice, an international conference held at Yale University in November 2011. This gathering provided framework and forum for MAVCOR fellows and invited scholars (from academy and museum), artists, architects, and practitioners from multiple fields and traditions to present related research for conversation and critique.

I am deeply indebted to artists Byron Kim and Alex Donis for their art, their ideas, their words, and their collaborative generosity. Equally, I heartily thank those authors invited to join this conversation-already-in-progress, taking us to new places, further illuminating key themes, and introducing new material. Those not already acknowledged here include Horace D. Ballard Jr., Mary Campbell, James Clifton, Finbarr Barry Flood, June Hargrove, Angie Heo, Yuhang Li, Ara H. Merjian, Haroon Moghul, Laurel C. Schneider, Isaac Weiner, Judith Weisenfeld, and Mary Weismantel.

At Yale University Press, Jennifer Banks is, from my perspective, the perfect editor, from the outset fully committed to the project and invested in its content. Heather Gold and Mary Pasti have skillfully and generously labored with her in realizing this volume. Insightful comments from the anonymous readers of the manuscript framed the book's revisions, strengthening every part. I also wish to acknowledge the staff of Princeton Editorial Associates for their fine work in producing the material object you hold in your hands.

Sensational Religion and MAVCOR, in relation to which it takes shape, would be impossible without the vision and support of the Henry Luce Foundation, the Yale Institute of Sacred Music (ISM), and Yale University. At the Luce Foundation, Lynn Szwaja and Michael Gilligan enthusiastically engaged, productively critiqued, gracefully nurtured, and generously funded the project. At Yale University, ISM director Martin Jean joined Szwaja and Gilligan in all these regards, offering collegial guidance and substance at every step. The administrative leadership and scholarly contributions of the university's deputy provost for the arts and humanities, Emily Bakemeier, have made this work and anticipation of the project's future iterations a pleasure through and through. Also at Yale, Jon Butler (former dean of the graduate school), Charles H. Long (former deputy provost), and Hans van Dyk (then associate director, Corporate and Foundation Relations) merit warmest thanks for their unflagging encouragement in MAVCOR's early conceptualization and planning stages.

Finally, I am grateful to my family, Roger Fallot and Anna Promey-Fallot, and the poodles, Lilith and Lucille, with them, for reminding me to take a hike, taste the ocean, feel the moon, smell the peonies—and to be amazed at the sensory wonder of it all.

Sensational Religion

1

Religion, Sensation, and Materiality

An Introduction

SALLY M. PROMEY

ensational Religion: Sensory Cultures in Material Practice is one outcome of a collaborative multiyear scholarly project in the emerging field of sensory culture studies. A sizeable, lively, and multidisciplinary literature maps the field's wide terrain at this juncture in its formation. At various points, the existing scholarship manifests the contributions of anthropology, art history, sociology, political theory, philosophy, history, religious studies, biology, ethics, and neuroscience.[1]

This volume is the first to consider the subject of sensory culture from the perspective of religious practice over a range of times and spaces, to provide material and historical ballast across this span to descriptive and theoretical literatures, and to reflect on relations between our historically situated subject and aesthetic and religious conflict.[2] Many of the authors represented here worked together over the course of nearly four years, meeting on three separate occasions for multiday seminars and critiquing each other's research projects.

This book investigates an interlocking set of concerns involving religion, sensation, and materiality. I mean the term *sensation* to signal three dimensions of this work. First, this volume examines the multisensory experiences and practices of religion in concrete instances, specific social contexts, and material objects. Second, within these particular instantiations it considers relations among materialities, embodiment, the senses, and cognition. Here sensation and cognition are intimately engaged and mutually constitutive aspects of bodily, corporeal existence rather than distinct and hierarchically arranged categories of experience. *Sensational Religion* is thus invested in the sense people make in lived practice, the interpretive worlds that both inform and derive from sensory phenomena. Under this rubric of making sense, the studies assembled here ask: How have people used and valued sensory data, and how have they shaped their material and immaterial worlds to encourage or discourage certain kinds or patterns of sensory experiences?[3] Third, some authors in this book explore religious sensation in its controversial sense, as when iconoclasm, censoring interventions, and accusations of blasphemy or sacrilege occur. Indeed I propose that these three dimensions of sensation are interconnected: that it is often precisely the sensory and sensual capacities of images and objects, as framed by the sense made of them in particular historical contexts, and especially in modernity, that elicit controversy.[4]

Importantly, furthermore, this volume lays out a set of related claims about the outcomes for visual and material religion of secularization theory.[5] This intellectual commitment places important aspects of the project squarely within a Western frame, aiming to illuminate its biases, by argument and example, and thus to describe and contribute to diminishing its formal, categorical, and interpretive grip. To summarize these claims, at the risk of oversimplification for purposes of argument and clarity: substantial aspects of the Enlightenment project aimed to protect art from the sensory excesses of material religion, to protect especially *fine* art from the day-to-day sensory and material muckiness of religious art and artifact, to abstract and elevate this protected and purified category of object in such a way as to disavow human kinships with the substance of that messiness and to neutralize its threat. Western narratives of modernity have inevitably been developmental ones, pressing religious people from idolatrous behaviors to the metaphysics of belief and in the process securing modern religion from corruption by sensitized, activated, and animated objects (the idols, fetishes, and totems of purportedly premodern, antimodern, or amodern others).

Anthropologist Talal Asad assembled important terms for this conversation in 1993 and again in 2003. Scholars of material religion have just begun to embrace the sensory implications and relevance of this work.[6] Political theorist William Connolly's reflections on Asad's earlier ideas get right to the point, underscoring the pervasive tendency among "secular, enlightened Europeans" to "treat belief as neatly separable from disciplinary practices, cultural routines, and the education of sensory experience."[7]

In 2007 anthropologist Webb Keane elegantly described Protestantism's divorce from Catholicism as a split primarily determined by disputes about the significance of materiality.[8] This particular smaller-scale break, between Catholics and Protestants, raggedly paralleled the tidy rift the Enlightenment postulated and presumed between religion and modernity. Voltaire, in 1764, had himself linked Catholic to "pagan" uses of images, and he was by no means alone in making this comparison and in seeking to distinguish modern rationalities from the (often sensory) fanaticisms and dogmatisms he identified with religious practice.[9] David Hume's *Natural History of Religion* similarly connected primitive religious forms to sensationalized material objects.[10]

My interest in this regard is fairly specific: the weight of secularization theory settled disproportionately on the material practice of religion. To a startling degree, modernist re-formations concerned properly constraining and transforming the material world.[11] Central to the "moral narrative of modernity," Keane suggests, "is the work of purification that aims to abstract the self from material and social entanglements."[12]

This volume focuses scholarly attention on precisely these material and social entanglements—and on their inextricable connections to human bodies, feelings, behavior, and belief. This work joins conversations—begun at least two decades ago, largely in anthropology and critical theory, but now claiming attention across the humanities as well as the social, natural, and physical sciences—about human capacities and their engagements with culture and with the natural and manufactured material universe. At Yale University and elsewhere, as collaborators in the Initiative for the Study of Material and Visual Cultures of Religion (mavcor.yale.edu), we have examined these subjects under the name "sensory cultures of religion," directing attention to the cultural construction of sensory apparati, ideologies, values, affects, and practices and the material objects they meet, make, and activate. This emphasis on *material* practice asserts the literal and figurative significance of materiality itself. It does so in general terms and also as secured in the character of particular materials, substances, and media. In using the word *material* as a modifier for practice, this volume points to the material construction of religious life stories, stories that simultaneously illuminate the social and political lives of objects and their interactions with and among human beings. *Sensational Religion* concludes with ruminations about relations between stuff and convictions of literal and figurative material transformations. For all these subjects, the contributing authors are, moreover, committed to considering the multilayered, interwoven, and cumulative construction of physical and interpretive contexts.

This book focuses on *material* and *visual* cultures of religion; it does not seek to provide a comprehensive overview of relations among all human senses and all religions. The task of the project has been broadly conceived (covering many centuries and more than five major religious traditions) but also carefully focused. *Sensational Religion* approaches these subjects from the perspectives of visual and material cultures of religion and then works to attend to the relations of visual and material cultures in religious contexts to multisensory engagements. Visuality is itself, after all, a multisensory phenomenon.[13] This volume represents an early stage in a larger conversation on religion, sensation, and materiality. I anticipate further research, for example, that will more effectively challenge the power of categorical terms like *religion* and *secular* in the imaginaries of the sensational(ized) and will provide tools for robust future investigations of multisensoriality and of historical sensory experiences resistant to existing scholarly facilities.

As this collaborative project began to achieve concrete form over the past few years, in the work of specific contributors, three interconnected themes emerged. The book's major parts, titled "Inhabitations," "Transgressions," and "Transformations," register these overlapping themes. On the opening page of each part I provide a brief introductory elaboration of the subject. In addition to the longer chapters gathered under these topics, shorter chapters clustered as "interludes" form mediating tissue of sorts between the adjacent thematic sections. These shorter pieces introduce focused reflections on particular subjects that elucidate or critique some of the complexities and perplexities of our themes. They also provide space for critics, curators, and practitioners to participate with historians and other academic scholars in these multidisciplinary conversations. The book's interludes appear in two parts: "Contested Grounds" and "Devotional Bodies." Each of the volume's five sections opens with its own pictorial commentary: a work of art, a photograph, a sensory instantiation of a theme.

Matter is all around us: we cannot escape it.[14] We are literally material beings in a material environment, populated with material objects, situated amidst the material stuff of nature, bound in intimate and more distant relations with other persons through shared material habits and habitats.[15] Objects, images, and a proliferation of material substances engage, shape, and interact with human bodies, events, and ideas just as profoundly, subtly, and emphatically as the words with which scholars generally exercise more comfortable interpretive familiarities. Pictures and things surround us, and people work with them, and they with people, to construct selves, communities, and worlds. The entities thus formed include, along a mutually invested continuum, *immaterial* compositions and worlds and thus embodied, unbodied, and imagined habitations of soul and spirit.

In the academy, the force exerted by historical ideas about modernity and religion has loomed especially large for the study of visual and material cultures of modern Western religions. In the twentieth century, as the disciplines most relevant to this volume took institutional shape, the secularization theory of modernity, harnessed to a developmental model of civilization, asserted a waning role for religion in Western cultural production.[16] Academics in the decade immediately past have directed considerable attention to dismantling the secularization paradigm, documenting religion's refusal to go quietly—or even to go at all. Moving into scholarly focus now is the extent and nature of the impact sustained under intellectual regimes that characterized religion as a particular kind of vestigial production, unsuited to modern nations.

If modernity's narration stumbled over the demographics of religion's persistence, material objects were star players in this problematic plot. What most clearly distinguished "primitive" peoples, practices, and times was their "superstitious" attachment to objects as fetishes and idols, their willingness to ascribe agency or other sorts of power to them, to worship them, to allow them to present and mediate the supernatural. Imagining the primitive in baseline reference to African "savages," such trajectories racialized sensation, emotion, and materiality and linked the three terms in this regard.[17] Race as a category is fully dependent on social, political, cultural, economic, and ideological interpretations of *sensed* perceptions of difference.

Seen through these lenses, the study of the religious stuff of premodernity or of "other" places and peoples did not falter—often quite the contrary: its pursuit, in fact, set up precisely the contrast necessary to sustain the conviction of modernist rupture. It should come as no surprise that students of medieval Christianity produced an early and especially robust literature on materiality and sensation.[18] The medieval period in this chronological schematic marks the moment before modernity, the moment before Christianity's great divide. For the medieval period, secularization theory predicts that primitive forms pertain. Asad, in fact, pushes off against his own astute studies of medieval Christianity to show ways that the secular is a product of Protestant Christian ideologies in modernity.[19] Few scholars, however, attended seriously over time to similar objects (to religious stuff) in modernity and postmodernity in the West; for the most part, these similarities went unremarked, submerged, or suppressed. When they *were* noted, they generally set off "folk," "outsider," "native," or "naïve" cultures from "modern" experience.[20] Purportedly premodern categories of object (fetish, idol, totem) made possible the very articulation of religion into modernity and now seem long overdue for reevaluation.[21]

The modern, and to some degree parallel, development of the category art lifted some objects and pictures out of the material realm and into the intellectual or abstract. Bolstered by Romantic theories connecting this special fine category of thing to imagination and even soul, this reclamation project dusted off the taint of fetish and repurposed certain kinds of artifacts for modernity, situating the aesthetic as a particular sort of refined, disinterested contemplation, not subject to the presumed vagaries and primitivisms of other material objects.

The pressure of the secularization paradigm repurposed religion, too, wrapped it up tight, shoved it inside, allowing it to expand again within the newly spiritualized human interior, where it now operated in proximity to the also relatively newly sequestered and constrained category of emotion.[22] Spiritualization attended aestheticization as each erected sturdy theoretical (often theological) barriers guarding art and spirit from incursions by material religion. Cultural evolutionary trajectories of the late nineteenth and early twentieth centuries thus demonstrated, if not the disappearance of religion altogether, then its "progress" to an "advanced" private and dematerialized state of interiority and invisibility. For some who followed this line of thinking, art occupied the place of religion, a new locus for spirituality, as religious dogmatism and orthodoxies seemed to this cohort to render impossible authentic spiritual expression in more traditional domains.[23] Grand civic arts projects, decorating the interiors and exteriors of public buildings in the United States and Europe, celebrated versions of this succession.[24]

Art history's twentieth-century contribution to this process of differentiation was the formalist construction of artistic modernism as an enterprise of innovation, individualism, and transgression characterized by a radical break with the past, its traditions, and traditional institutions. In its focus on form and its eagerness to set aside all sorts of cultural, historical, and social activity, including (especially) religion, modernist aesthetic formalism itself operated as a strategy of secularization. While Western art might derive stylistic innovation from its encounters with forms it understood as primitive, it first evicted the spirits from their material habitations. In his classic 1939 essay "Avant-garde and Kitsch," Clement Greenberg laid out the terms of this project—which would, as it turned out, be picked up and promoted by midcentury American liberal Protestant arts professionals who attempted to make this formula work to liberal Protestantism's own cultural advantage. These arts experts (people like Alfred Barr Jr., founding director of the Museum of Modern Art and president of the National Council of Churches Commission on Art) embraced Greenberg's definitions and valuations but aimed to rescue liberal religious art, and liberal religion itself, by linking both with Greenberg's avant-garde aesthetic. In modernist abstraction, so went this argument, liberal Protestant social and political currency might be regained through endorsement of a specific sort of high religious art deemed inhospitable to sentimental, material, commercial, and evangelical interests as well as to communist and socialist politics. Seeking to implement a strategy of opposition, containment, and replacement, the promoters of this new modernist religious aesthetic asked observant liberal Protestants to break and then to reform visual habits. They sought to substitute one sort of Christian image for another, denouncing the alternatives as idols of conformity and commerce.[25]

Barr's activities in this regard in the 1950s and 1960s are cast in noteworthy relief by Richard Meyer's work on Barr's earlier enthusiasm for Soviet retooling of Russian icons, protecting the icons as cultural patrimony and secular collectibles at a moment when actual Russian religious bodies, in the persons of priests and monks, were subjected to persecution and destruction.[26] Making icons into fine art effectively produced anesthetized objects—removed from multisensory religious contexts, purged of traces of contact with persons and activities that made original sense of them—purified for other purposes. A similar strategy attended later unsuccessful attempts by Western museum personnel to protect the Bamiyan Buddhas in Afghanistan from destruction by the Taliban. As Finbarr Flood has demonstrated, the efforts of the museum community failed in part because they were focused on aestheticization of these monumental objects, seeking to sanitize them of particular religious and political content and to redefine them to count among artifacts of world cultural patrimony.[27] It remains unclear whether other approaches might have had different outcomes, but this interpretive repossession and repositioning of the objects in relation to Western art market capital came across as elitist recolonization. These two examples do not represent the finest moments of Western high cultural institutions and their encounters with religious objects.

With its origins located in the conviction of a decisive rupture between past and present, many have pointed out the extent to which modernity thrived on a series of supersessionary binaries: sacred/secular, image/word, concrete/abstract, material/immaterial, exterior/interior, sensation/cognition, body/mind, emotion/reason, belief/knowledge, nature/culture, particular/universal.[28] Janet R. Jakobsen and Ann Pellegrini, for example, locate the dominance and compulsion of the secularization narrative in this "network of binary oppositions established by its central terms" and point to the ways in which "these distinctions are linked together in a mutually reinforcing manner."[29] These borders and binaries have been shaped by hierarchies and evaluations that pushed modern phenomena toward the purportedly more advanced right-hand term without much attention to the spaces between, the spaces most often occupied by objects and their sensory and affective fields.

Supersessionary patterns have been so deeply ingrained in scholarly habits that they sometimes replicate themselves in expectations about specific materials and how they should behave. Earlier writers on colonial American Puritan stone carving, for example, sketched progressions from one pictorial subject matter to another, with images on stones evolving to become more modern and less material in neat successions, from grim, purportedly judgmental skulls and crossbones to joyful soul effigies to more securely secular portrait stones.[30] In fact, these chronologies of change are not nearly as tidy as many asserted them to be; different sorts of images coexist over time, and portrait stones actively participated in devotional pieties of self-examination.[31] The first two forms, furthermore, skulls and crossbones and soul effigies, effectively represented two distinct chronological episodes in Puritan death rather than two points on a modernist cultural evolutionary trajectory.[32] The effigy asserted the ascent of the soul at the moment of death, the skull and crossbones projected hope for bodily resurrection at the end of time—and the portrait stone constituted a material invitation to anticipatory self-examination. Stones in Grove Street Cemetery in New Haven, Connecticut, provide graphic evidence to this effect in literally crowning skulls and crossbones with insignia of heavenly glory. Sometimes these images of skulls simultaneously seem to be in the process of combination with soul effigies or transformation from one to the other, perhaps in recognition of the longed-for reunion of body and soul at the biblical Last Judgment.

Ideas about the enlightened secular also operated as engines of imperialism, imagining a border between modernity and premodernity and driving the frequently colonized other to the far side of that divide. Modernity's concern to oust the idol and fetish and the superstitions these represented was in some fundamental ways *about* maintaining borders, about colonial engagements and encounters.[33] Fetish and idol dangerously threatened to breach the boundary between natural and supernatural, ontologies that ought to remain separate in a version of the modern in which, as Robert Orsi has observed, the "impure commingling" of matter and spirit constituted a species of the primitive.[34] In the fetish, power was ascribed to an object such that agency was not reserved for human subjects but was also resident in and through the material world. In defining other, "less advanced" religions, it was in large part the stuff they had and the powers invested in and exercised by that stuff that made the distinction stick.

One of cultural anthropology's most influential recent developments, as Daniel Miller relates in considering the work of Alfred Gell and Bruno Latour, reasserts the agency of the nonhuman universe: "Where material forms have consequences for people that are autonomous from human agency, they may be said to possess the agency that causes these effects."[35] Jane Bennett's articulation of a politics of "vital materiality" asserts the "capacity of things . . . to act as quasi agents or forces with trajectories, propensities, or tendencies of their own."[36] Asad maintains that "the power of things—whether animate or inanimate—is their ability to act within a network of enabling conditions. . . . Feeling, remembering, hoping are as physical as they are mental."[37] Scholars "need to show," Miller continues, "how the things that people make, make people"—and, I would add, how the things toward which we orient ourselves shape our perceptions of the environments we inhabit and the possibilities available to us.[38] This is true not only of constructed things themselves but of the very materials and media of construction, because these claim constitutive social, political, and cultural content and power, too.[39]

As Diana Coole and Samantha Frost suggest, for René Descartes, "I think, therefore I am" separated the active human mind from passive and inert matter and asserted an ontological distinction between the two.[40] His *Discourse on Method,* in which this phrasing appears, split thinking from sensation and mind from body.[41] In recent scholarship in many disciplines, "new materialists" like Coole and Frost experiment with theories that reinvest agencies, in varying degrees and of several sorts, in matter, in objects, and in media of production.[42] New materialists turn to the physical sciences to demonstrate that the immaterial cannot be so neatly divested of materiality and vice versa. Orsi's "impure commingling" would thus seem, in actuality, to be as much a characteristic of modernity as of premodernity. Many of the authors who contribute to this volume claim for their own work a relational theory of material agency, a theory that recognizes the active stance of medium (the basic stuff from which things are made) in shaping, containing, and constraining meaning, for example, or the liveliness in objects that meets, matches, and reforms human expectations for them.[43]

In his 2005 book *What Do Pictures Want?*, W.J.T. Mitchell conducts what he calls a thought experiment in which he posits images as living things—and argues that the most interesting consequence of this assumption is that the "question of their value (understood as vitality) is played out in a social context.... We ... don't just evaluate images," he continues: "images introduce new forms of value into the world, contesting our criteria, forcing us to change our minds. ... [Images] change the way we think and see and dream. They refunction our memories and imaginations, bringing *new criteria and new desires.*" We might well conclude, then, that images and objects, in their very materiality, also directly engage immaterial dimensions of human life. Mitchell contends, furthermore, that the lives of images are fundamentally social lives. No single individual controls the value or significance of an image or object; these material items of human manufacture periodically find themselves at the center of social crises, conflicts, and contentions as well as social cohesions of multiple sorts.[44] This is not surprising given the intimate involvements of images and objects with desires, values, memories, emotions, affects, and imagination.

It is a subsidiary thesis of *Sensational Religion,* subject to testing here and elsewhere, that contention about images and objects often concerns their appeals to sensation or sensory capacities. This proposal is not unrelated to their sometimes emphatic insistence on proximity to human bodily functions, discourses, and sensualities—and to Mitchell's assertion regarding their capacity to elicit "new criteria and new desires." Again the spill-off of secularization theory lays the ground for this conversation: the location of divinity or devotion in specific sensory objects and in sensual bodies reads in this context as a special kind of problem.

James Simpson's 2010 volume *Under the Hammer: Iconoclasm in the Anglo-American Tradition* provides an excellent synopsis of the work of earlier scholars on a number of these subjects. The Enlightenment substitutes the neutralizing, distancing faculty of taste for other powers of images and objects.[45] Taste (retaining its association with refined discrimination but oddly separated from its more immediately sensory significance) is, then, what distinguishes modern Europeans and their cohort from the primitive practices of discovered, classified, conquered, colonized, or missionized others. Just under the surface of the history of taste, however, the recurrent specter of iconoclasm refuses to permanently recede. "The Enlightenment does not so much reject the iconoclastic tradition," Simpson continues, "as adapt to it, and adapt it, by a massive work of image neutralization," by *transformation,* as we have argued here, by turning these objects into art. In one of his most provocative turns of thought on this subject, Simpson remarks that "the art collection, so characteristic of the age [of Enlightenment] and its cultivation of taste, is in part produced as a place of asylum from iconoclasm."[46]

Immanuel Kant, trained in the Reformation city of Königsberg, in his 1790 *Critique of Judgment* defined taste as "indifferent with regard to the existence of an object," as a matter of free and disinterested contemplation. "For . . . the ground of the pleasure," Kant maintained, "is placed merely in the form of the object for reflection in general, hence *not in any sensation of the object,* and also without relation to a concept that contains any intention."[47] Here Kant, in one strategic move, made possible the (modern) Protestant contemplation of the Catholic image in service of taste, all the while and simultaneously policing, subverting, and neutralizing the threat of the Catholic idol. Simpson concludes: "The category of the aesthetic is itself, in sum, a historical product of iconoclasm."[48]

Various Protestant clergy, theologians, and art theorists in the United States, for instance, repurposed major monuments of Catholic religious art as fundamentally, spiritually and aesthetically, Protestant. In a series of fairly audacious moves, in several historical moments and in pursuit of a modern, tasteful religiosity, American Protestants reclaimed religious fine art (Leonardo's *Last Supper* and Raphael's *Sistine Madonna,* for example) and the spiritual and cultural currencies it promised.[49] Key to these configurations, Protestants resituated and resited "formerly" Catholic materials, inventing new sensory contexts, climates, and channels for religious art and devotional practices (for example, in the home and in the natural landscape), thus reshaping the terms of encounter among Protestant audiences.[50] Far greater numbers of Protestants, in fact, colonized Catholic art than damaged or destroyed it.[51]

The history of the senses, the ways they have been defined, collected, ordered, numbered, and segregated, is a cultural history.[52] Only over time did the West achieve consensus about the number of senses. Plato, for example, did not draw a fast line between senses and feelings. In one numbering he counted pleasure, discomfort, desire, and fear among his senses. That we now number five senses we owe fairly directly to Aristotle, who proposed this tally for its ideal symbolic correspondence to that of the elements as he numbered them. So the five senses of sight, sound, smell, taste, and touch matched, at least numerically, the five elements of earth, air, fire, water, and quintessence, the substance that for Aristotle constituted the elemental quality of the heavens. For different allegorical and theological purposes, the first-century Philo numbered the senses seven, bringing the vocalizations of speech and the sense of the genital organs to Aristotle's five. This added up given the period's understanding that the senses, far from being merely passive receptacles for raw information, actively mediated communication and contact, with the eyes, for example, sending forth rays that grasped the objects toward which they were directed.

The third-century theologian Origen was not alone in proposing spiritual senses in correspondence with the physical ones.[53] By the middle ages, these spiritual or inward senses equated fairly closely with qualities we now think of as mental operations, like memory, imagination, fantasy, and common sense.[54] The most persistent voices of the Enlightenment changed all this, decisively separating the senses from mental capacities like cognition and intellection. Though John Locke trusted the senses as conduits of information, whereas Descartes was suspicious of their deceptions, both men classified the senses as natural, purely physical rather than cultural or spiritual, faculties. Theirs is the "scientific" understanding of sensory perception most familiar today, with its privileging of sight as the "sense of science." Scientific understandings of vision and hearing focused early attention on devising technologies that enhanced and recorded sights and sounds.[55] Perhaps not surprisingly, these technologies of replication facilitated the study of the two senses contemporary Western estimates gendered masculine and judged highest of the five. The absence of similar technologies for touch, taste, and smell have hampered efforts to think toward a more fully multisensory history.

Despite recognition of constraints produced by what Classen calls the "visualist regime of modernity," most of this volume's authors would agree that vision remains, with and among the other senses, a critical subject for historians and theorists.[56] Our aim here is not to supplant the emphasis on visuality but rather to assert the multisensory aspects and capacities of visuality itself. Western privileging of the eye is a centuries-long biological habit and cultural position, not merely an academic gambit. The question of how successfully to investigate "visual" practice when vision might be most fruitfully approached as fully engaged in a rounder human sensorium is a matter our project has considered. In embodied human perception, as distinguished from the products if not the practice of scholarly writing, one sense cannot be effectively isolated from the others. The senses are deeply intertwined, furthermore, not only among themselves but also with feeling, emotion, and affect as well as cognition.[57] Sensory experience involves embodied wholes, the simultaneous engagement of multiple, not always easily distinguishable, senses.[58] In the words of Tilley, "To see is not simply to be exposed to sensory data; it involves embodied interaction with the world. We see with the whole body just as we think with our body rather than part of it."[59]

Important to this collection of essays has been a desire not to perpetuate the bias that *sensory* cultures of religion concern mostly "non-Western," "less developed" practices occurring among people often formerly labeled primitive, or orientalized or exoticized in other ways. In looking at a range of traditions and expressions in various places and times, *Sensational Religion* hopes to show that sensory religious felicities are not the exclusive purview of any particular geography or chronology but that specific and differently inflected material and sensory practices, and reactions to them, can be located in a wide range of places and times. And so this book focuses attention, for example, on material spiritualities and sensitized artifacts in the United States and Europe as well as in Latin America and Asia.

In fact, this set of studies deliberately directs considerable attention to Western sensory contexts and histories. It does so in an effort to destabilize lingering notions of modern Western religious traditions (and various forms of Protestantism especially) as nonsensory interior affairs. Contrary to the situation introduced by secularization theory and its precedents (such as the Protestant reformations and ascendant strains of Enlightenment thought) in marking religious difference, the binary rift between modernity and premodernity on these issues is neither as easily and firmly located nor as extreme as many who have claimed to be moderns have asserted. The point is decidedly *not* that everything across time and space is the same but rather that scholars and intellectuals have drawn particularly hard categorical lines that cannot be defended when the evidence is scrutinized.

In Western modernity, Christianity, and especially Protestant Christianity, has prevailed not just in shaping a set of religious possibilities, in defining the contours of religion, but also in determining the "formations of the secular," as Talal Asad, Tracy Fessenden, and others have suggested.[60] Many cases explored in this volume illuminate precisely the sorts of sensory encounters and material experiences that Western modernity formerly claimed to discipline and subdue. I am interested in the ways practice resists and exceeds ideology, offering new avenues forward even, and perhaps especially, within Protestant modernity. My hope is that the individual essays assembled here begin to disentangle categorical binds. What I have sacrificed to this commitment to destabilization is the kind of chronological, geographical, and sensorial comprehensiveness to which this project might otherwise have aspired.

Importantly, moreover, I am not interested in simply reversing the terms of the argument, in staging modernity as a premodern sensorium or demonstrating the intellectual and (a)sensory sophistication of cultural/historical groups not generally granted modern ground. Instead, as a place to start, I have aimed to consider material practice and sensory cultures in specific instances. The authors assembled here share my conviction (1) that differences among and between groups and individuals over time are real differences *and* (2) that the gaps, fissures, and divides posited in the past, as well as mismatches of many lesser sorts, are generally not to be found precisely where ideologies have placed them.

In addition to inadequate global sweep, this book, or at least its introduction, might also be faulted for oversimplification of complex, even messy, historical ideas, forces, and inclinations. The narrative of secularization I have presented is, in at least two key ways, narrow and contrived. First, secularization theory rests on very particular strands of (mostly) Enlightenment thought. There were other threads and other thinkers. There were alternative ideas, often offered by the same key figures, ideas that did not fit so neatly within these ideological parameters. Descartes, for example, when writing as a scientist rather than a philosopher, had very different things to say about the senses and cognition; had Baruch Spinoza's earlier lead been more wholeheartedly embraced along these dimensions, the outcome might have varied considerably.[61]

Second, in streamlining for clarity my understanding of the impact of secularization theory on thinking about material religion, I run the risk of appearing to endorse the inaccurate impression that the secularization narrative succeeded in quashing material and sensory cultures of religion in the modern West. Although its disapproving scrutiny demanded reckoning, although some things look and behave differently for its force, secularization theory matched very poorly with actual experience on the ground. My conceptual and historical quarrel in this instance is not with the secular per se or with the processes of secularism over time but with the restrictive dimensions assigned by secularization theory to religion and to sensory materialities. I hold accountable for these outcomes neither the Enlightenment nor modernity in entirety but only those partial characteristics of Enlightenment thought and modernity selected and embraced by the secularization thesis, a thesis that advanced its own teleology and had real consequences. In actuality, this powerful theory represented a fairly narrow philosophical slice deduced from the wider range of possibilities and then applied (backward as well as forward in time), sorting modern from premodern, with religion (especially material religion) as a fulcrum.

Secularization theory held sway for close to two centuries as the paradigmatic narrative of modernity in the West. The set of historical events and ideas arrayed as evidence for secularization theory assumed the appearance of causality, so frequently and insistently were the same dots connected in the same sequence inside and outside the academy. In large part, the selective, repetitive, sequential hitching together of events and ideas has brought us to these particular instantiated impasses. We need new stories, adjusted to different sorts of material and sensory realities, to different versions of events, to deeper pluralisms (in William Connolly's sense of the term).[62]

This book argues that the "sense" secularization theory made of (religious) things obscured understanding of the lived engagements of both religions and things. The sensory styling of religion contributed to its location in and relegation to the past, rendering quaintly antique, for example, virtually all religions other than a peculiarly restrained version of Protestant Christianity. But while secularization's key presuppositions shaped the set choreography, it did not fully constitute or contain the dance.

Rather than demonstrate ways in which Western religion is not actually modern, it might yield more to consider that modernity is different along these dimensions than many scholars have formerly supposed. Practice and discourse resist and exceed one another, resist and exceed ideology. Secularization theory has created difficulties for material religion to which material religion in practice has rarely fully succumbed. Modern Protestant emphasis on the presumably more abstract word and on unmediated purportedly pure access to the divine has not eliminated its shaping of new sensory practices and its reshaping of old ones. By comparison with Catholicism, Protestant practice is differently embodied, not disembodied, differently materialized, not dematerialized.[63] At the most general level, Christian adherence to a theology of incarnation (a physical theory) mobilizes the material world; here divinity assumes a material body, invisible grace is rendered in visible and tangible signs, and the most holy sacraments take shape as divine investments in multisensory communication.[64]

A key aspect of the vitality of material is its capacity for transformation, for metamorphosis from one thing to another. One strategy by which human beings routinely accomplish material transformation is in turning stuff into words. Into this calculation, analogy introduces the reverse: metaphor often turns words into stuff and one object or thing into another. Within Protestant as well as Catholic Christianities, scriptural analogies and metaphorical imagination generate sensory, material, and hermeneutic connections across a wide array of pictures, objects, and practices; various audiences understand these connections to instantiate particular social relations, material agencies, and points of heightened access to spiritual realities. Christian scriptures here represent repositories of cultural knowledge not just about divinity but about divinity's relations to materials and perception, most fundamentally about life infused into matter—and also about the operations of both bodies and matter in getting things done. Here word and image/object are not binary equations but are mutually constituting entities: each shapes the other, enables the other, and both lay out a fluid, flexible matrix of symbols and tropes that, in their interlaced and replicated suggestions of iconographies, establish a set of possibilities for sensation, action, and imagination. These symbols and tropes are part of a cultural fabric; one is connected to another to another to another until this fabric apparently catches up everything. Further, because these tropes and symbols and materials (on their own terms) are often common to other religions and cultures, sometimes they net other fish too, leading to convictions of false or unstable similarities and dissimilarities (and especially of the professed "universality" of such symbols).

Although imagination, memory, and other cognitive functions may appear to abstract pictures (images and objects) from sensory moorings, pictorial things-in-time are part of the larger constellation of stuff that tangibly circulates within human life-worlds and in relation to sensing human bodies. Religion, with its robust sensorium of material practices, is a domain in which sensory segregation is especially difficult to maintain but where many have striven mightily to enforce and police it. As contributors to this volume, we pursue a working method that holds together the sensory and material in nonhierarchical relation, encouraging consideration of a wider human sensorium and configuring the material term to include close attention to specific materialities themselves and also to the ways that sensations and sensory properties situate human material bodies in connection to other bodies, material and immaterial, animate and inanimate.

The senses are themselves materially acquisitive, by which I mean that through sensory perception humans "acquire" things, collect them, locate them, remember them, adjust to them, make use of them. Sensation necessarily involves materiality; materiality implicates sensation. Neither replaces the other; neither consistently occupies the privileged position in interaction. And each communicates beyond itself to imagined, desired, and valued states or realms.

This study of sensory and material cultures has thus been constituted as a *relational* enterprise with respect to people and things. This relational model invites research built around strategies of multiplication, accumulation, and refinement rather than simple replacement or substitution. It also suggests useful reconfigurations of material agency itself as relational and contingent, as a matter of people and things in specific encounters and contexts.[65] The stakes in this examination of relations among religion, sensation, and materiality are high. The task at hand engages no less than a fundamental reorientation in understandings of religion and the intricacies and intimacies of personal, social, political, and cultural work accomplished in its sensory and material practice.

NOTES

1. See, for example, David Howes, ed., *The Varieties of Sensory Experience: A Sourcebook in the Anthropology of the Senses* (Toronto: University of Toronto Press, 1991); Constance Classen, *Worlds of Sense: Exploring the Senses in History and across Cultures* (London: Routledge, 1993); C. Nadia Seremetakis, ed., *The Senses Still* (Chicago and London: University of Chicago Press, 1996; originally published by Westview Press in 1994); Classen, *The Color of Angels: Cosmology, Gender, and the Aesthetic Imagination* (London and New York: Routledge, 1998); Leigh Eric Schmidt, *Hearing Things: Religion, Illusion, and the American Enlightenment* (Cambridge, MA: Harvard University Press, 2002); Howes, *Sensual Relations: Engaging the Senses in Culture and Social Theory* (Ann Arbor: University of Michigan Press, 2003); Howes, ed., *Empire of the Senses: The Sensual Culture Reader* (Oxford, UK, and New York: Berg, 2005); Elizabeth Edwards, Chris Gosden, and Ruth B. Phillips, eds., *Sensible Objects: Colonialism, Museums, and Material Culture* (Oxford, UK, and New York: Berg, 2006); and Howes, ed., *The Sixth Sense Reader* (Oxford, UK,

and New York: Berg, 2009). A considerable number of recent books, many of them part of David Howes's "Sensory Formations Series" with Berg publishers (Oxford, UK, and New York), deal with a particular sense among the Western five; see, for example, Carolyn Korsmeyer, ed., *The Taste Culture Reader: Experiencing Food and Drink* (2005); Jim Drobnick, ed., *The Smell Culture Reader* (Berg, 2006); and Constance Classen, ed., *The Book of Touch* (Berg, 2005). See also Veit Erlmann, ed., *Hearing Cultures: Essays on Sound, Listening, and Modernity* (Oxford, UK, and New York: Berg, 2004); Constance Classen, David Howes, and Anthony Synnott, *Aroma: The Cultural History of Smell* (London and New York: Routledge, 1994); Eve Kosofsky Sedgwick, *Touching Feeling: Affect, Pedagogy, Performativity* (Durham, NC, and London: Duke University Press, 2003); Sarah Ahmed and Jackie Stacey, eds., *Thinking through the Skin* (London and New York: Routledge, 2001); Susan Ashbrook Harvey, *Scenting Salvation: Ancient Christianity and the Olfactory Imagination* (Berkeley: University of California Press, 2006); Daniel Heller-Roazen, *The Inner Touch: Archaeology of a Sensation* (New York: Zone Books, 2009); David Morgan, *The Embodied Eye: Religious Visual Culture and the Social Life of Feeling* (Berkeley: University of California Press, 2012); and Scott McCredie, *Balance: In Search of the Lost Sense* (New York, Boston, London: Little Brown, 2007). Mark M. Smith, author of *Sensing the Past: Seeing, Hearing, Smelling, Tasting, and Touching in History* (Berkeley: University of California Press, 2007), is also editor of the "Studies in Sensory History" series of the University of Illinois Press; this series includes volumes by Constance Classen (*The Deepest Sense: A Cultural History of Touch* [2012]), and a forthcoming volume titled *Vision in History* by Rachael DeLue. Constance Classen and David Howes have embarked on a "Cultural History of the Senses" series with Berg publishers; both Classen and Howes are founding members of the interdisciplinary Centre for Sensory Studies at Concordia University (see www.sensorystudies.org). Also of note in this summary selection of works are several volumes in explicit relation to religion, materiality, or art in a particular time and place; see, for example, Alain Corbin, *Village Bells: Sound and Meaning in the Nineteenth-Century French Countryside*, trans. Martin Thom (New York: Columbia University Press, 1998); Leigh Schmidt's important volume *Hearing Things*, noted above; Isaac Weiner, *Religion Out Loud: Religious Sound, Public Space, and American Pluralism* (New York and London: New York University Press, 2014); Leo Mazow, *Thomas Hart Benton and the American Sound* (University Park: Pennsylvania State University Press, 2012); Margaret Olin, *Touching Photographs* (Chicago and London: University of Chicago Press, 2012); Patrizia Di Bello and Gabriel Koureas, eds., *Art History and the Senses: 1830 to the Present* (Aldershot, UK: Ashgate, 2010); and Alice E. Sanger and Siv Tove Kulbrandstad Walker, eds., *Sense and the Senses in Early Modern Art and Cultural Practice* (Aldershot, UK: Ashgate, 2012). A substantial literature also exists on sensory subjects in medieval Christian materialities, to which I refer in summary in note 18 below. In 1999 Leigh Eric Schmidt convened an influential conference, Religion and the Senses, at Princeton University; in April 2011, *American Historical Review* dedicated a forum to the subject of The Senses in History. Martin Jay wrote the forum's introduction, tracking this sensory turn in the discipline of history: Jay, "In the Realm of the Senses: An Introduction," *American Historical Review* 116, no. 2 (April 2011): 1–9.

2. See Wietse de Boer and Christine Göttler, eds., *Religion and the Senses in Early Modern Europe* (Leiden: Brill, 2013). This insightful volume offers a compelling perspective on sensory cultures of religious conflict in early modern Europe and is a useful, historically situated, companion to the work accomplished here.

3. *Making Sense of Religion in the Yale Archive,* an exhibition co-curated by Kati Curts, Olivia Hillmer, and Michelle Morgan, Sterling Memorial Library, October 4, 2011–February 3, 2012.

4. On our subject of sensory sensationalism, see also Dominic Janes's recent essay "Seeing and Tasting the Divine: Simeon Solomon's Homoerotic Sacrament," in *Art, History, and the Senses,* ed. Patrizia Di Bello and Gabriel Koureas (Aldershot, UK: Ashgate, 2010), 35–50. I thank Yui Suzuki for calling my attention to this book.

5. For earlier formulations of this argument, see Sally M. Promey, "'Return' of Religion in the Scholarship of American Art," a state-of-the-field essay, *Art Bulletin* 85, no. 3 (September 2003): 581–603; Sally M. Promey and Shira Brisman, "Sensory Cultures: Material and Visual Religion Reconsidered," in *Blackwell Companion to Religion in America,* ed. Philip Goff (Malden, MA: Wiley-Blackwell, 2010), 177–205; and Sally M. Promey, "Hearts and Stones: Material Transformations and the Stuff of Christian Practice in the United States," in *American Christianities,* ed. Catherine Brekus and W. Clark Gilpin (Chapel Hill: University of North Carolina Press, 2011), 183–213.

6. Talal Asad, *Genealogies of Religion: Discipline and Reasons of Power in Christianity and Islam* (Baltimore: Johns Hopkins University Press, 1993), esp. 72–77, and Asad, *Formations of the Secular: Christianity, Islam, Modernity* (Stanford, CA: Stanford University Press, 2003). See also David Scott and Charles Hirschkind, eds., *Powers of the Secular Modern: Talal Asad and His Interlocutors* (Stanford, CA: Stanford University Press, 2006).

7. William E. Connolly, *Pluralism* (Durham, NC: Duke University Press, 2005), 58.

8. Webb Keane, *Christian Moderns: Freedom and Fetish in the Mission Encounter* (Berkeley: University of California Press, 2007), and Promey and Brisman, "Sensory Cultures," 177–205. Literary theorist Anne Kibbey earlier proposed a similar argument: Kibbey, *The Interpretation of Material Shapes in Puritanism: A Study of Rhetoric, Prejudice, and Violence* (Cambridge, UK: Cambridge University Press, 1986).

9. Voltaire, entry for "Idol, Idolater, Idolatry," in *A Pocket Philosophical Dictionary,* trans. John Fletcher (Oxford, UK: Oxford University Press, 2011), 156–167. For a useful discussion of this entry, see James Simpson, *Under the Hammer: Iconoclasm in the Anglo-American Tradition* (Oxford, UK: Oxford University Press, 2010), 123. See also Promey, "'Return' of Religion," 581–603.

10. David Hume, *A Dissertation on the Passions; and the Natural History of Religion* in *Clarendon Edition of the Works of David Hume,* ed. Tom L. Beauchamp (Oxford, UK: Oxford University Press, 2007), 34–43. And see Jonathan Z. Smith, "Religion, Religions, Religious," in *Critical Terms for Religious Studies,* ed. Mark C. Taylor (Chicago: University of Chicago Press, 1998), 274, for discussion of Hume's place in this interpretive maneuver.

11. Promey, "'Return' of Religion"; Promey and Brisman, "Sensory Cultures"; and Promey, "Hearts and Stones."

12. Keene, *Christian Moderns,* 201.

13. For a recent essay on Alexander Baumgarten's understanding of sensation as a "complex assemblage," see Patrizia Di Bello and Gabriel Koureas, "Other than the Visual: Art, History, and the Senses," in *Art, History, and the Senses,* 4.

14. See Diana Coole and Samantha Frost, eds., *New Materialisms: Ontology, Agency, and Politics* (Durham, NC: Duke University Press, 2010), for a similarly framed argument.

15. Christopher Tilley, *The Materiality of Stone: Explorations in Landscape Phenomenology* (Oxford, UK, and New York: Berg, 2004), 2–4.

16. See this argument as developed in Promey, "'Return' of Religion."

17. Sara Ahmed, *The Cultural Politics of Emotion* (New York: Routledge, 2004), 3, and Jane Bennett, *The Enchantment of Modern Life* (Princeton, NJ: Princeton University Press, 2001), 117–118.

18. This rich literature deserves its own bibliographic essay. See, for example, the work of Caroline Walker Bynum, Linda Seidel, Jeffrey Hamburger, Robert Nelson, Bissera Pentcheva, and Jacqueline Jung.

19. See, for example, Asad, *Genealogies.*

20. In the late 1970s, for example, Stephen Wilson conducted an exemplary study of the material cults of saints in the urban churches of Paris's ten central arrondissements, but he designated the cults he studied as "popular" manifestations of religiosity: Wilson, "Cults of Saints in the Churches of Central Paris," in *Saints and Their Cults,* ed. Wilson (Cambridge, UK: Cambridge University Press, 1983), 233–260.

21. Numbers of scholars are taking steps in this direction. See, for example, William Pietz, "Fetish," in *Critical Terms in Art History,* ed. Robert S. Nelson and Richard Shiff (Chicago: University of Chicago Press, 2003 [1996]), 306–317; Bruno Latour and Peter Weibel, eds., *Iconoclash: Beyond the Image Wars in Science, Religion, and Art* (Karlsruhe, Germany: ZKM, 2002); W.J.T. Mitchell, *What Do Pictures Want: The Lives and Loves of Images* (Chicago: University of Chicago Press, 2005); Michael Taussig, *What Color Is the Sacred?* (Chicago: University of Chicago Press, 2009); Josh Ellenbogen and Aaron Tugendhaft, eds., *Idol Anxiety* (Stanford, CA: Stanford University Press, 2011).

22. See, for example, Colin Campbell, *The Romantic Ethic and the Spirit of Modern Consumerism* (Oxford, UK: Blackwell, 1987; paperback ed. 1989), 72–73; and Susan Stewart, "Remembering the Senses," in *Empire of the Senses,* ed. Howes (Oxford, UK: Berg, 2005), 59.

23. Nietzsche, Baudelaire, and Huysmans number among nineteenth-century writers whose thinking tends in this direction; for more on this subject, see Promey, "'Return' of Religion."

24. The Library of Congress in Washington, D.C., the Boston Public Library, and the New York Public Library constitute three examples.

25. See Sally M. Promey, "Taste Cultures and the Visual Practice of Liberal Protestantism, 1940–1965," in *Practicing Protestants: Histories of the Christian Life in America,* ed. Laurie Maffly-Kipp, Leigh Schmidt, and Mark Valeri (Baltimore: Johns Hopkins University Press, 2006), 250–293, and Promey, "Visible Liberalism: Liberal Protestant Taste Evangelism, 1850 and 1950," in *American Religious Liberalism,* ed. Leigh Eric Schmidt and Sally M. Promey (Bloomington: Indiana University Press, 2012), 76–96.

26. See Richard Meyer, "Revolutionary Icons: Alfred Barr and the Remaking of Russian Religious Art," in this volume.

27. Finbarr B. Flood, "Between Cult and Culture: Bamiyan, Islamic Iconoclasm, and the Museum," *Art Bulletin* 84, no. 4 (December 2002): 641–655.

28. On supersessionary thought, see Kathleen Biddick, *The Typological Imaginary: Circumcision, Technology, History* (Philadelphia: University of Pennsylvania Press, 2003). I am grateful to Shira Brisman for calling Biddick's work to my attention.

29. Janet R. Jakobsen and Ann Pellegrini, "Introduction: Times Like These," in *Secularisms,* ed. Jakobsen and Pellegrini (Durham, NC: Duke University Press, 2008), 6.

30. See, for example, Peter Benes, *The Masks of Orthodoxy: Folk Gravestone Carving in Plymouth County, Massachusetts, 1689–1805* (Amherst: University of Massachusetts Press, 1977), and Allan I. Ludwig, *Graven Images: New England Stonecarving and Its Symbols, 1650–1815* (Middletown, CT: Wesleyan University Press, 1966).

31. Sally M. Promey, "Seeing the Self 'in Frame'": Early New England Material Practice and Puritan Piety," *Material Religion* 1 (March 2005): 10–47.

32. I have elsewhere (in Promey and Brisman, "Sensory Cultures," 193) attributed to Lactantius, an early church author known to Puritans from both old and new England, the assertion

that a skull and two thigh bones constituted the minimum necessary remains for bodily resurrection. Although I learned this in graduate school and have heard other scholars mention it since, I have not been able to locate the original citation; I thus withdraw that aspect of the argument here. The point remains: the skull and crossbones both acknowledged mortality and anticipated the resurrection of the body.

33. Patricia Spyer, "Introduction," in *Border Fetishisms: Material Objects in Unstable Spaces,* ed. Spyer (London: Routledge, 1998): 1–11. In the West, the senses, like the materialities they mediate, have figured as part of the colonial enterprise. Conventional genderings and racialized ascriptions to these sensory codes have elevated sight and hearing as a white male prerogative, whereas the "lower," "animal" senses of taste, touch, and smell have been construed as the natural purview of women, children, and "others": Classen, *Color of Angels,* 6; see also Classen, *Worlds of Sense.*

34. Robert Orsi, remarks made in response to presentations at the Vibrant Materiality conference, Northwestern University, April 27, 2012. J. Michelle Molina organized this event to engage ideas presented in Jane Bennett's *Vibrant Matter: A Political Ecology of Things* (Durham, NC, and London: Duke University Press, 2010); see esp. viii–xi.

35. Daniel Miller, "Materiality: An Introduction," in *Materiality,* ed. Miller (Durham, NC, and London: Duke University Press, 2005), 11.

36. Bennett, *Vibrant Matter,* vii.

37. Asad, "Responses," in *Powers of the Secular Modern: Talal Asad and His Interlocutors,* ed. David Scott and Charles Hirschkind (Stanford, CA: Stanford University Press, 2006), 213.

38. Miller, "Materiality," 38, 43.

39. See, further, the introductory paragraphs to Interlude II of this book, "Devotional Bodies."

40. Coole and Frost, *New Materialisms,* 2, 7–9.

41. René Descartes, *Discourse on Method and Related Writings* (1637), trans. Desmond M. Clarke, Penguin Classics (London and New York: Penguin Books, 2003), 25; see also 24.

42. For many "new materialists"—Bennett, Coole, and Frost, for example—the parameters of material agencies are decidedly ethical ones.

43. Some have suggested that the scholarship of new materialisms fails to adequately address human relationalities. This perceived failure is by no means inherent to all versions of the enterprise. In many cases the distinction is artificial and highly selective. See Constance M. Furey, "Body, Society, and Subjectivity in Religious Studies," *Journal of the American Academy of Religion* 80, no. 1 (March 2012): 7–33. I am grateful to Kati Curts for pointing me toward this useful essay.

44. Mitchell, *What Do Pictures Want?,* 92–94; quotation from 92, italics added.

45. Simpson builds his case in terms very similar to those suggested six decades earlier by Stanley J. Itzerda in an essay titled "Iconoclasm during the French Revolution," *American Historical Review* 60 (1954): 25–26. For a key essay on the subject of taste and aesthetics, see Leigh Eric Schmidt, "Swedenborg's Celestial Sensorium," in *Sixth Sense Reader,* ed. David Howes (Oxford, UK, and New York: Berg, 2009), 151–181.

46. Simpson, *Under the Hammer,* 120–121.

47. Immanuel Kant, *Critique of the Power of Judgment,* in *Cambridge Edition of the Works of Immanuel Kant,* trans. Paul Guyer and Eric Matthews (Cambridge, UK, and New York: Cambridge University Press, 2001); quotations from 95 and 76, italics added.

48. Simpson, *Under the Hammer,* 133.

49. For an expanded account of two historical episodes in this process, see Promey, "Visible Liberalism."

50. This strategy of removal was by no means complete; Protestant groups also invented material and visual practices within their built environments of communal worship.

51. See Matthew Milner, "To Captivate the Senses: Sensory Governance, Heresy, and Idolatry in Mid-Tudor England," in *Religion and the Senses in Early Modern Europe,* ed. de Boer and Göttler, 307–327.

52. My summary narrative of sensory history in the next paragraphs owes almost everything to research accomplished by Constance Classen and David Howes. See especially Classen, *Color of Angels,* 6; see also Classen, *Worlds of Sense;* and see other works by Classen and Howes referenced in note 1 to this introduction. See also Alice E. Sanger and Siv Tove Kulbrandstad Walker, "Making Sense of the Senses," in *Sense and the Senses in Early Modern Art and Cultural Practice,* ed. Sanger and Walker (Farnham, UK: Ashgate, 2012), 1–16.

53. Classen, *Worlds of Sense,* 3. And see Paul L. Gavrilyuk and Sarah Coakley, eds., *The Spiritual Senses: Perceiving God in Western Christianity* (Cambridge, UK: Cambridge University Press, 2011).

54. Ibid.

55. Howes, *Sensual Relations,* 6.

56. Classen, *Color of Angels,* 1.

57. Recent scholarship in affect theory distinguishes affect from feeling or emotion; see, for example, Eric Shouse, "Feeling, Emotion, Affect," in *M/C Journal* 8.6 (2005), accessed April 1, 2013, http://journal.media-culture.org.au/0512/03-shouse.php.

58. It is worth further exploring Kati Curts's suggestion to me, in her review of this introduction, that the "diagnostic contests about which sensory regime actually reigns in modernity (the visual, the haptic, the aural, the spoken, etc.)"—as well, I would add, as the obsessive reiteration and enforcement of categorical boundaries between and among the Western canonical five senses—may be read "as yet another way that Christianity continues to 'order' not only analytic categories (religion/secular) but also human sensation."

59. Tilley, *Materiality of Stone,* 16.

60. Asad, *Formations of the Secular;* Tracy Fessenden, *Culture and Redemption: Religion, the Secular, and American Literature* (Princeton, NJ: Princeton University Press, 2007); and Gil Anidjar, "Secularism," *Critical Inquiry* 33, no. 1 (Autumn 2006): 52–77. Anidjar's essay illuminates connections of secularization narratives to discourses of orientalism.

61. See Benedict (Baruch) Spinoza, *Ethics,* trans. Samuel Shirley (Cambridge, UK: Hackett Publishing, 1992), 103. William Connolly describes a "minor Enlightenment" in the work of Spinoza and many others (including less pursued strains of "major" Enlightenment thinkers); see Connolly, "Europe: A Minor Tradition," in *Powers of the Secular Modern,* ed. Scott and Hirschkind, 75–92. Coole and Frost point their readers toward two helpful volumes on Spinoza's thought and related subjects in these regards: Jonathan Israel, *Radical Enlightenment: Philosophy and the Making of Modernity, 1650–1750* (New York: Oxford University Press, 2001), and Richard Tuck, *Philosophy and Government, 1572–1651* (Cambridge, MA: Harvard University Press, 1993). See also Anthony Synnott, "Puzzling over the Senses: From Plato to Marx," in Howes, *Varieties,* 70–71. In the first half of the twentieth century, Maurice Merleau-Ponty numbered importantly among those who offered alternatives to Cartesian views. Merleau-Ponty's work is now returning to favor among some scholars investigating perception, the body, and agentive objects.

62. William E. Connolly, *Pluralism* (Durham, NC, and London: Duke University Press, 2005).

63. For recent work on related subjects, see John Lardas Modern, *Secularism in Antebellum America* (Chicago: University of Chicago Press, 2011).

64. Susan Ridgely Bales, *When I Was a Child: Children's Interpretations of First Communion* (Chapel Hill: University of North Carolina Press, 2009), 73; see also Nicole LaBouff, "The Drama of Religious Experience in Elizabethan England: Bess of Hardwick's Memory Theater Embroideries," a lecture delivered at Yale University on February 19, 2013.

65. In addition to those already cited, I thank Jennifer Scheper Hughes for excellent conversations on closely related subjects.

PART ONE ✳ INHABITATIONS

Painters such as Mark Rothko and Jackson Pollock tackled subject matter that was too large for words. Content in my work (often, simply, the color of a thing) has tended to be idiosyncratic, sometimes too small for words. Our mother's skin is our initial universe. Though I often work from observation, I chose to remember and imagine my mom's skin color because I likened it to the grand kind of subject of the New York School of painters.   Byron Kim

This volume is organized topically and by association rather than by chronology, geography, or religious tradition. The parsing of subjects is somewhat arbitrary in the sense that most chapters might fit well under more than one of these rubrics. Despite this fluidity, the cumulative choices made have been purposeful and, I hope, suggestive of larger central issues.

The authors of the chapters in this initial part of *Sensational Religion* investigate sensory "landscapes" of personal, relational, and spatial sorts, internal as well as external to human bodies. The senses often seem to operate, in these chapters and in human life, as interface, membrane, or pivot between internal and external. In actuality, these interfaces are mutable. Internal and external are deeply intertwined, as are notions of subject and object, self and other, and thing and world.

Byron Kim's painting titled simply *Mother* seems a fitting object to open this part titled "Inhabitations," especially given that the artist depicts his mother's skin. In utero the human fetus encounters "mother" as its literal universe. Once a child is born, its mother's skin replaces one kind of haptic interiority with another, a different but still largely encompassing sensory surface and embrace. Skin is the sensory organ of touch. Some have suggested that touch is the most comprehensive of senses in that sight, sound, taste, and smell each has also to do with tactile impressions (of light on the retina, of sound waves striking the eardrum, of taste buds in contact with food or other substances, of odors reaching sensitive nasal passages). Most of the chapters in "Inhabitations" concern touch as well as sight.

Byron Kim, *Mother*, 1994. Oil on linen, 84 × 72 inches. © Byron Kim / Courtesy of the James Cohan Gallery, New York / Shanghai.

Four of these eight chapters consider sensory mediation and manifestation of spirit possession in several traditions and at different times and places. For reasons I have suggested in this volume's introduction, most of the authors of these chapters, but not all of them, deliberately take up the subject of spirit possession in modernity in the West or in conversation with the West. All four of these scholars focus attention on the places where spirit possession and material possession cross sensory paths and where each approaches questions of self-possession, of who or what is understood to inhabit, or co-habit within, human consciousness and corporeality. Each chapter considers the roles of material and performative objects in producing a sensational event.

The authors of the remaining chapters in this section extend the subject of inhabitation to include spaces, habitats, and habits of sensory engagement within them. These chapters explore the material framing of specific kinds of in-bodied spaces and of spatial boundaries felt and known. In one of these accounts, for example, the composite photograph, achieved by the superimposition of multiple images, elicits haptic imaginaries and becomes a locus of ideas about subjectivity, contingency, replication, saintliness, and social hierarchy. Other authors focus attention on the design and development of the "action office," along with desktop acts of religious display; the sensory politics of the night in the Jewish ghetto in Renaissance Venice; and the practical construction and artistic reiteration of the *eruv*. This latter topic raises the fascinating question of just how much sheer material it takes to make perceptible something that is essentially invisible.

Here issues of visuality, tactility, volition, and orientation (bodily, architectural, and environmental) coalesce. Each of these first eight authors queries and illuminates the sensory possession, marking, and interpretation of bodies, places, and neighborhoods.

SALLY M. PROMEY

2

Objects of Possession

Photography, Spirits, and the Entangled Arts of Appearance

PAUL CHRISTOPHER JOHNSON

It may be true that "photography was heir to the enlightenment project in its un-tiring urge to cancel the obscurity of the world," and in that sense was a disen-chanting machine tooled to expose the formerly mysterious and occult.[1] Yet surely that is only part of the story, since visual technologies also opened new vistas of en-chantment. Far from erasing spirit-possession practices with ideas of objective ocular truth born of the mid-nineteenth century, the birth and spread of photography helped populate the modern world with spirits and cause them to circulate. From one perspective this seems obvious enough: spirits depend on visual and material technol-ogies for their manifestation. They appear in and through bodies, things, images, and sounds. More surprising, perhaps, is the inverse point, that quests for congress with spirits took part in the rendering present of modern technologies of visualization and materialization, like photography, and of ensoniment, like phonography.[2]

Photographs are visual artifacts but also, at least prior to digital photography, material objects endowed with all the qualities of things: edges, shape, texture, solid-ity, and varying durability over time. For this reason photographs have not only visual but also haptic and even olfactory characteristics. As both an image and a thing, a photograph at once mediates something occurring elsewhere and else-when—a scene or person in a place and time different from the one in which the photograph is being viewed—and in the here-and-now, as an object that attracts my gaze, has weight in my hand, occupies space in a file, or pulls downward on the nail that secures it to the wall. The hybrid nature of being at once an image and a thing is important because it means that photographs have plural lives across multiple dimensions. One of these di-mensions is sensorial: the photograph is possessed of a visual life, a tactile life, and so forth. Another dimension is spatiotemporal: photographs enjoy a first life in relation to the time and place of their making and in relation to their framed subject, person or landscape. And they have many other possible lives enduring long after that person is dead or the landscape altered. The image-thing may circulate in new circuits of viewers or be variously archived or reproduced, reemerging a century later in a new time and place and graphic form. The plural lives of photographs are part of what has made them, since their invention, important religious tools. They work miracles of numination, rendering the departed present and animate again and again.

In the pages that follow, I consider the multiple lives of a photograph that depicts a nineteenth-century Afro-Brazilian possession priest—its social life, its ritual life, its legal life, its afterlives. Telling this story will help us reflect on the relation of religion and photographs and on the management of the religious lives of image-things. I raise the issue of "management" to signal that the coalition between photographs and spirits took shape within forceful systems of appearance—legal, social, and cultural. Photographs exerted agency and yet were far from free agents. A photograph depicting a priest's spirit powers, in this case, but also photographic powers of mediation, were constrained, regulated, and controlled. Yet it was also ritually put to work within those constraints. I explore these ideas by examining the photograph of Juca Rosa, the most notorious sorcerer (*feitiçeiro*) and spirit-possession priest of nineteenth-century Rio de Janeiro, Brazil. The photograph offers a window to a moment of social transformation and intersecting forces: the nineteenth-century abolition of slavery in Brazil and the "problem" of the assimilation and nationalization of former slaves and their religions, as well as the emergence of photography as a new technology of mediation as it was applied to Afro-Brazilian religions and to their policing. The goal is to show the relation between photography and spirit possession as intersecting and sometimes even symbiotic arts of metamorphosis, a conversion of powers unseen into things seen and heard, smelled and felt.

The Symbiotic Relation of Two Arts of Revelation

Two arts of revelation, spirit possession and photography, entered widespread public use in Brazil at around the same time, just after the middle of the nineteenth century, and their histories were closely entwined. In itself this crossing was not wholly unique. In France and the United States, for example, photography and possession were enmeshed, too, through photography's role in the popularization of spiritualism. "Spirit photography," the exposure of spirits behind or next to living subjects in portraits, was part and parcel of the expansion and public profile of spiritualism after 1860, beginning with William Mumler's images.[3] Spirit photography's influence, and then its debunking—Mumler in 1869, like Édouard Buguet in France in 1875, ultimately stood trial on charges of fraud—provided a descant to photographic portraiture in the period of the portrait market's rapid expansion from elite to middle-class use.

Like possession by spirits, photography offered a technology of memory work that was especially popular in the wake of wars and the abrupt mass mortality they caused: the Paris Commune of 1870–1871, the American Civil War of 1861–1865, the Brazil–Paraguay War of 1865–1870, and so on.[4] The early decades of photography transformed the idea of memory from an imprint of personal recollections and a consensual story cobbled together from various sources attributed with more or less legitimacy, including painted or written versions, into a "harder" idea of truth that simultaneously confirmed a world beyond. Photographs were considered to register what transpired independent of human perception; they showed not a report but what was objectively there. The first newspaper report on the camera in Brazil, from January 17, 1840, is suggestive of such optimism: "You would have to have seen it with your open eyes to have some idea of the speed and results of the operation. In less than nine minutes appeared the fountain on Paço Square, the plaza of Peixe, the monastery of São Bento, and all the other circumstantial objects, all reproduced with such fidelity, precision and detail, that one could easily see that the thing was made by the hand of nature itself, almost without the artist's intervention."[5]

This was especially the case in Latin America, where photography dovetailed with the enormous influence of Comtean positivism and its mantras of technological and scientific development in the effort to "catch up" with Europe and North America in the hierarchy of nations. The photo was a "form of expression adequate to the times of the telegraph and the steam locomotive."[6] "Order and progress," Auguste Comte's motto, eventually was even embossed on Brazil's first republican flag,[7] and photography was another signal technological advance in the march of national evolution.

Portraiture was fashionable in Brazil from the beginning. The first daguerreotype in Brazil was made in 1840, just a year after Daguerre had publicly announced his new technology in Paris. It was taken by Louis Compte, a French abbot who arrived in the Brazilian port of Salvador da Bahia on the ship *L'Orientale*.[8] Though photography was swift to arrive in Brazil, its rapid popularity was achieved in no small part because Emperor Dom Pedro II, whose reign lasted from 1840 until the end of the empire and the birth of the republic in 1889, was a science buff and genuine aficionado. At the age of fifteen, after having his daguerreotype printed in 1840 by Father Compte, he immediately purchased his own equipment. Later he commissioned daguerreotypes of all the royal family, and the new technology enjoyed a very public imperial imprimatur.[9] Because the court set the trends for the capital of Rio de Janeiro, virtually every family of means availed themselves of portraits as quickly as possible. The first portrait studio was opened in Rio in the same year, 1840. By the early 1860s, small, inexpensive cardboard-backed *carte de visite* photographs were in wide circulation among members of both the upper and the middle classes, and they were followed by the slightly larger "cabinet photographs," which were almost as popular as they were in Europe.[10] Some 90 percent of photographs taken in Brazil during this period were portraits, almost all of them in the carte de visite form and overwhelmingly devoted to the production and advertisement of "respectability."[11] They could be given to others, arranged in the salon, attached to one's front door, worn on the body, given to pay tribute, or used to arrange a rendezvous.[12] In 1870 there were 38 photographic studios operating in the central district of Rio; the number is hardly comparable with the 284 studios functioning in London at around the same time but is striking nonetheless.[13] The affordability of small photographs made them widely popular, and they transformed not only the social patterns of the living but also the relation to the dead. In Bahia, Brazil, for example, it became a common custom to photograph dead infants posed as still living and to refer to them as *anjinhos,* "little angels."[14] The photograph substituted for and rendered present the bodily presence of the departed. It was understood to retain something of the soul of the child.

Though by the turn of the twentieth century Brazil had become the center of Spiritism, a status it retains today, Spiritism did not migrate from France as quickly as photography.[15] Yet once its message began to circulate sufficiently, it found fertile ground. In part this was because it entered a society where possession by spirits and communications from the unseen world were common practices. The desirability of cultivating such communications was likewise familiar. The Brazilian anthropologist Gilberto Velho, for example, described the familiarity with the idiom of spirits and spirit possession as a "strong binding factor" for understanding otherwise heterogeneous Brazilian social experience.[16] Afro-Brazilian religions involving spirit possession, for example, were practiced, at least on occasion, by members of all ethnic groups and classes. There was widespread awareness of spirit mediumship and possession, even if it was in part coupled with representations of primitive "Africanness," at least among the upper classes. Spiritism offered the promise of Afro-Brazilian spirit-possession practices with none of the social liabilities; to the contrary, even if it was not quite respectable, it was thoroughly French, cosmopolitan, and à la mode.

Copies of Allan Kardec's *Le livre des esprits* (1857) were to be found in the capital by 1860 and were translated into Portuguese by 1866.[17] In Rio, early Spiritist groups like the Groupe Confucius, also called the Société des Études Spiritiques, were meeting by 1873. The monthly review *Revista espirita* was published beginning in 1875, and the large-scale Spiritist organization the Federação Espírita Brasileira convened at the beginning of 1884.[18] By the 1880s, Spiritism, alongside titillating reports of Afro-Brazilian feitiçeiros and *curandeiros* (healers), were everyday topics of newspaper pages as Brazil labored to define the proper limits of religion in the public sphere of the emerging republic.

I have not found evidence that spirit photography ever played an important role in Brazil, as it did in both France and the United States. However, a photo called *Portrait with Spirit,* taken by Militão Augusto de Azevedo in the then still-sleepy town of

São Paulo around 1880, depicts a satirically posed dandy with an Egyptian vase on his desk and an enormous white ghost hovering behind him. Although spirit photos may not have been taken in Brazil, there were certainly ironic "anti-spirit" photos emulating the infamous work of Édouard Buguet in Paris.[19]

Instead of through the phenomenon of spirit photos, in Brazil the co-emergence of photography and possession by spirits as linked technologies of remembering the dead took form through the early documentation and regulation of Afro-Brazilian spirit-possession practices. In the context of the waning decades of slavery and the positivist climate of order and progress, a period of defining and forming the modern republic, photography carried protoanthropological authority. Its authority, like that of anthropology, was based in the physical and temporal principle of the co-presence of the observing machine with the thing observed; like the anthropologist, the camera was *really there,* but without the biases or other frailties of the human eye. Like anthropology, the camera would help document, bound, and define human groups.[20]

Photography's role as a compiler of objective facts was applied to the juridical task of registering the religious lives of citizens, slaves, and former slaves—that is, of collecting and naming "the people." As elsewhere, in Brazil photography was central to the project of documenting and defining the nation, not only for recording and broadcasting its technological progress but for inventorying, ordering, demonstrating, and exerting control over national territory, "not just as an ally of science, but [as] an enactment of it," a control that appeared graphically in the 1882 *Anthropological Exposition* held at the Museu Nacional in Rio de Janeiro.[21] The exhibition of indigenous Brazilians, held up as both founders and sacrificial victims for the nation, was shot by Marc Ferrez, Brazil's most talented nineteenth-century photographer (and also the court photographer), and disseminated in the early photo magazine *Revista illustrada.*[22] Susan Sontag's words from a later time are nevertheless apposite to describe that vivid anthropological moment: "the most grandiose result of the photographic enterprise is to give us the sense that we can hold the whole world in our heads. . . . To collect photographs is to collect the world."[23]

It was also to gather and enforce the state, a point made clear with the first use by police of photographs of dissidents, collected in France to round up the rebels of the 1870–1871 Paris Commune,[24] while comprehensive photo albums of prison inmates were collected during the 1870s in Russia, the United States, and Brazil.[25] Nearer to my topic of the use of photographs to unveil religious motives and sentiments were the comprehensive photographic catalogs of the insane and "hysterics" assembled by Jean Charcot at his laboratory at the Salpêtrière Hospital in Paris, complete with its four-room "service photographique." The first volume of those images, *Photographic Iconography of the Salpêtrière,* appeared in 1876.[26] Charcot cast his photographs as documentary evidence expressing the spontaneous inner lives of his tormented patients, yet one cannot help but note the very performative, staged quality of these "objective" expressions, because patients were wheeled into the photographic lab and there given the props and cues for the revelations they would then proffer. The Salpêtrière's photographic service, it would seem, helped produce the very diseases it revealed.

The technology of photography was harnessed to the positivist vision of a transparently legible and fully governable world, a total world present in objective evidence, including the inner lives of persons. The total world became imaginable through the camera, among other new arts of appearance, making the camera not just a machine but also a moral artifact that set in motion manifold social, legal, and material effects. Within this new world, photographic portraiture helped to produce an image of "singular individuals endowed with interiority, and presented as though it were a fact."[27]

The manifestations of spirits, mediumship, and possession that occurred during the same period of photography's revelation of an objective evidential world would seem, then, to present a paradox. Given the apparent tension between the "religious" motives of spirit possession or mediumship and the documentary, rationalizing intent of photography, it cannot but seem contradictory, even anachronistic, to juxtapose spirit possession and photography as coeval and co-constitutive arts. But consider: spiritualists and other religionists applied the new scientific evidence provided by photographs to their own claims-making, as did the Catholic Church (see note 21): to take a very prominent example, Alfred Russell Wallace prefaced the third edition (1896) of *Perspectives in Psychical Research* with this ironclad assurance: "What are termed spirit-photographs . . . have now been known for more than twenty years. Many competent observers have tried experiments successfully." A decade later in 1908, the famous Italian criminal anthropologist Cesare Lombroso argued similarly, naming photography a "transcendental artistic power." Another decade passed and Sir Arthur Conan Doyle was still arguing the same.[28] Moreover, the followers of spirit photographers like Mumler in the United States and Buguet in France were hardly dissuaded by court testimony levied against the portraitists. Many were convinced that the spirits of the deceased appeared in spite of, or even through, practices intended to defraud clients. Photography did not disenchant the world. Rather it seems to have presented new prospects for enchantment, ones now fortified by hard visual evidence.

Another immediate objection will be that possession by spirits long predates photography's arrival in 1839. Does not possession as a phenomenon date to ancient times, to the sibyls of Greece, the demons of pagans against which the Pentecost of the New Testament defined itself, and the practices Europeans encountered on the West African coast when they arrived there at the end of the fifteenth century? To be sure. What was new in the second half of the nineteenth century was "spirit possession" as a discursive artifact, as a purportedly universal anthropological category in which diverse human societies could be joined, leveled, measured against each other. This is not the place to develop this point, but for a shorthand gloss we may take

Edward B. Tylor's 1871 *Primitive Culture,* which enshrined animism, the belief in spiritual beings, as the universal origin of religion.[29] Here was a juncture when "spirit possession" was anthropologically born, out of the same milieu and moment as spiritualism and photography.[30] The category of possession, like photography and Spiritism, served as a leveler: it funneled diverse histories and moments into standardized sets and common mise-en-scènes, pulling disparate figures and times into a familiar and contemporary form that rendered those persons, places, and times, if not equal, equivalent. Through them the world was made fundamentally *comparable.*[31]

Spirit-possession practices, like photography, enact a mimesis; they document something in the world, even as they are themselves a mode of experiencing, a mode of making, the world. Both are responses to and mediators of mortality: the spirits of Afro-Brazilian religions are deceased ancestors returned; photographs present a spirit presence, even in portraits of the living, freezing subjects to foreground their future demise. At the moment of being photographed, one becomes spectral, as a living trace of the future dead, or a "ghostly trace."[32]

We can think of spirit possession and photography as two forms of poiesis, both in Plato's sense of the kind of making that fights mortality and in Heidegger's sense of an emergence from one state to another, an ec-stasis or standing outside oneself. Spirit possession and photography are two arts, sometimes intertwined, of bringing forth or making what was hidden seen. Both are techniques of enlargement or extension of presence across space, even as a spirit's arrival and sudden departure, like the portrait of one beloved, indexes absence as much as presence. Or both absence and presence: "the advent of myself as other," to recall Barthes's memorable phrase.[33]

It was not clear how spirits or possessions would be documented once the enterprise of spirit photography was demystified for all but the most fervent devotees. With the luminous chimera silhouetted on Mumler's or Buguet's photo plates discredited, what was the look of a spirit's presence? More particularly, for my purposes here, what was its photographic look? What did the photographic look of the presence or possession of spirits *do?* To get at these issues, let us consider a conjunction between a moment of social upheaval and the spread of a new visual technology. The dramatic social change was the abolition of slavery in Brazil and its birth as a republic, along with the civil "problem" of the assimilation and nationalization of former slaves and their religions. The new technology was photography. Photography presented a new form of mediation between the public sphere and Afro-Brazilian religions. Spirit possession offered a form of mediation between Afro-Brazilians and the public sphere, too. My goal is to show the relation between photography and spirit possession as intersecting techne. To this end, I narrow my focus from the wide angle taken so far to look closely at a very specific entanglement of photographs, spirits, and law. The *spectral* and the phenomenon of "spirit possession" appeared as the conjoining of the photographic image-thing and management of the possessed at this key historical juncture.

The Case of Juca Rosa

The intersection of photographic documentation and possession by spirits may appear an arcane and obscure convergence. When we examine a widely publicized 1871 trial of an Afro-Brazilian sorcerer in Rio de Janeiro, though, it becomes difficult to avoid the conjunction of this unlikely duo. What was at stake at that moment was the question of whether Afro-Brazilians, slaves and former slaves, could become full citizens—accountable, contract worthy, rational, and autonomous but also sufficiently loyal to the nation that had once enchained them. The expansion of photography was coeval not only with the arrival and expansion of Spiritism in Brazil but also with the gradual emancipation of slaves from 1850 through 1888. Afro-Brazilians, slave and free alike, were understood as uniquely gifted in the arts of possession and, because also potentially subversive, uniquely in need of interpretation. There were state interests at stake in learning to read possession, in seeing and reforming the secret forces that lay under the skin, and, toward that end, in that inner life's anthropological documentation. Afro-Brazilians, in the age of gradual emancipation, would require strategic assimilation, containment, or marginalization—and, in any case, expanding policial and medical surveillance. What role would photographs play? Would photographic documentation of inner life indicate the sameness and equality of Afro-Brazilians, loyal citizens in the making, or catalog their essential difference as an irredeemable and politically dangerous other, an other occupied by foreign powers? The new truth-telling machine, joined to the emergent social sciences of anthropology and criminology, offered the promise of rendering internal states, mental capacities, even religious sentiments, in visual form.[34]

To set a broad-brush historical frame: in Brazil, emancipation was a long, drawn-out process. While slave shipping was officially illegal after 1836, at least *para inglês ver* (for the English to see), it continued with only partial disruption from the British navy until 1850. After 1850, the shipment of African slaves mostly ceased, but the institution of slavery and the internal trade in slaves continued, a great migration from the northeastern sugar zones of Bahia and Pernambuco to the burgeoning coffee plantations in the southeastern states of Rio de Janeiro and São Paulo. Slaves who fought in the war against Paraguay from 1865 to 1870 were offered their liberty, but the old institution's grip began to be loosened only with the 1871 "Law of the Free Womb," though the law was already hotly debated by 1868. Full emancipation was decreed with the "Golden Law" of 1888. The first of these laws bestowed freedom on the newly born; the second abolished slavery completely. At the precise moment when the Law of the Free Womb was being debated, and then passed, the most notorious nineteenth-century case of illegal fetishism was being tried in Brazil's capital, Rio de Janeiro.

The case of José Sebastião Rosa, known as Juca Rosa, has been masterfully documented by Gabriela dos Reis Sampaio, and I follow her work closely here, adding notes from my own reading of the archive.[35] First the bare bones: Juca Rosa was born of an African mother in 1834, father unknown. In his early adult years he earned a living as a tailor and a coachman. By the 1860s he had acquired a following as a possession priest of remarkable skill. In 1870 Rosa was anonymously denounced and then, following an investigation and trial, sentenced to six years of prison and hard labor, until 1877. For a full year prior to his sentencing, the story of the celebrity feitiçeiro was front-page news. The mere name *Juca Rosa* was a fulcrum for gossip about Afro-Brazilian religions and their place in the emerging nation. Central to the Juca Rosa "event" were issues of class, sex, and race conjoined most dramatically in accusations of José's deflowering of several white women and his marriage to a Portuguese *senhora*. Also present were issues of religion and national identity. Especially noted was Rosa's "theft" of Catholicism—the fact that he performed baptisms and marriages and used Catholic saints in an African possession religion, taking control of the look of the saints but then insidiously transforming them from within.[36]

That Rosa was routinely possessed by foreign spirits was also a subject of particular concern. As one newspaper article put it, "The sorcerer says he is inspired by an invisible power that is not God, nor any saint known to us."[37] Another public prosecutor, Antonio de Paula Ramos, summarized the matter as follows: that the defendant presented himself as master of supernatural powers; that, dressed in a "special manner" before the altar of Our Lady of the Conception, he celebrated crude ceremonies, then claiming to be inspired and infallible by virtue of this illuminated state—with "saint in the head"—and, as a result of this special status, received money and presents. Through claims of spirit knowledge, he "deceived [the] uncultivated, weak and superstitious spirits [of his followers]."[38]

A key part of the accusation, whether under the antiquated legal terms of sorcery or the new ones of fraud, rested on the issue of possession, the moment when Rosa donned a special outfit, assumed a new persona—"saint in the head"—and spoke in a supernatural voice and authority with which he deprived weaker spirits of their rational judgment and autonomy, whether in matters of goods or love. Here was a subversive "social adventurer," as he was called, taking over the national body by sabotaging its rational direction and assuming its controls from within, during a period of rupture, the crisis of emancipation.

Juca Rosa's Photograph

Juca Rosa's case is unique in the legal files of the period by virtue of its inclusion of a small-sized photograph (Figures 2.1 and 2.2) of the accused, found by the police in the home of one of his followers, and the use of the photograph in the process of acquiring depositions from witnesses.[39]

What can be observed about the photograph? Its material form is that of the carte de visite, the small portrait produced in sets of eight per photo plate and popu-

FIGURE 2.1. The photograph of Juca Rosa as I encountered it in the case file in spring 2010. Arquivo Nacional, Rio de Janeiro.

FIGURE 2.2. The same image of Juca Rosa as in Figure 2.1, digitally edited and reproduced in Gabriela dos Reis Sampaio, *Juca Rosa: Um pai-de-santo na Corte Imperial* (Rio de Janeiro: Arquivo Nacional, 2009), 188.

larized in the late 1860s. The distribution of such photo-cards would have been affordable for someone of Rosa's resources given his wide network of clients, at least some of whom were wealthy, though the bourgeois pastime of exchanging such cards must have been somewhat unusual for Afro-Brazilians. More surprising than the mere fact of Rosa's use of photo-cards is the pose he elected to depict, and crafted with care. Most cartes de visite exchanged in Brazil offered sober portraits of the subject, almost always alone, in noble dress and posed against one of several standard backdrops available in the many portrait studios. Portraits of slaves taken during the period had no poses or bucolic settings; rather, they were photographed in documentary, "anthropological" style, in plain unadorned garb and wielding the tools of their labor. Rosa's photograph, by contrast, portrays him and a companion standing on a proscenium painted with flowers, set against a bare white background, creating a space that is unusually open. The open space is filled by what can only be called a ritual situation or its imitation. A follower, João Maria da Conceição, kneels before Rosa on the proscenium —perhaps in homage, deference, or supplication or to graphically present a ritual hierarchy—and points toward him with a staff. Sampaio finds it likely that the staff was a drumstick called a *macumba,* as was the drum it struck to call down the gods in ritual events.[40]

And yet, despite the action conveyed by the photo, it is silent in its "fact making."[41] We know that Juca's clients possessed this photograph and that Rosa also had photos of all his clients. Their uses remain opaque to us. Still, the threats reported by one Leopoldina in her deposition hint that holding images of persons may have been a means of ritually controlling them. On this score, writes Mattjis van de Port, "The 'photographic real' was picked up in religious-magical practices, where it came to substitute [for] the body."[42] Photographs were even used in place of wooden body parts as ex-votos left in churches testifying to the occurrence of miraculous healings.[43] In that spirit, Rosa may have used carte de visite photographs of his devotees as proxies for their bodies. By ritually acting on a photograph for harm or benefit, he would affect the person pictured as well; several depositions state that Rosa admitted as much. Juca Rosa's photograph may also have served as a bodily proxy that extended his presence and power into clients' and devotees' homes.

The photograph held a quite different meaning for the police, as a testament to the performance of illegitimate ritual and potentially illegal practices. For the police investigation and then in the trial, the photo served as visual evidence of Rosa's possessions, the fact that he ritually engaged African spirits on behalf of clients from whom he then profited, with the issue of profit being key to the accusation of *charlatanism.*

The investigator and then the public prosecutor seem to have been little interested in the songs that were sung during the rituals, for example, or the foods that were prepared and offered to the saints. No descriptions of drums or icons or food entered the record. Rather, the investigation was resolutely focused on the question of Juca's posturing as one wielding spirits and able to exact undue fealty from his followers based on that power. Interrogations of Rosa's ritual family, moreover, emphasized the photograph as well. If the photograph helped to produce new modes of sociality and religious experience, its material form also neatly fit the procedures of "police work" as that bureaucratic system was coming into being.[44] The object's flat shape and flexible paper construction made it a congenial fit for the hand in interrogations and for the flat, rectangular shape of "the legal file" in the long term. This quality of the image-thing's material "fit" in the court file is what still today allows me access to the photograph, unlike anything else that may have been confiscated during Rosa's arrest. Thus there was a symbiosis between the photo and the surrounding text in terms of filing systems and bureaucratic institutions, two emerging technologies of the nation-state in 1871. The attraction of the photograph—not just as a revelatory thing but also as an archival thing, an evidentiary thing, a neat, compact, and clearly bounded thing —was at least part of what led authorities to focus on it in the case. But what, exactly, did it give evidence *of?*

At a specific moment in ritual gatherings in the home of one of his devotees (Henriqueta Maria de Mello), Rosa would retreat to a separate chamber in the company of a woman named Ereciana in order to change to his special attire of blue corduroy and silver fringe. Upon reemerging, he was transformed into a powerful authority named Father (*Pai*) Quimbombo; he would then fall to the floor and be "taken" (*tomado*) by a range of additional spirits—among them "Santo Zuza" and "Pai Vencedor."[45] The photograph depicting Rosa wearing the vestments of possession provided the evidence, and it was used to cue verbal depositions by witnesses confirming what transpired. Key to the investigation were descriptions of the process of Rosa's transformation from rational individual into a person possessed, wearing the garments that appear in the photograph.

Rosa never confessed. In his second interrogation, when asked about the special garments, he negated their ritual use. He claimed that they were a Carnaval costume ("mandou fazer essas vestimentas e as possuía para usar pelo Carnaval"). When asked to explain his possession of the photographs of many of his followers, he insisted it was just for play or a joke (*chalaça*). And of course, there were no "live" photographs of Rosa in the state most in question, that of being possessed.[46]

Before photographs of live ritual action in photojournalistic style, which emerged in the interwar period circa 1930, something as abstract as spirit possession could be read only from its external visual cues and their narration.[47] Without such an image, inspectors and prosecutors used Juca Rosa's portrait to try to discern the *look* of possession—evidence of one who works with a "saint in the head" (*santo na cabeça*). They found all the requisite parts of the accusatory narrative: "African" garments, primitive acts (indexed by bare feet), the tools for a drumming ceremony, unwarranted social hierarchy, hidden powers (associated with the mysterious sack hanging from Rosa's belt), and inexplicable Afro-Brazilian self-aggrandizement. Rosa had, after all, gone to a studio and carefully staged this portrait. *Who did he think he was?*

Why did Juca Rosa have the portrait made? One reason was likely for the solidification of his authority and the extension of his priestly presence. Other additional uses seem likely, especially in view of the small pouch Rosa hung from his belt as a symbol and source of material power. Sampaio points out the similarity to Central African *nkisi* (a spirit or the object that a spirit inhabits). I think this is not too far-fetched given that most enslaved Africans in Rio were taken from that region; Rosa's mother at least was very likely of Kongo ethnicity, especially given that the name Rosa adopted when possessed, Quimbombo, also suggests a Central African origin.[48] This possible nkisi might change how we think about Rosa's photos, both the ones he distributed and the ones he collected. A photograph of someone could be used against him or her via contagious magic, much as could a hair clipping, a piece of clothing, or the person's signature or written name. This is why Rosa had photos of his devotees and clients. Images, understood to contain something of the person they represent, could be used to exert power over someone, for good or ill. Photographs were religious tools that cut in at least two ways: they circulated a public persona, anchored memory, and solidified reputation and pedigree, but they were, and are, also ambiguous, dangerous things that had lives of their own and could be turned against the person so pictured.[49]

Conclusion: The Photograph as Ritual Tool

Both the spiritualists' and Juca Rosa's contentions that photographic portraits manifest and transmit power were correct, if not necessarily for the reasons given. Wittgenstein's notes on Frazer's *Golden Bough* remind us that it is not necessary to resort to "magical" explanations for the power of photographs, since actions we take toward them contain their own satisfaction—burning, kissing, arranging, or hanging photos creates an experience of emancipation, intimacy, or order.[50] This must have been so for Rosa's followers, who felt his presence near in his image. Photos circulate beyond the scenes of their making, granting them unintended powers. They make secret things potentially public, and their circulation cannot be easily managed. For practitioners of subaltern religions, there is a history of the threat posed by photography. For at least a century in Brazil, roughly from 1871 to the 1970s, photographs could be and were used as evidence in police cases against sorcery and, later, fraud. That memory persists in spite of Candomblé's recent popular acclaim and transformation into national "patrimony." Photographs were strictly forbidden during my initiation into Candomblé, for example, and photographs of states of possession were always forbidden. That does not mean that photos were completely banned. To the contrary, by 1890 stately portraits of temple founders graced the walls of ritual spaces as indexes of *axé* (transforming power) in the sense of the authority created by proper lineage, and also as advertisements of a given house's prestige. And the "possession shot" became standard by the late 1940s, as in this photo by Pierre Verger (Figure 2.3), and in a thoroughly evidentiary way.[51]

Here Verger's subject is in the midst of an initiation during which she learned to properly incarnate the god of love, beauty, wealth, and fresh water, Oxum. Note the portraits, including photographs, of prominent priestesses from the past that were hung on the wall behind the initiate. The photographs of former and current priestesses announce the prestige and tradition of the temple (*terreiro*) to the public and through them help to constitute the temple's legitimate genealogy (*axé*). The portraits are not only records of the past; they also circulate axé, as life-force, in the present.

The Juca Rosa photograph, likewise, was not just a document of past events, it was a vital actor in everything that transpired in the case. It was repeatedly animated by various frames of speech and action. One might even suggest, expanding further, that technologies of recording possession and playing it back to its actors, extending

FIGURE 2.3. One of many photographs of spirit possession taken by the French photographer Pierre Verger, this one shot at Candomblé Cosme, Salvador, Bahia, sometime between 1946 and 1953. Used with permission of the Fotos Pierre Verger ó Fundação Pierre Verger.

spirits' possible reach through secondary semiosis, began to play an important role in constituting what it means to "be possessed" in the age of mechanical reproduction. This was certainly true of Spiritism. Kardec, despite his misgivings about the premature promotion of spirit photography as evidence, incorporated photographic terms into his depictions of the appearance of spirits as "an image daguerreotyped on the brain" (in *Le Livre des mediums* [1861]). Or, as he wrote in *La Genèse* (1868), "As thought creates fluidic images, it is reflected in the perispital envelope as in a mirror; it is embodied and in a sense photographs itself there."[52]

In fact, spirits have never appeared but through techne of their unconcealing, whether bodies, cameras, or computers, and the manifesting materials are always changing, producing spirit possession differently over time. Michel Leiris, writing about the moment in which he took his possession photograph in 1931, describes the subject as a *poseur* speaking with a "voice like a phonograph."[53] But was he a poser before the Frenchman pointed his camera at him, or did his spirits begin to "pose" and speak like a phonograph when Leiris appeared carrying gear that would register and reproduce his spirits far from where they were first performed, extending his power to act across time and space almost infinitely?[54] Leiris recorded another moment when the magnesium flash of his colleague Marcel Griaule *caused* a spirit to appear in response to the apparent military danger.[55]

Or consider the words of a practitioner of Brazilian Umbanda residing in Portugal as she details her experience of possession:

> All my friends in the *terreiro* [temple of Candomblé] that see my *pomba gira* [female spirit] tell me how nice and funny she is, and how she helps women getting over their ailments. I have even asked them to take a photo of her when she incorporates me, so that I can have an idea what she looks like. I know it is my body, but one does not know what happens: the *time-lapse of incorporation* is like a blank. . . . I just feel a little trembling and dizzy afterwards, but at the same time one has a great feeling of peace and having done something worthwhile, being incorporated by such important entities. [Ana, 24, university student][56]

The famous photographer Pierre Verger offered yet another example: "The *adosu* [new initiate of Candomblé] can be compared to a photographic plate. He holds within the latent image of the god, at the moment of initiation imprinted on a virgin spirit innocent of any other imprinting, and this image reveals itself and manifests itself when all the right conditions are reunited."[57] Reaching beyond the Afro-Atlantic traditions, Tanya Luhrman interviewed a member of the Chicago Vineyard Church who described the vividness of his/her prayer life as "almost like a Power-Point presentation."[58]

The spirits and the Holy Spirit are now rendered present and interpolated through the conventions of the photographic view, a process that began in the time of Juca Rosa. These technological mediations of spirits do not diminish their religious significance, but they change it. Recently the anthropologist Katherine Hagedorn explored how Afro-Cubans performing in folkloric shows or documentary films requiring faked Santería rituals are often really possessed by the gods as they attempt to mimic their bodily movements.[59] Hagedorn is interested in how these stagings are infiltrated by the real, but it would seem that we could invert this to explore how "real" possession is increasingly infiltrated by media to become spectacular performance. Here again, Barthes's term "spectrum," combining spectacle and the return of the dead, as spectre, is apposite.

"What does my body know of Photography?," Barthes began his reflection on the splintering of his person into its images, each of which seemed to "freeze" and carry off a part of him into arcs of actions out of his control. His body no longer seemed to be quite his own, and it was not. He was, in part, a *zombi*—his body and its work become the captured property of other masters. Possession priests know this better than anyone, for their bodies are never solely "their own." The experience of losing ownership of one's body in both photography and spirit possession presents a symmetry and, at least sometimes, a symbiosis. Through the study of a photograph confiscated in 1871 I have tried to show that photography had dramatic effects on the making and regulation of a certain set of possession practices. Obviously, police, priests, tourists, ethnographers, and others came to know and regard possession differently through the agency of photographs. But, even more, photography and the photographic look of being possessed infiltrated religious practice itself as its meanings were increasingly experienced as if it were seen photographically and verbally narrated in photographic terms. Just as early photography was touched by the traces of spirits, spirit possessions were now summoned by flashbulb explosions, "time-lapse incorporation" exposures, carefully staged portraits on a proscenium, and PowerPoint presentations. Possession occurred using photographic techniques that enabled the gods to appear.

If Juca Rosa's body was confined, its portrait guarded a life of its own. It laid low for more than a century, but now it is going wild:[60] it hails me from a snug berth between old yellowed pages. Seeing an opening, it leaps out and runs, and now the drums are rising. With a single look back from under his silver-fringed cap, Pai Quimbombo burns the case file to dust and heads off to find new stages on which to appear, and act.

NOTES

1. Beatriz Jaguaribe and Maurício Lissovsky, "The Visible and the Invisibles: Photography and Social Imaginaries in Brazil," *Public Culture* 21, no. 1 (2009): 175–209, 177.

2. On photography and materializing spirits, see, inter alia, Fritz Kramer, *The Red Fez: Art and Spirit Possession in Africa* (London: Verso, 1987), 257. On spirits and phonography, see Stephan Palmié, "The Wizard of Menlo Park, the Ejamba of North Fairmont Avenue and the Dialectics of Ensoniment: An Episode in the History of an Acoustic Mask," in *Spirited Things: The Work of "Possession" in Afro-Atlantic Religions,* ed. Paul Christopher Johnson (Chicago: University of Chicago Press, 2013).

3. Crista Cloutier, "Mumler's Ghosts," in *The Perfect Medium: Photography and the Occult,* ed. Clément Chéroux, Andreas Fischer, Pierre Apraxine, Denis Canguilhem, and Sophie Schmit (New Haven, CT: Yale University Press, 2005), 20–28.

4. But more, photography revealed what the naked eye cannot see, presenting an *agenda of the invisible,* as Lissovsky put it: "The history of 1800s photography was marked by this agenda of the invisible: spirit portraits, the dissection of movement by Muybridge and Marey, the iconographies of the insane and the sickness of the soul (Hugh Diamond and the assistants of Jean Charcot), the inventories of criminal types, ethnographic photography," translation mine. In Maurício Lissovsky, "Guia prático das fotografias sem pressa," in *Retratos modernos,* ed. Cláudia

Beatriz Heynermann and Maria do Carmo Teixeira Rainho (Rio de Janeiro: Arquivo Nacional, 2005), 2. See also Ian Hacking, *Rewriting the Soul: Multiple Personality and the Sciences of Memory* (Princeton, NJ: Princeton University Press, 1995), 5.

5. From the daily *Jornal do comércio,* January 17, 1840, translation mine. The original Portuguese reads, "É preciso ter visto a cousa com os seus próprios olhos para se fazer ideía da rapidez e do resultado da operação. Em menos de nove minutos, o chafariz do largo de Paço, a praça do Peixe, o mosteiro de São Bento e todos os outros objetos circunstantes se acharam reproduzidos com tal fidelidade, preçisao e minuciosidade, que bem se via que a cousa tinha sido feita pela própria mão de natureza, e quase sem intervenção do artista."

6. Ana Maria Mauad, "Imagem e auto-imagem do Segundo Reinado," in *História da vida privada no Brasil,* vol. 2: *Império: A corte e a modernidade nacional,* ed. Luiz Felipe de Alencastro and Fernando A. Novais (São Paulo: Editora Schwarcz, 1997), 191, translation mine.

7. On November 19, 1889. "Order and progress" was derived from the phrase "*L'Amour pour principe; l'Ordre pour base; le Progrès pour but,*" which appeared as the epigraph on the title page of Auguste Comte's 1851 *Système de politique positive, ou traité de sociologie, instituant le religion de l'humanité* (Paris: Larousse). Robert Levine notes that even through the 1890s photography continued to be understood in Latin America as a "compiler of facts." Levine, *Images of History: Nineteenth and Early Twentieth Century Latin American Photographs as Documents* (Durham, NC: Duke University Press, 1989), 60. In Europe and the United States, by contrast, photography's use had shifted dramatically to take on the role of social critic in addition to the role of harvester of the "neutral" document, though as Susan Sontag noted, photography never is wholly stripped of the authority it gained as the register of something that was *really* there, no matter how creative and interpretive it becomes. Sontag, *On Photography* (New York: Farrar, Straus and Giroux, 1977), 11.

8. See Gilberto Ferrez and Weston J. Naef, *Pioneer Photographers of Brazil, 1840–1920* (New York: Center for Inter-American Relations, 1976), 14. Almost simultaneous with Daguerre and wholly independent of him, a French émigré who arrived in Brazil in 1824 named Antoine Hercules Romauld Florence appears to have also invented what he called "photographie" in the town of Vila São Paulo. That village, now called Campinas, is in the state of São Paulo. See, inter alia, Levine, *Images of History,* 7–9, and Mauad, "Imagem," 187.

9. Nancy Leys Stepan, "Portraits of a Possible Nation: Photographing Medicine in Brazil," *Bulletin of the History of Medicine* 68, no. 1 (1994): 137.

10. The small, 2.5- × 4-inch cartes de visite photos and the much less expensive wet-plate process used to make them were patented in Paris in 1854 by André Adolphe E. Disdéri and popularized after Napolean III had one produced in 1859. Eight shots would be printed from a single plate, making them much less expensive to reproduce than earlier portraits. They took both Europe and the Americas by storm in the 1860s, becoming a standard currency of social exchange and inspiring an early culture of celebrity with the circulation of photos of royalty. See Levine, *Images of History,* 24. Cabinet-cards, which eclipsed cartes de visite by the 1880s, were produced by the same process but were larger, 6.5 × 4.5 inches.

11. Jaguaribe and Lissovsky, "The Visible and the Invisible," 178.

12. Mattijs van de Port, *Ecstatic Encounters: Bahian Candomblé and the Quest for the Really Real* (Amsterdam: Amsterdam University Press, 2011), 85.

13. On Rio's data, see Mauad, "Imagem," 199. The comparative data between London and Rio appear in Pedro Karp Vasquez, *Dom Pedro II e a fotografia no Brasil* (Rio de Janeiro: Fundação Roberto Marinho, 1985), 20.

14. Vailati, as cited in van de Port, *Ecstatic Encounters,* 85.

15. Brazil's version of "Spiritism," as the religion is referred to in Brazil (not Spiritualism, as

it was called in its North American version), was very much the French sort, heavily dependent on the writings of Kardec and the tinge of French positivism.

16. Gilbert Velho, "Unidade e fragmentação em sociedades complexas," in *Duas conferências,* ed. Gilberto Velho and Otávio Velho (Rio de Janeiro: UFRJ Editora, 1992), 27, 34, 41. "Identificamos a crença em espíritos e em possessão como um forte fator aglutinador de um universo sociologicamente heterogêneo . . . da metrópole brasileira contemporânea."

17. Marion Aubrée and François Laplantine, *La table, le livre et les esprits: Naissance, evolution et actualité du mouvement social spirite entre France et Brésil* (Paris: J. C. Lattès, 1990), 110.

18. Ibid., 112–114; Emerson Giumbelli, *O cuidado dos mortos: Uma história da condenação e legitimação do Espiritismo* (Rio de Janeiro: Arquivo Nacional, 1997), 56, 61; David J. Hess, *Spirits and Scientists: Ideology, Spiritism, and Brazilian Culture* (University Park, PA: Pennsylvania State University Press, 1991), 86.

19. The Militão photograph *Portrait with Spirit* (1880) appears in Gilberto Ferrez and Weston J. Naef, *Pioneer Photographers of Brazil, 1840–1920* (New York: Center for Inter-American Relations, 1976), 69. Like Mumler in the United States, Buguet was accused of fraud for posing as a medium and pretending to produce spirits in his portraits. Upon interrogation, Buguet immediately confessed, explained how he had achieved the illusion, and, once freed, reopened his studio as an "anti-spirit" portrait shop where he offered portraits of the client with the overtly declared illusion of any spirit desired. His business card of 1875 read, "Photographie Anti-Spirite: Manipulation invisible. Le Spectre choisi est garanti. Illusion compléte." In Clément Chéroux, "Ghost Dialectics: Spirit Photography in Entertainment and Belief," in *The Perfect Medium: Photography and the Occult,* ed. Clément Chéroux, Andreas Fischer, Pierre Apraxine, Denis Canguilhem, and Sophie Schmit (New Haven, CT: Yale University Press, 2005), 50, and Cathy Gutierrez, *Plato's Ghost: Spiritualism in the American Renaissance* (New York: Oxford University Press, 2009), 69–71.

20. On the co-making of anthropology and photography, see Elizabeth Edwards, ed., *Anthropology and Photography* (London: Royal Anthropological Institute, 1992), especially the chapter by Christopher Pinney, "The Parallel Histories of Anthropology and Photography," 74–95. Spiritualism, too, claimed a positivist stance: "As a means of elaboration, Spiritism proceeds in exactly the same course as the positive sciences; that is to say, it applies the experimental method." Allan Kardec, *Genesis, the Miracles and the Predictions According to Spiritism* (New York: Spiritist Alliance, 2003 [1868]), 18.

21. The quote is from Stepan, "Portraits," 138. The issues of national evolution and progress appear in the choice of subject matter among nineteenth-century photographers in Brazil, who often favored shots of technological progress—a coffee plantation, a mine, a locomotive, a new tunnel, a modern city block—and national types—the slave, the Indian, the European immigrant family. João Vasconcelos argues that this new "programme of truth" applied to even domains recalcitrant to its logic. Thus the new Catholic assertion of papal infallibility (at the First Vatican Council, convened by Pius XI and ending in 1870) was accompanied by the evidence of the Virgin's apparition at Lourdes, which confirmed the change. Modern "disenchantment," Vasconcelos argues, was characterized not by the decline of religion per se but by its submission along with the rest of the world to the regime of evidence. João Vasconcelos, "Homeless Spirits: Modern Spiritualism, Psychical Research and the Anthropology of Religion in the Late Nineteenth and Early Twentieth Centuries," in *On the Margins of Religion,* ed. Frances Pine and João de Pina-Cabral (New York and London: Berghahn, 2007), 13–38.

22. Jens Andermann, "Espetáculos da diferença: A Exposição Antropológica Brasileira de 1882," *Topoi—Revista de história* 5, no. 9 (2004): 128–170. Noteworthy in the exposition was the absolute absence of persons of African descent in this museological and photographic casting of national origins.

23. Susan Sontag, *On Photography* (New York: Farrar, Straus, and Giroux, 1977), 3.

24. Ibid., 7. Disdéri took portraits of the dead in their coffins. With up to 40,000 deaths, spirit photography surged as an attempt to revive and retain those killed; the same occurred in the wake of World War I.

25. Lilia Moritz Schwarcz, "Além do enquadramento: Em Paris ou no Rio de Janeiro, fotos de presos revelam muito mais do que a identificação de 'vagabundos,'" *Revista de história,* 2011, accessed February 2, 2012, revistadehistoria.com.br.

26. Georges Didi-Huberman, *Invention de l'hystérie: Charcot et l'iconographie photographique de la Salpêtrière* (Paris: Macula, 1982). Didi-Huberman argues that police photography and medical photography can be seen as a compound medicojudicial program that gave birth to a field, and rubric, of *criminal anthropology.*

27. Patricia Lavelle, *O espelho distorcido: Imagens do individuo no Brasil oitocentista* (Belo Horizonte: UFMG, 2003), 24–25, translation mine.

28. Alfred Russell Wallace, *Perspectives in Psychical Research* (New York: Arno Press, 1975 [1896]), xiv. Cesare Lombroso, *After Death—What?: Spiritistic Phenomena and Their Interpretation,* trans. William Sloane Kennedy (Boston: Small, Maynard, 1909), 167. Doyle explained in detail how it worked: "Here, as in other tests, it is evident that we are dealing with a substance invisible to the eye, and one that is self-luminous, and which reflects upon photographic plates rays of light to the action of which our retina is insensible, and which is formed in the presence of certain mediums, or psychics, and has such photochemical energy as to enforce the development of its own image before other images, and also has a progressive development." Ibid., 261. Arthur Conan Doyle, *History of Spiritualism* (Cambridge, UK: Cambridge University Press, 2011).

29. For example. "In the year 1861, at the south of the Lake of Geneva, there might be seen in full fury an epidemic of possession worthy of a Red Indian settlement or a negro kingdom of West Africa." In the passage, Europeans, Amerindians, and Africans are drawn into the same comparative frame via "possession." Edward Burnett Tylor, *Primitive Culture* (New York: Harper, 1958 [1871]), 141. As George Stocking documented, Tylor considered "spiritualism" for his overarching rubric but found it already coopted by the popular movement. Tylor visited numerous spiritualist séances in London and was ambivalent about the veracity of the spirits he viewed in those sessions. Stocking also notes the interest of Radcliffe-Brown, another of anthropology's founding fathers, in mesmerism two decades later. George Stocking, "Animism in Theory and Practice: E. B. Tylor's Unpublished 'Notes on Spiritualism,'" *Man* 6 (1971): 88–104.

30. Or better, born again, since possession first was posited as a protoanthropological human universal by Hobbes. On this longer genealogy, see Paul Christopher Johnson, "An Atlantic Genealogy of 'Spirit Possession,'" *Comparative Studies in Society and History* 53, no. 2 (2011): 393–425.

31. Sontag shows how the material form of the photograph facilitates the arranging into rows, columns, and pages of various shots—Woodstock, Viet Nam, Prague, fashion, first communion, retirement, a burning house, the Eiffel Tower, skiing; all events, public and private, are equal currency in the powerful hands of the photographer. At least this was part of the myth and marketing of the camera. In *On Photography,* 11.

32. On photography and becoming spectral, see Roland Barthes, *Camera Lucida,* trans. Richard Howard (New York: Hill and Wang, 1994 [1981]), 14. On photography and the ghostly trace, see Sontag, *On Photography,* 9.

33. Poiesis gestures here especially toward Heidegger's idea of ecstasies as a breaking forth from one state into another and to Plato's idea in the Symposium of "making" as a quest for immortality. Michael Lambek used the term in his essay "The Sakalava Poiesis of History: Realizing the Past through Spirit Possession in Madagascar, *American Ethnologist* 25, no. 2 (1998): 106–127.

The idea of the photograph as "the advent of myself as other" appears in Barthes's *Camera Lucida,* 12. The phrase "photographic ecstasy" appears on the last page of the same work. Ibid., 119.

34. This was true not only of the moment of the birth of anthropology. Photography is still often viewed in these terms, as that which reveals the unseen. Mary Price quotes a contemporary photographer, Yousuf Karsh, and then criticizes his view: "Karsh says, 'This is the portrait of a harmonious soul revealing itself unconsciously in song.' But as an example of 'the invisible target,' the secret that can be surprised under the mask, it is too bland. That look of abstraction is characteristic not only of a harmonious soul but of a woman who has just begun to wonder whether she turned the stove off before leaving home." Mary Price, *The Photograph: A Strange, Confined Space* (Stanford, CA: Stanford University Press, 1994), 124.

35. Gabriela dos Reis Sampaio, *Juca Rosa: Um pai-de-santo na Corte Imperial* (Rio de Janeiro: Prêmio Arquivo Nacional, 2007).

36. Here is an example of the accusation of the "theft" of Catholicism: the lead inspector, Miguel José Tavares, wrote in the opening pages of the case file, "The audacity and perversity of these criminals goes to the point of involving our Holy Religion in its infamous practices, succeeding in substituting it with the most crude and abject superstition" ("A audacia e perversidade d'estes crimiosos chega ao ponto de involver a nossa Santa Religião em suas practices infames, consequindo substituila pela mais grosseira e abjecta superstição"). And, a few pages further on, "Rosa dares to make use of the images and names of the saints of the Catholic Church, in order to take advantage of even the religiosity of his victims, which he transforms into the crudest and vilest superstition" ("Rosa atreve-se a servir-se de imagens e do nome de Santos da Igreja Catholica, afim de aproveitar-se até da religiosidade de suas victimas . . . religiosidade que elle transforma na mais grosseira e vil superstição").

Not incidental in these discourses is the debate over what constitutes "religion." We might say it was being worked out in these documents. The defense lawyer, Fillipe Jansen de Castro Albuquerque Junior, rejected the notion that Rosa was guilty based on a what he called a specious opposition between "sorcery" and "religion": "This fame, this power, these wonders, when tolerated and not suppressed by the police, repeated over many years, will elevate these 'sorceries' to a 'belief' or 'religion.'"

37. "O feiticeiro . . . para tudo tem poder, porque o seu santo tudo sabe, tudo ouve e tudo conta. . . . O feiticeiro diz-se inspirado por um poder invisível que não é Deus, nem santo do nosso conhecimento." *Diário de notícias,* October 2, 1870. In Sampaio, *Juca Rosa,* 40.

38. One of these "weak spirits" was Leopoldina Fernandes Cabral, who told Tavares that even when she wanted to break free from Rosa's influence, she could not because he had threatened her, "telling her that if she does (leave), he, with the spirit that he ruled for good as for harm, would disgrace her and make her end up at Mercy Hospital." Sampaio, *Juca Rosa,* 99.

39. Despite the ample photographic documentation in João Reis's magisterial 2008 work on the ladino African priest in Bahia, Domingos Sodré, no comparable sort of incriminating photograph—a photograph used in the forensic process of unraveling secret ritual procedures—is present, nor am I aware of any other comparable photograph. João José Reis, *Domingos Sodré, um sacerdote Africano: Escravidão, liberdade e candomblé na Bahia do século XIX* (São Paulo: Companhia das Letras, 2008).

40. Sampaio, *Juca Rosa,* 185–189.

41. "Silences . . . enter the process of historical production at . . . the moment of fact making (the making of the *sources*)," not to mention in their assembly in an archive, their retrieval, and their narration. In Michel-Rolph Trouillot, *Silencing the Past: Power and the Production of History* (Boston: Beacon Press, 1995), 26.

42. Van de Port, *Ecstatic Encounters,* 87.

43. Martins, in ibid., 85.

44. Holloway finds that Afro-Brazilian religions were rarely directly policed in Rio during the nineteenth century except when they intruded on "what the white elite considered a necessary level of social peace and public calm." Thomas H. Holloway, "'A Healthy Terror': Police Repression of Capoeiras in Nineteenth-Century Rio de Janeiro," *Hispanic American Historical Review* 69, no. 4 (1989): 645. I would argue that the Juca Rosa case marked the beginning of the problematizing of Afro-Brazilian religions as emancipation neared and those religions would become part of "national" life.

45. Sampaio, *Juca Rosa*, 186.

46. Even two decades later, when Nina Rodrigues, the psychiatrist and first "anthropologist" of Afro-Brazilian religions, brought one young woman into his office during the 1890s and, first inducing hypnosis, caused her to be possessed by a god, there is no photographic record. Given the effort he made to control and document trance states, he almost certainly would have photographed her if he could have, but his documents are accompanied only by stills of statues and ritual implements.

Photographs of trance in ritual action began to be taken after 1930, enabled by higher-speed film, new repeating cameras made by Leica and Rolleiflex, and the flashbulb, a set of advances that generated the birth of "photojournalism." See Lisa Earl Castillo, "Icons of Memory: Photography and Its Uses in Bahian Candomblé," *Stockholm Review of Latin American Studies* 4 (2009): 17. To my knowledge, the first spontaneous photograph of spirit possession occurring in ritual action was published in the ethnographic of Michel Leiris. The photograph was taken in Ethiopia on September 27, 1932, and published in *L'Afrique fantôme*. Michel Leiris, *L'Afrique fantôme* (Paris: Gallimard, 1981 [1934], 388, plate 26.

47. The problem, as Juca's defense attorney pointed out, was that the police investigation and initial denunciation were all carried out within an antiquated legal framework, namely the Portuguese Filipino Code. Thus the issue of *feitiçaria* was foregrounded, though it was harnessed to nineteenth-century ideas about social contagion. The modern and "Brazilian" category was fraud (*estelionato*), hinging on the fact of profiting from the business. The judge agreed with the defense's argument that *feitiçaria* was an invalid legal category; nevertheless, he condemned Juca for the full term, based on the fact of his being a "*true* fraud." What is the role of the photograph here? Among other things, it serves as a hinge or shifter from the earlier Filipino code outlawing working with spirits to the modern Brazilian Criminal Code outlawing pretending to work with spirits for monetary gain. The new crime was not possession but rather fraud, *acting* possessed.

48. From *kingombo,* the Kimbundu term for okra. The word also appears in Cuba, as *quimbombó.* See Stephan Palmié, *The Cooking of History: How Not to Study Afro-Cuban Religion* (Chicago: University of Chicago Press, 2013), 307–308.

49. As the culture studies scholar of Brazil Lisa Earl Castillo suggests, the role of photographs is conflicted even in present-day Afro-Brazilian religion. Contemporary participants in Candomblé often seem to understand photographs to not merely represent or copy their subject but to retain the person's substance. On this score, Castillo cites Barthes, *Camera Lucida,* on the idea of the photograph as *Spectrum,* a spectacle that not only recalls but also reconjures the dead. Castillo, "Icons of Memory."

50. "To burn an effigy. To kiss the picture of the beloved. This is naturally not based upon a belief in a certain effect on the object which the picture represents. It aims at a satisfaction and also obtains it. Or rather it aims at nothing at all; we act in such a way and then feel satisfied" Wittgenstein's comments on Frazer are recounted and analyzed in Stanley J. Tambiah, *Magic, Science, Religion, and the Scope of Rationality* (Cambridge, UK: Cambridge University Press, 1990), 59.

51. Roger Bastide's classic 1953 essay on possession in Candomblé, for example, uses Verger's possession photos as evidence of the "complete modification" of the person, narrating the appearance of the gods (*orixás*), "as the photographs show." "When an individual is possessed by Ogum, it matters little whether male or female, their face immediately takes on a terrifying look, *as the photographs show;* the person incarnates brute force, the genius of war and the magic of domination." Bastide, "O cavalo dos santos," in Roger Bastide, *Estudos Afro-Brasileiros, 3. Série* (São Paulo: Universidade de São Paulo, 1953), 50–51, translation and italics mine. What is striking here is that *the photographs show* the complete and authentic transformation of the human being by virtue of the terrifying expression that appears on the face; the captions name only the god present, not their human carriers. It is as though no human subject or agent were present at all. The camera verifies the inner state, documenting the expression that shows the spirits' presence as plainly as it did in the studios of Mumler and Buguet. "Possession" became the favored subject by around 1950 and continued to be applied as visual evidence of an internal state. The "possession shot" remains the most desired target of camera-toting tourists visiting temples of Candomblé in Bahia today, setting up nearly routine confrontations between initiates and visitors based on contrasting notions of what photographs *are* and are *for,* a conflict over putative intent played out for probably the first time with Rosa's image in the police file.

52. Both citations appear in Chéroux, *The Perfect Medium,* 48.

53. In *L'Afrique fantôme,* 499.

54. Compare Barthes: "Once I feel myself observed by the lens, everything changes: I constitute myself in the process of 'posing,' I instantaneously make another body for myself." In *Camera Lucida,* 10.

55. Michel Leiris, *La possession et ses aspects théâtraux chez les Éthiopiens de Gondar* (Paris: Librairie Plon, 1958), 64.

56. Clara Saraiva, "Afro-Brazilian Religions in Portugal: Bruxos, Priests, and Pais de Santo," *Etnográfica* 14, no. 2 (2010): 275, italics mine.

57. Pierre Verger, *Notas sobre o culto aos orixás e voduns* (São Paulo: Editora USP, 1998), 83, translation mine.

58. Tanya M. Luhrmann, "How Do You Learn to Know That It Is God Who Speaks?," in *Learning Religion: Anthropological Approaches,* ed. David Berliner and Ramon Sarró (New York and Oxford: Berghan, 2007), 92.

59. Katherine J. Hagedorn, *Divine Utterances: The Performance of Afro-Cuban Santería* (Washington, DC: Smithsonian, 2001), 11.

60. I take the phrase "going wild" in this sense from Birgit Meyer, who writes of Protestants in Ghana who understand portraits of Jesus as possessing the possibility of "going wild" as hidden spirits use the eyes of the painting, even ones of Jesus, as tools for looking at and acting on humans. Meyer, "'There Is a Spirit in That Image': Mass-Produced Jesus Pictures and Protestant–Pentecostal Animation in Ghana," *Comparative Studies in Society and History* 52, no. 1 (2010): 100–130.

3

"Soft Warm Hands"

Nineteenth-Century Spiritualist Practices and the Materialization of Touch

MICHELLE MORGAN

Though it is often relegated to secondary status as a basis for knowledge, touch is a common subject in religious material culture. Jewish religious practices use a *yad*—which literally means "hand" in Hebrew—to point to and follow the scriptural lines of the Torah, ensuring that human flesh does not contaminate sacred scrolls while still signifying the possibilities of touch and contact. In Muslim, Hindu, and Kabalistic practices, the *hamsa,* or Hand of Fatima, works as an amulet to ward off the evil eye. Images of hands pressed together in prayer are a common Christian motif, reproduced everywhere from chalkware statuettes to bumper stickers. Each of these hands points, figuratively and literally, to a sum larger than its parts. If, as religion historian David Chidester, argues, "religious tactility is ultimately [about] the capacity to handle the challenges of living in the world, especially the challenges posed by what cannot be seen or heard," the hand and its representative correlates are chief vehicles for representing this touch-based capacity for religious belief and knowledge.[1]

In the United States during the nineteenth century, Spiritualism incorporated hands into its material practices as a means to convey a theory of touch. At its core, Spiritualism advocated direct contact with the spirit world, making, perhaps, its touch-centric practices less surprising.[2] Still, few scholars have taken Spiritualist touch seriously as a subject of inquiry. In his landmark study of Spiritualism, R. Laurence Moore claims that its downfall as a religious movement came from its lack of a philosophy.[3] Yet Spiritualists *did* have a philosophy—one not only embedded in belief and practice or simply a form of spiritual-scientific empiricism but one concerned with the body, the senses, materiality, and human perception as they participate in the production of religious knowledge. In fact, Moore quotes contemporaneous writers on Spiritualism, who repeatedly attested to the "sensuous materialism" and "truth by the testimony of the senses" that functioned as Spiritualists' operational framework, and he notes that theirs was a "religious faith based on seeing and touching."[4] Despite this apparent acknowledgment of Spiritualism's sensory-based theoretical claims, historians of Spiritualism have not often examined the material and sensory cultures that shaped that faith, more often stressing, at the expense of these embodied and sensory concerns, the technological, "scientific," and industrial objects and metaphors, such as the telegraph, that marked many Spiritualist practices and metaphors.[5] Yet sensory perceptions—in this chapter, touch specifically—were not simply the means through which belief and proof of the spirit world were made manifest materially but also functioned, with their attendant material cultures, as the very "stuff" of which that philosophy about the spirit world was constructed. Indeed, as Robert Cox argues, at the "core of Spiritualist experience . . . social boundaries of all sorts were conceived of and experienced with reference to the body and physical and emotional sensation."[6] These physical sensory frameworks cannot be separated so easily from the technological emphasis that figures prominently in both Spiritualists' practices and the secondary literature on the history of Spiritualism.

Spiritualism as most scholars recognize it was born in 1848 when Margaret and Kate Fox, two young girls living in Hydesville, New York, heard a series of rappings emanating, they claimed, from a murdered peddler who had died in their home.[7] Over the course of the nineteenth century it became a national and transnational movement and attracted millions of followers.[8] As in the case of any popular belief system, the reasons for Spiritualism's appeal and swift development are numerous, with cultures of sentimentality figuring prominently. Molly McGarry argues that Spiritualism tapped into and mediated tensions in the sentimental cultures familiar to most nineteenth-century people. In her view, increasing urbanization and industrialization during the nineteenth century made sentimental cultures of mourning—wearing black, braiding the deceased's hair into jewelry and other memento mori, and, not least, the expectation that people would move through the grieving process relatively quickly—inadequate for dealing with the pain those left behind felt after a loved one's death. With industrialization fragmenting communities that had previously shared the burden of mourning collectively, individuals found themselves lacking a wider support system and ill equipped to deal emotionally with the loss of family and friends.[9] Spiritualism offered the possibility that the dead had not completely departed but had simply crossed a threshold into another world.[10] Communication with this other world and those inhabiting it was the key tenet of Spiritualist practice. Reaching across the space that separated this sphere from the next meant finding new ways to facilitate contact; touch was foremost among Spiritualists' strategies.

This chapter charts the "stuff" that facilitated that contact as it appeared over the course of the century, looking at a variety of sensory materials that foregrounded touch and did so using the human hand as its instrument. Reports in newspapers, magazines, and Spiritualist books discuss otherworldly hands manifesting visually but also in a variety of touch-centric ways. Even in vision-centered spirit photographs, touch and hands commonly appeared. At midcentury, the planchette, a material object on which people would place their hands to facilitate communication with spirits, became the focus of a virtual media frenzy. Later in the century, William Denton's 1875 experiments at Paine Hall in Boston ushered in another touch- and hand-centered form through the materialization of paraffin spirit hands. Across this wide range of evidence, the sense of touch in Spiritualist practices demonstrates the relationship between sensory practices and materiality in the nineteenth century.

"Soft Warm Hands": Spiritualist Manifestations of Touch

Of all the images and objects left in the wake of Spiritualism, spirit photography has garnered the most scholarly and popular attention.[11] The ghostly images captured on photographic plates signified both a fascination with new technologies and concerns over the "other side." The possibility of proving the existence of spirits and communicating with them was not limited to the photographic medium, however. Samuel Morse's single-wire telegraph also became a metaphor for communication, and leading Spiritualist weeklies, such as the *Spiritual Telegraph,* made explicit the connections between technology and contact. Even the rappings that ushered in the era of Spiritualism were understood within the terms offered by Morse code.[12] While the historical literature on the relationships among photography, technology, and Spiritualism is rich, however, shifting attention to hands—a decidedly human instrument —allows us to focus on the undertheorized sensory material components of Spiritualist practices that coexisted in a framework parallel to explicitly technological ones.

In *The Book of Touch,* sensory history scholar and anthropologist Constance Classen writes: "Touch is not just a private act. It is a fundamental medium for the expression, experience and contestation of social values and hierarchies. The culture of touch involves all of culture. Yet at the same time we live in a society of the image, a markedly visual culture, in which, while there may be many representations of touch, there is often nothing actually there to feel."[13] Many nineteenth-century Spiritualists would have disagreed with Classen wholesale. Hands and touch were often figured in spirit photography and thus seem to confirm Classen's claim that Spiritualists required visible proof of the tactile (Figure 3.1). But this interpretation of spirit photography fails to listen to the voices of Spiritualists themselves. Epes Sargent, a prolific writer on all matters pertaining to Spiritualism, explicitly states the importance of hands and touch to Spiritualism, writing in the aptly titled *The Proof Palpable of Immortality* (1876): "One of the most common of the phenomena of Modern Spiritualism has been the appearance of hands, believed to be materialized by spirit power, and therefore called spirit-hands." Briefly discussing spirit hands molded from paraffin wax in

Denton's experiments in Boston (to which I will return later in this chapter), Sargent continues: "The experiment is a step in the same direction with spirit-photography, of the reality of which we have ample proof."[14] Sargent, in other words, noted that the "proof" of spirit photography was but one component of many other proofs—those that the manifestation of hands made both literally and figuratively "palpable" throughout the history of Spiritualism.

Even when Sargent is offering a deceptively straightforward account of the vision-privileging medium of spirit photography, touch figures centrally. He writes:

> Professor W. D. Gunning (1867) relates an instance in which a spirit-hand appeared on the photograph of a young girl. He says, "While sitting before the camera, she was smitten with partial blindness. She described it to me as 'a kind of blur coming suddenly over her eyes.' She spoke of it to the artist, who told her 'to wink and sit still.' In developing the plate, he noticed an imperfection, but did not observe it closely. He sat the girl again, and took a sheet of eight tintypes. She felt no blur over her eyes, and there was no blur on the pictures. The artist now examined the first sheet, and found hands on the face and neck of every tintype, eight in all!"[15]

"Smitten with partial blindness," the young girl in this narrative loses the sense most linked to the process of photography—vision. Her blurry vision is repeated or paralleled in the testimony of the photographer, who notices an "imperfection" on the original plate but remains, correspondingly, "blind" to it until later in the process of developing the image. What results are images of spirit hands touching the girl's face and neck, again in repetition. Touch and a concomitant loss of vision manifested in spirit photography through the hand are the constitutive proof, moreover, of the existence of spirits. Indeed, as art historian Michael Leja notes, many Spiritualists believed that it was not simply the presence of spirit hands *in* a spirit photo but precisely the figure of the spirit *touching* the sitter that proved to mid-nineteenth-century audiences that spirit photographs were not frauds.[16]

Beyond photography, nineteenth-century accounts of spirit hands are filled with examples of the felt, embodied, sensory qualities of tactile communication with those who had departed to the other side. Emma Hardinge Britten, a Spiritualist and the first historian of the movement, offers in *Modern American Spiritualism: A Twenty Years' Record of the Communion between Earth and the World of Spirits* (1869) countless descriptions of haptic spirit contact. In fact, during the moment of Spiritualism's "founding," she tells us, the Fox sisters were grasped by "cold hands."[17] From this early example in Hardinge Britten's compendium of spirit manifestations, descriptions of hands touching believers proliferated exponentially.[18]

Instead of looking to spirit photographs of hands as evidence of communication between this world and the next, however, Hardinge Britten accumulated and retold stories of séances she gleaned from both the Spiritualist and the mainstream press, such as one reported by the *Hartford Times* on March 18, 1853. In this account of a séance, a spirit asks a group of six people in attendance, "How many hands are on the table?" When they answer, "Twelve hands," the spirit replies that there are, in fact, thirteen:

> And there, sure enough, on that side of the table which was vacant, and opposite to the medium, appeared a *thirteenth* hand! . . . To make sure that we were not deceived or laboring under a hallucination, we counted our own hands, which were all resting in sight upon the table. There it was, however, an arm and a hand, the arm extending back to the elbow, and there fading into imperceptibility. . . .
>
> The hand . . . was seen to take the bell from the table and place it in the hands, first of one, and then of another of the party. At length it was placed in mine; but, slipping my hand over the bell, I grasped the hand that held it, desiring some more tangible knowledge of its character than that afforded by sight. It was a real hand—it had knuckles, fingers, and fingernails; and what was yet more curious (if possible) it was soft and warm, feeling much like the hand of an infant, in every respect but that of size.[19]

Virtually every component of hand manifestation and tactile contact is present in this account—the hand is "real" but not real, it is soft and warm, it can be touched and felt, and it visually fades. Most important, the author "desires more tangible knowledge than that afforded by sight." Rather than trust a visual "hallucination," the narrator must touch the hand presented to the group. Vision is presented as either inadequate or untrustworthy in matters of spiritual proof; although vision initially suffices (the séance's participants all see the hand, and speak of it, to "assure" each other of its "reality"), ultimately it is touch that must meet the material physicality of the hand.[20]

In other accounts, spirit touch manifests in conjunction with dazzling visuality. Leah Underhill (née Fox) wrote of an experience she had during a séance with Robert Dale Owen in which a female figure materialized, holding or illuminating from her palm a brilliant box of light. After requesting that the spirit touch her, she describes feeling a "human hand laid on my head"; moments later, she states: "I *felt,* and simultaneously *heard,* just behind the point of my [left] shoulder, a kiss imprinted. I could not, for any physical fact, obtain the evidence of three senses—sight, touch, and hearing —more distinctly than in this case I did."[21] The spirit figure remained ultimately indiscernible in face and personality to Underhill in this particular séance, drowned out from her visual field by the light emanating from its hand, but nonetheless it proved all the more real to her with its tactile, embodied contact.

If most spirit hands seemed quick to appease human desire for communication in relatively pleasant ways, others were not always so congenial. Hardinge Britten reprints several instances of spirit hands slapping, pinching, and hitting people, positioned in her text as a kind of spiritual tomfoolery but perhaps less welcomed by those whose bodies were painfully touched by these unearthly hands.[22] One story that made the print circuit, about the well-known Ohioan farmer-cum-medium Jonathan Koons, is representative. As in many nineteenth-century séances, the spirit hands at Koons's séance were asked to write. While watching the hand write with "a rapidity that no mortal hand can equal or come near to," one particularly intent séance participant held his head so close that the spirit rapped him on the nose with the pencil before continuing. The séance came to an end with "the hand . . . presented to each one in the room, and shaken by all save one, who was too timid to receive it. As before, it was deathly cold, but firm, and as solid . . . as a human hand."[23]

Words and images were also "written" on the bodies of mediums, though in these cases the hand that produced the writing was never visible, and neither were sensory perceptions beyond vision. Hardinge Britten tells of an individual whose friend had been shot through the heart; the friend asks "Miss Coggswell," a medium from Vermont, to help communicate with the departed: "There stood out boldly, raised above the ordinary surface of [her] arm, the figure of a human heart, clearly defined and painted in blood! But what was most remarkable of all was the very distinct appearance of a wound in the heart, as if made by a bullet."[24] The narrator of this account assures readers that "this medium has no disagreeable sensations in the production of these writings; and, if I mistake not, she has no peculiar sensations at all."[25]

Hardinge Britten's most fascinating example of spirits writing on mediums' bodies involves an "illiterate" house servant who manifested on her arm a picture of a shackled slave kneeling and praying, surrounded by the words "A Poor Old Slave"; this occurred in the presence of an individual the reader is meant to presume was Frederick Douglass.[26] Unlike the soft and warm (or, alternately, cold and solid) hands of spirits, and also unlike the temperamental pokes, pinches, and raps on the nose, the drawings and words do not appear to cause most of Hardinge Britten's mediums any harm or unpleasant sensations. This form of touch, in other words, is "senseless." It is the hand itself or its interaction with material objects that offers the physical resistance necessary to experience; words and images are hardly the only medium for the formulation of religious belief in Spiritualist practice.

Planchette; or, the Despair of Science

Spirit writing, of course, was not usually executed on the Spiritualist's actual body. In many instances ghostly hands penned messages from the spirit world while hovering over séance tables. Spirit writings also manifested through the mid-nineteenth-century explosion in the use of the planchette. Epes Sargent began the first of his histories of American Spiritualism, *Planchette; or, the Despair of Science* (1869), with the following claim: "The future historian of the marvelous cannot well avoid some mention of the planchette or 'little plank.' For his benefit, we will remark that the year 1868 witnessed the appearance of the planchette, in great numbers, in the booksellers' shops of the United States."[27] Twenty years after the Fox sisters realized a method for communicating with spirits through raps (which, of course, are another tactile, as well as auditory, phenomenon), the planchette arrived to facilitate further contact.

At first glance, the planchette (Figure 3.2) appears to be as exactly what it is: the precursor to the Ouija board plank used, in the popular game, since the turn of the twentieth century.[28] In this more contemporary form, as a plastic play piece in a children's game, this small board garners scant attention. During the mid-nineteenth century, however, the planchette caused considerable consternation and debate in both Spiritualist and scientific circles. According to Kate Field's *Planchette's Diary* (1868), a daily record of the author's early experiences with the planchette, it came to the public's notice in the United States through the English author and women's rights activist Henrietta Camilla Jenkin's novel *Who Breaks, Pays* (1861).[29]

Indeed, reports on the subject of the planchette proliferated throughout 1867–1869. The first mention in the American popular press appeared on November 30, 1867, in *Every Saturday: A Journal of Choice Reading*. The article, titled simply "Planchette," details the author's encounter with the "heart-shaped board" while vacation-

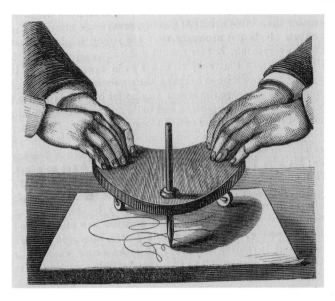

FIGURE 3.2. Planchette. From *Scientific American* (July 8, 1868).

ing in Scotland; the friend who introduced the author to the board claimed to have brought it "from America, where, he said, it was not only common, but was by many implicitly believed in as something preternatural."[30] This suggests (the author's ignorance notwithstanding) that the planchette had not yet garnered much attention in the mainstream press but was widely known in some circles. *Every Saturday* avoided passing judgment regarding whether the planchette could write out messages from the spirit world. However, this was not the case in the next report on the planchette, "A Three-Legged Impostor," which also appeared in *Every Saturday*.[31] From this point forward, the planchette found "her" way into scientific as well as popular circles, with an ambivalent article appearing in *Scientific American* (July 1868), a "five column . . . serious consideration" titled "Planchette: What Is It?" in the *Boston Journal of Chemistry* (September 1868), a tongue-in-cheek account of its "evil" intentions in the *San Francisco Daily Morning Chronicle* (November 1868), a skeptical piece in the *Ladies' Repository* (November 1868), a relatively positive review in the *Round Table* (December 1868), an "objective" account of its merits and demerits in *Putnam's* (December 1868), an admonishing and probably fictionalized account—presented as first-hand reporting—of its inherent capacity for fraud and deception in *Harper's New Monthly Magazine* (December 1868), and a nine-page diatribe against "superstitious" Catholics —who invested too much energy and concern in both Spiritualism and the planchette —in *Hours at Home: A Popular Monthly of Instruction and Recreation* (February 1869).[32] By the 1870s, a notice in *Every Saturday* remarked that the planchette had spread to India, where, the author surmised, "if it domesticate[s] itself as a god . . . it would not be at all surprising." Following that lead, *The Eclectic Magazine of Foreign Literature* used the planchette's supposed popularity in China as early as 1843 to argue that it was Chinese in origin (and that hence nothing good could originate from China).[33] This concern with the planchette is outlined here not to belabor the point that it achieved popular presence in public conversation during these years but to delineate the diversity of opinions about and frameworks within which the planchette was received, discussed, examined, and used.

Though its French and feminine suffix -*ette* caused most commentators to claim that the planchette probably came from France, what mattered to many nineteenth-century Spiritualists and non-Spiritualists alike was not necessarily its origins but the remarkable abilities it manifested. What matters for contemporary scholars of the sensory and material cultures of religion is the window the planchette provides into nineteenth-century Spiritualist beliefs about sensory perception and materiality. It was almost universally described as "heart-shaped," with two "pentagraph" wheels (the latest development in industrial technology, which allowed it to move quickly and with barely any force across a sheet of paper) and a hole (sometimes lined with India rubber) through which a lead pencil was placed, and much attention was given to the materials from which the board was made. Oak, mahogany, ash, pine, cedar— no wood seemed inadequate to the task at hand, and indeed, some reports mentioned that the diversity of materials from which it could be made allowed families in all income brackets to afford "a household god" (or "diabolical oracle") of their own, in some cases manufacturing planchettes out of "cigar-box lids."[34] As a human organ–shaped vessel made of organic material wedded to pentagraph wheels, the planchette embodied the simplest of handicrafts melded with sophisticated production techniques. Crucially, it was a *heart-shaped* instrument of writing and communication, mediating spiritual and textual contact between worlds. And, perhaps most important, the heart-shaped planchette functioned in Spiritualist religious practice as a material object that communicated not with Deity but with others *like the users* who had passed on.[35]

Yet something unique occurred with the planchette, anomalous to it out of all the instruments developed in Spiritualist practice to communicate with spirits during the nineteenth century and separate from the messages it scrawled out (moodily and petulantly at times, foolishly and inanely at others, and usually correct only half of the time, according to Spiritualists and skeptics alike). This simple board was, repeatedly and persistently, personified as a human entity and even accorded agency.[36] Field's introduction in *Planchette's Diary* set the tone for what presented itself over and over again as an anthropomorphic reading of the object: "Planchette emerged from her box. Mr. N. was no less curious than myself, and very soon we sat like two idiots, gazing intently upon the absurd creature, each with a hand upon her back."[37] In one newspaper article, the author tells us that he "purchased the fair siren . . . and even gave a little dinner-party in her honor."[38] And in almost every instance, regardless of genre, the planchette was not introduced by the article *the* in front of the noun but was usually named, like a female person, minus the article: simply "Planchette."

"Planchette," as the press reported widely, required not just the touch of human hands to work, however, but also the concerted will and intellectual effort of those near it. More specifically, it *responded* to individuals in ways quite distinct from the spirits themselves. Spirits might manifest, they might appear in photographs, they might even cause objects to move independent of any human faculty. Indeed, they often inhabited the planchette itself and scrawled out messages in various handwritings, depending on whatever spirit personality was possessing the board at any given minute. But the planchette was singular in that it not only required a confluence of all other Spiritualist phenomena to work—it served, that is, as the ultimate "instrument" bridging the agency of spirits, the agency of humans, and the agency of objects into one particular field of perception—but it was also repeatedly treated as an individual *separate* from the spirits working through it.

For example, planchettes were known to choose owners, working for some mediums and not others, usually developing attachments to individuals like prized pets. At times this led to awkward syntax and confusion for authors writing about the board as they struggled to keep the planchette's "identity" separate from that of the spirit speaking through it and the person touching it. In Spiritualist practice the planchette became something more than an object—it became a person, a thing with subjectivity and moods of its own, with distinctive calligraphies independent of the medium's; it was, again, heart-shaped, an "absurd creature" humanized by touch, dependent, even, on the human hand and thought to move and become an animate, even at times a thinking, object. The planchette, in other words, set and "conditioned" the limits of Spiritualist practice as it engaged and "sympathized" with materiality—not simply as evidence or proof of the materiality of the other side but as proof of the dependence on materiality to mediate that communication on this side as well.[39]

Sargent claimed as much, writing about materiality and spirit in *Planchette; or, the Despair of Science:*

> We know just as much about spirit as we do about matter. It is true that we know nothing of the essence of spirit: it is equally true that we know nothing of the substance or essence of matter. But perhaps the reader will say, "We cannot see spirit, and, therefore, we know but little about it." "Did it ever occur to the reader," asks a scientific writer, "that we cannot see matter either? When we look at any object, it is not the object, after all, that we see, but merely the image of it formed on the retina of the eye. When I look at a house a mile distant, the object that I really see is not a mile distant, but within the eye. I do not see the house at all, but I see an

image of light representing the house. Thus it appears that matter is just as invisible as spirit. We know some of the properties and laws of spirit, and this is precisely the extent of our knowledge of matter."[40]

Though in some ways Sargent's words sound like standard Spiritualist rhetoric designed to counter scientific claims about the lack of "evidence" Spiritualists provided for their beliefs, I take seriously here what Sargent has to say about spirit and matter, particularly because it occurs in a text that names the planchette in its title and questions the primacy of vision. Sargent rightfully questions the meaning of matter itself, positing that the privileging of sight and vision has led people to believe that they are seeing a real "thing" in the first place. Indeed other, more "scientifically minded," Spiritualists echoed his thoughts on spirit and matter in similar terms. The most prominent chemist of the antebellum period, Robert Hare, wrote and published extensively on the existence of "ponderable and imponderable matter," positing that spirits consisted of a form of matter beyond the grasp of current scientific understanding but not entirely beyond experiential witnessing through mediumship and other practices; Hare came to his conclusions after a much-publicized and (to the scientific community) scandalous conversion to Spiritualism.[41] Yet for most Spiritualists, it was the immediacy of touch, in conjunction with various manifestations of materiality, that established proof of the other side. Sargent's use of the planchette in a text ultimately only peripherally concerned with it further suggests the important role touch played in establishing a theory of matter, sensory perception, and religious or spiritual belief.

The question remains as to why the planchette was anthropomorphized to the extent that it was. The answer lies with industrialization and processes of production and commodity fetishism emerging during this period, particularly as they acted in conjunction with the Spiritualist aim to make contact with the dead. Moore warns against using "social and economic change" during the nineteenth century as an explanation for the rise of Spiritualism, arguing that although both "characterized the decade in which the Fox rappings first aroused public interest, [they] characterized all the other decades of the nineteenth-century as well."[42] It nonetheless seems that the anthropomorphizing of the planchette was part of a material- and sensory-based process that helped orient nineteenth-century individuals to these changes, especially as they met the challenges of producing, consuming, and using material goods and questioned the superficiality and glib cultures of sentimentality around death. Sentimental commodities were also produced, after all, because they were meant to signify outwardly what was largely an inward experience.[43]

For example, though supposedly more than "200,000" planchettes were manufactured and sold in the United States, they were also repeatedly presented as objects not of mass production but of craftsmanship.[44] To understand the significance of this, recall Field's animation of the planchette as an "absurd creature" upon whose back she and Mr. N. placed their hands. In her analysis of the "interior structure of the artifact," Elaine Scarry argues that "we routinely speak of certain artifacts as 'expressing the human *spirit*,' a statement that would be impossible to formulate in terms of bodily location . . . [since] many inventions exist that have no specifiable precedent in the body." Inversely, she tells us, the "shape of the hand and back" in Marx's work must also "be centrally described in terms of the bodily capacity for *labor*." Finally, Scarry argues that "by transporting the external object world into the sentient interior, that interior gains some small share of the blissful immunity of inert inanimate object-hood; and conversely, by transporting pain out onto the external world, that external environment is deprived of its immunity to, unmindfulness of, and indifference to-ward the problems of sentience." Such projection, Scarry claims, aims "*to deprive the external world of the privilege of being inanimate.*"[45] This transference or projection of indifference and unmindfulness onto an external object might help explain, in part, why the planchette was so often described as responding to questions in a silly, rude, or apathetic manner—as though the object was taunting people for their concerns in an increasingly commodified and commodity-filled existence. But it also demonstrates the remarkable adaptability of nineteenth-century users in imagining a hand- and touch-based communication that resisted the stressors of mass production and the commodification of sentimentality, grief, and mourning. Mediating between multi-ple worlds, the planchette represents the sensory and material practices of a belief sys-tem that was held in dynamic tension with the demands of a world many feared would become increasingly anonymous vis-à-vis mass production and commodification.

Wax Hands, the Thermodynamics of Touch, and Outward Contact

What happens, however, when the hands in question are physical, residual material objects or artifacts left behind by a spiritual entity? Turning to a body of materials closely aligned with spirit hands but given less focused attention in the Spiritualist press—paraffin or wax molds of spirit hands produced by nineteenth-century medi-ums—allows us to focus on relatively permanent artifacts of "proof" as they directly engage hands and touch. These iterations of hands are an associated but divergent form of the manifestation of spirit hands and the use of human hands for spiritual purposes, as seen in the hand contact needed to make the planchette function. Indeed it seems as though the longer Spiritualism persisted, the more it required palpable, material "proof" of the veracity of its claims.

Well known in the annals of Spiritualist manifestations are William Denton's experiments. Through the medium Mary Hardy, Denton conducted an experiment on the stage of Paine Hall in Boston in January 1875 during which a pair of spirit hands was created out of paraffin. When Denton took the stage, he aimed to publi-cally demonstrate something new—spirit hands molded of wax.[46] Denton was an accomplished geologist, and his early work, as explicated in his text *The Soul of Things,* focused on "reading" the "panorama" of distant locations and times by placing relics and geological specimens of those places and times in the hands of mediums who did not know the origins of the pieces they were holding.[47] By touching and holding these geological specimens in their hands, Denton's mediums—most notably his wife and sister-in-law—were able to visualize the histories of the places from which the specimens originated. Prior to his work in wax, Denton claimed to "have seen spirit-hands over and over again" and had even "taken impressions of them in flour and putty and clay."[48] But on this night, he produced via the medium Hardy what were touted as the first pair of spirit hands in wax.

Part of the allure of wax spirit hands was not only the residual proof they left in the wake of their manifestations—here, indeed, were material objects that could be exhibited and wondered over—but the supposed blending of spirit and medium that inhered in these molds. Functioning as veritable tactile portraits of contact between the spirit and profane worlds, wax hands were the culminating Spiritualist product of a theory of sensation and materiality developed over the course of the nineteenth century. The process by which spirit hands were molded is interesting, because it attests to the texture, detail, and thermal qualities of both the casting process and the resulting casts. Two buckets were set next to each other, one filled with hot water and one with cold, and paraffin was placed in the hot water in order to melt it. Alternately dipping a hand into the hot and then the cold water caused cumulative layers of wax to build up and harden, leaving a paraffin glove behind when the hand was removed from the mold. *The Encyclopedia of Occultism and Parapsychology* (1920) claimed that it took twenty minutes for a mold to be made thus, and that for preservation purposes the molds would be filled with plaster.[49] Finally, to discern the idiosyncrasies of any given mold, the wax was melted from the plaster, leaving the impression of the skin's surface—the *inside* of the wax mold and ostensibly the epidermal pattern unique to the owner of the hands—preserved on the outside surface of the cast hand. Holding a plaster cast of a spirit hand would produce a textural mingling of skin surfaces similar to that which would arise from holding hands with another living human.

In manufacturing spirit molds, the *Encyclopedia* asserted, "normal production" methods were "defied." Unlike the relatively straight fingers of human casts, in casts of spiritual hands "fingers are bent, wrists show, and the mould is fine and delicate, whereas those obtained from living hands are thick and solid." The production of spirit hand molds was also "remarkably quick." In the Denton experiment specifically, "the dish of paraffin was weighed before the mould appeared and after," a control test that apparently proved satisfactory, since "the difference corresponded to the weight of the mould." The writer of the *Encyclopedia* entry further remarked that "the plaster casts show a blend between the organism of the medium and the organising force which produces the materialization."[50] The ramifications for a theory of the sense of touch are profound. Not only dynamically melding spirit and material beings into one, the processes involved both hot and cold water as well as wax and made explicit the parallel thermal qualities repeatedly mentioned in earlier descriptions of the warmth and coldness of spirit hands. The interplay of interiority and exteriority made itself felt—the inside literally became the outside, with the resulting texture of the plaster further open to interpretation as individuals could touch and run their fingertips over the cast hand's veins, fissures, and bumps.

This sensuous play of spiritual contact and communication—in this case of external, objective physical existence if not internal, subjective, certitude—is even more poetic when set in contrast to traditional Christian iconographies of hands. Outside of Spiritualist practices, Christian iconography typically represents hands clasped together in prayer. The image of the praying hands holds its own kind of poiesis, as the sense of touch doubles back on itself, inwardly directing the palm against the palm, even as it signifies an outward reach toward God. But in Spiritualist iconographies of the hand, touch almost radiates outward, connecting to others both in the séance circle, as participants grasp each other's hands in a circle and maintain contact, and in the casts of spirit hands, where the material and the spirit are wedded to form one entity. Spiritualist touch is, in fact, a deeply outward-oriented process.[51] As Eve Sedgwick tells us in *Touching Feeling,* "Even more immediately than other perceptual systems . . . the sense of touch makes nonsense out of any dualistic understanding of agency and passivity; to touch is always already to reach out, to fondle, to heft, to tap, or to enfold."[52] The nineteenth-century Spiritualist seemed to credit, through material objects of touch that joined hands to spirit, a theory of sensory perception that attested to individuals' relationships to matter, spirit, and one another.

This philosophy of the sense of touch separated Spiritualists sharply from the empirically driven scientists of their day, even as they partook in the same positivist framework. While Spiritualists clearly engaged in a "religion of proof," their world was also one frequently engaged with the sense of touch in ways that incorporated touch *as* proof and not outside of it. Spiritualist touch, indicated and experienced through hands and various material mechanisms associated with hands, explained the most intimate details of Spiritualist practice and belief. More than smell, more than sight, more than taste, and more than sound, touch ordered the material world, animate and inanimate, and served as a bridge that connected virtually every experience Spiritualists had between this world and the next. Touch allowed nineteenth-century Spiritualists to reach back temporally, making "histories and bodies touch across time"; it offered a reading of the surface of the external world even as it enveloped and incorporated external phenomena inwardly through the very same actions and movements.[53] The sense of touch, most importantly, offered religious proof of another world; as Yi-Fu Tuan writes, "Touch is the sense least susceptible to deception and hence the one in which we tend to put the most trust. For doubting Thomas, seeing was not believing; he had to touch the wounds of the resurrected Christ to believe. The real, ultimately, is that which offers resistance. The tactile sense comes up *against* an object, and that direct contact, sometimes felt as harsh impingement, is our final guarantee of the real."[54] Forging a philosophy of materiality and the sense of touch, Spiritualists "proved" the existence of the other side through material objects and a theory of sensory contact in ways that differed fundamentally from those in the vision-driven, "empirical" world around them.

NOTES

1. David Chidester, "The American Touch: Tactile Imagery in American Religion and Politics," in *The Book of Touch,* ed. Constance Classen (New York: Berg, 2005), 62. For an account of similar representational strategies as they appeared in medieval thought and culture, see Marjorie O'Rourke Boyle, *Senses of Touch: Human Dignity and Deformity from Michelangelo to Calvin* (Boston: Brill, 1998).

2. Spiritualism's clearest antecedents germinated in the pseudosciences of animal magnetism and mesmerism, the revivals of the Second Great Awakening, and Swedenborgianism. On Mesmerism generally, see Robert Darnton, *Mesmerism and the End of the Enlightenment in France* (Cambridge, MA: Harvard University Press, 1968). For mesmerism in the United States, see David Schmit, "Re-Visioning Antebellum American Psychology: The Dissemination of Mesmerism, 1836–1854," *History of Psychology* 8, no. 4 (2005): 403–434.

3. R. Laurence Moore, *In Search of White Crows: Spiritualism, Parapsychology, and American Culture* (New York: Oxford University Press, 1977), 36.

4. Ibid., 19.

5. Ibid., 18, 28. See also John Lardas Modern, *Secularism in Antebellum America* (Chicago: University of Chicago Press, 2011), 15, 222–223 279–301. Though Modern rightfully suggests that we should understand American spirituality as a "depend[ence] upon the promises of immediacy in an increasingly mediated world," and though he even ties this to phrenology and a "way of theorizing affect" (13), he nonetheless largely bifurcates Spiritualist sensory, material, and technological practices. The exception is Robert Cox, who examines the intersection of affect and physical sensation in Spiritualist practices in *Body and Soul: A Sympathetic History of American Spiritualism* (Charlottesville: University of Virginia Press, 2003). Cox illustrates the kinds of "impressions" and embodied contact made possible by sympathetic communication between the spiritual and the mundane world, as well as the heightened acuity of touch in some subjects as vision and hearing receded, but he does not explore the cosmological significance of touch in depth.

6. Cox, *Body and Soul,* 80.

7. The Fox sisters are typically credited in contemporary histories with ushering in American Spiritualism, but contemporaneous texts considered earlier origins. Emma Hardinge Britten noted the case of Nelly Butler, an apparition who conversed with people and demonstrated what appear to have been early Spiritualist phenomena in Maine in 1880. See Hardinge Britten, *Nineteenth Century Miracles: Spirits and Their Work in Every Country of the Earth* (New York: Lovell, 1884), 487–495. An 1851 pamphlet names the previous inhabitant of the Fox cabin, "Mr. Michael Weekman," as the true progenitor of spirit communication. See J. B. Campbell, *Pittsburgh and Allegheny Spirit Rappings, Together with a General History of Spiritual Communications throughout the United States* (Allegheny, PA: Purviance, July 1851), 8–9. Several authors claimed that at

least twenty-two years before the Fox sisters "founded" Spiritualism, the "Seeress of Prevorst" in Germany had outlined the same basic tenets; a succinct account of this view can be found in Epes Sargent, *Planchette: or, the Despair of Science* (Boston: Roberts Brothers, 1869), 141–152.

8. Anne Braude and Molly McGarry argue that the lack of a central organization and a diversity of practices make it is almost impossible to tell how many individuals claimed to be Spiritualists during the nineteenth century. I see that fluidity as productive rather than problematic because it expands the number of historical actors affected by its tenets. See Anne Braude, *Radical Spirits: Spiritualism and Women's Rights in Nineteenth-Century America* (Bloomington: Indiana University Press, 1989), 25–31, and Molly McGarry, *Ghosts of Futures Past: Spiritualism and the Cultural Politics of Nineteenth-Century America* (Berkeley: University of California Press, 2008), 3.

9. McGarry, *Ghosts of Futures Past,* 21–28. Both Braude and McGarry attest to the feminist and human rights components of Spiritualist practices, as well as their appeal. Future research would be well served to investigate the relationship between the Spiritualist movement's radical politics and what Candy Gunther Brown argues are the "empathetic" and "compassionate" components of touch that have been traditionally ignored in studies of American religions, particularly around healing and therapeutic cultures. See Gunther Brown, "Touch and American Religions," *Religion Compass* 3–4 (2009): 770–783. Alternately, Russ Castronovo argues that Spiritualist practices "stag[ed] interiority" in a way that "engendered an ideal citizenship supposedly free of material considerations" and "popularized the suspension of historical awareness." While Castronovo's argument is compelling, he primarily examines representations of Spiritualism in fiction. See Castronovo, *Necro Citizenship: Death, Eroticism, and the Public Sphere in the Nineteenth-Century United States* (Durham, NC: Duke University Press, 2001), 104–105.

10. Shaker practices functioned similarly. See Sally Promey, *Spiritual Spectacles: Vision and Image in Mid-Nineteenth-Century Shakerism* (Bloomington: Indiana University Press, 1993).

11. Jennifer Tucker, *Nature Exposed: Photography as Eyewitness in Victorian Science* (Baltimore: Johns Hopkins University Press, 2005); Cox, *Body and Soul,* 2003); Clément Chéroux, Andreas Fischer, Pierre Apraxine, Denis Canguilhem, and Sophie Schmit, eds., *The Perfect Medium: Photography and the Occult* (New Haven, CT: Yale University Press, 2005); Cathy Gutierrez, *Plato's Ghost: Spiritualism in the American Renaissance* (New York: Oxford University Press, 2009); and Michael Leja, *Looking Askance: Skepticism and American Art from Eakins to Duchamp* (Berkeley: University of California Press, 2004). For work on Spiritualism, sound, and hearing, see Leigh Eric Schmidt, *Hearing Things: Religion, Illusion, and the American Enlightenment* (Cambridge, MA: Harvard University Press, 2000).

12. For a nineteenth-century account using this analogy, see William Crookes, F.R.S., *Researches in the Phenomena of Spiritualism* (London: J. Burns, 1874), 95. See also Jeremy Stowlow, "Techno-Religious Imaginaries: On the Spiritual Telegraph and the Circum-Atlantic World of the 19th Century," Working Papers of the Institute on Globalization and the Human Condition, McMaster University, Hamilton, Ontario, March 2006, http://globalautonomy.ca/global1/servlet/Xml2pdf?fn=RA_Stolow_Imaginaries; Werner Sollors, "Dr. Benjamin Franklin's Celestial Telegraph; or, Indian Blessings to Gas-Lit American Drawing Rooms," *American Quarterly* 35, no. 5 (Winter 1983): 459–480; and Cox, *Body and Soul,* 87–89.

13. Constance Classen, "Fingerprints: Writing about Touch," in *The Book of Touch,* ed. Classen (New York: Berg, 2005), 1–2.

14. Epes Sargent, *The Proof Palpable of Immortality; Being an Account of the Materialization Phenomena of Modern Spiritualism. With Remarks on the Relations of the Facts to Theology, Morals, and Religion* (Boston: Colby and Rich, 1876), 220.

15. Sargent, *Proof Palpable,* 139. This story was repeated much later, in James Coates's *Photographing the Invisible.* Coates does not repeat the blurred vision of the sitter but describes the hands that touched the girl's face and neck in some detail: "a pair of hands clasped round the sitter's neck, the right hand coming on the chin and the left partly thrust under the girl's collar. The hands are shown up to the wrist, and then fade away." See Coates, *Photographing the Invisible: Practical Studies in Spirit Photography, Spirit Portraiture, and Other Rare but Allied Phenomena* (Chicago: Advanced Thought Publishing, 1911), 153.

16. Leja, *Looking Askance,* 35–41.

17. Emma Hardinge Britten, *Modern American Spiritualism: A Twenty Years' Record of the Communion between Earth and the World of Spirits* (New York: Self-published, 1869), 38.

18. Indeed, there is an auspicious absence of discussion about the role of spirit photography in her text. Hardinge Britten treated Mumler's photographs many years later, in *Nineteenth Century Miracles.* My hunch is that she sought to distance herself from the spectacle wrought by Mumler's photographs and subsequent fraud trial; this hunch is substantiated by Sargent's discussion in *Proof Palpable,* where he notes that different editions of his book will track his shifting thoughts on the veracity of Mumler's photographs, at first expressing skepticism, then redacting that skepticism, and so on. Hardinge Britten appears to have held Sargent in high regard. She reprinted a lengthy and laudatory review of Sargent's *Planchette; or, the Despair of Science* from the British periodical *Spiritualist* in her *Nineteenth Century Miracles.* See Hardinge Britten, *Nineteenth Century Miracles,* 463–464.

19. Hardinge Britten, *Modern American Spiritualism,* 106, italics in original.

20. It is difficult to imagine these spectacles outside of our contemporary ideas about "phantom limbs," but although the phenomenon was well known long before the advent of Spiritualism, S. Weir Mitchell did not give that particular sensation its name until the Civil War. See N. J. Wade, "The Legacy of Phantom Limbs," *Perception* 32 (2003): 517–524, and Daniel Heller-Roazen, *The Inner Touch: Archaeology of a Sensation* (New York: Zone, 2009), 253–270.

21. Leah Underhill, *The Missing Link in Modern Spiritualism* (New York: Thomas R. Knox, 1885), 349–351.

22. Hardinge Britten, *Modern American Spiritualism,* 268, 376.

23. Ibid., 314–315. For other examples of spirit hands, see John W. Edmonds, George T. Dexter, and Nathaniel P. Tallmadge, *Spiritualism* (New York: Partridge and Brittan, 1853), 23; Sargent, *Planchette,* 36, 45, 59, 89, 117, 127, 134, 139, 206, 207, 231, 286, 395; and Robert Dale Owen, *The Debatable Land between This World and the Next* (New York: G. W. Carelton, 1871), 351–353, 376–380.

24. Hardinge Britten, *Modern American Spiritualism,* 172.

25. Ibid., 172. Another medium, Mr. Foster, also was known to manifest words on his arms. He is treated at length in Owen, *The Debatable Land,* 386–390, as well as in Sargent, *Planchette,* 119–120. Hardinge Britten includes an anecdote in *Nineteenth Century Miracles,* 539–540, regarding a young female medium who would manifest bite and teeth marks—painfully—on her upper arms.

26. Hardinge Britten, *Modern American Spiritualism,* 196. This story is also recounted in Cox, *Body and Soul,* 20. Douglass was familiar with Spiritualism and, as one scholar has noted, made prominent use of Spiritualist metaphors of communication in his writing. See Paul Gilmore, *Aesthetic Materialism: Electricity and American Romanticism* (Stanford, CA: Stanford University Press, 2009), 111–142.

27. Sargent, *Planchette,* 1.

28. "Fads and Fancies: The Ouija Craze," *Current Literature* 10, no. 3 (July 1892): 417; "A Fortune Telling Apparatus: Ouija, the Latest Craze in Paris, Brings Queer Spirit Message," *Washington Post,* October 27, 1907, M2.

29. Kate Field, *Planchette's Diary* (New York: J. S. Redfield, 1868), 81–83, and Henrietta Camilla Jenkin, *Who Breaks, Pays* (Philadelphia: Frederick Leypoldt, 1863), 168. Field's claim that Jenkin introduced American audiences to the planchette is corroborated by an August 1868 article in *Lippincott's Magazine*. See "My Acquaintance with Planchette," *Lippincott's Magazine of Literature, Science and Education* 2 (August 1868): 217–218.

30. "Planchette," *Every Saturday: A Journal of Choice Reading* 4, no. 100 (November 30, 1867): 691–692.

31. "A Three-Legged Impostor," *Every Saturday: A Journal of Choice Reading* 5, no. 126 (May 30, 1868): 696–699.

32. "What Is Planchette?" *Scientific American* 19, no. 2 (July 8, 1868): 17–18; *The Boston Journal of Chemistry* 3 (September 1868), n.p.; "Planchette," *Daily Morning Chronicle* (San Francisco), November 18, 1868, 2; "Planchette; or, Spirit-Rapping Made Easy," *Ladies' Repository* 29 (November 1868): 369–371; "Planchette," *Round Table* 203 (December 12, 1868): 385–386; Sidney Hyde, "Planchette in a New Character," *Putnam's Magazine* 2, no. 12 (December 1868): 724–732; Charles H. Webb, "The Confessions of a Reformed Planchettist," *Harper's New Monthly Magazine* 38, no. 223 (December 1868): 99–107; and "Planchette at the Confessional," *Hours at Home: A Popular Monthly of Instruction and Recreation* 8, no. 4 (February 1869): 346–354.

33. "Foreign Notes," *Every Saturday: A Journal of Choice Reading* 2, no. 24 (December 14, 1872): 672, and Herbert A. Giles, "Mesmerism, Planchette, and Spirtualism in China," *Eclectic Magazine of Foreign Literature* 29, no. 4 (April 1879): 490–496. Sargent mentions the use of the planchette in China in the year 1843 as well. See Sargent, *Planchette,* 398.

34. "Planchette," *Daily Morning Chronicle,* 2, and "Planchette at the Confessional," *Hours at Home,* 347.

35. For a discussion of the correspondence between hearts, stones, materiality, and communication, see Sally Promey, "Hearts and Stones: Material Transformations and the Stuff of Christian Practice," in *American Christianities: A History of Dominance and Diversity,* ed. Catherine A. Brekus and W. Clark Gilpin (Chapel Hill: University of North Carolina Press, 2011), 183–213.

36. Field, *Planchette's Diary,* 27–28, 42, and "A Three-Legged Impostor," *Every Saturday,* 697.

37. Field, *Planchette's Diary,* 9.

38. "A Three-Legged Impostor," *Every Saturday,* 697.

39. My thinking about the animation of objects and the correspondence between materiality and human sympathy is shaped by Bill Brown, "Thing Theory," *Critical Inquiry* 28, no. 1 (Autumn, 2001): 1–22.

40. Sargent, *Planchette,* 195.

41. Robert Hare, *Experimental Investigation of the Spirit Manifestations* (New York: Partridge and Brittan, 1856), 368–396. See also Robert Hare, Letter to the National Intelligencer, Robert Hare Papers, American Philosophical Society, Mss.B.H22, undated Box 4. Hare's thoughts on slavery and that topic's relationship to Spiritualism are briefly treated in Cox, *Body and Soul,* 146–161.

42. Moore, *In Search of White Crows,* 102.

43. See, for example, Lori Merish, *Sentimental Materialism: Gender, Commodity Culture, and Nineteenth-Century American Literature* (Durham, NC: Duke University Press, 2000).

44. Sargent, *Planchette,* 398; "My Acquaintance with Planchette," *Lippincott's,* 3.

45. Elaine Scarry, *The Body in Pain: The Making and Unmaking of the World* (New York: Oxford University Press, 1985), 283–285, italics in original. David Chidester also posits that the

"principal theorists of modernity," Marx and Freud, "were theorists of tactility . . . in touch with resistance." See Chidester, "American Touch," 61.

46. Sir Arthur Conan Doyle claimed that a paraffin mask was made, while Epes Sargent claims that it was a pair of hands. See Doyle, *The History of Spiritualism,* vol. 2 (New York: George H. Doran, 1926), 165, and Sargent, *The Proof Palpable,* 220. Lewis Spence also notes that it was a pair of hands. See Spence, *The Encyclopedia of Occultism and Parapsychology* (New York: Dodd, Mead, 1920), 716.

47. William and Elizabeth M. F. Denton, *The Soul of Things; or, Psychometric Searches and Discoveries* (Boston: Walker, Wise and Company, 1863).

48. Sargent, *Planchette,* 134.

49. Leslie Shepard, ed., *Encyclopedia of Occultism and Parapsychology,* vol. 2 (Detroit: Gale Research Company, 1978 [1920]), 716.

50. Ibid. Hereward Carrington, a member of the Council of the American Society for Scientific Research and the Society for Psychical Research in London, published a text in 1907 detailing the methods whereby various Spiritualist claims to materialization could be debunked. Like the wax hands that served as "proof" of the existence of spirits, Carrington's descriptions outline the multiply tactile and sensory qualities he deployed to expose them as frauds—testimony, perhaps, to the fact that science is not yet completely held to the regime of the eye. See Carrington, *Physical Phenomena of Spiritualism* (Boston: Herbert B. Turner, 1907), 225. The ways Spiritualists used unveiling fraud as part of their operational logic has recently received fascinating treatment. See David Walker, "The Humbug in American Religion: Ritual Theories of Nineteenth-Century Spiritualism," *Religion and American Culture* 23, no. 1 (Winter 2013): 30–74.

51. This outward orientation might be more in keeping with the Jewish and early Christian *orans* posture, though no direct relationship, to my knowledge, exists.

52. Eve Kosofsky Sedgwick, *Touching Feeling: Affect, Pedagogy, Performativity* (Durham, NC: Duke University Press, 2003), 14.

53. Carolyn Dinshaw, *Getting Medieval: Sexualities and Communities, Pre- and Postmodern* (Durham, NC: Duke University Press, 1999), 2–3.

54. Yi-Fu Tuan, "The Pleasures of Touch," in *The Book of Touch,* ed. Constance Classen (New York: Berg, 2005), 78, italics in original.

4

Possessions and the Possessed

The Multisensoriality of Spirits, Bodies, and Objects in Heian Japan

YUI SUZUKI

Recently I participated with my mother, who was in search of healing, in an Esoteric Buddhist fire rite (*goma*) at a small Tendai Buddhist temple in Saka-guchi, Japan. As the ritual opened, the great *ajari* master (*dai ajari*), dressed in white, walked into the center of the worship hall and seated himself in front of an elaborate altar.[1] Directly behind the altar stood a large wooden statue of the Buddhist deity Fudō Myōō (S: Acala [nātha], Figure 4.1). The ritual, dedicated to Fudō, activates the powers of this benevolent but wrathful deity "with the prayers of the spiritually pure priest" and "the meritorious faith of the worshippers."[2]

Throughout the ritual, the priest read out each of the prayers the participants had written on pieces of wooden goma sticks. Just prior to the ritual, along with my mother and other participants, I too had written my prayer request, for my mother's healing. After the ajari master read out each wish, he threw the goma sticks into the burning fire, one after another. As participants we knew that the burning of these sticks symbolically immolated the negative effects that hinder happiness. Throughout the process, led by an apprentice priest, we repeatedly chanted a mantra to Fudō: *Nōmaku sanmanda bazaradan senda makaroshada sowataya un tarata kanman.*[3] As I recited the mantra, I watched the fire crackle and grow larger. Grayish-white smoke swirled around the dancing flames, completely obstructing the view of the Fudō deity behind the altar. I gazed, instead, at the beads of sweat collecting slowly on the back of the master's neck as he chanted his prayers and methodically threw the remaining sticks onto the hearth. My own chanting vibrated in my ears and vocal chords, blending with other sensations: the rhythmic beating of the drums that accompanied the mantric chants; the smell of the sandalwood incense wafting in the air, mixing with that of the burning wood; and the warm heat of the fire piercing the cool air of the temple.

FIGURE 4.1. *Fudō myōō, the Immovable One,* twelfth century. Japanese cypress wood with polychrome and gold; joined woodblock construction; height 38⅞ inches (98.8 centimeters). Special Chinese and Japanese Fund, 05.220a–c. Photograph © 2014 Museum of Fine Arts, Boston.

As the rite drew to a close, the great ajari master stepped down from the central altar and walked among the congregation, transferring the powers of Fudō to each one of us. When the priest came by, he tapped his wooden prayer beads a few times on my head and on my shoulders. Though his touch was light, I immediately felt the weight of the beads and imagined the energy of Fudō entering my body. I glanced over and saw my mother's face and shoulders soften and tears of relief roll down her cheeks as she received Fudō's blessing. The experience transformed us in deeply emotional and spiritual ways.

As an art historian working with Buddhist statues, I have emphasized the primacy of Buddhist *images* in the context of ritual and devotional practices. While participating in the fire ritual, however, the central image of Fudō became secondary, at least visually, during that moment as the ritual brought forth a heightened activation of all my sensory perceptions. It was, more accurately, an experience of synaesthesis, which the Byzantine scholar Bissera Pentcheva describes as the simultaneous experience of the senses.[4] This experience pressed me to reconsider the role objects played in Heian-period (794–1185) Buddhist practices, which have been my principal field of scholarly interest. Pentcheva argues that in current scholarship on medieval art there is a tendency for scholars to obsess about "making things visible fueled by optical visuality."[5] Perhaps a different kind of framework is necessary for thinking about Heian Buddhist art and ritual objects as well.

This chapter reassesses what has been excluded from the histories of the visual. I argue that heightened moments of Heian apotropaic and healing rituals reveal a complex multisensorial social network of exchanges that take place between spirits, people, and objects.[6] The first section of the chapter examines beliefs and anxieties of laypeople in the Heian period about the invisible spiritual forces that caused many grievances outside the laity's immediate control. The second section addresses the synaesthetic experience that Buddhist objects imparted in the context of multifaceted rituals to remove these spiritual obstacles.

Heian Anxieties and Fears over Spirit Entities

The Heian period witnessed the introduction of a rich pantheon of Buddhist deities and complex ritual practices, resulting in the large-scale construction of imperial and aristocratic temples and the creation of two- and three-dimensional icons. For Heian elites, commissioning Buddhist images and ritual performances not only served a spiritual purpose but also aimed to achieve an array of this-worldly goals, from securing professional success and healing illness to ensuring safe childbirth. Properly harnessing the powers of propitious deities through magical rituals, Buddhist and non-Buddhist alike facilitated the acquisition of these practical benefits.

Efficacious Buddhist rites were characterized by their complex commingling of spiritual and this-worldly benefits. For the Heian lay community, removing spiritual and physical obstacles was about conquering the malicious workings of spirit entities in order to shift the balance of nature from chaos to harmony and from defilement to purity. The Medicine or Healing Buddha (J: Yakushi, S: Bhaiṣajyaguru), one of the most popular Buddhist deities in the Heian period, was widely sought after not only for his healing powers but also because practitioners considered him particularly effective in vanquishing malevolent or vengeful spirits (onryō).[7] Heian elites ordered rituals and prayed fervently to their gods in order to prevent these spirits from bringing disorder to their lives.

The Heian belief in the spirit realm consisted of an immensely complex classification of spirit entities, including onryō, demons (oni, ki), august spirits (goryō), local natural deities (kami), and so forth. By the ninth century, the belief that such spirits caused disease and other natural calamities was widespread among the populace and the aristocratic society. Early Heian official histories note that a spirit pacification ceremony took place in 863 in the garden of the Greater Palace to drive out epidemics and other calamities from the Heian capital. The populace believed that disease gods and vengeful spirits caused these misfortunes:

> The spirits named are Sudō Tennō, Iyo Shinno, Fujiwara no Yoshiko, the inspector, Tachibana no Hayanari, and Fun'ya no Miyatamaro. All of these were executed and have become vengeful spirits and demons. For some time now pestilence has ranged and the number of dead is exceedingly high. Throughout the realm, it is believed that the disasters are the result of their spirits. They are spreading from the capital and home provinces to the outer provinces. Every summer and autumn placation rites are held without respite.[8]

These words, from *Authentic Account of Three Generations in Japan* (*Nihon sandai jitsuroku*), demonstrate that spirits were understood as the major causes of natural disasters and required regular subduing through government sponsorship of spirit pacification rites.

Official ninth-century documents increasingly noted one type of malicious spirit entity: *mono-no-ke*.[9] *Later Chronicle of Japan, Continued* (*Shoku nihon kōki*), from 869, documents the frequent appearance of mono-no-ke between the years 837 and 845 CE.[10] The *Chronicle* tersely mentions them by stating that strange occurrences on the imperial palace grounds had been determined to be the "workings of mono-no-ke." The *Chronicle* also notes that in order to pacify mono-no-ke, the court ordered Buddhist rites of repentance, including sutra recitations (*tendoku*, mainly the *Great Perfection of Wisdom Sutra* and the *Medicine Master Buddha Sutra*) to be performed at the emperor's residential compound.[11] At this historical moment, any strange and inexplicable phenomena perceived as inauspicious and potentially threatening to the emperor were understood to be the workings of mono-no-ke.

Although *mono-no-ke* is often translated into English as "possessing spirit" or "evil spirit," its etymological origins reveal that possession of this sort was an amorphous and ambiguous concept.[12] The root word in *mono-no-ke,* represented by the graph *mono* 物, derives from *tama* 魂. This tama can be translated as "spirit" or something intangible, formless, and invisible.[13] The graph mono 物 was also interchangeable with the graph mono 鬼, or "demon," as well as something "hidden from this world."[14] The root word *ke* 怪 (sometimes interchanged with the root word 気), denoted a "certain sense or perception." Thus mono-no-ke was formless and strange, a mysterious and hidden presence.

The fact that these spirits could not be seen heightened people's anxieties about them. In the absence of visibility, other senses had to be used to facilitate their detection. It was possible for mono-no-ke to communicate to the living through dreams, where they appeared in human form. The more prevalent means of interaction, however, was for the mono-no-ke to possess a human body or object. Their presence was invisible to the eye but could be sensed, and they often produced a sensation described as a feeling of "eeriness."[15] In the classic Heian novel *The Tale of Genji,* the protagonist Genji spends the night with his lover Yūgao in an isolated house and perceives something strangely disturbing and eerie.[16] During the night he is terrified by "noises of invisible things walking and coming up behind him, though he could not see them."[17] Many other accounts describe the amorphous and ineffable quality of mono-no-ke; their invisibility gave them their power and rendered them especially frightening.

From the late ninth century onward, mono-no-ke evolved into something more specific, becoming almost synonymous with any life-threatening situation faced by an individual, such as a prolonged or incurable illness.[18] The court diaries written during the tenth and eleventh centuries reveal that Heian elites regarded mono-no-ke as demons and volatile spirits, often of deceased political rivals that bore a grudge toward the living.[19]

Spirit Possessions and Power Plays

Across a number of cultures and periods, the ability to possess human bodies has been a feature associated with spirits and demons; this phenomenon has often been regarded as a marginal cultural experience. According to Lesley Sharp, many anthropologists interpret spirit possession as a phenomenon that allows people of lesser social status to temporarily assert themselves without being held accountable for their actions; the possessing spirits, rather than the ones possessed, are responsible for their unruly behavior.[20]

In Heian Japan, however, spirit possessions were not relegated to a subordinate social group, nor were they gender specific.[21] Malicious spirits often plagued Fujiwara no Michinaga (966–1027), one of the most illustrious court politicians of the tenth century. His contemporary, the court noble Fujiwara no Yukinari (972–1027), for example, noted in his diary several instances when Michinaga was attacked by a spirit or was accosted by another demonically possessed individual. According to Yukinari, a lady-in-waiting stricken by a menacing spirit (*jaryō*) once tried to attack Michinaga.[22] Yukinari further notes in his diary that earlier in the year, Michinaga himself had been temporarily possessed by a volatile spirit that made him gnash his teeth and squint his eyes in a fit of rage; this spirit was that of his dead political rival, Fujiwara no Korechika, whom Michinaga had deposed.[23] Yukinari's observations demonstrate that people in positions of power were quite vulnerable to possessions by malevolent spirits due to their precarious political situations.

The fact that Heian literature records so many of these spirit possessions at the time of the Fujiwara family's domination of political power illuminates the contradictory and complex workings of autonomy and power among those who wielded it. During Michinaga's time in the eleventh century, conflicts between high-ranking nobles vying for political gain became increasingly frequent, even among the Fujiwara families. With these power struggles, concerns over the vengeful spirits of political adversaries who plotted against them also increased. Many believed that defeated members of rival factions would become malicious spirits and wreak havoc on the living.

Those in power were as fearful of curses cast by the living as of those cast by the dead. Mimi Yiengpruksawan demonstrates that Michinaga was terribly afraid of curses as well as vengeful ghosts and often blamed them for his illnesses.[24] The prevalence of spirit possessions and the sponsoring of various types of rituals by high-ranking members of the Heian court indicate that spirits and the phenomenon of possession were not at all marginal experiences of the weak and powerless.[25] In fact, the eleventh century's unsettled political climate made powerful people such as the ruling members of the Fujiwara family particularly vulnerable and susceptible to attacks by spirit entities.

Spirits and the Synaesthetic Experience

Anthropologist Daniel Miller describes the theological preoccupation of many religions (including Buddhism) as being centered on their critique of materiality. Miller states, "Truth comes from our apprehension that this [materiality] is mere illusion. Nevertheless, paradoxically, material culture has been of considerable consequence as the means of expressing this conviction."[26] It is only through material objects and sensorial experiences that spirituality can be properly expressed and attained.

The same paradoxical condition can be applied to the Heian belief in spirits in that people used ritual objects in sensory ways to engage with invisible spirit entities and to render them less powerful. In other words, not only were material objects sensual extensions of the body and part of a merging of mind, body, and objects;[27] invisible, formless entities were also a fundamental component of this complex universe. In order to make their invisible presences known, spirit entities depended on human bodies and material objects. To communicate their wills and demands, they attached themselves to human bodies, temporarily inhabited them, spoke through them, and made their hosts ill or induced them to manifest strange behaviors. These spirits, in turn, could be subjugated by higher spiritual powers, and they responded to specific auditory and visual stimuli.

A detailed description of a series of rituals performed in 1008 for the safe childbirth of Fujiwara no Shōshi (988–1074) reveals how spirits were inextricably and paradoxically connected to material objects and to the human experience of embodiment.[28] Standard practice in dealing with demonic forces involved calling on the services of numerous religious specialists. These included Buddhist priests who could perform Esoteric Buddhist rites (genza/genja or ajari), mediums (known as yorimashi), and Yin-Yang masters (onmyōji). An account of the events leading up to, during, and just after Shōshi's labor, as described by Murasaki Shikibu in her diary, mentions the active participation of all three types of ritualists.

Shōshi, an imperial consort, was provided with a full cast of eminent Buddhist priests who performed elaborate rituals before and during her labor, as well as after her child's birth, to keep malignant forces at bay. Even for a middle-class woman, such specialists (though their numbers were much fewer) were employed during labor, as depicted in a scene from Illustrated Legends of the Kitano Shrine (Kitano tenjin engi emaki) (Figure 4.2). One scene from the scroll shows a bird's-eye view of a Heian middle-class residence where a woman is deep in labor, slumped against her wet nurse, who supports her in a tight embrace. A female medium wearing a white kimono is seated in front of them. Nearby, another female attendant, dressed in blue, appears to sprinkle some white matter on the woman in labor. In the adjacent room, a man clad in brown holds up his hand as if making sacred symbolic hand gestures (mudras) as he chants. Out on the veranda, another man is twanging the strings of a bow while a Yin-Yang master, dressed in black, performs divination in the garden in front of an altar that displays a row of white paper streamers.

Carrying Emperor Ichijō's potential heir to the throne, Shōshi was considered an easy target for malignant spirits, especially those of her political foes, who had plotted her downfall. She was also vulnerable to curses cast by jealous rivals. Her political position as the mother of a future emperor made her pregnancy doubly treacherous. Expense was not an issue when it came to ensuring the well-being of Shōshi and the unborn child. Shōshi's father, Michinaga, spent a hefty fortune commissioning

FIGURE 4.2. Childbirth scene from "The Human Realm," handscroll 8 (sections 24–26), in *Illustrated Legends of the Kitano Shrine,* early thirteenth century. Ink and color on paper. Kitano Tenmangū, Japan.

many Buddhist statues and sponsoring rituals to ensure Shōshi's safe delivery. According to Michinaga's diary, in the seventh month of 1008, Michinaga had a white sandalwood statue of the Medicine Buddha made. An entry from the following year mentions that while Shōshi was pregnant he commissioned life-sized golden statues of Buddhist deities, including Shaka, Monju, and Fugen, and sets of seven Yakushi and six Kannon statues. He also dedicated life-size polychromed images of the Five Great Wisdom Kings and the six heavenly deities.[29]

Eminent Buddhist priests frequently performed the tantric five-altar rite, dedicated to the Five Great Wisdom Kings (*Godaison*), featuring Fudō and four other Esoteric deities of fearsome countenance. Because the rite was specifically designed to subdue evil forces with the fierce powers of the mystic kings, it was often employed to pray for safe childbirth.[30] Shōchō, the compiler of the iconographical and ritual manual *Asabashō,* for example, notes that the main purpose of the ceremony was to expel "impending difficulties."[31] A month before Shōshi's actual delivery, at his Tsuchimikado mansion Michinaga sponsored this elaborate ritual, led by Buddhist priests of high standing from the temples Kannon'in, Jōdoji, and Hosshōji.[32] It is conceivable that the life-sized polychromed statues of the Five Great Wisdom Kings mentioned in Michinaga's diary were used in this spectacular ceremony. The service was also held to consecrate and transform certain objects, including Shōshi's sash, with the purifying powers of the Five Great Wisdom Kings. Immediately after the ceremony, the priests presented the consecrated objects to the empress for her protection.[33] Here we have an instance of what Paul Johnson has called "multiple valences of possession." Certain objects come to possess powers of a higher order; in turn, the "possessed" objects mediate these powers to the persons who gain possession of the coveted commodities.[34]

Several ritual specialists presided over Shōshi's birthing, and each had a different role to perform. Each provided points of contact between humans and spirits. Calling in a Yin-Yang master signified not that the birthing was in any way unusual but rather that it was a time of great vulnerability. Yin-Yang diviners were regularly engaged for service to discern the presence of harmful spirit entities during a Heian birthing because mono-no-ke possession was likely to occur at such a time. Murasaki Shikibu mentions that several reputed Yin-Yang masters were present during Shōshi's birthing.[35] Yin-Yang masters were not usually involved in the actual pacification and exorcism of mono-no-ke, but if possession was suspected, Yin-Yang masters performed divinations to diagnose the specific types and identities of the possessing spirits. The appropriate rituals to appease them could then be performed.[36] For instance, Fujiwara no Yorimichi once summoned renowned Yin-Yang masters Kamo no Mitsuyoshi (939–1015) and Abe no Yoshihira (954–1026) to perform divinations so that they could identify the spirit entities causing his long-term afflictions.[37]

Colors carried specific symbolic meanings and transformative qualities. In the case of an impending birth, it was customary for the birthing woman and her attendants to wear white attire and to equip the delivery room with white furnishings.[38] Murasaki Shikibu writes in her diary that when Shōshi's labor pains began, a white-curtained dais was prepared for her, and she and her attendants were dressed in white (Figure 4.3).[39] Her bedding as well as interior furnishings such as curtains, hanging blinds, and screens were also prepared in white; these were used to contain Shōshi and the activity of childbirth.[40] They were also employed to separate and define the spatial boundaries between the pure and the defiled. According to Karen Gerhart, in Japan the color white symbolized purification and was often worn to counteract the pollution caused by death.[41] In the case of Shōshi's labor, childbirth was considered a kind of blood defilement, and the screens that sequestered Shōshi were means not only to provide privacy to the imperial consort but also to contain the defilement, preventing it from spreading and contaminating others. Meanwhile, the white robes both protected and purified Shōshi and her ladies-in-waiting.

Buddhist priests were usually the ones who dealt directly with subjugating mono-no-ke. For Shōshi, celebrated priests called by their venerable titles Ajari (Venerable masters) were brought in from the renowned Shingon and Tendai Buddhist temples to attend to the menacing spirits. These priests performed rituals that enabled the

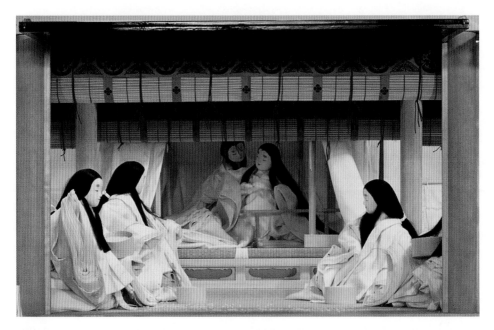

FIGURE 4.3. A royal birthing and rice-throwing (*uchimaki*). Photograph © Costume Museum, Kyoto, Japan.

mono-no-ke to enter the bodies of yorimashi, who were always female.[42] The responsibilities of the yorimashi included being receptacles to temporarily host the mono-no-ke and, if necessary, providing mouthpieces for the spirits, who wanted to make their tribulations known to the living.

By the power of mystic incantations, a skilled priest lured the malignant spirits into the bodies of the mediums, whether the spirits were simply hovering in the room or had already latched onto the laboring woman. The mediums, therefore, were positioned not too far from the birthing, but partitioning screens were used to sequester them and to keep them away from the vulnerable Shōshi (Figure 4.4). Seven female mediums assisted the imperial consort, ready to temporarily host in their own bodies any malicious spirits that might attack Shōshi. A priest was assigned to each medium, in charge of transferring any possessive spirits from the empress to the medium if necessary. The author of *A Tale of Flowering Fortunes* (*Eiga monogatari*) wrote, "Each of the possessed mediums was put inside the enclosure of folding screens, where the attendant miracle workers shrieked incantations in unison."[43] Murasaki Shikibu conveys the clangor and violence assaulting the senses just after the baby was born:

> What awful wails of anguish came from the evil spirits at the moment of
> birth.... Holy Teacher Chisan was in charge of Miya no Naishi's enclo-

FIGURE 4.4. Female mediums (*yorimashi*). Photograph © Costume Museum, Kyoto, Japan.

sure; he was thrown to the ground by evil spirits and was in such distress that Holy Teacher Nengaku had to come to his aid with loud prayers. It was not that his powers were on the wane but that the evil proved so very persistent. The priest Eikō was in charge of Lady Saishō's substitute and he became hoarse from chanting all night; when none of the women asked to accept the spirits were able to do so, there was uproar.[44]

Although Murasaki does not identify the spirits by name, they were generally regarded as deceased political rivals of Michinaga and Shōshi, who had been waiting for the moment to assail the weakened mother and her newborn baby.

The Esoteric Buddhist rite employed to expunge evil spirits was called *kaji* (S: *adhiṣṭhāna*) and was first introduced to Japan from China in the ninth century by Kūkai. According to Pamela Winfield, "Doctrinally speaking, *kaji* refers to the mutual empowerment between self and Buddha that characterizes tantric deity yoga." When practically applied, "*kaji* is said to occur when a trained master concentrates and extends Buddha's universal energy to a receptive subject for healing purposes."[45] Kaji, like all other Esoteric Buddhist rites, involved a complex sequencing of symbolic acts using what Buddhism calls the Three Mysteries—mind, word, and body. The ritual practitioner, focusing on a painted or sculptural image of an Esoteric deity (such as Fudō), continually performed a series or combinations of mudras, recited mystic syllables (mantras), and invited the deity to enter the purified ritual space and the body of the practitioner so that the deity's merits could become one with him.[46]

It is worth noting here that a different kind of possession takes place during the performance of an apotropaic healing ritual, such as kaji. Here possession is not the forceful intrusion of a malignant entity. Instead, the higher deity-entity is enticed, or invited, to enter the body of the practitioner and extend his all-encompassing powers. Geoffrey Samuel, in a 2008 article, demonstrates that this type of possession outlines a relationship between "spirit-entity, mind-body, or the psycho-physical complex."[47] According to Samuel, it is not as simple as "becoming one with the deity"; rather, as he eloquently puts it, it is a kind of reshaping that takes place in the consciousness of the religious practitioner during the ritual act in which he attempts to pattern his mode of being after the specific deity.[48]

In kaji, certain Buddhist ritual objects functioned as effective tools manipulated by the priests at critical junctures to act as catalysts for exorcism.[49] These objects, therefore, were crucial in helping to alter the mind-body of the practitioner during certain sections of the ritual. The *vajra*, sometimes translated as "adamantine" or "diamond," is an essential ritual tool used in tantric Buddhist practice, and it comes in various types, as single-, three-, and five-pronged shapes (Figure 4.5). Its origin is said to be the Vedic god Indra, who holds a single-pointed vajra in his hand.[50] Esoteric or tantric Buddhism lends the vajra a diverse and rich symbolism. Like the diamond, the vajra's hardness represents the indestructible Buddhist Law and encompasses the victorious power it has over delusion and malevolent forces.[51] It is also a thunder-and-lightning weapon symbolic of awakening and enlightenment by the rays issuing from the body of Vairocana, the Cosmic Buddha.[52] Moreover, the single-pronged vajra is seen as a protector of the Buddhist teachings and a destroyer of demons.[53]

Similarly, practitioners employed stringed prayer beads (Figure 4.6) during kaji. According to Esoteric Buddhist interpretations, prayer beads materially manifested the *dharmakāya*, the unconditioned Buddha-body. Such sacred objects "embodied the original, underlying order of the cosmos" and, like the vajra, "empowered the humans that used [them] with the Buddha's powers."[54] When the Buddhist prayer beads were held during the chanting of prayers, the sound of prayer and the tactile quality of the beads were intimately linked. In this sense, prayer beads should be considered material presences of sound. As a "visual residue of aurality,"[55] a string of prayer beads is an object that was (and still is) rubbed between the hands to make specific sounds and to mark key moments during the ritual, producing a multisensory experience.

Once the priests succeeded in transferring malignant spirits to the mediums and sequestering them there, the primary objective for the exorcist was to detach the mono-no-ke from the mediums' bodies and send these evil spirits back to the spirit world. The interminable recitation of sacred prayers, which entailed the continuous

FIGURE 4.5. Single-pronged vajra (*tokko sho*), late twelfth century. Gilded bronze, 1 × 1 inch (2.54 × 2.54 centimeters). Eugene Fuller Memorial Collection, Seattle Art Museum. Photo: Susan A. Cole.

chanting of mystical incantations (mantras and *dharanis*), accomplished this final expulsion, weakening the spirit's hold on its host. Mantras and dharanis were known to have a powerful dispelling effect on mono-no-ke and other types of demonic spirits. The ninth-century Shingon Buddhist master Kūkai once explained that mantras and dharanis worked like medicine in that they were effective cures for demonic spirits. These magical sounds were fundamental Buddhist teachings that had the power to transform all who heard them, including demons, into powerful protective spirits.[56] As such, they were "sources of illocutionary force, magical utterances, set apart from ordinary speech by the ritual setting."[57] In addition to the magical function of the mystic syllables, Kathryn Linn Geurts, in discussing West African notions of embodiment, reminds us that "words are not only information or knowledge but also sound, so in addition to their meaning, words have a physical force which operates not only at the site of the ear and mind but throughout the entire body."[58] Similarly, Murasaki Shikibu writes that throughout Shōshi's labor, "Buddhist priests warded off mono-no-ke with the ceaseless chanting of loud spells." She also remarks, "It was quite terrifying to hear the priests, their voices hoarse with such praying and wailing as if to call up the very manifestation of Fudō."[59] The resonating sounds of the priests' voices must have had a powerful emotional and somatic effect on all those present.

FIGURE 4.6. Buddhist prayer beads (*nenju*), thirteenth–fourteenth century. Collection of Nara National Museum, Nara, Japan.

In addition to the commanding presence of Buddhist priests who chanted and lured the spirits with ritual objects, other specialists at the birthing site augmented the priests' exorcism of mono-no-ke. Male attendants from the court continuously twanged bows as an auditory deterrent with magical powers over the pesky spirits (Figure 4.7). Such twanging, called *meigen,* was often performed during labor or just after a baby's birth, at the baby's first bathing ritual.[60] In fact, Heian-period practitioners considered twanging so effective that it was regularly performed at the palace to

FIGURE 4.7. Male attendant twanging his bow (*meigen*). Photograph © Costume Museum, Kyoto, Japan.

protect the emperor.[61] The particular resonance created by the plucking of the bow-string was perceived to have a repelling effect on mono-no-ke.[62] The childbearing scene from the *Illustrated Legends of the Kitano Shrine* shows a man twanging his bowstring (see Figure 4.2). The man (most likely a male servant of the household) carefully positions himself on the veranda, making sure to turn his back *away* from the childbearing scene and the interior of the house. He plucks his bow without using an arrow in an attempt to disperse the spirits out of the house and keep others from entering. Similarly, when Shōshi gave birth to Prince Atsuhira, the performance of meigen was an elaborate affair; twenty men, ten of Fifth and ten of Sixth Rank, stood in two lines and twanged their bows throughout the baby's evening bath.[63]

Throughout the birthing, Shōshi's ladies-in-waiting also assisted in perpetually warding off harmful spirits, who responded negatively to tactile as well as to aural sensations. Yin-Yang masters often practiced *sanmai* (also known as *uchimaki*), the customary ritual practice of throwing rice at invisible entities to scare them away. Rice, the sacred food offering to the kami since ancient times, was understood to have purifying properties. Murasaki Shikibu recounts the chaotic scene of rice raining down on Shōshi and her ladies-in-waiting (see Figure 4.3).[64] In the birthing as depicted in the *Illustrated Legends of the Kitano Shrine* (see Figure 4.2), a female attendant throws rice at the woman in labor. In addition, in *The Tale of Genji Scrolls*

FIGURE 4.8. Scene from chapter titled "The Flute" (*Yokobue*), in *The Tale of Genji Scrolls* (*Genji monogatari emaki*), twelfth century. Ink and color on paper. Collection of The Tokugawa Art Museum. Photograph © The Tokugawa Art Museum Image Archives/DNP Art Com.

(*Genji monogatari emaki*), a scene from the chapter titled "The Flute" (*Yokobue*) shows Yūgiri's wife Kumoinokari nursing her baby in the middle of the night. As she cajoles the baby, her wet nurse holds a large platter of rice that had been prepared to disperse the mono-no-ke threatening the baby (Figure 4.8).[65] In the novel, Kumoinokari admonishes Yūgiri for raising the shutters and letting a wandering spirit into the house, thereby waking the baby.[66] During such vulnerable moments as birthing and nursing a baby, the magical and efficacious properties of rice functioned as tactile deterrents to mono-no-ke; the rice sanctified the space encroached upon by the malignant spirits.

A quintessential example of rice throwing, and one that most vividly conveys the paradoxical relationship between spirits and objects, is a story recorded in the late Heian compilation known as *Tales of Old and New* (*Konjaku monogatari shū*). In Chapter 27 this narrative recounts an episode in which a wet nurse encounters some spirits that live in a dilapidated house. She throws rice at the ten spectral men on horses and manages to disperse them. The next morning, she discovers traces of blood on the rice.[67] It is not only the symbolic and magical property of the rice but also its very materiality and tactility that give it certain efficacies over invisible entities.

Conclusion

Heian ritual specialists and their participants performed a wide range of ritual activities to counter the malicious workings of malicious spirits. Such performances suggest pronounced anxieties over invisible but real things beyond one's immediate control. They also show repeated efforts to maintain a healthy equilibrium in a universe where the boundaries between humans and spirits were seamless and context contingent. The political climate of the late Heian period exposed the extremely volatile positions of power maintained by ruling members of the Fujiwara families, which they believed made them vulnerable and particularly susceptible to spirit possessions. At the same time, their wealth and power gave them easy access to potent objects such as Buddhist images, as well as to ritual performances and religious specialists for vanquishing and purifying negative forces.

These objects and practices expose the intangible spirit world as forming an integral part of Heian reality and its rich sensorium, one that required constant negotiation between the material and the immaterial to maintain a harmonious cosmic order. In this way, the Heian sensorium brings to light a complex network of spirits, stuff, and bodies in a world fully saturated with multisensorial exchanges. Malign spirits were controllable through the careful manipulation of objects, human bodies, and powerful deities by male and female ritual specialists. Such dynamics reveal the senses as salient channels for the experience of the immaterial, both demonic and divine.

NOTES

1. Romanized terms appearing in parentheses next to their English translations are Japanese. When referring to both Japanese and Sanskrit terms, I use (J:) and (S:), respectively. In Japanese Buddhism, *ajari* comes from the Sanskrit term *ācārya,* meaning "master" or "teacher." In Japanese Tendai Buddhist practice, the rank of "Great Ajari" is given only to a Tendai priest who has fulfilled the thousand-day ascetic training on Mount Hiei, known as *kaihōgyō* . Catherine Ludvik, "In the Service of the Kaihōgyō Practitioners of Mt. Hiei," *Japanese Journal of Religious Studies* 33, no. 1 (2006): 121.

2. Ian Reader and George J. Tanabe Jr., *Practically Religious: Worldly Benefits and the Common Religion of Japan* (Honolulu: University of Hawai'i Press, 1998), 66.

3. In English, "Homage to the all-pervading Vajras! O Violent One of great wrath! Destroy! *hûm trat hâm mâm.*" Translation from Hugo Deslippe, "Fudo Myo-o," accessed September 1, 2013, http://www.japanese-buddhism.com/fudo-myo-o.html.

4. Bissera V. Pentcheva, "The Performative Icon," *Art Bulletin* 4 (December 2006): 631. As Bissera notes, the experience of synaesthesis does not equate with the modern notion of synesthesia, in which one sense (e.g., sight) is experienced as another (e.g., smell).

5. Ibid., 636.

6. Daniel Miller, ed., *Materiality* (Durham, NC: Duke University Press: 2005), 11. In this context Bruno Latour's "network of agents" is relevant in my work, as is Miller's.

7. On the apotropaic powers of Medicine Buddhas, see Yui Suzuki, *Medicine Master Buddha: The Iconic Worship of Yakushi in Heian Japan* (Leiden: Brill, 2012).

8. Quoted in David T. Bialock, *Eccentric Spaces, Hidden Histories: Narrative, Ritual, and Royal Authority from* The Chronicles of Japan *to* The Tale of the Heike (Stanford, CA: Stanford University Press, 2007), 137.

9. Bialock notes that references to spirit possession in national histories significantly increased in the ninth century. For example, *Later Chronicle of Japan, Continued* records no fewer than thirteen references to mono-no-ke. Ibid., 136.

10. *Shoku nihon kōki* is a twenty-volume historical text that covers the years during Emperor Ninmyō's reign (833–850). *Shoku nihon kōki,* in *Kokushi taikei,* vol. 3 (Tokyo: Yoshikawa Kōbunkan, 1966).

11. The pacification ceremonies were held in the inner palace (*dairi*), including the Shishinden, Jōneiden, and Seiryōden. Ibid., 68, 156.

12. Later Heian literature and court diaries often used the term *jaki* (bothersome demon or spirits) interchangeably with *mono-no-ke.*

13. Takemitsu Makoto, *Nihonjin nara shitte okitai mononoke to Shinto* (Tokyo: Kawade Shohō Shinsha, 2011), 9–10; Yamaori Tetsuo, *Nihonjin no reikonkan* (Tokyo: Kawade Shohō Shinsha, 1994), 39–40; and Sasama Yoshihiko, *Oni to mono-no-ke no bunkashi* (Tokyo: Yūshikan, 2005), 153–154.

14. Sasama, *Oni to mono-no-ke,* 6.

15. For example, the narrator of the *The Great Mirror* (*Ōkagami*) recounts how Fujiwara no Kaneie's (929–990) death resulted in his move to a residence called Nijōin, notorious for having an "eerie" atmosphere. Though Kaneie never saw any spirits in this house, the *Ōkagami* recounts the strange occurrences he encountered there, including how he experienced "invisible hands" slamming down all the shutters he had raised. Helen Craig McCullough, trans., *Ōkagami: The Great Mirror* (Princeton, NJ: Princeton University Press, 1980), 163.

16. Murasaki Shikibu, *The Tale of Genji,* trans. and ed. Royall Tyler (New York: Penguin Books, 2001), 65.

17. Ibid., 69.

18. The term *jaki* (bothersome demon) is also commonly recorded in court diaries and is often used interchangeably with *mono-no-ke.*

19. Hayami Tasuku, *Jujutsu shūkyō no sekai* (Tokyo: Hanawa Shobō, 1987), 94.

20. Lesley Sharp, "The Power of Possession in Northwest Madagascar," in *Spirit Possession: Modernity and Power in Africa,* ed. Heike Beherend and Ute Luig (Madison: University of Wisconsin Press, 1999), 5.

21. And cf. Doris Bargen's argument, in analyzing the classic Heian novel *The Tale of Genji,* that spirit possession was a female strategy or "weapon" used to counter male strategies of dominance. Bargen, *A Woman's Weapon: Spirit Possession in* The Tale of Genji (Honolulu: University of Hawai'i Press, 1997), xix.

22. Yukinari's diary *Gonki*'s entry of 1000.12.16 noted this incident. See Fujimoto Katsuyoshi, "Fujiwara no Michinaga no 'Mono-no-ke kan,'" *Aoyama Gakuin Women's Junior College* (1998): 24.

23. *Gonki* entry, 1000.5.25, ibid., 22–23.

24. Mimi Hall Yiengpruksawan, "The Eyes of Michinaga in the Light of Pure Land Buddhism," in *The Presence of Light: Divine Radiance and Religious Experience,* ed. Matthew T. Kapstein (Chicago: University of Chicago Press, 2004), 246.

25. Sharp, "The Power of Possession," 4. Sharp claims that this paradigm (spirit possession as a marginal experience for the weak and powerless) is exemplified by the works of I. M. Lewis. See I. M. Lewis, "Spirit Possession and Deprivation Cults," *Man* 1:3 (1966): 307–

329; *Ecstatic Religion: An Anthropological Study of Spirit Possession and Shamanism* (Baltimore: Penguin Books, 1971); *Religion in Context: Cults and Charisma* (Cambridge, UK: Cambridge University Press, 1986).

26. Miller, *Materiality,* 1.

27. Carl Knappett, "Photographs, Skeuomorphs, and Marionettes: Some Thoughts on Mind, Agency, and Object," *Journal of Material Culture* (2002): 98–99.

28. Shōshi was the imperial consort to Emperor Ichijō (r. 986–1011). The most detailed account of Shōshi's childbirth scene is recorded by Murasaki Shikibu, the renowned author of *The Tale of Genji.* See Richard Bowring, trans., *Murasaki Shikibu: Her Diary and Poetic Memoirs* (Princeton, NJ: Princeton University Press, 1982), 51–73.

29. *Midō kanpakuki,* 1008.7.14 entry (on the sandalwood Yakushi). 1009.10.13 entry on the many statues commissioned by Michinaga. See Nishio Masahito, *Yakushi shinkō: gokoku no hotoke kara onsen no hotoke e* (Tokyo: Iwata Shoin, 2000), 80–81.

30. Hayami, *Jujutsu shūkyō* (Tokyo: Hanawa Shobō, 1987), 100–102. Hayami quotes from the *Asabashō,* which states, "The Five-Altar Rite is practiced to vanquish enemies." In 903, Fujiwara no Onshi (Yasuko) gave birth to Prince Yasuakira, second son of Emperor Daigo.

31. Yamaori, *Nihonjin no reikonkan,* 172.

32. The Five-Altar Rite for Shōshi was performed by Shōsan, the Gonsōjō of Kannon'in (who manned the Fudō altar), and Keien, the Daisōzu from Hōjūji, who manned the Gōzanze altar. It was customary for Heian elite women to return to their parents' homes to give birth. As Fujiwara no Michinaga's daughter, Shōshi resided at his Tsuchimikado mansion during the latter months of her pregnancy.

33. Bowring, *Murasaki Shikibu,* 42–43.

34. Paul Johnson, comments made at MAVCOR Fellows Seminar, August 14, 2010.

35. Bowring, *Murasaki Shikibu,* 57. Murasaki Shikibu writes, "Those known for their divining skills had also been ordered to attend; surely not a spirit in Japan could have failed to prick up his ears."

36. Shigeta Shin'ichi, *Heian kizoku to Onmyōji* (Tokyo: Yoshikawa Kōbunkan, 2005), 2.

37. Ibid., 435. Because Yin-Yang masters determined that the probable cause of his affliction was an angry god (*kami*), the curse of an enemy, or mono-no-ke, several types of rituals were performed for Yorimichi.

38. See, for example, section 3, "Shiei jiben gaki" (Hungry ghosts that prey on newborn babies) in the "Scroll of the Hungry Ghosts" (J: *Gaki zōshi,* Tokyo National Museum; originally belonged to the Kawamoto family). In this scene female attendants assist a middle-class Heian woman through the birthing process. All the women are wearing white, while a hungry ghost preying on the newborn baby goes unnoticed.

39. Photograph provided by the Costume Museum, Kyoto, Japan. The scene is taken from *The Tale of Genji* and shows Princess Akashi giving birth to her son, but it is very similar to Murasaki Shikibu's description of Shōshi's labor. The same applies to Figures 4.4 and 4.7.

40. McCullough, *Ōkagami,* 163.

41. Karen Gerhart, *The Material Culture of Death in Medieval Japan* (Honolulu: University of Hawai'i Press, 2009), 198, n.b. 4; 205, n.b. 35.

42. There are instances in which yorimashi were young children.

43. William McCullough and Helen McCullough, trans., *A Tale of Flowering Fortunes: Annals of Japanese Aristocratic Life in the Heian Period* (Stanford, CA: Stanford University Press, 1980), vol. 1, 272.

44. Bowring, *Murasaki Shikibu,* 55–57.

45. Pamela D. Winfield, "Curing with *Kaji:* Healing and Esoteric Empowerment in Japan," *Japanese Journal of Religious Studies* 32, no. 1 (2005): 108.

46. Michael Saso, *Tantric Art and Meditation* (Honolulu: Tendai Educational Foundation, 1990), 15.

47. Geoffrey Samuel, "Possession and Self-Possession: Spirit, Healing, Tantric Meditation, and Āveśa," *Diskus* 9 (2008) (online journal of the British Association for the Study of Religions): 5.

48. Ibid., 6.

49. Ikeda Kikan, ed., *Makura no sōshi: Murasaki Shikibu nikki* (Tokyo: Iwanami Shoten 1962), 66, 326. According to Carmen Blacker, female mediums often held such ritual paraphernalia as powerful spirit lures. Carmen Blacker, *The Catalpa Bow: A Study in Shamanistic Practices in Japan* (London: George Allen and Unwin, 1975), 147–148. In the Heian novel *The Pillow Book* (*Makura no sōshi*), the author, Sei Shōnagon, explains how a priest used ritual objects such as vajras and prayer beads to exorcise baleful spirits from the sick person's body to that of the female medium. Sei Shōnagon, *The Pillow Book,* trans. Meredith McKinney (London: Penguin Books, 2006), 24, 251.

50. Anne Nishimura Morse and Samuel Morse, *Object as Insight: Japanese Buddhist Art and Ritual* (Katonah, NY: Katonah Museum of Art, 1995), 122.

51. Dale E. Saunders, *Mudrā: A Study of Symbolic Gestures in Japanese Sculpture* (Princeton, NJ: Princeton University Press, 1985), 184–185.

52. Saso, *Tantric Art,* xi.

53. Fabio Rambelli, *Buddhist Materiality: A Cultural History of Objects in Japanese Buddhism* (Stanford, CA: Stanford University Press, 2007), 155.

54. Ibid., 62.

55. A term used by Sven Ouzman to explain the nonvisual, aural aspects of southern African (San) rock engravings. "Seeing Is Deceiving: Rock Art and the Non-visual," *World Archaeology* 33, no. 2 (2001): 241.

56. On the power of mantras, see Ryūichi Abé, *The Weaving of Mantra: Kūkai and the Construction of Esoteric Buddhist Discourse* (New York: Columbia University Press, 1999), 337–339.

57. Bialock, citing the linguist John Austin, in *Eccentric Spaces,* 361.

58. Kathryn Linn Geurts, "Consciousness as 'Feeling in the Body,'" in *Empire of the Senses: the Sensual Culture Reader,* ed. David Howes (Oxford and New York: Berg, 2005), 176.

59. Bowring, *Murasaki Shikibu,* 51.

60. According to Murasaki Shikibu's diary, the twanging of the bows was performed during the Ceremony of the First Bath (*Yudono no gishiki*). Bowring, *Murasaki Shikibu,* 56–57, 61. Another example of meigen to scare mono-no-ke is described in the Yūgao chapter of *The Tale of Genji,* where Genji orders a palace guard to twang his bowstring after encountering a spirit. Tyler, *The Tale of Genji,* 67.

61. To protect the emperor, imperial bodyguards called Takiguchi performed meigen. These men also performed during certain purification rites, when they would twang their bowstrings to drive away evil spirits. Takemitsu Makoto, ed., *Suguwakaru Nihon no jujutsu no rekishi* (Tokyo: Tokyo Bijutsu, 2008), 76–77. Carmen Blacker, by contrast, argues that when a spirit medium twanged the strings of a bow, it was a way for the medium to summon or "cajole the presence of a malicious spirit." See Blacker, *Catalpa Bow,* 107.

62. Meigen is still practiced today at the birthing of an imperial prince, and also at many major shrines during the annual spring Setsubun festivals, such as at Matsuo Shrine and Tsuruoka Hachiman Shrine.

63. Bowring, *Murasaki Shikibu,* 61.

64. Ibid., 55.

65. In the novel, Yūgiri is woken from a dream by a commotion, and when he arrives at the scene (his wife nursing their baby), he finds the women scattering rice to exorcise malign spirits. Tyler, *The Tale of Genji,* 702, n.b. 16.

66. Ibid., 702–703.

67. *Konjaku monogatari shū,* fasc. 27, no. 31, in *Nihon koten bungaku taikei,* vol. 25 (Tokyo: Iwanami Shoten, 1975), 518–519.

5

Tethering Djinns

Sensation, Religion, and Contention in Popular Turkish Media

PERIN GUREL

On December 25, 1956, a meteor collided with the Earth, bringing death and destruction in its wake. The collapse of the surface infrastructure in Istanbul led to the resurgence of hidden species, including giant rats, Byzantine ghosts, and tribal djinns. Nothing has been the same since then. Now we live in a twenty-first century we could never have imagined. Will you be able to survive the online multiplayer computer game Istanbul Kıyamet Vakti (IKV, Istanbul Apocalypse)?

In 2007 Suat, a young Turkish worker in Germany, became plagued by hallucinations. High-tech body scans showed no signs of physical illness; the psychiatric drugs the German doctors had prescribed were not working. Worse yet, something seemed to be blocking Suat's phone conversations with his mother and the beautiful young bride he had left in his village. Frustrated and suicidal, he returned to Turkey. Before he went to his village, a friend helped him locate a sheik in Istanbul who discovered the cause of his sickness through divination: a djinn, long in love with Suat's new wife, not only had been haunting him in Germany but also had taken his place in his village home. Suat died a sudden death in Istanbul in a hotel bathroom. When the old sheik and his whole family, except for a little girl, also died unexpectedly, some neighbors suspected the sheik of practicing magic. But the village women who watched a young bride give birth to a half-djinn baby with twisted feet knew better. Do you dare expose yourself to what they saw by watching the horror movie *Musallat* (The Haunting)?

These are high-tech stories of twenty-first-century djinns, creatures that have dominated the Turkish religiofolkloric imagination for centuries. The two cultural products introduced above both contain djinns and claim to be some sort of "first" in Turkey. IKV, Turkey's first massively multiplayer online computer game (MMOG), was launched in 2006. Similarly, the producers announced that *Musallat,* a successful

89

2007 Turkish horror movie, was the first movie in which djinns were visually repre-sented in the world cinema. The Turkish press lauded both IKV and *Musallat* for their attempts to combine technology with cultural authenticity. Their production and reception, however, show how such contemporary djinn tethering comes with technological, financial, and imaginative difficulties at the production stage and with religiocultural complications at the level of reception.

Despite the common association of djinns with "possession" in the English lan-guage, this chapter uses *tethering* or *binding* to underline the precariousness of such representations and interpretations in media. Intended meanings, affects, and sensa-tions regularly threaten to dissolve or backfire during the production and consump-tion of high-tech djinn media. The quality of design and special effects at the pro-duction stage and the extratextual connections read in by the audience influence reception. The multisensory embodied experience of immersion that is essential to the success of video games and movies is marked by instability.

What pleasures and anxieties operate in the making and consumption of virtual djinns in contemporary Turkish media, and how do these sensations relate to extra-textual discourses about Turkishness and religion? Finding the answer requires study-ing basic, almost reflexive emotions and motions (such as the thrill gained from demolishing a virtual enemy in the computer game or an involuntary gasp following a shock-cut in the horror movie) alongside "higher-level" religious and sociocultural pleasures and anxieties experienced by the consumers. One must also compare the ideas and motivations guiding the production of these cultural works with their cha-otic reception, particularly as consumers negotiate the various levels of perceived reli-giosity and authenticity in each text, often using their multisensory experience of immersion and any lingering feelings as benchmarks. This study, therefore, involves close readings of comments volunteered by audiences and gamers online, participant observation in Turkish Internet cafes, and interviews with key cultural producers, as well as close readings of the texts themselves.

Building on on-site and online research conducted in Turkey and the United States in the winter of 2010 and the summer of 2011, this chapter argues that Turkish popular culture has entered an era in which it can materialize djinns via technological innovation by tethering them to human-made forms in the service of a nationalist cul-tural economy of "authenticity" and "strategic Westernization." Strategic Westerniza-tion is a nationalist doctrine of reform prescribed on the assumption that a country —in this case, Turkey—must "catch up" technologically, economically, and politically with the Western world while retaining its Turkishness.[1] As explored in the brief historical sketch below, djinns have long been part of Turkish folklore and Islamic teachings; realistic media representations of them, however, are the result of a new post-1980s neoliberal media regime. Earlier strategic Westernizers often sought to prove the nonexistence of djinns by propagating a secular, materialist worldview in their texts. Post-1980s cultural producers, on the other hand, have been more likely to fold djinns into strategic Westernization projects by producing profitable, technologically novel, but culturally "authentic" representations in new media. Djinns' presence in vernacular culture is also essential to the economic success of popular Turkish cultural products using them. The preexisting emotional constellations Turkish consumers bring to djinn media help further the multisensory experience of immersion and produce lingering effects, even where technology fails.

Far from a simplistic story of cultural imperialism versus cultural nationalism, the tethering of djinns to new Turkish media in the early twenty-first century is marked by transculturation, that is, cultural exchange and change across power differentials.[2] Tethering djinns is about the search for visual authenticity in a world saturated by the outputs of Hollywood products: representations of "authentic" Turkish djinns come to be haunted by popular Hollywood monsters, such as goblins and aliens, as early as the conception stage. It is also about money, know-how, and technologically "making do" in a country that has experienced a major but still precarious economic boom under a neoliberal government that is not afraid to speak the language of religion.

More than mere "entertainment," stories of twenty-first-century djinns provide a safely "apolitical" space for continuing public negotiations over the forms religion can and should take in the neoliberal public sphere, as well as the proper modalities and commitments of strategically Westernized Turkishness. Although the producers I have interviewed have not cited religion as a key motivating factor or subsumed any religious message and significance in the context of their search for "authenticity" or Turkishness, these products were marketed, consumed, and interpreted in complex ways once they were in the public sphere. They sparked multiple debates on the complex ideological triad on which contemporary Turkish identity has precariously teetered since at least the early twentieth century: Islam, modernization / strategic Westernization, and Turkishness.[3] These discussions and controversies tended to cluster around the multisensory aspects of the audience's engagement with each text, specifically around the complex experience of immersion and affective contamination, which build upon immediate psychological and physiological experiences as well as lingering thoughts, emotions, and sensations.

Religion, Fear, and Representation

Persian, Arabian, and Indian folk stories featuring djinns as a leitmotif, some of which were later collected in the famous *One Thousand and One Nights,* made their way into the Turkish language and mixed with the pre-Islamic tradition of folk tales about spirits called *peri* early in Turkish history. The Qur'an has also had a substantial influence; it mentions djinns multiple times and confirms their existence as a separate group of beings parallel to humans. According to the Qur'an, djinns are made of "the smokeless flame of fire" (15:27), in contrast to humans, who were created from "an altered black mud" (15:26). The Qur'an maintains that, on the day of reckoning, God will gather all beings together and chastise djinns for having led many humans astray (6:128).[4] Although djinns have long been sources of fear and awe for humans, the phrase *ins wa jinn* (humans and djinns) occurs frequently in the Qur'an, pointing to the parallels between the two creatures: djinns were created to worship God, just as humans were; they both possess free will; and both will be held accountable for their beliefs and actions (51:61).

The Qur'an and the hadith tradition, which builds on the reported narratives of the Prophet, give few clues as to the appearance and behaviors of djinns. They are invisible, even to Prophet Muhammad, in Surat Al-Jinn, Chapter 72 of the Qur'an, which depicts a group of djinns who accept Islam upon hearing the Prophet's recitation of the Qur'an. In the Qur'an, djinns are also depicted as unwilling and powerful slaves to the Prophet Solomon, for whom they construct palaces, places of worship, and everyday objects (38:37–38). This servitude ends only when Solomon dies, although the stories of *One Thousand and One Nights* tell of evil and powerful djinns (*ifrit*) locked in bottles, lamps, and rings for centuries by the seal of Solomon. In terms of appearance, one hadith states that "the jinn are of three types: a type that has wings, and they fly through the air; a type that looks like snakes and dogs; and a type that stops for a rest then resumes its journey."[5] Other ahadith repeat that djinns may take the shape of snakes.[6] The depiction of djinns in miniatures and manuscripts, although likely influenced by such theological descriptions, has taken a track of its own.

Djinns inspired material and visual culture in various ways in the pre-nineteenth-century Ottoman Empire and its neighbors. Perhaps most conventionally, they were the focus of amulets and talismans, apotropaic objects intended to ward them off. Amulets against djinns include powerful verses such as Ayat Al-Kursi, a famous verse of the Qur'an, and are sometimes marked with the seal of Solomon. Significantly, djinns themselves have also been the subjects of artistic depiction, allowing for imaginative chimeras. The thirteenth-century *Kitab 'Ajā'ib al-makhlūqāt wa Gharā'ib al-Mawjūdāt* (Marvels of Things Created and Miraculous Aspects of Things Existing), by famous Arab cosmographer and natural historian Al-Qazwini, was reproduced several times in Ottoman Turkey through the centuries; it depicts djinns as humanoids of various colors with the heads of dogs, camels, and elephants.[7] Fifteenth-century miniatures, now in the Topkapi Palace Libraries, by a Central Asian artist with the pen name Mehmed Siyah-Kalem, depict djinns as dark, horned, humanoid demons.[8] Siyah-Kalem's djinns share their unnatural coloration, horns, heavy bracelets, arm links, and chains with a famous 1568 Shi'a image depicting Imam Ali's defeat of an army of djinns (Figure 5.1). In all of these images, djinns are dressed sparsely, if at all, pointing to their wild nature in contrast to that of the civilized and impeccably clothed humans. Significantly, in such images humans tether djinns rather than the

FIGURE 5.1. Unknown artist (Ahsan-ol-Kobar), *Imam Ali Conquers Jinn,* 1568. Golestān Palace, Tehran.

opposite; this is apparent in their depiction as slaves in chains (or in the presence of the seal of Solomon) as well as in humans' ability to fashion these chimeric depictions of them.[9]

In the nineteenth-century Ottoman Empire, long besieged by Western imperial forces, the impulse to materialize (and thus control) djinns merged with the rise of "strategic Westernization," that is, the defensive borrowing of Western institutions and inventions with the aim of buttressing national power. Authors of novels and stories written in the realistic Western idiom increasingly began to draw attention to djinns, not as potential threats to individual salvation but as dangerous secular hoaxes. Ömer Seyfettin's 1919 short story "Perili Köşk" (The Haunted Mansion) (1919) exemplifies this strain of materialist writing. The story depicts a family in a rented mansion pestered by a spirit. Although the rest of the family is terrified, the well-educated father refuses to believe in any apparition he cannot feel with his hands. When he finally catches and touches the white specter that had been haunting the mansion's grounds, the tenant understands that what he has just felt with his fingers is not an otherworldly djinn but an ordinary white sheet worn by a human. That human turns out to be their landlord, who is trying to scare tenants away in order to profit from the large deposits paid by new renters. By removing the sheet, the father teaches a lesson to his family and the readers about their presence on a secular Earth: "Ben dünyada ecinni filan yoktur, demez miyim?" ("Haven't I told you that there are no djinns etc. in the world?").[10] Just as trapping djinns in material objects was the first step to mastering them in old manuscripts, in this story, materializing the djinn becomes the first step to unmasking it as a human-made fiction.

The post-Ottoman Turkish state directly inherited its project of strategic Westernization from rationalist intellectuals like Seyfettin, whose works continue to be a staple of elementary school curricula. Between his inauguration as president in 1923 and his death in 1938, Mustafa Kemal Atatürk, the founder of republican Turkey, implemented a series of reforms motivated by an ideology that combined nationalism and statism with strategic Westernization, commonly referred to as Kemalism. A central part of the Kemalist plan was bringing Islam under state control and eradicating "irrational ideas, magical superstitions, and religious beliefs that provided obstacles to economic and social progress."[11] Atatürk emphasized the essential irreconcilability of irrational superstition with Turkish strategic Westernization and nationalism: "Social life dominated by irrational, useless, and harmful beliefs is doomed to paralysis," he lectured. "Progress is too difficult or even impossible for nations that insist on preserving their traditions and beliefs lacking in rational bases."[12] Under Atatürk's lead, Kemalists waged a war against "superstitious" content in cultural texts; this religio-political battle entrenched a dichotomy between belief in djinns and progress that still haunts Turkish culture.[13]

Leftist and nationalist cultural producers continued this didactic project as the century progressed, even though it became evident, as early as the 1954 publication of Mahmut Makal's compendium of Anatolian folk beliefs, *Memleketin Sahipleri* (The Masters of the Country), that the state had not been able to untether humans from djinns' rule. According to Makal, superstitions about djinns, spirits, and magic dominated Turkish life and operated as the "real" masters of the country. In the 1970s and 1980s, populist films used djinn sightings either as comedy tropes mocking the backwardness and naiveté of uneducated Anatolians or as dangerous hoaxes. Films containing fake djinns, such as the 1976 *Süt Kardeşler* (Milk Siblings), featured popular comedians and sought to entertain and inform, privatizing and broadening the appeal of the Kemalist civilizing project.[14]

Materializing Djinns Neoliberally

Following the dismantling of the statist economy after the coup of 1980 and the rise of new independent media outlets in the mid-1980s and 1990s, Turkey experienced yet another iteration of djinns in popular culture. The coup brutally suppressed leftist movements, but it also paradoxically led to a "broadening [of] the [discursive] road," the effects of which resonated in Turkish media.[15] Issues deemed marginal or too coarse by the state now found airplay on the new private TV channels. Religion gained increasing influence in politics and a greater visibility in the public sphere, even as more and more Western, especially American, cultural products began streaming into Turkish homes.[16] "A synthesis has been realized between the West and Islam," declared President Turgut Ozal boldly in 1991. "This synthesis has ended the identity crisis of the Turk."[17] According to Ozal, the ideal Turk would now be both "a believer and open to all kinds of innovations."[18] This late modern synthesis of belief and strategic Westernization proved popular yet was sufficiently unstable that new identity crises and contentions emerged in its wake.

Differences between earlier depictions of djinns and the new generation of djinns in Turkish popular culture are profound, marking a new regime of antimaterialism and a playful attitude toward "superstitions." In the literary arena, magical realist novels like *Sevgili Arsız Ölüm* (Dear Shameless Death) (1983) by Latife Tekin and *The Bastard of Istanbul* by Elif Shafak (2006) have incorporated djinns into their texture as realistic characters. In popular culture, too, djinns have shed their educational roles to become formidable enemies. In the cult horror novel *Zifir* (Darkness) (2007), the MMOG IKV (2005), and the horror movie *Musallat* (2007), djinns are not cast as hoaxes to be revealed but as very real forces with which the modern world has to reckon. They are often incorporated into modern urban landscapes as opposed to being merely projected onto a backward Anatolia. Most interestingly, in these new cultural products djinns are not simply impediments to progress, strategic Westernization, and nationalism. On the contrary, their digital creation functions as a metonym for Turkish technological progress.

Outside the bounds of the state, in an increasingly globalized market economy, djinns are used to mark technological innovations even as they provide an aura of authenticity to the cultural products they inhabit. Thus they function in a renewed productive tension with ideas about the West, Turkish national identity, and Islam. Despite claims to "authenticity," the visualization of djinns is regularly haunted by popular Western representations of mythological beings like elves and goblins. Although cultural reformers of the early and mid-twentieth century sought laughter as a way of alleviating Turkish citizens' "irrational" fear of djinns, the contemporary cultural producers I have interviewed seek to avoid laughter because it would mark their technological failure vis-à-vis the United States, the center of the global media industry. Such visualization and materialization attempts are also complicated by the Islamic and folkloric preconceptions of the audience. In contrast to the top-down paternalistic cultural economy of the early twentieth century, in the information age the cracks between production and consumption, intentions and use, the textual and the extratextual become hypervisible as audiences talk (or type) back.

IKV, officially launched in 2006, is the brainchild of Mevlüt Dinç, a senior programmer who, following years of work in the United Kingdom, returned to Turkey to contribute to the development of the gaming field in the country in 2000. Building on Dinç's interest in carrying historic Istanbul to virtual reality, IKV is set in an alternate Istanbul, shaken and forever altered by a meteor that struck in 1956. This virtual Istanbul is plagued by previously hidden creatures like giant rats, werewolves, rat men, warlike Byzantine ghosts, and tribal djinns, against which the humans must fight for the soul of the city while also banding with and against each other. Like other MMOGs, IKV asks its players to design a character, go on missions, and battle creatures to gain new strengths and acquire new weapons and objects. What differentiate this game from the wildly popular *World of Warcraft,* however, are its Turkish setting and interface and the emphasis on Turkish cultural elements in the stories and missions.[19] The aim, according to Dinç, was to create "the feeling of a Turkish game" and to reflect "the cultural heritage of Turkish society." "All characters represent our own culture," he noted in a phone interview, "in their names, language, and mannerisms." The use of djinns served precisely this purpose.[20]

The promotional materials for the game describe djinns as tribal beings of low intelligence, cowards when alone but dangerous in groups. We learn that djinns emigrated to the surface of the earth once the meteor destroyed their underground habitations. Djinns breed rapidly, but they also sustain a high degree of intertribal violence. However, they can band together against humans. A promotional screenshot shows a small, muscular, dark green creature with yellow eyes, pointed features, and medieval European regalia (Figure 5.2). In fact, these creatures, original designs by IKV's Turkish artistic team, closely resemble the depictions of goblins in Western culture, exemplified in fantasy role-playing games such as *Magic: The Gathering* and *Dungeons and Dragons* and in video games such as *World of Warcraft.* Although djinns are both smart and shape shifting in traditional Turkish folklore, the IKV djinns do not seem to have these attributes. They are crude warriors with medieval weapons, not ethereal entities with the ability to cast spells and twist human limbs. As Dinç also notes, djinns are not the only antagonists in the game, which also contains werewolves, rat men, giant spiders, and other monsters with which djinns are cast together.

Because they are called djinns, however, IKV's djinns function awkwardly in a culture with the expectation that djinns transcend or exceed goblins in terms of such characteristics as invisibility, supernatural powers, and the ability to shift shapes and to harm humans by suddenly striking them and twisting their faces and limbs. In one forum discussion, for example, an IKV player joked that a technological flaw that misshaped his avatar and hampered its movement was the result of "Cin çarpması," or being struck and twisted by djinns. Others readily joined in on the joke.[21] In the

FIGURE 5.2. Istanbul Kıyamet Vakti, screen shot with djinn. Courtesy of Mevlüt Dinç and Sobee, Istanbul.

summer of 2010, the goblinlike djinns sparked more expansive discussion in one of the game forums:

> Yener096 [23 July 2010 17:27]: Hey, I gotta say something. Why does IKV say djinns are fairytale creatures? Our religion states clearly that something like this exists. I saw it in the [advertising] fragment, it says fairytale creatures. (Please write something).
>
> Yener096 [27 July 2010 16:50]: Comments pls.
>
> Dadawa [27 July 2010 19:49]: Like you say, such a thing is mentioned in our religion and in many religious books. But this is a game. Don't you think it would be weird for it to have a religious element?
>
> ScorpioN [05 Aug 2010 17:22]: As if there aren't other subjects to open, you are talking about this.
>
> Paranoyak [28 Sept 2010 13:30]: Yeah, well, maybe they should have the call to prayer in the mosque at Eminönü too :) This is a game not reality don't lose yourselves in it so much :)
>
> Maviakrepikv [30 Sept 2010 13:52]: Then there are no werewolves either :d
>
> [...]
>
> celik2626 [24 Oct 2010 17]: Do you think the djinns there look like they are being used by the devils? If it comes to that they should make a dabbe [a horror movie] version of the game and we should see the djinns in the mirror :D[22]

It is important to note that a pause occurred before any others responded to the question of Yenero96. There was also considerable resistance to and mockery of his or her concern. However, this was not the only time that IKV's superficially religious aspects, seen as a part of the Turkish mise-en-scène by the producers, came under religious scrutiny. The historic mosques of this virtual postapocalyptic Istanbul, for example, became the target of another debate. Although a player mentioned the possibility of the call to prayer jokingly in the discussion above, in February 2011 the possibility was brought up as a serious request, with some players insisting that it was necessary and others dismissing it as silly.[23] Some players also expressed distress that some of the missions are related by a pig-headed humanoid wearing a 1950s-style business suit, while others mocked such concerns. Whenever religious elements are inserted into the discussions in the forums, some players assert that religion has no place "in a game" and think the discussion is not worthwhile, whereas others suggest the opposite, as does a player with the nickname eLeaNoR, who finds the topic "normal and IMPORTANT" because "we live in a Muslim country."[24]

More posts on the forum, however, seem to have centered on immediate sensational concerns caused by such things as technological problems. As an MMOG, IKV creates a sensory universe combining visual (i.e., graphics), auditory (i.e., music and sound effects), and tactile features, such as the feeling of clicking a mouse repeatedly in combat. Like many MMOGs, the game employs three-dimensional graphics on a two-dimensional grid. The player can see his or her avatar as well as control it through an isometric third-person view. All computer games aim for perceptual and psychological immersion in which the senses of the player become submerged in the game world.[25] The experience of immersion goes beyond the visual to a holistic "feel" of the game, which has as much to do with the quality of the graphics as with that amorphous quality aficionados call "gameplay," the immediacy with which the character can traverse the world of the game.[26] In other words, a game without obvious lag time is likely to allow for a smoother "sensory-motoric immersion" experience.[27]

Based on my research in game forums and Internet cafes, IKV contains glitches that often result in a reduced sense of immersion and increased frustration. Players I have asked to test the game in Internet cafes have compared the graphics and gameplay unfavorably with those of Western MMOGs. Granted, these comments were from players with no emotional commitment to this particular game. Advanced and committed aficionados of IKV, however, also report setbacks that reduce the sense of immersion: invisible characters with only their shadows showing, characters or monsters that appear in places that they are not supposed to show up, spells that do not work, and creatures that keep on moving even though the computer says they are dead.[28]

The most often-repeated complaint is "lag," the amount of time that passes between a player's actions (such as a mouse click) and the manifestation of those actions on the screen (such as a spell). A forum commenter put it this way: "Lag is a problem.

We are embarrassed to keep saying this. I don't want to believe that your foundation is this bad. Because of these simple but annoying mistakes, the game appears crappy."[29] Another player responded that he or she had also complained about the same thing, and the production team "threw it into the wishing well—maybe it will get fixed around 2028."[30] The concept of lag is important because it has connotations of in-adequate "strategic Westernization" and supports the feeling that Turkey has not yet "caught up" with the West in technological proficiency. The second player's response sets up a symbolic equivalence between the lag in the game and Turkish digital technology: it operates fatalistically, through such things as wishing wells, and therefore with immense delays.

According to IKV's designer, Mevlüt Dinç, the Turkish computer game industry has indeed not yet "caught up" with the West and is even far behind ostensibly Eastern countries like Korea.[31] Given IKV's difficulties with immediate sensational experiences (i.e., gameplay), the cultural pleasures and nationalist commitments are essential to the game's continued success and its ability to boast of more than 700,000 registered players who make time investments that far exceed those made by fans of other types of media, such as movies. The kinds of sociocultural immersion and inter-activity IKV provides does motivate people to return to the game despite continued technical glitches.

First, like many MMOGs, IKV creates an online community but, unlike many, a Turkish-speaking (or rather Turkish-typing) one. In addition to the social element, the time and money invested to improve characters foster the sense of real-world importance and identification with the game. Most important, IKV allows for cultural interactivity with a Turkish life-world that combines an imagined past (i.e., the 1950s setting) and a postapocalyptic future. Cultural interactivity, according to online game developer Michael Sellers, is a "form of game play [that] involves giving the player a new historical or cultural perspective or articulating previously tacit cultural knowledge."[32] Many IKV players note that the "cultural" stuff, like the Turkish soundtrack, the sight of familiar buildings in Eminönü, and the Turkish names and titles of the characters, make the game more enjoyable. Cultural interactivity and immersion also lighten the discourse around some of the "humiliating" technical problems the game seems to harbor. In the lag example, shame felt regarding the persistence of the lag is softened through humor referring to the status of Turkish technology and super-stitions about wishing wells: a shared frustration with structural difficulties. The same can be said about the player who documented his avatar's technologically driven dis-tortion on the forum and joked good-humoredly with others that it must have re-sulted from being struck by djinns.

Despite occasional contestations around the IKV djinns' Islamic accuracy, this online community, so far, seems to have accepted the task of sporadically butchering small, pointy-featured tribal djinns. Underlying that acceptance is a tacit folkloric recognition: although IKV's djinns may resemble Western goblins, it is equally significant that they do not resemble Western genies. Many Western and Asian computer games include "genies," marked by turbans and tails of smoke, as do some of the role-playing games cited above.[33] The fact that IKV makes its djinns more similar to goblins than to genies (an Orientalist invention built on Western readings of *One Thousand and One Nights*) is another telling example of cultural immersion. Surprisingly, Western goblins are visually more similar to the depictions of djinns in Islamic manuscripts than are Western genies. This transcultural overlap is also implicitly articulated in Turkish translations of the Harry Potter books and films, in which house elves are called "cin" (djinn) and goblins are rendered "cin-cüce" (djinn-dwarf). Thus, despite the asserted peripherality of Islamic theology and/or early miniatures to the IKV project, the game's developers, in creating their djinns, have employed a cultural prerogative that reflects the force of local folklore vis-à-vis a Western-dominated visual culture industry. By tethering (Turkish) djinns to the bodies of (Western) goblins and bypassing (Orientalist) genies, IKV claims a hybrid linguistic and visual cultural space that is informed by what Turkish consumers will recognize as "Turkish," if not necessarily "Islamic."

Interestingly, a green sinewy goblin is also the kind of image one would find online in search of a "real" djinn. Internet legend has it that a group of youngsters unwittingly took a picture of such a creature in a cave in Saudi Arabia (Figure 5.3). The image has been passed around transnationally among Muslims for over a decade via photocopies, e-mails, and websites as well as conventional media. In 2004 Turkish journalist Ali Murat Güven revealed in an article he wrote that this sighting was a

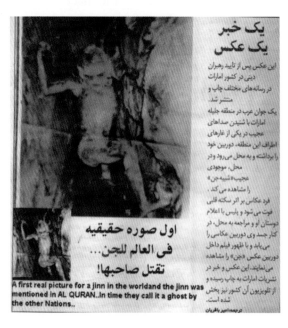

FIGURE 5.3. Unidentified newspaper clipping with "real" djinn. Courtesy of Murat Güven.

FIGURE 5.4. Murat Güven and the "real" djinn. Courtesy of Murat Güven.

hoax after discovering that the "djinn" in this photo was actually a plastic goblin in an English tourist shop called Crystal Quest in Cheddar Gorge.[34] The newspaper for which Güven worked printed multiple pictures of the so-called djinn, allowing readers to zoom in on its online version to see the truth for themselves. The paper also printed a picture of Güven grabbing the djinn's leg, smiling, and gesturing toward the audience (Figure 5.4). For an audience weaned on Ömer Seyfettin's "Perili Köşk," depicting a wise tenant who unmasks a djinn hoax by touching the djinn, this tactilely materialist pose would be deeply resonant.

In an e-mail to me, Güven stated proudly that this article had become one of the most "clicked" news articles in Turkish Internet history and noted its importance in "furthering the presence of a rationalist Muslim civic society" suspicious of "urban legends."[35] In addition to writing his article in Turkish, Guven also sent e-mails in English to Muslim reporters and bloggers across the Middle East, asking them to not continue to spread this hoax. However, unlike Seyfettin, he did not take a strictly materialist and secular position. Instead of claiming that djinns do not exist, he argued that they are made out of fire and therefore cannot be seen by human eyes or cameras. In his letter to a popular Muslim site, Güven also argued that belief in such hoaxes might do damage, in the West, to the image of Muslim cultures.[36]

Musallat

If Güven located the evolution of Turkish Islam in the unmasking of a plastic djinn, the creators of *Musallat* aimed to push the borders of Turkish film technology by deliberately building an artificial djinn. Attempting to materialize djinns "for the first time in Turkish and world cinemas" was quite a challenge for *Musallat*'s director, Alper Mestçi, and assistant director and director of special effects, Cem Gül.[37] The team had decided to produce a Turkish horror movie with a djinn as the main antagonist, and they set about figuring out whether, how, and how often to show the djinn in the movie. "Genies" had already been represented in the world cinema, of course, as had demons and various other monsters and fantastical creatures, some of which were called "djinns."[38] Mestçi and Gül, however, recognized none of the Western djinns and genies as authentic and were unaware of Middle Eastern filmic visualizations such as that in the 1988 Egyptian film *Ta'wīzah*, which depicts a horned, papier-mâché djinn.[39] They set out to watch horror movie after horror movie both to ascertain the veracity of *Musallat*'s claim to being a first in the world and to get clues as to how they might technologically achieve a realistic depiction.

To make sure that their scenario seemed authentic and plausible, they spoke with family and friends and read about djinns in books as well as online. For example, the main plot, of a djinn falling in love with a young girl at a Turkish bath and attaching himself to her for life, had a precedent in Internet lore. For the technical aspects of the creation of a monster, the team studied Hollywood movies and paid attention to monsters such as Jason and Freddy Kruger as well as orcs from the *Lord of the Rings* series. They worked with conceptual artists to decide on the depictions of the djinn and the half-djinn baby that is born of the union of the woman and the djinn. They settled on a tall, sinewy, bald, dark green creature with pointed ears and beastlike legs and feet and a pointy-eared, flesh-colored infant with twisted feet.

The team decided to create a creature that would not be "scary" per se but "creepy," "between being and non-being." The creature had to be different from the orcs and goblins of Western cinema, because those monsters had weapons and clothes and no spiritual or supernatural facilities. "They die when you cut them," Gül explains. By contrast, their djinn would have no need for clothes and no need to protect itself from the elements, and it would be impossible to kill with a sword, unlike IKV's djinns. The team also studied images from Islamic manuscripts online, such as the works of Al-Qazwini and Siyah-Kalem, but found them unsatisfactory because they were "not scary enough." The creature they came up with was built on oral and Internet folklore more than had been previous visual representations, Western or Eastern. However, it was necessarily haunted by them: the team worried, for example, that a tall, bald, dark green creature like the one they created might remind viewers of a Hollywood-style alien. Thus, in avoiding the stocky green goblins of American cinema in favor of a tall, ethereal creature, they risked running squarely into the boundaries of another Western visual import.

The special effects regime that propelled Hollywood to global prominence has long constituted an "Achilles heel" for the Turkish movie industry, which typically depends on cultural immersion for its successes.[40] Like several other contemporary high-tech movies with "Turkish" themes, such as the 2004 space comedy *G.O.R.A.* and the 2012 historical epic *Fetih 1453* (Conquest 1453), *Musallat* set out to challenge this binary. The monster was built transnationally and through a combination of special-effects makeup and computer-generated imagery (CGI). The conceptual designs were sent to a studio in Los Angeles, where silicone prosthetics were made for the actor playing the djinn to wear on his eyes, teeth, ears, nose, and spine. Three hours of special-effects makeup preceded CGI to make the actor playing the djinn appear thinner, taller, and more spectral than he really was.

The "first time" aspects of this transnational technological collaboration became a big part of the publicity effort to draw viewers to the film in a country in which horror movies historically have had a very limited market. The news items advertising the movie explained how the prosthetics and the lenses were made in Hollywood with the best materials and the most advanced technology. Similarly, the media announced that parts of the movie were filmed with the same technique used in the Hollywood blockbuster *The Matrix.*[41] According to the publicity, *Musallat* was worth seeing not only because it was the first film in the world to depict djinns and was based on "a real story" but also because it was a first in Turkey for its technology.

Gül, however, is very open about how difficulties regarding technology and resources put limits on the quality of the representation. In the film a djinn in love with a Turkish worker's wife takes his place in the man's village, driving him insane at his German workplace and trying to keep him away from the village. In the meantime, the djinn sleeps with and impregnates the worker's wife. Building on urban legends of sex with djinns, the team decided to take the story to the next level and show the result of such a union: a half-djinn infant that the village women immediately recognize as a djinn at the time of birth and stab with a pair of scissors. The conceptual artists designed a deformed baby with twisted feet, protruding spine, and pointy ears, which was then made out of silicone in Turkey (Figure 5.5). Gül notes that the materialization of the baby was unsuccessful and delayed because it was the first time the Turkish group the filmmakers hired had produced a whole baby for special effects. The team, however, felt that the baby must be shown because otherwise *Musallat* would resemble the cult movie *Rosemary's Baby,* in which the actors behave as if a hideous creature has been born offscreen. "In the twenty-first century, we had to be able to show this. Saying, 'Ahh, so scary' and stuff wouldn't have worked; it would have made the audience laugh!" says Gül. Because they were unsatisfied with the quality of the product, the team had to use a great deal of blood to cover its imperfections. Because the dummy's motorized limbs appeared mechanical and soon malfunctioned, the team used ropes to move the baby's limbs; Gül digitally removed the ropes in the editing room. The director could barely show the baby's twisted legs—key elements of the materialization of the legend—because the legs did not move, despite plans to the contrary. Gül was particularly displeased with the size of the head vis-à-vis the body because it

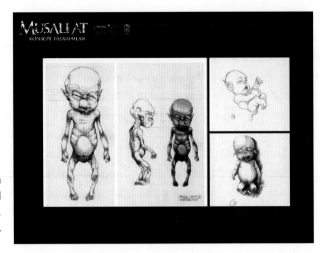

FIGURE 5.5. Mustafa Kural, *Djinn Baby,* conceptual design for the film *Musallat.* Courtesy of Cem Gül.

differed from the conceptual designs and gave the baby proportions resembling those of a three-month-old.

The impulse to materialize *Musallat* stemmed from a conviction that "it [was] about time," and thus from a sense of competition with the West and other Muslim countries—the latter imagined as stereotypically as the former. Although the mainstream media celebrated *Musallat's* materialization of djinns as a first in the world, unofficial reviewers criticized this choice for reducing the horror. A blogger argued that the dummy baby and its djinn father were huge strategic mistakes: "In *Musallat,* fear is fearlessly materialized. We can say that this materialization, in some ways, damages the atmosphere of tension. Because if you depict a djinn, you will reduce people's fear instead of increasing it. It is well known that humans are more afraid of what they cannot see."[42] The blogger's comments imply a tacit reference to Turkish classics like "Perili Köşk," in which the materialization of a djinn equals its elimination as an otherworldly menace. That unseen threats are more powerful is, of course, also a horror movie truism. Cem Gül is not entirely in disagreement with such arguments. The team had decided to show the djinn "partially out of stubbornness," but instead of going along with the storyboard that called for the djinn to make repeated appearances, they decided to signal the presence of the djinn most of the time through other markers, such as hallucinatory effects, CGI cockroaches, discordant sounds, and visual distortions. In the movie, the djinn appears only twice in its real form. Once, when the village women murder his baby, we see him lose his disguise briefly out of anger and sadness, and we see him in the mirror once again right before he kills Suat. The reduction in the materialization impulse was due to the fact that the team was seeking a creature "between being and non-being," as previously noted. However, it was also due to technological limitations. The team had imagined creating the djinn fully through 3-D animation, but they soon realized that they could not create a realistic enough creature and risked making the audience laugh. Thus they decided to use a combination of CGI and special-effects makeup, or a "morph," as is common in Hollywood. They also found it technologically impossible to exactly follow the storyboard. Many scenes simply seemed "ridiculous" when shot. Thus they cut out or changed scene after scene, creating a film that is, according to Gül, "a little more simple, not too scary, but at least serious."

In making these decisions the team was practicing "pragmatic aesthetics," that is, putting "technical and budgetary compromises to artistic effect," as many horror film producers do.[43] Some of the most celebrated low-budget horror movies use budgetary and technical compromises aesthetically, but *Musallat's* special-effects director views their compromises as having structural (not individual) roots, as a symptom of the Turkish film industry. The budget, he notes, was not all that small for a Turkish horror movie; the problem was a lack of Hollywood-style know-how, as exemplified by the malfunctioning three-month-old-looking "newborn."

The idea of an Islamic ban on making images or sculptures never came up in my discussions with producers about the materialization of djinns. In other words, iconophobia was not a determining factor for the production team, despite the religious undertones of the film. This does not mean, however, that there was no fear: fear of technological insufficiency, fear of lack of support, and fear of laughter clearly plagued the production process. Anxiety about creating laugher instead of fear was particularly acute in *Musallat,* because earlier examples of Turkish horror movies from the 1970s regularly bear the brunt of laughter on YouTube. For classical Turkish cinema produced between 1950 and 1980 (referred to as *Yeşilçam*), horror film, in particular, "emphasize[d] in part what Yeşilçam is not and cannot be."[44] *Musallat* generally succeeded in overcoming that particular curse of Turkish horror movies and managed to both scare and enchant its audience. It brought over 350,000 viewers to the box office in a country where horror movies usually claim around 50,000 viewers. It covered its production costs—more than 1,000,000 Turkish lira (approximately US$800,000 in 2007)—and even made a tidy profit. On the whole, Cem Gül is happy that *Musallat* was "saved from becoming a ridiculous movie."

As in the case of a computer game, multisensory immersion is important for a horror movie—a genre defined by the type of emotional and physiological responses it is supposed to elicit. *Musallat* makes extensive use of conventional Hollywood codes of horror, including jump-cuts, claustrophobic and canted framing, dizzying camera angles, extremes of dark and light, unnatural movements, distorted high-angle point-of-view shots implying the djinn's gaze, and discordant sounds. It uses the abject through nauseating images of blood, gore, creepy bugs, lust, pregnancy, and disease. It takes viewers on a rollercoaster ride from a horrifically antiseptic Berlin to a crooked and cramped Istanbul to a claustrophobic village and forces them to confront the ritual washing of a dead body, the purple-blue veins of a pregnant belly almost bursting at the seams with a monstrous baby, and the twisted faces and limbs of multiple victims. In line with horror's work as "a body genre," *Musallat* courts the immediate haptic sensations of shock and disgust.[45] However, it also aims for a deeper extratextual, religiocultural horror that transcends the film's immediate cinematographic wizardry.

Musallat's mobilization of preexisting fears of djinns in Turkish culture helps explain its success almost as much as its directors' use of pragmatic aesthetics. In the case of a horror movie like *Musallat,* immersion depends on extratextual codes, discourses, and performances preceding and following the actual viewing of the film. These include ad campaigns using multiple media, newspaper articles, trailers, and word-of-mouth marketing, such as, in the case of *Musallat,* the (unfounded) urban legend that the studio retained an imam to protect the actors with prayers during filming, which circulated ahead of the movie's release. These build up audience fears and anticipation on the way to the cinema and compound the cultural and religious preconceptions and expectations a viewer brings to the movie. Such pre-sensations, in turn, are activated in the dark movie theater and merge with the visual and aural codes the movie projects. Ideally, the anxiety continues to haunt the viewer after the experience of viewing. Successful horror movies manage to evoke a lingering "affective contamination" as the film's key moments are remembered and its possibilities are applied to the viewer's life.[46] A movie like *Musallat* must make an example of its protagonist and antagonist, pointing to the real-life possibility that a malignant djinn is perhaps watching the viewer in the present, real-time moment. In a consumer-capitalist economy, the movie must also prepare the audience for its own sequel, such as the 2011 *Musallat 2.*

As in the case of computer games, cultural immersion is important for the Turkish film industry, which must consistently compensate for technological weaknesses by promising local affects.[47] Just as *Musallat*'s advertising exploits nationalistic commitments and the ideology of strategic Westernization by emphasizing its supposed "first-time" status and "authenticity," its cinematography urges viewers to connect the film to familiar extratextual events and texts. *Musallat* encourages extratextual connections in plot as well as cinematography. The film starts with news-style interviews with ordinary individuals (probably not professional actors) filmed via steadicam, referencing a realistic documentary aesthetic. All of the witnesses say something about how scared they have been since an unspecified horrible event. Some try to anxiously make light of the situation; others simply refuse to comment. The grainy daytime documentary then leads into a credits sequence, shot with low-key lighting, depicting the ritual washing of a dead body in moonlight through fractured close-ups and extreme close-ups as the distorted sound of the Muslim call to prayer echoes in the background. The film suddenly cuts to a fly-on-the-wall camera in a well-lighted modest living room in Germany. We watch Suat making tea using a kettle and a tea bag, chatting with a friend about how much he misses his village, including the Turkish-style tea made by his mother. Cultural sensations and anxieties are evoked as Suat imbibes the inferior Western tea. The "real" tea is out of reach, just as are his wife's body and his mother's warmth.

As the audience will realize only toward the end of the film, the vulnerable dead body being washed in the opening sequence belongs to Suat, murdered by his djinn rival. From the film's onset, Suat's disempowerment has been fixed. The ritual washing scene also foreshadows a key moment of the film, the origin of all its crises: the djinn watching the body of Suat's future wife as she bathes as a young girl in a Turkish bath. As Gül also comments, underneath the supernatural horror, *Musallat* courts broader gendered cultural themes: exile and alienation in the West, isolation in an Anatolian village, and the violation of a man's honor as his wife's body is brought to ecstasy and agony by an Other.

The reception of *Musallat* shows an interaction between the film's ability to function as a distinct "embodied event," using technical codes and special effects to produce immediate changes in the viewers' "embodied minds," and its ability to evoke lingering extratextual religiocultural anxieties.[48] As of August 2013, *Musallat* held a rating of 5.9/10.0 on the international website Internet Movie Database (IMDb), where it has been reviewed in English ten times. Nine out of ten of these comments are from Turkey; the latest comment is dated March 2010. On the other hand, the film has a 7.1/10.0 rating on the Turkish equivalent of IMDb, Sinemalar.com, where it has garnered 1,099 short reviews in Turkish. Around 1,360 users have marked it as a "favorite"; the latest three comments, from August 16, August 8, and August 7, 2013, reveal an ongoing discussion about the quality of Turkish horror movies and their use of "real" religious elements, such as djinns.

Whether in English or Turkish, most of these online commentaries refer to the film's use of cinematic codes, often comparing the film's special effects favorably to those of other Turkish movies. Turkish viewers also articulate the importance of their own preexisting religiocultural fears in driving their enjoyment of the film. The following comment, for example, was posted in English to IMDb and seeks to relate the viewer's Turkish/Muslim experience of cultural immersion to the experience of potential non-Turkish visitors:

> I watched the film and I liked it. Because this movie is not identical to
> other Turkish horrors. Subject is interesting, acting is surprisingly good
> and the directing is quite successful. And also this subject is very gruesome
> for Muslim audiences. Because there are a lot of legends and tales about
> Cins [djinns] in Turkish Culture. In the first part of the movie many ques-

tions are taking shape in the watcher's mind. And all the questions are answered by the director in the second part of the movie. The leading actor Burak Özçivit is pretty successful. The special effects are remarkable. And the sequence of events in the movie are inspired by true events. At last everybody must see this film.[49]

The commentator is pleased with the pragmatic aesthetic choices made by the film's directors. However, even Turkish reviewers who are critical of the acting and the special effects note that the extratextual aspects of the movie make it truly scary, demonstrating the importance of cultural immersion to *Musallat*'s success. Many viewers, both critical and positive, refer to the religious reality of djinns and their understanding that the film was "based on a true story" in their ratings. Almost all of the reviewers on Sinemalar.com refer to other Turkish horror movies, Hollywood, and/or their own perceptions of the reality of djinns in judging the film. The commentators also use *Musallat* as an opportunity to discuss Turkey's stage on the road to strategic Westernization and its ability to reproduce the "authentic" in an era marked by Hollywood's near monopoly on commercial film production. In addition, as in the case of IKV, the film helps consumers launch "apolitical" discussions on the possible uses and exploitation of religious sentiments. Religious aspects make the film scarier for almost all commentators, but some insist that these should not be used because they play with deep sensibilities and leave lingering effects (i.e., affective contamination): "Is it right to make films with religious elements? That is up for debate. Because you know it is real and, whether you want it or not, it comes to your dreams or somehow it enters your subconscious and you cannot forget it."[50] This question was repeated and answered in multiple ways on Sinemalar.com, and the discussion continues online.

In many ways, the depictions of djinns in contemporary Turkish popular culture amount to a tethering of djinns for human purposes, echoing Solomon's Qur'anic mastery over djinns, even when djinns emerge triumphant in the actual (human-made) narrative. Fear beyond the merely reflexive, however, is never an ahistorical force; human fears are made and contested in specific contexts. In Turkey the drive to represent djinns is deeply connected to the project of strategic Westernization, debates over the role of Islam in the public sphere, and the general sense of being in competition with the rest of the world economically, culturally, and technologically. Just as Solomon's djinns helped convince the Queen of Sheba of his cultural and religious superiority, modern Turkish djinns work hard to convince Turks and others of national authenticity and competitive technological expertise. In doing so, they reveal important anxieties and pleasures residing in the borderlands of the secular and the religious, production and reception, Westernization and authenticity, and the sensational, in both senses of the term.

NOTES

1. Perin Gurel, "Wild Westernization: Gender, Sexuality, and the United States in Turkey," Ph.D. dissertation, Yale University, New Haven, CT, 2010.

2. For more on "transculturation," see Mary Louise Pratt, *Imperial Eyes: Travel Writing and Transculturation* (London: Routledge, 1992).

3. See, for example, Ziya Gökalp, *Türkleşmek, İslamlaşmak, Muasırlaşmak* (Turkification, Islamification, and modernization) (Istanbul: Toker, 1997 [1918]).

4. For more, see Perin Gurel, "Djinn/Genie," in Jeffrey Andrew Weinstock, ed., *The Ashgate Encyclopedia of Literary and Cinematic Monsters* (Farnham, UK: Ashgate, 2014).

5. Reported by al-Tahhaawi in *Mushkil al-Athaar,* 4/95, and by al-Tabaraani in *al-Kabeer,* 22/214, reproduced in "Jinn According to the Qur'an and Sunnah," in *Muttaqun Online,* accessed April 21, 2012, http://muttaqun.com/jinn.html.

6. Sahih Muslim, Book 026, Hadith 5557, accessed April 21, 2012, searchtruth.com.

7. Zakarīyā ibn Muḥammad al-Qazwīnī, *'Ajā'ib al-makhlūqāt wa-gharā'ib al-mawjūdāt* (Marvels of things created and miraculous aspects of things existing), National Library of Medicine, Turning the Pages Online, accessed April 21, 2012, http://archive.nlm.nih.gov/proj/ttp/qazwini_home.html.

8. Mine Haydaroğlu, *Ben Mehmed Siyah Kalem: İnsanlar ve Cinlerin Ustası* (I, Mehmed Siyah Kalem: The master of djinns and humans) (Istanbul: Yapı Kredi Yayınları, 2004).

9. It is doubtful that a *longue durée* cultural memory with regard to such Islamic depictions exists in contemporary Turkey, although resemblances explored later in this chapter may point to this possibility. These few images, however, are widely available online at Turkish sites and form a possible "authentic" visual source for producers to tap into, in addition to Hollywood genies, other "Western" creatures like goblins or aliens, and the mainly linguistic archive provided by folklore.

10. This and all other translations from Turkish are my own.

11. Metin And, "Atatürk and the Arts, with Special Reference to Music and Theater," in *Atatürk and the Modernization of Turkey,* ed. Jacob M. Landau (Leiden: Brill, 1984), 215–232, quote on 215.

12. Quoted in Niyazi Berkes, *Development of Secularism in Turkey* (Montreal: Routledge, 1964), 465.

13. Perin Gurel, in "Sing, O Djinn!: Memory, History, and Folklore in *The Bastard of Istanbul,*" *Journal of Turkish Literature* 6 (2009): 59–80, elaborates some of this history, particularly as it pertains to literature.

14. Although djinns occasionally appeared in a comedic context in traditional Ottoman shadow puppetry (i.e., Karagöz-Hacivat plays), they functioned as real characters, not as hoaxes to be unveiled.

15. Erik J. Zurcher, *Turkey: A Modern History* (New York: I. B. Tauris, 2003), 298.

16. Nurdan Gürbilek, *Vitrinde Yaşamak: 1980'lerin Kültürel İklimi* (Living in the store windows: The cultural climate of the 1980s) (Istanbul: Metis, 2001).

17. Nicole Pope and Hugh Pope, *Turkey Unveiled: A History of Modern Turkey* (New York: Overlook, 1998), 170.

18. Ibid.

19. *World of Warcraft* is currently the world's most popular MMOG, with over ten million subscribers across the world. *World of Warcraft Statistics* and Survey Poll, *Squidoo,* n.d., accessed August 13, 2012, http://www.squidoo.com/world-of-warcraft-statistics.

20. Mevlüt Dinç, phone interview by author, Istanbul, July 12, 2011.

21. "Cinler Seklimi Kaydirdi" (Djinns misshaped me), IKV Forum, accessed July 12, 2011, http://www.ikvonline.net/4565-cinler-%C5%9Feklimi-kayd%C4%B1rd%C4%B1.html.

22. "IKV'de Cinler" (Djinns in IKV), IKV Forum, accessed April 21, 2012, http://forum.istanbuloyun.com/viewtopic.php?f=61&t=30460.

23. "IKV'de ezan sesi duyabilecek miyiz?" (Will we get to hear the call to prayer at IKV?), IKV Forum, accessed April 21, 2012, http://forum.istanbuloyun.com/viewtopic.php?f=46&t=53552&start=0.

24. Ibid.

25. Staffan Björk and Jussi Holopainen, *Patterns in Game Design* (New York: Cengage Learning, 2004), 206.

26. Many game scholars prefer the term *ergodicity* to *gameplay* and define it as "nontrivial effort required by the reader to traverse the text." Espen Aarseth, *Cybertext: Perspectives on Ergodic Literature* (Baltimore: Johns Hopkins University Press, 1997), 1.

27. Björk and Holopainen, *Patterns in Game Design,* 206.

28. "Oyundaki Hatalar" (Mistakes in the game), IKV Forum, January 16, 2012, http://forum.istanbuloyun.com/viewtopic.php?f=46&t=86161.

29. Ibid.

30. Fahrenheit, response to "Oyundaki Hatalar," IKV Forum, January 16, 2012, http://forum.istanbuloyun.com/viewtopic.php?f=46&t=86161.

31. Dinç, phone interview.

32. Michael Sellers, "Designing the Experience of Interactive Play," in *Playing Video Games: Motives, Responses, and Consequences,* ed. Peter Vorderer and Jennings Bryant (Mahwah, NJ: LEA, 2006), 9–21, quote on 21.

33. Philipp Reichmuth and Stefan Werning, "Pixel Pashas, Digital Djinns," *ISIM Review* 18 (2006): 46–47, https://openaccess.leidenuniv.nl/bitstream/handle/1887/17085/ISIM_18_Pixel_Pashas_Digital_Djinns.pdf?sequence=1.

34. Ali Murat Güven, "'Efsane Cin' Enselendi" ("The legendary djinn" has been caught), *Yeni Şafak,* October 5, 2004, http://yenisafak.com.tr/arsiv/2004/ekim/05/tarih.html.

35. Ali Murat Güven, e-mail to author, July 31, 2012.

36. Ali Murat Güven, letter to Anvari.org, accessed April 21, 2012, http://www.anvari.org/fun/Farsi/Jinn_Picture.html.

37. Cem Gül, interview by author, Istanbul, August 3, 2011. Subsequent quotes drawn from the same interview.

38. Mark Allen Peterson, "From Jinns to Genies: Intertextuality, Media, and the Making of Global Folklore," in *Folklore/Cinema: Popular Film as Vernacular Culture,* ed. Sharon R. Sherman and Mikel J. Koven (Logan: Utah State University Press, 2007), 93–113.

39. Ibid., 96–97.

40. Savas Arslan, *Cinema in Turkey: A New Critical History* (New York: Oxford University Press, 2011), 163.

41. "Musallat'a Hollywood Makyajı, Matrix Tekniği Uygulandı" (Hollywood makeup, *Matrix* technique applied to *Musallat*), *DivxPlanet,* December 12, 2011, http://divxplanet.com/index.php?page=haber&sid=90.

42. "*Musallat* Film Eleştirisi" (*Musallat* film critique), *Selcuk Hoca,* November 16, 2007, http://www.selcukhoca.com/musallat-film-elestirisi/.

43. Thomas M. Sipos, *Horror Film Aesthetics: Creating the Visual Language of Fear* (Jefferson, NC: McFarland, 2010), 29.

44. Arslan, *Cinema in Turkey,* 163.

45. Linda Williams, "Film Bodies: Gender, Genre, and Excess," *Film Quarterly* 44, no. 4 (1991): 2–13.

46. Anna Powell, *Deleuze and Horror Film* (Edinburgh: Edinburgh University Press, 2005), 4.

47. Arslan, *Cinema in Turkey,* 79.

48. Powell, *Deleuze and Horror Film,* 234, 80.

49. CuneytBaskaya, "Alper Mestçi is in a good way of horror," IMDb, August 23, 2008, http://www.imdb.com/title/tt1077091/reviews.

50. Ceylan62, "*Musallat* Hakkinda" (About *Musallat*), Sinemalar.com, October 9, 2011, http://www.sinemalar.com/kullanici/ceylan62/yorumlari/0/3/.

6

Shadowy Relations and Shades of Devotion

Production and Possession of the 1886 Smith College Composite Photograph

KATI CURTS

In July 1886, John T. Stoddard published an article in the journal *Science* featuring a set of recently completed composite photographs. That same year a group of women at Smith College put on a play written by their classmate Zulema A. Ruble in celebration of their impending graduation. The principal protagonist of both productions was the same: a representation of the Smith College Class of 1886. This representative figure was initially generated in photographic form by superimposing the negatives of all forty-nine members of the graduating cohort with the aid of new camera technology and techniques. It was then personified and performed in writing, verse, and dramatic form by the graduating class. The Smith women christened the image Composita, and her visage quickly garnered high praise among classmates and critics alike (Figure 6.1). However, the graduating class was not the only thing being celebrated; so, too, was the photographic process that brought Composita into the world. The *New York Times* reported that this composite captured "a face of wonderful beauty, strength and refinement" by way of a "new and remarkable process." During the years 1885 and 1886 alone, *Science* published more than ten articles about new uses of and methods in composite photography. It was, indeed, a time of commencement for the Smith women as well as for this emerging photographic technique.[1]

This chapter traces the story of the Smith College Class of 1886 composite photograph as it was exposed in scientific publications and circulated among the image's component sitters—as a picture and play of both scientific classification and class devotion. It explores how the contours of Composita took shape and the ways in which this photographic possession and performative subject accommodated sensual and sensational inhabitation. But why should students and scholars of *religion* care about Stoddard's pictures or Ruble's play? The question cuts to the heart of definitional and

"Composita" 1886

LOVELL PHOTO.—NORTHAMPTON. MASS.

FIGURE 6.1. John T. Stoddard, "Composita" of Class of 1886. Composite photograph created from negatives taken by the Lovell Brothers of Hardie and Lovell, Northampton, Massachusetts. Courtesy of Smith College Archives, Smith College, Northampton, Massachusetts.

methodological concerns in studies of religion as well as ongoing discussions about the choices scholars make in nominating and analyzing sources—about what can and cannot properly be examined under the rubric "religion." Scholars and students in the field of religious studies have, in recent years, ably demonstrated the material and discursive formation of religion as an analytic category forever reshaped and reproduced in concert with other epistemological categories and amid a tangled historical and cultural terrain. A first- and second-order category, a term of scholarly analysis and an operative framework in popular discourse and public life, religion has proven to be not only plural but also exceedingly porous. This is to say that religion and whatever it is distinguished from, typically that which is "secular," have been shown to be much less distinct than often assumed.[2]

In taking up the Smith College Class of 1886 composite photograph within the interpretive matrix of *Sensational Religion,* I want to suggest that studies of the sensory cultures of religion(s) can usefully entertain questions about the blurry outlines of the religious and the secular. Following Talal Asad's proposal that these co-constitutive categories are best pursued indirectly through their "shadows," I approach questions of the religious and the secular through their hazy historical relations and offer a narrative of the production and possession of Composita as an allegory for the practices and products of that-which-is-deemed-religious and that-which-is-not. Through this historical allegory of the recondite relations imbuing the religious and the secular, the scientific and the devotional, I consider how scientists and students, images and imaginings confront multiplicity and division amid desires for identity and association, for singularity and sociality. I narrate how they layer upon, touch, blend, expose, obscure, and shadow one another. What follows, then, is an attempt to "speak otherwise" about the intimate connections between and among humans and things as they negotiate the misty margins of religion and the secular.[3]

I begin by discussing the creation of the 1886 Smith composite through Stoddard's commentary on the subject as well as composite photography's historical and genealogical connections to related scientific and aesthetic projects. Attending to the profoundly social and material consequences of composite photography's seemingly immaterial conceptualizations, I then turn to the ways in which the image circulated among and was repossessed by the women who haunted its shadows. I consider the ways the college's graduating class embodied the composite photograph and interrogate the historical and cultural processes by which Composita came to serve as an icon of femininity and whiteness. In so doing, I suggest that the composite photograph reproduces not only a collegial camaraderie but also a class-based devotion to a particular kind of civilizing mission. Throughout, I demonstrate how composite photographs are constituted as profoundly multisensory objects; these superimposed images help to expose the ways in which embodiment is never unmediated but is rather deeply situated within historically and culturally constructed relations of power. I further suggest that studies of these power relations can contribute to a longer history of feminism and religion in the United States. Ultimately, I argue that this particular photoperformative form exposes a multilayered history—of photographic process and devotional play, of educating middle-class women and professionalizing scientific men, of picturing bodies and embodying pictures.[4]

Stoddard, Producing the Composite

As a long-time professor of chemistry and physics at Smith College, John Tappan Stoddard was interested in instruments and techniques developed for the study of perspective and visualization. He experimented with X-ray imaging and designed his own camera for the creation of composite photographs (Figure 6.2). Although Stoddard produced a number of composites for Smith College in the 1880s and 1890s, his 1886 composite took on special significance, primarily due to (what he perceived to be) its contributions to methodological precision in composite creation. Like other scientific men of the era, Stoddard presented his composite photographs as "pictorial averages" that required a precise method for an exacting result. For, Stoddard explained, "only those composites which are made according to the same method of adjustment can be properly compared as types." The creation of "types" was important precisely because of the need to compare and to differentiate—criminal from credible, ruse from religion, sham from science—which was itself typical of the late nineteenth century.[5]

Stoddard's concern for this typological comparative imperative also emerged from a long history of composite projects, photographic and otherwise. Over the course of the Enlightenment and into the nineteenth century, composite creations inhabited the boundaries of antiquarianism, whimsy, oddity, and science. By the late nineteenth century, two forms and practices were most commonly (and simultaneously) going by the name composite. The first closely resembles what today might be more commonly referred to as collage or photomontage. This kind of composite emerged as artists and photographers began to graft together separate images of clouds with landscape photos as a way to produce a more pleasing image, particularly given the limitations of the wet collodion negative's sensitivity to blue light and its tendency to overexpose sky tones. These composite assemblages were often then rephotographed, and one account of the practice suggested that it was this final rephotographic act that distinguished the resultant image as a composite.[6]

Nineteenth-century scientists, too, discussed methods for producing a composite, including the employment of entertainment technologies like prisms, magic lanterns, stereopticons, panoramas, and stereoscopes. Stoddard himself referred to the stereoscope as a tool for creation of an ephemeral composite but argued that it and other means of such composite creation needed to be improved in order to yield "an

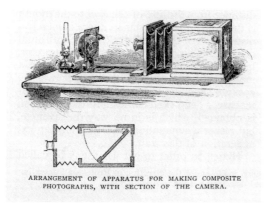

FIGURE **6.2.** "Arrangement of Apparatus for Making Composite Photographs, with Section of the Camera," from John T. Stoddard, "Composite Photography," *Century Illustrated Monthly Magazine* 33, no. 5 (1887): 753. Courtesy of Smith College Archives, Smith College, Northampton, Massachusetts.

ARRANGEMENT OF APPARATUS FOR MAKING COMPOSITE PHOTOGRAPHS, WITH SECTION OF THE CAMERA.

objective and permanent result" for comparative, scientific practice. Indeed late nineteenth-century discourse rarely explicitly identified as composites the products of processes like that of the stereoscope, for they were often perceived as limited and less secure versions of the pictorial averages otherwise sought by nineteenth-century scientists. Instead the *composite* moniker was given to another photographic production, one typified by the works of Francis Galton. The nephew of Charles Darwin and an infamous nineteenth-century eugenicist, Galton was well known at the time for his use of multiply exposed photos created by superimposing the negatives of several portraits, and Stoddard's 1886 creations, in form and practice, adhered most closely to this latter, Galtonian form.[7]

Said to have originated in an 1876 conversation between Galton and Herbert Spencer, the superimposed form of composite imagery explicated, in social Darwinist style, particular "types," or average features characteristic (and even definitive) of particular classes of human beings. As other studies of composite photography have usefully demonstrated, Galton's procedures and pictures of composite creation were deeply implicated in the production and study of criminality and eugenics in the nineteenth and twentieth centuries. Historians of visual culture have likewise linked these photographic forms to the ways in which "looking itself is a racial act and being looked at has racial effects." Employing photographic practices to identify, classify, and categorize bodies into a biotheological Great Chain of Being, scientists and eugenicists approached these composites as a visible mean, Stoddard's "pictorial average," generated through the objectifying gaze of a (white, male) researcher. Attempting to ascribe an evidentiary basis to racism, these scientists linked photography to biological racialism.[8]

As recent scholarship has noted, however, including several chapters in this volume, vision and visuality are not and need not be understood as disembodied sensations. Even when photographers enacted techniques that apparently attempted disembodiment or an erasure of the body, they did so, at least in part, because the photographic image in nineteenth-century discourse was often assumed to be implicitly indexical to a broader range of the human sensorium. Photographers like Stoddard proposed a seemingly immaterial figuration as an attempt at photographic purification—a way to expose the final, essential features entangled in presumably ever-embodied forms even as they simultaneously materialized human types. In other words, composite photography did not always or only attempt an erasure of the body for a floating head. Rather, a history of composite photography, in its links to physiognomy and anthropometric measurements, attests to the ways in which pictured faces and forms were made to be violently dis/embodied through a robust sensory racialization and sensationalizing process reproduced by and made to be held within the apparent truth of a composite photograph. To propose that the composite photograph is only visual, then, is to ignore or needlessly separate the practices of creation from the image; such a tactic supposes process severed from product. As Stoddard's commentary about the 1886 composite attests, however, methods of creation are precisely inseparable from the result.

Stoddard's argument, first advanced in the pages of the journal *Science,* primarily sought to distinguish between two technical processes in the creation of his composites (Figure 6.3). Both images were created from the same negatives of the class of 1886. Their difference, Stoddard explained, lay in the photographic process; a better method made for a more accurate average. The figure on the left, Stoddard's preferred image, thus avoided the pitfalls of what he referred to as the "disfigurement" of the one on the right, that is, the appearance of multiple mouths and imposing eyes. This is to say that the question was, for Stoddard and his fellow scientists, how to appropriately align the multiple exposures in order to render the most definitive and unified image of this collective subject. In producing a composite, Stoddard explained, the photographer had to decide whether to select the eyes as the point of intersection among the combined portraits or whether to adjust them according to the average ratio of the distance from eyes to mouth. In Stoddard's process, the figure on the left represented the distance ratio method, the one on the right the eye-oriented one. To align the eyes, for Stoddard, was to risk disfigurement as well as a kind of falsity in figuration. Stoddard explained his preference for the processes and production of the picture on the left thus: "Composites made in this way lose something of the deepeyed, earnest expression, which is the result of superposing all the eyes of the components on exactly the same points. This loss, however, is a real gain in the truthfulness of the composite portrait, for the deep, dark eyes do not represent the average, but rather a summation, and hence exaggeration of earnest expression."[9] Stoddard's preference suggests the ways in which composite photos served as embodied sensory and sensationalized photographs. He implicitly challenged a simplistic regime of the visual, forcing and enforcing a more robust sensory inhabitation in the composite, one that he suggested is more truthful. Without the careful practice and control of photo-

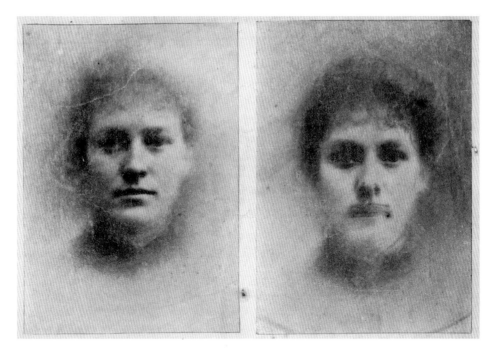

FIGURE 6.3. "Composite Portraits of Some Smith College Students," detail from a photographic plate published in *Science* 8, no. 182 (1886). Courtesy of Smith College Archives, Smith College, Northampton, Massachusetts.

graphic technology and technical expertise, Stoddard argued, the composite holds a distinct potential for exaggeration and imbalance, which risks spilling out and disfiguring the otherwise precisely rendered Smith student—blemishing the ideal and spurring questions about distinctions between hoodlum and holy. In order to attain the true over the tainted, Stoddard advocated a method that resisted ocular alignment and its apparent tendency to exaggerate.

This concern with surplus was noteworthy for scientists and scholars like Stoddard in the closing decades of the nineteenth century. Immigration had increased the country's population, but according to some it did so in seemingly troublesome ways. Rural America appeared to be disappearing as the urban landscape swelled with new residents relocating from less populated areas of the country. Catholics and Jews streamed into cities along the eastern seaboard during the second half of the century as the country industrialized, challenging what had been largely presumed by many to be a decidedly Protestant nation. A changing labor market promised class mobility but often ended in inescapable sweatshop conditions. Popular revivals swept the nation in the 1870s and 1880s, and, after two decades of Reconstruction, freed blacks continued to mobilize oppositional discourses against a reemerging white American nationalism. In the decades following the Civil War, the best-selling book in the country, after the Bible, was Josiah Strong's *Our Country*. Published in 1885 when visions of North–South reunification of whites were heralded and a postwar nationalism sanctified racial segregation and conflated Protestant Christianity, whiteness, and American identity, Strong's polemic extolled the perils of excessive immigration, religious enthusiasm, unhygienic standards, alcohol, and other concerns ostensibly related to city life. It was the immigrant, the drunk, the primitive, and the feminized that threatened America's righteous future, Strong asserted. Only the ongoing reproduction of a "mighty Anglo-Saxon race" with its powers of civilization—notably its masculine virility, Christian charity, and English language—could save the United States from the excesses afflicting it. *Our Country* likewise contributed to increasing discourse on the missionary obligation of white Protestants. It was, argued Strong, the duty of (white) American Christians to go forth into the rank interiors of the hulking American city as well as across the vast globe with missionary zeal, intent on bringing light to the dark edges of the world.[10]

For Stoddard, as for Strong, the "center" was to be reformed and maintained through a restoration of focus, balance, and truthfulness, redeeming the ideal amid the excess, in order to comparatively adjudicate principled from profligate. To appropriately and clearly render this refined center through a composite's central features, Stoddard concerned himself particularly with issues of measurement and distance— the "density" of photographic negatives, ratios of facial markers, optical distances from camera lens to negative, times of exposure, the velocity of silver salt's chemical reaction, and the many dimensions and directions provided for the construction of an appropriate camera for composite creation. Amid such exacting procedures, any exaggerating tendencies were made to be ever on the periphery, and indeed, in Stoddard's composite, the periphery is where the layers pile up indeterminately, where bodies in negative exposure blur together amorphously. Similar to concerns for maintaining suitable scholarly distance from and measured responses to objects of study, it was necessary for Stoddard, the scientific photographer of human typologies, to achieve proper balance through assiduous practices of measurement, calculation, temporal delay, and an appropriately mediating distance.[11]

Concern for balance and measurement was further arresting for educators, like Stoddard, who were tasked with educating young women at institutions like Smith College, for this was also a time at which debate about women's access to higher education was articulated by both its supporters and its critics through recourse to education's effect on bodily fitness. Opponents argued that the energy necessary for intellectual activity would divert vitality away from women's reproductive organs. The danger posed by educating women was not only to their own bodies and (presupposed) families but also to a nation apparently overrun by births of the wrong kind—those among black and immigrant populations. Critics charged that these precocious young women were threatening the preservation of the "white" race.[12]

In response, supporters of women's education in this period crafted housing, curricula, and administrative affairs to combat these concerns. Though intent on delivering a liberal arts education comparable to that of Amherst College, an all-male school nearby, Smith College implemented the "cottage system" to ensure that students were brought up in a supervised, homelike environment. Appropriate food, hygiene, rest, and exercise were prescribed for each student, and a system of rigorous physical exams was administered to counter the critics. Precursors to the later, highly controversial, twentieth-century "posture photos," these exams were often quite invasively administered and provided elaborate measurements of each student's body. In a student's first and third years, data were collected on her breath (the strength and capacity of her lungs), height, weight, hair color, eye color, "temperament," whether she wore corsets, if she had ever "taken gym," her birthplace, her father's occupation, the nationality of her parents and grandparents, and if she had any hereditary diseases. Measurements were similarly recorded of each woman's waist, "wingspan," vision, hearing, head circumference, chest (in repose and expanded), hips, knees, calves, ankles, instep, elbows, wrists, and on and on. This information was compiled regularly to attest to the fitness of the students, and Smith College frequently reported that students' health improved over their tenure at the college; gaining weight and girth was proof, according to the school and education advocates, that Smith's education did not weaken the constitution of women. Stoddard's 1886 "pictorial statistic" contributed to this proliferation of data concerned with the assessment of both the bodies of women and the social body they presumably bred.[13]

In the remaining pages of this chapter I consider Stoddard's preferred composite of the class of 1886 as it was taken up, circulated among, and encountered by the women ostensibly depicted therein. In the process, two things become increasingly edifying for studies of sensory cultures. The first is that Stoddard's photographic frame was never entirely controlling or containing. The second tempers the first, because repossession and inhabitation of the composite by the Smith graduating women was always and ever ambivalent, attesting to the class's own historically and culturally situated context as well as to the challenges, shadows, and shades of devotional practice.

Composita, Possessing a Devotional Icon

As much as scientists sought to deploy the composite photograph as a tool to "discover" and compare human types, their ability to capture their subjects was bounded by the composite's not quite controllable, fuzzy framework. The performative and mediating role of Stoddard's preferred composite was most explicitly embraced through its unique acceptance among its component sitters. The Smith College Class of 1886 adopted the image as a kind of mascot, personified and embodied through Composita, a figure who played a number of important roles for the Smith women, particularly around the date of graduation. Reclaiming, in part, the objectifying gaze suggested by composite photography's role in the scientific and anthropological discourse of the day, the Smith women collectively inhabited Composita through an ambivalent process of communal repossession. "She" appears in students' letters to one another and was displayed as the first card amid pages of student portraits in class photo albums (Figure 6.4).[14]

A figure of collective devotion as graduation threatened to disperse the intimate relations forged among the Smith students, Composita served as the "embodied soul of 'Eighty-Six." She was featured as the subject of a graduation toast and publically lauded as the devotional body of the class, "bits that were human / being clustered together and forming a woman." She was proclaimed the students' own, a form and figure of belonging that was beloved by the class:

> We give her expression and feature and tone
> A bit of ourselves—and we feel her our own.
>
> "In Union is strength," is a saying that's trite,
> And yet the ethical principle's right.
> We've proved it with four years' experience dear,
> Should Composita shake now, Ah wont it be queer?
>
> Then bound firm together we'll buffet the storm,
> We'll laugh at the weather, be it cold, be it warm,
> Let it rain, let it shine, we'll sink or we'll swim,
> But we'll hold fast together, heart to heart, limb to limb.
>
> The years of our quiet College life are now numbered.
> The lessons are over, the bond must be sundered,
> Composita scattered with rustle and whirl,
> And yet where'er flying we're parts of our girl.

For the Smith women, Composita signified the loving devotion of classmates, friends, and intimates on the eve of their departure from one another.[15]

Composita not only served as a kind of mascot for the Smith graduating women in toasts, poems, and letters; she was also given the titular role in the senior class commencement performance. This ostensibly ethnographic "type" was thus further recovered as the primary protagonist in a play written by Zulema A. Ruble, a member of the senior class and long-time student of classical languages. Ruble composed her play, *Composita: A Drama in Three Acts,* for the Senior Dramatics, a graduation production given in June of 1886. In it Ruble reclaimed and reinterpreted Composita, embracing her as a figuration of class unity. In her telling, the image of Composita—who in the

FIGURE 6.4. Photograph Album of Emma L. Bradley, Smith College Class of 1886. Courtesy of Smith College Archives, Smith College, Northampton, Massachusetts.

drama gained a Christian name (so to speak), "Octogenta Sex" (Eighty-Six)—was represented and reaffirmed as the spirit and soul of the class (Figure 6.5).

The play centers on a reception in Hades given by Persephone in Composita's honor. Escorted into the depths of the underworld by Hermes from her comfortable room at Smith College, Composita attends the party, but like all shades in the underworld, she must also face the judgment of the gods, in her case Minos, Aeacus, and Rhadamanthus. The gods, rather than evaluating her themselves, however, determine that they will instead observe the verdict given by a group of scientists and mathematicians also in attendance. The figures Composita meets at Persephone's party include many of the classic canonical figures from nineteenth-century collegiate curricula—Homer, Socrates, Sappho, Hannibal, Archbishop Whately, Mr. Hill (described as the "author of a manual of punctuation"), PolyCon (the shade of Political Economy), and PolySci (the shade of Political Science). Ruble's show of academic acumen and intellectual prowess, though, focused most notably on three figures: Euclid, Gottfried Wilhelm Leibnitz, and Isaac Newton. As divinely ordained experts, these three scientists set out to examine and appraise Composita. Euclid puzzles over her dynamism and shape, insisting that she should rather have taken the form of a truncated cone.

FIGURE 6.5. "Composita Octogenta Sex," handbill for the Class of 1886's Senior Dramatics, June 19, 1886. Courtesy of Smith College Archives, Smith College, Northampton, Massachusetts.

Leibnitz deploys a new apparatus, a "microcosm-scope," to investigate Composita's "unanimity." However, it is Newton who, with a tool described as a "soul prism," ultimately destroys Composita's unified form, severing her forty-nine "constituents" into disparate entities. Within the three acts of the play, Composita is obliged to undergo one last observation and assessment by scientific men, a final exam that shatters her into pieces (Figure 6.6).

As the three scientists attempt to reassemble the protagonist from her now scattered components, Composita is transformed into a kind of sinful Humpty Dumpty. For when the men try putting her back together again using Leibnitz's crystal lens, a tool that would ostensibly restore the unity of her soul, Composita is at once crystallized. No longer an apparently dynamic, embodied composite photograph, Composita is transformed into a "helpless and motionless statue." Ruble presented this monumentalized entombment as the Smith College version of Lot's wife, for what has apparently wrought Composita's statutory conviction is her "soul-destroying crime" of cramming, the ultimate undergraduate abomination. Composita's offense is rung out in chorus as "the dreadful crime, the awful crime, the impious crime of cramming," or what the scientists variously deem the involvement of the soul in evil, a "sin,"

Ye 23ᵈ day of June
Yeare — 1886

a "constitutional defect," "some microbe in her soul." In criminalized Composita, the rogue's gallery is closer than otherwise presumed. Heralded as perfection and yet immensely and imminently perilous, Composita carried and was made to carry within her all the potentiality and precariousness of the figure of the nineteenth-century bourgeois white woman. Composita, the soul of '86, was "for a saint too human / Yet too saintly for a woman," as one member of the class of 1886 succinctly wrote amid graduation ephemera in her scrapbook. Yet as Stoddard's photographic lens met Leibnitz's crystallizing one head on, Ruble's account also suggested an implicit, if ambivalent, critique of comparative typology as compositional internment. In an attempted reversal of roles, Ruble widened the angle of vision to include her observer as combination and separation were shown to coincide and collide.[16]

Animated and rendered full-form in Mary Eastman, the Smith student awarded the drama's leading role, Composita was not only imagined as a kind of multiplied, collective woman but was also singled out, at least insofar as only Eastman performatively inhabited the devotional body of Composita. Casting decisions are not detailed in the class records, and questions remain about why more than one woman did not play the role, not to mention whether Composita's dramatic separation was multiply cast or not. Nevertheless, it appears that Ruble and her colleagues similarly sought

Stoddard's pictorial average. In allotting Eastman the role as "everywoman" of the Smith College Class of 1886, they perpetuated a foreclosure of the particularities of their own indeterminate margins. A print, presumably of the Composita image, held in the Smith College Archive illustrates this ambivalence. On the reverse of this *carte de visite,* "Mary Eastman" is written across the top, and in a different hand, likely the archivist's, the description "Composita 1886" is written and then crossed out. Although it is not evident when precisely each of these markings was made, such (re)inscriptions point toward the ways in which Eastman was made to stand in metonymically and historically for the communal form of Composita. It is also suggestive of the challenges Ruble and her colleagues, as well as later historians, faced in attempting to repossess the composite image without also reasserting such universalizing presumptions.[17]

This marked and re-marked image attests to the limits of multiplicity in form and feeling, thought and expression, that Composita was imagined to represent. However, it also manifests the ways in which certain subjects were afforded the apparent privilege of inhabiting her form while others were unable to or disallowed from doing so. Class of 1886 member Harriet M. White, in a letter she wrote to the class just after graduation, obliquely conveyed her own ambivalent perception of this fuzzy figuration of class dynamics, embodied devotion, and performative privilege: "I enjoy life immensely, and while I'd like to see '86 better represented than in the *Composita,* would not for worlds, be this-year's Smith freshman." This simultaneous appreciation and apprehension for her class and its representation in Ruble's play serves as a useful reminder about the power relations embodied by the Smith "type," its objectification by a scientific man, and its use as typological "woman" of the late nineteenth century.[18]

Envisioning and inhabiting types is always a matter of power dynamics. Vision itself is related to and complicit with questions about the power to see and the violence implicit in such visualizing practices. This vision is never disembodied, and these sensorial and sensationalized relations must be relentlessly interrogated. In drawing out Composita's production and repossession, I suggest that it is necessary to attend not only to the warm and fuzzy devotion among these women but also to the violence embedded in her figuration. For Ruble and her fellow students, Composita may have been reclaimed as a kind of pluralist project, a move away from the cyclopean vision of the camera(man) toward their own misty marginalization. But as Donna Haraway reminds, such perspective is never unproblematic or easily learned. It is always partial, if also uniquely situated: "The positionings of the subjugated are not exempt from critical re-examination, decoding, deconstruction and interpretation; that is, from both semiological and hermeneutic modes of critical enquiry. The standpoints of the subjugated are not 'innocent' positions." To speak of the embodied nature of all vision, of a never disembodied head, is to attend to the situated knowledges embedded within the photographer *and* the composite subject(s). Composita, in Ruble's play, may serve as one form of knowledge from below, to continue using Haraway's language, as evidence that the Smith students were "savvy to modes of denial through repression, forgetting, and disappearing acts—ways of being nowhere while claiming to see comprehensively . . . to be on to the god-trick and all its dazzling—and therefore, blinding—illuminations." But Composita, too, performed her own kind of violent erasure in effulgent obfuscation. Even as the photo represented for many the devotion shared between and among the Smith women and reclaimed relations otherwise rendered peripheral by Stoddard, Composita also shaped and shadowed the traces of virtue and vice that the feminine body was imagined to hold within it. The composite woman, in scientific discourse and in the graduation drama, became a kind of blurry figure-ground, a partly concealed map of the ideal white woman of financial and educated means. A figure of polysemous devotion to class, Composita was also a photo-performative figure, always already embodied in racialized, feminized form—a figure over which much violence was wrought in white supremacist discourse of the late nineteenth century.[19]

In the final moments of Ruble's play, Hermes—Composita's tour guide of Hades and now her apparently forlorn suitor—laments Composita's fate and proclaims her criminalizing sin the result of self-defense:

> Ah, Composita, ... Thy soul so pure, methought, could not endure the
>   analytic prism's test nor Leibnitz' crystal lens. And thou art a criminal;
>   thou, a monument, stiff and stark! . . . Composita, couldst thou have
>   escaped the crime? Is an earthly college course possible without this
>   dire defect? O that I had the *faculties* to tell me this! Nay, 'tis false, 'tis
>   false! Back into Tartarus vile Suspicion! I tell thee her action was not
>   *free.* I fly to high Olympus, there
> Before the throne of Zeus to swear
> Her provocation was intense,
> She wrought the deed in self-defence!"[20]

So even as Ruble reinscribed an objectification of the female form by powerful, scientific men and offered an embodied portrait of white womanhood in nineteenth-century popular discourse, she also insisted that the shade's "sin" be seen as a structural problem, one generated by and necessitated through the strategic negotiations of earthly conditions. In Hermes' rhyming verse, Ruble professed the inescapablility and intensity of Composita's provocation, even while compelling the question about which so much is at stake: who is the self that needed defending here? As ever, this inhabited devotional body in communal repossession is deeply ambivalent, a blurry construction and a locus of destruction, a scene for self-defense in the face of structural limitations and a site for purifying discourse and racialized violence.

Shades of Saintliness and Sin

In *The Varieties of Religious Experience,* William James likened his notion of saintliness to a composite photograph, asserting, "The collective name for the ripe fruits of religion in a character is Saintliness. . . . and there is a certain composite photograph of universal saintliness, the same in all religions, of which the features can be easily traced." Like James's desire here for easily traceable features of saintliness, scientists like Stoddard sought ready characteristics that would allow for straightforward distinctions between the consecrated and the criminal. Of concern for these scientific men was the potential for excess. Stoddard sought precision in methods of balance and distance in order to render a unified and comparable "type" amid the superfluous. For James, too, saintliness was ripe fruit, perhaps all too near its ruin. Like Stoddard, James was concerned with overly enthusiastic devotion, too-intense asceticism, or the "frenzy of self-immolation" that this lapsed-Protestant professor (if not professing Protestant) saw as characteristic of some Catholic saints. Thus, although James is well known for his attempts to reassert the value of the apparently marginal and marginalized religious person who was pathologized as diseased or delusional by so many of his contemporaries in the study of psychology, James's composite photograph of saintliness, like Stoddard's idealized "pictorial average," universalized his Protestant type.[21]

Composita, as saint and sinner, a pictured body and embodied picture, figured a history of violent acts and ideas, even as the women of the Smith College Class of 1886 attempted to eschew deterministic, seemingly hegemonic discourses. As they sought to counter gender limitations, they remained circumscribed by particularizing class- and race-based boundaries. However, theirs was not the only Composita. In 1958 Alice Cone Perry, a graduate of the Smith College Class of 1913, compiled the results of 134 questionnaires she sent out that year for use in a skit at her class reunion. The resultant play was an interview with "Composita Smith Average," who was purportedly chosen "by a committee of experts as the 'Outstanding Normal Member of the class of 1913 of Smith College.'" For over seventy years, Composita's components had multiplied while simultaneously insisting on normative form, this time performatively inhabited by Margaret Bryan Washburn. It was, though, a different questionnaire, compiled just a year before Perry's class of 1913 Composita in 1958, that has come to live in infamy. It became the basis of Betty Friedan's 1963 book *The Feminine Mystique,* published in part to counter ongoing claims that higher education made women into unfit and unhappy housewives. Though Friedan's questionnaire did not take up the Composita brand, it, too, advanced and even compelled an ambivalently universalist (re)form on behalf of white, middle-class subjects.[22]

The 1886 Smith College composite photograph figures a multilayered history. It pictures tenuous, sensitive, and sensual invocations of communal relations and material practices, of gazes meeting and bodies touching, both carefully and violently.

Composita's photographic contours and performative construction suggest devotional icons and sensational types as deeply ambivalent and multiply mediated compilations. As picture and play, this composite helps demonstrate the ways in which humans and things are embedded in and constituted through entangled sensory and sensationalized relations and offers a locus for the historical interrogation of proper sociality in plurality. A history of the Smith College Class of 1886's composite and its shades of devotion—to science and methodological precision, to friends and intimates, to class and to race—also allegorizes the shadowy relations of the religious and the secular as they are made to merge and emerge historically.

NOTES

I am grateful for the generous support and critical insights of Emily Johnson, Alex Kaloyanides, Sarah Koenig, Christopher Kramaric, Michelle Morgan, and Shari Rabin, as well as participants in the Initiative for the Study of Material and Visual Cultures of Religion, who heard and provided feedback on earlier versions of this project. Special thanks go to David Walker for his unfailingly gracious reading and crucial feedback and to Professors Kathryn Lofton, Sally Promey, and Laura Wexler for their expert advice and guidance at various stages in the development of this chapter.

1. Smith College is a women's college in Northampton, Massachusetts, whose first class entered the school in 1875. The composites published in Stoddard's article were made from photographic negatives of individual portraits taken by John Lyman Lovell of Hardie and Lovell, a Northampton photography studio. John T. Stoddard, "Composite Portraiture," *Science* 8, no. 182 (1886): 89–91; Zulema A. Ruble, *Composita: A Drama in Three Acts* (Canton, IL: Canton Register, 1887); and "Truths and Trifles," *New York Times*, July 16, 1886. For more on the ways in which the Smith 1886 composite was characterized and its relationship to later photographic processes, see also Adam Greenhalgh, "Risky Business: Chance and Contingency in American Art around 1900," Ph.D. dissertation, University of Maryland, College Park, 2012.

2. For analyses of the historical formation of the category of religion, see, for example, Talal Asad, *Genealogies of Religion: Discipline and Reasons of Power in Christianity and Islam* (Baltimore: Johns Hopkins University Press, 1993), 1–54; Jonathan Z. Smith, "Religion, Religions, Religious," in *Critical Terms for Religious Studies,* ed. Mark C. Taylor (Chicago: University of Chicago Press, 1998), 269–284; and Tisa Wenger, *We Have a Religion: The 1920s Pueblo Indian Dance Controversy and American Religious Freedom* (Chapel Hill: University of North Carolina Press, 2009), 1–16. For examinations of religion and the secular, see, for example, Talal Asad, *Formations of the Secular: Christianity, Islam, Modernity* (Stanford, CA: Stanford University Press, 2003), 1–66; Janet R. Jakobsen and Ann Pellegrini, "Times Like These," in *Secularisms,* ed. Jakobsen and Pellegrini (Durham, NC: Duke University Press, 2008), 1–38; and Ann Pellegrini, "Feeling Secular," *Women and Performance* 19, no. 2 (2009): 205–218.

3. Asad, *Formations of the Secular,* 16, 62–66. My reference to "speaking otherwise" is meant to evoke allegory's etymology, coming as it does from the Greek *allegoria,* meaning "speaking otherwise." For another approach to the study of religion via allegory, see, for example, Richard J. Callahan, Kathryn Lofton, and Chad E. Seales, "Allegories of Progress: Industrial Religion in the United States," *Journal of the American Academy of Religion* 78, no. 1 (2010): 1–39. For a related discussion of composite photography's historical relevance to the study of "visual piety," cf. David Morgan, *Visual Piety: A*

History and Theory of Popular Religious Images (Berkeley: University of California Press, 1998), 40–43.

4. I use the language of *devotion* and *icon* throughout this chapter to describe—as process and product—the relations between and among John Stoddard, the Smith College Class of 1886, composite photography, performative enactment, and Composita. A number of scholars have importantly and usefully linked the term *icon* (via the Greek *eikon*) to longer genealogies of *image*. In English usage, dating from the sixteenth century it was most often used as a simile, as a figure of speech in comparing two things. By the nineteenth century it was being deployed in reference to a portrait or a picture, especially for illustrations in natural history books and for paintings of holy figures. Charles S. Peirce, in the late nineteenth century, used the term as one of his three classifications for signs (icon, index, and symbol) in his development of semiotics. By the mid-twentieth century, *icon* was extended to celebrities and popular entertainment figures, graphic representations in computing, and commercial branding practices.

A genealogy of *devotion* is more difficult to recite here, even in brief, because, despite increasingly bountiful genealogical work on terms of analysis in the study of religion, no scholarship has appeared yet to treat this term/concept specifically. Although etymological investigation should largely be taken as a starting point for further study, it is useful to note that *devotion* comes from the Latin noun *devotio,* which is derived from the verb *devovere,* itself having originated in the late sixteenth century and meaning roughly "to consecrate" or "to vow formally." An archaic use of this verb form was also used to "invoke or pronounce a curse upon." The ambivalent relation here between consecration and curse suggests a potential etymological springboard for my use of the term, even as the *Oxford English Dictionary* (OED) offers two present-day definitions of devotion that are also close to my usage: "love, loyalty, or enthusiasm for a person or activity," as well as "religious worship or observance." However, I am suggesting that the singular individual or activity invoked in the OED's current definition of the term may—at least in the production and possession of Composita—dissolve into a portrait of group relations. Such an ambivalent etymological-definitional profile prompts consideration of the ways in which devotional practices and objects of devotion may not always (or ever?) be individuated or singularly contained but are rather historically situated amid the faded contours of religion and the secular, the individual and the communal, and perhaps also the consecrated and the cursed.

For more on the genealogy of *icon,* see, for example, Margaret R. Miles, "Image," in *Critical Terms for Religious Studies,* ed. Mark C. Taylor (Chicago: University of Chicago Press, 1998), 160–172; W.J.T. Mitchell, "Word and Image," in *Critical Terms for Art History,* 2nd ed., ed. Robert S. Nelson and Richard Shiff (Chicago: University of Chicago Press, 2003), 51–61; and David Morgan, "Image," in *Key Words in Religion, Media, and Culture,* ed. Morgan (New York: Routledge, 2008). For more on the intersection of religion, iconicity, and brand making in American religious history, see, for example, David Chidester, *Authentic Fakes: Religion and American Popular Culture* (Berkeley: University of California Press, 2005); Kathryn Lofton, *Oprah: The Gospel of an Icon* (Berkeley: University of California Press, 2011); and Jennifer Connerley, "Friendly Americans: Representing Quakers in the United States, 1850–1920," Ph.D. dissertation, University of North Carolina, Chapel Hill, 2006. For more on the etymology and definitions of *icon* and *devotion,* see, for example, *Oxford Dictionary of English,* s.vv. "devote," "devotion," and "icon"; *Oxford Dictionary of Word Origins,* s.vv. "icon" and "vote"; and *Dictionary of Critical Theory,* s.v. "icon."

5. Stoddard, "Composite Portraiture," 90. On Stoddard's academic interests and tenure at Smith College, see Henry Weather Tyler, "John Tappan Stoddard (A Tribute)," *Hampshire Gazette,* December 18, 1919; Mary Louise Foster, "John Tappan Stoddard," *Smith College Weekly,* December 17, 1919; "Smith College: President Neilson's Tribute to Professor Stoddard," n.d.; and

"Obituary: Prof. John T. Stoddard," n.d., all of which are housed in John Tappan Stoddard Papers 42, box 1026, Smith College Archives (hereafter all references to the Smith College Archives are cited as "College Archives"). For additional composite photos taken by Stoddard as well as composites of other college students, prison inmates, and others collected by Stoddard and his colleagues, see Smith College Department of Physics Records 52, box 1253, College Archives. For more on late nineteenth-century concerns with identifying and distinguishing between sincerity and deception, see, for example, David S. Walker, "The Humbug in American Religion: Ritual Theories of Nineteenth-Century Spiritualism," *Religion and American Culture* 23, no. 1 (2013): 30–74; Stephen Mihm, *A Nation of Counterfeiters: Capitalists, Con Men, and the Making of the United States* (Cambridge, MA: Harvard University Press, 2007); James W. Cook, *The Arts of Deception: Playing with Fraud in the Age of Barnum* (Cambridge, MA: Harvard University Press, 2001); and Karen Halttunen, *Confidence Men and Painted Women: A Study of Middle-Class Culture in America, 1830–1870* (New Haven, CT: Yale University Press, 1986).

6. A longer genealogy of composite creation might usefully be traced at least as far back as Mannerist artists like Giuseppe Arcimboldo, through satirical illustrations like George Spratt's early nineteenth-century personifications of fashionable activities and occupations to photographic innovations like those depicted in Oscar Rejlander's 1858 creation *The Two Ways of Life*, which assembled and exposed more than thirty photographic negatives to depict a mid-nineteenth-century allegory of virtue and vice. Later photographers and painters like William Notman and artists under his employ rendered collagelike creations similar to Reijlander's composites, which were sometimes referred to as combination prints. These kinds of composites were often used especially to depict large groups through the assemblage of previously taken individual photos that were cut and pasted together atop painted scenery or previously photographed spaces— often both—before being photographed again to create a new, singular image. The resultant image was frequently reproduced en masse because it could be expected that most if not all of the individuals in the final photograph would order a print of the composite. For more on related artistic and scientific practices from the sixteenth century to the nineteenth, see, for example, James A. Secord, "Scrapbook Science: Composite Caricatures in Late Georgian England," in *Figuring It Out: Science, Gender, and Visual Culture,* ed. Ann B. Shteir and Bernard Lightman (Hanover, NH: Dartmouth College Press, 2006), 164–169; Michel Foucault, *The Order of Things: An Archaeology of the Human Sciences* (New York: Vintage, 1994); Susan M. Pearce, *On Collecting: An Investigation into Collecting in the European Tradition* (New York: Routledge, 1995); Arthur MacGregor, *Curiosity and Enlightenment: Collectors and Collections from the Sixteenth to the Nineteenth Century* (New Haven, CT: Yale University Press, 2007); and Eilean Hooper-Greenhill, *Museums and the Shaping of Knowledge* (New York: Routledge, 1992). For additional analysis of Rejlander's other photographic work as it relates to genre painting and photography of the laboring poor and to cartoons of the "street urchin type," see Stephanie Spencer, "O. G. Rejlander's Photographs of Street Urchins," *Oxford Art Journal* 7, no. 2 (1984): 17–24. For more on Notman and composites like his, see, for example, Russell J. Harper and Stanley Triggs, *Portrait of a Period: A Collection of Notman Photographs, 1856–1915* (Montreal: McGill University Press, 1967), and Robert Taft, *Photography and the American Scene: A Social History, 1839–1889* (New York: Dover, 1938), 358–359. For an appeal to iterative photographic practice as essential to composite creation, see William J. Broecker, ed., *International Center of Photography: Encyclopedia of Photography* (New York: Crown, 1984), 115.

7. For debate regarding the potential composite qualities and ephemeral nature of stereoscope images, see, for example, John T. Stoddard, "Composite Photography," *The Century Illustrated Monthly Magazine* 33, no. 5 (1887): 757; Joseph Jastrow, "Composite Portraiture," *Science* 6, no. 134 (1885): 165–167; and Francis Galton, "Composite Portraits, Made by Combining

Those of Many Different Persons into a Single Resultant Figure," *Journal of the Anthropological Institute of Great Britain and Ireland* 8 (1879): 132–144. It is perhaps also worth stating directly that the characteristic of permanence insisted on by scientists like Stoddard is likewise related to studies of religion in the late nineteenth century, when scholars, theologians, practitioners, and believers negotiated and attempted to come to terms with that-which-is-epistemologically-and-ontologically-concrete. By the late seventeenth century, religion was increasingly approached through the study of natural history, where practices of measurement were heralded for their verifiability and objectivity. Study of this "religion of nature" was considered an exercise in reasoning, a way to better clarify and calculate the universal structure of nature governed by divine laws evinced in and made accessible through the surrounding world and the very nature of mankind. For more on the constitution of "natural religion" and subsequent discursive moves toward a "science" of religion, see J. Z. Smith, "Religion, Religions, Religious," 269–284. Galton, along with Alphonse Bertillion, is largely responsible for popularizing a photographic procedure and product, distinct from other contemporaneous collagelike forms and practices of composite creation, that has come to be known as the mug shot. For more on Galton and the emergence of the mug shot, see, for example, Allan Sekula, "The Body and the Archive," *October* 39 (1986): 3–64, and Jonathan Finn, *Capturing the Criminal Image: From Mug Shot to Surveillance Society* (Minneapolis: University of Minnesota Press, 2009), 1–30.

8. Shawn Michelle Smith, *Photography on the Color Line: W.E.B. Du Bois, Race, and Visual Culture* (Durham, NC: Duke University Press, 2004), 11, 47. For accounts of the origin of Galton's photography, see Galton, "Composite Portraits," 132; Walter E. Woodbury, *The Encyclopaedic Dictionary of Photography, Containing Over 2,000 References and 500 Illustrations* (New York: Scovill and Adams Company of New York, 1899), 133; and Bernard E. Jones, ed., *Cassell's Cyclopaedia of Photography* (New York: Arno, 1973), 136–137.

9. Stoddard, "Composite Portraiture," 90.

10. Josiah Strong, *Our Country: Its Possible Future and Its Present Crisis* (New York: American Home Missionary Society, 1885); Edward J. Blum, *Reforging the White Republic: Race, Religion, and American Nationalism, 1865–1898* (Baton Rouge: Louisiana State University Press, 2005), 1–19, 214–226; and Beryl Satter, *Each Mind a Kingdom: American Women, Sexual Purity, and the New Thought Movement, 1875–1920* (Berkeley: University of California Press, 1999), 21–27, 36–39. The passage during this period of the first federal immigration legislation—the Page Act of 1875 and the Chinese Exclusion Act of 1882—further attests to concerns about ostensibly excessive immigration (of particularly racialized groups) during this period.

11. It is worth explicitly noting that the power dynamics involved in who is made to stand before the camera to be captured in composite form is similar to scholarly tendencies in the study of religion to emphasize the embodied religious practice of religiously and racially marginalized groups. The feminine figuration of enthusiastic religiosity, frequently in the form of weak or writhing bodies, evinces a similar tendency. These variously minoritized subjects have been, and frequently continue to be, approached by scholars as rife with surplus tendencies, possibilities, and potentialities. For related critiques of such trends, see, for example, Ann Taves, *Fits, Trances, and Visions: Experiencing Religion and Explaining Experience from Wesley to James* (Princeton, NJ: Princeton University Press, 1999); Wenger, *We Have a Religion;* Kathryn Lofton, "The Perpetual Primitive in African American Religious Historiography," in *The New Black Gods: Arthur Fauset and the Study of African American Religions,* ed. Edward E. Curtis IV and Danielle Brune Sigler (Bloomington: Indiana University Press, 2009), 171–191; Tracy Fessenden, *Culture and Redemption: Religion, The Secular, and American Literature* (Princeton, NJ: Princeton University Press, 2007), 111–136; Fessenden, "'Woman' and the 'Primitive' in Paul Tillich's Life and Thought: Some Implications for the Study of Religion," *Journal of Feminist Studies in Religion* 14, no. 2

(1998): 45–76; Satter, *Each Mind a Kingdom,* 21–56; and Elizabeth A. Castelli, "Women, Gender, Religion: Troubling Categories and Transforming Knowledge," in *Women, Gender, Religion: A Reader,* ed. Castelli with the assistance of Rosamond C. Rodman (New York: Palgrave, 2001), 3–25.

12. Margaret A. Lowe, *Looking Good: College Women and Body Image, 1875–1930* (Baltimore: Johns Hopkins University Press, 2003), 1–3, and Satter, *Each Mind a Kingdom,* 27–36.

13. Lowe, *Looking Good,* 7, 13–28. For more on the twentieth-century controversy over "posture photos" taken primarily among Ivy League and Seven Sister schools, see, for example, Ron Rossenbaum, "The Great Ivy League Nude Posture Photo Scandal," *New York Times,* January 15, 1995; David Yosifon and Peter N. Stearns, "The Rise and Fall of American Posture," *The American Historical Review* 103, no. 4 (1998): 1057–1095; and Patricia Vertinsky, "Physique as Destiny: William H. Sheldon, Barbara Honeyman Heath, and the Struggle for Hegemony in the Science of Somatotyping," *Canadian Bulletin of Medical History* 24, no. 2 (2007): 291–316.

14. Emma L. Bradley, album, n.d., Class of 1886 Records 80, box 1429, College Archive (hereafter all references to the Class of 1886 Records will be denoted by "Class Records"). For additional historical and theoretical consideration of the "gaze," see Margaret Olin, "Gaze," in *Critical Terms for Art History,* ed. Robert S. Nelson and Richard Shiff (Chicago: University of Chicago Press, 2003).

15. Ruble, *Composita,* iii, and Mary Eastman, "Toast: The Class of '86, Composita," Commencement Exercises, Class Records, box 1425, College Archive.

16. Ruble, *Composita,* 31–48, and Abby Maria Bennet Slade, scrapbook, Class Records, oversize box, College Archive. For a related analysis of representations of stillness and motionlessness as forms of self-possession rather than passivity in New Thought novels written by female authors in the 1880s and 1890s, see Satter, *Each Mind a Kingdom,* 111–149.

17. Photograph, Smith College Department of Physics Records 52, box 1253, College Archives.

18. Harriet M. White, "Class Letter of 1887," Class Records, box 1426, College Archives.

19. Donna Haraway, "Situated Knowledges: The Science Question in Feminism and the Privilege of Partial Perspective," 1988, in *Blackwell Reader in Contemporary Social Theory,* ed. Anthony Elliot (Malden, MA: Blackwell, 1999), 290–297. For more on the role of white womanhood in white supremacist discourse, see, for example, S. M. Smith, *Photography on the Color Line,* 109; Fessenden, *Culture and Redemption,* 111–136, 161–180; and Satter, *Each Mind a Kingdom,* 21 56, 181–216.

20. Ruble, *Composita,* 38, italics in original.

21. William James, *The Varieties of Religious Experience: A Study in Human Nature* (New York: Barnes and Noble Classics, 2004), 163, 239–240, and Wayne Proudfoot, introduction to James, *The Varieties of Religious Experience,* xxi–xxv.

22. Alice Cone Perry, "A Real Treat," 1958, Class of 1913 Records, box 1821, College Archives, and M.E.P., "Lo! Now Has Come Our Joyful'st Feast," in *The Big Bass Drum: "Inside Nineteen Thirteen,"* ed. R. E. Porters, 45th Reunion Edition, August 1958, Class of 1913 Records, box 1821, College Archives.

7

The Spirit in the Cubicle

A Religious History of the American Office

KATHRYN LOFTON

At Herman Miller good design is a shibboleth.   Herman Miller News Release, January 25, 1965

In December 2009, Rich Sheridan, chief executive officer of the Ann Arbor, Michigan, software firm Menlo Innovations, posted a blog entry to his company's site declaring that office cubicles "kill." He wrote that cubicles "kill morale, communication, productivity, creativity, teamwork, camaraderie, energy, spirit, and results." When AnnArbor.com ran an article about his post under the title "Death to Cubicles," thousands responded with concurring accounts of soul-crushing discomfort within cubicle walls. In reply to this skirmish of posts, a leading producer of cubicles, Herman Miller Inc., waded into the fray. In his original post, Sheridan had alluded to Herman Miller, pointing to Ann Arbor as the birthplace of the cubicle death trap. Indeed, under the auspices of the Ann Arbor–based Herman Miller Research Corporation, designer Robert Propst had developed the cubicle design in the early 1960s, calling his innovation the Action Office (AO) (Figure 7.1). Fifty years later, Herman Miller's public relations officials answered Sheridan's screed with corporate care and certainty. First, they extended sympathies to those who had testified to their unhappiness with this product; second, they supplied a reasoned defense of their design, emphasizing the critical consumer agency that everyone ought to possess. "For us, the best places to work give people a choice of where to work and how to work," Herman Miller reminded its buyers. "If wide-open spaces suit the kind of work you do, go for them." The cubicle was a business's design choice on behalf of a worker's privacy: "People will always need privacy, and organizations around the world have found the good old cubicle a wonderful way to organize heads-down work and minimize distractions."[1]

This chapter tackles the simultaneity of suffering and freedom occurring within that infamously generic space, the office cubicle. Through his blog post, Rick Sheridan gave voice to the pervasive feeling that the banal cubicle conveys malignant onto-

FIGURE 7.1. An advertisement for the Action Office, circa 1978–1980. Courtesy of the Herman Miller Inc. Archive, Zeeland, Michigan.

logical consequences. The thousands who replied to Sheridan's post shared an opinion so common that it is a cultural jeremiad: the cubicle degrades the spirit. In its containment of individuals, the cubicle divests humans of their humanity. Through its individual encasement, it denies individuals connections to others; through its right-angle seating and desk, it restricts movement and denies healthy embodiment. The cubicle might then be understood as a place that denies sensorial experience, limiting the physical freedom and interactive opportunities of its confined occupants. But in his original propositions on behalf of the Action Office, Robert Propst focused on this disconnection as precisely his problem to solve: "The mind is no better than what the five senses convey or divert from it," he wrote in 1965. "We knew that the ability to concentrate depends on a delicate balance between the escape from distraction and the pulse-beat of bustle and involvement." Propst sought to create a careful sensorial equilibrium for office workers, a space where they could be disciplined in their work while also mobile to whatever new innovation or connection that work might spark. "The maximum use of our senses is the most compelling reason for grouping people together in offices, grouping offices together in single large buildings, and putting many large buildings together in compact communities," Propst wrote.[2] His job, as he understood it, was to maximize this maximal context: to design spaces for the human mind to flourish alongside and with other minds.

This was a democratic proposition offered in an era of counterculture, a dream in which every worker occupied a kingdom equal in form to that occupied by everyone else. If earlier office layouts reiterated a status hierarchy among workers, Propst proposed instead that there should be a "hierarchy of values in the organization of interior spaces." The space of the Action Office would be a space in which individuals could flourish on the premise that they possess possibility equal to that of everyone else. How, exactly, did Propst imagine that his Action Office offered such possibility for flourishing? And why did it fail to occur? The purpose of the Action Office was, in the words of its designers and producers, "serious and profound," directed toward the single goal of making an office "the best possible environment for thinking."[3] It is tempting to make ironic hay of such sentiment, assuming that any claims on behalf of your best self are advertisements seeking to sell you a product. How could a product enlighten or enliven its purchaser—or her *mind*—when the facts of commodification invariably entrap the purchaser into the supplicating role of consumer? In its missionary claims for the mind of the masses, the Action Office could have been the apotheosis of capitalism, a mountebank selling talk of the mind's salvation for the price of your physical freedom.[4] A review of documents from the Herman Miller Archive suggests, however, that such a conclusion occludes the religious valence of corporatism in American history. Herman Miller argued that the office cubicle was a space for the denial of sensory experience but also that it would provide a new sensory landscape, one in which the mind would be focused and the body at ease. I pause on Herman Miller's seriousness in this task, to consider the aspirational outset of the Action Office as an object in the history of religion.

To some observers it might seem as if there is nothing *less* religious than a cubicle; the cubicle is, by such reckoning, a fascist containment of bodies, not a frame for spiritual experience. In reply I propose three ways in which the cubicle invites analysis by scholars of religion: first, its history includes a specific denominational origin that is revealing about the moral community Herman Miller Inc. sought to be and create; second, its design included propositions for and manifestations of spiritual rejuvenation for the laboring body; and third, the space created by the cubicle offered territory for personal ritual expression and religious identity within the broader matrix of industrial capitalism. These three aspects of the cubicle do not make it a religious object. Rather, they make the cubicle a critical object in the sensorium of modern experience: aesthetic, religious, economic, sensorial, and otherwise.

My research into Herman Miller echoes ongoing scholarly efforts to analyze the conjunction of American religious history and American business life.[5] In this exploration of the Action Office at Herman Miller, I will focus more on product development within a given corporation than do those other studies. The majority of current scholarship emphasizes the ways that self-identified religious groups engage and reply to capitalist experience through their own corporate developments, alternative economic practices, or communitarian associations. In this chapter I emphasize product development in an effort to spotlight the interactive concomitance between technological innovation, aesthetic prescription, and religious ideation. Although my case study here is narrowed to a particular product line offered by a specific company in the mid-twentieth century, I argue that it is impossible to observe an example of technological innovation in the modern period that does not also include an aesthetic prescription and religious sentiment; likewise, the aesthetic mandate almost always includes the deployment of innovative technology and recommendation of some kind of communal revision relevant to religious studies.

The case of Herman Miller makes this conjunction powerfully apparent. The story of the Action Office includes ample invocations of technological innovation and aesthetic cool. This conjunction had already powerful genealogical roots in modernism in Europe, where designers had sought to convert the abstractions of that movement into new architectures and home decor for the common people. Religious thought simmered beneath the surfaces of these innovators and their propositions, as in the case of the Dutch artistic movement known as De Stijl, in which participants like Piet Mondrian produced canvases and furniture that exhibited their commitments to pure abstraction, mathematical precision, and a form of visual harmony that they described as spiritual, with deference to the Theosophical readings many of them had done. Religion appeared in European modernism as a sort of reclaimed iconography, as in the case of the April 1919 Bauhaus Manifesto written by Walter Gropius, which was printed with a woodcut by Lyonel Feininger of a Gothic cathedral rendered in Cubist style on its cover.[6] In the cultures of modernism, religion may not have been practiced in ways recognizable to the modernists' Renaissance or Baroque forebears; nevertheless, those iconoclastic modernists repurposed religion as a potent repository of symbols, as well as a set of important metaphysical provocations, in their effort to provide a universal aesthetic for the social revolutions of modernity. For many, modernism itself—in its simple lines, democratic optimism, and creative hauteur—became a kind of spiritual ideal, a religion of pure abstraction, unmoored from archaic authority or ecclesiastical rule.

Herman Miller would play a central role in the popularization of European modernism in America, a popularization that transpired amid overwhelming suburbanization and the expansion of the post–World War II military–industrial complex. Town planners, developers, and builders—like William Jaird Levitt and his building company, Levitt and Sons—plotted utopic microcosms in new suburbs like that of Levittown, Pennsylvania, which reached completion in August 1957 and became synonymous with the phenomenon of high-volume tract-house development for moderate-income families on the urban periphery.[7] In the United States modernist design became the language of the new social mobility, corporate power, and populist prosperity. "Harnessed firmly to the American dreams of home ownership, consumerism, and democratic freedom, modernism's utopian promise came closest to being realized not in Europe but in the United States," museum curator Judith A. Barter has observed, "not at the hands of Gropius's million socialist workers, but through the workings of the marketplace and the hopes and desires of countless consumers."[8] Through the fusion of technological advances, machine manufacture, aesthetic revisions, and millennial ambition, Herman Miller brought the concept of "good design" into every home as a material and spiritual possibility. Herman Miller became an evangel for modernism, and the Action Office was, as we shall see, its most significant missionary tool.

The Setting

Promotional materials for the Action Office consistently invoked the reputational specter of its producer, "an unorthodox furniture company in Zeeland, Michigan." Company publicists argued that the Action Office was "typical of Herman Miller design, but Herman Miller, Inc. is probably typical of no other furniture manufacturer in the world." What made Herman Miller so different? "Few corporations its size open important meetings with readings from the Bible, yet build their sales on a shining reputation for iconoclastic modern design."[9] Through its own promotional work and market success, Herman Miller circulated as a company that tied experimental form with pious utilitarianism. Contributing to its appeal was its rural Midwestern ties; rather than having its headquarters in the modernist meccas of Los Angeles or New York, Herman Miller originated in southwestern Michigan and kept its headquarters there. As one 1965 news release rhapsodized:

> Yet Zeeland (population 4,000) is still home, and the parent plant, a handsome new building set down literally in the middle of a pasture surrounded by a herd of cattle, is staffed by descendants of the solid Dutch burghers who once matched the waterfall flitches on the suites of furniture. At noon the lunchpails come out, full of mama's cooking, and at 3:30 o'clock (having been there since 7 o'clock), they all go home to get in some fishing or swimming or to tend the chickens and fields before the sun sets.[10]

For buyers hesitant about newfangled design and technological change, this pastoral image endorsed the product as one born of common folk with nostalgic values, not modernist aesthetes designing for absinthe and free love. The marketed portrait of Zeeland conformed to its own self-understanding. Located just outside Grand Rapids,

Zeeland was a main settlement for the second wave of Dutch immigrants to the United States during the antebellum era. In 1847 two groups emigrated to the United States after they had been prevented in the Netherlands from worshiping in a Reformed church free from state domination. As their churches expanded in Michigan, the battles they fled continued in the Netherlands, largely under the leadership of Abraham Kuyper (1837–1920), a Dutch theologian and political leader who opposed the liberalizing tendencies within the Dutch Reformed Church.[11] Kuyper authored theological tenets associated with a movement called Neo-Calvinism.

Three elements of Kuyper's theology connected to economic developments within the Dutch Reformed diaspora. First, his followers possessed an aversion to experimental or mystical forms of religion, preferring instead to restrict their interests to the doctrinal and practical aspects of religion. Second, Kuyper's Neo-Calvinism included Hyper-Covenantism, an elaboration of the historic Calvinist doctrine of God's covenant with humanity. For Kuyper's followers, this Hyper-Covenantism interpreted the covenant not as a primarily soteriological obligation but as a primarily *cultural* one. Kuyper understood the covenant established between God and human beings as one that obligated followers to manifest their faith in the material world. Third—and related to the second and first elements—Kuyper made significant contributions to the formulation of the principle of common grace, focusing on the role of God in everyday life. Kuyper wrote, "Oh, no single piece of our mental world is to be hermetically sealed off from the rest, and there is not a square inch in the whole domain of our human existence over which Christ, who is Sovereign over all, does not cry: 'Mine!'"[12] The theology espoused by Kuyper heavily influenced Dutch immigrants in Michigan, offering justification for the development of intensely cohesive communities, as well as a disproportionately large share of the American furnishings industry.[13] As critics of Gilded Age material excess, the Dutch Reformed encouraged plain living; even wealthy Reformed parishioners lived in homes distinguished by their frugality and austerity. The furnishings produced in southwestern Michigan provided a hand-hewn earnestness coordinate with Kuyper's theological perspective.

In 1923 D. J. De Pree, the grandson of Dutch émigrés, purchased his employer, the eighteen-year-old Michigan Star Furniture Company. He renamed it Herman Miller in honor of his father-in-law and financial backer. Within a short period of time, De Pree began to look for new talent to develop an aesthetic more salable to the expanding middle-class marketplace. He hired New York–based designer Gilbert Rohde (1894–1944) to serve as his initial adviser on new product development. Like those trained at the Bauhaus School (1919–1933) in Germany, Rohde asserted that manufacturers had a responsibility to offer the public well-considered designs to meet their needs rather than continuing to mass-produce established styles that were, he argued, no longer relevant to a changing way of life.[14] Not long after Rohde's death, De Pree read a *Life* magazine article that promoted a storage unit designed by architect

George Nelson (1908–1986) that appeared, when closed, to be merely a flat wall with small circular bits of hardware to open its multiple rectangular units.[15] By the time Herman Miller issued its 1948 catalog, Nelson had already imprinted the company with his vision, articulating five principles that he said guided their work:

- What you make is important.
- Design is an integral part of your business.
- The product must be honest.
- You decide what you will make.
- There is a market for good design.[16]

Through Nelson's stewardship, Herman Miller produced iconic home furnishings designed by Ray and Charles Eames, Harry Bertoia, Richard Schultz, Donald Knorr, and Isamu Noguchi. Despite the seeming diversity of this contributing roster, Herman Miller sustained a coherent aesthetic because of Nelson's insistence on his principles of material honesty, domestic usability, and the marketability of thoughtful design.[17] Likewise, even when D. J. De Pree transferred management of the firm to his sons Max and Hugh in 1960, he remained "the spiritual head of the firm." Although a descendent of Kuyper's Reformed theology, De Pree himself was a lay Baptist minister and quoted biblical passages to describe the importance of shared work, democratic decisionmaking, and well-made goods. A 1965 press release emphasized the material effects of this biblical management: "Religion is not only a way of life for the De Prees but a way of business. Honesty in the use of materials is as natural to them as is fairness in dealing with people."[18]

To be clear, then: it would not be correct to describe Herman Miller in 1960 as a Dutch Reformed outfit. It possessed an interdenominational staff from the outset. What I seek to emphasize is the community context in which Herman Miller developed an egalitarian managerial ethos and commitment to the particularities of ergonomic comfort in every facet of human performance. "Herman Miller employees take pride in their work and their plant," a press release raved. "Their communication with management is direct, and frequently by first name, and management shares the increased earnings obtained through those increased efficiencies suggested by its workers." Working at Herman Miller was always a *job,* but Herman Miller's leadership also suggested that employees gleaned social meaning from this particular employment. "Over the years, the De Prees have been a strongly religious family, and old virtues survive in the corporate culture," wrote one reporter for a 1981 profile in *Fortune* magazine. George Nelson, always a relative outsider to this Midwestern enclave, described his Herman Miller bosses as "thoughtful, socially conscious, good to employees, hardworking." He concluded, "They embody all the Boy Scout virtues." Herman Miller's annual meetings began with a prayer. Alcohol was neither served at company functions nor allowed on expense accounts. Top executives referred to their "stewardship" of their products, their "covenant" with their employees. Head salesman Joe Schwartz elaborated this profile of corporate culture, invoking their religious past: "Herman Miller's financial strategies were heavily influenced by their Calvinist traditions; by moral values they were very frugal. Up until we went public, Herman Miller never built a building unless we had the cash to pay for it."[19] These common rites and practices contributed to Herman Miller's public profile as a communitarian company open to innovation—if that innovation coordinated with its principles of design and social well-being.

The Problem

By the late 1950s, D. J. De Pree had decided that Herman Miller ought to enter more actively into the market for office furnishings. Until the 1960s, the design of large-scale offices depended on the labor management theories of Frederick Winslow Taylor (1856–1915). Taylor's *Principles of Scientific Management,* submitted to the American Society of Mechanical Engineers for approval in 1910 and subsequently published in 1911, was immediately applied in every center of industrial labor in the world. The resultant "Taylorism" had two essential aspects: first, the careful breakdown of each work activity into its smallest constitutive units, and second, the precise study of the time it took to complete each unit. The work station of any employee was optimally located within an open-plan configuration of desks arranged in a square formation, with higher-level management occupying private offices that framed the edge of that square. "Transferred to architecture, Taylorism was seen as legitimizing functionalism as a theory and practice linked to industrialism," explained twenty-first-century designers Iñaki Ábalos and Juan Herreros.[20]

In the years prior to World War II, the prevalence of the Taylorist office began to diminish as more participatory styles of management became fashionable. The development of comprehensive heating and air conditioning systems, fluorescent lighting, and the suspended ceiling made the physical workplace a more malleable one. And the popularization of psychology influenced many managers to begin to conceive of the workplace as a site not only of productivity but also of social ecology. It was in this vein that Herman Miller invited Robert Propst, an independent business consultant from Colorado, to work for the company under the auspices of the Herman Miller Research Corporation. "By 1959, the company's management had concluded that the company should assume a greater responsibility for the total environment in which men work and live," he would later recount. To that end, Propst began to study the office as a space of "working, learning, living and healing."[21] After several years of interviews and site visits, Propst reported his findings with dismay: "Today's office is a wasteland. It saps vitality, blocks talent, frustrates accomplishment. It is the daily scene of unfulfilled intentions and failed efforts. A place of fantasy and conjecture rather than accomplishment. It fosters physical and mental decline and depresses capacity to perform. It is the equivalent of doing business on clay tablets in an age of the computer and instant communication."[22] The problem with the contemporary office was connected to the changes in the work done by offices. "In the last fifty years, activity has moved from tasks of the hand to tasks of the mind in a dramatic contrast of ratios," Propst wrote. "Life in an office rarely deals with the actual object, actual money or, often, even people in the flesh."[23] Offices transact information, not things, Propst explained, such that "thinking is the primary role of the human being in today's office." However, offices did not engender thought. Workers were, he ranted, "surrounded by papers they never read and people they never really influence, and they frequently live in a blizzard of involvement well beyond their ability to relate and implement."[24] If the office was a place for thinking, it failed to foster productive thought; it was a confused sector of bothersome interaction and overabundant information.

Propst narrowed the problems facing office design to two sensorial aspects: sight and posture. "There is a direct relation between seeing objects and taking action on them," Propst argued, pointing to piled papers and the excess of reference materials in offices as telltale signs of disarrayed minds. How a desk looked to the worker affected how the worker could think.[25] Likewise, the working positions of office employees affected their performance. "Existing office environments can be criticized for providing only one primary work posture," Propst wrote, suggesting that this limited physicality had two problematic consequences.[26] First, this singular posture was deleterious to health. "Being seated in multi-hour stretches results in a noticeable drop off in mental capacities because of the resulting imbalance in physical activities," Propst wrote. "Sedentary living is hazardous to health, dampens creativity and results in minimum work performance." Second, a seated posture presupposed seated conversations, "with natural inclinations toward relaxation and diversion." Propst argued that standing conversations had more "economy and dispatch than seated ones." The office required some level of social engagement. "Involvement is an essential need, a good idea . . . to be part of, visible, wanted, needed, recognized, part of the family of activity." Yet that involvement needed to be precisely right: neither too lingering nor too abbreviated, neither too restful nor too removed from the immediate tasks at hand. The right design would admit the mind–body connection and "produce the highest productivity with minimum fatigue."[27] Rather than rigidity and entrapment, the office systems advocated by Herman Miller were meant to promote variability, flexibility, and substantive sociability. As the history of the cubicle now turns to Robert Propst, it becomes a less obviously religious story: Propst was neither explicitly religious himself nor comfortable in the Christian atmosphere of Zeeland. Yet departure from denomination does not mean a departure from the imperatives of religion; it merely means that these imperatives will be transfigured into new modes of articulation and experience.

The Solution

Rather than isolated pieces of furniture, Propst sought to develop office landscapes in which each element functioned in a systematic way. This "allows maximum flexibility for the individual to change instantly, easily and economically his own work arena of multi-posture work stations, paper-handling, information retrieval and communications," promotional materials explained, reiterating that the Action Office is a *system* by which corporations and the individuals in them might express their particular needs and personality.[28] Propst would not use the word *desk*. Rather, in his office *human performers* would work at *free-standing units* in their *work stations*. Propst designed extensions of the thought process, systems by which individuals enacted their labors with coherent physicality and sensorial attention. "Every element of the Action Office system is designed with people in mind," one brochure explained. "Edges and corners are rounded. Basic finishes are neutral colors, found to be the most relaxing for your eyes. Accent colors, provided by fabric covers on many components, create visual interest and excitement. Individual work stations can be modified easily, and work surfaces can be adjusted to different heights."[29] Central to the sale of the system was its smooth materiality and physical adjustability. To arrive at this ideal, Propst auditioned a first Action Office design (AO1), which included a stand-up work surface and open-sided work areas (Figure 7.2). The AO1 group included a high desk with an appropriate-level perch, movable shelf units for quick recovery of filed items, low mobile conference tables, and freestanding units specially designed for typing. The AO1 components had no drawers but instead had shallow wells fitted with molded plastic trays for pencils, rubber bands, and paper clips. The overall look of AO1 was a powerful mix of old and new, with aluminum, wood, and laminate materials combining to suggest evocations of old office furnishings formatted for a new efficiency. Propst imagined that the AO1 pieces would never be perfectly clear of paper, and he encouraged a "meaningful clutter of information" that was ostensible rather than secreted in drawers or cabinets. "Display becomes part of the furniture system."[30] AO1 appeared in December 1964.

It promptly failed. As Joseph N. Schwartz, Herman Miller's marketing manager, told *Home Furnishings Daily* in 1969, "Quite frankly, Action Office I was a disaster mainly because people did not understand it." Responses to AO1 suggested that the product was neither familiar enough to be recognizable nor strange enough to intrigue buyers. The furnishings seemed too heavy to be as mobile as promised and not up to George Nelson's expected modernist standards. Propst immediately returned to research, and Herman Miller promoters began to think about how to sell the next in-

A
new
world
to work in

ACTION OFFICE
If you're a stand-up worker, come in and see
Action Office. If you're a sit-down worker,
come in and see Action Office. If you like to
straddle or perch while you work, come in
and see Action Office.
You see, we made Action Office just for you.

Dealer Signature

Researched and developed by Robert Propst,
Director of Herman Miller's Research Division.
Design by George Nelson.

Action Office Ad Mat #1

FIGURE 7.2. A 1964 advertisement for the first Action Office (AO1). Courtesy of the Herman Miller Inc. Archive, Zeeland, Michigan.

novation that he produced. Later Joe Schwartz would explain that they were "determined to ensure comprehension by presenting the theory behind the product and showing how it can solve the problems of change in the office."[31] The major difference between AO1 and the resulting Action Office 2 (AO2) was the difference that would define the transformation of the object, namely that freestanding units were replaced by integrated furniture elements. In other words, AO2 included walls (Figure 7.3).

"The new concept, Action Office II (AOII), is, in the most simplistic terms, a planning tool which provides a coherent system of components utilizing walls, easily

FIGURE 7.3. A photograph from a 1973 brochure shows an Action Office installation at the Banque Hervet offices in Fussy, France. Courtesy of the Herman Miller Inc. Archive, Zeeland, Michigan.

connectable panels, wall-hung, panel-hung, and free-standing furniture," Herman Miller announced in 1968.[32] Like AO1, AO2 was meant to be totally flexible—the word "modular" appeared constantly in the promotional materials (Figure 7.4). Modularity referred to the fact that the system's shelves, filing units, and all other components were completely interchangeable. This modularity occurred within a grid, the distinguishing aspect of which was a series of panel-hung, wall-hung, and free-standing units. With AO1 Propst had begun to theorize about singular office spaces but also about the relationship of one work station to another (Figure 7.5). With AO2 this arrangement of the office as an entire landscape became central to its sale. In 1960 the German-based Quickborner Team revolutionized the practice of office planning through the concept of *Bürolandschaft* (office landscape). Rather than straight alleys of identical desks, *Bürolandschaft* recommended that the office be more like an English garden, whose apparently natural order had been developed by Capability Brown (1716–1783) in the late eighteenth century. Similarly, the Quickborner Team developed patterns in office layout that might have been devised by the workers themselves had they approached the problem with the requisite overview.

"Office planning has frequently treated human beings as a hydraulic quantity of sideless, senseless particles," Propst wrote, invoking the mathematics of Taylorism. In

Modularity and flexibility

A facility based on change

The ability to change and adapt to new demands is absolutely essential. Moreover it will be necessary to accomplish such adaptations with ease, as they are often a regular feature of office life. This facility is particularly important to an expanding company where unplanned growth can eventually work as inhibition to the rate of further growth.

Panels and components

Action Office is a system that is based on a modular grid, the basic components of which are a series of panel-hung, wall-hung and free-standing units.

Modularity means that shelves, filing units and all other components are completely inter-changeable, also that future additions to the range of Action Office components will be easily incorporated into existing Action Office installations. And of course modularity ensures that everything fits perfectly, so that space is used economically and efficiently.

Panels can be of varying heights, and three width sizes. They may be flat or curved, open or with panels of glass that let through light but not sound. In addition, all panels are available in a wide choice of fabrics and colours. Beneath the outer fabric the panel itself may be sound-absorbent board, or pin board for display areas.

It is to these panels that most of the other components in the system will be attached. These include work surfaces, storage units, shelving, display surfaces, as well as lighting.

Sign system

There is also a sign system, co-ordinated with other components, to identify traffic routes, departments and individuals. The signs are designed to enable them to be suspended from the ceiling, clipped to the top of panels, or fixed directly to the panel face.

Electrical accessories

It is worth noting too, that the modularity of the system has been carried right through to include lighting fixtures and electrical power strips, which can also be easily re-sited.

Colours and materials

Panels and components are neutral, with dark tone trim and accessories. This basic principle means that the system survives changes in fashion and taste. In addition, panels and work surfaces are available in oak veneer finish.

Colour is introduced in the form of fabric-covered panels, pin boards and storage unit doors. Fabrics can be chosen from the Herman Miller range, or supplied to the customer's own specification. Rods and clips are also provided, for attaching fabric hangings to standard panels.

10

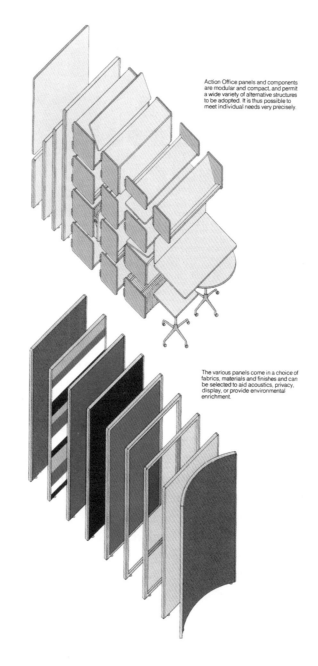

Action Office panels and components are modular and compact, and permit a wide variety of alternative structures to be adopted. It is thus possible to meet individual needs very precisely.

The various panels come in a choice of fabrics, materials and finishes and can be selected to aid acoustics, privacy, display, or provide environmental enrichment.

FIGURE 7.4. A 1978 brochure explains the modularity of the Action Office. Courtesy of the Herman Miller Inc. Archive, Zeeland, Michigan.

FIGURE 7.5. A 1966 drawing illustrates the ideal landscape design for the Action Office system. Courtesy of the Herman Miller Inc. Archive, Zeeland, Michigan.

AO2 individuals occupied working landscapes that recognized their variability and dynamism. The long regimented rows of desks that marked the classical office bullpen were replaced by small groupings in looser arrangements. The separating panels "provide as much or as little 'territoriality' or enclosure privacy as a person or task requires" (Figure 7.6).[33] AO2 did not inhibit individual need; it was an articulation of individual need:

> Inside these spaces—which can be moved and reformed at will—each worker is provided with his precise needs through a system of furniture components designed by Herman Miller, Inc. Called Action Office II, the system provides a variety of work surfaces—file bins, storage units, shelves, carrels, display panels, and chalk boards—to fill all job demands. Since, to some degree, the worker knows his own requirements best, he can add or subtract from his equipment simply by requisitioning the necessary components.[34]

Herman Miller distributed catalogs that included images of the "system vocabulary," suggesting that AO2 was like a set of Legos with which office workers might play. It could be arranged in any number of ways to respond to workers' particular preferences and physical needs.

FIGURE 7.6. An advertisement for the Action Office 2, circa 1978–1980. Courtesy of the Herman Miller Inc. Archive, Zeeland, Michigan.

And what if a worker found it dispiriting to face a wall rather than a window or other workers? "People who are facing the Action Office 2 panels are normally facing information, storage and display," Propst replied. "By facing information and display rather than a blank wall, the age old problem of people facing walls is eliminated because we are really not facing a wall but the day-to-day information with which we work." Herman Miller extolled the personalization possible with such panels. The austere quality for which cubicle-filled offices are now criticized was entirely intentional: "We tried to create a low-key, unself-conscious product that was not at all fashionable," Propst reflected. "We wanted this to be the vehicle to carry other expressions of identity. That's why we provided tackboards and all kinds of display surfaces." When a member of the sales staff for the original cubicle design brought a plastic gorilla to decorate his workspace, management briefly looked askance at such a garish additive to their sleek, plain structure. But Propst insisted that this was exactly the kind of thing that had been intended by the design itself.[35] The human performer was to provide the action of this office. The cubicles were dully colored because the worker afforded the color; the design was simple because the worker presented the drama (Figure 7.7). The limited territory of quiet the system provided was a staging area where the worker's ideas could be born.

FIGURE 7.7. A 1978 brochure for the Action Office illustrates how this system would accommodate computer systems. Courtesy of the Herman Miller Inc. Archive, Zeeland, Michigan.

The Sale

AO2 entered the marketplace in 1968. Its sheer appearance would not be enough to allow the potential buyer to make sense of its new components and modular language. As marketing director Joe Schwartz remarked, "We had to educate people about a *concept,* not just a *product.*" Rather than spending money on large ads, booklets, and catalogs, Herman Miller instead hosted seminars for people who worked in, owned, rented, or managed facilities. The Herman Miller Seminar Series was offered first in the Union Bank Building in downtown Grand Rapids, but it quickly became a traveling road show to which hundreds of thousands of people came to learn how to build more efficient offices using the latest fusion of technology, aesthetics, and optimism for the human performer. At these seminars every attendee left with a copy of *The Office: A Facility Based on Change,* a volume written by Robert Propst and circulated first as a mimeographed pamphlet simultaneous to the release of AO1 in 1964. The book was 8 × 11 inches in size, with large-font type, a sparsely modern graphical layout, and multiple black-and-white photographs squarely arranged near short, koanlike utterances about the history of the office, the relationship between the office space and its human performers, the challenges confronted in office space, and, most important, in the second half of the book a description of a product that would resolve the quandaries raised in the first half. Colloquially known as the Red Book, it was a booklet for an era in which every tract seemed to offer a new view with a new look for a new world. "The real office consumer is the mind," Propst preached. "The subject starts there. More than anything else, we are dealing with a mind-oriented living space."[36]

Revolutionary imperatives pervaded Propst's writing and the promotions surrounding the release of the Action Office. The new office was not just a new product in a clogged marketplace; it was a product that would unclog the marketplace. "Our buildings, furnishings and services have to be revisualized and revitalized," Propst said. "The office as an institution will no longer be able to ignore the new master." This naming of the problem and proclamation of the necessary reform echoed throughout the history of modernist design. In 1919 Walter Gropius exclaimed, "The old forms are in ruins, the benumbed world is shaken up, the old human spirit is invalidated and in flux towards a new form. We float in space and cannot perceive the new order." Forty-five years later, Propst conceived of a new order, a new design for the human spirit to reclaim itself. I am intrigued by this move from condemnation to reformation and by the particular locutions upon which it relied. In the history of religions, such grumbling critique and bright-eyed optimism harkened to the discursive patterns surrounding the Reformation, in which reformers constantly insulted Catholicism, developing protests into new doctrines that emerged as the sectarian network known as Protestantism. Likewise, among the promotions and prescriptions surrounding the Action Office, Herman Miller criticized old offices for their "encrusted routine and procedures," as well as for their "rigid" hierarchical structures. "The traditional office confines the occupant to rigid forms and work formats," an *Action Office Workbook* chides, emphasizing that by contrast the AO2 is "simply expedience with a choice."[37]

The Action Office was, as advertisements repeatedly argued, a new world in which to work (see Figure 7.2). The reformation of the office would "upset the inflexible and status seekers," but Herman Miller expected that the Action Office would "elate a sizeable group of men who want their office to serve their mental effort rather than their egos." This was the good news that Herman Miller spread with an unmitigated certitude. If the Action Office was to work, everyone in it had to share its principles. Everyone had to want to "come to terms with modularity" and accept the ferocious persistence of change. Also, if the Action Office was to work, "The whole system has to play; if any element is resistant, adjustment is inhibited." Change was intrinsic to the system, but the system would not work if its star players—its human performers—did not recognize and invest in a daily practice of change. This meant, on the most basic level, that workers had to participate in shifting their panels themselves, moving the entirely movable components of the system vocabulary as often as possible to create new connections, new visual landscapes, and new postures. It also meant, on a more ontological level, that the work that workers did in the Action Office had to be compatible with such a sense of change. "Change as a continuous rather than an occasional force, is recognized in the Action Office concept," Propst emphasized. "Change in the ebb and flow of assignments. Changes in individual responsibility. And in the organization's direction."[38] If the human performers in the Action Office were not in action, the Action Office would become a cubicle.

The Result

In *Knocking on Heaven's Door: American Religion in the Age of Counterculture* (2003), Mark Oppenheimer identified 1968 as a critical year to this history. "Sometime between the Summer of Love in 1967 and the Woodstock festival in 1969, or between the death of King and the deaths at Kent State, even the conservatives began to dress down, talk more informally, and listen to different music," he wrote. Just as quickly as it appeared, however, the counterculture changed. "By the mid-1970s," Oppenheimer argued, "the counterculture had become the culture." Oppenheimer suggested that this quick change from countercultural critique to mainstream culture was in part due to the fact that the counterculture was largely an aesthetic effect more than a political or theological one. To be sure, "This aesthetic change could, itself, be subversive."[39] But it was also likely that this change could be transfigured into a commodity form devoid of metaphysical dissent, like a peace necklace inlaid with diamonds or a Kabbalah bracelet worn by someone who had never read the *Zohar*.

The release of AO2 occurred in 1968. By 1985 it was named "Best Design of the Past 24 Years, 1961–1985" by the Industrial Designers Society of America. In the intervening years, everything changed for Herman Miller. To fund the production of AO2, the De Prees decided that Herman Miller would become a publicly owned company. In 1970 they sold 197,000 shares at $13.75 and raised $2.5 million for production. The contract furniture business grew by leaps and bounds, and although Herman Miller's designs spawned many less expensive imitations from companies like Steelcase, it retained its reputation as the originator of facility management, and funds garnered by Herman Miller from the Action Office allowed it to further develop the field of ergonomics, resulting in its enormously popular Aeron chair. But the wild success of the Aeron chair presumed a worker still huddled in a singular location, stuck in a certain posture in front of a computer monitor. The dream of multiple postures was replaced by the dream of a comfortable support system for the seated worker's back.

The Action Office itself did not live up to its modular dream—or rather, its occupants did not experience its prescribed possibilities. High real estate costs led companies to cram cubicles into office buildings without the English garden effect of the hoped-for AO2 landscape. AO2 had hinged connectors that could form any angle, yet by the mid-1970s those had been replaced by permanent brackets that lacked such inherent variability. Herman Miller research found that workplaces had not been using the hinges to change office spaces (citing, among other reasons, the fact that computer and phone cable setups were too complex to shift easily). In general, Propst's forms became more often replicated than his prescribed functions. Companies crammed more workers into smaller spaces and took advantage of the Action Office system's huge potential for savings and tax breaks, since tax laws permit businesses to write off the depreciation of cubicles much more quickly than that of traditional office furniture. "The dark side of this is that not all organizations are intelligent and progressive," Propst reflected toward the end of his life. "Lots are run by crass people who can take the same kind of equipment and create hellholes. Barren, rat-hole places." According to data compiled by the International Facility Management Association, the average workspace has dwindled by fifteen square feet in sixteen years, a diminishment of one foot of personal space per year between 1994 and 2010.[40] The history of the cubicle—like the histories of the prison and the asylum offered by Michel Foucault—began as a Christian proposition for bodily asceticism and became a contribution to the carceral network. "The carceral texture of society assures both the real capture of the body and its perpetual observation," Foucault described. "It is, by its very nature, the apparatus of punishment that conforms most completely to the new economy of power and the instrument for the formation of knowledge that this very economy needs."[41]

Propst carried no guilt for the disaster born of his dream. Speaking from his Redmond, Washington, home in 1998, he said, "I don't even feel faintly guilty about Dilbert. The things expressed in that comic are the very things we were trying to relieve and move beyond. It was a Dilbert world even back then. Everything we worked toward tries to express something more interesting."[42] That "something more interesting" was a commodity promoting a new sensorial world, but it was also a circulating ideology against a desensitizing sterility. There are many cynical views of the perpetuation of this sterility in office life, such as those offered in Scott Adams's comic strip *Dilbert* (1989–present) or the 1999 film *Office Space*. But there are also cultural works that present its sensory stultification as its possibility for meditative revelation, as depicted in David Foster Wallace's posthumously published novel *The Pale King* (2011). Today perhaps the strongest element of Propst's original vision to have survived is the way that cubicles function as spaces of individual expression. Workers do add color to their cubicles, adding themselves through accessories and objects, pinning to their bulletin board panels their personal pictures, and drinking from their personalized mugs. In the cubicle, then, we could find a space of inordinate individuality, where workers—be they Hindu, Buddhist, or Roman Catholic—could build a shrine to someone someplace else, a possible private sensorium of religion within the hum and sheen of the modern office. Such desktop acts of individual religious identity indicate the limits of the cubicle to define the self within as mere office performer and hypo-thetically remind workers of spaces they occupy—and conceive—beyond the cubicle.

But the cubicle is also where workers do sit, day after ritual day, making these hours of their lives the rungs of a ladder nobody seems able to escape with ease. After all, that cubicle also signifies ambition—dreams to move from one form of anony-mous labor to slightly more marked ones, to sit in dignity and earn benefits to propel you and your family into better futures, to offices with corner windows and distin-guishable furniture, purchased for a higher price from the same Herman Miller com-pany (an Eames chair, perhaps, with an accompanying Noguchi table). The cubicle is a shuttering, spiritless trap; the cubicle also presents an opportunity to pursue a spir-ited rise. "What is most relevant here is that mass culture cannot be entirely located at either end of the authenticity spectrum," Celeste Olalquiaga has written. "It nei-ther fully supports authenticity nor wholly abolishes it, but rather maintains an in-termediate, fluctuating position in which certain aspects of authenticity adapt to modernity."[43]

Accounts of religion invariably demonstrate the strange emergence of authen-ticity as a metric of meaning in the modern period. In such a vein, the story of the Action Office and the Herman Miller Furniture Company includes generational shifts familiar to the early years of new religious movements. The religious history of America is littered with upstart operations that go bankrupt, and there are docu-ments galore of utopian communities that become ghost towns, such as the Moravi-ans of Bethlehem, Pennsylvania, or the believers in the Amana Colonies of Iowa or the Oneida community of upstate New York. These self-sufficient towns of egalitar-ian labor underwent constraint, over time, to limited manifestations as packaged consumer goods such as Oneida flatware, Amana refrigerators, and Moravian cook-ies.[44] The story of the Action Office, however, is not a story of utopian socialists seek-ing alternative refuge from nineteenth-century industrialization. It is the story of a spiritually conscious capitalist body seeking incorporation in the postindustrial twentieth century.

As a result, the history of Robert Propst and his Action Office is a story more about the religious valences in corporate practice than it is about the denominational facts of the southwestern Michigan community that gave birth to Herman Miller. It is the fusion of a Neo-Calvinist civility with De Pree's dissenting Baptist pugnacity that created a community of producers equally complicit in the products they mass-produced to create equal access to more humane working environments. And al-though Herman Miller has a singular story in the ranks of modernism, what has been observed here about its fusion of populist aesthetics, revamped technology, and prac-tical religion can be quickly discerned in any number of companies, as recent studies of Apple, IKEA, and Wal-Mart have suggested.[45] *Corporation* is just another word for *sect*. And sects produce any number of creeds, codes, and ideas about committed community. The story of the Action Office is an example of the incorporation of the self into corporate narratives of sensorial freedom. It is also an example of the social worlds conceived through consumer products by companies dreaming on our material and spiritual behalf. The sensorium of religion in the modern period cannot be understood without analysis of the individual and the community produced in and through such market forms and processes.

NOTES

I acknowledge Gloria Jacobs and Linda Baron at the Herman Miller Inc. Archive for their enthusiastic assistance with this research, as well as audiences at Hamilton College, Heidelberg University, the John C. Danforth Center on Religion and Politics at Washington University, and the University of Illinois, Urbana-Champaign, for their thoughtful feedback on earlier versions of its argument. Special appreciation is extended to Darren Dochuk, Jonathan Ebel, Marie Griffith, Mark Jordan, Dana Katz, S. Brent Plate, Sally Promey, Leigh Schmidt, and Tara Ward for their provocations.

1. Nathan Bomey, "Death to Cubicles, Menlo Innovations CEO Rich Sheridan Says," AnnArbor.com, December 30, 2009, http://www.annarbor.com/business-review/death-to-cubicles-menlo-innovations-rich-sheridan-says/#.UCaFnqNLfyI, and Randall Braaksma, "'Do Cubicles Kill?' That Depends," January 7, 2010, http://www.hermanmiller.com/discover/do-cubicles-kill-that-depends/#more-3319.

2. Reprint of Robert L. Propst, "Change and Opportunity: The Action Office," *Contract,* January 1965, Pubs 7824, Herman Miller research archive (hereafter HMIA).

3. Reprint of a conversation with Robert Propst, *Architectural and Engineering News,* 1965, Pubs 7645, HMIA, and Herman Miller News Release, January 25, 1965, News, HMIA.

4. Max Horkheimer and Theodor W. Adorno, "The Culture Industry: Enlightenment as Mass Deception," in *Dialectic of Enlightenment,* by Horkheimer and Adorno (London: Verso, 1997), 120–167.

5. Richard J. Callahan Jr., Kathryn Lofton, and Chad E. Seales, "Allegories of Progress: Industrial Religion in the United States," *Journal of the American Academy of Religion* 78, no. 1 (March 2010): 1–39; Darren Dochuk, "Blessed by Oil, Cursed with Crude: God and Black Gold in the American Southwest," *Journal of American History* 99, no. 1 (2012): 51–61; Katherine Carté Engel, *Religion and Profit: Moravians in Early America* (Philadelphia: University of Pennsylvania Press, 2009); Sarah Hammond, "'God Is My Partner': An Evangelical Business Man Confronts Depression and War," *Church History* 80, no. 3 (September 2011): 498–519; Kathryn Lofton, *Oprah: The Gospel of an Icon* (Berkeley: University of California Press, 2011); and Mark Valeri, *Heavenly Merchandize: How Religion Shaped Commerce in Puritan America* (Princeton, NJ: Princeton University Press, 2011).

6. Hans Janssen, *Mondrian / De Stijl* (Ostfildern, Germany: Hatje Cantz, 2011); Mark C. Taylor, *After God* (Chicago: University of Chicago Press, 2007): 205–217; Maurice Tuchman, *The Spiritual in Art: Abstract Painting, 1890–1985* (New York: Abbeville, 1995); and Barry Bergdoll, Leah Dickerman, Benjamin Buchloh, and Brigid Doherty, *Bauhaus, 1919–1933: Workshops for Modernity* (New York: Museum of Modern Art, 2009).

7. For an assessment of the history and anthropology of Levittown, Pennsylvania, see Dianne Harris, ed., *Second Suburb: Levittown, Pennsylvania* (Pittsburgh: University of Pittsburgh Press, 2010).

8. Judith A. Barter, "Designing for Democracy: Modernism and Its Utopias," in *Shaping the Modern: American Decorative Arts at the Art Institute of Chicago, 1917–65,* Museum Studies series (Chicago: Art Institute of Chicago, 2001), 16–17.

9. Herman Miller News Release, January 25, 1965.

10. Ibid.

11. James Bratt and Christopher Meehan, *Gathered at the River: Grand Rapids, Michigan, and Its People of Faith* (Grand Rapids, MI: Grand Rapids Area Council for the Humanities and Eerdmans, 1993).

12. Abraham Kuyper, "Sphere Sovereignty," in *Abraham Kuyper: A Centennial Reader,* ed. James D. Bratt (Grand Rapids, MI: Eerdmans, 1998), 488. On Kuyper, see James Bratt, *Dutch Calvinism in Modern America: A History of a Conservative Subculture* (Grand Rapids, MI: Eerdmans, 1984); James Bratt, "Abraham Kuyper's Calvinism: Society, Economics, and Empire in the Late Nineteenth Century," in *Calvin Rediscovered: The Impact of His Social and Economic Thought,* ed. Edouard Dommen and James Bratt (Louisville, KY: Westminster John Knox Press, 2007).

13. From the time of the Centennial Exposition in Philadelphia in 1876 to the beginning of the Great Depression, the Grand Rapids furniture community considered itself the center of the furniture universe. Christian G. Carron, *Grand Rapids Furniture: The Story of America's Furniture City* (Grand Rapids, MI: Public Museum of Grand Rapids, 1998).

14. Phyllis Ross, "Merchandising the Modern: Gilbert Rohde at Herman Miller," *Journal of Design History* 17, no. 4 (2004): 359–396.

15. "*Life* Presents . . . Storage Wall," *Life* 18, no. 4 (January 22, 1945), 63–71.

16. Joe Schwartz, *How Design Happened at Herman Miller* (Zeeland, MI: Herman Miller, 2006), 24. On the critical writings of George Nelson, see John Harwood, "The Wound Man: George Nelson and the 'End of Architecture,'" *Grey Room* 31 (Spring 2008): 90–115.

17. For an overview of Herman Miller design, see John R. Berry, *Herman Miller: The Purpose of Design* (New York: Rizzoli International, 2004).

18. Herman Miller News Release, January 25, 1965.

19. Ibid. and Ann M. Morrison, "Action Is What Makes Herman Miller Climb," *Fortune* (June 15, 1981).

20. Iñaki Ábalos and Juan Herreros, *Tower and Office: From Modernist Theory to Contemporary Practice* (Cambridge, MA: MIT Press, 2003), 183. On Taylorism, see Stanley Abercrombie, "Office Supplies: Evolving Furniture for the Evolving Workplace," in *On the Job: Design and the American Office,* ed. Donald Albrecht and Chrysanthe B. Broikos (New York: Princeton Architectural Press, 2000), 80–97.

21. Robert L. Propst, "The Action Office," *Human Factors: The Journal of the Human Factors and Ergonomics Society* 8, no. 4 (August 1966): 299; *Action Office 2 Workbook, 1968–1972,* Pubs 9484, HMIA. Much of this research is available in the Herman Miller Archive in Zeeland, including an elaborate questionnaire focused on soliciting replies to this set of basic queries: "What, for example, is the purpose of an office? What is the nature of work in offices? What are the factors that influence the health and productivity of people who use offices? How can materials, designs, space, activities, and human factors be interrelated to improve the net result of their interaction?" Propst, "The Action Office," 300.

22. "The Action Office," Herman Miller brochure, 1964, BROC A016, HMIA.

23. Propst, "Change and Opportunity."

24. Herman Miller brochure, 1978, BROC A019, HMIA; and Propst, "Change and Opportunity." Propst echoed his contemporary Eliot Noyes, who worked as consultant director of design at IBM. IBM was not simply a maker of business machines, Noyes argued in a 1966 inter-

view; rather, it was in the business of controlling, organizing, and redistributing information: "If you get to the very heart of the matter, what IBM really does is to help man extend his control over his environment." John Harwood, "The White Room: Eliot Noyes and the Logic of the Information Age Interior," *Grey Room* 12 (Summer 2003): 13. IBM would be among the first companies to invest in Action Office furnishings.

25. Robert Propst, "Human Productivity in Offices," 1961, BROC A062, HMIA. "The human body is no longer postulated as the agent of space in either pictorial or sculptural art," Clement Greenberg asserted in 1958. "Now it is eyesight alone." In *Eyesight Alone* art historian Caroline A. Jones considered this sensorial emphasis, encouraging analysis of modernism to take up its invitation to visualization: "At its narrowest, the modernist visibility might describe the aesthetic protocols required by a specific abstract painting—what may and may not be seen there according to an art world expert. At its broadest, it involves the way cities are laid out in grids to manipulate urban light and shade, with streets widened to provide clear thoroughfares for managing fire and controlling urban unrest." Caroline A. Jones, *Eyesight Alone: Clement Greenberg's Modernism and the Bureaucratization of the Senses* (Chicago: University of Chicago Press, 2005), xvii.

26. Robert Propst, "Human Productivity in Offices: Research Division, Project #4," 1962, BROC A063, HMIA.

27. Robert Propst, "Human Productivity in Offices," 1961; "Local Publicity Release," Sales Aids Information, December 1964, BROC A015, HMIA; Propst, *The Office: A Facility Based on Change* (Elmhurst, IL: Business Press International, 1968), 25; and Propst, "Human Productivity in Offices," 1961.

28. Joe Schwartz, *How Design Happened at Herman Miller* (Zeeland, MI: Herman Miller, 2006), 40. Schwartz details the emergence of the Action Office on pp. 39–58. Herman Miller News Release, September 17, 1968, News, HMIA.

29. Herman Miller brochure, 1978–1980, BROC A010, HMIA.

30. "Local Publicity Release," 1964.

31. "Hard N.Y. Drive Starting for Action Office II Line," *Home Furnishings Daily,* 1969, BROC A099, HMIA.

32. Herman Miller News Release, September 17, 1968.

33. Propst, *The Office: A Facility Based on Change,* 27, and Herman Miller News Release, September 17, 1968.

34. Reprint of article from *Progressive Architecture,* November 1969, Pubs 7734, HMIA.

35. *Action Office 2 Workbook, 1968–1972,* and Yvonne Abraham, "The Man Behind the Cubicle," *Metropolis* (November 1998), http://www.metropolismag.com/html/content_1198/no98man.htm.

36. Schwartz, *How Design Happened at Herman Miller,* 58. Nearly every early promotion of the AO2 included this small advertisement: "This data is well defined and documented in an easy-to-read book entitled 'The Office—A Facility Based on Change' written by Bob Propst and published by Business Press International. Hard Bound, single copy press in the USA is $9.95. Quantity prices are available by writing the publisher." Propst, *The Office: A Facility Based on Change,* 19.

37. Propst, *The Office: A Facility Based on Change,* 29; Gropius, quoted in *Modernism 1914–1939: Designing a New World,* ed. Christopher Wilk (London: V&A Publications, 2006), 11; "The Action Office," Herman Miller brochure, 1964; Herman Miller brochure, 1973, BROC A093, HMIA; Herman Miller brochure, 1969, BROC A027, HMIA; and *Action Office 2 Workbook, 1968–1972.*

38. Herman Miller News Release, January 25, 1965; Propst, *The Office: A Facility Based on Change,* 71, 63; and "The Action Office," Herman Miller brochure, 1964.

39. Mark Oppenheimer, *Knocking on Heaven's Door: American Religion in the Age of Counterculture* (New Haven, CT: Yale University Press, 2003), 6, 27.

40. Abraham, "The Man Behind the Cubicle." See also "The Numbers," *Spirit: Southwest Airlines Magazine* (November 2011): 35.

41. Michael Foucault, *Discipline and Punish: The Birth of the Prison* (New York: Vintage, 1977), 304.

42. Abraham, "The Man Behind the Cubicle."

43. Celeste Olalquiaga, *The Artificial Kingdom: On the Kitsch Experience* (Minneapolis: University of Minnesota Press, 1998), 19.

44. "The Oneida Story," http://www.oneida.com/aboutoneida/the-oneida-story/; Amana: The Simple Truth about Us," http://www.amana.com/content.jsp?pageName=ourAmanifesto; and Salem Baking Company, "Moravian Cookies," all accessed August 6, 2013, http://www.salembaking.com/product/moravian-cookies/. For more on the utopian impulse in American history, see Donald E. Pitzer, ed., *America's Communal Utopias* (Chapel Hill: University of North Carolina Press, 1997).

45. On spirituality and design at IKEA, see Lauren Collins, "House Perfect," *New Yorker* (October 3, 2011): 54–65; at Apple, see Walter Isaacson, "Design Principles," Chapter 26 in *Steve Jobs* by Isaacson (New York: Simon and Schuster, 2011); and at Wal-Mart, see Bethany Moreton, *To Serve God and Wal-Mart: The Making of Christian Free Enterprise* (Cambridge, MA: Harvard University Press, 2009).

8

Sensing the City

Night in the Venetian Ghetto

DANA E. KATZ

In his 1936 essay "The Work of Art in the Age of Mechanical Reproduction," Walter Benjamin describes the shifts in human sense perception associated with the advent of new media such as film and photography. Though he seeks specifically to apprehend the modern through an examination of the reproducible image, Benjamin observes that his reception theories have a longer history. He posits that architecture "since primeval times" has participated in a complex network of sensory information, arguing:

> Buildings are appropriated in a twofold manner: by use and by perception
> —or rather, by touch and sight. . . . On the tactile side there is no counter-
> part to contemplation on the optical side. Tactile appropriation is accom-
> plished not so much by attention as by habit. As regards architecture,
> habit determines to a large extent even optical reception. . . . For the tasks
> which face the human apparatus of perception at the turning points of
> history cannot be solved by optical means, that is by contemplation,
> alone. They are mastered gradually by habit, under the guidance of tactile
> appropriation.[1]

Benjamin contends that long before the art of photography or the landscape of modern urbanism, inhabitants of the built environment received architecture in a state of distraction. It is not attentiveness that makes humans order their architectural occupancy. It is habit. Habit catalyzes the aesthetic encounter as the spaces of everyday life stimulate the senses. Habit guides the body through architectural space, the quotidian qualities of the encounter evoking a bodily response. Habit naturalizes urban onlookers to wander within that which they do not quite see.

Benjamin reminds us that the built object cannot be captured exclusively with the eyes. As three-dimensional objects on a habitable scale, buildings preclude full visualization. Katherine Fischer Taylor notes that "the impossibility of ever *seeing* a building in a single synthetic view" makes optical appropriation unachievable.[2] The architectural experience requires the contemplative capacities of opticality and the materialist impulses of tactility to render a building intelligible on a spatial scale. Vision and touch become interconnected sensoria in the act of perception. Constituents in a reciprocal spatial relationship, sight and touch nevertheless obey distinct laws of perception. Their differences are measured in distance. While sight permits viewers direct access to an object without proximal contact, touch requires closeness and connection. Viewers are able to keep the object of their gaze in sight without the need for physical engagement; touch alternatively demands bodily proximity. Such distinctions remain an issue of boundaries. Elizabeth Harvey states that sight, like hearing and smell, "extend[s] the body beyond its own boundaries," whereas touch breaks down those physical barriers to insist on the corporeal and the contiguous.[3] Architecture creates the conditions for visual detachment and tactile closeness no matter on which side of its walls you stand. The physical embodiment of the wall defines the space within and its exclusivity from without. Through its irreducible separation and touchable materiality, the wall emblemizes the city and the senses that sustain it.

This chapter explores the architectural wall as it implicates the seeing and touching bodies it houses. Here I study sight and touch to interrogate sensing as a mediator of urban experience, to query the boundaries erected around the senses. Whereas Benjamin mined human sense perception for its cognitive and haptic possibilities, I seek instead to understand the representations of sight and touch erected around walls and the protean qualities of their construction. I study buildings and bodies to identify how the spatial experience of a wall structures vision and affects the shape of touch. If architecture, as Benjamin suggests, stimulates the visual and the tactile conditions of perception, the Jewish ghetto of early modern Venice offers a unique venue for pursuing the limits of the senses of space. In 1516 the Venetian Senate founded the ghetto as a state-controlled institution with specific spatial and temporal dimensions (Figure 8.1). The ghetto changed the urban physiognomy of Venice when authorities confined Jews to compulsory housing on the city's periphery.[4] Jews were free to traverse Venice's streets, squares, and canals during the daytime hours but were compelled to return to their segregated space at sunset. Ghettoization evolved as a nocturnal pursuit grounded in fears surrounding the senses. Venetians locked Jews up at dusk and guarded ghetto gates at the moment when vision was occluded and suspicion of cutaneous contact between Christians and Jews was at its highest. Threats to the body and the soul were thought to multiply as the sky turned black as pitch, when nighttime transgressions were invisible to the naked eye. "Because the darkness of the

FIGURE 8.1. The Ghetto Nuovo, established in Venice in 1516. Photo by Dana E. Katz.

night offers everyone the possibility of doing evil," declared Venice's Council of Ten, the city had to defend the boundaries of night from potential unruliness.[5] The Venetian ghetto was at the center of this sensorial politic because the fear of the Jew, as I will argue, was most concentrated at night.

Night Vision

Venice was singular in its nocturnal sociability. The lagoon city shimmered with the illuminations of the night sky, creating a unique setting for pious and political encounter. Crepuscular processions filled the city streets and canals during major civic celebrations, most notably during Christmastide and Carnival season.[6] Night provided the appropriate solemn atmosphere in which to observe the feasts and festivals of the Catholic liturgical calendar and to commemorate momentous events in Venetian history. After a Saturday sunset in July 1592, a cross section of the city assembled around the classically inspired votive church sited on the Giudecca in celebration of the Feast of the Redeemer. Venice's doge and senators initiated the evening proceedings by walking across a specially fabricated pontoon bridge from the Zattere to Giudecca en route to the mass held at the Church of the Most Holy Redeemer (Il Redentore, Figure 8.2). This church, famously executed by Palladio, and the annual celebrations surrounding its construction acknowledged Venice's gratitude for deliverance from the devastating plague that had struck the city beginning in 1575, killing over fifty thou-

FIGURE 8.2. Andrea Palladio, Il Redentore, Isola della Giudecca, Venice. Photo by Dana E. Katz.

sand inhabitants.[7] The departed pestilence inspired the erection of ecclesiastical architecture as well as the creation of numerous history paintings that further documented the feast's civic significance. Joseph Heintz the Younger, in a painting dated 1648, depicts the doge attended by prominent ecclesiastics and patricians on the steps of the church (Figure 8.3). The northern artist incorporates anecdotal details of the feast, including a group of nobles exiting *gondole,* a boy wrestling a dog, beggars asking for alms along the embankment, and a young girl losing her shoe to the waters. In the eighteenth century, Gabriel Bella located the feast later in the night, with a full moon rising above the bridge-bound procession (Figure 8.4). His bodies in motion emblemize the city and animate its nocturnal rites and rituals. Bella saturates the canvas with the colors of night and spectacle. These early modern works orient reception in space and time. Concentrating the city's constituency around the watery surroundings of Palladian architecture, the Feast of the Redeemer promoted new understanding of the nocturnalization of urban space, whose specific parameters derived from the Venetians embodied in it.

However spectacularly Venice reflected the lights of the night, access to that nocturnal city was limited. Obstruction was manifold, based in part on the conceptual distance that class, gender, and ethnicity wrought on constructions of urbanity. Jews were particularly vulnerable to night-wrapped Venice. On March 29, 1516, the Senate required Jews to leave their homes in the city's various districts and move behind the walls of the Ghetto Nuovo (Figure 8.5). The edict proclaimed:

FIGURE 8.3. (Top) Joseph Heintz the Younger, *Procession of the Redentore,* ca. 1648. Museo Correr, Venice. Courtesy of Alinari / Art Resource, New York.

FIGURE 8.4. (Bottom) Gabriel Bella, *Eve of the Feast of the Redeemer,* eighteenth century. Fondazione Querini Stampalia Onlus, Venice. Courtesy of the Fondazione Querini Stampalia Onlus.

FIGURE 8.5. Aerial view of the Venetian ghetto complex as it appears today. From 1516 to 1797, walls enclosed the Venice *ghetti*. Courtesy of Davide Calimani.

> To prevent the Jews from going about all night, provoking the greatest dis-
> content and the deepest displeasure on the part of Jesus Christ, be it deter-
> mined that . . . two doors shall be made. These doors must be opened in
> the morning at the sound of the *marangona* [the bell rung at sunrise], and
> in the evening they shall be shut at the twenty-fourth hour [sunset] by
> four Christian guards. . . . If by chance any Jew is found by officials or pub-
> lic servants outside the Geto after the hours specified above, they shall be
> bound to arrest him at once for his disobedience.[8]

The mandate stipulated that the Jews would be locked into the ghetto at night behind iron gates and watched by Christian guards twenty-four hours a day. The establishment of the ghetto compelled Jews to submit to uninterrupted surveillance and enforced curfews. It created a sequestered space that prevented them from infiltrating Christian society after the evening bells tolled.[9]

In early modernity, night possessed an element of the horrific and the sublime; that is, the darkness of the night induced both demonic acts of violence and spiritual visions.[10] The nocturnal vignettes of Paolo Uccello's Corpus Domini predella of 1468, representing the desecration of the eucharist, incorporate both aspects of night. The artist situates the Jews' bloody attempt to destroy the host and the Christians' recovery of it within a vast nightscape, replete with a crescent moon above (Figures 8.6 and 8.7). Here darkness is made to reaffirm eucharistic truth and fortify Christian faith while perpetuating the notion of the Jew as demonic.[11] Christian allegations of Jewish nighttime violence were not unusual in the Renaissance. According to a ritual murder case in Trent in 1475, a guard testified that he heard the Christian child

FIGURE 8.6. (Top) Paolo Uccello, scene 2, detail from *The Desecration of the Host,* Corpus Domini predella, 1468. Galleria Nazionale delle Marche, Urbino. Courtesy of Erich Lessing/Art Resource, New York.

FIGURE 8.7. (Bottom) Paolo Uccello, scene 3, detail from *The Desecration of the Host,* Corpus Domini predella, 1468. Galleria Nazionale delle Marche, Urbino. Courtesy of Erich Lessing/Art Resource, New York.

FIGURE 8.8. *Ritual Murder of Simon of Trent,* late fifteenth century. Parrocchia di San Martino, Cerveno. Photo by Dana E. Katz with the consent of the Ufficio Beni Culturali Ecclesiastici della Diocesi di Brescia.

Simon Unferdorben screaming from the Jewish Samuel Ebreo's house at night (Figure 8.8).[12] The veil of darkness additionally incited Jews in sixteenth-century northern Italy to engage in the carnivalesque acts of dancing and gambling on the eve of a young Jewish boy's circumcision. Civic statutes in Padua and Cremona, for example, reveal how Jews fused sacred ceremonies with profane nocturnal Jewish rituals during the night of the circumcision *veglia* (vigil).[13] Close of day affected other Jewish rites as well. In Venice and cities including Ancona and Mantua, the establishment of ghetto coffeehouses in the seventeenth century initiated a new form of piety inspired by the silence and isolation of the twilight hours.[14] Following Maimonides' *Hilchot Talmud Torah* (3.13), in which he states that "it is only at night that a man acquires most of his wisdom," the study of Torah became a nocturnal endeavor.[15] Maimonides emphasizes that "a person who desires to merit the crown of Torah should be careful with all his nights, not giving up even one to sleep."[16] Coffee and its capacity to instill wakefulness in those who imbibe it created an innovative form of nighttime study and male sociability outside the home that further perpetuated fears of Jewish violence. The strict nighttime curfew established in Venice for the ghetto inhabitants sought primarily to prevent such nocturnal abuses, thereby assuaging Christian fears and Christ's discontentment.

The containment of Jews behind ghetto walls and gates implicates architecture in a system of binaries that mapped the boundaries of faith. The partitioning of space in Venice epitomized a paradoxical process of communal belonging. As Ania Loomba suggests, "The outsider is not safely 'outside' at all," to denote "the fragility as well as strength of the boundaries between communities."[17] Such boundaries were not in fact fixed. Instead, perimeters manifested a form of social production that was never securely set, "always in process, and always constituted within, not outside, representation."[18] Maintaining boundaries was a necessary practice of daily life; to exceed them made Jews dangerous in the eyes of Christians. Yet how Venetians represented and experienced those boundaries differed markedly throughout the day. In the autobiography *The Life of Judah,* the seventeenth-century Venetian rabbi Leon Modena describes the permeability of the ghetto walls during the daytime hours, when the gates remained open: Jews ventured out to work, shop, gamble, visit Christian friends, and teach Christian children, while Christians entered the ghetto compound in search of loans and trade.[19] After nightfall, however, the Venetian government restricted contact between Jews and Christians. The safe conducts conferred on Jews repeatedly specified that they could not leave the ghetto after hours without pecuniary penalty and imprisonment. The establishment of the Venetian ghetto promoted commercial interactions during the day, when the ghetto remained open, and prohibited social interrelations at night, when guards closed the ghetto gates. Closure and aperture of the ghetto complex were inseparable and mutually constitutive conditions of confinement, interconnected categories essential to the stabilization of Venice's social geography and economic prosperity.

The walls surrounding the ghetto complex thus played an integral role in the spatial production of nocturnal Venice. When senators passed legislation in 1516 that mandated the Jews' segregated housing in the Ghetto Nuovo, they emphasized the spatial integrity of the walls enclosing the complex: "Furthermore, two high walls shall be built to close off the other two sides [of the ghetto], which rise above the canals, and all the quays attached to the said houses shall be walled in."[20] When authorities expanded the ghetto with the establishment of the Ghetto Vecchio in 1541, the Cinque Savi alla Mercanzia required the city to "connect with walls along the right and left side [of the ghetto]; in this wall a door shall be made to enter and exit; this wall shall continue along the boundaries of the said ghetto . . . , in order that there is no exit along the Cannaregio other than the door."[21] On August 3, 1560, Jewish residents in the overcrowded Ghetto Nuovo submitted an appeal to the Cinque Savi to move to the Ghetto Vecchio. The magistrates approved the request with the condition that the windows, balconies, and doors of the Jews' homes abutting Christian houses be walled in and a wall be erected "of equal height and length" so as to block the Jews' view.[22] The spatial arrangement of ghetto enclosure was maintained by the walling up of available surface that gave Jews access to the night. The high walls of ghetto homes completed this enclosure. In June 1758, for example, the Cattaveri charged Domenico Gregorin Murer to renovate the collapsing façade of Simon and Salamon Germani Todeschi's Ghetto Nuovo apartments, the documents specifying that the "new walls [of the façade] were necessary in carrying out the enclosure of the aforementioned ghetto."[23]

The walls composing the ghetto denoted sharp separation. In general, walls imply isolation. They inhibit passage. Richard Sennett writes that the wall "is an urban construction which literally closes in a city."[24] Indeed, Venice's ghetto walls configured enclosure on an urban scale. When the sky went dark, Jews were locked into the ghetto behind fortified walls and encased within the high walls of their tenements. The construction of ghetto walls constituted an idea of the city based on the spatial restrictions of communal incongruity. In his seventh-century *Etymologiae*, Isidore of Seville distinguished the physical boundaries of community from their symbolic representation: "A city is so-called on account of its inhabitants rather than its walls."[25] Here the idea of the city takes on a human dimension as the physiognomies of community are set apart from spatial considerations. The emphasis on the communal collective in Isidore's definition stands in marked contrast to the material places of the city mapped in early modern Venice, which present space as a physical location. Community in Venice evolved not only as a result of lineal and affinal relations but also as a mark of spatial incorporation. The idea of community was built on boundaries that distinguished the incorporated Christians from the city's disenfranchised outsiders. Social fissure and urban fragmentation gave rise to the concept of community in Venice to situate and temporalize the city's geographical constraints.[26]

Walls were a prominent feature of the early modern city. Yet how Jews traversed (or transgressed) those boundaries presented particularities symbolic of enclosure. Walls, for instance, surrounded the Jewish quarter of mid-fifteenth-century Candia, the capital of the Venetian colony of Crete, which Venice ruled from 1211 to 1669. The Judaica was situated inside city walls in an area of the island that had little appeal to Venetians or Greeks because the neighborhood was vulnerable to outside invasion and adjacent to a tannery that emitted fetid odors and waste (Figure 8.9). Although Venice's Maggior Consiglio had compelled Jews to reside within the perimeters of the Judaica in 1334, walls did not delineate the contours of that quarter until the fifteenth century.[27] In the fifteenth century, Venetian officials increased the number of walls demarcating the urban spaces of the Jewish quarter of Candia when accusations circulated that Jews had sensory access to ecclesiastical ceremonies. According to archival documents, Dominicans living in the monastery of Saint Peter the Martyr alleged that Jews could see from their windows and balconies "all the way into the space of the church and over the altar . . . and through the entire monastery . . . and this could also bring about a risk for the souls of the monks of this monastery."[28] To alleviate this

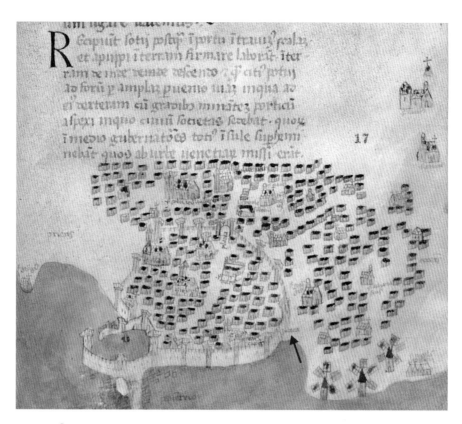

FIGURE 8.9. Cristoforo Buondelmonti, *Map of Candia*, in *Descriptio insulae Candiae*, 1419, with an arrow indicating the location of the Judaica added to the original by the author. Biblioteca Medicea Laurenziana, Florence, Ms. Plut. 29.42, ca. 17r [1429]. Courtesy of the Ministero per i Beni e le Attività Culturali.

concern, Venetian authorities obliged the Jews of Candia to erect, at their expense, "a wall from stone and limestone . . . high enough that they are able to fill in the space and to block their view."²⁹ This wall visualized social marginality by dividing inside from outside, pious from perfidious. Whereas the coastal wall defined the outside perimeter of the Jewish quarter and circumscribed the older section of the city, this high wall was erected inside the Judaica to obstruct the Jews' view and leave them out of sight of their Dominican neighbors. It protected the privilege and privacy of the friars, but it never prohibited passage. Instead, the walls of the Candia Judaica were porous, unaccompanied by guarded gates. They defined the separation of the Jews' surroundings, but they neither limited access nor restricted movement.

"It is thus obvious," writes David Jacoby, "that the principle of compulsory residential segregation physically implemented in the colonies preceded by about two centuries its application in Venice and may have served as a precedent for the creation of the Venetian Ghetto in 1516."³⁰ Jewish populations in the Venetian colonies were often differentiated residentially from Christian neighborhoods. As the Cretan city of Rethymno delineated the perimeters of its Jewish quarter with crosses, colonial Candia erected walls to mark the constricted space of Jewish segregated housing. However Candia delimited the spaces of Jewish occupancy, the walls of that enclosure remained perforated. In fact, Venetian officials in 1464 required the Candiote Jews to pay for the enlargement of the Judaica gate in order to facilitate the free passage of merchants, Jews and others, in and out of the Jewish quarter. The Judaica walls denoted division, but their social construction never intended isolation. The walls in Candia's Jewish quarter represented an urban district of compulsory residence that continually heralded relations outside its segregated space.

The Venice ghetto, on the contrary, defined exit and entrance through a system of surveillance regulated by bolted gates and watchful guards. In Venice an economy of vision developed around ghetto walls to insist on an isolation that was closely bound up with the night. The wall initiated a partitioning process "related to the isolation between two opposites."[31] It constructed the space where identity drew its limits. In his architectural treatise *De re aedificatoria* (ca. 1452), Leon Battista Alberti stresses that a city plan must incorporate walls to frame the urban landscape: "The best means of dividing a city is to build a wall through it. This wall, I believe, should not run diametrically across the city but should form a kind of circle within a circle."[32] Venetians did not follow Alberti's urban plan of walled concentric circles. Venice was unusual in that it was an open city that did not rely on defensive fortifications. The city wall, which Henri Pirenne describes as a "*privilege* which [no medieval city] lacked," for it symbolized civic status and independence, was not essential to Venice's urban image.[33] The waters of the lagoon gave Venice the impression of a self-contained world impregnable to outside invasion. Venetians may not have used the wall defensively to demarcate city limits, but officials did employ walls internally to striate spaces of difference. Ghetto walls were a principal feature of that difference. The walls partitioned space as they structured the lives of those folded within their geometries. What mattered was not necessarily that Jews were out of sight after dark but rather that their compulsory and segregated confinement was made conspicuous throughout the day and night. Ghetto walls colonized the eye, their elevation visualizing the Jews' marginalized presence in the city. Whereas buildings on Venice's fragile lagoon ground traditionally rose only three or four floors in the early modern period, the walls of the ghetto tenements soared with acute perpendicularity up to nine stories. The demographic pressures of the community caused Jews to build upward, constructing multistory and multifamily structures anomalous within the Venetian skyline.[34] The ghetto walls stood implacably high to divide the constituent members of the city and to signify protection from the night. Such walls, soaring and under surveillance, became the key tool in stimulating vision against night's miasma to defend the senses of space.

Cutaneous Contact

The prominence of ghetto walls functioned to realign urban disparities. Walls articulate the oppositional relationship of the interior and exterior worlds to enforce a sense of distance and separation. Erected to construct detachment, walls nonetheless lay claim to their vulnerabilities and expose the conflicting elements of their social construction. Indeed, walls provoke paradox in that the points of differentiation between the walls' two faces are also their common points. In their liminal position between inside and outside, they open themselves through direct contact to what lies beyond their perimeters.[35] It is the approachability of walls, the urge to scale them or to find their perforated points, that distinguishes their architectonic allure. It is the stories narrated at the threshold of enclosure, "between a (legitimate) space and its (alien) exteriority," that determine walls' contradictions.[36] Spaces that delimit can also appropriate. Walls that separate can also be crossed. The act of drawing boundaries challenges the very nature of the operation and underlines the spatial stories that polarize and cohere community in the same discursive moment.[37]

The walls of the Venice ghetto may well have defined the nocturnal limits of community, but they also told stories of their own permeability. Such walls created an architectural skin around Venice's Jewish corpus to enforce separation from Christians after nightfall. Yet these walls also remained distinctly porous. As Marin Sanudo observes in his contemporary chronicle, the establishment of ghetto enclosures came with manifold exemptions. Sanudo specifies that on July 29, 1516, only four months after the Senate founded the Ghetto Nuovo, legislation passed that permitted Jewish doctors to leave the confines of the ghetto in order to visit patients and attend medical gatherings late into the night.[38] Levantine and Ponentine Jewish merchants residing in Venice's *ghetti* also received special dispensation from the Cinque Savi alla Mercanzia to have nighttime access to the seas for their commercial needs. When the government granted Jews privileges to stay outside the ghetto after curfew, authorities stipulated that they were to avoid "forbidden" spaces, presumably referring to brothels and the houses of respectable Christian women. The ghetto gates that swung open at night to allow in wealth and prosperity from maritime trade and to allow out succor for the infirm shut tight to guard against sexual contact between Jews and Christians. Illegal business practices instituted a bureaucratic paper trail, with infractions enforced by secular authorities; however, illicit sexual activity in a community defined by rigid endogamy ignited communal fears that destabilized categories secular and sacred.

The anxiety around sex centered on the sense of touch. Touching, specifically interfaith touching, was a form of sexual transgression that collapsed religious boundaries and spatialized social controls. When physical relations between Christian and Jew became proximate, authorities advocated prophylactic campaigns of segregation.

For example, in 1423 Franciscan friar Bernardino da Siena sermonized a series of pro-hibitions, directly reiterating the terms of canon law, that proscribed immediate phys-ical contact between Christians and Jews: "It is a mortal sin to eat or drink with Jews"; "It is a mortal sin to seek the help of a Jewish doctor"; "Christians are not allowed to bathe in the company of Jews"; "It is a mortal sin for Christians to socialize with Jews in their homes"; "It is a mortal sin for Christians to act as wet nurses or otherwise help to raise the children of the Jews or serve as midwives for them, even to wash the new-born child."[39] Bernardino's codes of conduct provided moralizing instruction that in-sisted on the physical separation of Christians and Jews during the day's routines and rituals. Civil authorities in Venice did not always enforce these injunctions, which prompted Patriarch of Venice Cardinal Lorenzo Priuli in 1596 to advocate analogous interdictions that perpetuated injunctions against touching. In a memorandum is-sued to the Venetian government prior to the renewal of the Jews' charters of sojourn (*condotta*), Priuli urged officials to disallow Jews from eating with Christians; hiring Christians to work in Jewish homes as "servants, or under any other name"; soliciting Christian wet nurses to suckle Jewish children; and inviting Christians "of either sex" into the ghetto at night.[40] The *condotte,* which Priuli found too lenient and in practice readily abused, had from their inception specified that Jews could not hire Christians to work in their homes under penalty of a pecuniary fine and imprisonment for the Jews involved as well as temporary banishment for the implicated Christians.[41]

Regulations over conditions of contact correlated not only with canon law but also with the dictums of *ius commune.* For example, the *De Iudaeis et aliis infidelibus* of Marquardus de Susannis, published in Venice in 1558, treats the dangers of illicit sexual behavior between Christians and Jews in a judicial handbook that combines common law and canon.[42] De Susannis understood the carnal communion of Jew and Christian legally as an insult against Christianity. Jews, in his opinion as jurisconsult and ambassador for the Republic of Venice, maintained the status of "enemies of the cross and blasphemers of the name of Christ"; therefore, he deemed the sexual union of a Jew and a Christian a violation of the holy, a pollution of the Christian corpus. As Kenneth Stow explains in his study of the *De Iudaeis,* "When Christian men have sex-ual relations with Jewish women, they commit the same crime that is committed by having relations with a nun, namely, that of insulting both baptism and Christian-ity."[43] To prevent such abuses of faith, de Susannis underscores the important func-tion that dress served in distinguishing Jews from Christians. Lawyers, as well as ecclesiastics, thought that if Jews were visibly recognizable through, for example, the use of badges, veils, or head coverings, Christians would avoid overly familiar contact with them.[44] De Susannis's judgment on dress was not innovative for the period; the precedent had originated in Canon 68 of the Fourth Lateran Council (1215): "It some-times happens that by mistake Christians mingle with Jewish or Saracen women, and Jews and Saracens with Christian women. Therefore, lest they, under the cover of error, find an excuse for the grave sin of such mingling, we decree that these people [Jews and Saracens] of either sex and in all Christian lands and at all times be readily distinguishable from others by the quality of their clothing."[45] As a symbolic marker of Jewish difference, distinguishing garb endured as a legal imperative in early modern common law in part because it helped resolve questions of intent. If there was no doubt that a Jew and a Christian were ignorant of their crime, de Susannis concludes that they could not be indicted for "sexual relations with an infidel."[46] Judges commuted their penalty to the crime of fornication. The sartorial marking of the Jew, however, made it difficult to plead ignorance. The distinctively dressed Jew found guilty of carnal misconduct with a Christian could instead be charged with "the intent of causing opprobrium to the faith," which carried a penalty of death and loss of property.[47]

The *De Iudaeis* addresses variations in penalty, the punishment contingent on the intent and identity of the accused. Sexual intercourse among members of the opposite faiths was an ecclesiastical crime; nevertheless, canon law did not set a punishment for the crime. Judges most often sentenced the defendants following the guidelines of local statutes, turning to common law if the community in which the crime occurred did not treat interfaith intercourse in its registries. In Venice local statutes explicitly addressed the consequences of this sexual crime, nearly a century before Jews had settled permanently in the archipelago. Maintaining sexual boundaries became a legislative imperative in Venice, where the touching of an opposite-sexed outsider prompted swift justice. As early as July 19, 1424, the Venetian government unanimously passed legislation that forbade sexual relations between Jewish men and Christian women. The penalty for such an act depended on the Christian woman's station. Authorities fined a Jew 500 lire and sentenced him to six months in jail when he was found with a prostitute from the Rialto. The pecuniary fine remained the same when a Jew had carnal relations with a Christian woman of higher social stature, additionally subjecting him to one year in prison.[48] The *Avogadori di Comun* also penalized Christian men who had sexual relations with Jewish women. Venetian statutes could not tolerate the carnal communion of Jew and Christian, which polluted the civic body as well as the Corpus Christi.

Sennett associates the alienations implicit in the Jew's touch with claims of contagion; Jews were thought to spread syphilis, leprosy, plague, and other diseases.[49] Despite chimerical allegations circulating Europe that indicted Jews as agents of pollution, the *noli me tangere* policy in Venice had less to do with anxieties over the touch of infectious contagion than with suspicions over miscegenation. Venetians, in fact, placed Jews in contiguous contact with Christians and contagion when permitting Jewish doctors to leave the confines of their ghetto enclosure, day or night, to care for the health of the civic body. The Cattaveri even temporarily released Jews from the ghetto during times of plague, thereby sanctioning a Jewish presence throughout the city when infection was at its most concentrated.[50] Concerns over bodily proximity involved not solely the risks of infection but also, more specifically, the sexual constructions of touch. The cohesion of the Christian corpus in Venice required spatial reinforcement to protect the sexual boundaries of the city and the bodies, Jewish and Christian, that set those boundaries in motion.

The barriers established around the ghetto consigned sex to a patrolled status contained behind brick walls. Those walls, nonetheless, did not abate fears of the Jews' sexuality in Venice or in early modern Europe more generally. The Jews' sexualized bodies aroused constant scrutiny. For instance, Jewish women were thought to be sexually suspicious, with enhanced libidos that triggered an uncontrollable attraction to Christian men. Long before Shakespeare's famed Jewess Jessica threatened Christian bloodlines with her desirable beauty, medieval theologians rendered Synagoga, the collective image of the Jewish community, as a personified woman seducing Christianity.[51] The carnality of Synagoga displayed in medieval thought and art cogently suggests feminine wantonness. As Sara Lipton argues, Synagoga, the archetypal Jewess, is "perversely and destructively fertile, [and] has brought forth progeny only to doom them to Hell by her unwifely and immodest behavior."[52] The seductive qualities of Synagoga render her a shameful temptress difficult to repress in the sexual imagination of Christian society. Contemporary Jewish women provoked similar fascinations that enticed the minds of Christian men. Thomas Coryat, the English visitor who wrote of his Venetian travels in 1611, describes the Jewish women he encountered in the ghetto:

> In the roome wherin they [Jews] celebrate their divine service, no
> women sit, but have a loft or gallery proper to themselves only, where
> I saw many Jewish women, whereof some were as beautiful as ever I
> saw, and so gorgeous in their apparel, jewels, chaines of gold, and rings
> adorned with precious stones, that some of our English Countesses do
> scarce exceede them.[53]

Shakespeare perhaps never set eyes on the Venetian Jewess that served as his play's muse, but the English contemporary Coryat lingers over her body with thick description to reveal the temptation of her physical appearance. Coryat scrutinizes this bedecked and bejeweled beauty from head to toe to unveil a Jewess socially inscribed with the carnality of Synagoga. English diarist John Evelyn likewise references the physicality of the Jewish women he observed at a wedding in the Venetian ghetto on March 24, 1646. His brief description centers on the bride, "clad in White, sitting in a lofty chaire, & covered also with a white vaile," but his eye wanders to the "very beautifull Portuguez-Jewesses, with whom we had some conversation."[54] The exotic beauty of the Jewess seduces Christian senses. It was the temptation of the irredeemable body beneath her beauty that Venetian authorities attempted to thwart through collective punishment and residential enclosure. The nighttime lockdown of Jews within ghetto walls acted to avert sexual forays *entre* Jew and Christian. Preventing carnal contact between Christians and Jews was hardly original to cinquecento Venice. What was new was the use of architecture to prohibit it. The fortified and surveyed ghetto walls prevented midnight trysts turned transgressions, infidelities turned blasphemies. Ghettoization sought to control carnal lusts under the cover of darkness, thereby precluding the possibility of miscegenation. Domestic detachment impeded the temptation to touch.

City officials sought to bind the sexed corporeality inhabiting Venice through the strategic segregation of space.[55] The ghetto provided the order and organization to polarize the sundry bodies of Venice by limiting the mobility of the Jews' bodies on the nocturnal streets. If night provided the fertile ground for sexual encounter, the ghetto controlled the bodily world of Venice against intimate contact. The city that restricted the nighttime movement of Jews through high walls and guarded gates also gave urban expression to the Jews' corporeal presence. The ordering of social space in Venice situated Jews within an architecture of embodiment that in fact reinscribed their bodies (physically, socially, discursively) into the larger urban form. The ghetto contained the Jews' contested bodies as those bodies then projected themselves onto the sociocultural cityscape of Venice. A reciprocal relationship materialized between the body and the city. As Elizabeth Grosz explains, "The city is made and made over into the simulacrum of the body, and the body, in its turn, is transformed, 'citified,' urbanized as a distinctively metropolitan body."[56] Bodies and cities are inextricably linked to reveal the social construction inscribed in their material makeup. Architectural treatises from antiquity onward acknowledge the reciprocity of body with building. Vitruvius, for example, anthropomorphizes architecture in Book Three of *De architectura* to reveal the proportions of the human body beneath the harmony of the temple structure, while modern architectural theory, such as that espoused by Finnish architect Juhani Pallasmaa, embeds the body in its environment: "I experience myself in the city, and the city exists through my embodied experience. The city and my body supplement and define each other. I dwell in the city and the city dwells in me."[57] The city engenders an indivisible relation to the body, even when that body is marginal. Venice, for example, cultivated, as it controlled, the corporeality of the Jew. The ghetto's walled boundaries that subordinated the Jews' bodies could not contain those bodies continually or completely. Walls can never fully sequester bodily mobility. Boundaries, though established as observed limits, are actualized only through the act of passage, and Jews articulated the transience of their bounded strictures when accessing Venice's urban life after dark.

Entry to the evening outside ghetto walls often ended with carnal consequences. The Cattaveri permitted Jews only brief encounters with nocturnal Venice, requiring them to return to the ghetto at a specific hour of the night. At times Jews transgressed the stipulations of their licenses. In September 1609, Rachel Hebrea Cantarina, accompanied by her brother Marco and father Jacob, was granted permission to leave the ghetto after curfew to sing in the homes of respectable members of society. Instead of entertaining nobles with song, Rachel and her family were found eating, drinking, and behaving dishonestly with Christian commoners. The magistrates viewed the incident as an affront to God and a bad example to all and amended Rachel's nighttime privilege to include a proviso that all three members of the Cattaveri must unanimously approve any future request for leave submitted by the female performer. Modification of this proviso transpired over time; nevertheless, the details of that license never impressed Rachel, who in June 1613 was found singing around Venice *in gondola* at night without proper permission.[58] The nocturnal anxiety Rachel provoked motivated civic and moral censure when she gained unregulated contact with the darkened streets. It was the allure of her sonorous voice in the context of a metropolitan center that delighted in leisure that gained her access to the night and made magistrates tolerant of her transgressions. She personified the seductive powers of Synagoga with a recognizable carnality that threatened proscriptions to touch. Rachel's night flights unequivocally destabilized the boundaries city officials had so carefully spelled out in statutory definition and in architectural applications to the urban form. Despite legislative exclusions prohibiting Jews' physical contact with the world outside the ghetto, in the darkness Rachel rediscovered her siren powers of voice and her delicacy of touch when encroaching on Venice's sexualized borders. In this case, the law could not prohibit the very mingling it sought to restrict.

The porousness of ghetto walls that provided Rachel a path to Venice's ordered nightscape disquieted city officials. Pier Cesare Ioly Zorattini documents a case in which a Jew "*secretamente*" returned to his family in the ghetto at two in the morning after escaping the *lazzaretto,* the mandatory quarantine for Venice's plague-stricken on a small lagoonal island.[59] Here the ailing Jew traverses the Venetian night to journey from one form of confinement to another. This story animates the permeability of Venice's compulsory enclosures. Once again the walls of the ghetto are breached, this time to allow a Jew to reenter its shadowy perimeters. In his 1596 memorandum to city officials, Cardinal Lorenzo Priuli addressed the ghetto's structural frailties when accusing Jews of exiting ghetto enclosures by night through unfortified windows and unguarded quays. Specifically, he alleged that such architectural apertures gave Jews nocturnal access to Venice during which they would impregnate defenseless Christian women and later steal the newborn children to raise them (as Jews) in the ghetto.[60] Trial records also reveal the permeability of the ghetto night as Jewish men left the confines of *clausura* to engage in *commercio carnale*. In 1715 authorities accused (but later acquitted) Zacaria da Pesaro Ebreo of engaging in sexual relations with a Christian woman named Matia Cantona in a dark courtyard near the Ponte dal Aseo, and in 1717 Abram Treves Ebreo dal Zante and Vita Almeda Ebreo were found living outside the ghetto in the home of a Christian woman, who allegedly received payment for her sexual services.[61] The ghetto, established to control the Jews' sexed corporeality through a system of surveillance that protected the innocence of Christians by night, also heightened anxieties about the Jews' sexualized mobility. As Priuli's claims suggest, the ghetto's tall tenements never mitigated the sexual politics embodying Jews; instead, they catalyzed fantasies of the Jews' furtive touch. In Venice the ghetto evolved as an institution of exclusion that regulated Jewish sexuality, but such an exclusion of sexuality itself became a sexual act in that it aroused in the Christian imagination an explicit world of Jewish carnality.

Senses of Space

Machiavelli writes in *The Prince,* "In general, men judge more by sight than by touch. Everyone sees what is happening, but not everyone feels the consequences. Everyone sees what you seem to be; few have direct experience of who you really are."[62] For Machiavelli sight and touch occupied a sensory hierarchy that did not necessarily align with the ocularcentric traditions of Greek philosophy.[63] Hellenic models provided sight higher sensorial status, due in large part to the corporeal associations of tactility. Touch relies for perception not on localized receptors but on the sensitivities of the skin enwrapping the entire body. Tactile stimulation accentuates the material impulses of the flesh, heightening the bodily desire for physical contact with the outside world. In Machiavellian terms, the power to touch shaped human subjectivity. Sight might provide the discerning eye a view to the intention and integrity of a man, but, as the philosopher observes, it is only through the physically proximate connection to touch that one might truly know a man. Seeing and touching, perhaps inherently antithetical, become entwined experiences of the bodily sensorium. Perception emerges from the desire to see and to feel. As Walter Benjamin reflects on the sensorial applications of architecture, he likewise concludes that building exploits the sensory involvements of the visible and the tactile to insist on a reception based on distraction. Architectural appropriation comes to light only out of focus with an emphasis on the hand–eye mechanisms of haptics. With its appeals to the tactile imagination, architecture enlivens our kinesthetic impulses and our need to experience the proximities and intimacies of space. Certainly navigating the Venetian nightscape, armed with candles and oil lanterns, required an acute sense of sight. Investments in looking, however, became shortsighted when vision was occluded at day's close and impetuousness pervaded the early modern night sky. There in the darkness the contours of buildings blurred and rested bodies turned restless. And as those bodies moved through space they provoked associations both sensual and contentious as fantasies of interfaith touching broke down nocturnal boundaries and carnal desires filled the night air.

I am grateful for the support provided by the Gladys Krieble Delmas Foundation and Reed College. I also thank Erin Hazard, Kathryn Lofton, Sally Promey, Benjamin Ravid, and Kenneth Stow for their insightful suggestions and careful critiques, as well as Akihiko Miyoshi for his generous assistance with the visual material.

1. Walter Benjamin, *Illuminations,* ed. Hannah Arendt (New York: Schocken, 1968), 240.

2. Katherine Fischer Taylor, "Architecture's Place in Art History: Art or Adjunct?" *Art Bulletin* 83, no. 2 (June 2001): 342.

3. Elizabeth D. Harvey, ed., *Sensible Flesh: On Touch in Early Modern Culture* (Philadelphia: University of Pennsylvania Press, 2003), 2. See also Sander Gilman, *Inscribing the Other* (Lincoln: University of Nebraska Press, 1991), 29–49.

4. On the history of the Venetian ghetto, see Ennio Concina, Ugo Camerino, and Donatella Calabi, *La città degli ebrei: Il ghetto di Venezia, architettura e urbanistica* (Venice: Albrizzi Editore, 1991). See also Donatella Calabi, "The 'City of Jews,'" in *The Jews of Early Modern Venice,* ed. Robert C. Davis and Benjamin Ravid (Baltimore: Johns Hopkins University Press, 2001), 31–49; Umberto Fortis, *The Ghetto on the Lagoon: A Guide to the History and Art of the Venetian Ghetto (1516–1797),* trans. Roberto Matteoda (Venice: Storti Edizioni, 1988); Riccardo Calimani, *The Ghetto of Venice,* trans. Katherine Silberblatt Wolfthal (New York: M. Evans, 1987); Roberta Curiel and Bernard Dov Cooperman, *The Venetian Ghetto* (New York: Rizzoli, 1990); Richard Sennett, *Flesh and Stone: The Body and the City in Western Civilization* (New York: W. W. Norton, 1994), 212–251; and Vivian B. Mann, ed., *Gardens and Ghettos: The Art of Jewish Life in Italy* (Berkeley: University of California Press, 1989).

5. Archivio di Stato di Venezia (ASVe), Consiglio di Dieci, Deliberazioni miste, reg. 14 (1450–54), fol. 18r, December 16, 1450. See also Elisabeth Pavan, "Recherches sur la nuit venitienne à la fin du Moyen Age," *Journal of Medieval History* 7 (December 1981): 346.

6. Giustina Renair Michiel, *Origine delle feste veneziane* (Milan: Annali universali delle scienze e dell'industria, 1829), vol. 2, 33–34. On Venetian feast culture, see Edward Muir, *Civic Ritual in Renaissance Venice* (Princeton, NJ: Princeton University Press, 1981); Biana Tamassia Mazzarotto, *Le feste veneziane: I giochi popolari, cerimonie religiose e di governo* (Florence: Sansoni, 1980); Susanne Tichy, *Et vene la mumaria: Studien zur venezianischen Festkultur der Renaissance* (Munich: Scaneg, 1997); and Giuseppe Tassini, *Feste, spettacoli, divertimenti, e piaceri degli antichi Veneziani* (Venice: Filippi, 1961).

7. On the Feast of the Redeemer and its architecture, see Francesco Basaldella, *La festa del Redentore: Storica festa nazionale veneziana* (Venice: Quaderni di cultura giudecchina, 2000); Tracy Elizabeth Cooper, *Palladio's Venice: Architecture and Society in a Renaissance Republic* (New Haven, CT: Yale University Press, 2005), 228–257; and Deborah Howard and Laura Moretti, *Sound and Space in Renaissance Venice: Architecture, Music, Acoustics* (New Haven, CT: Yale University Press, 2009), 114–128.

8. ASVe, Senato, Terra, registro 19, fols. 78r–79r, March 29, 1516. See also David Chambers and Brian Pullan, eds., *Venice: A Documentary History, 1450–1630* (Oxford, UK: Blackwell, 1992), 338–339.

9. The Senate adjusted the Jews' curfew to accommodate the change in season. See Benjamin Ravid, "Curfew Time in the Ghetto of Venice," in *Medieval and Renaissance Venice,* ed. Ellen E. Kittell and Thomas F. Madden (Urbana: University of Illinois Press, 1999), 241; reprinted in *Studies on the Jews of Venice, 1382–1797* (Aldershot, UK: Ashgate, 2003). On early modern Italian ghettos beyond Venice, see, for example, Stefanie B. Siegmund, *The Medici State and the Ghetto of Florence: The Construction of an Early Modern Jewish Community* (Stanford, CA: Stanford Uni-

versity Press, 2006), and Kenneth R. Stow, *Theater of Acculturation: The Roman Ghetto in the Sixteenth Century* (Seattle: University of Washington Press, 2001).

10. On night in the medieval and early modern periods, see Craig Koslofsky, *Evening's Empire: A History of the Night in Early Modern Europe* (Cambridge, UK: Cambridge University Press, 2011); A. Roger Ekirch, *At Day's Close: Night in Times Past* (New York: W. W. Norton, 2005); Bryan D. Palmer, *Cultures of Darkness: Night Travels in the Histories of Transgression* (New York: Monthly Review Press, 2000); and Jean Verdon, *La nuit au Moyen Age* (Paris: Perrin, 1994).

11. On the presence of Jews in Uccello's Corpus Domini predella, see Marilyn Aronberg Lavin, "The Altar of Corpus Domini in Urbino: Paolo Uccello, Joos Van Ghent, Piero della Francesca," *Art Bulletin* 49, no. 1 (1967): 1–24, and Dana E. Katz, *The Jew in the Art of the Italian Renaissance* (Philadelphia: University of Pennsylvania Press, 2008), 16–39.

12. Regarding the alleged ritual murder of Simon of Trent, see R. Po-chia Hsia, *Trent 1475: Stories of a Ritual Murder Trial* (New Haven, CT: Yale University Press, 1992); Wolfgang Treue, *Der Trienter Judenprozeß: Voraussetzungen, Abläufe, Auswirkungen, 1475–1588* (Hannover: Hahnsche, 1996); Anna Esposito and Diego Quaglioni, *Processi contro gli ebrei di Trento (1475–1478): I processi del 1475* (Padua: CEDAM, 1990); Iginio Rogger and Marco Bellabarba, eds., *Il principe vescovo Johannes Hinderbach (1465–1486) fra tardo Medioevo e Umanesimo* (Bologna: Edizioni Dehoniane, 1992); Gianni Gentilini, *Pasqua 1475: Antigiudaismo e lotta alle eresie, il caso di Simonino* (Milan: Medusa, 2007); and Katz, *The Jew in the Art of the Italian Renaissance*, 119–157.

13. Elliott Horowitz, "The Eve of the Circumcision: A Chapter in the History of Jewish Nightlife," *Journal of Social History* 23, no. 1 (Autumn 1989): 45–69.

14. Elliott Horowitz, "Coffee, Coffeehouses, and the Nocturnal Rituals of Early Modern Jewry," *AJS Review* 14, no. 1 (Spring 1989): 17–46.

15. Moses Maimonides, *Hilchot de'ot = The Laws of Personality Development; and Hilchot Talmud Torah = The Laws of Torah Study* (New York: Moznaim, 1989), 206–207.

16. Ibid.

17. Ania Loomba, *Shakespeare, Race, and Colonialism* (Oxford, UK: Oxford University Press, 2002), 18.

18. Stuart Hall, "Cultural Identity and Diaspora," in *Identity: Community, Culture, Difference,* ed. Jonathan Rutherford (London: Lawrence and Wishart, 1990), 222.

19. Mark R. Cohen, *The Autobiography of a Seventeenth-Century Venetian Rabbi: Leon Modena's Life of Judah* (Princeton, NJ: Princeton University Press, 1988), 5–6.

20. Chambers and Pullan, *Venice*, 339.

21. ASVe, Collegio Notatorio, reg. 24, fols. 176v–177v, July 20, 1541, and ASVe, Inquisitorato alle Arti, busta 102, filza "Casi tra li Ec.mi Ss.ri Cattaveri con li Ec.mi Ss.ri Cinque Savi sopra le case delli ghetti di Hebrei," fols. 12r–15v. See also Giambattista Gallicciolli, *Delle memorie Venete antiche profane ed ecclesiastiche* (Venice: Domenico Fracasso, 1795), vol. 2, 309–310, section 946. For a full transcription of the archival document, see Benjamin Ravid, "The Religious, Economic, and Social Background and Context of the Establishment of the Ghetti of Venice," in *Gli Ebrei e Venezia: Secoli XIV–XVIII,* ed. Gaetano Cozzi (Milan: Edizioni Comunità, 1987), esp. 251–252.

22. ASVe, Inquisitorato alle Arti, busta 102, fols. 21r–24v, August 3, 1560.

23. ASVe, Ufficiali al Cattaver, busta 278, June 14, 1758.

24. Richard Sennett, "The Open City," *Urban Age* (November 2006): 3.

25. As quoted in Stephen J. Milner, "The Florentine Piazza della Signoria as Practiced Place," in *Renaissance Florence: A Social History,* ed. Roger J. Crum and John T. Paoletti (New York: Cambridge University Press, 2006), 83.

26. This analysis was informed by my spatial study of Renaissance Mantua. See Dana E. Katz, "Spatial Stories: Mantua and the Painted Jew," in *Rabbi Judah Moscato and the Jewish Intellectual World of Mantua in the 16th–17th Centuries*, ed. Giuseppe Veltri and Gianfranco Miletto (Leiden: Brill, 2012), 199–225.

27. David Jacoby posits that the Jews residing in Candia during the Byzantine period most likely selected the location of the Judaica, along the seawall on the Bay of Dermata or "Bay of Hides," because the Jews themselves played an important role in the tanning industry. In Byzantium, he suggests, Jewish residential segregation in Candia (Greek, Chandax) was voluntary. Segregation became compulsory in the early fourteenth century under Venetian rule. By 1423 Venetian authorities were prohibiting Jews from acquiring real estate outside the Judaica and compelled them to sell any property previously purchased. David Jacoby, "Jews and Christians in Venetian Crete: Segregation, Interaction, and Conflict," in *Interstizi: Culture ebraico-cristiane a Venezia e nei suoi domini dal Medioevo all'età moderna,* ed. Uwe Israel, Robert Jütte, and Reinhold C. Mueller (Rome: Edizioni di storia e letteratura, 2010), 248–261. See also Maria Georgopoulou, *Venice's Mediterranean Colonies: Architecture and Urbanism* (Cambridge, UK: Cambridge University Press, 2001), 192–210; Joshua Starr, "Jewish Life in Crete under the Rule of Venice," *Proceedings of the American Academy for Jewish Research* 12 (1942): 59–114; David Jacoby, "Venice and the Venetian Jews in the Eastern Mediterranean," in *Gli Ebrei e Venezia: Secoli XIV–XVIII,* ed. Gaetano Cozzi (Milan: Edizioni di Comunità, 1987), 29–58; and Zvi Ankori, "From *Zudecha* to *Yahudi Mahallesi*: The Jewish Quarter of Candia in the Seventeenth Century," in *Salo W. Baron Jubilee Volume,* 3 vols. (Jerusalem: American Academy for Jewish Research, 1974), vol. 1, 85.

28. ASVe, Duca di Candia, busta 32, Memoriali, fasc. 44/4, fols. 334v–35r, July 8, 1450. I thank Sonia Sabnis for translating this document. See Maria Georgopoulou, "Mapping Religious and Ethnic Identities in the Venetian Colonial Empire," *Journal of Medieval and Early Modern Studies* 26, no. 3 (1996): 483.

29. Ibid.

30. Jacoby, "Venice and the Venetian Jews in the Eastern Mediterranean," 37.

31. Resmiye Alpar Atun and Naciye Doratli, "Walls in Cities: A Conceptual Approach to the Walls of Nicosia," *Geopolitics* 14 (2009): 109.

32. Leon Battista Alberti, *On the Art of Building in Ten Books,* trans. Joseph Rykwert, Neil Leach, and Robert Tavernor (Cambridge, MA: MIT Press, 1988), 118.

33. Henri Pirenne, *Medieval Cities: Their Origin and the Revival of Trade,* trans. Frank D. Halsey (Garden City, NY: Doubleday, 1956), 107, italics in original.

34. On Venice's ghetto skylines, see Dana E. Katz, "The Ghetto and the Gaze in Early Modern Venice," in *Judaism and Christian Art,* ed. David Nirenberg and Herbert Kessler (Philadelphia: University of Pennsylvania Press, 2011), 233–262, and Katz, "'Clamber Not You Up to the Casements': On Ghetto Views and Viewing," *Jewish History* 24, no. 2 (June 2010): 127–153.

35. On the spatial theories of boundary, see also Henri Lefebvre, *The Production of Space,* trans. Donald Nicholson-Smith (Oxford, UK: Blackwell, 1991), esp. 86–87, and Michel de Certeau, *The Practice of Everyday Life,* trans. Steven Rendall (Berkeley: University of California Press, 1984), 126–130.

36. De Certeau, *The Practice of Everyday Life,* 129.

37. See Katz, "Spatial Stories," 203–204.

38. Marin Sanudo, *Venice: Città Excelentissima: Selections from the Renaissance Diaries of Marin Sanudo,* ed. Patricia H. Labalme and Laura Sanguineti White, trans. Linda L. Carroll (Baltimore: Johns Hopkins University Press, 2008), 340–341. See also Ravid, "Curfew Time," 243.

39. Franco Mormando, *The Preacher's Demons: Bernardino of Siena and the Social Underworld of Early Renaissance Italy* (Chicago: University of Chicago Press, 1999), 170.

40. ASVe, Senato, Terra, filza 141 (m.v.), January 30, 1596.

41. See, for example, the *condotte* found in the following archival sources: ASVe, Senato, Terra, filza 141 (m.v.), January 30, 1596, and ASVe, Compilazione delli Leggi, busta 187, Ebraica Stamperia Ebrei, filza 1, fol. 296, January 11, 1767. On Christians entering the ghetto after nightfall, see Ravid, "Curfew Time," 251–253.

42. On Marquardus de Susannis and the *De Iudaeis et aliis infidelibus,* see Kenneth R. Stow, *Catholic Thought and Papal Jewry Policy, 1555–1593* (New York: Jewish Theological Seminary of America, 1977).

43. Stow, *Catholic Thought and Papal Jewry Policy,* 100.

44. On the sartorial restrictions placed on the Jews of Venice, see Benjamin Ravid, "From Yellow to Red: On the Distinguishing Head-Covering of the Jews of Venice," *Jewish History* 6, nos. 1–2 (March 1992): 179–210; reprinted in *Studies on the Jews of Venice, 1382–1797* (Aldershot, UK: Ashgate, 2003).

45. Robert Chazan, *Medieval Stereotypes and Modern Antisemitism* (Berkeley: University of California Press, 1997), 100.

46. Stow, *Catholic Thought and Papal Jewry Policy,* 107.

47. Ibid., 106.

48. ASVe, Compilazione delle Leggi, busta 188, July 19, 1424. See also Giambattista Galicciolli, *Delle memorie Venete antiche profane ed ecclesiastiche* (Venice: Domenico Fracasso, 1795), vol. 2, 291–292, section 907, and Benjamin Ravid, "The Legal Status of the Jew in Venice to 1509," in *Proceedings of the American Academy for Jewish Research* 54 (1987): 185–187.

49. Sennett, *Flesh and Stone,* 225–227.

50. See ASVe, Sanità B. 2, Capitolare I (1485–1574), fol. 43, and ASVe, Consiglio di Dieci, Comune, reg. 5, 1529, fol. 116v. See also Benjamin Ravid, "New Light on the Ghetti of Venice," in *Shlomo Simonsohn Jubilee Volume,* ed. Daniel Carpi et al. (Tel Aviv: Tel Aviv University, 1993); and Lisa Pon's forthcoming work on Venice's *lazzaretto* (the mandatory quarantine for those of the city stricken with the plague on an island in the lagoon) and ghetto.

51. On Jessica's willful female sexuality, see Lisa Lampert, *Gender and Jewish Difference from Paul to Shakespeare* (Philadelphia: University of Pennsylvania Press, 2004), 138–167. On the seductive powers of Synagoga, see Sara Lipton, "The Temple Is My Body: Gender, Carnality, and Synagoga in the *Bible Moralisée,*" in *Imagining the Self, Imagining the Other: Visual Representation and Jewish–Christian Dynamics in the Middle Ages and Early Modern Period,* ed. Eva Frojmovic (Leiden: Brill, 2002), 129–163.

52. Lipton, "The Temple Is My Body," 135.

53. Thomas Coryat, *Coryat's Crudities* (Glasgow: James MacLehose, 1905), 372.

54. John Evelyn, *The Diary of John Evelyn,* ed. E. S. De Beer (Oxford, UK: Clarendon Press, 1955), vol. 2, 477.

55. On the sexual politics of segregation, see David Nirenberg, "Conversion, Sex, and Segregation: Jews and Christians in Medieval Spain," *American Historical Review* 107, no. 4 (October 2002): 1065–1093.

56. Elizabeth Grosz, "Bodies-Cities," in *Sexuality and Space,* ed. Beatriz Colomina (New York: Princeton Architectural Press, 1992), 242.

57. Vitruvius, *Vitruvius: Ten Books on Architecture,* trans. Ingrid D. Rowland (New York: Cambridge University Press, 1999), 47–48. See also George Dodds and Robert Tavernor, eds., *Body and Building: Essays on the Changing Relation of Body and Architecture* (Cambridge, MA: MIT Press, 2002). For Pallasmaa's phenomenological insights on architecture, see Juhani Pallasmaa, *The Eyes of the Skin: Architecture and the Senses* (Chichester, UK: John Wiley and Sons, 2005), 40.

58. Ravid, "Curfew Time," 247.

59. Pier Cesare Ioly Zorattini, *Processi del S. Uffizio di Venezia contro ebrei e giudaizzanti, 1682–1734* (Florence: Leo S. Olschki, 1994), vol. 12, 114. I thank Lisa Pon for sharing this reference with me.

60. ASVe, Senato, Terra, filza 141 (m.v.), January 30, 1596.

61. ASVe, Ufficali al Cattaver, busta 128, fasc. "1715," July 15, 1715–September 11, 1715, and ASVe, Ufficali al Cattaver, busta 128, fasc. "1717," September 22, 1717. For further examples, see Carla Boccato, "Processi ad ebrei nell'archivio degli ufficiali al Cattaver a Venezia," *La rassegna mensile di Israel* 41, no. 3 (March 1975): 175, and Pier Cesare Ioly Zorattini, "Jews, Crypto-Jews, and the Inquisition," in *The Jews of Early Modern Venice*, ed. Robert C. Davis and Benjamin Ravid (Baltimore: Johns Hopkins University Press, 2001), 101.

62. Niccolò Machiavelli, *The Prince*, Chapter 18, in *Selected Political Writings*, ed. and trans. David Wootton (Indianapolis: Hackett, 1994), 55.

63. See Martin Jay, *Downcast Eyes: The Denigration of Vision in Twentieth-Century French Thought* (Berkeley: University of California Press, 1993).

9

The Materiality of the Imperceptible
The Eruv

MARGARET OLIN

After Pompey had approached the heart of the temple, the center of adoration, and
had hoped to discover in it the root of the national spirit, to find indeed in one central
point the life-giving soul of this remarkable people, to gaze on a Being as an object
for his devotion, on something significant for his veneration, he might well have
been astonished on entering the arcanum to find himself deceived so far as some
of his expectations were concerned, and, for the rest, to find himself in an empty
room.   G.W.F. Hegel, "The Spirit of Christianity and Its Fate"

The telephone and telegraph wires in Warsaw are, through bribes, supplemented so
that they form a complete circle, which turns a city into an enclosed area in the sense of
the Talmud, like a courtyard, so that even the most pious can move within this circle
on Saturday carrying odds and ends like handkerchiefs.   Franz Kafka, *Tagebücher*

Franz Rosenzweig thought of the Jewish community as temporal, a community of generations that he contrasted to a spatial notion of community attributed to Christianity. Similarly, Abraham Joshua Heschel referred to the
Sabbath, Judaism's central holiday, as the "architecture of time." Both thinkers not
only implicitly relegated the matter that fills space to a lower order of existence but
also discouraged sensory perception in general. Jews and anti-Semites alike commonly attribute to Judaism an antagonism to the body and to its visual perception,
with respectively positive or negative associations.[1] Certainly the stress on time un-
derlies Hegel's mystified reaction to the invisibility of the deity's representation and
encouraged his characterization of Judaism as antivisual, an anti-Semitic prejudice
now largely discredited.[2]

It is, however, not possible to separate time from the space within which it passes
and from the abundance of visible, tactile material that it uses. Hegel's empty space
presupposes a series of interlocking hierarchical spaces and activities in which not
only objects but also people are increasingly and rigorously excluded until, at its cli-

max, the empty Holy of Holies excludes everyone but the high priest.[3] The series of all too visible spaces and one's carefully laid out route through them contributes to the imagined visitor's shock over the invisible content at its apogee. Modern eyes can appreciate an "empty room" through the experience of minimal art, meditation practices, and spare modernist architecture that exalt the invisible as a corollary to the notion of a visible so powerful that little of it is necessary to make its impact. An empty space carved out for spirituality can be stirring, a rich metaphor for practices either deeply spiritual or artistic.

But of what is a circle of telephone poles a metaphor? The spatial practice described by Kafka does not involve an empty space circumscribed by the elaborate architecture of the Temple. It is not empty but full of miscellaneous stuff—an open space in which everyone, secular or pious, wanders about carrying odds and ends. Although it is rigorously bounded, it excludes no one. Yet in everyday life in neighborhoods in Europe, the United States, and even in Israel, this practice has given rise to a great deal of opposition, fantasy, and art. In its own way Kafka's description of a Jewish practice full of everyday stuff is perhaps as telling in relation to Jewish spatial practice as is Hegel's description of the Holy of Holies.

Even the Most Pious

The territory negotiated by Kafka's pious folk belonged to a phenomenon known as the *eruv,* or "Sabbath boundary." Orthodox Jewish law does not normally allow the transportation of objects between a private space and a public space or for any distance within a public space on the Sabbath, a prohibition based loosely on the biblical imperative to "do no work" on that day. An eruv is meant to enhance the Sabbath by helping fulfill the biblical command that the Sabbath be "a joy," a commandment that the injunction against carrying would seem to contravene. The inhabitants of private dwellings constructed around a common shared courtyard could form a partnership allowing them to regard themselves as living together in one home for the purpose of carrying. In the absence of a courtyard, the eruv boundary fixed the problem by conveniently adding symbolic doors and gates that could turn a whole neighborhood into a private space. On the Sabbath one could now carry anything that one could carry in one's own home throughout the entire eruv. Because the Talmud is itself the source both of the strict interpretation of the law against work on the Sabbath and of its amelioration in the eruv, some regard this "structure" as typical of the Rabbinic corpus's characteristic mediation between strictures and joy.[4] The writer of a letter commenting on a controversy of an eruv in London called the eruv a "magic schlepping circle."[5]

As a border, the eruv has something unique to communicate about space. Borders can have a material presence, either unfriendly, like the ugly walls and checkpoints that mark the borders between some territories and countries, or friendly, like the internal borders that welcome visitors as they enter a district, state, or town. Other borders, like the boundaries of a parish or school district or an aldermanic ward, are discoverable only through specialized maps, usually downloadable from the website of the city hall, the school district, or the church. Yet all of these borders are, from time to time, contested or defended, sometimes with passion.

The eruv is another matter. While it, too, can arouse passion and anger and stir the imagination, it usually does so among people who never intend to use it and whose activities are in no way affected by it. Perhaps even more interestingly, although this border, like that of the parish, is for the most part invisible, its invisibility is qualitatively different from that of a parish or school district: the eruv border is not unmarked; it uses a great deal of material that marks every inch of it. Camouflaged and noticeable at the same time, the eruv engages a discourse of visibility and invisibility and does so in a language of very ordinary material things. An understanding of the material nature of the eruv does not center on religious iconography but rather on spatial demarcation, a performance around a quintessential product of conceptual street art, a drawing in space. As a religious sign, the eruv invites a wide range of interpretations. Whether made of materials through the construction of an eruv or art about it, or in words through description, argumentation, or litigation, these interpretations place into question other borders: between perceptibility and imperceptibility, between the trivial and the momentous, and between modern religious spatial practices and the material and mundane contexts in which they take shape.

An Enclosed Area in the Sense of the Talmud

Although eruv practice dates at least to the Talmud, a tractate of which is devoted to it, and myth has it dating back to King Solomon, the tendency to conceive the eruv primarily in terms of its barely perceptible boundaries is recent. Like many Jewish practices, the eruv makes symbolic use of food, a mixture of which designates the partnership.[6] The provision of common food as a symbolic shared meal gave expression to social relationships already encouraged by the design of the shared courtyard: for twenty-four hours a week it conceptually turned one of the homes into a pantry and a courtyard of homes into a single courtyard home.

Food was perhaps the eruv's first material. For many centuries, the major complications faced by the members of eruv groups pertained to the food rather than the space. The issue was not related to its appearance or taste but to the allowable kinds and amounts of food or where it could be kept. Moses Maimonides, in the code of law he compiled in the twelfth century, recommends that the food be made visible so that children will learn the law of the eruv, and beginning in medieval Europe, the eruv was a matzo that hung in the synagogue.[7] Since then, however, the discourse of the eruv has become increasingly focused on the boundary of the space that is transformed into a private dwelling, not on the bread that cements the pact. This development corresponds to the changing nature of Jewish living arrangements. Few obstacles stand in the way of managing an eruv if most Jews live in courtyards, or even in an entire town, if surrounded by an unbroken wall. It becomes difficult, however, to apply rules meant for courtyards opening into alleys to small German medieval towns whose houses have yards in back and front doors that open directly onto narrow streets.[8] Currently, Jews tend to live among others in unwalled cities where a neighborhood or an entire city must first be visibly transformed into a courtyard before it can serve as an eruv. At present, the word *eruv* usually signifies the boundaries of an eruv, or "sabbath territory," as Charlotte Fonrobert terms it.[9] The bread itself has devolved into one or more boxes of matzos, replaced once a year, that now often languish unseen on a high shelf in an unnoticed office (Figure 9.1).[10]

Telegraph Poles Form a Complete Circle

The boundaries of the eruv are as unnoticeable as the matzos. Indeed, the eruv is architecture's minimum. In terms of materials and physical labor, it might seem to be a budget director's dream. Preexisting construction is almost the only kind that comes into play in the Mishneh Torah. Although the cost to establish, maintain, or repair an eruv can reach a figure as high as $25,000, to turn a city neighborhood into a courtyard even now often involves little more than the reinterpretation of an existing structure as a "gate."[11] Some of the areas that may be treated as a private domain within which one is permitted to carry are "an alley which has a side-post or a crossbeam" or "a city surrounded by a wall at least ten handbreadths high, with gates which are closed at night."[12] When a new gate is built, it tends to be unobtrusive. A tiny addition can effect a redefinition. A board that extends between two balconies in adjoining courtyards, for example, may, depending on accessibility, serve as an entrance so that the inhabitants of the two courtyards can establish a single eruv.[13] Only if all of the formations cannot be made to connect is it necessary to build.

What an eruv may save in physical labor, it often makes up for in mental labor and detailed research. Eruv planners have to contend with knotty definitions of what, in an urban center, counts as a "courtyard" or "alley" in the Talmudic sense.[14] A window low enough to step into can count as an entrance, but if it is too high a ladder is necessary to turn it into an entrance. How high is a matter of speculation.[15] The program of the eruv is the entire urban neighborhood, and its building materials consist of the appropriated accumulation of urban life. The construction of an eruv requires an investigation of urban systems whose meticulousness rivals that of many an architectural project. Natural boundaries like a shoreline or a slight depression in the earth and artificial boundaries like fences, walls, and utility wires must all be redefined as inter-

FIGURE 9.1. Box of matzos in the office of Rabbi Jason Rappaport, Slifka Center for Jewish Life, Yale University, New Haven, Connecticut, 2010. Photo by Margaret Olin.

connecting "gates" to attain a complete and unbroken courtyard that takes into account traffic and pedestrian patterns and the routes of freeways and other major roads and plazas.[16]

The material that effects the transformation of secular public land into private property for religious purposes twenty-four hours a week, like the pumpkin that turned into Cinderella's coach, is humble. Certainly the eruv is no work of high art. It is closer to what Claude Lévi-Strauss called bricolage.[17] Whereas the utilitarian engineer has specialized tools made for every project, the bricoleur uses what he has at hand to attack problems that arise. The bricoleur who assembles an eruv acquires the parts at the hardware store or uses what he finds on the street to create the semblance of a basic post-and-lintel construction. The essential characteristic of a post (*lechi*) is that it must be directly under a lintel (*koreh elyon*) and point up at it. Hence, if an electric wire extends from the top of a pole, it can act as a lintel. If the wire, as is more common, extends from the side of the pole, another kind of wire, usually monofilament (fishing) line, can be placed above the pole to serve as the lintel (Figure 9.2). Otherwise, directly beneath the electric wire one may attach to the pole a lechi composed of a wooden rod or a rubber PVC conduit, indistinguishable from those used

FIGURE 9.2. Eruv boundary, New York City, 2012. Photo by Margaret Olin.

by the electric company (Figure 9.3). A wire or line may be attached to a wall, in which case a thick painted line of rubberized sealant (a material used, for example, to seal cracks in an asphalt driveway) may serve as a lechi.[18] Only if there is no pole to transform into a lechi and no other piece of the built environment to serve instead, such as a fence, is it necessary to put up a separate pole for the eruv.

Much of this effort is in the service of camouflage, to prevent the eruv from intruding into the urban setting. Hence the lines are inconspicuous.[19] Even those who use the eruv cannot be expected to see them. The author of one of the most often-quoted guides to constructing an eruv mentions his own difficulty in identifying one on the street.[20] One needs a map to avoid straying accidentally outside, and even the map often needs such voluminous annotation that a verbal description of the route could easily replace it. "Starting from 156 Conrad and going toward Ray Rd.," advises a helpful note, "it is best to walk only on the right side of the street (side with houses), keeping the poles between you & the street" (Figure 9.4).[21]

Yet every week the eruv must be checked and any loose fishing line or a missing lechi fixed. Otherwise the eruv is "down," and it is forbidden to carry. Therefore another set of materials brings the imperceptible eruv to light. Placed on the top of the conduit where it meets the electric cable or fishing line, a rubber tip like that at the bottom of a chair leg or a cane serves as the capital of a column—or the top of the wooden rod may be painted white (Figure 9.5). This symbolic link between the column and the architrave identifies a wire as part of the eruv. When a fishing line is

FIGURE 9.3. PVC conduits on a utility pole, New Haven, Connecticut, 2010. The power company's conduit is on the left; the one on the right is an eruv "lechi." Photo by Margaret Olin.

FIGURE 9.4. (Top) Annotated map of the New Haven, Connecticut, eruv, 2012.

FIGURE 9.5. (Bottom) Eruv lechi, Ann Arbor, Michigan, 2010. Photo by Margaret Olin.

used, little flags made of anything from tape to shiny tinsel to bits of cloth adorn it near the pole to help the eruv checker see the wire (Figure 9.6). These flags, inconspicuous compared to other miscellaneous contraptions and items such as tied-together shoes that wind up on utility wires, help maintain a careful balance between camouflaging the eruv for most people and keeping its components clearly visible to the checker. Users of the eruv trust a means of communication such as the Internet or a map to stay informed about its status and location. To them, the eruv itself remains conceptual, accessed primarily by reading, a cartographic version of one of Benedict Anderson's "imagined communities."[22]

The eruv's appropriation of the mundane for religious purposes has inspired artists. From the slender lines in Alan Cohen's photographs taken in Me'a She'arim, Jerusalem, and their thin, curling flags emanates a delicate, almost ethereal aura, as if they were on an undetermined spiritual mission (Figure 9.7). Fiber artist Ben Schachter's embroideries of eruv maps reveal the beauty of these drawings in space, the result of meditation on rules given from the beyond, their reasons not fully understood (Figure 9.8). Spirituality, in these cases, suggests a nonspecific, secularized sense of higher things. When, however, in 2007 the British artist Mark Wallinger shaped a border of fishing line inspired by the eruv into a perfect circle like that Kafka imputes

FIGURE 9.6. Eruv, New Haven, Connecticut, 2010. Photo by Margaret Olin.

FIGURE 9.7. Alan Cohen, *Ha Me'agel near Me'a She'arim Street, Jerusalem*. Photograph from the series *Improbable Boundaries*, 2009.

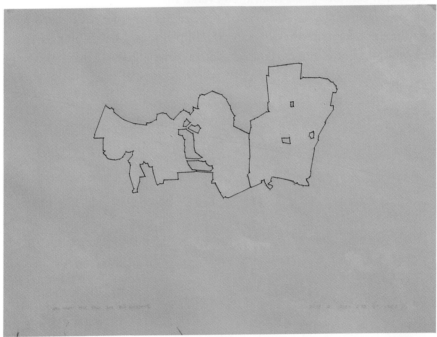

FIGURE 9.8. Ben Schachter, *Five Towns Eruv*, 2010. Acrylic and thread on paper, 20 × 30 inches.

to Warsaw for his installation *Zone*, created for Skulptur Projekte Münster, the effect for which he strove was implicitly Christian. Passers-by, he wrote, would "only notice it if they look upwards towards 'higher things.'" He described it as a "transcendent de-marcation," comparable to the "walls of monasteries [that] separated the sacred from the secular."[23]

The sensory deprivation of this spatial practice does not make the eruv ethereal to most of its users. On Friday afternoons a website pronounces it "up" or "down," as if it were a machine. It is pragmatic. Its ethereal invisibility depends on the use of the most mundane constituent parts. Furthermore, a close look suggests that the invisibility of the eruv carries a good deal of baggage. Indeed, the eruv is all about carrying, and thus about baggage. In his novel *The Yiddish Policemen's Union,* which envisions a Jewish state in Alaska, Michael Chabon draws out the absurdity that someone might see in the practice:

> Landsmann has put a lot of work into the avoidance of having to under-
> stand concepts like that of the eruv, but he knows that it's a typical Jewish
> ritual dodge, a scam run on God, that controlling motherfucker. It has
> something to do with pretending the telephone poles are doorposts, and
> that the wires are lintels. You can tie off an area using poles and strings and
> call it an eruv, then pretend on the Sabbath that this eruv you've drawn—
> in the case of Zimbalist and his crew, it's pretty much the whole District—
> is your house. That way you can get around the Sabbath ban on carrying in
> a public place, and walk to shul with a couple of Alka-Seltzers in your
> pocket, and it isn't a sin. Given enough string and enough poles, and with
> a little creative use of existing walls, fences, cliffs, and rivers, you could tie
> a circle around pretty much any place and call it an eruv.[24]

Chabon's perspective on the eruv brings out its workaday character as a machine that needs to be kept well oiled and running. It also suggests the disjunction between its large scale and its seemingly paltry aims. The entire city has to be reorganized and a large labor force employed so that the pious can pocket Alka-Seltzer on Saturday. The novel embroiders on the ridiculous character of these arrangements involving trucks as well as workers, a command central, and a full-time project director, Zimbalist the "boundary maven." Through his hero, Landsmann, Chabon gently mocks the strange ways in which Jews set up their communities and the considerations that guide them when they are left to their own devices.

Chabon's mention of the eruv echoes that of Kafka, escalating Kafka's sniffling pious into sufferers of headache, heartburn, and acid indigestion. Both authors contrast an expansive complex arrangement to the petty result at which it aims. A short aphorism that may also have had to do with the eruv could express what Kafka thought of this practice: "The true way is along a rope that is not spanned high in the air, but only just above the ground. It seems intended more to cause stumbling than to be walked along."[25] Certainly the passage suggests a tightrope, but Kafka may also have had eruvin in mind. Read with his comment about handkerchiefs, and keeping in mind the notion that an eruv is a guide, the aphorism expresses Kafka's belief in the irrationality of the law. The complex set of rules devised by Talmudic rabbis about carrying during the Sabbath and their just as complicated rules devised to ameliorate the situation created by the first set, with multiple stipulations and seemingly trivial consequences, do seem intended to make people stumble rather than to guide them. The best descriptor for the eruv, conceived this way, is "Kafkaesque."[26]

Unsurprisingly, when its supporters propose an eruv, they rarely mention handkerchiefs or other optional items that suggest physical comfort but rather refer to religious necessities. They will use the eruv "to bring a Talis or Siddur to Shul, or a Sefer to a class or Shiur, or to carry glasses," explains the "Halichot of Eruv" published by the Boston eruv association, adding, only far down on the list, "house keys or other permitted items necessary for Shabbat."[27] The good deed of pushing a wheelchair is frequently mentioned. Where women play an important role, the emphasis is on strollers. Expressing his delight at the success of his fifteen-year effort to institute an eruv in northwest London, David Schreiber wrote: "Even now, when I visit Ner Yisrael, I get a real kick out of counting the number of strollers parked outside."[28] Often an icon of a woman pushing a stroller signifies whether the eruv is "up."[29] The things that are carried within the eruv are themselves symbolic, constituting a barometer of the relations within the community; to denigrate these things is to denigrate those who carry them.

The Bribe

Kafka was not nearly as well informed about the eruv as Chabon would be, but he was right that it is necessary to have, if not a "circle," then at least an unbroken circuit of symbolic gates. Gaps must be filled, necessitating cooperation with utility companies, since the eruv must obtain permission to attach light wires or strings to their poles to complete a circuit. Kafka goes further, however, by suggesting not only the triviality of a law that prohibits carrying handkerchiefs but also the sneakiness of the work-around, a bribe: "the most pious," it seems, with handkerchiefs on their minds, are willing to bribe officials for mundane material concerns. The Jewish community, however, does not have to bribe the city. What it does is even more improbable: the Jewish community must rent an entire neighborhood, or a whole city, for the purpose of carrying (handkerchiefs) on the Sabbath.

What Kafka called a bribe is actually a feature of the eruv's discourse that ensures the participation of nonorthodox Jews and non-Jews in the community. Whether the eruv is perceptible or not, and even if it requires no building and no modification of a single railing, pole, or wire, the rules of the partnership require that its members rent the homes of non-Jewish owners in the courtyard for the Sabbath for the purpose of carrying. In larger eruvin, the secular authorities often play this role, granting permission sometimes informally, sometimes with a proclamation.[30] Charlotte Fonrobert has argued that the rabbis of the Talmudic period, who shaped the laws of the eruv and included the necessity to rent homes symbolically from non-Jewish neighbors, intended from the beginning to weld the Jewish people in a neighborhood into a community, to claim a Jewish territory, and to regulate relationships between Talmudic Jews and others, including Jews who do not recognize the eruv as well as non-Jews, in a proto-Diasporic living situation.[31]

Currently, permission to carry costs the eruv at Yale University a dollar per year, paid to the chief of police of New Haven, Connecticut; three centuries ago, the same privilege cost the Jews of Altona, Germany, 12 Marks, a not inconsiderable sum.[32] On a local level, neighbors may be drawn into plans for an eruv. The eruv boundary may not run through, but rather must run around, a Jewish neighborhood, or an eruv in a heterogeneous community must obtain the consent of nonparticipating locals to allow the eruv of the orthodox Jewish community to include their fences within its boundaries. In Philadelphia, an eruv committee celebrated the completion of their eruv in the courtyard of a seminary, where its members thanked the priests for permission to affix the last line to their fence.[33] Such ceremonies suggest that because it shares its space with others, this almost imperceptible boundary can be a powerful symbol of tolerance and multiculturalism in Diasporic communities. Indeed, some cite the Talmud in reference to the communal aims of the laws concerning the eruv. Rabbi Yehoshua said, "Why do we mix together the courtyards [build eruvin]? In order to follow peaceful ways . . . and through the eruv the people will make peace."[34] Thus, while the simple line of the eruv surrounds and defines the complexity of urban space, engaging the symbolism that normally attends an intricate architectural program, it also defines the complex human community within.

The relation between the eruv community and the surrounding non-Jewish or non-eruv community is at the root of the eruv's dialog about perception. The imperceptible eruv has to make its existence known by asking for public acceptance, even where it might seem unnecessary. Indeed, the painstakingly unobtrusive nature of eruvin in the Diaspora suggests that the relations represented by the eruv are often far from harmonious. The building of an eruv can touch off a bitter controversy. Non-Jews may fear that Jews are getting special privileges and may find visible eruv structures unsightly. They may not wish their property lines to contribute to Jewish purposes. "What could Jews say, if Christians planted Christ images or their ilk in front of their houses?" wrote a citizen of Wandbek, Germany, in 1882, thus setting off a multiyear battle over eruv structures.[35] More recently, a similar comment about an eruv posted by a reader in an online Connecticut newspaper began: "Imagine some Christian group put a bunch of crosses on public property."[36] Many battles over the eruv have taken place or are taking place in courts in the United States, Great Britain, and Canada, with varied outcomes.[37] Battle lines form, however, not only between Jews and others but also between Jews who use the eruv and those who do not. Satmar Hasidim object to most modern urban eruvin vociferously, fearing that they will lead to violations of the Sabbath. Reform or secular Jews sometimes fear that an eruv may attract orthodox Jews to their neighborhoods. A skit in a comedic news show about eruv litigation played upon this fear.[38] Indeed, the very interest in camouflaging the eruv suggests that the seeming innocence of this construction masks potential divisiveness.

It follows that a Jewish state, such as Michael Chabon's imaginary Jewish state in Alaska, should have no reason to hide an eruv boundary. And indeed, in Israel, where the chief rabbinate authorizes an eruv in every town, the eruv flag, tucked unobtrusively near a pole in a North American eruv, waves over the street in Jerusalem, attached to distinctive eruv poles observable everywhere in the country (Figure 9.9). Nevertheless, even there Jews draw up battle lines. Satmar Jews are not the only orthodox Jews to object. Haredi Jews, who accept the eruv but not the authority of the chief rabbinate, construct their own eruvin; they often incur opposition from both other orthodox and secular Jews.[39] A neighborhood can get tangled in competing, overlapping eruvin. Similarly, as a ubiquitous symbol of the community, the eruv can play a symbolic rhetorical role in relations between Jews and Arabs. Some artists visualize this agonistic character of public life in Israel and Palestine bleeding into the thin wire of the eruv. For her *L'erouv de Jerusalem* (1996), the French conceptual artist Sophie Calle interviewed Arab and Jewish inhabitants of Jerusalem, asking them to show her public places that they regarded as private. In the installation, photographs of eruv poles around Jerusalem surround a map marked with stories and photographs of the places shown Calle by her interviewees.[40] Other than the fact that the places and their stories all exist within the eruv, they have nothing ostensibly to do with it. Yet the stories all concern boundaries: A girl does not leave her private space to enter the street where, as she can see from her window, a boy sits on a bench hoping that she will come to talk to him. Someone looks across a border with the knowledge that to cross it would literally mean stepping into a minefield. Outer borders become inner limitations, and to cross them is a liberating experience: a young man crosses a border from his own space into that of the other to engage in activities forbidden in his own society. To peruse these stories about people and pictures of deserted public spaces is to become aware that Calle's interviewees live in a society where life is saturated in the awareness of impassable borders for which the porous eruv boundary is a sign.

The delicate eruv line itself takes on new meanings in more directly political works. The eruv wire that moves invisibly through the American city quietly dominates the changing landscape of the occupied territories in Dani Bauer's photographs taken in Modiim, Israel, in 2008. His triptych *Sans personne à qui parler* (2008) is titled in direct response to Calle's installation. It shows eruv poles traversing desolate lands that once housed Palestinian fields and villages. Here there is indeed no one to talk to, no one to tell stories about private lives and internal constraints. Constraints are all too external: the only signs of human life are the

FIGURE 9.9. Me'a She'arim neighborhood, Jerusalem, 2012. Photo by Margaret Olin.

typically red-roofed settlements with solar panels, surrounded by eruv poles that might as well be barbed wire (Figure 9.10). Avner Bar Hama, however, uses the fragility of the eruv's lines to express his sympathy for those on the settlers' side. In many of his works the eruv surrounds all of Israel and symbolizes the fragility of the entire Jewish state. His *Gush Katif—Mutual-Responsibility—Guarantee* celebrates and mourns greater Israel in the form of a map, Israel's borders marked by eruv poles, where Gaza (Gush Katif) is effaced, and in photographs that represent eruvin, to grieve and protest the eviction of the settlers from the region. In *Mutual-Responsibility of the Country* (2006), the words of Deuteronomy 11:12—"It is a land the Lord your God cares for; the eyes of the Lord your God are continually on it from the beginning of the year to its end"—are emblazoned on the map of Israel surrounded by eruv poles. But these words are in the process of being effaced, crumbling along with the dream of a greater Israel (Figure 9.11). The eruv poles, Bar Hama writes, function not as a (transparent) border but "as a wall that isolates the people of Israel from the rest of the nations."[41] Rather than enabling Jews to live among others, in Israel the eruv forces them to dwell apart. The border may appear open, but in reality the gates are closed.

Imperceptibility may encourage malleability in a sign. The eruv can be regarded as ethereal and spiritual and suggestive of a higher reality. Or it can be seen as a devious way for Jews to try to rearrange public utilities and urban neighborhoods to achieve for

FIGURE 9.10. Daniel Bauer, *Sans personne à qui parler III*, 2008. Photograph.

FIGURE 9.11. Avner Bar Hama, *Mutual-Responsibility of the Country,* 2006. Digitally altered drawing and photograph.

themselves mysterious, materialistic, or trivial ends that suggest small-mindedness. The eruv's practitioners often regard it as a merely practical amenity, a utilitarian machine no more spiritual than an acoustical aid in a synagogue. Yet all recognize that an imperceptible border can be as strong and even coercive as a fence or a wall, and the fear of what invisibility can hide is often greater than the fear aroused by a visible threat. Perhaps that mystery constitutes the appeal of the practice. But it also explains Kafka's bemusement concerning the eruv and even Hegel's antipathy toward the empty Holy of Holies: that some important religious practices might not always demand beauty or art, or even prized implements, but that they might do with just any stuff, or with no stuff.

NOTES

1. On the relation between physicality and perception in the discourse of Jewish visuality, see Margaret Olin, "Jewish Art and Our National Past Time," *Images: A Journal of Jewish Art and Visual Culture* 3 (2010): 83–101.

2. See Margaret Olin, *The Nation without Art: Examining Modern Discourses on Jewish Art* (Lincoln: University of Nebraska Press, 2001), esp. 3–18.

3. On the Temple in Jerusalem and its hierarchies, see Jonathan Z. Smith, *To Take Place: Toward Theory in Ritual* (Chicago: University of Chicago Press, 1987), 47–73.

4. On rabbinical authority and compliance, see Jacob Neusner, *A History of the Jews in Babylonia* (Leiden: Brill, 1968), vol. 3, 243–252.

5. Calvin Trillin, "Drawing the Line," *New Yorker* (December 12, 1994): 50–62, quote on 60.

6. On the Rabbinic interpretation of the eruv, see Charlotte Elisheva Fonrobert, "Neighborhood as Ritual Space: The Case of the Rabbinic Eruv," *Archiv für Religionsgeschichte* 10 (2008): 239–258, and Fonrobert, "The Political Symbolism of the Eruv," *Jewish Social Studies,* n.s. 11 (2005): 9–35. My understanding of Rabbinic intentions in establishing eruvin is informed by these and other of Fonrobert's extensive studies.

7. Moses Maimonides, *The Code of Maimonides,* trans. Soloman Ganz and Hyman Klein (New Haven, CT: Yale University Press, 1961), vol. 3, 205. A container of matzos still hangs in synagogues, for example in HaAri synagogue in Tzfat, Israel. One scholar has proposed the (controversial) theory that this practice may inadvertently have reinforced anti-Jewish blood libels. Israel Jacob Yuval, *Two Nations in Your Womb: Perceptions of Jews and Christians in Late Antiquity* (Berkeley: University of California Press, 2006), 236–239.

8. For the medieval transition in eruv discourse toward explicit discussion of contemporary urban spaces, see Micha Perry, "Imaginary Space Meets Actual Space in Thirteenth-Century Cologne: Eliezer Ben Joel and the Eruv," *Images* 5 (2011): 26–36.

9. Charlotte Fonrobert, "Diaspora Cartography: On the Rabbinic Background to the Contemporary Ritual Eruv Practice," *Images* 5 (2011): 14–25.

10. The practice of an annual (as opposed to a weekly) deposit of bread is long-standing, attested to, for example, in a twelfth-century work by an associate of the French Talmudic authority Rashi. Kristin C. S. Zapalac, "'With a Morsel of Bread': Delineating Differences in the Jewish and Christian Communities of Regensburg before the Pogrom of 1519," in *Infinite Boundaries: Order, Disorder, and Reorder in Early Modern German Culture,* ed. Max Reinhart (Kirksville, MO: Sixteenth Century Journal Publishers, 1998), 285. Yuval points to an earlier, Italian source. Yuval, *Two Nations in Your Womb,* 236–239.

11. The webpage of an eruv in the San Fernando Valley cites a bid of $25,000 for the replacement of the monofilament lines of the eruv, although eventually, according to the site, it was able to do the job for less. Accessed July, 2012, http://www.valleyeruv.org/.

12. Maimonides, *The Code of Maimonides,* vol. 3, 200.

13. Ibid., vol. 3, 217.

14. See Perry, "Imaginary Space Meets Actual Space." Perry's source is Victor Aptowitzer, *Sefer Rabiah: Dezisionen, Novellen und Responsen zum Talmud von Rabbi Elieser ben Rabbi Joel ha-Levi,* vol. 1 (Berlin: Meḳiẕe Nirdamim, 1913), 393–402.

15. Maimonides, *The Code of Maimonides,* vol. 3, 213–221.

16. Many manuals exist for the purpose of constructing eruvin. A recent one is Yosef Gavriel Bechhofer, *The Contemporary Eruv: Eruvin in Modern Metropolitan Areas* (Jerusalem and New York: Feldheim, 1998).

17. Claude Lévi-Strauss, *The Savage Mind,* trans. George Weidenfeld and Nicholson Ltd. (Chicago: University of Chicago Press, 1966), 16–36. Eyal Weitzmann also compares the eruv to "a giant-scale act of urban bricolage." Weitzmann, "The Subversion of Jerusalem's Sacred Vernacular," in *The Next Jerusalem: Sharing the Divided City,* ed. Michael Sorkin (New York: Monacelli, 2002), 122.

18. Thanks to Adrian Kohn and Divya Menon-Kohn for information about the eruv in Waltham, Massachusetts, where such lechi made of sealant appear.

19. The "What's Up with That?" column in *Time Out New York* once tried to answer the question of a puzzled onlooker who noticed the fishing line. "Eruv: Sabbath String," *Time Out New York,* September 15, 2009.

20. Bechhofer, *The Contemporary Eruv,* 67.

21. Quoted from the New Haven eruv interactive map, accessed July 2012, http://www.nheruv.org/EruvIII.htm.

22. Benedict Anderson, *Imagined Communities: Reflections on the Origin and Spread of Nationalism* (London and New York: Verso, 1991).

23. Quoted from the project website, accessed July 2012, www.skulptur-projekte.de/kuenstler/wallinger. See also Katharina Steinmann de Oliviera, "Grenzen: Mark Wallingers 'Zone,'" *Kunst und Kirche* 4 (2008): 21–23.

24. Michael Chabon, *The Yiddish Policemen's Union* (New York: Harper, 2007), 110.

25. Franz Kafka, *The Basic Kafka* (New York: Pocket Books, 1979), 236.

26. For a work of art based on these implications of Kafka's aphorism, see Suzanne Silver, "Kafka in Space: Parsing the Eruv," *Images* 5 (2011): 66–67.

27. "The Halakhot of Eruv," adapted from the manual of the Cleveland, Ohio, eruv, accessed September 2011, http://www.bostoneruv.org/halachot.htm.

28. David Schreiber, unpublished manuscript, December 2010, n.p.

29. See www.eruvstatus.com, accessed September 2011.

30. Rules for large urban areas containing practicing and nonpracticing Jews and gentiles are referenced frequently in the Mishneh Torah in particular. Maimonides, *The Code of Maimonides,* vol. 3, 236, paragraph 23, concerns rules pertaining to the transfer of property for the purpose of an eruv without the knowledge of some of those who benefit from the transfer.

31. Fonrobert, "The Political Symbolism of the Eruv" and "Diaspora Cartography."

32. Peter Freimark, "Eruw/'Judentore,'" in *Judentore, Kuggel, Steuerkonten: Untersuchung zur Geschichte der deutschen Juden, vornehmlich im Hamburger Raum,* ed. Peter Freimark, Ina Lorenz, and Günter Marwedel (Hamburg: Hans Christians, 1983), 19–21. This lengthy essay is a fount of information on eruvin practices in eighteenth- and nineteenth-century German lands. I am grateful to Rabbi Jason Rappaport for information about the New Haven eruv and to Timothy Guinnane for information about monetary values in eighteenth-century Altona.

33. Bonnie Squires, "Ribbon Tying: Completion of the Main Line Eruv," *Philadelphia Jewish Voice,* December 2006.

34. Jerusalem Talmud, eruvin 83:2. Cited on the website of the West Hartford eruv, Young Israel of West Hartford, accessed September 2011, http://1.yiwh.net/index.php/en/home/the-eruv.

35. Freimark, "Eruw/'Judentore,'" 36.

36. Posted by DingDong, *New Haven Independent,* July 31, 2012, 1:14 p.m., accessed October 2012, http://www.newhavenindependent.org/index.php/archives/entry/eruv_fits_early_into_route_34_plans/.

37. Some examples: Non-Jews opposed the Palo Alto eruv. Orthodox Jews opposed the Flatbush eruv. Secular and reform Jews have filed suit in opposition to an eruv in Northampton, New York. Accessed October 2012, http://www.paloaltohistory.com/the-eruv-debate.php, http://eruvonline.blogspot.com/2011/07/flatbushwilliamsburg-eruv-imbroglio.html, and http://dockets.justia.com/docket/new-york/nyedce/2:2012cv03760/332881/.

38. "The Thin Jew Line," an episode of *The Daily Show,* a series on Comedy Central, March 23, 2011.

39. Peggy Cidor reports on one such conflict in the neighborhood Kiryat Hayovel that began with the construction of an illegal eruv by Haredi. Cidor, "High Stakes," *Jerusalem Post,* October 18, 2007. See also Yechiel Spira, "Arrest Made in Kiryat Yovel Eruv Sabotage Attack," *Yeshiva World News,* February 19, 2010, which reports on a dispute between secularists and Jerusalem's Kiryat Yovel neighborhood.

40. Sophie Calle, *L'erouv de Jérusalem* (Arles: Actes Sud, 2002).

41. Avner Bar Hama, "Eruv—Mutual-Responsibility—Guarantee," *Images* 5 (2011): 93.

INTERLUDE ONE ✳ CONTESTED GROUNDS

Ad Reinhardt, another New York School painter, has especially influenced me because his black paintings were meant to be the ultimate paintings and they seemed to encompass everything or nothing at all. Reinhardt was the greatest proponent of art having no content but art content. My friend Tom Finkelpearl and I went to the Met one day to test Reinhardt's assertion that there are no religious objects in the fine art museum, i.e. once the religious object becomes art by virtue of its context in the art museum it loses all its meaning as a religious object. I performed 108 prostrations beneath a large Buddhist mural. Meanwhile Tom, pretending that he was a stranger to me, asked a guard what I was doing. The guard informed him that I was just one of those people who often come to the museum to worship and leave offerings and that the staff had to clean up after them. Byron Kim

The following set of short chapters explores the introduction of unexpected, unwelcome, or prohibited objects, performances, and bodies. Six authors consider subjects including the uses of insistently ritual and devotional objects in ostensibly secular institutions, multisensory secular art in avowedly religious institutions, audible religion in civic spaces and residential neighborhoods, the art of one religious tradition in the architectural precincts of another, and the sensory neutralization by a Western arts professional of religious objects from the Soviet state. Each case here concerns strategies of ritual practice, exhibition, or display in the United States and/or Europe in modernity.

Two chapters examine sonic Islam and its implications for interpreting the American public soundscape. Both suggest that many in the West consider Islam to represent a premodern religious sensorium rather than a differently modern set of sensory practices. In this context, sound collapses distinctions between public and private in "disrespecting" conventional Western regulatory boundaries. Modern American Muslim practice thus appears to run counter to the purported inward turn of religion in modernity.[1]

Byron Kim with Assembly of the Buddha Sakyamuni, *at the Metropolitan Museum of Art, New York,* 1996. Photo by Tom Finkelpearl.

The spaces of religious practice and belief, even within a particular local group in a particular tradition, are inherently pluriform spaces. What constitutes "religion" or "spirituality" varies from person to person, and the politics of religious communities and practices manifest complex terms of engagement. When social, civil, and spatial circles expand to include wider populations (religious and otherwise), the sensory calculus of values and desires around these subjects multiplies and intensifies, too.

SALLY M. PROMEY

NOTE

1. For further reflections and earlier supporting arguments, see Talal Asad, *Formations of the Secular: Christianity, Islam, Modernity* (Stanford, CA: Stanford University Press, 2003), esp. "Introduction: Thinking about Secularism," 1–17, and 21–40 from Chapter 1: "What Might an Anthropology of Secularism Look Like?"; William E. Connolly, *Pluralism* (Durham, NC, and London: Duke University Press, 2005), esp. 55; and David Scott and Charles Hirschkind, eds., *Powers of the Secular Modern: Talal Asad and His Interlocutors* (Stanford, CA: Stanford University Press, 2006), esp. the contributions by William E. Connolly ("Europe: A Minor Tradition," 75–92) and Talal Asad ("Responses," 206–241).

10

Conversations in Museums

JAMES CLIFTON

I first considered the issue of the exhibition of religious art in secular museums in curating an exhibition at the Museum of Fine Arts, Houston, titled *The Body of Christ in the Art of Europe and New Spain, 1150–1800* (1997). I noted in the introduction to the catalog that although early modern European religious art has long been collected in the United States, its iconography and original ecclesiastical and devotional functions have been elided in a process of aestheticization that has valued form over subject. Thus, while individual labels in the permanent exhibition spaces of "encyclopedic" museums might address Christian subject matter, the paintings are hung with little regard to that subject matter, and they fit into an overarching narrative of a history of artistic style. I felt that bringing together works from diverse times and places that are not ordinarily exhibited together in a museum would help to recuperate some of the meaning and original function of those works as well as to demonstrate the persistence and consistency of certain subjects that might not otherwise be readily apparent to museum visitors.[1] In a subsequent essay that drew on visitors' comments on the exhibition, I considered the matter of religious art in secular museums further and expressed concern that the museum, by exhibiting the Christian works, might be complicit in supporting and perpetuating a particular religious ideology, that is, that it might be seen as endorsing a Christian narrative, Christian doctrine, and the cult status of the objects. But I concluded that the museum has a primary and overriding obligation to the objects themselves and that not to address the religious element in religious art would be to offer a mutilated view of the objects and the history of image making.[2]

I would like to extend and redirect my considerations here by placing greater emphasis on the objects themselves, making an "objectual turn," as it were. The transformation of historical objects entailed by their removal to a museum has been well noted,[3] but the implication is that the role of the objects in this transformation is entirely passive. How might we identify and analyze a more active role for displaced objects? I suggest that objects are active interlocutors in a three-way conversation along with museums and visitors to museums—a kind of *sacra conversazione,* if you will[4]—and that, like the objects and the viewers, museums themselves stand to be transformed by this interaction.

Chris Arthur, referring to religious objects as "religious data," has wondered "whether it is possible to convey the non-material dimension of religion through material objects" that are exhibited in a museum, and whether it is "legitimate to present such data as *intrinsically* interesting, rather than as referring beyond themselves."[5] Posited here is a semiotic structure in which the objects function as signifiers and the signifiers are necessarily of less interest than the signified: a semiotic means to an end in the making of objects and a semiotic means to an end in the reception of objects. I have approvingly likened the idea of "religious data" to Michael Baxandall's reference to pictures in general as "material and visible deposits left behind by earlier people's activity."[6] But the notion assumes the passivity and secondary status of objects and thus overlooks their inherent force.

Over the past several decades, a "new materialism" has developed in which studies of objects and things in a variety of disciplines have—albeit with considerable debate and dissension—tended to emphasize their active functioning in matter, space, and time (rather than as more or less transparent signifiers, for example), blurring the inanimate and animate even to the point of stark anthropomorphization: objects and things have or appear to have—one imagines—not only histories, (social) lives, and biographies but also agency, intentionality, desires, loves, thoughts, wills—in short, personhood.[7] In Arjun Appadurai's succinct formulation, it is "the idea that persons and things are not radically distinct categories."[8]

Religious artworks self-evidently undergo changes of meaning or significance in their displacement into a museum—into a place for which they were not intended.[9] Of course this particular kind of displacement is only a more salient one of many that an object undergoes over the course of its existence, and significant displacements need not be physical at all but can be caused by a shift in context over the course of time. One might think of the changes to Leonardo's *Last Supper*—its displacement into new contexts—as the structure around it was repurposed from refectory to facility for Napoleonic soldiers to museum. When a religious object comes into a museum it is, in many instances, the moment of a decisive step, albeit perhaps neither the first nor the last, in its becoming an artwork at all, in its transformation from ecclesiastical and/or devotional object to artwork. The change to the artwork—in its substance rather than its accidents, one might say—is enormous, to be sure.[10] Stanley Idzerda, speaking of the origins of the French museum in the late eighteenth century, coined a relevant and suggestive phrase: "iconoclasm . . . without destruction." He quoted a

Commission des Monuments member's recommendation in 1793 that a scepter from the royal tombs of Saint Denis be preserved for the new Louvre museum "not as a scepter, but as an example of fourteenth-century goldsmith work." Idzerda asserts, "Immure a political symbol in a museum and it becomes merely art."[11] Similarly, Constance Classen, noting the prohibition against touching in the modern museum, has described displayed artifacts as "imprisoned in their cases, corrected by cleaning and restoration, silenced and isolated."[12] But to accept such a change as definitive and complete underestimates the residual effects of the objects' former lives and the power of museum visitors to breach those imprisoning walls and invoke or revive the lingering, slumbering, or moribund symbolism of these objects (or even invent new symbolism)—quite possibly facilitated and even encouraged by the museum itself. Furthermore, the move into a museum and the consequent transformation of the object are not necessarily permanent. Often temporary exhibitions include objects—paintings, sculptures, reliquaries, and so on—that, after the exhibition, will return to their ongoing role in explicitly religious contexts. Just as vestiges of the museum may remain with them when they return to ecclesiastical life—they have been rebranded as artworks, after all—vestiges of the church are particularly strong with them during their Babylonian exile in the museum, and they must, per force, have an impact on the museum itself.

One can speak of a dialog between object and subject (that is, the viewer) just as much as one can speak of a dialog between text and reader, and, as Michael Ann Holly has pointed out, this dialog not only can be cast in historical terms but is also susceptible to change: "Of course the 'answers' [when the past 'answers back'] alter as the dialogue between subject and object changes through different times and places."[13] But as religious objects enter a museum, and especially as they are exhibited together, we might expand this dyadic dialog to a larger conversation, now including not only multiple objects in conversation with each other but also the museum itself, not as simply the venue for such a conversation but also as a participant in the conversation. (In *museum* I include all the human agents responsible for its activities, as well as its architecture, its programs, its position within various social contexts, and so on.)

The museum's active role in shaping, and therefore participating in, such a conversation was evident in an exhibition in the summer of 2011 at the National Gallery, London, *Devotion by Design: Italian Altarpieces before 1500,* curated by Scott Nethersole.[14] It consisted largely of works in the National Gallery's collection, as well as in the Queen's collection and that of the Courtauld Gallery, and thus brought together objects that might ordinarily be interspersed with other kinds of works of the period, including secular works. Room 4, called "Sacred Space," unique among the exhibition galleries, was particularly interesting (Figure 10.1). Eight altarpieces were arranged along the walls of this rectangular space, placed on or above raised platforms of proportions and designs resembling those of altars. Alone but for some church furnishings on one

FIGURE 10.1. *Devotion by Design*, Room 4, National Gallery, London, 2011. © The National Gallery, London.

end wall was Signorelli's *Circumcision*. Two low benches were set up perpendicular to the axis of the room and close together, like pews in a church. Sacred music of the period, with no visible source, played quietly. The didactic text for the room explained —perhaps justified—the arrangement, lighting, music, and extra objects:

> This room evokes the interior of a Tuscan church around 1500. The lowered lighting, sacred objects and music create an atmosphere for contemplation. On the high altar are the two candlesticks and altar cross stipulated by church law for the celebration of the Mass. The early 15th-century Tuscan crucifix is a processional cross, of a type that would have been detached from its staff and placed on the high altar after being processed. The different forms and styles of the altarpieces in this space suggest how the decoration of a church might evolve over time.

In some sense, the arrangement of this space and the museological intention behind it were like those of period rooms that one finds in museums worldwide, although ecclesiastical period rooms are rare and museums rely on the vague but useful notion of "evocation." Here the evocation included "creat[ing] an atmosphere for contemplation"—an atmosphere that was implicitly just as present in the National Gallery in 2011 as it would have been in a hypothetical Tuscan church in 1500 (perhaps even more so, because hearing a highly skilled performance of sacred music in a church, though it might seem a quintessential experience, was a relatively uncommon one at that time).[15] Were museum visitors invited to contemplation—a term put to serious mystical use in the early modern period—in the museum? It is perhaps worth pointing out the obvious: that this quasi-religious space in the museum was prompted by the religious objects that occupied, and were in conversation with, that space.

The museum brought other objects into the conversation in the gift shop at the end of the exhibition (Figure 10.2). There one could find together on one small wall, *inter alia,* rosary beads priced from £5 to £25; bracelets with roundels of saints, Christ, and Mary; cross pendants made of green stone; miniature triptychs; a variety of crosses; and scented candles with the ambitious name of "Inspiratus" and the hopeful description of "an uplifting blend of aromatic spices." The potential reception of these objects—like that of the paintings—remained ambiguous, flexible, and ultimately determined by the viewer/consumer rather than by the maker or the museum. Rosaries can function as fashion accessories just as easily as they can function as devotional aids.[16]

Also in the summer of 2011, the museum-goer in London could visit *Treasures of Heaven: Saints, Relics, and Devotion in Medieval Europe* at the British Museum. The presence of relics in a secular museum offered a less subtle provocation than that of,

FIGURE 10.2. *Devotion by Design* gift shop, National Gallery, London, 2011. Photo by James Clifton.

say, the Italian altarpieces by Fra Angelico, Piero della Francesca, Andrea Mantegna, and Luca Signorelli in *Devotion by Design*—all regulars of the encyclopedic art museum.[17] Relics and reliquaries occupy a peculiar place in the history of art or the history of objects and have gained requisite attention in discussions of the materiality of religion.[18] They had originally been experienced by touch as well as by sight, not simply because they are three-dimensional objects that have been handled in the course of their use but also by virtue of their putative supernatural force. The perceived power of a relic could be conveyed to the votary by touch even through the reliquary, which itself gained force through its special physical relationship with the relic. In the case of a secondary, or contact, relic, whose virtue derives from physical contact with a holy figure, the chain of power transference could extend across space and time from saint to contact relic to reliquary to votary. The inclination to touch sacred relics was evident in a photograph included in a montage of still images playing on a video monitor toward the end of *Treasures of Heaven;* it showed votaries touching the Plexiglas case covering the casket housing a small part of the skeleton of Saint Therese of Lisieux when it was touring the United Kingdom in 2009. (One wonders if a similar inclination led to greasy handprints on some of the cases in the British Museum exhibition.) Even if most votaries are not in a position to touch relics, the *potential* for a tactile experience can operate as an extension of their visual experience. Many secular collected objects were also experienced by touch in cabinets of curiosity and museums well into the nineteenth century, as Fiona Candlin and Constance Classen have pointed out,[19] and the modern prohibition against touching in the "pseudo-sacred space of their museum-temples," in Classen's words, has had the effect of increasing the secular reverence for both classes of objects.[20] But the isolation of relics, with the Plexiglas cases acting as a doubling of the reliquaries in which they are already housed, may simultaneously augment the objects' special status and the viewers' longing to experience their sacred force, even in the context of a secular museum.[21] Of course visitors were free to touch, kiss, or otherwise engage in religious *frottage* with the relic-related gifts in the gift shop situated at the end of the exhibition, which may have provided an outlet for pent-up tactile yearning.

The slide show in *Treasures of Heaven* introduced elements of the modern and the secular into the exhibition, discoursing further on the role of objects in maintaining the presence of the dead. Included along with Saint Therese's reliquary were slides of Pope John Paul II's funeral and his blood reliquary, Lenin's tomb, flowers outside Buckingham Palace commemorating Princess Diana's passing, and Diana's engagement ring, which was subsequently put to the same purpose by Prince William and Kate Middleton, as well as several more anonymous and personal memorials.[22] The inclusion in the exhibition of representations of such relics, which have their own, somewhat different, fascination, was a statement by the museum—an interpolation into the conversation about and with relics—on the nature, function, and meaning of the medieval relics with which the images of modern relics were juxtaposed, as well as on the relationship between sacred and secular, inserted provocatively as a tiny crack in the monolithic presentation of a millennium and a half of exclusively premodern religious objects. Some of the religiously minded visitors may have disagreed with the museum's implicit position, but, as Alexander Nagel has pointed out, in the history of collecting and displaying together relics, reliquaries, marvelous natural objects, and works of human artifice, even before the modern era, the distinction between sacred and profane has often been blurred.[23]

But here I would like to draw attention to an appendix of sorts to the exhibition that suggested, perhaps, a subtext for the visitors' experiences. It was an advertisement—placed in the liminal space between exhibited relics and gifts for sale—for an upcoming exhibition at the British Museum, *Hajj: Journey to the Heart of Islam*. The advertisement explained that the exhibition "will explore the sacred pilgrimage to Mecca, known as Hajj. Objects . . . will reveal the purpose, history and context of this significant journey for Muslims, from its beginnings to the present day. Discover [there it switched to the imperative] the rituals that take place, the experiences of the pilgrims and the sheer operation behind this extraordinary event which attracts over three million pilgrims each year." So we would discover someone else's religious experiences. But in larger type we were told (again in the imperative), "Experience more spiritual journeys." By implication, in *Treasures of Heaven* we had experienced a spiritual journey. But had we simply experienced vicariously someone else's long-past spiritual journey by "discovering" their religious experiences, or was our visit to the museum exhibition itself a spiritual journey?[24]

The museums' positions with respect to visitors' spiritual engagement with exhibited objects at the British Museum and the National Gallery—and, of course, at many other institutions as well—are profoundly, and to my mind intriguingly, ambiguous. Each of the interlocutors in these conversations among objects, museum, and viewers brings to the conversations different strengths or sources of authority: the objects have their aura (historical, aesthetic, sensuous, value-based, and so on); the museum has its control over the circumstances (sensory, spatial, textual, and so on) under which objects are apprehended by viewers and thus over the conditions of conversation; and the viewers (and would-be touchers) have their ability to respond to exhibited objects in an entirely idiosyncratic manner, which may or may not have been encouraged by the objects and the museum. None of the interlocutors controls the conversation as a whole, which remains, in Umberto Eco's phrase, an "open work."

NOTES

1. James Clifton, "Introduction," in *The Body of Christ in the Art of Europe and New Spain, 1150–1800,* exhibition catalog, Museum of Fine Arts, Houston (Munich and New York: Prestel, 1997), 11–15.

2. James Clifton, "Truly a Worship Experience? Christian Art in Secular Museums," *Res* 52 (Autumn 2007): 107–115. For the viewer's response to the important National Gallery, London, exhibition *Seeing Salvation: The Image of Christ* (2000), see Graham Howes, *The Art of the Sacred: An Introduction to the Aesthetics of Art and Belief* (London: I. B. Tauris, 2010), 45–58.

3. See, for example, Barbara Kirshenblatt-Gimblett, "Objects of Ethnography," in *Destination Culture: Tourism, Museums, and Heritage,* by Kirshenblatt-Gimblett (Berkeley, Los Angeles, and London: University of California Press, 1998), 17–78.

4. Because the traditional meanings of *conversation* include wordless coexistence and interactions, the term need not be considered metaphorical here.

5. Chris Arthur, "Exhibiting the Sacred," in *Godly Things: Museum, Objects, and Religion,* ed. Crispin Paine (London and New York: Leicester University Press, 2000), 9, 2, italics in original.

6. Michael Baxandall, *Patterns of Intention: On the Historical Explanation of Pictures* (New Haven, CT, and London: Yale University Press, 1985), 13, and Clifton, "Truly a Worship Experience?," 110.

7. For an introduction to the material, see Fiona Candlin and Raiford Guins, eds., *The Object Reader* (London and New York: Routledge, 2009), esp. 1–18 ("Introducing Objects").

8. Arjun Appadurai, "The Thing Itself," *Public Culture* 18 (2006): 15.

9. In Karin Dannehl's outline of object biographies—production, distribution, consumption —the collecting of objects after their initially purposed consumption represents a return to distribution, and their collecting by a museum, with consequent interpretation and presentation, represents an extended consumption stage. Dannehl, "Object Biographies: From Production to Consumption," in *History and Material Culture: A Student's Guide to Approaching Alternative Sources,* ed. Karin Harvey (London and New York: Routledge, 2009), 127–129.

10. One change to its "accidents" is a subsequent *lack* of change in perpetuity; that is, the museum environment is designed specifically to retard, if not eliminate, physical change to the object entirely, what Appadurai, in "The Thing Itself," 16, calls "the corrosion of history" and "the corrosive effects of history and context."

11. Stanley J. Idzerda, "Iconoclasm during the French Revolution," *American Historical Review* 60 (1954): 25–26, cited by Miguel Tamen, *Friends of Interpretable Objects* (Cambridge, MA, and London: Harvard University Press, 2001), 62–63.

12. Constance Classen, *The Deepest Sense: A Cultural History of Touch* (Urbana: University of Illinois Press, 2012), 177–178.

13. Michael Ann Holly, "Responses to Mieke Bal's 'Visual Essentialism and the Object of Visual Culture' (2003): Now and Then," *Journal of Visual Culture* 2 (2003): 240.

14. Scott Nethersole, *Devotion by Design: Italian Altarpieces before 1500,* exhibition catalog, National Gallery, London, 2011.

15. Even if the playing of sacred music in the gallery only evoked rather than replicated conditions of viewing circa 1500, however, it signaled a special space to the visitors by its departure from customary museum practice. Of course, because sound effects of various sorts are not unprecedented in exhibitions, the more jaded museum visitor might have thought, "Ah! the sacred music, in its departure from customary museum practice, is evoking for me the experience of an Italian church circa 1500," thus becoming too conscious of the museological technique, perhaps, to be susceptible to the creation of an atmosphere for contemplation, although the meta-didactic text itself clues in the unwary visitors as well.

16. Noted by Eduardo Fernández in conversation, November 2, 2011.

17. Although the British Museum is not an art museum as such, the exhibition's other venues, in Cleveland and Baltimore, were both art museums.

18. For a recent treatment, see Caroline Walker Bynum, *Christian Materiality: An Essay on Religion in Late Medieval Europe* (New York: Zone Books, 2011), as well as Martina Bagnoli, Holger A. Klein, G. Griffith Mann, and James Robinson, eds., *Treasures of Heaven: Saints, Relics, and Devotion in Medieval Europe,* exhibition catalog, Cleveland Museum of Art; Walters Art Museum, Baltimore; and British Museum, London (New Haven, CT, and London: Yale University Press, 2010).

19. Fiona Candlin, *Art, Museums, and Touch* (Manchester, UK: Manchester University Press, 2010), 58–90, and Classen, *The Deepest Sense,* 136–146, 176–178.

20. Classen, in *The Deepest Sense,* 145, who sees the increased proscription against touching objects as a result of increased reverence for them in the nineteenth century, but the reverse is true as well. Alexander Nagel, in "The Afterlife of the Reliquary," in *Treasures of Heaven,* ed. Bagnoli et al., 214, sees modern conservation as an adaptation of late medieval conservation practices developed for image relics. For the museum-as-temple metaphor, see Carol Duncan and Alan Wallach, "The Universal Survey Museum," *Art History* 3 (1980): 448–469, and Carol Duncan, *Civilizing Rituals: Inside Public Art Museums* (London and New York: Routledge, 1995).

21. Perhaps surprisingly, the apparent English propensity for touching objects, including religious ones, when offered the opportunity, which was discussed in the nineteenth century and subsequently, has been attributed to Protestantism, because Protestants ascribed no supernatural force to objects and thus respected them less than did Catholics. See Candlin, *Art, Museums, and Touch,* 81.

22. I am grateful to Anna Harnden of the British Museum for clarifying the content of the *Treasures of Heaven* video piece in conversation.

23. Nagel, "Afterlife of the Reliquary," 213. Nagel's essay in the *Treasures of Heaven* catalog, which considers both religious and secular relics and reliquaries from the Reformation to the late twentieth century, corresponds functionally to the video piece in the exhibition itself, extending, complementing, and even challenging the exhibition's treatment of premodern objects.

24. As it happened, there was nothing in *Hajj* (a fine exhibition, at the British Museum in early 2012) that explicitly suggested that the exhibition visitor was on a spiritual journey; it was an exhibition *about* journeys, both physical and spiritual. Phrases such as "Muslims believe . . ." and "In the Islamic tradition . . ." in the didactic texts established the museum's ideally objective, ethnographic position, and the occasional implicit acceptance of the belief position (e.g., "Pilgrims respond to God's call . . .") was presumably used for the sake of conciseness, although the posted floor plans of the exhibition with the direction of Mecca indicated struck a curious note.

11

Revolutionary Icons
Alfred Barr and the Remaking of Russian Religious Art

RICHARD MEYER

The temporal existence of an artwork is not bound by its moment of production or by the life or death of its creator. Works of art may be rediscovered and reactivated—if also repressed or refused—by later viewers and cultural contexts. As the Renaissance art historians Alexander Nagel and Christopher Wood write,

> No device more effectively generates the effect of a doubling or bending
> of time than the work of art, a strange kind of event whose relation to time
> is plural. The artwork is made or designed by an individual or a group of
> individuals at some moment, but it also points away from that moment,
> backward to a remote ancestral origin, perhaps, or to a prior artifact, or to
> an origin outside of time, in divinity. At the same time it points forward
> to all its future recipients who will activate and reactivate it as a meaning-
> ful event. The work of art is a message whose sender and destination are
> constantly shifting.[1]

As it persists over time, the artwork may become newly relevant to later works and social-historical worlds. Contrasting the study of art history to that of literature, music, and dance, Thomas Crow has observed that the "unique, physically sensible pattern" of the work of art links the time of its making to that of our viewing in a peculiarly vivid manner. For Crow, art is distinguished by its status as an expressive object "from the past that arrives in our midst like a traveler through time."[2] Building on this line of argument, I propose that the category of contemporary art might include not only newly produced works by living artists but also those "time travelers" that arrive "in our midst" from earlier moments and historical contexts.

215

In this chapter I consider a particularly vivid example of such time travelers. The objects at issue here—medieval Russian religious icons—traveled great conceptual and political distances in the early twentieth century when they were appropriated by the Soviet state in the aftermath of the October Revolution. And, as we shall see, it was not only the Soviets who redefined the icons but also American museums wishing to display the works as aesthetic achievements rather than as religious relics. One viewer who proved especially adept at charting the distances traveled by the Russian icons was Alfred H. Barr, the director of the Museum of Modern Art in New York from 1929 to 1943 and a visitor to postrevolutionary Russia as early as 1927 (the tenth anniversary of the Revolution). What follows is a close reading of Barr's own account of the icons.

"Revolutions have as a rule not been kind to religious art."[3] With this memorably understated line, Barr opens his essay on Russian icons in the February 1931 issue of *The Arts* (Figure 11.1). To make the claim concrete, Barr points to the destruction of Catholic relics under Henry VIII and Oliver Cromwell, the Calvinist burning of "Dutch and Flemish primitives" in the sixteenth century, and the destruction of church sculptures during the French Revolution. To these examples Barr counterposes the Bolshevik case:

> The Russian revolution has pursued a far more enlightened program,
> though not without certain curious contradictions. Lenin himself was
> not interested in art—in fact he confessed a distaste for cubism—but
> both he and Trotzky [*sic*] recognized the importance of preserving works
> of art, however ruthless they may have been in the destruction of human
> lives. The fact that the Winter Palace was not sacked after its capture in
> 1917 is strong evidence of the discipline—and historical consciousness—
> of the men who directed the October Revolution at its very inception.[4]

Barr praises Lenin and Trotsky for preserving works of art rather than, in the manner of previous revolutionaries, defiling them. In this sense, Barr follows the pro-Soviet tone of the Boston Museum of Fine Arts, which presented an exhibition of Russian icons in 1930 and declared, "The Soviet revolution made all the icons of the Greek Church the property of the Russian government and the government undertook immediately to collect and care for them. They have been swept into the various museums but in most cases not before they have passed through the Central National Restoration Workshops which have been set up at Moscow within the walls of the Kremlin."[5]

Where both Barr and the *Bulletin of the Museum of Fine Arts* present the Soviet government as benevolent in their treatment of religious art, alternative accounts offer a starkly different version of the same history. Writing in the *Art Journal* in 1961–

THE ARTS

WHERE SHALL WE PUT LAUTREC? BY DANIEL
CATTON RICH—RUSSIAN ICONS BY ALFRED
H. BARR, JR.—MUSIC—BOOKS—EXHIBITIONS

50 cents a copy   **FEBRUARY, 1931**   *$4.00 a year*

PUBLISHED NINE TIMES A YEAR, FROM OCTOBER TO JUNE INCLUSIVE

FIGURE 11.1. Cover, *The Arts* 17, no. 5 (February 1931).

1962 (which is to say, in the midst of the Cold War), the American scholar Leo
Teholiz wrote, "The Bolsheviks ravaged the churches in Russia after the 1918 October
Revolution. They burned, pillaged, destroyed, and confiscated church property, including hundreds of objects of religious art. Icons were defaced and defiled. The Bolsheviks originally set out to destroy and trample into the ground all 'religion' but only
managed to scratch the surface during the period of the 1920's."[6] Though Barr's article
mentions the "ruthless . . . destruction of human lives," it does not dwell on the dispar-
ity between the preservation of religious icons by the Soviet state and its persecution
of religious clergy, including the imprisonment, torture, and execution of more than a
thousand priests in the years following the Revolution. While the revolutionaries are
lauded for their "discipline and historical consciousness," the church is repeatedly crit-

icized for its "general indifference . . . toward the artistic and archaeological value of its icons and frescoes," an indifference that was made manifest in the "oily soot" that blackened the paintings over centuries of exposure to candlelight and oil lamps in poorly ventilated churches.[7] Throughout the article Barr positions the icons as aesthetic objects in need of study and preservation. In one stroke, he effectively removes them from the multisensory practices they activated in their ecclesiastical contexts and frames their intended religious function as antimodern and uncivilized. On his account, the church's "neglect" of the art formerly in its care stands in for wider practices of barbarism:

> Whatever one's religious beliefs, it can scarcely be denied that the Russian church from a social point of view often worked for evil. It encouraged superstition of the most primitive order. Icons were worshipped almost as fetishes and employed for all manner of magical as well as devotional purposes. Rasputin's power would have been impossible in a more enlightened religious tradition. Politically the church as a body was often aligned with the forces of oppression. As late as 1912 the entire clergy of the country was mobilized by the government in an attempt to suppress liberal tendencies in the Duma elections. These facts are not irrelevant when one learns of certain objections raised against the exhibition of icons now on view at the Metropolitan Museum.[8]

The Soviet government organized this Metropolitan Museum show of Russian icons at the request of the Boston Museum of Fine Arts, where the exhibition was mounted prior to its presentation in New York's premier art museum. Legal challenges from the American government nearly precluded the exhibition from being seen in either museum because, as Barr notes, "So far as our State Department is concerned, the Russian Government is officially non-existent."[9]

In both Boston and New York, the exhibition provoked protests among Russian-born Americans (many of whom had fled or been forced into exile after the Revolution), who argued that the icons had been confiscated illegally by a godless regime. In its coverage of the protests, the *New York Times* cited a letter sent by the National League of Americans of Russian Origin to the president and trustees of the Metropolitan Museum. The letter posed the following questions to the museum's board: "Do you realize with whom you are trafficking when borrowing the Russian icons from what some people choose to call the Soviet Government? Can you fully grasp the measure of indignation which policies of this sort arouse in the minds of right-thinking Russians?"[10]

The Metropolitan's official response avoided the ethical issues raised by the questionable provenance of the icons. The museum insisted that the works were secular rather than sacred ("These icons are old paintings. They come from various museums and galleries in Russian cities. Some of them have long been museum pieces illustrating the history of Russian art"). From reading the Metropolitan's letter, one would hardly know that these objects ever had a religious function at all. The assistant director of the Metropolitan, Joseph Breck, likewise told the *New York Times* that the American public was fortunate to have "an extraordinary opportunity to see a large exhibition of Russian icons hitherto practically impossible to see outside Russia. To those of us who have never studied in Russia, they come as practically an unknown art." Breck situates the icons within the realm of visual study and aesthetic contemplation. Notice how the sensory appeal of the icons is reduced to a strictly visual form of attention. Breck continues, "The icons carry on the tradition of Byzantine art and are especially notable for their beauty of color and pattern and the richness of their gold ornamentation."[11] Color, pattern, and ornamentation are prized in their own right, all but abstracted from the holy purpose to which they were originally put.

In his article on Russian icons, Barr bluntly criticized the double standard whereby those who objected to the exhibition at the Metropolitan Museum "have continued to tolerate the presence in our museums of Flemish, Spanish, and Italian primitives, many of which were removed from their original chapels by none too pious means." Barr further denounced the protestors as "for the most part counter-revolutionary Russians from whom sympathetic interest can scarcely be expected."[12]

Given that Barr has often been characterized as apolitical (or, more precisely, as depoliticizing) in his approach to modern art, his defense of Soviet cultural policy in 1931 comes as something of a surprise. The urgency of Barr's voice in the "Russian Icons" essay may be attributed in part to the recentness of his firsthand encounter with Soviet culture. Barr's 1927–1928 trip to Moscow and Leningrad involved a dynamic engagement with contemporary art, film, theater, and artists but also with medieval religious icons. As scholar Sybil Kantor has noted, "Barr's diary has as many entries on viewing icons as on viewing modern art."[13] During the trip Barr visited several collections of Russian icons and sought out reproductions of them for research and teaching purposes. By his own account, he grew increasingly "eager to see and talk icons; a great new field is opening up, if only material (books and photographs) were available here. I spent the afternoon in a vain hunt for books. Found a set of Grabar [Igor Grabar's multivolume *History of Russian Art*] for 40 rubles but the plates are bad."[14]

Barr found better reproductions when he visited the Soviet Central State Restoration Workshops, the government agency charged with the study and restoration of prerevolutionary art.[15] Barr was especially impressed by "the recovery of ikons which goes on from year to year since the founding of the state laboratory by Igor Grabar. The cleaning methods resemble [the] Fogg's enlightened policy." This was high praise from Barr given that the conservation practices of the Harvard museum (which Barr knew well from his doctoral studies) were among the most advanced in the world at the time. Barr notes the irony of the fact that the Russian conservation of the icon paintings had been "made possible through the anti-religious policy of the Soviet [state]."[16] Rather than destroying the icons as counter-revolutionary, Grabar and his workshops repurposed them as part of the cultural heritage of a newly secularized, nonreligious nation. The icons were meant both to celebrate the visual brilliance of Russian culture and to stand, by way of contrast, as a sign of the premodern past that the Soviets had transcended.

In addition to repairing the icons and in some cases attributing them to an individual hand for the first time, the Restoration Institute also produced copies of particularly important or fragile works (Figure 11.2). According to Barr, "Six of the oldest and most valuable icons are represented in the exhibition [at the Metropolitan] by copies which are technically miraculous. They were made within the last four years by the same expert craftsmen who cleaned the originals."[17]

It is no longer the icons themselves but rather the technical perfection of their twentieth-century copies that qualifies, from Barr's perspective, as "miraculous." In the exhibition catalog, Grabar (who organized the show on behalf of the Soviet government) expanded on the wondrous effect of the facsimiles:

> These copies have not been made in the usual way. They constitute a new
> type of archaeological facsimile; for they reproduce exactly not only the
> general character of the originals and the impression conveyed by them,
> but their whole make-up, their structure, their technical peculiarities, even
> their defects, and this at the exact stage of exposure to which the originals
> have been brought. A copy of this kind may almost be said to replace the
> original; when the two have been compared, it has often been impossible
> for experts and students of ancient Russian to distinguish the copy from
> the original.[18]

The almost perfect copy might also be said to be an almost perfect displacement of the work's original multisensory devotional function. The "expert craftsmen" who made painted facsimiles of the icons after the 1917 Revolution were doing so in the name of socialist policy, not religious practice. In effect, the communist state sought to uncouple the icons from their sacred context and use and present them, newly restored and museum ready, as the rightful patrimony of the Soviet people.[19]

After devoting the first third of his essay to the fate of Russian icons since the Revolution, Barr offers a stylistic history of their development from the eleventh century through the seventeenth. In tracing this history he does not argue for the works as sources for modernist painting—whether by Malevich, Matisse, or any number of other artists for whom such a connection might be adduced. "Russian Icons" pro-

FIGURE 11.2. *The Vladimir* Mother of God, twentieth-century copy by Bryagin of eleventh-century icon, Figure 1 in Barr, "Russian Icons," *The Arts* 17, no. 5 (February 1931).

poses no genealogy of modernism. For Barr at this point, at any rate, the twentieth-century relevance of the icons resided not in their stylistic influence on contemporary art but in their material and symbolic reclamation by the Soviet state. The socialist repurposing of prerevolutionary painting provided the contemporary context for Barr's art-historical analysis.

Barr concludes the essay by discussing a work from his own collection that bridges the gap between premodern past and postrevolutionary present—an enamel box top painted in the Stroganov style of a seventeenth-century Russian icon (Figure 11.3). "The subject," Barr writes "is the Soviet Trinity—Soldier, Worker, and Peasant—surrounded by factory chimneys and Fordson tractors (but they are really St. Theodore the Stratelate, St. Demetrius of Thessalonika, and St. Nicholas of Myra, unwittingly masquerading in honor of St. Marx)."[20] Though refashioned into a properly proletarian subject, the painted box top brings with it the imprint of religious iconography that cannot be entirely stamped out. Purchased on the street for a few rubles by an American visitor to Moscow in 1928, the box top bespeaks the persistence of the prerevolutionary past in the (then-)present moment. The saints "mas-

FIGURE 11.3. *The Soviet Trinity—Soldier, Worker, and Peasant,* enamel box top, Figure 19 in Barr, "Russian Icons," *The Arts* 17, no. 5 (February 1931).

querading in honor of St. Marx" embody Soviet political ideology even as they point back to the history of the Russian Orthodox Church and its devotional practices.

Finally, it is worth remembering that these figures were reproduced in the pages of an American art magazine and that Barr's English-language commentary on them was occasioned by the concurrent exhibition at the Metropolitan Museum of Art. The works on display in the exhibition could not be extricated from the political and interpretive conflicts they provoked in 1931. The history of Russian icons from the eleventh century through the seventeenth was still being written—and rewritten—in the twentieth.

NOTES

1. Alexander Nagel and Christopher S. Wood, *Anachronic Renaissance* (New York: Zone, 2010), 9.

2. Thomas Crow, "The Practice of Art History in America," *Daedalus* 135, no. 2 (Spring 2006): 70–71.

3. Alfred H. Barr Jr., "Russian Icons," *The Arts* 17, no. 5 (February 1931): 297–313, 355–362, quotation from 297.

4. Ibid., 297

5. P.H., "The Exhibition of Russian Icons," *Bulletin of the Museum of Fine Arts* 18, no. 169 (October 1930): 90.

6. See Leo Teholiz, "Religious Mysticism and Socialist Realism: The Soviet Union Pays Homage to the Icon Painter Andrey Rublev," *Art Journal* 21, no. 2 (Winter 1961–1962): 76.

7. Barr, "Russian Icons," 303.

8. Ibid.

9. Barr credits the American Russian Institute with overcoming these challenges by "courageously assum[ing] legal responsibility" for the show. Ibid.

10. Letter from J. J. Lissitzyn, general secretary of the National League of Americans of Russian Origin, to the president and trustees of the Metropolitan Museum, as cited in "Russian Icon Show Stirs New Protest," *New York Times,* January 11, 1931, 36.

11. Ibid.

12. Barr, "Russian Icons," 303.

13. Sybil Kantor, *Alfred H. Barr, Jr. and the Intellectual Origins of the Museum of Modern Art* (Cambridge, MA: MIT Press), 165.

14. Barr, "Russian Diary," as quoted in Kantor, *Alfred H. Barr, Jr.,* 165.

15. During their visits to workshops, Barr and Abbott purchased multiple photographs of icons, several of which were used to illustrate Barr's 1931 essay in *The Arts.*

16. Letter from Alfred Barr to Paul Sachs, as cited in Sybil Kantor, *Alfred H. Barr, Jr.,* 164.

17. Barr, "Russian Icons," 305.

18. Igor Grabar, "Introduction: Ancient Russian Painting," in *A Catalogue of Russian Icons Received from the American Russian Institute for Exhibition* (New York: Metropolitan Museum of Art, 1931), xi–xii.

19. Teholiz describes the complex process whereby religious icons could be repurposed as Soviet cultural patrimony: "From one point of view, the Soviet authorities seem to allay their fears and direct concern about the deceptive and fraudulent quality of religion, and from another viewpoint, religious art really was not 'reactionary,' or an 'opiate,' but instead it could be appreciated as a work of art. It could be discussed as an example of a national folk art and appreciated for its decorative beauty, elements of design and harmony of color; and the church buildings and other historical monuments acknowledged as fine examples of the building tradition of the Russian nation. It might even be possible to link together the past and the present: the development of past art forms, trends, styles in the different arts, the folk art, monumental art, religious art, applied art, architecture, sculpture and the fine arts, to show how all of these ultimately evolved through the centuries into what is today considered "the people's art"—the art of socialist-realism. In the final process of its development, those qualities which the Soviets consider decadent, formalistic and bourgeois would have been conveniently cast off." Teholiz, "Religious Mysticism and Socialist Realism," 77.

20. Barr, "Russian Icons," 362.

12

Sonic Differences
Listening to the Adhan *in a Pluralistic America*

ISAAC WEINER

It should have been a mere formality. In 2006 Steve Elturk, president of the Islamic Organization of North America, planned to convert an existing office building in Warren, Michigan, into a mosque and Islamic education center, but he first had to obtain a variance from the city's Zoning Board of Appeals. What should have been a relatively straightforward process dragged on for months as city officials manufactured numerous reasons to deny Elturk's request. At a series of public Planning Commission hearings in March and April, standing-room-only crowds gathered to voice their opposition to the proposed center. Their complaints ranged from objections to noise and traffic to more amorphous concerns about how the mosque would affect the character of the neighborhood. One irate resident even went so far as to issue a warning that worship at the mosque might include animal sacrifice. Sharing these concerns, the planning commissioners delayed voting on Elturk's application for as long as they could, until they were forced to relent under threat of litigation and a U.S. Justice Department investigation. Even then, they attached one final condition to their approval. Elturk would have to agree never to install a loudspeaker or other amplificatory device to the building for the purpose of broadcasting the Islamic call to prayer. Though he had never expressed any intention to do so, the city officials went out of their way to make clear that they would not put up with any noise. Sound marked the limit of what they would tolerate.[1]

The Warren case was far from an isolated incident. The *adhan,* or Islamic call to prayer, echoes as one of the most distinctive features of Islamic cities and towns with its interruption of daily routines five times a day. But in the pluralistic spaces of American public life, it has often emerged as a source of contention. Zoning boards have regularly used concerns about noise to block the construction of new Islamic centers. Many American Muslim leaders have responded, like Steve Elturk, by forswearing any intent to broadcast the adhan publicly. "It's not a critically important aspect of our faith," Victor Begg, the founder of the Muslim Unity Center in West Bloomfield, Michigan, explained. "In these days and times, we've got enough problems. I don't know why we should bring on unnecessary ones." Like many American mosques, the Muslim Unity Center has turned its loudspeakers inward, avoiding unwelcome attention by incorporating the adhan into its communal prayer service.[2]

Other American Muslims have insisted more strongly on the importance of broadcasting the call to prayer publicly. In 1979 the leaders of a mosque in Dearborn, Michigan, even went to court to defend their right to amplify the adhan after neighbors complained to the police. They argued that their practice was "in strict accordance with the tenets of the Moslem faith" and thus protected under the First Amendment of the U.S. Constitution. They accused the complaining neighbors of anti-Islamic bigotry. The neighbors insisted that their complaints had nothing to do with religion. They claimed to be upset because the adhan regularly awakened them early in the morning, and they saw no reason to treat it differently from any other source of acoustic annoyance, whether religious or not. Here, as in many cases, it proved exceedingly difficult to distinguish "legitimate" complaints about noise from "illegitimate" complaints about particular noisemakers. In his decision Judge Thomas J. Brennan tried to strike a compromise by requiring the city to define noise more precisely in terms of an exact decibel measurement, but the mosque's leaders later complained that city officials had selected a maximum level that they knew would restrain broadcast of the prayer call. Once again, sound marked the limit of what an American community proved willing to tolerate.[3]

In some cases, however, the adhan has met with approval as well as opposition. In the small city of Hamtramck, Michigan, an independent political entity almost completely surrounded by Detroit, a mosque generated controversy in 2004 when it petitioned the Common Council for permission to broadcast the call to prayer. A historically Polish-Catholic enclave, Hamtramck has received an influx of Muslims over the past few decades. Despite vocal opposition from some of the city's long-time residents, the Common Council decided to rewrite its antinoise ordinance in order to expressly exempt the adhan and other "reasonable means of announcing religious services" from its provisions. Citing their commitment to multiculturalism, toleration, and religious freedom, council members went out of their way to accommodate its broadcast. And in an unusual special election, Hamtramck residents ultimately voted to affirm the council's action, a decision that was invested with great symbolic significance. In fact, over the course of the Hamtramck dispute, the adhan became as much a symbol of American-style pluralism as a normatively sanctioned Islamic ritual. This public auditory practice came to offer an important means for Hamtramck Muslims to claim a place for themselves *as Muslims* in their new community.[4]

These disparate examples, from the same metropolitan area, indicate that the adhan has elicited a wide range of responses when broadcast in American cities, and disputes about its public call have played out in different ways. But despite their varied outcomes, these cases all indicate how central auditory practices have been to the ongoing project of negotiating religion's sensory and material place in American society. When Americans have managed their religious differences, they frequently have done so in response to particular sonic manifestations. As sounds such as church bells and prayer calls have emanated from the more traditional spaces to which modern religion has been confined, they have been heard by diverse listening audiences, who have interpreted their meaning and message in very different ways. When residents in Warren, Dearborn, or Hamtramck encountered Islam, they did so not as an intellectual abstraction but as a set of particular embodied practices and material engagements. For them, responding to religious diversity was not a matter of resolving theological or doctrinal differences, as scholarship on religious pluralism has often presented it, but of engaging with different kinds of religious mediations, of making sense of the new sounds that were entering their shared city streets.

Past studies of sensory religion have paid particular attention to visual displays of public piety. These cases offer a critical reminder that as we work to recapture the multisensoriality of contemporary religious life, we must attend to sound alongside other forms of sensory and material mediation. We still have much to learn about the auditory modes through which Americans have publicly practiced their faith and about how these sonic practices have mediated contact among diverse religious adherents. Surely it is true that the senses cannot easily be segregated, especially in the case of religion, and my attention to sound is meant neither to diminish the importance of sight nor to suggest that the two stand in mutual opposition. Yet it is also important to consider why sound has so often marked the limit of what communities have been willing to tolerate. What is it about the particular properties of sound that have made it so conducive to conflict?[5]

In the adhan disputes discussed above, complainants repeatedly described sound as distinctly transgressive, as particularly difficult to contain or to control. While neighbors could choose whether to enter a house of worship, they felt as though they could not regulate what they heard in public places. They could not choose whether to join the acoustic community constituted by the adhan's call. As this religious sound spilled over into city streets, it crossed and collapsed the symbolically significant boundaries between public and private, broadcaster and receiver, self and other, in ways that seemed to distinguish it from visual displays. Sociologist Nilüfer Göle has described the minaret and the veil as the "mute symbols of Islam," silently attesting to Islamic public presence.[6] But the adhan called out to passersby, soliciting their attention and demanding some kind of response. Although neighbors might have been able to shut their eyes to the growing diversification of their communities, they did not think that they could shut their ears quite so easily. They could not maintain their distance. "Vision is a spectator," the American pragmatist John Dewey once wrote, "hearing is a participator."[7]

Some non-Muslim listeners responded enthusiastically to the adhan precisely for this reason. They interpreted its call as a challenge to reach out to and actively engage with their new neighbors, to forge new relationships across religious boundaries. Religious polyphony might be loud, they maintained, but it need not sound cacophonous. For them, living in a diverse society required one to put up with a little bit of noise. Others went even further and expressed their hope that Christians, too, might learn to hear the adhan as an invitation to pray. "Wouldn't it be great if all of us practiced our faith in the way that our new neighbors are?" a Hamtramck civic activist asked me.[8] In this aural display of public piety, she heard not a threat to be contained but a model to be emulated. As its sound spilled over onto Hamtramck's streets, she hoped that her Christian coreligionists might respond, too, not as eavesdroppers but as active listeners. It was precisely its insistent demand for attention, she seemed to imply, that gave the adhan its power. For these enthusiasts, the adhan could generate a space for reconfiguring and reimagining collective identities, for promoting more pluralistic visions of common life.

For its opponents, on the other hand, the adhan was something to be resisted precisely on account of its propensity to cross social and geographic boundaries. When neighbors complained about the adhan as noise, they asked the civic authorities to protect them from unwanted exposure to religious difference. Their complaints aimed to reinscribe the imagined lines that separated discrete religious communities from each other and to reinforce a clear distinction between self and other. Noise restrictions offered them a means of policing religion's boundaries and containing the threat posed by sound's promiscuousness. When religion grew too loud, they suggested, it could become mere noise, and thus subject to careful regulation.

Even as they sought to silence the adhan, however, their complaints often had the unintended effect of making more audible the sounds of their own religious practices. That is, the adhan was often compared to church bells, and this analogy invited the adhan's opponents to note that Christians, too, had their own ways of publicly broadcasting their faiths. Disputes about the adhan inevitably became as much about different forms of auditory practice, therefore, as about whether religion should be kept quiet altogether. These controversies forced Christian complainants to pay greater attention to their own particular material engagements and sensory forms. In other words, if part of what it means to be a religious modern is to progress from material practice to inward belief, these disputes offered yet another reminder that, to paraphrase Bruno Latour, we have perhaps never been as modern as we presumed.[9]

1. Steve Elturk, interview by author, July 24, 2007, and Minutes of the Planning Commission of Warren, Michigan, March 13, 2006.

2. Victor Begg, interview by author, July 23, 2007.

3. *Dearborn v. Hussian et al.,* no. 79-933979-AR (Wayne County Ct., June 3, 1980), and Mary Klemic, "Moslems Protest Curb on Noise," *Dearborn* (MI) *Times-Herald,* November 6, 1980.

4. In the broader book project on which this chapter is based, I analyze the Hamtramck dispute in greater depth. I also trace a longer history of complaints about religious noise in the United States. See Isaac Weiner, *Religion Out Loud: Religious Sound, Public Space, and American Pluralism* (New York: New York University Press, 2014).

5. On the study of sound and religion in America, see Isaac Weiner, "Sound and American Religions," *Religion Compass* 3, no. 5 (September 2009): 897–908. See also Weiner, "Sound," in "Key Words in Material Religion," special issue, *Material Religion* 7, no. 1 (2011): 108–115.

6. Nilüfer Göle, "Mute Symbols of Islam," *Immanent Frame,* January 13, 2010, accessed September 20, 2011, http://blogs.ssrc.org/tif/2010/01/13/mute-symbols/.

7. John Dewey, *The Public and Its Problems* (New York: H. Holt, 1927), 219.

8. Sharon Buttry, interview by author, October 30, 2007.

9. Bruno Latour, *We Have Never Been Modern* (Cambridge, MA: Harvard University Press, 1993).

13

Art and Sensory Contention in a Christian Seminary

KATHRYN REKLIS

*T*he Institute for Art, Religion, and Social Justice is a project of Union Theological Seminary that AA Bronson and I founded in 2009. The institute's mission is to explore the relationship between art and religion through the lens of social justice by commissioning and supporting contemporary art projects and practices. Since its founding the institute has sponsored two site-specific exhibitions, two lecture series, two performance events, and three artist residencies. In what follows, I reflect on some of the challenges and unexpected serendipities of staging artistic projects in a residential Christian seminary.

We launched our first project, an exhibition titled *compassion,* on-site on November 19, 2009, and it was on view until January 14, 2010. Artists Marina Abramović, Bas Jan Ader, Michael Bühler-Rose, Alfredo Jaar, Terence Koh, Gareth Long, Yoko Ono, Paul Mpagi Sepuya, Chrysanne Stathacos, and Scott Treleaven exhibited work curated by AA Bronson, who situated the art in various locations around the buildings of Union Theological Seminary. To see the entire exhibit required the visitor to undertake a kind of artistic and ritual pilgrimage through the often-overlooked historic buildings (Figure 13.1).

Perhaps due to naïveté or simply willed ignorance on our part, we were surprised at the reactions our first exhibition generated. The frenzy of mounting the exhibition and planning the opening and closing receptions took the place of more measured consideration of what would happen in between the two receptions: namely, that a residential seminary community would interact with these pieces in the flow of daily life. Or rather, they would encounter these pieces and choose to interact with them, to resist them, to protest them, or to incorporate them into their mundane experiences.

FIGURE 13.1. Chrysanne Stathacos, *Rose Mandala Mirror (Three Reflections for HHDL),* 2006. Glass, mirror, roses, dimensions variable. Courtesy of Matthias Herrmann. Part of the exhibition *compassion,* curated by AA Bronson for the Institute for Art, Religion, and Social Justice at Union Theological Seminary, New York, November 2009–January 2010, seen from the top of the seminary's rotunda staircase.

One of the most controversial pieces was, tellingly, perhaps one of the least viewed. Michael Bühler-Rose contributed a video installation, *I'll Worship You, You'll Worship Me* (2009), which recorded a Hindu bathing ritual performed on a glass front facing the camera so that the experience of the viewer was as the object of the ritual purification (Figure 13.2). It played on a loop on a small flat-screen TV on the second floor of the seminary rotunda, really a small landing on part of a grand spiral staircase at what used to be the seminary's main entrance. This is an out-of-the-way spot. Few actually used the stairs during the exhibition because the entrance at the foot of them was closed to the public at the time. On the floor above the landing is a hallway lined with classrooms, and on the ground floor just across from the staircase is the entrance to the library. Many people traverse these spaces, but few would find their way past the video to view it unless they were to go there deliberately. But the film had sound: the very distinct sound of ritual bells rung persistently, a kind of incessant liturgical chant. We received more complaints about the bells than about any other piece. It was fairly obvious that most of the people complaining had not actually bothered to see the work, because almost no one mentioned its religious content; they simply complained about, or demanded an end to, the "noise."

The bells in the video were a kind of aural intrusion into the expected sensory atmosphere of the seminary. The work was disruptive not so much because it was a depiction of a Hindu ritual in a Christian space (though AA received at least one direct

FIGURE 13.2. Michael Bühler-Rose, *I'll Worship You, You'll Worship Me,* 2009. Single-channel DVD version, 12 minutes. Courtesy of Michael Bühler-Rose. Still image from a video installation that was part of the exhibition *compassion,* curated by AA Bronson for the Institute for Art, Religion, and Social Justice at Union Theological Seminary, New York, November 2009–January 2010.

complaint about the "pagan" video) but because it disrupted the expected order of an educational space. Seminarians could hear the bells every time they entered or exited the library and when walking between classes. Although the bells were not audible inside the library or a closed classroom, their presence in these transitional moments confused, or even angered, unsuspecting passersby. This sense of communal frustration was only compounded by the fact that few people actually knew what they were hearing. However, some must have taken the time to track down the offending sound, because we had a daily battle with unknown antagonists who turned the volume down or off. It became a kind of regularly repeated ritual for us to walk by the video and return the volume to its intended setting.

The freedom that members of the seminary community apparently felt to "adjust" the exhibition was another completely unexpected challenge of working in a nontraditional exhibition space. Marina Abramović exhibited another film installation, *8 Lessons on Emptiness with a Happy End* (2008), which was run on a loop off DVD on a large flat-screen TV mounted directly opposite the main chapel doors in what serves as a narthex or lobby space. The film had minimal sound and depicted a group of Thai child soldiers playing "war" inside and outside a small cabin, ending with a bonfire of their rifles (Figure 13.3). The screen fit perfectly into a nook that bore a memorial plaque in honor of the chapel's benefactor. Most of the plaque was obscured by the screen, except for the words, etched in stone, "For the Glory of God," which were perfectly framed above the screen. Although we did not know ahead of time that Abramović's work would fit so well in this space, the unintended irony of the juxtaposition added significantly to the experience of the work and lent it a "religious" valence that it did not possess in and of itself.

The presence of the screen so close to the chapel, moreover, made it unavoidable by anyone entering or exiting the space and created other unintended juxtapositions for members of the worshiping communities who met there. Union students would turn the video off because it interfered with their experience of daily chapel, and we agreed to close the exhibit on Sundays because other religious groups rented the chapel for services and did not want the video playing during their services. In this case, the content of the video did come up against the theological identity of the space. But the contestation of the space was less about content than, as in the case of Bühler-Rose's video, about disruptions of experience.

It is interesting to compare Abramović's video and its perceived intrusions into the liturgical or theological space of the chapel with the installation that shared the narthex space. Yoko Ono exhibited *Whisper Piece* (2001), a set of six white one-by-one-inch pin-on buttons that each bore one of the words *Breathe, Dream, Remember, Respira, Sueña, Recuerda*. The artist donated three thousand of these buttons, and we displayed them in a simple wooden bowl on a simple wooden stand directly in the middle of the narthex equidistant between the chapel doors and Abramović's video

FIGURE 13.3. Background: Marina Abramović, *8 Lessons on Emptiness with a Happy End,* 2008. Video, color, sound. Courtesy of Sean Kelly Gallery, New York. Middle ground: Yoko Ono, *Whisper Piece,* 2001. Set of six buttons, each 1 × 1 inch, with three thousand buttons displayed in a wooden bowl on a wooden stand. Courtesy of Matthias Herrmann. Two parts of the exhibition *compassion,* curated by AA Bronson for the Institute for Art, Religion, and Social Justice at Union Theological Seminary, New York, November 2009–January 2010, viewed from the seminary's chapel doors into the chapel narthex.

installation. A small sign encouraged visitors to take a button of their choice. No one in the community complained about this exhibit, and it was probably the work that was spoken of most appreciatively. Perhaps this was simply because Ono was the artist most people had heard of (I do not want to underestimate the "cool" factor in getting to take home a button by Yoko Ono as a souvenir from seminary). But I also think it was least protested because it was least intrusive to the expected sensory experience of the space. A simple wooden bowl set on a simple wooden stand in the middle of a narthex looks like a bowl that might hold holy water at the entry to a Catholic church. Regular participants in liturgical forms of Christian worship would not be surprised to find something of that size and shape in that particular setting. On approaching it, they might be surprised to discover buttons instead of water, but even the physical gesture of dipping one's hand into the bowl and retrieving a button would not be unlike that of blessing oneself with holy water.

I do not mean to imply that the content of the works displayed did not cause alarm. We left two books at different points along the pilgrimage where people could leave comments, and we had a few like "What does this have to do with Jesus?" But for the most part, the objections that seminary members expressed were directed toward the sensory and material aspects of the exhibition: what the art sounded and looked like, where it was spatially located, how it interacted with the other material and sensory expectations of the space. These concerns may have masked deeper uneasiness with the content of the artwork, but they also spoke directly to the challenges of presenting work in a nontraditional context. And this was not just any nontraditional context but that of a residential, multidenominational, Christian seminary. People live, work, study, and worship at Union, which means that they respond to the many uses of the space differently than they would if the space had only one use. What felt disruptive or out of place outside the chapel may not have been noticed in an administrative corridor; what frustrated library users coming and going late at night may have been tolerated in the much noisier refectory.

We have less direct insight into what nonseminary visitors experienced when they walked through the exhibition, but one has to imagine that the specific setting substantively reshaped the experience. One might have had to wander a considerable way through some confusing administrative wings to discover a rather small print by Paul Sepuya containing two head-and-shoulders images of a young white male emerging from a faded white background, with a black hand resting on his shoulder in one image and on his forehead and left eye in the other. When found, it appeared modestly hung in a simple fashion between two administrative offices, so the visitor stood there looking at it, perhaps overhearing a conversation about financial aid or new budget software. If visitors explored the exhibit during lunch hours, they would have had to linger on the edges of the refectory where students were eating lunch to appreciate AA Bronson and Terence Koh's exhibit, a short text describing an action in which a white dove is released into the refectory rafters (each of us witnessed guests and seminary residents searching for the dove). Occasionally a small group of visitors would stand in front of the Abramović video while the gospel choir led chapel behind them—or they might have arrived at that installation only to discover that the chapel leaders had turned the video off!

If these strange sensory and spatial juxtapositions challenged seminary members and spectators to think about the space and art they were encountering differently, so much more did these experiments change the way the artists themselves think about their work. We intentionally invited artists who do not usually describe their work as "religious" or "spiritual" to participate in our programming. In accepting our invitation, they embraced the challenge to think about their work—and experience talking about their work—in a different way. We noticed this difference most explicitly in the two lecture series we hosted (in the fall of 2010 and the spring of 2012). Though we had little success in turning out many audience members from the seminary (indeed, most of our audience was composed of art students from the downtown art schools and Columbia as well as the broader artist community of New York City), the visiting artists expected to speak to a "seminary audience" in a "seminary space." We did not usually tell them that few seminary students would probably be there! Many artists have told us that talking in this space, however they construed it in their imaginations, was the most interesting work they had done recently. The opportunity to think differently was a kind of nonsectarian grace they had not even known they were seeking.

We have tried not to assume that we know what kinds of new interactions, commonalities, or alliances might be formed between "art" and "religion." We have tried to avoid any of the formalist or metaphysical claims that both are the heritage and were the downfall of many earlier conversations about art and religion. By focusing on "social justice" as a motivation and theme for both artists and religious practitioners, we have tried to clear space for the unexpected, including the controversial and the illuminating. Often in our work, as in other spaces, contemporary "art" and "religion" have circled around each other warily, missing each other just as I always seemed to miss the unnamed malefactor who kept turning off the volume on Bühler-Rose's video. I suspect part of these spatial and sensory disconnects occurred because many seminarians are more comfortable speaking about God than about art. Maybe I should have simply sat in a chair and waited all day so I could finally talk to my "noise offender." Maybe we could have productively conversed about art and divinity and social justice. Or at least we might have settled on some happy volume for the chanting of the Hindu bathing ritual.

14

Complicated Candy

Sensory Approaches to the Controversy over Sweet Jesus

HORACE D. BALLARD JR.

On March 30, 2007, artist Cosimo Cavallaro confronted William Donohue, the president of the Catholic League, on CNN's *Anderson Cooper 360°*. The object of contention was *Sweet Jesus* (Figure 14.1), Cavallaro's six-foot-tall chocolate sculpture of a crucified nude. *Sweet Jesus* was to have been the focal point of an installation called *My Sweet Lord,* to be displayed in the window of THE LAB Gallery in midtown Manhattan.[1] As taxis, tourists, and theatergoers rambled past during the last week of Lent, *Sweet Jesus* would serve as a reminder of the approaching Christian feast day of Easter. But within forty-eight hours of Donohue's learning of the installation, Cavallaro received death threats, the exhibition was scrapped, and Matt Semler, creative director of THE LAB, resigned his position after summing up Donohue's statements as "a Catholic fatwa." Edward Cardinal Egan, archbishop of the Archdiocese of New York, condemned the "ugliness" of *My Sweet Lord* as "one of the worst assaults on Christian sensibilities ever."[2]

Neither the public nor objectors saw *Sweet Jesus.* Knowledge of the installation was conveyed solely through fiery rhetoric, the same kind of blind bombast that had propelled Donohue's protest of Chris Ofili's *Holy Virgin Mary* in 2000. It thus seems appropriate to view the controversy over *Sweet Jesus* as an equally important event in the ongoing conversation surrounding the public display of artistic work deemed religious in the contemporary moment.

Donohue's outbursts mentioned none of the specifics of the installation's display. Molded from two hundred pounds of Swiss chocolate and suspended by clear wire over the outline of a cross chalked on the floor, *Sweet Jesus* was to be visible for just seven hours during Holy Week: one hour per day, from 6 p.m. to 7 p.m. On Easter Sunday, the installation would be on view from midnight to 1:00 a.m. to mark the moment when many Christians believe an angel rolled the stone away from the

FIGURE 14.1. Cosimo Cavallaro, *Sweet Jesus,* 2005. Dark Swiss chocolate, 6 feet tall. Courtesy of Sarah Cavallaro.

mouth of Jesus's tomb. Although detractors claimed that the nude statue would be in plain view of children passing to and from school and that millions would be shocked as they passed by the statue unexpectedly on their way to work, these critiques were unfounded. Proactively censored for its perceived public indecency, *Sweet Jesus* would have proved rather demure. Thus the first question we might ask regarding the installation is, what was the big deal?

In a volume on sensory religion and material practice, one useful approach is to position Cavallaro's installation within the sociopolitical history of food art. During the mid-nineteenth century, food became a familiar medium for public sculpture in the United States. Chef d'oeuvres of butter, sugar, corn, fruit, and other agricultural products at national fairs and international exhibitions helped advance ideologies of American exceptionalism and bounty.[3] Food sculpture at the turn of the twentieth century signified the Americas' growing prestige as global economic engines. In the wake of the Spanish-American War, for example, patriotic propaganda declared the reconciled United States "'a new Eden': a garden so fertile it could feed the world." Food art bore testimony to this gospel of progress.[4] Conversely, the display of agricultural abundance *to be seen but not eaten* made visible cultural anxieties surrounding U.S. policies on industrial versus agricultural labor, neoimperialism, national determinism, and shifting categories of citizenship.

Cavallaro, an artist who had come to notoriety in the late 1990s for his public installations involving cheese, probably knew something about the history of food sculpture in the Americas. In fact, he made *Sweet Jesus* at a postmodern moment when numerous works of public art interrogated the relationships among politics, memory, and chocolate. In closest chronological proximity, the performance installations of Janine Antoni, April Banks, Song Dong, Gerhard Petzl, and Emma Staite traced the process from cacao berry to candy bar in order to epitomize the artist's task of creation within humanity's destructive commodification of the natural world. Did *Sweet Jesus* lay claim to similar critiques? What were Cavallaro's stated aims and intended functions for the statue and its installation?

The following exchange between Anderson Cooper and Cavallaro launched CNN's *360°* segment and provides clues to the artist's intentions:

> COOPER: Cosimo, I want to start by asking you what your intention was with—with this—this piece of art.
>
> CAVALLARO: My intention was to celebrate this body of Christ, and in a sweet, delicious, tasteful way.
>
> COOPER: Why—why use chocolate?
>
> CAVALLARO: Because it's a substance that I like. And it's sweet. And I felt that the body of Christ, the—the meaning of Christ, is about the sweetness.
>
> COOPER: Were you trying to shock, I mean, to—to cause attention? Often —usually, when Christ is shown, he's wearing some form of clothing. This is a naked Christ, which has also caused some concern.
>
> CAVALLARO: No more than the religion, the way they use it. I was just using it as an iconic figure. I mean, that my intention was to shock people? No. I was—my intention was to have them taste the—and feel what they're looking at in their mouth.[5]

Here a conversation beginning with a question about intentionality quickly shifted to one of sexual legibility and public decency. Though Cavallaro situated his intentions within the sensory affect of the work's medium, Cooper quickly bypassed materiality in favor of the ostensibly shocking: "a naked Christ." The statue's candied perishability disappeared from the view of the censor, subsumed in a firestorm over Jesus's penis. As Bryan Cones suggests, "Our modern obsession with genitalia prevents us from appreciating the full significance of [*Sweet Jesus*] and shuts down any intellectual conversation about this piece."[6] If we resituate chocolate at the heart of the controversy, approaching the work's medium not merely as foodstuff but as a complicated historic commodity, we come to the realization that chocolate was never *just* chocolate within the context of the work. For Cavallaro, chocolate was the vehicle for conveying the "sweetness" of divine love.

In a statement about the work, Cavallaro connected his personal experience of chocolate with "the mystical/transcendental quality and rushes of memory associated with the Catholic 'Wafer' received during Holy Communion."[7] By equating the communion wafer (a fascinating sculpted commodity in its own right) with chocolate, Cavallaro positioned *Sweet Jesus* within a Catholic discourse of theological transubstantiation, the process by which the Eucharistic elements are transposed from bread and wine to the edible flesh and blood of Christ. For Cavallaro, the contrition inspired by Christ's suffering was infused with the sensation of consuming chocolate: its taste, smell, and tactility. The sculpture became a visual metaphor for the words of the Psalmist: "Taste and see that the Lord is good" (Psalm 34:8). *Sweet Jesus* negotiated the poles of theological mystery and public art within a sociopolitical sensorium of secular political power and sacred ritual. In casting the sculpture as an exercise in "remembering," Cavallaro's *Imago Dei* turns the bittersweet blend of individual suffering and grace into public atonement. In the spatial geography of midtown Manhattan—an area of twenty-four-hour-a-day, seven-day-a-week, streaming information, crowds, street vendors, Wi-Fi visuality, multiple languages, and cultural transmissions of every degree—Cavallaro's decision to use a perishable, edible substance can be read as a desire to keep the enduring, miraculous nature of Christ's sacrifice center stage.

Nor should we discount chocolate's complicated global history. The chocolate we enjoy today is intrinsically "modern," bearing little resemblance to the thick, bitter medicine prepared by Meso-American women for priests, warriors, and guests in pre-Hispanic Mexico. From its first introduction into the Western market, chocolate existed as a transgendered, transnational substance with specific customs surrounding its preparation and enjoyment. Its colonial roots linked Meso-American communities with early modern Europe, pantheistic belief systems with Christianity, brown-skinned Central and South American laborers with lighter-skinned bourgeois consumers, and ecologically rich equatorial nations with the economic powers of Europe and North America. When the Spanish conquistadors arrived in the Americas, they brought with them a diet structured along lines of class and race. They recreated in New Spain a diet that duplicated the one they had known at home, "ensuring their continued good health, high status, and Christian consciences."[8] Indigenous foods gained acceptance among the elite only when they appeared to be Creole adaptations of Spanish dishes. With no prior Old World equivalent, chocolate was slow to be interpolated into the European diet. By the early seventeenth century, however, the Chinese porcelain trade, as well as the founding of European ceramic centers, spurred the process of modifying liquid cacao into melted chocolate by the addition of sugar and sweet spices, accompanied by new sets of hollowware and serving utensils. The beverage became fashionable among those at the pinnacle of New Spain's social hierarchy, and its popularity was transferred to the aristocratic classes of Europe when

New World elites returned to their mother country with their *mestizo* progeny and domestics.[9]

In the eighteenth and nineteenth centuries, the chocolate bar was popular with U.S. Army generals due to its caloric count and low cost. By World War I, chocolate had undergone a transformation in gender. The substance morphed from a drink or superfood prepared for (largely) male enjoyment to the focal point of an industry predicated on constructions of courtship, gift economies, childhood treats, and female consumption. Marketing campaigns in the first half of the twentieth century promoted chocolate as a tool that the well-heeled gallant used in the wooing of high-class women.[10] Chocolate's use as the object of exchange in a social transaction between men and women (in which the sex act proved the desired outcome) shifted the power of discretionary consumption to women.

Contemporary portrayals of chocolate consumption echo concerns over transgressive, sinful pleasure. Advertisements for chocolate are full of words such as "sin," "temptation," and "wickedness." A 1995 Suchard Chocolat ad with the caption "C'est une épreuve que le Seigneur nous envoie" (It is a test that the Lord sends us) affirmed that chocolate's associations with religion were alive and well. The film *Chocolat* (2000) brought chocolate and religion into conversation again as Cartesian dualities rather than as part of the synonymous relationship they share for Cavallaro. The film's ending declares chocolate a pleasurable, "safe sin," one that can "tame the heart of the every woman." This plot point becomes racially charged when we realize that the marketing of chocolate remains almost exclusively directed to middle-class white women.[11]

Though Cavallaro did not intend that audiences would eat *Sweet Jesus,* he insisted that viewers metaphorically "taste . . . and feel what they are looking at, in their mouth." Such an overt invitation to "digest" the cultural ramifications of the work proved too much for many critics. It was easier for some to disparage Cavallaro's grand gesture than to actively contemplate the rich interplay among commodity culture, spirituality, and fetish in the contemporary moment. *Sweet Jesus* could have been the catalyst for substantive conversations about phallocentric desire and feminine consumption. Instead, knowledge of chocolate's delicious pleasures turned critics into iconoclasts, imbuing pirated images and descriptions of the statue with idolatrous power. Unbeknown to Donohue and others, they were engaged in a kind of guilty *scopophilia* in which the triune pleasures of looking, imagining, and tasting necessitated the need for emotional relief from "the erotic associations between complexion and commodity" that inform chocolate as a simulacrum for skin.[12]

The formal aspects of *Sweet Jesus* lend additional complexity. Cast of dark Swiss chocolate atop a metal armature, the sculpture's facial features neither phenotypically stereotype a particular race nor placidly idealize. The eyes appear small, the nose long and hooked, and the lips thin and slightly frowning. The forehead protrudes but remains unlined. The hairline is high on the crown of the head, and the hair is pulled back in a short ponytail. If the statue had been displayed, the viewer would have been confronted with a sizeable question: What does it mean if the body of Christ is dark but racially illegible? Did Cavallaro's Jesus have a model? Were viewers meant to read these facial characteristics as an amalgam of traits and think of *Sweet Jesus* as, *e pluribus Unum,* an everyman, or were they meant to consider the sculpture as a teleological mestizo figure bridging the peculiar histories of colonialism, imperialism, and slavery in both the Roman Empire and the Americas? And if, as author bell hooks suggests, images of dark-skinned male bodies suspended for public consumption are politically charged with the history of lynching and other extrajudicial methods of punishment, to what end does *Sweet Jesus* engage with *theodicy,* the concept of discerning the presence of a Christian divine will in a fallen world? On these issues both artist and critic remained silent. One may suppose, then, that the "indeterminacy" of *Sweet Jesus* projected a phenomenological and psychological viscosity over the entire installation's materiality and purpose—"a troubled verisimilitude" that arguably proved confusing and threatening to its critics.

The breviloquence of *My Sweet Lord* and the controversy it inspired between artist and critic spanned a period of two days (seven if we allow for short articles buried in weekly and monthly periodicals), and its dissipation proved too dispassionate to warrant the notice of many scholars. Articles, blogs, and pundits clamored for fiery, emotional statements from religious conservatives yet shied away from the broader ramifications that could have reconstituted the nature of discourse around sacred objects and their conscious and unconscious political agendas. In reinvigorating the conversation about *Sweet Jesus,* this chapter raises questions in order to ascertain the types of dialogical encounters about economic imperialism, theological aesthetics, race, and gender that the artwork *might have had* with its viewership. The histories and approaches raised in these pages view the chocolate materiality of the work and its multisensory "consumption" as more subversive, and more intriguing, than its nudity. With so many questions and postcolonial contingencies still unresolved, perhaps Donohue was right to fear Cavallaro's chocolate Jesus—not for its simple nudity but for its complicated religious and historical *jouissance.*

NOTES

1. THE LAB Gallery, located in the Roger Smith Hotel, is situated at the intersection of 47th and Lexington.

2. See "Chocolate Jesus Sculpture Angers Catholic Group," *New York Times,* March 31, 2007; Bryan Cones, "Sweet Jesus," *U.S. Catholic* 72 (June 7, 2007): 6, 50; Lisa Miller, "Sweet Jesus," *Newsweek* 149, no. 16 (April 16, 2007): 16.; "I'm Coo-coo for Cocoa Christ!," www.artscandal.com, May 7, 2009.

3. Pamela H. Simpson, "A Vernacular Recipe for Sculpture: Butter, Sugar, and Corn," *American Art* 24, no. 1 (2010): 22–23. Scholars credit the sugar-paste model of Greenwich Village

at the 1855 Crystal Palace, the bas-relief butter sculpture *Dreaming Iolanthe* at the 1876 Philadelphia Centennial Exposition, and the Liberty Bell made of oranges at the 1893 World's Columbian Exposition with the transformation of food art from crafty display technique to chef d'oeuvre.

4. Simpson, "A Vernacular Recipe for Sculpture," 25.

5. "Chocolate Jesus Sculpture Angers Catholic Group," *Anderson Cooper 360°*, March 39, 2007, transcription mine.

6. Cones, "Sweet Jesus," 50.

7. Proposition Gallery, "Chocolate Saints . . . Sweet Jesus," online press release, accessed December 5, 2010, http://www.theproposition.com/exhibition-archive/chocolate-saintssweet-jesus/.

8. Rachel Laudau and Jeffrey M. Pilcher, "Chiles, Chocolate, and Race in New Spain: Glancing Backward to Spain or Looking Forward to Mexico?" *Eighteenth-Century Life* 23, no. 2 (1999): 63–64.

9. Sophie and Michael Coe, *The True History of Chocolate* (London: Thames and Hudson, 2000), 7.

10. Sarah Moss and Alexander Badenoch, *Chocolate: A Global History* (London: Reaktion Books, 2009), 110–118

11. Ibid., 116.

12. Michael A. Chaney, *Fugitive Vision: Slave Image and Black Identity in Antebellum Narrative* (Bloomington: Indiana University Press, 2008), 69. Chaney uses this phrase to discuss the relationality between the gaze of a slave master and an abolitionist. I could not resist using it here.

15

Space Invaders

The Public, the Private, and Perceptions of Islamic *"Incursions" in Secular America*

HAROON MOGHUL

I have worked closely, for much of the past decade, with American Muslims, individually and institutionally. Over this time I have seen many American Muslims internalize popular opinions of Islam and reflect these internalizations in their material and sensory practices. This chapter considers how American Muslims have adjusted their enactments of Islamic piety—a phrase intended to include embodiments, representations, and other expressions of religiosity—in the context of the "Ground Zero mosque" project, properly known as Park51, and in the "space" of air travel.

So Much Islam, So Few Muslims

A 2011 Pew study on religion in American media found that 33 percent of religion news stories that year were about Islam, although fewer than 2.5 million Americans are Muslim.[1] Why such lopsided concern? The undeniable effect of the September 11 attacks and the ongoing "war on terror" offer partial explanations. But there is also a tendency to perceive Islam as a threat to the binary constructions (secular and sacred, modern and traditional, public and private) upon which modern society depends.[2] These binaries endorse Western Christianity (and Protestantism especially) as normative, although, of course, Western Christianity's supposed maturity and modernity are themselves products of contingent histories.[3]

For various reasons, some of them discussed elsewhere in this volume, religion itself is seen as a threat to this binary, and "Islam has been represented in the modern West as peculiarly so (undisciplined, arbitrary, singularly oppressive)."[4] As such, in American media Islam is frequently treated as, or invoked as, an exception to the sort of modern and secular societies that Christianity purportedly enables.[5] Islam can thus be presented as a religion any embodiment of which represents a threat to the secular political and social order upon which Western civil discourse is founded and depends. Therefore, when an embodiment of Islam does not *appear* to conform to this order, the embodiment, or even Islam itself, is deemed to stand outside of or in opposition to modernity and the values associated with it: secularity, individuality, rationality, and the like.[6] Further, the embodiment, or Islam itself, may be perceived as a transgression of or incursion into secular space and therefore threatening to that space and the very concept of secularity.

To better understand this concern, I turn to Talal Asad, who defines secularism not as "an intellectual answer to a question" but "an enactment by which a *political medium* . . . redefines and transcends particular and differentiating practices of the self."[7] To complicate matters, Islamic tradition has identified the material enactment of certain practices, from dress to forms of worship, as inseparable from piety.[8] That is to say, Muslims rarely understand Islam to be exclusively a matter of private belief. Much as Asad has identified within secularism concerns for and advocacy of certain practices of the self, Islam, too, can be described as a project of self-construction. Not unlike Christians, Muslims traditionally inscribe morality within certain rituals, community and social relations, and adherence to visible norms. Moreover, these physical and material embodiments of Islam respond to, and thus simultaneously construct and confirm, certain kinds of spaces. Mosques, for example, are spaces reserved for performing specific forms of worship, and the *hijab* is a means by which a Muslim woman enters a nondomestic space and is identified as a Muslim while in that space.

The danger here is that in a rapidly globalizing world, the perceived incompatibility of key physical and material practices of Islam with Western constructions of the sacred and the secular, and concern for the maintenance of boundaries between the two, may lead some Muslims to conclude that Islam is incompatible with secular spaces and secular societies, as it has led some in the West to believe. More optimistically, the greater visibility of Islam and Muslims in the West may lead to a broadening of Western understandings of religion and a shift in our conceptions of the sacred and the secular. In this short reflection I consider how the anxieties and fears of Islam focus on particular material enactments of Islam, beginning with the physical and spatial choreographies of Muslim prayer.

There are primarily three types of Muslim prayer: *dhikr,* the repetitive invocation of God; *du'a,* supplication; and *salat,* ritual prayer. Salat is my immediate concern. Salat should be performed during five defined periods of the day; it includes standing, bowing, sitting, and prostrating; it may be performed congregationally; and it should be performed facing Mecca. Further, one must be ritually pure to perform salat. The ritual ablution, or *wudu',* involves washing the hands, face, arms, and feet. The observance of wudu' is accommodated at mosques; in their absence, Muslims seek spaces that can accommodate wudu'. Finally, on Fridays the midday salat is shortened to include a sermon for a service known as *salat al-jumu'ah,* which is considered mandatory for adult Muslim males. Because it falls on a weekday, salat al-jumu'ah can be difficult to perform in Western societies.

The nature of and responses to salat interest me in part because salat is a gender-neutral practice: male and female Muslims pray in nearly exactly the same way. Although there are no legal restrictions on performing salat publicly in the United States, I have heard many American Muslims describe how publicly performing salat has come to feel culturally transgressive. They consequently make efforts to pray almost anywhere except in public. For example, an investment banker in New York City told me that while at work, he prays in the custodial closet rather than in his cubicle. What can explain such anxieties?

Muslim If You Do, Muslim If You Don't

Recent estimates set the numbers of Muslim residents of New York City at between 600,000 and 800,000, many of whom work in Manhattan. Speaking generally, the city offers inadequate facilities for wudu' and salat. On occasion I have seen taxi drivers lay prayer rugs on the trunks of their cabs, creating a prayer area that is visible to the public but nonetheless on private property. This option is inadequate for those Muslims who wish to perform salat out of immediate public view and of course cannot address the challenge of salat al-jumu'ah.[9]

Considering the caution many Muslims now associate with public embodiments of Islam, the demand for mosques is not surprising. Efforts to secure dedicated prayer spaces, however, have backfired in unexpected ways. The initiative to establish such a space at the University of Michigan, for example, included a plan for wudu' facilities. Critics interpreted this as an attempt to "Islamize" a public university.[10] The same allegation was directed against the Park51 project, the so-called Ground Zero mosque.[11] The project, announced in late 2009, envisioned a mosque and community center in lower Manhattan. Many New York Muslims greeted this plan with cautious optimism given that the number, size, and quality of spaces for prayer in the city fall far short of demand. This holds for several reasons.

First, although the majority of Muslim New Yorkers live outside Manhattan, many work in that part of the city. This complicates fundraising for Manhattan mosques because observant Muslims need prayer spaces close to work *and* close to home, where they also often need schools and other communal religious structures. Second, securing a space in Manhattan large enough to accommodate growing congregations can be prohibitively expensive.[12] Third, the need for wudu' facilities further taxes the situation; potential prayer spaces require the installation of specific and expensive amenities, such as foot-washing stations. Fourth, a single mosque would be inadequate for Manhattan's Muslims because worshipers cannot be more than one or two subway stops from their prayer space in order to make attending salat al-jumu'ah feasible on a regular work schedule.

Beyond providing a place for prayer, the Park51 project promised other badly needed spaces, some of which New York Muslims had not imagined might cater to them, such as a gymnasium with a swimming pool, several restaurants, and a theater. My reflections here are based on my work with the Park51 project as an independent consultant (from June to August 2010), as well as on conversations with American Muslims during the period of greatest public controversy, from May to November of 2010.

The Park51 project drew intense opposition in many quarters. This, in turn, affected how Muslims saw and understood the project and contributed to widespread unease with the project among these Muslims. Non-Muslim author and blogger Pamela Geller played a significant role in driving the controversy. Her blog, *Atlas Shrugs,* called for protests against the "Ground Zero victory mosque," establishing a meme that would haunt the project going forward.[13] Critics suggested that past Muslims built mosques to commemorate their victories over their enemies. This unfounded and ahistorical assertion dogged the Park51 project, leaving proponents with the felt "responsibility" to prove otherwise.[14] Muslims, too, numbered among those who questioned Park51's purpose and wondered who its primary audience would be.

Should Park51 be an Islamic center or a "neutral" community center? Could it be both, and if not, which community should it serve? Could Park51 incorporate both a mosque and "secular" institutions, and if so, on what bases? Park51's developers had initially proposed locating the mosque in the planned structure's basement, providing for more efficient movement of persons, especially during salat al-jumu'ah. However, because most readings of Islamic law assert that a mosque extends upward in space indefinitely, a basement location would be impossible.[15] This then led to a proposal to place the mosque on the top floor. A mosque on the top floor of a thirteen-story tower, however, fed directly into the rhetorical fabrication of a so-called Muslim victory monument triumphantly overlooking Ground Zero.

Some on the development team then proposed building a multifaith worship space rather than a mosque, but many New York Muslims considered this solution no more than surrender to Islamophobia; further, multifaith worships spaces, too, have their opponents. As the summer dragged on, the Park51 project became increasingly expensive to pursue; more time and resources were devoted to responding to hostile critics than to establishing the project in whatever form. This reinforced the desire among some on the development team to focus on a multipurpose project in place of a more narrowly conceived "Islamic Center," because the former would make additional revenue streams available.

Recall, for example, the developers' proposed inclusion of a gym and swimming pool operating on a fee-based membership model. Some Muslim New Yorkers, who looked forward to gender-segregated recreational facilities, greeted this proposal with enthusiasm. However, critics of the project alleged that gender-segregated recreational spaces were indicative of "creeping Shari'ah," a Muslim "plot" to take over Western societies by quietly introducing Shari'ah in Muslim spaces and then to expand from these spaces to encompass society more generally. (Similar accusations had been leveled against the University of Michigan for its inclusion of a Muslim prayer space.)

In order to dispel these unfortunately potent criticisms, some working on the project suggested that recreational facilities include mixed-use hours alongside male- and female-only hours. However, securing Shari'ah-compliant financing, as would be required in the case of a mosque, for a space that would also include mixed-gender swimming spaces represented an apparently insurmountable challenge in this highly charged context. To make such an accommodation *in order to* enable access to gender-segregated time slots could be a compelling point in a nuanced discussion of Muslim community institutions appropriate to Western contexts, but the levels of unease, heat, and threat surrounding Park51 prohibited the full exploration of creative possibilities.

Flying while Muslim

Western Muslims perhaps most frequently express anxiety when it comes to praying in airports and on airplanes. Consider that new security screenings, in place since the September 11 attacks, require travelers to arrive at an airport several hours in advance. This regulation is taken by many American Muslims to apply specifically to them, and arriving at the airport earlier than usual increases the likelihood that a Muslim will have to perform salat while at the airport or on the airplane because salat must be performed at set times of the day. For those of us, myself included, who have been stopped and detained, nearly prevented from boarding aircraft, or awkwardly interrogated on return from trips abroad, this creates significant anxieties.

One legal aim of airport security mandates random selection rather than racial, ethnic, or religious profiling. However, Muslims have personally reported that they experience a higher rate of temporary detention than do many other travelers. This is equally true for Muslims who do not wear headscarves, keep beards, or originate in countries stereotypically identified as Muslim (South Asia and the Middle East, for example). In the context of the current anxiety around Islam, the Transportation

Safety Administration itself participates in the creation of a fictitious "monolithic" Islam. A generic suspicion of Muslims contributes to flattening distinctions among disparate individuals, advocating a horizontal categorical Islamic identity.

Praying at an airport or on an airplane would not seem remarkable to many travelers coming from, going to, or familiar with Muslim-majority countries. But considering how awkward the public performance of salat already is, especially for Muslims who have just gone through a security screening during which the least evidence of Islam could have constituted a rationale for a "random" detainment, performing salat in the airport is extraordinarily uncomfortable. For the Muslim traveler, the likelihood that one will need to publicly perform salat is inseparable from whether the airline or airport in question would accept such embodiments of Islam. This may be one reason why a number of young American Muslims have shared with me their preference to fly on airlines based in Muslim-majority countries.

Islamic Airspace

Bob Smietana, a writer for *The Tennessean,* has closely tracked opposition to Islam and Muslims in his state and has noted that what began as opposition to a single mosque project in Rutherford County, Tennessee, has now extended to include other manifestations of Muslim life in the area. A network of activists, led by anti-Muslim "intellectuals" such as Frank Gaffney and Robert Spencer, has shifted its energies beyond mosques to individual embodiments of Islam. The latest issue concerns whether public schools can and should make accommodations for students to perform salat during the school day.

Given current demographics, it is likely that such questions will become more common and that the challenge posed by embodiments of Islam in supposedly neutral "secular" spaces will become increasingly significant in the United States. By considering how Islam is accommodated and consumed in the context of air travel, I suggest that certain religious practices can be public, visible, material, or aural/audible without necessarily implying a deliberate challenge to appropriate boundaries of the secular state. Christians in the United States have certainly found workable and welcome public spaces for free exercise of their faith in the context of disestablishment, including provisions for Christian student groups to meet on public school campuses. I posit that American First Amendment rights, shaped in the context of a historical response to an explicitly Protestant Christian frame, can be extended to creatively engage Islam as well (as has already been done in the case of multiple religious traditions relatively new to this nation). The responses to material embodiments of Muslim piety in air travel that I examine may also suggest ways that we will *see* and *hear* Islam as the world becomes more globalized and the presence of Muslims in Western society becomes more and more unremarkable.[16]

Flying from and to the United States on airlines affiliated with Muslim-majority countries, I have noted various accommodations to the practice of Islam, including *qibla* markers indicating the direction of Mecca; spaces set aside within larger aircraft for salat; audio recordings of the *du'a as-safar,* or traveler's supplication, included in preflight announcements; and, on younger fleets, software that enables the passengers to read and listen to the Qur'an through their seat-based entertainment systems. But the range, frequency, and type of these accommodations vary. On Pakistan International Airlines, the du'a as-safar is read in the original Arabic and translated into Urdu and English, Pakistan's national and official languages. On a number of Gulf airlines, such as Emirates, Etihad, and Qatar Airways, the du'a as-safar is included in preflight announcements but is not translated into English, although all other Arabic announcements are translated into English. It may be that such a du'a might be perceived to be offensive to English-speaking passengers, although this assumes that all Arabic-speaking passengers are Muslim or do not mind *hearing* expressions of Muslim belief, whereas English-speaking passengers are not Muslim or do not want or need the supplication to be read in a language other than Arabic.

Further, such accommodations do not hold across all airlines originating in Muslim-majority countries. Turkish Airlines, for example, does not include the du'a as-safar in its preflight announcements; as the nation's flag carrier, Turkish Airlines is perhaps keen to maintain a kind of corporate secularity. Still, Turkish Airlines' onboard entertainment system offers "spiritual music" as well as audio recordings of the Qur'an by Turkish reciters. I know of no North American or Western European airlines that make such accommodations to religion. They may strike the average American as unusual and even antiquated, and their availability on a fast-growing carrier such as Turkish Airlines may seem paradoxically premodern. Yet such accommodations to Islam may well become more ordinary, inviting us to rethink how we construct the boundaries between public and private, secular and sacred.

Anxieties about Islam affect *how* Muslims embody their faith and also constrain them in so doing. The current prevalence of public conversation and contention affects American Muslims directly and will frame instantiations of Islam, individually and collectively, in coming years. We can expect more such conversations in the future as we begin to ask how a Western Islam will take shape, how it will appear, how it will sound, and what its material and physical enactments, individual and collective, will mean for the specific boundaries between sacred and secular, private and public, upon which many Western self-understandings depend.

NOTES

1. "Religion in the News: Islam and Politics Dominate Religion Coverage in 2011," *Pew Forum for Public Life,* February 23, 2012, http://www.pewforum.org/Government/Religion-in-the-News—Islam-and-Politics-Dominate-Religion-Coverage-in-2011.aspx#about.

2. Lynne Gerber, *Seeking the Straight and Narrow: Weight Loss and Sexual Reorientation in Evangelical America* (Chicago: University of Chicago Press, 2011), 4.

3. John Locke criticized Catholicism for being too "outward" a faith. Much of our concept of public, neutral space and private religion can be traced to some of Locke's ideas, for example, his contention that "a private subjective conscience [is] the sole route to salvation," and that is "the purpose and function of faith." Jean Bethke Elshtain, *Sovereignty: God, Self, and the State* (New York: Basic Books, 2008), 128–129.

4. Talal Asad, *Formations of the Secular: Christianity, Islam, Modernity* (Stanford, CA: Stanford University Press, 2003), 9–10.

5. Gil Anidjar, *Semites: Race, Religion, Literature* (Stanford, CA: Stanford University Press, 2008), 53.

6. Asad notes that the study of religion, too, operates on a similar binary: "These familiar themes suggest that 'religion,' whose object is the sacred, stands in the domain of the non-rational." Asad, *Formations of the Secular,* 22.

7. Ibid., 5, italics in original.

8. Asad writes, "It is their attachment to Islam that many believe commits Muslims to values that are an affront to the modern secular state." Asad, *Formations of the Secular,* 159.

9. One of the few pieces on such problems is Wajahat Ali's essay "My Awkward Moments in Muslim Prayer," Salon.com, February 23, 2011, http://www.salon.com/2011/02/24/awkward_moments_muslim_prayer/singleton/.

10. The Southern Poverty Law Center (SPLC), among others, noted how Muslim requests for footbaths to accommodate one of the requirements of wudu' were taken by anti-Muslim hate groups to represent evidence of the surreptitious implementation of Shari'ah, what is sometimes called "Islamization." Leah Nelson, "Anti-Muslim Activists Gather in Tennessee to Warn of Shari'ah," SPLC blog, November 12, 2011, http://www.splcenter.org/blog/2011/11/12/anti-muslim-activists-gather-in-tennessee-to-warn-of-shariah-takeover/.

11. Nor should this be seen as exclusive to the "Ground Zero mosque" project. An article in *The Tennessean* explores a sustained effort in Rutherford County, Tennessee, to stop the construction of a mosque and deny Muslim students accommodations for prayer at (public) schools. "Fight against Islam Stretched beyond Murfreesboro Mosque," *The Tennessean,* August 5, 2012, http://www.tennessean.com/article/20120805/NEWS06/308050052/.

12. I went to New York University as an undergraduate in 1998, at which time roughly twenty to twenty-five persons regularly attended salat al-jumu'ah services. Today that community accommodates upward of three hundred persons per week. During the summer of 2010, the Park51 project opened a temporary prayer space at 51 Park Place, and within several weeks it had reached its maximum legal capacity (of approximately six hundred persons) for salat al-jumu'ah.

13. The meme continued for quite some time after that. See Pamela Geller's blog entry "Protest the Ground Zero Victory Mosque," *Atlas Shrugs,* January 6, 2011, http://atlasshrugs2000.typepad.com/atlas_shrugs/2011/01/protest-the-ground-zero-victory-mosque-january-12thmark-your-calenders.html.

14. See, for example, Jim Meyers, "Hamid: Ground Zero Mosque Islamic Victory Symbol," *Newsmax,* August 18, 2010, http://www.newsmax.com/InsideCover/groundzeromosquetawfik/2010/08/18/id/367823.

15. Salat can be performed almost anywhere; Muslims perform salat at home, at work, outdoors, or in any number of buildings. Mosques provide dedicated worship spaces that meet several conditions: they must regularly hold all five prayers for congregational service, they must be used for no other purpose, they must have no other buildings above or below them, and they

must be financed in accordance with Islamic law. (That is, the source and structure of the funding, as well as the activities funded, must comply with certain principles and restrictions.)

16. The weekend edition of *Financial Times,* August 4–5, 2012, features a second-page story ("Fasting Sets Muslim Competitors a Higher Challenge") on how Muslim Olympians at the London 2012 games accommodated fasting in the Islamic lunar month of Ramadan in their competitions and training. I expect the frequency of such articles to increase as Muslims become increasingly visible throughout the West.

PART TWO   ✳   TRANSGRESSIONS

The visual artist Alex Donis specializes in the most unlikely, even impossible, of amorous pairings—Jesus French-kisses Lord Rama, Mother Teresa and pop star Madonna smooch, an Aztec warrior embraces Christopher Columbus, Che Guevara tenderly connects with Cesar Chavez, the Virgin of the Immaculate Conception caresses Our Lady of Guadalupe. Donis renders religious, historical, and political icons into multiethnic couplets of desiring bodies. In so doing he explores the corporeal and sensory capacities of iconic figures often rendered as formless ideologies. Most of these images he produces in oil and enamel on light boxes, displayed upright and thus simulating stained glass. Their arrangement in a semioval shape suggestive of a Christian apse reinforces their devotional resonance. Though the erotic activity in Donis's pictures is rarely more explicit than a kiss, the artist's work repeatedly has been met with threats of violence, acts of vandalism, and institutional censorship. The opening artifact for "Transgressions" features Donis's *Jesus and Lord Rama* from his *My Cathedral* series of 1997. The series poses fundamental questions about the potential limits of religious imagination, intimacy, ethnicity, sexuality, sensation, and fantasy.[1] The range of responses, from the smashing of glass to the erection of alternate altars dedicated to "tolerance, love, and acceptance," suggests that these "limits" themselves are rapidly shifting targets, dependent on specific individual or communal vantage points.

In some cases not examined in this volume but discussed elsewhere by its authors, an "imagined" sensory or sensual assault attracts so much ardor that a potentially more provocative feature is masked or ignored. Chris Ofili's *Holy Virgin Mary,* for example, found itself in the midst of a firestorm of debate when William Dono-

---

Alex Donis, *Jesus Christ and Lord Rama,* from the *My Cathedral* series, 1997.

257

hue of the Catholic League and New York City Mayor Rudolph Giuliani accused the artist of smearing elephant dung on the Mother of God. In actuality, the artist limited his use of elephant dung to two round "feet" on which the six-foot high panel rested and to a third carefully shaped orb that seems to signify a breast. In no place did he "smear" her with excrement as accusers claimed, and the British artist, of Nigerian heritage, explained the use of this medium in relation to its purported African significance in relation to fertility. Far more problematic in context but virtually ignored in the controversy were the attached pornographic magazine cutouts; these depicted female genitalia and buttocks, in many cases touched and pulled apart by fingers. The artist had extracted these images from explicitly pornographic serial publications and had then attached them, collagelike, to the surface of the canvas. Most detractors had not actually seen the image in person; if they had seen it at all, they had not seen the life-scale original itself but had viewed postage stamp–sized reproductions in which the cutouts were not easily visible. In many such newer, especially American cases, it is often Catholics who have become the iconoclasts, earning a reputation that had been, since the Reformation, more characteristically reserved for Protestants.

The chapters that appear in "Transgressions" grapple at greater length and to somewhat different ends with subjects raised under "Contested Grounds." Here "transgression" concerns not just infractions and perceptions of infractions, but also the crossing of literal and figurative "things" over real or ideational thresholds. This part of the book explores, as well, transgressions of gendered and racialized bodies in self- or other-inflicted acts of violence and repression.

The obstacles and limits encountered here, variously impassable or ultimately navigable over time, include habits, assumptions, convictions, values, affects, and their sensory manifestations and apparatus. Sometimes scholars and other "modern" practitioners have perceived violations where none existed. Examples include Byzantine icons presumed to have been targets of iconoclasts but actually worn away by material practices of devout touching, kissing, or rubbing, as well as the frequent representation of the features of Muhammad in Iranian coffeehouses. The authors of these "Transgressions" chapters explore multisensory practices of resistance to dominant political and religious regimes; artistic and philosophical uses of sensation to assert ecstatic and ethereal states paradoxically understood to transcend the senses; sensationalized depictions of martyrdoms; the impact of Western secularization theory on popular Islam, communities of affect, and sensory religiosity in post-1979 Iran; and a hitherto undocumented instance of African American Protestant women in the 1930s organizing interracial, interfaith groups of individuals and institutions to confront racism by exhibiting black art in affluent white secular commercial spaces. What is common to each chapter is the mediating or precipitating role of sensory materialities, art and artifacts, in larger religious, political, economic, and cultural negotiations, often ones also concerning gender, race, and nationality or transnationality. In some meaningful way each chapter in *Sensational Religion* might justifiably appear under the heading "Transgressions." The term is key to the genealogy of this project and to an overarching thesis that highlights the sensory and sensual as special pressure points in perceptions of the transgressive behaviors and categorical challenges of material religion.

SALLY M. PROMEY

NOTE

1. Richard Meyer contributed substantively to this paragraph on the work of Alex Donis; these words should be considered part of a conversation initiated by Meyer and his prior scholarship on Donis.

Ironically, in regard to Donis's series, depictions of similarly intimate relations, close bodily embraces and "heavenly" kisses, between Christ and Ecclesia (or the "true church"), for example, abound in earlier Christian devotional literatures.

16

Praying for Grace
Charles Ellis Johnson's Synesthetic Skin

MARY CAMPBELL

This promise [of polygamy] is yours also, because ye are of Abraham, and the promise was made unto Abraham.... Go ye, therefore, and do the Works of Abraham; enter ye into my law, and ye Shall be Saved.   Doctrine and Covenants 132:31–32

Whenever I see a pretty woman, I have to pray for grace.   Joseph Smith Jr.

Shortly before he died, Charles Ellis Johnson (1857–1926) turned his camera on himself (Figure 16.1). It was not the first time that Johnson had experimented with self-portraiture. A professional photographer and stereographer, Johnson made the occasional self-portrait over the years. In general, however, Johnson focused his lens—or, in the case of his stereographs, his lenses—on the world around him. In turn-of-the-century Utah, this world was largely religious. A member of the Church of Jesus Christ of Latter-day Saints (LDS), Johnson had married into the prophet Brigham Young's family in 1878 and became one of the Mormon church's favorite photographers during the 1890s. The Temple, the Tabernacle, portraits of enormous polygamous families—Johnson shot all of these turn-of-the century LDS attractions and more. As one of his own advertisements proudly declared, the Johnson photography studio and store stood as an "Information Bureau [for] everything about Utah and the Mormons" (Figure 16.2).

What about this late self-portrait, though? The term "information bureau" certainly does not seem to apply here. In stark contrast to Johnson's pictures of prophets and apostles and even his other self-portraits, this image does not immediately reveal its subject. At first glance, this stereograph presents the viewer with little more than an empty dressing room. We see a sink, a clothing or towel rack, a vanity table with mirrors, a brush, and a comb. An Eastern-looking rug covers most of the floor, and three chairs crowd the space. To our far right, a doorknob and a thin edge of wood suggest that the door stands partially ajar. Johnson himself hovers at the other edge of the frame. We have to look closely to find him there, cloistered to the far left of the

FIGURE 16.1. Charles Ellis Johnson, untitled self-portrait, ca. 1926, stereo-view. Courtesy of L. Tom Perry Special Collections, Harold B. Lee Library, Brigham Young University, Provo, Utah.

two pictures and seemingly sliced in half by one of the vanity's mirrors. Peering at his small, partial figure tucked off to the side, one wonders whether this picture qualifies as a self-portrait at all. Did Johnson realize that he was including himself in the view? Did he intend to? Does it matter?

The questions do not stop here. Why, for example, would Johnson choose to shoot this scene as a stereograph? The primary allure of stereography, after all, is the illusion of three-dimensionality that it creates. Reproduced in a book, a stereograph looks like nothing more than a set of nearly identical photographs. Inserted into a viewer, however, a stereo-card like Johnson's unfolds into an all-encompassing environment. Press your face to the stereoscope's mask, adjust the card to the proper distance, and suddenly the outside world drops away. Instantly the card triggers your binocular vision, prompting your mind to knit the two images together into a single, three-dimensional view. This view flickers slightly, the effect of the pulse of your optical nerves as they struggle to hold the two pictures together. Other than this faint beat, however, stereo-views tend to appear strangely still. One confronts a set of full, frozen bodies through the stereoscope's twin lenses. More than that, one becomes acutely aware of one's own body. Part of the fascination of stereography is the way that it seems to "reskin the eye" in all five of the senses, especially touch. As the writer and

stereo-enthusiast Oliver Wendell Holmes so eloquently declared in 1859, the medium allows us to "clasp an object with our eyes, as with our arms, or with our hands."[1]

Returning to Johnson's stereograph, what exactly is the viewer supposed to clasp here? Empty chairs? Mirrors? A view of the artist that we can only partially see? What does Johnson's fragmented, three-dimensional view of himself reflected in a mirror in a vacant room ultimately offer? As this chapter argues, here the viewer finds an allegory of stereography itself. As we examine those chairs and especially that vanity, we discover both an image of Johnson and a picture of his medium, a vision of the stereoscope and its ability to reincarnate the viewer into a radically enhanced body produced solely through the eyes. In addition to this, we find a religious body in Johnson's image. In this stereographic self-portrait, we eventually see not just Johnson and even Oliver Wendell Holmes but also Joseph Smith Jr. The original prophet, seer, and revelator of the Mormon church, Smith entertained his own dreams of the body fundamentally transformed through sight. We find these dreams here. In visualizing stereography's capacity to transmute looking into bodily being, Johnson simultaneously restates Smith's most audacious theological innovation: the belief that polygamy could replace God's grace as the path to salvation. Gazing at this image, I argue, we experience polygamy's physical impulse to divinity as well as its eventual loss.

Johnson's image might be enigmatic, but one thing is clear: the picture invites the viewer in. Sliding the card into the stereoscope, we find ourselves on the threshold of a room filled with empty chairs. Seen stereoscopically, these chairs appear strikingly solid, even tactile. As mentioned above, the image's three-dimensionality calls out to the viewer's own body, our body—in this case, by encouraging us to imagine settling our full weight onto one of those wooden seats. The chair in the foreground restates this aspect of the medium's appeal even more explicitly. Turned toward the picture plane, this chair overtly offers the viewer a place to sit. It is as though this stereograph actively wanted us to step into its pictorial space, as though it were literally urging us to pull up a chair and gaze into its mirrors.

Interestingly, we can see only a portion of these mirrors from our spot at the door. One assumes that the vanity originally had three glasses, but looking at the image through the stereoscope, we see only two. In this respect, this section of Johnson's image resembles a stereo-card before the viewer slides it into the stereoscope. Like all stereo-views, Johnson's truncated shot of the vanity is composed of two pictures divided by a thick line; like all stereographs, this vanity offers us a view made of two slightly different scenes. Examining this image, we find a set of nearly twinned pictures that, like all stereographs, promises to give us a second body if we will simply arrange our first according to the requirements of its viewing apparatus—here that vanity and chair. In keeping with the picture's sense of doubling, the body on offer here is dual, too. Peering through first the stereoscope and then the vanity, we discover an image of Johnson and, at the same time, the suggestion that we might be able to see our own stereographic reflection in the image's conjoined mirrors.

In this way Johnson's image stands as both a self-portrait and an allegory of stereography itself. Indeed, returning to Oliver Wendell Holmes, Johnson's work seems to restage Holmes's famous account of the medium. An early fan of stereo-views, Holmes popularized them as a form of home entertainment in 1861 when he invented a hand-held version of the stereoscope. Two years before, Holmes had published his seminal essay "The Stereoscope and the Stereograph" in the *Atlantic Monthly*. In this article Holmes praised the way that stereography seemed to endow the viewer with a second body, a body produced solely by the eyes. Lifting the stereoscope to his face, he wrote, "I pass, in a moment, from the banks of the Charles to the ford of the Jordan, and leave my outward frame in the arm-chair at my table."[2] Abandoning his actual anatomy for the pleasures of the stereoscope's synesthetic skin, Holmes delighted in his newfound ability to "*creep* over the vast features of Rameses . . . , *scale* the huge mountain-crystal that calls itself the Pyramid of Cheops . . . , *pace* the length of the three Titanic stones of the wall of Baalbec, . . . and then . . . *dive* into some mass of foliage with my microscope."[3] As this passage reveals, Holmes found a surrogate body in the stereo-cards he collected. He discovered an alternate corporeality that, judging by his ecstatic litany of verbs, appeared to provide him with satisfactions just as great, just as *physical,* as the pile of bones and tissue that he left behind in his chair in Cambridge. The fact that Holmes described his rebirth into stereographic being as a passage to the Holy Land only reinforces this sense of monumental, if not outright sacred, transformation.

We seem to see an echo of this transformation in Johnson's self-portrait. Gazing at this image, it is as if we had walked into Holmes's study and discovered both his armchair and his table. His "outward frame" is missing, of course, but we find a trace of his new, prosthetic body in Johnson's figure in the mirror. It is as though we catch both Johnson and Holmes passing through to the world of the stereoscope in this picture. We seem to watch them here as they trade ordinary physical existence for the substitute joys of stereography's amplified eyes. As Holmes himself opined, solid bodies no longer matter in the realm of the stereograph. Once the stereographer has flayed an object for its three-dimensional appearance, Holmes declared, he is free to "leave the carcas[s] as of little worth."[4] Studying Johnson's picture, one wonders whether those worthless physical remains include the viewer's original body as well. An outmoded corpse, *this* body has no place in Johnson's self-portrait, at least not directly. As an image of both the stereographer and his medium, this picture instead presents us with a dream of that body radically alchemized through sight.[5]

In this respect, Johnson's self-portrait confronts the viewer with another dream —another dream of bodies become much more through the workings of a massively enhanced eye. Here the dream belongs to Joseph Smith Jr., the founder of the Mormon church. Smith might initially seem like an odd match for Holmes. Smith, after all, made his name as a prophet, whereas Holmes held himself out as a visual tourist. Holmes might have reveled in the way that the stereoscope allowed him to simultaneously sit in a chair in Massachusetts and "loo[k] down upon Jerusalem from the Mount of Olives."[6] It was Smith, however, who dedicated his life to the pursuit of a new Holy Land. And yet, just like Holmes, Smith found a way out of ordinary existence through his eyes. For Smith as for Holmes, transcendence began with vision. As Mormonism's first "prophet, seer, and revelator," Smith staked both his church and his identity as God's chosen one on his ability to see the divine in an extremely literal, even stereographic, way.

Later in life, Smith would claim that his existence as a holy seer had begun in 1820. He did not officially found the LDS church, however, until 1830, the same year that he published the *Book of Mormon.* According to Smith, an angel named Moroni had led him to this new bible seven years earlier. Not only was this text buried in a hillside, however; it was written in an unrecognizable language that Smith described as "Reformed Egyptian."[7] In order to transcribe the sacred document for his secular audience, Smith had to use the translating device that accompanied the book's golden plates. Known as the "Urim and Thummim," this tool consisted of two stones that, according to Smith's mother, "connected with each other in much the same way as old fashioned spectacles."[8] The Urim and Thummim, in other words, were a pair of holy glasses; they were an optical apparatus that allowed Smith to see the English text of the biblical record that he sought to translate. With the plates on the table next to him, Smith would place the two stones into his hat, submerge his face in the stuffy, woolen-scented darkness, and wait until a vision of the English words appeared (Figure 16.3). As Smith's brother William recounted, "When Joseph received the plates he also received the Urim and Thummim, which he would place in a hat to exclude all light, and with the plates by his side he translated the characters."[9] Or, as Smith's early assistant in translation, Martin Harris, explained to a local newspaper, "By placing the spectacles in a hat and looking into it, Smith interprets the characters into the English language."[10] In account after account, the key elements of this translation story remain the same: stones for seeing, hat to enclose the face, and finally, the sequence of hallowed images rising up to meet Smith's eyes.[11]

In a fundamental way, then, Smith produced the *Book of Mormon* with the aid of a divine stereoscope. Like Holmes seated in his chair in Cambridge, Smith placed his face in a sort of mask, stared into lenses, and waited for a picture to emerge. Under these conditions, Smith became, like Holmes, a tremendously enhanced eye—a fact that he recognized and that, moreover, delighted him. Returning home with the sacred plates and stones for the first time, for example, it was the latter that excited him most. "I can see any thing," he crowed to his mother, "they are Marvellus [*sic*]."[12] Smith had previously described his use of seer stones in similar terms. A common part of rural folk magic, seer stones provide a clear precedent for the Urim and Thummim, a sort of magical antecedent to Smith's sacred translators.[13] Smith eventually replaced the Urim and Thummim with these older, magical rocks, staring at them in his hat in order to complete his translation of the *Book of Mormon*.[14] Using a seer stone for the first time, Smith "discovered that time, place, and distance were annihilated; that all intervening obstacles were removed, and that he possessed one of the attributes of the Deity, an All-Seeing Eye.'"[15]

We see more than a little bit of "The Stereograph and the Stereoscope" in this account.[16] Thirty years before Holmes published his essay, Smith spoke with awe about an amazing optical device that could transport him from America to the Holy Land in the blink of an eye. Whether Smith received his viewing apparatus from an angel or instead invented it himself à la Holmes seems less important here than the sheer pleasure both men took in their newfound power to "see any thing" through the latest in visual gadgetry. At base, Smith and Holmes (and perhaps even the angel Moroni) shared the nineteenth century's general taste for optical toys.[17] If, as Smith claimed, his translation of the *Book of Mormon* ushered in a new era of direct commu-

FIGURE 16.3. Anonymous, *Joseph Smith, Jr., Translating the Golden Plates*, n.d. Courtesy of Images of the Restoration: Mormon Art (www.imagesoftherestoration.org). Used with permission.

nication between humanity and God, modern visual technology now had an important role to play in the exchange.[18]

So, too, did the body that this technology produced. This is another critical similarity that connects Holmes and Smith. As discussed above, Holmes did not just become an exalted eye with his stereoscope. Instead he also assumed a magnificent body—a synesthetic proxy body that crept and scaled and paced and dived all over the globe with an intensity—even a promiscuity—that far exceeded the capacity of any actual human physique. Visual transcendence bleeds immediately into physical gratification in Holmes's description of stereography. His essay persistently links the joys of enhanced seeing with the satisfactions to be found in the eye's massively enhanced body.

We discover a similar movement from the visual to the corporeal in Smith's religious metamorphosis. On one hand, the Urim and Thummim transformed Smith into a prophet by transmuting him into a set of hallowed eyes. By his own account, Smith became a full-blown seer and a revelator when he gazed into his holy stereoscope. Whether he actually used the Urim and Thummim to translate the *Book of Mormon* from a set of golden plates or instead drew the book's story from his own imagination is irrelevant here. As soon as Smith buried his face in his hat in search of a new bible, he pronounced his divine right to see the sacred and therefore to speak for God. In addition to this, however, he claimed the religious authority that would eventually allow him to create a radically new body for both himself and his followers. As he avowed in 1843, one of the benedictions that God revealed to him was the blessing of polygamy. "This promise [of polygamy] is yours also," Smith announced, "because ye are of Abraham, and the promise was made unto Abraham. . . . Go ye, therefore, and do the Works of Abraham; enter ye into my law, and ye Shall be Saved."[19] According to Smith, God had chosen him to restore both biblical truth *and* an Old Testament body—meaning a polygamous body—to nineteenth-century America. As the literal and theological descendants of Abraham, the original Mormons were to find their salvation through plural marriage.[20]

It is important to realize just what Smith meant by "salvation" in this context. In most Christian faiths, the term denotes deliverance from sin and its consequences. To be saved in this sense is to have been lifted out of the realm of human transgression and folded into the fullness of an everlasting divine presence. As a result, traditional notions of salvation depend on the existence of a stark divide between the human world and the space of God. Because the sacred exists at a radical remove from the secular, humans can make the leap from one plane to another only through the intervention of God's grace. Human beings might be able to work toward their soul's salvation within this theological framework, but they cannot generate it themselves. Ultimately, that power rests exclusively with God.

Mormon polygamy disrupted this conventional conception of salvation. When Smith instructed his followers that they would be saved through polygamy, he did not mean that plural marriage would draw them closer to God by invoking his grace. Instead he meant that polygamy would literally make Mormon men gods.[21] According to Smith's theology, the faithful, polygamous Mormon male was destined to become a deity in his own right. By adhering to Mormonism's covenants, he was to attain the stature and power of the God of the Old and New Testaments. Smith taught his Latter-day Saints that God had a body just like a man's; that man was God's actual, physical offspring; and that devout Mormon husbands would eventually populate their own planets in the afterlife by having heavenly children with their multiple wives.

Critically, Smith emphasized that deification would come only to those who practiced polygamy on earth. In Smith's religious cosmos, neither the unmarried nor the monogamously married could become gods in the afterlife. "For these angels did not abide my law," Smith declared, "therefore they cannot be enlarged . . . and from henceforth are not Gods, but are angels of God for ever and ever."[22] In order to attain godhood, in other words, Mormon men had to begin the divine work of populating their future kingdoms in the here and now. As the Mormon leader Jedediah M. Grant preached in 1853, "[If] you want a heaven, go to and make it."[23] With plural marriage, the Saints pursued their heaven-making to the utmost. By marrying and having children with more than one woman, polygamous Mormon men sought to initiate their divine existence on earth.

In this respect, plural marriage effectively relocated the primary site of Christian grace. Whereas the New Testament finds human salvation in Christ's body, Mormon polygamy embedded salvation in the male Saint's body. According to Smith, the LDS devout no longer needed to merit grace passively through Christ's suffering on the cross. Instead they could now create their own grace by assuming the polygamous biblical bodies that God had revealed to them.[24] Early in his career as a prophet, Smith had reputedly confessed to suffering from the weaknesses of his own body. "Whenever I see a pretty woman," he is rumored to have admitted to a friend, "I have to pray for grace."[25] Through polygamy, Smith effectively transformed this sort of physical need *into* grace. Casting an expansive male sexuality as the origin of sacred creation and man's eventual deification, Smith alchemized desire into divinity, erotic impulse into the engine of man's own world-building salvation.[26]

Like Holmes and his stereoscope, then, Smith ultimately forged a new body for his male Saints. Like Holmes and his stereoscope, Smith stared into lenses (his divinely delivered stones), passed to a holy land, and ultimately found a magnificently amplified corporeality there. This new body might have belonged to the world of religion rather than the realm of popular entertainment. Smith's new soma might have set itself to the task of sexualized heaven-building, whereas Holmes's ranged over the wonders of the world. Just like Holmes, however, Smith reincarnated himself through sight. As a seer and a revelator, he radically reimagined the potential of the male body by shattering the constraints of ordinary vision.

If we read Johnson's self-portrait as an allegory of stereography, then, should we not also see it as an allegory of early Mormonism—as a picture not simply of the stereographer but also of Smith's original, polygamous dreams? Lifting the stereoscope to our eyes, we find an invitation to step through a doorway, sit down, and assume the body that beckons from just beyond the vanity's double mirrors: Johnson's body, the stereoscope's synesthetic body, but perhaps also Smith's polygamous body—that new, holy flesh that vowed to pull the Mormon devout through to heaven even as it called heaven down to earth. Has the figure in Johnson's image already passed through to this sacred realm? It looks out at us here from its double mirrors—mirrors that we can now read as a visual echo of both Holmes's stereoscope and Smith's Urim and Thummim, his seer stones. Three months before he recorded his revelation on polygamy, Smith spoke again about these holy stones. As he declared, "The place where God resides is a great Urim and Thummim," "a globe like a sea of glass and fire, where all things for their glory are manifest, past, present, and future, and are continually before the Lord."[27] For Smith, the Urim and Thummim were literally heaven: their prosthetic gaze constituted the very space of God. As deities in the making, Smith's polygamous devout were presumably destined to inhabit such stereoscopelike spaces themselves one day, the sort of space that Johnson already occupies here. Studying his small figure in the mirror, then, we seem to encounter both Holmes's account of stereographic rebirth *and* Mormonism's ultimate theological promise: its vow to reincarnate faithful men as gods of both the body and the eye.

It is worth mentioning that the LDS church ultimately had to break this promise, at least at it applied to the here and now. Mormon polygamy might have presented the male Saints with an intoxicating vision of physicalized divinity. The larger nation, however, remained horrified by the specter of LDS plural marriage—so horrified, in fact, that the federal government waged an all-out legal war on the Mormons in order to force them to abandon the practice. Between 1854 and 1890, Congress and the federal courts stripped Mormons of a whole host of constitutional protections, including not just their right to religious freedom but also their right to vote, to hold public office, to hold property, and to be free of unreasonable searches and seizures.[28] Although the LDS devout held out for almost four decades, they eventually caved under this federal firestorm. In 1890 the fourth LDS prophet, Wilford Woodruff, made an announcement. "Acting," as he declared, "for the Temporal salvation of the Church," he instructed the Mormons to renounce polygamy.[29]

As we can now see, the Saints disavowed much more than an unorthodox family structure when they relinquished plural marriage.[30] In disclaiming polygamy, they abandoned the central doctrine of Smith's theology: that potent dream of the male body's sexualized capacity to do nothing less than make its own heaven. When the country broke the Saints to monogamy, therefore, it forced the Mormons to choose their church's temporal salvation over Smith's visceral fantasy of man's ability to initiate his own salvation in the here and now. In this way, the nation compelled the Saints to cede their fundamentally alapsarian vision of existence; it forced them to relocate their heaven to the realm of an imagined hereafter. In this "trauma of surrender" the church never actually renounced plural marriage as a religious doctrine.[31] Smith's original polygamy revelation remains a part of Mormon scriptures, and, as the Mormon historian Jan Shipps writes, "The LDS church still quietly seals devout widowers to additional wives."[32] Although church authorities now work doggedly to stamp out polygamy as a temporal practice, they refuse to abandon the belief that they themselves will eventually become polygamous gods in the afterlife. In this refusal, contemporary Saints live, as they have since 1890, in a state of deferral. Straddling the stark divide between their beliefs and their actions, postpolygamy Mormons find themselves consigned to a place of waiting—waiting for godhood, waiting for their bodies to reassume the divine glow of world-making, waiting to escape an earthly life that now stands at a fundamental remove from a heaven that beckons from just beyond.

This brings us back to Johnson's self-portrait one last time. Johnson, after all, belonged to a fundamentally different religion than did Smith or even Smith's successor prophet and Johnson's own father-in-law, Brigham Young. Smith was assassinated in a prison cell in Illinois forty-six years before Wilford Woodruff advised his followers to abdicate plural marriage. Young died seventeen years before Woodruff's mandate. Johnson, on the other hand, was thirty-three the year that the LDS church officially reverted to monogamy. This means that Johnson was a part of that first group of Mormons who had to stand by and watch as their church relinquished its attempts to initiate man's deification in the here and now. Johnson himself was not a polygamist.

Even as a monogamist, however, he belonged to a transitional generation of Mormons —the generation that had to acclimate itself to a faith that no longer linked the secular and the sacred in the body of man.

We see traces of this acclimation in Johnson's self-portrait, traces of its scars. Studying Johnson's reflection in the mirror, for example, we eventually realize just how truncated it appears, how dismembered even—half a face, an amorphous blur of black suit, the barest suggestion of a hand. For all of this stereograph's offers of a body, we do not fully find one here. What we do find is an eye: a single eye that stares out at us from only one of the stereograph's two images. There is no second eye to be found in the entire portrait. Even as he pictured himself in a medium that creates a sense of embodiment through a trick of binocular vision, in other words, Johnson cast himself as Cyclops, as he who has only one eye. In so doing, he effectively depicted himself as a man doubly alienated from physical existence. Not only is the better part of Johnson's figure missing from this stereograph; his reflection lacks the ocular equipment necessary to create a proxy body out of sight.

In addition to this, Johnson appears strikingly flat here. Even after one inserts the stereo-card into the stereoscope, Johnson himself looks two-dimensional, thin. Whereas those chairs and the table and even the sink at the back of the room expand into stereoscopic fullness, Johnson's form remains sandwiched on a single plane. This is because the image on the right includes only one of the vanity's three mirrors and almost nothing of Johnson himself. In order to generate the appearance of three dimensions, this section of Johnson's stereograph would have to contain four mirrors between its two halves, whereas here it has only three. Examining this picture through the stereoscope, the viewer sees a single scene with two mirrors. Those glasses, however, and Johnson within them, look flat and two-dimensional because they do not work stereographically. There simply is not enough—and especially not enough of Johnson himself—to allow us to seize this portion of the image "with our eyes, as with our arms, or with our hands."[33] The double mirrors that we see through the stereoscope still trope stereography's ability to reproduce three-dimensional bodies. Studying this image both in and out of the stereoscope, we even receive a lesson in how stereography works, how it fools or fails to fool our eyes. That said, the medium's magic does not extend to Johnson. Because we see him with only one eye, we do not grasp him as a physical body in relation to our equally physical bodies. We might know how the stereographic illusion should function, but we cannot experience it here. Just as Johnson exists as Cyclops in his self-portrait, so, ultimately, do we. Just like Johnson's partial figure, we find ourselves also disembodied, disenchanted.

Like Johnson's generation of Saints, then, we stand fallen before this image, fallen out of embodiment and into a space of flat approximation, a realm of division and deferral and waiting. Shot during the period after the Mormons were forced to relinquish their dream of corporeal godhood to the realm of an imagined hereafter, this image struggles to conjure a body that now recedes beyond reach—stereography's body, Johnson's body, and, of course, Smith's body—that audacious theological fantasy of a male body capable of making its own heaven without God's intervention. Even as Johnson's picture reenacts this fantasy, it suggests that the dream is just that: a dream, the lingering echoes of a belief come fundamentally undone. In this way the body that animates Johnson's self-portrait also haunts it. Gazing at the image, we see Smith's body and eye exalted within the Urim and Thummim. At the same time, however, we see the abject corpse that Holmes spoke of, that "carcas[s] . . . of little worth." Here this carcass does not sit slumped in Holmes's chair but instead stares out at us from the mirror. Shattered, split, and stripped of its capacity for transcendence, it confronts us with the fractured remains of Smith's original theology: a flattened approximation of a body that used to be.

NOTES

1. Oliver Wendell Holmes, *Soundings from the Atlantic* (Boston: Ticknor and Fields, 1864), 142.

2. Ibid., 154.

3. Ibid., 153–154, italics mine.

4. Ibid., 162.

5. The fact that we see a doorknob at the images' stereographic suture line only intensifies this sense that Johnson's self-portrait also depicts the medium's ability to transform seeing into bodily experience. Situated directly between the doubled pictures, this stereographic join becomes invisible as soon as the viewer adjusts the stereo-card to its proper position. This doorknob, in other words, sits at the very locus of the images' illusion of depth. It hovers at that critical point where the two photographs come together to spark the viewer's binocular vision, and with it his sense of existing as a physical presence within a three-dimensional space. With this doorknob, Johnson's image claims the capacity to make a world, remake the viewer's body, and then swing the door open to both.

6. Holmes, *Soundings from the Atlantic,* 154.

7. Richard Lyman Bushman, *Joseph Smith: Rough Stone Rolling* (New York: Knopf, 2005), 65. According to Charles Anton, the professor of classical studies at Columbia College who examined a copy of this script, it actually contained a "'singular medley' of Greek and Hebrew letters with other strange marks, with 'sundry delineations of half moons, stars, and other natural objects, and the whole ended in a rude representation of the Mexican zodiac.'" Ibid.

8. In the words of Smith's mother, the Urim and Thummim consisted of "smooth three-corned diamonds set in glass." D. Michael Quinn, *Early Mormonism and the Magic World View* (Salt Lake City: Signature Books, 1998), 171, quoting Lucy Mack Smith, *The Biographical Sketches of Joseph Smith, the Prophet* (New York: Arno, 1969), 101.

9. Quinn, *Early Mormonism,* 170.

10. Ibid., 169, quoting the Rochester *Gem,* September 5, 1829.

11. See, for example, Quinn, *Early Mormonism,* 170, quoting "The Mormonites," *New Hampshire Gazette,* October 25, 1831: "In 1831, a Mormon missionary preached that Smith had found 'two stones with which he was enabled by placing them over his eyes and putting his head in a dark corner to decypher [sic] the hieroglyphics on the plates.'" See also Quinn, *Early Mormonism,* 173, quoting David Whitmer, *An Address to All Believers in Christ* (Richmond, MO: Self-published, 1887), 3: "Joseph Smith would put the seer stone into a hat, and put his face in the

hat, drawing it closely around his face to exclude the light; and in the darkness the spiritual light would shine. A piece of something resembling parchment would appear, and on that appeared the writing." Interestingly, the Mormon church now downplays the role of the Urim and Thummim in Smith's translation process, at least when it comes to visual depictions of the event. Despite the consistency and clarity of the written record, all church-approved pictures of Smith translating feature him seated at a desk, pen in hand, studying the golden plates intensely. In its contemporary incarnation, in other words, the LDS church takes pains to present its first prophet as an academic rather than as a folk magician or, alternately, as an early stereoscope lover.

12. Lucy Mack Smith, *The Biographical Sketches of Joseph Smith,* 101, quoted in Bushman, *Rough Stone Rolling,* 60.

13. For a discussion of the use of seer stones in nineteenth-century folk magic, see John L. Brooke, *The Refiner's Fire: The Making of Mormon Cosmology, 1644–1844* (Cambridge, UK: Cambridge University Press, 1994), 31, and Quinn, *Early Mormonism,* 30–65.

14. Quinn, *Early Mormonism,* 171.

15. Ibid., 152.

16. We also see more than a little bit of Ralph Waldo Emerson. In Smith's declaration that the Urim and Thummim destroyed the human limitations of space and time, effectively endowing him with God's own sight, we find an echo of Emerson's 1836 essay "Nature." "I become a transparent eye-ball," Emerson wrote. "I am nothing; I see all; the currents of the Universal Being circulate through me; I am part or particle of God." Ralph Waldo Emerson, "Nature," in *The Spiritual Emerson: Essential Writings,* ed. David M. Robinson (Boston: Beacon, 2003), 25. Smith's seer stones concretized this transcendent eye. With the Urim and Thummim, he effectively channeled Emerson's visual transcendence into a fantastic invention that, while still overtly sacred, would likely have also appealed to Edward Muybridge and Henry Ford.

17. Other examples of such toys include the zoetrope, the thaumatrope, the phenakistoscope, and the praxinoscope.

18. See Laurie Maffly-Kipp, introduction to *Book of Mormon,* by Joseph Smith Jr. (New York: Penguin, 2008), xxi.

19. *Doctrine and Covenants* 132:31–32.

20. Nineteenth-century Mormons saw nothing metaphoric in their declaration that they were God's chosen people. In the words of Johnson's father-in-law, Brigham Young, "The Elders who have arisen in this Church and Kingdom [Mormonism] are actually of Israel." Young, *Journal of Discourses,* ed. G. D. Watt, 26 vols. (Salt Lake City: Deseret Book Company, 1966), vol. 16, 75. In this respect, the LDS church took the well-worn trope of an American Zion and gave it an articulation that was as concrete as any it had seen since John Winthrop declared his congregation to be a city upon a hill in 1630.

21. Mormon men, but not Mormon women. While nineteenth-century LDS polygamy effectively deified male Saints, it cast plural wives in a spiritually subservient role. As the religious scholars Colleen McDannell and Bernard Lang observe, "A woman achieves her sense of godhood by participating in her husband's eternal priesthood. Because of this, she is permitted to 'bear the souls of men, to people other worlds,' and to 'reign for ever and ever as the queen mother . . . of numerous and still increasing offspring.'" McDannell and Lang, *Heaven: A History* (New Haven, CT: Yale University Press, 1988), 319, quoting Duane S. Crowther, *Life Everlasting* (Salt Lake City: Bookcraft, 1971), 147, 339.

22. *Doctrine and Covenants* 132:16–17.

23. Edwin Brown Firmage and Richard Collin Mangrum, *Zion in the Courts: A Legal History of the Church of Jesus Christ of Latter-day Saints, 1830–1900* (Urbana: University of Illinois Press, 1988), iv.

24. For an excellent discussion of the changing Mormon conceptions of grace, see Brooke, *The Refiner's Fire.*

25. Fawn M. Brodie, *No Man Knows My History: The Life of Joseph Smith, the Mormon Prophet,* 2nd ed., rev. and enl. (New York: Alfred A. Knopf, 1971), quoting Wyl Wilhelm, *Mormon Portraits, Joseph Smith the Prophet, His Family and His Friends* (Salt Lake City, 1886), 55.

26. See *Doctrine and Covenants* 132:61: "If any man espouse a virgin, and desire to espouse another, and the first give her consent, and if he espouse the second, and they are virgins, and have vowed to no other man, then is he justified."

27. *Doctrine and Covenants* 130:8, 7.

28. For a fuller discussion of the legal respone to Mormon polygamy, see Mary K. Campbell, "Mr. Peay's Horses: The Federal Response to Mormon Polygamy, 1854–1887," *Yale Journal of Law and Feminism* 13 (2001).

29. Despite Woodruff's announcement, the actual status of Mormon polygamy would remain confused for roughly another twenty years. Although most Saints followed Woodruff's directive, or "First Manifesto on the Saints," for example, many assumed that this announcement applied only to new marriages and therefore did not dissolve polygamous unions contracted before 1890. Moreover, even after Woodruff's successor, Joseph F. Smith, issued a second manifesto in 1904, church authorities continued to authorize certain plural marriages. For all of this confusion, however, the effect of Woodruff's "First Manifesto" was instant and acute. As Jan Shipps writes, "Whatever else it did, the Manifesto announced that the old [LDS] order would have to pass away." Shipps, *Mormonism: The Story of a New Religious Tradition* (Urbana: University of Illinois, 1985), 115. Or, in the words of Gordon and Gary Shepherd, "At a certain point Mormonism had to bend or be broken. Mormon leaders chose to bend." Shepherd and Shepherd, *A Kingdom Transformed: Themes in the Development of Mormonism* (Salt Lake City: University of Utah Press, 1984), 202.

30. Meaning, of course, unorthodox in the Western context. In other cultures, polygamy remains a common marital arrangement.

31. Shipps, *Mormonism,* xv.

32. Ibid.

33. Holmes, *Soundings from the Atlantic,* 162.

17

"The Best Hotel on the Boardwalk"

Church Women, Negro Art, and the Construction of
Interracial Space in the Interwar Years

BETTY LIVINGSTON ADAMS

In October 1937 a select group of white and black women received a postcard (Figure 17.1) on which to make room reservations—single or double—for the upcoming two-day interracial conference in Asbury Park, New Jersey. The postcard was eye-catching. On one side was a colorful photograph of the oceanside Hotel Berkeley-Carteret, on the other the imprimatur of the venerable Federal Council of Churches of Christ in America (FCC). The postcard strikingly displayed the luxurious accommodations that awaited guests at "the best hotel on the boardwalk."[1] What the postcard did not disclose was the liminal space the equal number of black and white Protestant women would occupy for two days in October or the full identity of the sponsoring group. When the 140 delegates from twelve Northern states and the District of Columbia arrived at the Berkeley-Carteret they could not miss the opulence of the grand hotel, which had lost none of its luster despite the devastation of the Great Depression. Nor could they miss the exhibit of "primitive" African art and the sculpture, paintings, and photographs of "New Negro Art" prominently placed to be viewed by all hotel guests.[2] Indeed, for hotel guests and passersby the visual sensation created by the fine art display was rivaled only by the visual and spatial juxtaposition of black and white churchwomen in implicitly secular and white space.

In this chapter I explore the use of visual and material culture, particularly fine arts, by the Church Women's Committee of the FCC's Commission on Race Relations during the interwar years. Organized in 1926, the Church Women's Committee (CWC) incorporated products of the New Negro Art Movement into a moveable, living tableau intended to stimulate and educate as it catalyzed women into action in the cause of race relations and social justice. These white and black upper- and middle-class women challenged prevailing discourses on race, space, and religion through art exhibits and interracial conferences in a program of applied theology and

HOTEL BERKELEY-CARTERET. ASBURY PARK. N. J.

FIGURE 17.1. "The Best Hotel on the Boardwalk," postcard showing Hotel Berkeley-Carteret, Asbury Park, New Jersey, issued by the Federal Council of Churches of Christ in America, 1937. Presbyterian Historical Society, Presbyterian Church (U.S.A.), Philadelphia, PA.

religious education. They embedded African American images and objects and black and white bodies in public space to "promote interracial goodwill and cooperation through united thought and action." Determined to "face frankly the problem of race relations" and find a "solution in the light of Christian teaching," they challenged the structure and effect of racialized space by making the aestheticized and corporeal presence of African Americans visible. Considered bold, if not radical, by some, this intersensorial practice was intended to position race relations as a religious topic. The CWC incorporated innovative techniques of the consumer market and practices of social science into a gendered religious framework to articulate a renewed Protestant "enthusiasm for human welfare and belief in the Fatherhood of God."[3]

Even as they engaged in traditionally gendered activities like luncheons, teas, conferences, and art exhibits, the churchwomen appeared to Northern clergy as all too willing to challenge pastoral prerogatives and denominational conventions. Southern white churchwomen had their own reservations about their Northern Protestant sisters who trespassed spatial and social boundaries meant to reify racial differences and protect white supremacy. Wary of the churchwomen's transgressive program "to deal with the problems of race relations, establishing justice, fair play, and interracial goodwill," entrenched religious forces eventually undermined the CWC's program of racial equality.[4] Though they fell short of their goal of promoting a religious vision suited to a modern, multiracial society, the CWC expanded the religious discourse beyond personal piety and helped to define race relations as a religious issue.

Post–World War I America was riven by labor unrest, racial violence, and social dislocations. The national landscape had changed dramatically with the transformation from an agricultural to an industrial economy and the migration of black and white citizens from rural to urban areas. South to North and East to West, cities and towns mushroomed seemingly overnight. Labor and racial clashes increased as groups competed for space and place in the rapidly changing social order. Racial and industrial violence in the North rivaled the mob violence and lynchings that had long characterized the South. To many, the economic and social upheavals signaled a loss of national identity and a diminution of Protestant leadership. In the wake of war and the remapping of the nation's political, social, and racial geographies, liberal and conservative religious institutions were reluctant to address racial and economic discrimination or the spread of Jim Crow segregation in public spaces, including Northern churches. The limits of American Protestantism were all too clear as mainline denominations stood by silently and defined race relations as "outside" their purview and lodged more immediately within the social domain. In the midst of such profound changes, black and white Protestant men focused on control and avoidance rather than on immoral structures and systems, while white churchwomen chafed under denominational practices that limited their autonomy and black churchwomen pressed for institutional responses to racial and economic injustices.[5]

Beginning in the mid-1920s, white and black women of the CWC attempted to "arouse the conscience" of Christians in the area of race relations and to redefine the boundary between religion and society. The Church Women's Interracial Conference Movement became a site for fashioning a distinct public role for Protestant women in a society in need of reconstruction. They would mold personal attitudes for "justice and fair play in all relations of life," "stimulate right community attitudes and action," and, they hoped, become "a great power" in their communities.[6]

The CWC grounded its program of gendered leadership and religious education in a liberal theological belief in the immanence and personality of Jesus and the burgeoning field of social science. The women found support for their religious activism in the writings of George Haynes, African American secretary of the FCC's Commission on Race Relations and an ordained minister with a Ph.D. in sociology from Columbia University. Haynes contended that it was possible to create an "interracial mind," one educated to counter the increasing separation of the races in social, civic, and public life. Haynes believed that race consciousness, like class or caste consciousness, led to social distance; however, because race consciousness was a "phenomenon," like public opinion, it was amenable to change through education. Christian principles and American enthusiasm would create a sensory field of "happy experiences and memory . . . within and between groups" and eradicate the color line.[7] The CWC believed it was uniquely suited to fashion this principle into a religious practice, for "interracial action must be preceded by interracial thinking."[8]

The CWC proposed a new role for religious women in interwar America, one based not on domestic devotion but on public activism. With a program centered on interracial conferences they would stimulate religious groups "to deal with the problem of race relations, establishing justice, fair play, and interracial goodwill." The Church Women's Interracial Conference Movement would be a "new stage of progress in grappling with interracial problems by religious forces." In concert with Protestant women of all denominations, they would lead in the reconstruction of the national landscape by formulating "methods, plans, and programs for possible action by local women's groups in the local churches of their communities." As a national religious women's institution, one not supported—or constrained—by denominational boards, the CWC would look to the "hearts of . . . women" for support.[9] They were modern, liberal churchwomen with a mission that transcended racial or sectarian boundaries.

"Enjoying the privilege and opportunities" of the male-led FCC, these Protestant women felt empowered to exercise spiritual authority in public space. They hoped to create an autonomous public role for women, one that would locate their work in "every community where there are members of more than one race" and not, insignificantly, beyond the reach of pastoral and denominational control.[10] Through the Interracial Conference Movement they would present a practical—and gendered—solution that would transform religious practices with an updated Kingdom of God theology and free America to come (in)to its senses by eliminating the divide between thinking and feeling, sacred and secular, black and white.

From the mid-1920s to the end of the 1930s, the CWC sponsored three national interracial conferences, more than half a dozen regional conferences, and numerous local interracial conferences and meetings. Interracial conferences, the coming together of "representatives . . . of the two great races which together hold the future of American civilization in their hands" and "spokesmen [*sic*] for thirty-one denominations and organizations whose membership number millions of American women," would be the mechanism for solving the most controversial social and political issue of the day, the problem of the color line.[11] In recapping her experience at the Second General Interracial Conference in 1928, one African American conferee wrote, "That was an interesting group of women who met . . . to discuss the church and its relation to the inter-racial question. . . . [A] more representative body . . . would be hard to find. And for two days . . . they carried out a most crowded program of breathtaking scope. . . . and you rather felt breathless from rushing so fast and so far into the realm of applied religion and social science and the race question and reports of what has been done and what can be done, and what yet remains to be done."[12]

Despite the intensity of the sessions, the CWC ensured that each interracial conference maintained a "deeply spiritual nature . . . throughout by the touching beauty of the music and the inspiration of the prayers."[13] The 1927 Philadelphia-area conference on discrimination in employment, housing, health, and education ended with an inspiring Sunday-morning service at which "a Quakeress spoke[,] emphasizing the abundant life as the experience which white and colored people may have as they strive for amicable contacts." One white delegate rated the conference she attended "the deepest spiritual experience" of her life and "a glimpse of the Kingdom of God."[14]

Churchwomen began to incorporate productions of the New Negro Art Movement into their program following the First General Interracial Conference in 1927. Under the auspices of CWC members in Chicago, the Chicago Woman's Club and the Chicago Art Institute sponsored "The Negro in Art Week," an exhibition that featured forty contemporary paintings of the New Negro Art Movement, three pieces of sculpture, drawings, decorative art, and the Blondiau Collection of African sculpture and metalwork from the Belgian Congo. The women also included lectures, poetry readings, and musical concerts as part of the exhibition.[15] Sharing the liberal Protestant belief in the beneficent effect of the fine arts on character, these Northern women also recognized that art exhibits provided an avenue for women's public practice of religion in a secular culture.

A year earlier the William E. Harmon Foundation had announced the first awards for distinguished achievement by Negroes in literature, music, business, science, education, religion, race relations, and the fine arts. One of the foundation's goals was "to bring about a wider interest in Negro art as a contributing influence in American culture." In a joint venture between the FCC and the Harmon Foundation, the administrative duties for the juried fine arts competition and exhibition were assumed by Race Relations Commission Secretary George Haynes, thus placing the CWC within the ambit of this exciting and modern cultural movement.[16]

In the aftermath of World War I, African Americans exhibited a militancy and racial consciousness that ushered in a "New Negro aesthetic." For African American philosophy professor and contemporary culture critic Alain Locke, this aesthetic was the cultural representation of the "new freedom and dignity" embodied by African Americans in the "Harlem Renaissance."[17] The artistic themes and strategies pursued by black artists were wide ranging, from portraiture with modern depictions of the body to sensuous nude sculptures to genre paintings of everyday life and epic stories and abstractions. The 1929 Harmon exhibition broadside depicted the variety of artistic representations in works by Richmond Barthé (*Tortured Negro*), Malvin Gray Johnson (*Swing Low, Sweet Chariot*), and Charles Dawson (*The Quadroon Madonna*) (Figure 17.2). The representational variety notwithstanding, the visual rhetoric was an unmistakable challenge to the prevailing racial discourse.[18] For the CWC, as for the

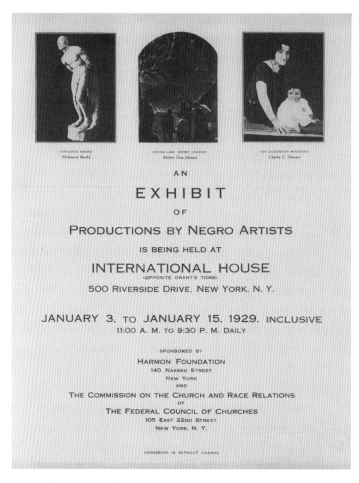

FIGURE 17.2. *An Exhibit of Productions by Negro Artists,* held at International House, New York, sponsored by the Harmon Foundation and the Commission on the Church and Race Relations of the Federal Council of Churches, broadside, 1929. Reproduced across the top are *Tortured Negro* by Richmond Barthé, *Swing Low, Sweet Chariot* by Malvin Gray Johnson, and *The Quadroon Madonna* by Charles C. Dawson. Presbyterian Historical Society, Presbyterian Church (U.S.A.), Philadelphia, PA.

shapers of the Harlem Renaissance, this iconography was to be an antidote to the minstrel trope that dominated racial thought and popular culture.

From 1928 to 1933 the Harmon Foundation sponsored five juried art exhibits at the International House and the Art Center in New York City, where annually two to three thousand black and white visitors viewed fine art images and objects. The New York show was followed by a six-month traveling tour that carried the art productions to communities around the country, North and South, especially to those cities and towns from which winners hailed and where churchwomen's interracial committees could add the New Negro Art exhibit to their race relations program.

At a time when professional galleries were few in number, churchwomen in the Interracial Conference Movement reached out to their network of women's clubs and religious organizations to generate publicity and ensure an interracial audience. White and black residents in cities and industrial towns from Hartford, Connecticut, to Youngstown, Ohio, Nashville, Tennessee, and Saint Louis, Missouri, were able to view New Negro Art along with residents of Chicago and Atlanta. Exhibits were held in churches, YWCA centers, and high school gymnasia, sites art historian Mary Ann Calo describes as "non-professional contexts, in which inadequate attention had been paid to hanging, lighting, and other variables that would enhance the aesthetic experience of the work rather than display it."[19] Despite the site deficiencies, the exhibits asserted the visual and physical presence of African Americans in public space, space that throughout the 1920s and 1930s was increasingly designated as *white* space. With support from the CWC in New York, local churchwomen coordinated advance publicity and mailed invitations to an equal number of black and white viewers. The women followed up on each showing with a survey on racial attitudes. In connection with the 1927 Negro art exhibition in Chicago, for example, they distributed ten thousand pamphlets, four hundred posters, and one hundred invitations in advance of the show and a survey on racial attitudes afterward.[20] By creating new contexts for viewing fine art productions by African Americans and by increasing the conditions for wider publics to witness African American audiences viewing fine art, the churchwomen hoped to alter the reception of blacks in public space and thereby engender interracial thinking, especially among whites. The power of visual images in the right context, they believed, would lead to transformation on the personal level and empowerment on the national level. The result would be a new era in race relations.

Generally the fine arts exhibits combined "primitive" African art, which had taken the art world by storm at the turn of the century, and artistic productions that constituted the New Negro Art Movement of the 1920s.[21] In keeping with the format of the 1927 Chicago exhibit, no distinction was made in terms of media, provenance, technique, or interpretation. Rather the pieces were arrayed in linear fashion, beginning with "primitive" African art objects and ending with sculptures, paintings, etchings, and photographs by twentieth-century professional and amateur artists.[22] The spatial arrangement presented a narrative of the "evolution" of African Americans in the cultural progression from Africa to urbanization and modernity in America.

Here was iconography for a modern religious temper. New Negro Art represented "self-liberation" and an aesthetic instantiation of individualism, along with the power of liberal religion and modern science to solve social problems. Here with representations of black life in mediated space, white and black Americans could "meet upon one of the highest levels of life, upon the level of a common recognition . . . in the field of intellectual, artistic, spiritual endeavor."[23] The sensorial experience of view-ers with the images and objects of a New Negro Art exhibit represented, at least for the moment, life moving from conflict to harmony and the embodiment of the "inter-racial mind," one educated to counter racial segregation in social, civic, and public life. Protestant women saw themselves as leaders in this transformational process. Whereas negative attitudes and discrimination limited human development, the CWC averred, "Religion at its best imposes upon us the responsibility for recon-structing our social order so that every person will have larger opportunity for maxi-mum development."[24] "Christian women," they maintained, "by organized effort and personal influence in church, community and home should be the strongest force in building and maintaining attitudes of fundamental respect for human personality."[25] For the CWC the success of Negro art exhibits was less about the artwork and more about the work of the artists and its effect on attitudes and the structure of public space.

This was not art for art's sake. Art in this context was to serve higher social, po-litical, and spiritual purposes. For the CWC the value of Negro art lay in the oppor-tunity to establish interracial contacts "for the purpose of spreading information as to what the Negro is doing in the Fine Arts."[26] By this formulation, the women be-lieved, creating a space for self-expression by black Americans would stimulate the spiritual growth of white Americans. The convergence of modern culture and mod-ern religion would present a visual argument against racial discrimination and map a new site for women's religious activism in the era of Jim Crow. The primary focus in art exhibits was on the "social and biographic at the expense of the aesthetic," and ex-hibition catalogs were often no more than a checklist of the works displayed.[27] Much to the chagrin of the professional black artists who entered the Harmon competi-tion, press releases highlighted the biographies of "janitors, waiters, and sign paint-ers" who hailed "from all sections of the country" and were "compelled to carry on their art in spare time."[28]

In 1930, for example, William H. Johnson, a twenty-nine-year-old native of Florence, South Carolina, living in New York City, was the first-place winner in the Harmon Foundation juried exhibition for his painting *Self-Portrait* (Figure 17.3). The press release did not provide a critical discussion of Johnson's winning work or men-tion his training at New York's National Academy of Design or his three years in France. Instead it portrayed Johnson as "one of our coming great painters. *He is a real modernist.* He has been spontaneous, vigorous, firm, direct; he has shown a great thing in art—*it is the expression of the man himself.*"[29]

Following the 1928 Harmon exhibition, one art critic lamented, "Some dis-appointment was expressed that this assembling of Negro work gave no more of the

SELF-PORTRAIT   *William. H. Johnson*

EXHIBIT OF FINE ARTS
by
American Negro Artists

Presented by the
Harmon Foundation
and
The Commission on Race Relations
Federal Council of Churches

FIGURE 17.3. *Exhibit of Fine Arts by America Negro Artists,* presented by the Harmon Foundation and the Commission on the Church and Race Relations of the Federal Council of Churches, exhibit catalog cover, 1930. Reproduced at the top is *Self-Portrait* by William H. Johnson. Presbyterian Historical Society, Presbyterian Church (U.S.A.), Philadelphia, PA.

special experience and psychology of the Negro than it did." Others characterized the entries as derivative and imitative, displaying none of the racial or African idioms the white art world demanded.[30] Indeed, the self-portraits, sculptures, and depictions of middle-class domesticity that black artists submitted for juried exhibitions portrayed a slice of African American life that disappointed those looking for expressions of modernist, primitive, or racialist images. Many African American artists in the 1920s were "figurative painters" working in a representational style that did not include overtly religious, political, or work-related themes. Those who created such pieces rarely submitted them for Harmon shows. Rather the portraiture and genre pieces depicted the varied experiences of black artists living and working in different locations. Such images were part of a representational discourse of resistance that contradicted racist caricatures common during the interwar years. Nonetheless, for black artists as well as their cultural critics, the conflation of religion, art, race, and public space was problematic.

In 1931 the Harmon Foundation exhibition moved from the International House on Riverside Drive to the Art Center on East Fifty-sixth Street. The exhibition catalog, the most elaborate ever, reflected a turn in the New Negro Art Movement and the public response to it. The catalog cover featured a photograph of Sargent Claude Johnson's award-winning sculpture *Chester* and the frontispiece Laura Wheeler Waring's *Mother and Daughter* (Figures 17.4 and 17.5). Inside were thirty-one sepia reproductions of modern paintings and sculptures, along with photographs of pieces by nineteenth-century African American artists Edward M. Bannister and Henry Ossawa Tanner. The catalog also included essays that sought to interpret the artistic moment. Art Center Director Alon Bement applauded the exhibition for "the beginning of race consciousness.... It was the feeling of the judges that this fourth exhibition may be said to mark the real appearance of the Negro in the field of visual art." Alain Locke pointed to the sensorial quality of the black experience in the "consciously racial surface" of sculptures by Richmond Barthé, the "striking stylistic analy-

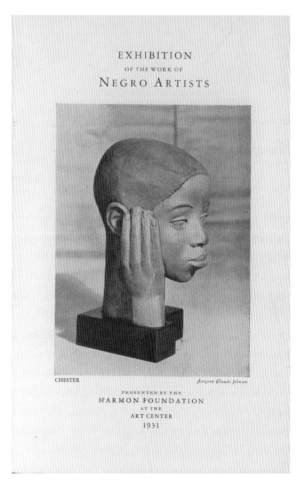

EXHIBITION
OF THE WORK OF
NEGRO ARTISTS

CHESTER

Sargent Claude Johnson

PRESENTED BY THE
HARMON FOUNDATION
AT THE
ART CENTER
1931

FIGURE 17.4. *Exhibition of the Work of Negro Artists Presented by the Harmon Foundation at the Art Center,* New York, exhibit catalog cover, 1931. Reproduced at center is *Chester* by Sargent Claude Johnson. Presbyterian Historical Society, Presbyterian Church (U.S.A.), Philadelphia, PA.

MOTHER AND DAUGHTER   *Laura Wheeler Waring*

*All the photographic work for this catalogue and the Exhibition has been done
by James L. Allen, 213 West 121st Street, New York, N. Y.
Negro photographer*

FIGURE 17.5. *Exhibition of the Work of Negro Artists Presented by the Harmon Foundation at the Art Center,* New York, exhibit catalog frontispiece, 1931. Features *Mother and Daughter* by Laura Wheeler Waring. Presbyterian Historical Society, Presbyterian Church (U.S.A.), Philadelphia, PA.

sis" of Sargent Johnson, and "the design structure and motives" of Aaron Douglas and William H. Johnson, who "indirectly reflected the idioms in the modernist style."[31]

For the CWC the change in venue to an arts-specific space signaled a change in their relationship to the visual images and objects. The Art Center "placed the exhibit on a definitely professional basis." Although the new location increased the number of viewers and attracted art critics and gallery owners eager to capitalize on the successful showing, the women wondered how "the value of the interracial contacts might be continued."[32] It was important that the visual/material narrative of New Negro Art as a marker of modernity and liberal Christianity not be replaced by art critics and gallery owners eager to create their own version of a modern American identity.[33]

Context mattered. What was a matter of aesthetics for Alain Locke and art critics was for these women one of religious practice. To maintain control of its narrative, the CWC encouraged women's organizations to advertise the touring exhibits widely. More significantly, they fostered closer cooperation with women in religious organizations. Whether national, regional, or local, interracial conferences were designed to inspire others to "grow" interracial committees to "solve our racial problems in the all-embracing and tolerant spirit of Christ" and, in the process, "contribute to the possible solution of world problems." Those cities and towns in which churchwomen established interracial committees were designated "forward-looking" communities.[34]

At the same time that the interracial conferences were gaining importance, the expansion of the color line in the North and Midwest was complicating the churchwomen's reality. Finding suitable conference sites became more difficult. Conference locations had to provide ample space for concurrent and plenary sessions as well as group meals, informal fellowship, and overnight lodging. Dinners, luncheons, teas, and opportunities for personal interaction were central to the conference experience. Remarking on the conference schedule, a delegate noted, "There is tea at five . . . and we dress for dinner, and eat together at various tables throughout the conference trying to break up our relations and know as many as possible." To assure nondiscriminatory and courteous treatment of all delegates at all events, the women thoroughly interrogated hotel proprietors and conference managers prior to negotiating a contract.[35]

For the CWC, visual representations and spatial arrangements were integral to the "new stage of progress in grappling with interracial problems by religious forces." The "close informal contacts between delegates in small groups and in personal conversations, and . . . a spirit of fellowship" reified the new religious spirit and provided the moral language for race relations discussions. When the women gathered, secular space was temporarily transformed into sacred space and fine art into religious iconography to stimulate a "greater spirit of fellowship and cooperation between the races . . . [an] imperative in religious organizations which have proposed belief in Christ's teaching of brotherhood."[36] In this way, black and white churchwomen hoped to model a new Christian practice by making racial issues religious issues and by unifying sacred space and public space.

In spite of the women's sacred desire to enact the Christian teaching of "brotherhood," they encountered profane resistance. Finding accommodations that met both their ethical and their fiscal criteria became more difficult in the late 1920s and 1930s with the intensification in the virulence and extent of Jim Crow racial segregation. As more women became involved in the CWC's Interracial Conference Movement and placed racial discrimination within a religious framework, they felt empowered to challenge racial discrimination in public spaces. The CWC received numerous requests from women's organizations with national constituencies seeking assistance in erasing the color line. After the National Association of Deans of Women contacted the CWC regarding the hotel situation in the nation's capital, for instance, local churchwomen were advised to visit hotels and compile lists of those open to meetings of interracial groups. Following a successful exchange with another interracial women's group, the local hotel management promised that "they will not close the doors to Negro delegates." Women in Fort Wayne, Indiana, reported that a meeting with the president of the Interurban Railroad had elicited his commitment "that there should be no further discrimination against Negroes." When the Federation of Women's Boards of Foreign Missions could not persuade the proprietor of one Atlantic City, New Jersey, hotel to change his policy, they moved to another "where Negro delegates were accepted." While the Congregational Council in Seattle "brought hotel proprietors to terms," Presbyterian women were forced to make other arrangements for their biennial conference in Pittsburgh following a change in hotel management.[37]

Fearful that national groups with interracial constituencies would abandon the practice of securing headquarters sites for conferences, the CWC declared the "time ripe for concerted action" against hotels and restaurants "where Negroes are refused admittance." The matter of hotel and meeting arrangements was on the agenda at the Third General Interracial Conference held at Oberlin College in June 1930, where the women discussed "Tomorrow in Race Relations." The conference adopted a resolution for approval and dissemination by the FCC Executive Board that read in part, "We, the Church Women's Committee . . . believe that a greater spirit of fellowship and cooperation between races is imperative in religious organizations which have professed a belief in Christ's teaching of brotherhood." The resolution called upon Protestant leaders to demand "general observance of certain fundamental courtesies which should be shown alike to all members. . . . No official function should be held unless all delegates can be included on equal terms."[38]

Although the FCC Executive Board had earlier ordered its own "united survey . . . and joint action" on the subject of discrimination, the women's resolution was "not given much consideration." One board member expressed "very strong sentiment against it," effectively dooming approval. Undaunted, the churchwomen concluded that the resolution "would have educational effect" even if not approved. They distributed copies to women's groups, including white women's groups in the South, "for study and report as to their feeling."[39]

Throughout the 1930s, Jim Crow segregation in public space intensified. In 1935, for instance, every large hotel in New York City refused to hold the National Urban League's anniversary dinner. That same year the National Conference of Social Work was forced to move its conference to Atlantic City from Washington, D.C., in order to ensure equal treatment of all members. African American delegates to the 1936 International Council of Religious Education meeting in Cincinnati had to room at the local YMCA after the headquarters hotel refused to honor their reservations.[40]

In response to its inquiry regarding hotel and conference arrangements, the CWC received numerous reports of racial discrimination, including one from the Student Volunteer Movement requesting assistance with hotels and restaurants in New York City. Succumbing to pressure to address the problem of the color line at its doorstep, the FCC reluctantly convened a "Special Group Called to Consider the Matter of Hotel Arrangements in New York City." The committee recommended that religious organizations patronize only hotels that did not discriminate and, timidly, proposed consideration of legal action if necessary.[41]

When the 140 black and white churchwomen convened on the Jersey shore in 1937, they were aware that the spatial juxtaposition of an equal number of black and white women and New Negro Art in secular (and implicitly white and affluent) space created a synesthetic experience that extended beyond the luxurious Hotel Berkeley-Carteret. As at previous conferences, the New Negro Art exhibit was "an important feature." Although the Harmon Foundation had suspended sponsorship of fine art exhibits four years earlier, it provided prize-winning pieces and photographs of New Negro Art from its private collection. Also on display were pieces of African art from the Newark (New Jersey) Museum lending collection.[42] The display was arranged so that the viewer's gaze moved from the wood and bronze sculptures, musical instruments, ebony and ivory carvings, and other pieces of African art to the modernistic sculptures, portraits, and photographs of New Negro Art, ending at a map of the United States that pinpointed the locations of churchwomen's interracial committees, sites of urban growth and African American migration that had so profoundly changed the political and cultural landscape. The exhibit was strategically placed so as to be visible to conference delegates as well as hotel guests and passersby. The latter "showed a great deal of interest; looked at the exhibit and asked questions about it and the sponsoring organizations."[43]

The presence and visibility in public space of middle-class black women *in the flesh* and the aesthetic presentation of black life and experience on canvas reinforced the theme of the two-day religious conference, "The Next Chapter in Racial Understanding." Although the conference sessions were "a real spiritual inspiration . . . giving much interesting information," the art exhibit and the corporeal presence of a number of white and black women fulfilled a larger purpose. The aesthetics aimed to move viewers "from exotic curiosity to true understanding of black culture, and from distortion of black identity to recognition of its beauty."[44] By challenging the status quo on race and space, religion and gender, the CWC hoped to create an "interracial mind" among delegates as well as hotel guests. The scales of reference of images and objects to physical bodies, from the representational to the corporeal, were central to their social justice activism.

A month later, a similar gathering of 165 black and white churchwomen, also carefully selected and racially balanced, from thirteen Midwestern and Western states convened at the North Shore Hotel in suburban Evanston, Illinois. With the same theme, topics, and traveling art exhibit as the New Jersey conference, the women re-created the tableau of aesthetic and physical bodies for the meeting in suburban Chicago. Prior to the CWC conference, the tony North Shore Hotel had been used for interracial meetings when only two or three African Americans were in attendance. This time, the CWC gleefully noted, "They had a considerable number and everything went very smoothly."[45]

"Liberal, democratic, and Christian"—these were the markers of modernity that black and white Northern Protestant women claimed for themselves and desired for their country.[46] They envisioned an inclusive America, one in which gender and racial barriers to the development of individual personality were removed. By their assessment, the major impediment to America's realization of full democracy and modernity was racial intolerance, the product of un-Christian attitudes and ways of thinking.

Who better to arouse the conscience of the nation and usher it into religious modernity than these newly enfranchised Protestant women, self-proclaimed representatives of the two great races that would shape American civilization? Their plan of action was straightforward. The sensorial experience created by the aestheticized presence of black Americans on canvas and by the corporeal presence of black and white bodies on an equal plane would mold women's attitudes, and they, in turn, would lead in the creation of just communities. As the women's intentional and intense interaction at conferences suggests, they did not privilege aestheticized black bodies over corporeal ones. However, as liberal Protestants they placed great faith in the mediated power of images. With a redirected gaze and a retrained mind moving from the representational to the corporeal, they believed that personal liberation and communal reconstruction would inevitably follow.

Unfortunately for the CWC, theirs was not a shared vision. Never adequately funded or fully supported by the FCC, the CWC had to rely increasingly on outside contributions to cover the costs of research and the publication of material as well as to provide administrative support for interracial committees. As the Depression deepened in the 1930s and the FCC's budget was severely constricted, the CWC was forced to suspend its sponsorship of national and regional interracial conferences. In 1941 the FCC effectively dissolved the CWC by integrating its members into other areas. FCC executives would not commit to retaining any of the African American members in its newly configured operations.[47]

In one of its final acts, the nearly moribund CWC commissioned a painting by Aaron Douglas to publicize the sixteenth annual observance of Race Relations Sunday in 1938 (Figure 17.6). The eleven-by-seventeen-inch poster with Douglas's signature depicting the rising star of freedom and the stylized figures of African Americans on a journey to modernity transmitted the CWC's intertwined discourses of race re-

FIGURE 17.6. *Race Relations Sunday, February 13, 1938, Introducing Interracial Week, Church, School & Community Observances,* Department of Race Relations, Federal Council of Churches, New York, poster. Image at poster's center is a reproduction of an Aaron Douglas painting commissioned for this purpose. Presbyterian Historical Society, Presbyterian Church (U.S.A.), Philadelphia, PA.

lations, religion, and modernity in a portable and durable image. A smaller version of the poster became the standard cover for distributing material of the Commission on Race Relations to religious groups and social agencies, including those in the South.[48]

With the privileges and opportunities afforded by the FCC, the CWC had been free to operate as a national organization without deferring to the denominational or regional prejudices of the better-financed women's missionary boards. Though it had early expressed the importance of "do[ing] nothing that can be misunderstood by the southern group," Southern white women had restricted the dissemination of material by the CWC to missionary organizations. Now the CWC found itself out of step with white Northern missionaries, who were eager to assert their own independence and mend denominational ties across regional boundaries. Consequently, when the United Council of Church Women announced in 1942 that it would "carry forward the program formerly developed by the Women's Committee," the CWC was without allies.[49] There seemed to be no place for its vision of interracial and gendered religious activism. African American artists would make a similar discovery as the products of the New Negro Art Movement were excluded from the national canon of modern art.[50]

The CWC's Interracial Conference Movement highlights the possibilities and limitations of religious activism. Though these Protestant women ventured boldly where others feared to tread, they were unable to overcome the social and political structures of early twentieth-century America or to escape its binary constructions. Hamstrung by their subordinate position within the FCC and the Commission on Race Relations, the CWC lacked the resources or authority to expand race relations beyond the black/white formulation or to meaningfully address the social and economic conditions of Mexican and Asian Americans, for example. Further, their desire to include Catholic and Jewish women in the CWC was rejected by the FCC, for which ecumenism remained a Protestant endeavor. Not until the cataclysm of World War II would the Protestant vision expand beyond the binary axes.

Even the CWC's use of visual and material culture had its limitations. These women who spoke with a pronounced upper-middle-class accent carefully managed the sensorial experience of the Interracial Conference Movement, from site selection to the arrangement of paintings, images, and objects, to fit a class-bound narrative. There is no evidence, for example, that the CWC included in its exhibits the more radical cultural products of New Deal realism. The 1930s shift in visual and material representation celebrated a more vernacular and working-class reality of race, class, and gender. Though the churchwomen's incorporation of fine art into its program of religious education was short-lived, they succeeded in bringing wider attention to African American artists and to the value of fine arts in religious education.[51]

Although they did not realize their interwar goal of modern, just communities, the black and white women of the CWC expanded the religious discourse of the time with their mapping of images, objects, and bodies in public space. Believing in an immanent God who cared about social order and human systems, they embodied an early civil rights advocacy.

NOTES

1. National of Council of Churches Papers, RG 18, Box 56, Folder 13, Presbyterian Historical Society, Philadelphia, PA (hereafter cited as NCC Papers and PHS). It is worth remarking that the Protestant women's group chose a postcard with the image of a luxury hotel rather than one with a religious symbol or message. On the commercial production of religious ephemera, including postcards, see Colleen McDannell, *Material Christianity: Religion and Popular Culture in America* (New Haven, CT, and London: Yale University Press, 1995).

2. Minutes of the Church Women's Committee on Race Relations, December 6, 1937, NCC Papers, RG 18, Box 56, Folder 12, PHS (hereafter cited as CWCRR Minutes).

3. Initially, CWC membership was restricted to female officers of the FCC's constituent boards and organizations; representatives of interracial organizations like the YWCA were accepted as members at large. CWCRR Minutes, September 18–19, 1928, NCC Papers, RG 18, Box 56, Folder 13; CWCRR Minutes, February 28, 1927, NCC Papers, RG 18, Box 56, Folder 11; CWCRR Minutes, October 29, 1928, NCC Papers, RG 18, Box 56, Folder 11; and Summary of Findings, Second General Interracial Conference of Church Women, Eagles Mere, PA, September 18–19, 1928, NCC Papers, RG 18, Box 56, Folder 13.

4. The women grounded their program in a practical theology that stressed practices and action rather than doctrine. CWCRR Minutes, March 26, 1928, NCC Papers, RG 18, Box 56, Folder 11.

5. On religion, race, and gender in the early twentieth century, see Gail Bederman, "'The Women Have Had Charge of the Church Work Long Enough': The Men and Religion Forward Movement of 1911–1912 and the Masculinization of Middle-Class Protestantism," *American Quarterly* 41 (September 1989): 432–465, and David M. Reimers, *White Protestantism and the Negro* (New York: Oxford University Press, 1963).

6. Findings of the Women's Committee, May 4–9 and 8–9, 1929, NCC, RG 18, Box 56, Folder 13.

7. George Edmond Haynes, *The Trend of the Races* (New York: Council of Women for Home Missions and Missionary Education Movement of the United States and Canada, 1922), 96–98, 168–169; Haynes, "The Church and the Negro Spirit," *Survey Graphic* 6 (March 1925): 695–697, 708–709; and Haynes, "Changing Racial Attitudes and Customs," *Phylon* 2 (1st quarter 1941): 28–43. On sensory fields, see David Howes, "Introduction: Empires of the Senses," in *Empire of the Senses: The Sensual Cultural Reader,* ed. David Howes (Oxford, UK, and New York: Berg, 2005), 1–15.

8. *Church Women in Interracial Cooperation,* Pamphlet 7, December 1926, prepared by the Continuation Committee of the Interracial Conference of Church Women held at Eagles Mere, PA, September 21–22, 1926, p. 5, NCC Papers, RG 18, Box 56, Folder 13.

9. Ibid., 1. CWCRR Minutes, November 1, 1926, NCC Papers, RG 18, Box 56, Folder 11.

10. CWCRR Minutes, May 26, 1939, NCC Papers, RG 18, Box 56, Folder 12, and *Church Women in Interracial Cooperation,* 1.

11. Press release, Federal Council of Churches, [1928], NCC Papers, RG 18, Box 56, Folder 13.

12. Gloria T. Hull, ed., *The Works of Alice Dunbar-Nelson* (New York: Oxford University Press, 1988), vol. 2, 230–231.

13. *Church Women in Interracial Cooperation*, 1.

14. CWCRR Minutes, May 2, 1927, NCC Papers, RG 18, Box 56, Folder 11, and *Church Women in Interracial Cooperation*, 2.

15. Lisa Meyerowitz, "The Negro in Art Week: Defining the 'New Negro' through Art Exhibition," *African American Review* 31 (Spring 1997): 7–90, and Mary Ann Calo, *Distinction and Denial: Race, Nation, and the Critical Construction of the African American Artist, 1920–1940* (Ann Arbor: University of Michigan Press, 2007), 72–74.

16. Harmon Foundation Award Flyer, Leaflet 5, January 1926, NCC Papers, RG 18, Box 60, Folder, 13, and Gary A. Reynolds, "An Experiment in Inductive Service: Looking Back at the Harmon Foundation," in *Against the Odds: African-American Artists and the Harmon Foundation,* ed. Gary A. Reynolds and Beryl Wright (Newark, NJ: Newark Museum, 1989), 27–43.

17. Alain Locke, "The American Negro as Artist," in *The New Negro: Readings on Race, Representation, and African American Culture, 1892–1938,* ed. Henry Louis Gates Jr. and Gene Andrew Jarrett (Princeton, NJ, and Oxford, UK: Oxford University Press, 2007), 543, and Calo, *Distinction and Denial,* xi.

18. The literature on African American art of the 1920s and 1930s is extensive. See, for example, Richard J. Powell, *Black Art and Culture in the 20th Century* (London: Thames and Hudson, 1997); Andrea D. Barnwell and Kirsten P. Buick, et al., "A Portfolio of Works by African American Artists Continuing the Dialogue: A Work in Progress," *Art Institute of Chicago Museum Studies* 24 (2): *African Americans in Art: Selections from The Art Institute of Chicago* (1999): 180–219, 265–267; David Krasner, *A Beautiful Pageant: African American Theatre, Drama, and Performance in the Harlem Renaissance, 1910–1927* (New York: Palgrave Macmillan, 2002); Henry Louis Gates Jr. and Gene Andrew Jarrett, "Introduction," in *The New Negro,* 1–20; and Lauren Rebecca Sklaroff, *Black Culture and the New Deal: The Quest for Civil Rights in the Roosevelt Era* (Chapel Hill: University of North Carolina Press, 2009).

19. Calo, *Distinction and Denial,* 71. The Harmon Foundation's role was controversial in the interwar years and has remained so. For a contemporary assessment, see Romare Bearden's 1937 indictment, "The Negro Artist and Modern Art," in *The New Negro,* 371–372. For a historical analysis, see Calo, *Distinction and Denial,* 146–159.

20. Lisa Meyerowitz, "The Negro in Art Week," 81.

21. For a sampling of the ongoing sensation generated by African art, see Sheldon Cheney, "Darkest Africa Sends Us Art," *New York Times,* February 13, 1927, SM7; "'Primitive' and Otherwise: American Folk Art—Seascapes and Waterfronts Art in the Home," *New York Times,* September 27, 1931, X11; H. I. Brock, "Black Man's Art: From Africa Come Primitive Objects That Reveal a Story of Culture," *New York Times,* May 5, 1935, SM10; and Edward Alden Jewell, "Old Culture Seen in African Exhibit," *New York Times,* November 28, 1935, 33. For a critique of modernist appropriation of African art forms, see Calo, *Distinction and Denial,* 12.

22. Meyerowitz, "The Negro in Art Week," 75–90. Like many art historians, Meyerowitz ignores the religious element that informed the visual and spatial arrangement of the "New Negro" exhibitions. On the Harmon Foundation's influence, see Beryl Wright, "The Harmon Foundation in Context: Early Exhibitions and Alain Locke's Concept of Racial Idiom of Expression," in *Against the Odds,* 13–25 and Calo, *Distinction and Denial,* 23–66.

23. The words were spoken by Rabbi Stephen Wise of the Free Synagogue of New York at the Third Annual Harmon Awards ceremony. Dean Shailer Matthews of the Chicago Divinity School delivered the address to winners in Chicago. Press release, February 13, 1929, NCC Papers, RG 18, Box 60, Folder 13.

24. Report, Interracial Committee of the Oranges, [1935], NCC Papers, RG 18, Box 59, Folder 16.

25. CWCRR Minutes, January 30, 1933, NCC Papers, RG 18, Box 56, Folder 12. On liberal Protestant religious optimism and Jesus as the "perfect embodiment of personality," see Richard Wightman Fox, *Reinhold Niebuhr: A Biography* (New York: Pantheon Books, 1985), and Fox, "The Niebuhr Brothers and the Liberal Protestant Heritage," in *Religion and Twentieth-Century American Intellectual Life,* ed. Michael J. Lacy (Cambridge, UK: Woodrow Wilson International Center for Scholars and Cambridge University Press, 1989), 94–115. See also Ina Corinne Brown, *Training for World Friendship: A Manual in Missionary Education for Leaders of Young People* (Nashville: Cokesbury, 1929).

26. Press release, February 25, 1931, NCC Papers, RG 18, Box 60, Folder 13.

27. Calo, *Distinction and Denial,* vii.

28. Press releases, Harmon Foundation, December 21, 1930, and February 14, 1931, NCC Papers, RG 18, Box 60, Folder 13.

29. Press release, Harmon Foundation, January 4–5, 1930, NCC Papers, RG 18, Box 60, Folder 13, italics mine. On the lack of critical artistic assessment of Harmon exhibitions, see Gary A. Reynolds, "American Criticism and the Harmon Foundation Exhibitions," in *Against All Odds,* 107–119.

30. F.L.K., "American Negroes as Artists: In an Exhibit Which Is the Outgrowth of the William E. Harmon Awards in Fine Arts," reprinted from *Survey Graphic,* September 1928, NCC Papers, RG 18, Box 60, Folder 13, and David Levering Lewis, "The Politics of Art: The New Negro, 1920–1935," in *Prospects: An Annual of American Cultural Studies*, vol. 3, ed. Jack Salzman (New York: Burt Franklin, 1977), 237–261.

31. *Exhibition of the Work of Negro Artists Presented by the Harmon Foundation at the Art Center,* 1931, NCC Papers, RG 18, Box 60, Folder 13; Harmon Foundation press releases, February 14, 1931, and February 17, 1931, NCC Papers, RG 18, Box 60, Folder 13; and Wright, "The Harmon Foundation in Context," 21–24.

32. CWCRR Minutes, January 26, 1931, NCC, RG 18, Box 56, Folder 11. On the crowded viewing space and poor lighting at the International House and the superior setting of the Art Center, see Reynolds, "An Experiment," 35.

33. On the interwar contestation over the definition of a national art form, see A. Joan Saab, *For the Millions: American Art and Culture between the Wars* (Philadelphia: University of Pennsylvania Press, 2004).

34. CWCRR Minutes, January 26, 1931; CWCRR Minutes, November 24, 1930, and January 30, 1933, NCC Papers, RG 18, Box 56, Folder 12.

35. Gloria T. Hull, ed., *Give Us Each Day: The Diary of Alice Dunbar-Nelson* (New York: W. W. Norton, 1984), 264, and CWCRR Minutes, January 26, 1931.

36. CWCRR Minutes, March 30, 1931, NCC Papers, RG 18, Box 56, Folder 11.

37. For information on the incidents, see the following CWCRR Minutes: for Washington, D.C, see November 25, 1929, May 26, 1930, and September 29, 1930; for Fort Wayne, see May 27, 1929; for Atlantic City, see January 27, 1930; and for Seattle and Pittsburgh, see September 28, 1931, NCC Papers, RG 18, Box 56, Folder 11.

38. Oberlin Conference Findings, June 20–22, 1930, and CWCRR Minutes, November 25, 1929, April 28, 1930, and March 30, 1931, NCC Papers, RG 18, Box 56, Folder 11.

39. CWCRR Minutes, May 25, 1931, NCC Papers, RG 18, Box 56, Folder 11, and "Note sent to women's publications, and denominational representatives on Women's Committee," October 29, 1931, NCC Papers, RG 18, Box 56, Folder 11. Some months earlier the FCC Executive Board had refused to endorse the CWC's antilynching resolution because "ministers could not be expected to take this type of leadership." CWCRR Minutes, September 29, 1930, NCC Pa-

pers, RG 18, Box 56, Folder 11. No doubt a reluctance to transgress the prerogatives of pastors as well as a disinclination to alienate male-dominated denominational boards that funded the FCC influenced the board's decision in this instance as well.

40. For the National Urban League and National Conference of Social Work, see CWCRR Minutes, November 25, 1935; for the International Council of Religious Education, see September 28, 1936, September 23, 1934, and September 28, 1936, NCC Papers, RG 18, Box 56, Folder 12.

41. Members of the special group included CWC Secretary Katherine Gardner, Commission on Race Relations Secretary George Haynes, and FCC President Samuel McCrea Cavert, along with representatives of affiliated organizations. The group served as a clearance committee on hotel arrangements for the thirteen national religious and social work organizations that made up the FCC membership. CWCRR Minutes, May 17, 1937, NCC Papers, RG 18, Box 56, Folder 12, and Minutes of the Meeting of the Special Group Called to Consider the Matter of Hotel Arrangements in New York City, November 16, 1937, NCC Papers, RG 18, Box 11, Folder 4.

42. For a description of the collection acquired in 1928, see "Darkest Africa Sends Us Art," *New York Times,* April 29, 1928, XX19.

43. CWCRR Minutes, December 6, 1937, NCC RG 18, Box 56, Folder 12.

44. Calo uses the phrase to assess New Negro Art in general. Calo, *Distinction and Denial,* 46. For a formulation of aesthetics that connects a valued quality, perception, responses, and experiences, see Sally M. Promey, "Taste Cultures: The Visual Practice of Liberal Protestantism, 1949–1965," in *Practicing Protestants: Histories of Christian Life in America, 1630–1965,* ed. Laurie F. Maffly-Kipp, Leigh E. Schmidt, and Mark Valeri (Baltimore: Johns Hopkins University Press, 2006), 250–293.

45. CWCRR Minutes, January 31, 1938, NCC Papers, RG 18, Box 56, Folder 12; see also CWCRR Minutes, December 16, 1937, NCC Papers, RG 18, Box 56, Folder 12.

46. *Church Women in Interracial Cooperation,* 1–2.

47. CWCRR Minutes, September 28, 1936; January 27, 1941; March 2, 1942; and November 18, 1942, NCC Papers, RG 18, Box 56, Folder 12.

48. Scrapbook, NCC Papers, RG 18, Box 56. Initiated by the FCC in 1923 in response to racial violence, Race Relations Sunday was intended to encourage interaction among black and white Protestants in the North and the South. Preparing material for the observance was one of the first projects undertaken by the women on the Commission on Race Relations. Haynes, "Changing Racial Attitudes," 28. For discussion of Aaron Douglas and his art, see Amy Helene Kirschke, *Aaron Douglas: Art, Race, and the Harlem Renaissance* (Jackson: University Press of Mississippi, 1995); Kirschke, "The Fisk Murals Revealed: Memories of Africa, Hope for the Future," in *Aaron Douglas: African American Modernist,* ed. Susan Earle (New Haven, CT, and London: Yale University Press, 2007), 115–135; and Renee Ater, "Creating a 'Usable Past' and a 'Future Perfect Society': Aaron Douglas's Murals for the 1936 Texas Centennial Exposition," in Earle, *Aaron Douglas,* 95–113.

49. On relations with Southern women, see "To Dear Member of the Church Women's Committee," May 26, 1939, NCC Papers, RG 18, Box 56, Folder 12; CWCRR Minutes, February 24, 1930, NCC Papers, RG 18, Box 56, Folder 11; and CWCRR Minutes, June 24, 1929, NCC Papers, RG 18, Box 56, Folder 11. On the United Council of Church Women's disinclination to assume a group as large as the CWC, see CWCRR Minutes, October 6, 1942, NCC Papers, RG 18, Box 56, Folder 12.

50. On the complicated interaction of art, race, nationalism, and American modernism, see Calo, *Distinction and Denial;* A. Joan Saab, *For the Millions: American Art and Culture be-*

tween the Wars (Philadelphia: University of Pennsylvania Press, 2004); Lauren Rebecca Sklaroff, *Black Culture and the New Deal;* and Richard J. Powell, ed., *Rhapsodies in Black: Art of the Harlem Renaissance* (Berkeley: University of California Press, 1997).

51. In 1950 the National Council of Churches, successor organization to the FCC, created the Department of Worship and Arts to encourage the appropriation of art as a religious practice. See Promey, "Taste Cultures," 250–293.

18

Aestheticizing Religion
Sensorial Visuality and Coffeehouse Painting in Iran

MINOO MOALLEM

There is no manager more powerful than consumption, nor, as a result, any factor more powerful—albeit indirect—in production than the chatter of individuals in their idle hours.   Gabriel Tardé, *Economic Anthropology*

Coffeehouse painting is a genre of popular painting that depicts Islamic and cultural myths and stories in Iran. The resulting paintings are performative (theatrical and cinematographic), sensorial in their performance (combining voice, sound, vision, and taste), and aesthetic (using figures, colors, and architectural spaces). They make ethical claims and moral judgments about religious and cultural events. Artists and patrons sometimes call this painting style "imaginative painting." Because most of these images were displayed in the spaces of coffeehouses, *naqashi-ye qahveh khaneh-yee* (painting of the coffeehouses) is their more common name.[1] This painting style is both visual and auditory because it is linked to the performative traditions of *pardeh khani, Ta'zieh,* and *naghali,* or musical and poetic narration and the performative retelling of passion plays and tales based on a *naghal's* (storyteller's) interpretation of popular emotions—sadness, pride, heroism, mourning, vengeance, and so on—and their embodied knowledge of stories. Naghals were mostly men; only very recently have a few women begun to be trained by male naghals.[2]

Coffeehouse painting originated among anonymous painters and became popular in the early twentieth century during the Qajar era. Although Iranian modernist painting invested in the imitation of European traditions—including the portrayal of kings and the suppression of the sacred in modernity's self-image—coffeehouse painting was intimately connected with the depiction of the sacred in the imaginations of ordinary painters, storytellers, and religious performers.[3]

In twentieth-century Iran, coffeehouse painting became a site of consumption of cultural and religious myths, images, and stories that brought sound, image, color, figuration, and performance into the same frame of reference while crossing the boundaries of the secular and the religious.[4] The explosion in popular urban art forms inspired by coffeehouse painting at the time of the Iranian Revolution of 1979 brought together material culture, religious meanings and images, and political aesthetics. Coffeehouse painting and performance engaged with revolutionary activities in complex ways, and the form thus resonates with notions of "vital materiality" that challenge the assignment of activity to people and passivity to objects.[5]

The rise of religious and diasporic tourism in postrevolutionary Iran contributed to the vast commoditization of this urban popular art. The expansion of globalization and new media technologies have extended the local spaces of coffeehouses (qahveh khaneh) into the Internet's virtual and representational spaces. Here the sensory and performative visuality of these paintings enables the aestheticization of the nation not only as an imagined community but also as a gendered community of affects.[6]

Coffeehouse painting, furthermore, continues to influence Iranian rap, hip-hop, and political graphic art, facilitating the convergence of the religious and the secular, the modern and the traditional, the aesthetic and the political, and the imaginary and everyday life, pressing for a radical critique of modernization or modernist theories of art and religion in Iran. The current digitization of coffeehouse painting and its popularity among Iranian diasporic communities present an important opportunity to further an aesthetic analysis that accounts for the sensory mediation of objects in linking social identification, cultural belonging, and religious affiliation.

This chapter focuses on the sensory mediation of qahveh khaneh painting from the local spaces of coffeehouses to the virtual spaces of the Internet. I argue for recognition of the sensorial visuality of these paintings since they create sensorial bonds between Iranian culture and Shia Islam through the activation of objects, icons, sounds, songs, stories, colors, and spaces that provoke affect and emotion.[7] Iranian culture has a particular relationship with Islam. Because Arabic is the language of Islam and, with the exception of an Arab minority, most Iranians do not speak Arabic, other representational forms and material objects play a significant role in popular Shia Islam. Here objects, artifacts, and their performance contribute to the creation of a community of affect beyond textual Islam. In this context, coffeehouse paintings display cultural hybridity and mélange, invoking mythical and spatial memories that transgress the linear temporality of modern nationalism.

I locate coffeehouse paintings in the spaces of coffeehouses, where they historically emerged as a form of popular urban art. By focusing on the themes of four paintings of Javad Aghili, a prominent contemporary coffeehouse painter, I elaborate on the sensorial visuality of these paintings and their significance in the formation of viewing citizens as both producers and consumers of sensory relations. Shia Islam images, meanings, and stories are crucial not only in their textual and discursive materiality but also in influencing people's affective and sensual relationships with material objects and visual images. Elizabeth Castelli's suggestion that religion is a "troubled" category because it is inherently unstable is directly relevant to its situation in modern

Iran.[8] What is problematically called religion, in this case Shia Islam, cannot be understood either in isolation from other cultural meanings and practices or without interrogating the realm of senses and affects enacted and experienced through the mediation of material objects.[9]

The experience of sensation in these paintings, I argue, challenges abstracted notions of modern citizenship because the producers, the viewers, the consumers, and the performers are influenced by the sensory and mimetic experience these paintings provoke. In other words, these paintings function as sites of mediation and mediatization; they parse relations between their own subjects and forms and the historical and cultural contexts within which the images are produced, circulated, and consumed. At this juncture, visual and material religion illuminates the construction of identities, affinities, and affects associated with cultural perceptions and experiences. I ask how and in which ways sensorial visuality and aesthetics are mobilized to create modern and postmodern forms of gender identity, belonging, and citizenship. These paintings constitute both sites of knowledge and ways of life; they elicit and frame the (ethical) construction of the self as a work of art. Aesthetic analysis thus promises to elucidate cultural and religious subject formation as well as the formation and transformation of "structures of feeling" at a particular historical moment.[10]

From Islamic Art to Coffeehouse Painting

In Iran, the rise of modernist art (either in its Orientalist gaze, where it is generally labeled Islamic art, or in its nationalist gaze, where art attains autonomy) has marginalized popular forms of cultural representation. Popular forms of artistic production, existing beyond the space of museums and art galleries, have succumbed to the notion of a homogeneous public, Oriental, Islamic, or national. The modernist or modernizing secularist cultural trajectory and its evaluation of coffeehouse painting as vulgar, popular, folk, and kitschy, and thus unworthy of scholarly attention, have thwarted analysis that brings the politics of material and visual culture into conversation with affective and performative religious practices.[11] In this context, the separation of affective and religious aesthetics has also undermined the theoretical linkages between these realms.[12]

Historically, both the study of "Islamic art" and the modernizing project of the Iranian state invested in Westernization and modernization to create political attachments to modern forms of citizenship. With the separation and marginalization of religious images and practices, the space of the coffeehouse, mosque, or *tekkiyeh* (performative communal religious places, separate from mosques) became privileged spaces for the lower middle classes to retain collective cultural meanings and cultural memories, the repetition, reinvention, and consumption of which aided this population in addressing its sense of despair and marginalization. In my view, attachment to what Lauren Berlant describes as the "virtual but sensual space of commons" was formed in the margins of state institutions.[13]

Given that coffeehouse painters were not considered artists according to the modern definition of art, most of them did not have the means to survive. They pursued occupations as stone workers, construction workers, tile workers, and so on to make a living. Their connection to the working classes and the illiterate urban poor influenced their genre of painting. The sensorial engagement of both coffeehouse painters and people who related to this genre of painting and the aesthetics of religion shows that religious meanings and practices go beyond the textual, interpretive, and institutional notions of the religious elite and involve visual, sensual, and auditory connections to space and place. In this context, the notion of time is subordinated to that of space, the timelessness of stories, and the circularity of life in space. The performance of painting is accompanied here by the singing and crying of the painter, and the audience is reminded of the experience of *rowzeh khani* and *nowheh khani* (rhythmic lamentation and the recitation of the tragedy of Karbala).[14] Javad Azadmehr, in his memories of Mohammad Moddaber, a prominent coffeehouse artist, writes, "I have seen Moddaber with a boom (painting) in one hand and a handkerchief in the other hand. He would sing a nowheh while painting and cried into the handkerchief. People cried with him if they were present at his painting session."[15]

At the time of the Iranian Revolution, the convergence of this multisensory form—including visual, auditory, and performative notions of religious narrative—with oppositional politics, challenging the Pahlavi regime, shaped popular uprisings and the events of the revolution. It also continues to inspire religious oppositional movements.[16] The incorporation, suppression, or museumization of affective popular practices in the postrevolutionary era has not precluded their potential for new forms of political mobilization. In addition, the commercialization of coffeehouse painting for diasporic consumption has acquired new value in the transnational marketplace. As commodities eliciting the sensorial visuality of Iranianness or Persianness, some of these paintings have become a significant part of Iranian immigrants' living-room or small business décor. This form of art sustains the desire for the sound, color, stories, and space of the homeland. Although there has been some analysis of the significance of popular art in the Islamization and stylization of the Iranian Revolution of 1979 and its aftermath, there is still a dearth of scholarly attention that focuses on the specific material, aesthetic, and visual practices of Shi'ism in Iran.[17]

Coffeehouses as Liminal Fields of Play

The narration and recitation of Islamic and Iranian epic stories, including the stories of the Shahnameh (the Book of Kings), through the mediation of *pardeh* (large paintings on tissue or any other material) took place in public and in the mostly male spaces of coffeehouses. Some of these public male spaces included the *zoorkhaneh* ("house of strength," a traditional gymnasium for men) and coffeehouses.[18] In modernized Iran these spaces became arenas of affective and imaginative connection to a form of subordinated masculinity common to Shia Islam and pre-Islamic Iranian notions of manhood. Coffeehouses played a significant role in mediating between the artists or storytellers and consumers through the display of these paintings.

Historically, coffeehouses as sensory urban spaces have been destinations of fascination for male Orientalists, tourists, and travelers.[19] Western travelers have commented on these spaces as sites of male bonding and everyday leisure. These tourists often provide robust descriptions of the sound and smell of the hookah, the techniques of smoking, the pleasure of drinking tea (which has through the years become more popular than coffee in these "coffeehouses"), the male homosocial and homoerotic relations, and the ease with which these spaces integrate strangers. For example, in an account of his travel to Iran, Michael Carroll writes, "After that first evening when I met Hassan, I became a regular customer at the tea house. It was pleasant to be recognized when I went in, to sit down without embarrassment and to be served my tea without asking for it, with a special number of sugar lumps that the attendant never forgot. My pipe would follow immediately, with a cheerful grin from the kalianboy."[20] Carroll refers to the pleasures of drinking and smoking in the coffeehouses as soon as he learns how to "gurgle and bubble in the jar."[21] Other travelers comment on the spatial and architectural specificity of coffeehouses, describing them as unique Oriental spaces where local men meet early in the morning and late in the evening, especially in the big cities.[22]

The existence of coffeehouses and the consumption of coffee in Iran go back to the Safavid era (1501–1722). A number of travelers to Iran reference coffeehouses in their chronicles. For example, French jeweler Sir John Chardin, in his *Travels in Persia, 1613–1677*, went beyond reporting the consumption of coffee alone:

> These houses were heretofore very infamous places; they were served and entertain'd by beautiful Georgian Boys, from ten to sixteen Years of Age, dress'd after a Lewd Manner, Having their hair ty'd in Wefts, like the Women; they make 'em Dance there and act and say a thousand immodest Things, to move the beholders, who caus'd these Boys to be carry'd, everyone where he thought proper; and this fell to the Lot of those who were nothing else in Reality, but Shops for Sodomy, which was very terrible to Wise and Virtuous People.[23]

Labeling coffeehouses "shops for sodomy," Chardin constructed Western masculinity as "wise and virtuous" and Persian masculinity as its opposite. Although for the Western traveler qahveh khaneh represented sites of sexual perversion and male homo-sexuality, for coffeehouse painters the places provided spaces for networking and transacting business. According to Hassan Ismaeelzadeh, a well-known coffeehouse painter, "Mostly the ties of friendship were fastened in these places and always the coffeehouse was a resort place for thousands of workers, jobless people, and petty em-ployers, and every day coffeehouses witnessed the conclusion of hundreds of con-tracts between workers and contractors."[24]

Although the transformation of coffeehouses from the seventeenth century to the twentieth requires careful historical analysis, coffeehouses continued to be called qahveh khaneh in Farsi even when tea became popular in Iran and replaced coffee.[25] With the expansion of urbanism in the late nineteenth and early twentieth centuries, the number of coffeehouses started to increase in many urban areas, providing men of the popular classes with a space for drinking tea, having conversations, exchanging business information, or simply having a quiet or entertaining time. Traditional cof-feehouses, which serve different patrons depending on class, ethnicity, and urban lo-cation, are separate from modern coffee shops. Although modern coffee shops and tea shops have increasingly replaced coffeehouses, there are still a number of coffeehouses that continue to accommodate male clients, some dominated by minority groups (especially the Azari minority) and others patronized by a specific segment of urban professionals such as bakers, builders, barbers, butchers, and so on. In the bazaar areas of various Iranian cities (especially big cities), a number of coffeehouses serve the *bazaari* (those who work in the bazaar), often sending tea to various stores and their guests. The Farsi term *qahveh khaneh* is not used for modern coffee shops; instead, the English phrase is used to distinguish these urban spaces as inviting the middle and upper middle classes and providing gender mixing, cosmopolitan fashion, and food.

Coffeehouses not only functioned as places of friendship and networking for men but also provided space for the consumption of tea, tobacco, stories, and paint-ings by bringing image, spectacle, and experience into the same multisensory context. As mediatic spaces, qahveh khaneh participated in the circulation of information and welcomed painters, poets, and naghals to take part in the production and reproduc-tion of visual and oral cultural meanings. The space of qahveh khaneh slowly became a place for the circulation of popular art and popular culture. Some qahveh khaneh owners turned into urban cultural entrepreneurs and art dealers mediating between numerous anonymous painters and their clients. In addition, they took charge of ordering paintings to decorate the walls of qahveh khaneh as well as for theatrical performances of pardeh khani and naghali. Naghali is the live performance of epic or religious stories. The performer/storyteller, or naghal, uses spoken words, poetry, songs, and gestures to dramatize the narration of the story. He also uses a painting or a painted curtain to visually and virtually communicate with his audience. Although not all coffeehouse spaces were mediatic, a significant number of them became privileged spaces for the circulation of popular culture and art as they supplemented the formation of modern citizenship with forms of citizenship invested in the multisensory viewing of popular and religious cultural meanings and practices.[26] These mediatic qahveh khaneh spaces became very popular in urban and cosmopolitan areas, creating modest havens for those social classes marginalized by the modernizing and modernist culture of the local elite with its investment in new urban spaces, including art galleries, museums, theaters, and cinemas.

Soon after the establishment of a modern nation-state in Iran with the coup d'état of Reza Shah in 1921, the culture industry gradually became centralized and fell under the control of the modern nation-state. With the expansion of new urban entertainment spaces such as theaters, cinemas, and cabarets, the modernizing state became hostile to qahveh khaneh and challenged these gathering spaces under the rubric of concern for public hygiene, cultural normativity, and urban security.[27] Citing the prominent coffeehouse painter Hussein Gullar Aghasi, Hadi Seyf writes: "The government started to use excuses to destroy Qahveh khaneh culture. Sometimes they would say that the buildings were too old, other times they would say that the naghals were confusing people with their ambiguous discourse, other times they would point to the display of paintings on the walls as accumulating dust and against public hygiene, but people knew that they were against people who were getting together in Qahveh khaneh."[28] With the rapid modernization and Westernization of urban spaces in the mid-twentieth century, a number of mediatic coffeehouses lost their function and appeal as sites of popular art and theater. However, the coffeehouse invocation of carnal memory through the visual and auditory representation of historical or mythical events continued to influence notions of a subordinated masculinity.[29] Coffeehouse invocation nonetheless persisted through poster and graphic art, political murals, and decorative artwork.

Coffeehouses are increasingly disappearing from the urban scene; those that survive are mostly used by men of lower classes. The replacement of *qahveh* (coffee in Farsi) with the English word *coffee* and *khaneh* with *shop* indicates the spatial and semiotic transformation of these spaces. In modern Iran, *khaneh* is used to depict one's residence or one's family house (a place where one lives with his or her *khanevadeh*, or family) and *shop* to describe a commercial public space. The use of *khaneh* to denote coffeehouses displays the liminality of these spaces as public and private, commercial and intimate, and for leisure and business.

The Ethnopoetics of Qahveh Khaneh Paintings

Modernist artistic rhetoric valorizes the individual artist and asserts the ideal immunity of the work of fine art to commoditization. Coffeehouse paintings were produced by anonymous painters for public or popular consumption and exchanged for money or other nonmonetary goods or even donated by the painters to religious spaces. The painters used any materials to which they had access, including glass, wood, silk, cotton, walls, ceramics, and herb or mineral powders mixed with oil to produce three principal colors. These painters were not professional artists but had other occupations and mostly painted in the evenings out of personal interest. They did not have systematic knowledge of design, illustration, and perspective systems. According to Javad Aghili, coffeehouse painting was learned and transmitted through popular and embodied male traditions of "*zanu be zanu* / knee-to-knee" mentorship.[30] It also stemmed from popular visual memory that was mobilized in relation, if not in reaction, to modern oculocentrism and the privileging of vision over the other senses.[31]

The painters were not necessarily familiar with religious texts but picked up their stories from oral culture, especially from the narrators. As Gullar Aghasi stated, "We selected certain Shahnameh stories. We picked stories that related to the people's pain and healed their burning desires while teaching them about *gheirat* [male honor and dignity] and *ibrat* [learning from the others' experience of suffering by bringing them to life]. We did not care about what the original story was about; sometimes we just painted what the naghals or storytellers wanted us to depict."[32]

To my mind, the most interesting aspect of these paintings is their significance in mapping out the landscape of religious and cultural affects that rely on ethical principles. These are defined by aesthetic and affective styles influenced by religious practices and issuing from the everyday lives of people. Indeed, the concept of ethnopoetics in reference to a narrative that is perceived as a form of action in its performative and aesthetic effect may be useful in describing this genre of painting.[33]

The painters' attachment to the notions of good and bad, just and unjust, right and wrong, and beauty and ugliness mediated their depiction of religious stories. In sum, the artists embraced painting as a form of prayer. Given that this kind of work was either ordered for tekkiyeh, imamzadeh, or holy shrines or dedicated to these spaces, these painters did not care about payment, saying, "This is our share."[34] The artists produced most of the paintings to narrate their emotional connection with particular stories or religious events and to provide a venue for their own desire to make aesthetic moral judgments about these events, expressing their views through visual imagery as they depicted a particular character or an emotional mood, displaying cruelty, compassion, or revenge. As Aghili noted in my interview with him, "We left our imagination open to depict anything that we liked and we felt emotional about, including images of the prophet or the imams or Shia religious figures. We did not feel any prohibition against depicting religious figures."[35]

The visual and auditory mixing of sounds, colors, and images of Iranian culture with Islamic-Shia narratives in a coffeehouse painting was crucial in creating cultural continuity. While the modern nation-state under the Pahlavi regime invested in pre-

Islamic Persian traditions to construct national unity and modern citizenship, these painters focused on the cultural and visual hybridity of Iranian and Islamic traditions.[36]

Coffeehouse painters' field of action belied modern notions of art as autonomous from other cultural activities and rituals. These painters either dedicated their work to religious communal spaces or took orders from a wide range of groups, from storytellers and moviemakers to ordinary people requesting their portraits from coffeehouse owners. They combined a range of techniques appropriated from multiple artistic traditions, including bringing together the details of miniature painting with the realism of portrait painting and the arts of calligraphy, poetry, and storytelling. They were selective in what they depicted, but most told tragic stories. Although those painters who lived in Tehran or major Iranian cities like Isfahan and Mashhad had the opportunity to sell their work, most painters in small towns, according to Seyf, "came to the work as a *gharib* [stranger], [and] created art anonymously."[37] Given that these painters did not have connections to the emerging networks of art and art dealership in modern Iran, their paintings were bought from them inexpensively and sold for high prices in international markets; most of the painters lived and died in poverty.

Currently the material and visual culture that characterizes this genre of cultural production goes beyond coffeehouse painting and consists of various kinds of works, including poster art targeting religious tourists along with paintings that are specifically made for Iranian diasporic consumers (bought and sold mostly in the Tehran Friday Market), focusing on the feasting ceremonies, Iranian love stories, or epic stories from the Shahnameh.

Ascending or Descending? The Razm, the Bazm, and the Night of Me'râj in the Paintings of Javad Aghili

Coffeehouse painters mostly depicted three major themes: the *razm,* or the heroic and tragic battles both pre-Islamic and Islamic; the *bazm,* or the feasting and entertaining ceremonies; and religious events and stories.[38] The recurring themes in these paintings are not necessarily related to the choices of the painters but rather to the stories that were frequently told and retold, memorized, and remembered through *naghali* (storytelling), coffeehouse performances, poetry, and miniature painting. An analysis of the historical context within which this tradition of painting became popular and of the repetitious retelling of certain religious and national events and stories, especially tragic stories, would be outside the scope of this chapter. Also, the depiction of these stories and events cannot be separated from the social and cultural context within which the painters configured, refigured, or perhaps disfigured what they painted.

In this section I focus on four specific works by Javad Aghili (one of them a collaborative painting) to further elaborate the notion of sensory visuality in coffeehouse painting. The four paintings included in this chapter are available to the public via Aghili's website. The themes of these paintings are neither unique to Aghili nor limited to a single version of a painting but were rather borrowed from cultural and religious accounts and stories imitated and repeated by many coffeehouse painters.

Aghili's background is different from those of many of the coffeehouse painters in that he is a highly educated engineer. Like other coffeehouse painters, however, he started painting not as a job but out of a passion to express his sensory connection to cultural and religious narrative. As he noted when I spoke with him, most of his paintings came out of an affective and embodied connection with religious events and stories.

Me'râj

Aghili's *Me'râj,* or *Night of Ascendance* (Figure 18.1), brings religious tales into conversation with aesthetic judgment by linking the popular traditions of coffeehouse painting with the elite traditions of miniature painting. According to Aghili, this particular painting emerged at an emotional and spiritual moment when he was celebrating the night of Me'râj. The "night of ascendance" (the 27th of Rajab in the Me'râj Islamic lunar calendar) refers to the journey of the prophet from Mecca to Jerusalem, where he ascends to the heavens and meets with earlier prophets before being taken into paradise and the presence of God. Although there is a brief reference in the Qur'an to this event, there is no consensus among Muslim theologians about the precise status of the journey as visionary or corporeal experience. However, the subject has attracted the visual imaginations of poets and painters in Iranian, Indian, and Turkish traditions of miniature painting. In Persian miniature painting and poetry this is one of the most poetically and visually depicted religious events. According to historical accounts, Me'râj occurs when the prophet experiences a moment of rejection and hardship in the community and proves his legitimacy as the last prophet of the monotheistic religions.

Although the event of Me'râj is depicted and recounted in detailed and multilayered ways in various Islamic accounts, the most striking aspects of Aghili's version are his depiction of the Prophet Mohammad without a veiled face and his feminization of both the angel Gabriel and Buraq (a winged mythical horse).[39] This painting differs from miniature depictions in Aghili's introduction of the lion as an Irano-Shia symbol and his feminization of Buraq and Gabriel.[40] In literary and biographical accounts, Buraq is sometimes described and depicted as masculine and sometimes as feminine. The lion nonetheless is a motif that is largely used in decorative art, carpets, and mosaics; it symbolizes majesty, power, and masculinity in Iranian culture.[41] A

FIGURE 18.1. Javad Aghili, *Me'râj*, painting, 100 × 70 centimeters. Javad Aghili Personal Collection. Used with the permission of the painter, Mr. Javad Aghili.

number of scholars argue that this symbol came to Shia Islam from a pre-Islamic Iran under the Safavid dynasty and that the symbol functions to collapse the meaning of the king and the holy man into the notion of the shah. However, according to Najmabadi, the gradual integration of the lion and the sun as symbols of state power under the Safavid dynasty, along with their modification and formalization under the late Qajar and Pahlavi dynasties, deemphasized religious connotations.[42] In my view, the return to the lion motif without the sun may signify a reconfiguration of the lion as a more ambiguous symbol representing masculinity, because he descends to the earth with the possibility of ascendance only through the mediation of Buraq.

The presence of the winged Buraq—a mixture of human, animal, and bird that carried the prophet on its back along with the angel Gabriel and other angels flying through the skies—has been a recurring pictorial representation in Islamic art and poetry.[43] The feminization of Buraq and the angel Gabriel in this painting constructs femininity as liminal and transitional, for both angels and Buraq constitute vectors mediating heaven and earth. This painting, in my view, provides a space for the inhabitation of masculinity surrounded by femininity as concealed, transitional, and intermediary—a hybrid creature, between angel, human, animal, and bird. Although domesticity and docility were on the rise in modernizing Iran, this painting has be-

AESTHETICIZING RELIGION **307**

come a dwelling-place of Islamic liminal creatures and feminized angels who facilitated the ascent of the prophet (depicted as a male human subject) to the heavens. The night of ascendance and the inhabitation of the pictorial and the poetics of the night may here display a world of ambiguity and liminality in the face of modern humanism and reproductive heteronormativity.

In this work Aghili depicts the prophet with a human face. This represents a divergence from miniature painting of the seventeenth century forward, though there is evidence that the prophet was depicted with a human face in Persian miniatures in earlier centuries.[44] In my interview with the artist, Aghili noted that he and other coffeehouse painters depicted anything that they liked and with which they felt an emotional bond, including images of the prophet or the imams or other Shia religious figures. In his view, the coffeehouse painters did not feel any prohibition against depicting religious figures.

As for the visual depiction of religious figures and stories, although I agree with Laura Marks that aniconism was the visual culture within which Islam arrived in Iran in CE 632, Shi'ism has never submitted itself to the iconographic prohibition and suspicion of images of Islamic orthodoxy, which has distinguished the art and crafts of Iran from those of other Islamic countries.[45]

Historically, the convergence of painting and religion in Iranian culture goes back to Mani (CE 216–276), the prophet who was believed to be an extraordinary painter and the illustrator of Arjang.[46] In addition to the coffeehouse style of painting, other forms of painting and engraving, including *shamayel sazi* (the imaginary depiction of Shia imams, especially Imam Ali), are popular throughout Iran.[47] Many shrines and sanctuaries in Iran, moreover, have a number of shamayels donated by anonymous artists.[48] In sum, the figural depiction of religious personages continues in contemporary Iranian culture. This form of investment in the visual and figural display of religion has reconciled the premodern and the modern, paving the way for what could be called a hybrid postmodern visual culture.

The Razm

The popularity of coffeehouse painting coincided with the formation of a modern culture of consumerism in Iran. This form of consumerism relied on new notions of domesticity and gender identity in the context of Iranian modernization and Westernization. Although this process included the male elite, it excluded many men of the lower middle class and the working class and subjected them to a form of authoritarian modernization. I have argued elsewhere that tragedy, as a genre grounded both in myth and in history, reconstituted itself here as a site of resistance displaying a certain loss of willpower for men.[49] Walter Benjamin distinguishes between *Tragödie* and *Trauerspiel* as two radically distinct forms, one grounded in myth and the other in history.[50] In the context of Iran, the fusion in coffeehouse painting of the pre-Islamic myth of Siavash and the Shia tragedy of Imam Hussein, one mythical and the other historical, enables emotional inwardness as well as ceremonial lamentation in ways that demand a spectatorial response.

Aghili, along with a number of other coffeehouse painters, also depicts the myth of Siavash and the tragedy of Karbala. The representation of these events brings the pre-Islamic and the Islamic together to create a modern notion of Iranian tragedy depicting men's sacrifice and heroism and demanding both an aesthetic and an emotional attachment to the spectacle.

As Hassan Ismaeelzadeh, another well-known coffeehouse painter, has noted, "In the battle scenes of our paintings, defeat has no meaning. We have come to prove our sincerity by depicting nobilities and magnanimities. Is Imam Hussein really faced with defeat in the battle of Karbala? Of course not, the one who has protected the oppressed for such a long time can never be faced with defeat. Our master the commander of martyrs is alive; death belongs to those we have cursed for more than a thousand years."[51]

The aesthetic embodiment and emotional inhabitation of mythical and religious tragedies depicted through martyrdom and self-sacrifice for the sake of community created space for men of marginalized classes to express their sense of despair, disappointment, and loss in the face of a modernizing and Westernizing state that suppressed religious aesthetics and figuration. Through this cultural aesthetic field most deprived classes could see themselves in this articulation of culture and could express themselves in the modern formation of citizenship. The imaginative and material making of space through coffeehouse painting provided an intermediary space, a space beyond the domestic space and the domesticity of culture in modernity that required self-sacrifice along with a tragic presence for men.

The Myth of Siavash

Figure 18.2 shows Aghili's own depiction of the myth of Siavash. In popular culture Siavash, a pre-Islamic hero, is commemorated as the symbol of innocence, a man unjustly killed in exile in the land of Turan, Iran's adversary. A number of painters, including Aghili, have painted not only the beheading of Siavash by the enemy but also Siavash's attempt to pass unscathed through fire to prove his innocence against accusations of treason. In the depiction of the myth of Siavash, some coffeehouse painters combine text with image, using both Arabic and Farsi.[52] For example, in Mohammed Farahani's version, the scripts were made by a calligrapher acknowledged in the painting. The painting is performative because, in the painting itself, the artist renders different audiences, in this case women and soldiers, who watch and witness the event. Although this is a pre-Islamic story, in some versions of this painting the flag is

FIGURE 18.2. Javad Aghili, *Siavash,* painting, 100 × 70 centimeters. Javad Aghili Personal Collection. Used with the permission of the painter, Mr. Javad Aghili.

painted green with the famous statement of Nasro Minallah-e-Wa Fathun Qareeb, "With the help of God, victory is not far."

The Tragedy of Karbala

One of the recurring themes in coffeehouse painting is the depiction of the day of Ashura (the tenth day of Muharam in the lunar calendar) and the tragedy of Karbala, in which the martyrdom of Imam Hussein along with members of his family, friends, and companions is situated. Most of these paintings are of a larger scale and sometimes painted collaboratively to depict a series of events in the tragedy of Karbala.[53] In their depiction of Ashura (Figure. 18.3), Aghili and Abbas Blookifar (another coffeehouse painter) create a performative scene with multiple happenings, temporalities, characters, and stories in one painting. The audience is asked to participate in the painting by witnessing the cruelties of the enemy and by identifying with the army of Imam Hussein. Aghili and Blookifar render the enemies of Imam Hussein as mean humans; they depict the gazes and bodily gestures of the imam's family and friends as beautiful, innocent, and gentle. Such a portrayal of faces enables *souratkhani* (face reading), which enabled *naghals* or storytellers to

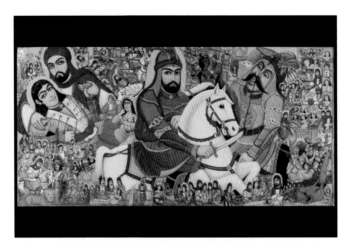

FIGURE 18.3. Javad Aghili and Abbas Blookifar, Ashura painting, 330 × 156 centimeters. Javad Aghili Personal Collection. Used with the permission of the painter, Mr. Javad Aghili.

home in on particular characters through the dramatization of their feelings and emotions as they are depicted in the painting.[54] Again the painter combines Iranian and Islamic motifs.

In this painting Aghili and Blookifar depict various characters in a cinemato-graphic way through color, facial expressions, the sizes of their bodies, and the context within which the story was taking place. Indeed the strength and popularity of visual media, including the film industry, in Islamic Iran have roots not only in miniature painting and poetry but also in the religious performance of *ta'zieh* (the dramatic per-formance of the tragedy of Imam Hussein and the event of Karbala) and qahveh khaneh painting. In my view, a number of contemporary Iranian directors (Majid Majidi, for example) continue this form of aesthetic judgment in their films by dis-tancing popular Shi'ism from state religion because of its concern for social justice for the least privileged classes. In other words, popular Shi'ism continues to provide space for the least privileged classes to voice their concern for social justice, while religion, in this case Shi'ism, is increasingly used by the state elite to consolidate the power of the state and the ruling classes. The commercialization of these paintings, on the one hand, and their incorporation into the Islamonationalist agenda of the Iranian state and religious tourism, on the other, have influenced their production, circulation, and consumption as transnational commodities.

According to Hadi Seyf, Mohammad Moddaber, another well-known qahveh khaneh painter, reinvented and mixed pre-Islamic Iranian traditions with Islamic tra-ditions: "When Mohammad Moddaber got a taste of the repulsiveness and bitterness of his era and matured, he revisited Siavash, he turned the fire of Siavash and the red-ness of its flames into a *golestan* [orchard], he dressed up Siavash in green garb so he could shout out his innocence and his liberation. He was the one who took Rostam to the court of Suleiman [Solomon]."[55] These two paintings, as well as similar works by other coffeehouse painters depicting the tragedy of Karbala and the myth of Siavash, were mostly displayed in the coffeehouses. The participation of the audiences and their identification with the recurring appearance of good and evil gave life to an aesthetic-historical discourse that became politicized along with the emergence of an Islamic subject at the time of the Iranian Revolution of 1979.[56]

Given that the language of the majority of Iranians is not Arabic, as I have already indicated, there has been more reliance on the affective, performative, and visual expressions of Islam and its everyday practices involving sound, sight, and storytelling rather than on the hermeneutic and textual experience of religion. However, these practices did not take shape outside the Iranian modern historical context but rather provided space for the expression of desires and beliefs that did not fit with the dominant and hegemonic values of the modernist/modernizing and Westernizing nation-state. In other words, coffeehouse painting provided a public space where bodies, objects, artifacts, and stories converged with each other to create a web of connections, an assemblage in the terms of Deleuze and Guattari, a collective force for action.[57]

The depiction of tragic events such as the myth of Siavash and the tragedy of Karbala relied on notions of manhood based on bravery, heroism, generosity, patience, and courage and included the depiction of images that were attached to religious and national Shia parables and stories. These paintings, along with the space of coffeehouses, resisted the hegemonic masculinity of the modernized male elite that relied on Westernization, heteronormativity, and respectability.

Aghili's depictions of the myth of Siavash and the tragedy of Karbala affectively mediate myths, stories, and religious events: that is, they display tactility and bodily pain or pleasure as felt by both the painters and the audiences. These paintings, in my view, function as "actants," as things that make other things happen.[58] The performative aspects of these paintings gradually created a powerful field of oppositional political action that was closed to the gaze of the West and the Westernized elite and influenced the visual and auditory culture of the Iranian Revolution of 1979. While modern notions of a hegemonic masculinity were becoming central in defining modernized and Westernized gender identities, these alternative notions of masculinity filled the gap by reviving the aesthetic Islamic and pre-Islamic cultures grounded in the visual, mythical, oral, and historical narratives of the past, including the stories of Shahnameh and the Shia retelling of historical events.[59] The loss of premodern notions of manhood to modern hegemonic masculinity is commemorated in these paintings. The failure of the modernizing state to create a public sphere that included disenfranchised classes created an opportunity for coffeehouses to shape an "intimate public," in Lauren Berlant's terms, where "one senses that matters of survival are at stake and that collective mediation through narration and audition might provide some routes out of the impasses and the struggle of the present."[60] The hypermasculinity of Jahel (an urban male character who was part thug and part hero) and his ambiguous relationship to premodern notions of manhood, which were extensively incorporated in the entertainment industry, especially in the particular genre of film-e Farsi in prerevolutionary Iran, are examples of this tension.[61] This affective and aesthetic bonding, along with the subordinated model of masculinity, found an expression in the formation of an Islamic subjectivity and an Islamic nationalist masculinity around the time of the Iranian Revolution of 1979. As I have argued elsewhere, this form of identity relied on the notion of a warrior masculinity that was supplemented by the emphasized femininity of the veiled sister justifying gender hierarchy, gender segregation, and gender complementarity.[62]

The Bazm

In depicting two distinct topics—the bazm, or feasting ceremonies that involve dancing, playing music, and so on to celebrate pleasure and bliss, and the razm, or the battlefield—coffeehouse painters recreate gendered notions of space by depicting women as the main players of the bazm, with men taking center stage in the razm. Bazmi paintings include festive rituals with women dancing and playing music.

In most of these paintings (Figure 18.4), the artists represent female characters as types, who most often dance and play ceremonial music; such imagery has been extensively commercialized and consumed by Iranian diasporic communities. With the expansion of Iranian diasporic tourism to Iran and the longing for a multisensory representation of Iranian culture beyond miniature painting, these paintings have found new market appeal.

The framing of the gendered dichotomy of the bazm (feasting, mostly feminized) and the razm (fighting, mostly masculine), not necessarily in opposition but as an entanglement of love, pleasure, and the moral battle between good and bad in everyday life, is influenced more by Iranian Sufi traditions and pre-Islamic Manichaeism. The popular commercial consumption of this particular theme among Iranians in the diaspora to decorate households, ethnic stores, and restaurants may in part have to do with the prohibition of public dancing and singing by women under the Islamic Republic and the diasporic commemoration of the homeland through the sensorial visuality of feasting, dancing, singing, and playing music.

Coffeehouse painting continues to resist the hegemony of sight or vision in going beyond vision to bring into the same frame of reference spatial practices, representations of space, and representational space, in Henri Lefebvre's terms.[63] The paintings have the capacity to make space a place, meaning that the paintings function as actants, or vital objects provoking a connection to the past, while involving an affec-

FIGURE 18.4. Javad Aghili, *Woman Playing Daf*, painting, 80 × 60 centimeters. Javad Aghili Personal Collection. Used with the permission of the painter, Mr. Javad Aghili.

tive and aesthetic spatial engagement. This aesthetic provocation is open to instability and chance, retelling, reordering, and reimagination.[64] In this case, the space of the coffeehouse and the spatiality of coffeehouse painting suspend the linear temporality of the nation to produce representational spaces inhabited by artists as well as popular classes. Indeed these painters self-fashioned their manhood and masculinity in the face of either a secular or a religious state or certain configurations of transnational Islam that suppress and contain sensational religiosity.

The Viewing Citizen and the Digitization of Qahveh Khaneh Painting

The transformation of most of the mediatic coffeehouses from urban social spaces to representational spaces relying on abstract forms of masculinity and constructions of femininity as concealed, abjectified, and othered paved the way for the parallel presence of affective communities of men as consumers of sensual experiences of pain and pleasure. The aestheticization of religion is certainly not a form of apolitical formalism but is rather a site for understanding both the performative and the political. In other words, social subjects as viewing or even visionary citizens relate emotionally and corporeally to aesthetic forms and sensory mediations as they inform and are informed by religion as both cultural memory and political knowledge.

The move to depict religious events by a number of other coffeehouse painters has opened up these events and stories to the imagination of artists, narrators, and ordinary citizens, because none of these painters had religious education or were systematically educated about textual or clerical religion. They depicted religious stories and events not as forms of abstraction but as an expression or release of their feelings and attitudes toward memorizing and eliciting certain religious stories and events. Furthermore, their paintings became "vibrant matters," or things with the ability to generate vitality animating the virtual (Deleuze), giving everyday practices of religion an affective and ethical sensibility.

With the expansion of new media and cyberspace and the circulation of images via websites, the transactions between the national and the transnational in terms of what is produced in one location and received in another location have both deemphasized and broadened spatial practices by replacing them with conceptualized or representational spaces. In this context, the multisensory experience of visual media has challenged the inhabitation of space and become central to the production and reproduction of space. Coffeehouse paintings spatialize Iranian immigrant households because these images redeploy sensorial sites of identity and belonging, bringing the sounds, smells, tastes, stories, and aesthetic design of the homeland to the times and spaces of various diasporic locations. Coffeehouse paintings, as sites of local and spatial practices of religion, transgress the perceived prohibition of the depiction of religious figures in transnational Islam. Indeed the desacralization of religious figures into consumable cultural icons changes the nature of religiosity and religious practice. However, the investment in the ocularcentric world of Internet transmission makes the corporeal and multisensorial experience of paintings less relevant and more subordinated to cosmopolitan and transnational Islam.

Indeed the aesthetic as a means of sensorial engagement offers a window into the understanding of religion in general and Shi'ism in particular. Recent attempts to attach this genre of painting to Islamic nationalism and the Islamic state, especially in poster art, have aimed to preserve the national heritage. These gestures, along with the commodification of this genre of painting for diasporic consumption, contribute to the genre's transformative aspects. The new accessibility of the religious imaginary, as opposed to its suppression in either secular nationalism or textual or clerical Islam, opens up religion to various forms of imagination, interpretation, a multiplicity of judgments, and contestation. This form of the secularization of religion and the production of a religious material and visual culture goes beyond the dichotomies of secular/religious, reason/emotion, and masculine/feminine. It also has the potential to bring aesthetics and politics into conversation with subjectivity and sensation. In authorizing artistic freedom to make aesthetic judgments about the significance of pleasure and pain, love and passion, tragedy and death, and the presence of injustice in everyday life, coffeehouse painting continues to be a potential source of popular religious contestation. The transformation of qahveh khaneh painting in poster art, advertisements, and digital media and its articulation into diasporic consumer practices is already changing the nature of haptic space.

NOTES

I am indebted to Sally Promey for her careful reading and her helpful comments on this chapter as well as for organizing a number of workshops at which I had the opportunity to discuss my work with other participants. I thank Mia Mochizuki and Richard Meyer for their comments on an earlier draft of this paper. I also thank my research assistant, Nina Torabzadeh, as well as Ahmad Moallem and Azadeh Bahmanpour for their help. My deepest thanks to Javad Aghili for agreeing to talk to me about this tradition of painting and for giving me permission to include several of his paintings in this chapter.

1. In this chapter I use *qahveh khaneh painting* and *coffeehouse painting* interchangeably.

2. The alternative usage for naghali is naqqali; for naghal, the parallel alternative is naqqal. See http://www.youtube.com/watch?v=OftE6oScdcI&feature=plcp (accessed January 3, 2013) for one of the first performances by a female naghal.

3. Hamid Keshmirshekan refers to the coffeehouse artists as "traditional." His analysis of the work of some of these painters during and after the Iranian Revolution is informative. See Keshmirshekan, "Contemporary Iranian Art: The Emergence of New Artistic Discourses," *Iranian Studies* 40, no. 3 (2007): 335–366.

4. The paintings come in different scales and dimensions. The larger paintings are as tall as a large curtain or a wall and have been used in the coffeehouses as screens enabling the performative storytelling of naghals as they recited the dramatic lamentation of the Karbala parable or pre-Islamic Persian epics.

5. Jane Bennett, *Vibrant Matter* (Durham, NC: Duke University Press, 2010), 119.

6. I also like Jacques Rancière's notion of a community of sense because it cuts out of time and space and brings together practices, forms of visibility, and patterns of intelligibility. See Rancière, "Contemporary Art and the Politics of Aesthetics," in Rancière, *Communities of Sense* (Durham, NC: Duke University Press, 2009), 31.

7. The concept of haptic space suggested by Laura Marks as "space that invites not distant contemplation but intimate involvement" is useful for understanding what I call sensorial visuality. See Marks, *Enfoldment and Infinity: An Islamic Genealogy of New Media Art* (Cambridge, MA: MIT Press, 2010), 54.

8. Elizabeth Castelli, *Women, Gender, Religion: A Reader* (New York: Palgrave, 2001), 4.

9. For a critique of the secularization of modernity and modernist art and its consequences for visual cultures of religion, see Sally M. Promey, "The 'Return' of Religion in the Scholarship of American Art," *Art Bulletin* 85, no. 3 (September 2003).

10. In Raymond Williams's terms in reference to the culture of a period or generation. Williams, *The Long Revolution* (London: Broadview, 1961), 64–65.

11. The modernist tradition of Saqqakhaneh painting, emerging in the 1960s (and problematically called neotraditionalism by Keshmirshekan), incorporated religious motifs borrowed from coffeehouse painting to give modernist painting a local color and a sense of national uniqueness. Coffeehouse painting, however, is not reducible to this form. See Hamid Keshmirshekan, "Neo-traditionalism and Modern Iranian Painting: Saqqa-khaneh School in the 1960s," *Iranian*

Studies 38, no. 4 (2005): 607–630. See also Fereshteh Daftari, "Another Modernism: An Iranian Perspective," in *Picturing Iran: Art, Society, Revolution,* ed. Shiva Balaghi and Lynn Gumpert (New York: L. B. Tauris, 2002).

12. Jane Bennett argues that affect "refers to how moods and aesthetic sensibilities influence ethics and politics as much as do words, arguments, and reasons." Bennett, *Vibrant Matter,* 61.

13. Lauren Berlant, *Cruel Optimism* (Durham, NC: Duke University Press, 2011), 228.

14. In Shia Islam, *Karbala parable* or *Karbala tragedy* refers to the martyrdom of Mohammad's grandson Imam Hussein and his family in their struggle against the oppressive rule of the Umayyad caliphs.

15. Cited by Hadi Seyf, *Coffee House Painting* (Tehran: Cultural Heritage of Iran, 1990), 49.

16. During the Iranian Revolution of 1979, political slogans such as "We shall not live under the oppressive conditions" used a lamentation style of nowheh khani to provoke a sensory and emotional attachment to Islamic oppositional politics. Also, the Iranian reform movement, sometimes called the Green Movement, juxtaposes sensorial visual colors, figures, sounds, and events of Shia Islam with oppositional politics to challenge the current Islamic regime in Iran.

17. For an analysis of the graphics of the Iranian Revolution, see Michael Fischer and Mehdi Abedi, *Debating Muslims: Cultural Dialogues in Postmodernity and Tradition* (Madison: University of Wisconsin Press, 1990). Fischer and Abedi refer to the influence of miniature paintings on the revolutionary poster arts, but they do not take into consideration the influence of qahveh khaneh painting on the revolutionary graphic art of 1979. Elsewhere I have argued that the parable of Karbala as well as Ta'zieh (the Shia passion plays) played a significant role in the formation of an Islamic revolutionary subject and a warrior masculinity during the revolution of 1979. See my book *Between Warrior Brother and Veiled Sister: Islamic Fundamentalism and the Politics of Patriarchy in Iran* (Berkeley and Los Angeles: University of California Press, 2005).

18. Some of these paintings were displayed in the sanctuaries (*imamzadeh*) or the *tekkiyyeh* (religious community spaces, separate from mosques, used for religious performances and rituals such as passion plays in the month of Muharram).

19. See also Samuel G. Benjamin, *Persia,* 3rd ed. (London: T. Fisher Unwin, 1891).

20. Michael Carroll, *From a Persian Tea House: Travels in Old Iran* (London and New York: Tauris Parke, 1960), 21.

21. Ibid.

22. Rudi Matthee, "Coffee in Safavid Iran: Commerce and Consumption," *Journal of the Economic and Social History of the Orient* 37, no. 1 (1994): 1–32. See also Willem Floor, *The History of Theater in Iran* (Chicago: Mage, 2005).

23. Sir John Chardin, *Sir John Chardin's Travels in Persia* (New York: Cosimo Classics, 2010 [1724]), 242.

24. Cited by Kazem Chalipa in his preface to *Coffeehouse School Painter* by Hassan Ismaeelzadeh (Tehran: Nazar Research and Cultural Institute, 2007), 147.

25. For an extensive historical account of this transformation, see Rudi Matthee, "From Coffee to Tea: Shifting Patterns of Consumption in Qajar Iran," *Journal of World History* 7, no. 2 (1999): 199–230.

26. Not all forms of pardeh khani took place in the space of coffeehouses. Street corners or central locations in rural areas were also privileged spaces for pardeh khani.

27. Willem Floor refers to the occasional closing of coffeehouses as early as 1858 to discourage popular discussion of oppositional politics. Floor, *The History of Theater in Iran,* 99.

28. Seyf, *Coffee House Painting,* 34, my translation.

29. This form of masculinity was influenced by premodern notions of *gheirat* (honor), *az khod gozashtegi* (selflessness), *zoor* (physical strength), *lutigari* (generosity), *entegham* (vengeance), and *javanmardi* (mindful manhood), along with and sometimes in opposition to modern hegemonic heteronormative models of masculinity.

30. Javad Aghili, interview by author, August 14, 2011.

31. For a historical analysis of oculocentrism or ocularcentrism, see Martin Jay, *Downcast Eyes* (Chicago: University of Chicago Press, 1993).

32. Cited by Seyf, *Coffee House Painting,* 31, my translation.

33. Dennis Tedlock, *The Spoken Word and the Work of Interpretation* (Philadelphia: University of Pennsylvania Press, 1983), and Dell Hymes, *Now I Know Only So Much* (Lincoln: University of Nebraska Press, 2003).

34. Seyf, *Coffee House Painting,* 31, my translation.

35. The belief in the uniqueness of the relationship between the sacred figures and the believer, including the visual, sonic, and verbal expression of such love and affection, has a long history in Iranian Sufi traditions. Rumi's poetic depiction of the encounter between Moses and the Shepherd is a magnum opus of such freedom of expression and imagination.

36. As I have argued elsewhere, Orientalist discourse dichotomized a civilized Persia and a barbaric Islam. Persian Orientalists believe that Persia was highly civilized before it adopted Islam. This discourse was incorporated into Iranian modern nationalism and continues to be at the core of Iranian nationalism, especially among diasporic communities.

37. Seyf, *Coffee House Painting,* 192, my translation.

38. For a list of the common religious events in these painting, see Ismaeelzadeh, *Coffeehouse School Painter,* 147.

39. According to the Sufi scholar Shaykh Muhammad Hisham Kabani, the imagined world is between that of human bodies on earth and that of angels. See Kabani, *Angels Unveiled: A Sufi Perspective* (Chicago: Kazi, 1995), 226.

40. According to Vesta Sarkhosh Curtis, the Iranian mythic hero Rustam is depicted as the son of a lion in Persian poetry and miniatures. See Curtis, *Persian Myths* (London: British Museum Press, 1993), 40.

41. In Iranian Shi'ism, the lion symbol refers to the Imam Ali. In popular culture, Imam Ali is called the "lion of god" (*shir-e khoda*) and is admired for his generosity, courage, bodily strength, and ethical commitments to *haq* (justice). According to Anna Caiozzo, the lion is also associated with Mithra (the ancient Persian god). See *Réminiscences de la royauté cosmique dans la représentation de l'Orient médiéval* (Cairo: Institut Français d'Archéologie Orientale, 2011), 21.

42. For an extensive discussion of this transformation, see Afsaneh Najmabadi, *Women with Mustaches and Men without Beards: Gender and Sexual Anxieties of Iranian Modernity* (Berkeley and Los Angeles: University of Califronia Press, 2005), 63–96. Although Najmabadi's discussion is very informative, it lacks an interrogation of the European reconfiguration of these symbols in the Orientalist accounts of Persianness.

43. According to Sir Thomas Arnold, "It was particularly in illustrated copies of the works of the Persian poets that pictures of Buraq made their appearance." Arnold, *Painting in Islam* (New York: Dover, 1965), 117–122, quote on 120. Buraq continues to be depicted in popular art. In recent events in Egypt and in several murals, Buraq has been depicted as epitomizing the journey of revolution and freedom. See Mona Abaza, "The Buraq of Tahrir," *Jadaliyya* (May 2012), http://www.jadaliyya.com/pages/index/5725/the-buraqs-of-tahrir.

44. Depicting the prophet's face was a common practice in Persian painting. Medieval Iranian and Islamic miniaturists produced many versions and sometimes used the same image of Mohammad's face (see Arnold, *Painting in Islam,* 117–122). Also, *Jami'at-Tawarikh,* by Rashid

as-Din, a Persian historian, includes a number of illustrations depicting the prophet Muhammad's face in the early Mongol period. See Rashid as-Din, *Histoires des Mongols de la Perse, ecrit en persan par Rashi eldin* (Paris: Imperimerie Royal, 1836). *Miraj Nameh* (a famous book of illustrations by a Turkish artist and painter from the fifteenth century) includes Muhammad's face. See "Me'râj ii, Illustrations," *Encyclopaedia Iranica* online, http://www.iranicaonline.org/articles/meraj-ii-illustrations. Furthermore, according to the same entry in the *Encyclopedia Iranica,* the prophet's face veil emerges under Safavid rulers not as a prohibition but as propaganda because the Safavid king Shah Ismai'l claimed divinity for himself, and thus the use of the veiled face may have functioned to fuse his identity with the identity of the prophet.

45. Marks, *Enfoldment and Infinity,* 52.

46. For more information on the pre-Islamic artistic traditions and the Islamic carvings and paintings in Iran, see Shurideh Ghasi, "Imam 'Ali Mirrored in Art: On the Occasion of Moharram Month," *Tavoos Quarterly* 5 and 6 (Autumn 2000–Winter 2001): 1–3.

47. With the rise of religious tourism in Iran, a number of posters depicting Shia imams have acquired new value and are bought and sold around the holy places, including the tomb of Imam Khomeini in Tehran.

48. The references to Islamic painting, or "Mohammeden painting," by a number of Orientalist scholars, including Sir Thomas Arnold, is a reduction given the cultural hybridity of these paintings and their continuation in modern popular culture. However, the focus on religious symbols, icons, or phantasmatic motifs of these paintings and sometimes their comparison with Christian art has enabled a wealth of scholarship on this topic.

49. Minoo Moallem, "Ethnicité et rapports des sexes: Le Fondamentalisme islamique en Iran," *Sociologie et Sociétés* 24, no. 2 (Fall 1992): 59–71.

50. Walter Benjamin, *The Origin of German Tragic Drama* (London: Verso, 1963), 16.

51. Cited by Chalipa, preface to *Coffeehouse School Painter,* 136.

52. The Iranian epic poet Firdausi made a conscious attempt to not use any Arabic word in his Shahnameh, where the myth of Siavash is preserved and remembered. The modern Iranian state, in its attempt to construct an Iranian national identity, also returned to the pre-Islamic past, devaluing Arabic words as Farsi became the official national language under the Pahlavi regime. Arabic words have gained purchase again with the establishment of an Islamic Republic in Iran.

53. A number of prominent coffeehouse painters have depicted the tragedy of Karbala and the day of Ashura. Examples include Mohammad Moddaber, Gullar Aghasi, Hassan Ismaeelzadeh, and Abbas Tekkieh. The large scale and detailed portrayal of the events of Karbala opened up the reading of these paintings to those who relied on oral culture for commemoration.

54. For more information on souratkhani, see Dr. Jaber Anasseri, *The Sultan of Karbala: A Chronicle of the Martyrdom of Imam Hosein and a Survey of Rituals Commemorating This Tragic Event in Iran* (Tehran: Zarrin and Simin Books, 2003).

55. Cited by Seyf, *Coffee House Painting,* 55, my translation.

56. I have already written extensively about this subject (in *Between Warrior Brother and Veiled Sister*).

57. See Gilles Deleuze and Félix Guattari, *Mille plateaux-capitalisme et schizophrénie* (Paris: Editions des minuit, 1980).

58. Bruno Latour mobilizes the term "actant" to talk about the source of action (human or nonhuman); Bennett calls this "thing-power" (Bennett, *Vibrant Matter,* xvii).

59. I borrow the notions of hegemonic and subordinated masculinity from R. W. Connell, *Gender and Power* (Stanford, CA: Stanford University Press, 1987).

60. Berlant, *Cruel Optimism,* 226.

61. Film-e Farsi refers to a prerevolutionary genre of filmmaking in Iran that combined singing, dancing, and half-naked women arousing the sexual fantasies of young urban men.

62. Moallem, *Between Warrior Brother and Veiled Sister.*

63. Henri Lefebvre, *The Production of Space* (Oxford, UK: Blackwell, 1991).

64. Doreen Massey refers to Levin's concept of "productive incoherence" as well as Derrida's notion of risk and chance in talking about space and spatiality. See Massey, *For Space* (London: Sage, 2005), 151.

19

Piety, Barbarism, and the Senses in Byzantium

VASILEIOS MARINIS

In this chapter I examine the intentional defacement of sacred art in Byzantium. I refer here not to the destruction of images by iconoclasts in the eighth and ninth centuries but rather to subtler interventions performed after the completion of the works of art.[1] These include graffiti, the scraping of paint for quasi-medicinal and magical use, and the erasure of faces of heretics and persecutors of Christians, especially in manuscripts (Figures 19.1–19.5). I propose that, rather than being the results of intellectually deficient barbarism, these were acts of piety and expressions of the Byzantine understanding of the sacred and its material manifestations.[2] As such, I place them in the context of people's exchanges with the spiritual world, actions that often involved the whole sensorium. These exchanges were based on the belief that materiality could and did partake in the essence of the prototype.

In a homily delivered on March 29, 867, in the cathedral of Hagia Sophia in Constantinople at the inauguration of a mosaic of the Virgin that still survives in the apse, Patriarch Photios described the image as follows: "The Virgin is holding the creator in her arms as an infant. Who is there who would not marvel, more from the sight than from the report, at the magnitude of the mystery? . . . For even if the one introduces the other, yet the comprehension that comes about through sight is shown in very fact to be superior to the learning that penetrates through the ears. . . . No less—indeed much greater—is the power of sight."[3] In arguing for the primacy of vision over hearing and the other senses, Photios entered into a long and pervasive tradition in Greek thought going back to Plato and Aristotle.[4] Perhaps unsurprisingly, modern scholarship on the senses in Byzantium has concentrated on vision and almost exclusively on how "art," both pagan and Christian, was perceived by its audiences.[5] Yet, whatever the Byzantines thought about their religious images, they rarely, if ever, thought of them primarily or exclusively as "art."[6] Whatever artistic merit

FIGURE 19.1. *The Entombment of Christ and the Marys at the Tomb,* Crypt of the Hosios Loukas monastery, eleventh century. Photo by Vasileios Marinis.

might have been noticed in an image was subservient to its perceived function. According to the author of the life of Saint Andrew *en te Krisei,* "The icon's divine beauty rests not in form or the beautiful colors of the figure, but is seen in the inexpressible blissfulness of the represented virtue"; that is, the real value of an icon rests in its inner essence.[7] Moreover, the Byzantines did not simply look at images but interacted with them in a variety of ways. This interaction was often reciprocal. The insistent focus on the optical perception of Byzantine religious art has been the rather unfortunate by-product of the textual sources scholars have used, namely theological and philosophical treatises as well as *ekphraseis,* formal rhetorical descriptions—in other words, works of high literature that come as close as possible to our contemporary notion of art criticism.[8] Yet such texts do not convey common attitudes toward images, just as an exhibition review in the *New Yorker* does not reflect the opinion of most casual museumgoers, not to mention the general public. For the purposes of this chapter I rely mainly on hagiographical sources.

FIGURE 19.2. *Saint Barbara* (ca. 1000) with eleventh-century graffiti, Santa Maria della Croce, Casaranello gallery, Casarano, Italy. Photo by Linda Safran.

The eighth-century vita of Saint Stephen the Younger contains the following story. Stephen's mother, Anna, approaching menopause without giving birth to a male child, frequented the famous sanctuary of the Mother of God in Blachernai in Constantinople. There she stood in front of the icon of the Virgin and submitted her request for a son. One night, after she had performed her prayers and prostrations, she fell asleep and saw the Mother of God, "in appearance similar to the icon," who struck her in the loins and told her that she would bear a son.[9] There are two noteworthy features of this story. First, the appearance of the Virgin in the vision was "similar" to that of her icon, not vice versa. As in so many other hagiographical texts, it was the image that dictated the imagination and validated the original.[10] Second, through the metonym of a vision, the image came into physical contact with the petitioner. Byzantine authors often repeated that they found their images "lifelike," a statement that had rightly perplexed modern critics.[11] That is, until Robert Nelson made his astute observations on the subject. Nelson argued that the Byzantines "described their religious images as 'life-like,' implying thereby not our aesthetic category of naturalistic,

FIGURE 19.3. Katholikon in the gallery of the Hosios Loukas monastery on Mount Helicon near Distomo, Greece. Photo by Vasileios Marinis.

but literally lifelike, that is, living or alive."[12] Thus, according to hagiographical sources, which often reflect popular perceptions, images moved, talked, listened, touched, became angry, bled, and even attacked when threatened. According to a story preserved in the chronicles of the medieval Russian pilgrims, the maker of a mosaic of Christ in Hagia Sophia boasted that he had made Christ as he was in real life. The angered icon responded, "And when have you ever seen me?," after which the artist was paralyzed.[13] A "Saracen" soldier threw his weapon at an image of the military saint George, who made the missile turn and hit the soldier in the heart.[14] During iconoclasm, a certain Leo struck an icon of the Virgin with a sword; blood gushed immediately from the Virgin's breast.[15] Such stories conflated the signifier and the signified. In the words of Charles Barber, they underlined "the narrow divide that separates the icon from its subject, quite clearly affirming that what happens to the icon affects its subject."[16]

The sensory exchange with the spiritual world did not end with the saint's image. An icon was often but one of the accoutrements of a saint's shrine, along with the relics, the tomb or casket, the lamps, the perfumed oil, and so on.[17] For example, a man

FIGURE 19.4. *The Crucifixion and Iconoclasts,* Chludov Psalter, fol. 67r, c. 850–875. State Historical Museum, Moscow.

with bowel pains approached the coffin of the tenth-century Saint Nikon and prayed for a cure. He was overcome with a sudden thirst, grabbed the oil lamp that hung over the coffin, drank its contents, and was cured.[18] Even more astonishing were the practices in the shrine of Saint Artemios in Constantinople. Men with growths in their genitals lay prostrate on Artemios's tomb; by pressing their afflicted parts against the tomb, they were healed.[19]

Such close encounters, however, could also produce collateral casualties. Images have been worn out by repeated kissing over a long period of use. One example is the image of Christ in a late eleventh-century manuscript now at Dumbarton Oaks (ms. 3) (Figure 19.6). Christ's face and hand, the two areas to which people still direct their veneration today, are much more flaked than the rest of the image.[20] Christians might also have been responsible for intentional damage to images. The crypt under

FIGURE 19.5. *The Martyrdom of Saint Polyeuktos,* Walters Ms. W. 521, fol. 56v, second quarter of the eleventh century. Courtesy of the Walters Art Museum, Baltimore.

the Katholikon, or main church, of the monastery of Hosios Loukas was decorated in the eleventh century with a series of Passion scenes on the side walls and portraits of saints on the vaults. The fresco *The Entombment of Christ and the Marys at the Tomb* still bears signs of later interventions (see Figure 19.1). On the right side of the composition, the eyes and mouths of the two Marys and the eyes of the angel who points to the empty tomb have been scraped. Yet the surviving faces of the people on the left side of the same image are intact.[21] The saints' images on the vaults display the same discrepancy. In the Middle Ages the monastery of Hosios Loukas was an important pilgrimage destination, especially famous for the tomb and relics of its founder, Luke, a local holy man who performed many healing miracles.[22] The crypt housed his tomb. Pilgrims seeking deliverance from ailments continued to visit and venerate the tomb even after the relics were removed to the Katholikon.[23] It is in the context of this

FIGURE 19.6. *Christ,*
Dumbarton Oaks ms. 3, fol.
39r, late eleventh century.
© Dumbarton Oaks, Byzantine
Collection, Washington, D.C.

building as a healing center that we need to seek the interpretation of the acts of defacement we have seen.

The use of plaster from sacred images for magical and quasi-medicinal use is known from written sources. In a letter to Louis the Pious, the iconoclast Emperor Michael II (r. 820–829) wrote the following: "This too we declare to your Christ-loving affection that many clerics and laymen . . . have become originators of evil practices. . . . Some priests and clerics scraped the paint of images and, mixing it with the eucharistic bread and wine, let the communicants partake of this oblation after the celebration of the Eucharist."[24] Similarly, in the seventh-century account of the miracles of the medical saints Cosmas and Damian we read the following story:

A certain woman depicted the saints Cosmas and Damian on all the walls of her house, being as she was insatiable in her desire of seeing them. She then fell ill. Perceiving herself to be in danger, she crawled out of bed and, upon reaching the place where the most wise saints were depicted on the wall, she stood up leaning on her faith as upon a stick and scraped off with her fingernails some plaster. This she put into water and, after drinking the mixture, she was immediately cured of her pains by the visitation of the saints.[25]

Historians habitually cite such stories to illustrate the serious abuses that led to the iconoclasm crisis in Byzantium (730–787 and 815–843). Iconoclasm was primarily a religious movement that denied the holiness of images and considered their veneration idolatrous.[26] Iconophiles, the party that promulgated the reverence of icons, responded with the Second Council of Nicaea, also known as the Seventh Ecumenical Council, which took place in that city of Asia Minor in 787. The council codified the Orthodox position on the matter, which has since been followed by all Chalcedonian churches. The Nicaea II definition of images, very much Neoplatonic in character, claimed that "the honor given to an image is transferred to its prototype."[27] The council strove to elucidate the difference between the icon and the prototype: "The image resembles the prototype, not with regard to the essence, but only with regard to the name and the position of the members which can be characterized. When one paints the image of a man, he does not seek to find his soul in the image."[28] Based on such definitions, a number of scholars have viewed the story of the miraculous healing through the drinking of the icon's plaster as an example of the confusion between the sign and the signified or, as Kitzinger puts it, "a complete identification of picture and prototype,"[29] which is characteristic of the preiconoclastic superstitions that Nicaea II sought to dispel. Such scholarship assumed a clear division between an educated elite and the uneducated general populace, to whom "superstitious" behavior was usually attached. And yet that same miracle is quoted in the Acts of Nicaea II as an example of the powers of icons (iconophiles used miracle accounts as another means to justify icon veneration).[30] Curious as this may sound, the council never claimed that the image was inconsequential. The image is different from the prototype "in essence," but it is still holy by its association with (or by its likeness to) the prototype. In an explicit statement, the council decreed that "whoever venerates the icon, venerates in it the person (*hypostasis*) of the one depicted."[31] Theodore of Stoudios (d. 826), a major iconophile theologian, claimed that there was "a likeness of *hypostasis*" between image and prototype[32] and that the divinity is in the icon "through a relative participation, because [the icon] shares in the grace and honor [of the depicted divinity]."[33] Hence, according to such iconophiles as Leontios of Neapolis and Theodore Abu Qurrah, when an image is damaged and loses its likeness to its prototype, it should be destroyed.[34]

The tenth-century vita of the fictional Saint Andrew the Fool recounted a relevant story in which the likeness of icons to their prototypes was obscured. A woman, despairing of her unfaithful husband, approached a certain magician called Vigrinos. Vigrinos visited her house and performed a series of rituals in front of her icons. The woman's husband indeed stopped desiring others, but his wife started having very disturbing dreams. In one of them she saw her icons covered in excrement and giving off an incredible stench. She sought the advice of a pious man called Epiphanios, who was able to break the spell. The author of the vita explained that Vigrinos's magic managed to "defile and neutralize the holy icons" because he "secretly spread on them his pulverized excrement,"[35] thus altering the likeness of the icons to their prototypes. As a result, the sharing of miraculous properties ceased.

The notion that materialities partook of divine grace permeated all aspects of Byzantine religiosity. It had a critical biblical precedent. In Mark 5:25–34 the woman with the issue of blood touches Christ's cloak and is immediately healed.[36] Early Christian and Byzantine hagiography is filled with characters whose attitudes are similar to that of the woman with the issue of blood. According to the tenth-century life of Saint Nikon of Sparta, when people heard the of the saint's death

> one could . . . see the roads flowing with people. . . . Wherefore desiring to show the heat and fervor of their faith, those flowing in thus undertook to do something boorish and coarse. And one hastened to carry away something from the squalid locks of the blessed one's head, another something from the hairs in his beard, still another a patch from his old cloak and his goatskin outergarment. And it was a great and illustrious thing for all to carry away some one of the things touching the skin of the holy remains, for relief of sufferings and every sort of disease.[37]

Notice again the tension between the author's distaste for the behavior of the crowd and his admission that even ordinary objects that touched the saint's body— the so-called contact relics—effected cures. We cannot dismiss such phenomena as merely exaggerations of the simple-minded. After all, at every celebration of the Divine Liturgy the Eucharistic bread and wine turned into the body and blood of Christ, a potent manifestation of the relationship between materiality and the sacred.[38] This connection was further emphasized, starting in the middle of the twelfth century, by the image of the *Melismos* (literally "Fraction").[39] This composition featured the Christ child lying on a paten set on the altar, surrounded by clergy and ready to be sacrificed. The *Melismos* created an intense visual correspondence between the ritual acts of the celebrants and their symbolism by virtue of its location in the main apse of a church, directly behind and above the altar.

If the official theology promulgated the sacredness of materiality, promoted a devotion that encompassed multiple senses, and entailed tactile engagement with objects of veneration, the proliferation of graffiti in Byzantine churches should not be surprising. The study of graffiti in Byzantium is still in a nascent stage. The little scholarship on the topic that exists has concentrated on individual monuments or areas.[40] Therefore, my suggestions are necessarily preliminary in character. Here I focus on the most common textual graffiti, those that spelled out prayers (see, for example, Figure 19.2).[41] Such graffiti were scratched into every wall surface of a church building, including the sanctuary. Although there was great variety, the majority of these inscriptions repeated such formulaic prayers as "Lord help your servant" or "Prayer of your servant" or "For the remission of sins of your servant." Occasionally they concluded with the name of the male or female supplicant, his or her title, and a date. Longer prayers were unusual. In addition to textual graffiti there were pictorial ones, often of boats or vessels, a variety of animals, and more rarely of Christ, the Virgin, or a saint.

What was the function of such graffiti? Véronique Plesch, writing about late medieval texts in northern Italian chapels, has argued that inscribing words on a sacred image is both a devotional act, an insertion and immersion into the depicted saint's flesh, and a ritual act, repeated and symbolic, that crosses the liminal threshold of the pictorial surface.[42] Catherine Jolivet-Lévy, in her examination of Byzantine examples from Cappadocia, claimed that the images on which graffiti are incised act as intermediaries between supplicant and saint and, ultimately, Christ. The graffiti themselves assure physical contact with the saint.[43] These observations are certainly correct, yet they consider only part of the evidence. Graffiti were frequently incised in areas of a church that contained no images (see Figure 19.3); many were addressed to Christ and the Virgin but not to a specific saint;[44] and rarely did a graffito correspond to the image on which it was inscribed. I therefore suggest that the graffiti were meant primarily to ensure the supplicants' permanent presence close to sources of divine grace, such as the relics of the martyrs under the altar, and inside a sacred space, something that guaranteed liturgical and extraliturgical commemoration. The supplicants inscribed their prayers not only into the painted body of a saint but also into the masonry flesh of the building itself, which was rendered sacred through the rituals celebrated there. Indeed, when a church was completed, the bishop performed a lengthy two-day consecration rite that culminated in the deposition of martyrs' relics under the altar.[45] Proximity to such holiness had momentous soteriological implications. Already in the fourth century, Basil, bishop of Caesarea (d. ca. 379), claimed that the body of a martyr sanctified the place where it was buried and those that gathered together around it.[46] And Gregory, bishop of Nyssa (d. after 394), placed the tombs of his relatives near relics of the Forty Martyrs of Sebasteia so that, at the time of resurrection, they might find themselves in confident and helpful company.[47]

How to secure such a presence depended on the means and social status of each individual. The extreme expression of this attitude was burial inside a church, something prohibited by canon law.[48] For example, the two churches in the monastery tou

Libos housed twenty-nine imperial and aristocratic tombs dating from the tenth century to the fifteenth. Such tombs were decorated with sculptural ornament, images of the deceased that bore their names, and lengthy poems that again named them and appealed to the visitor to pray for their souls.[49] An epigram commissioned by Irene Palaiologina to decorate the now-lost tomb of her husband, John II Doukas Komnenos Angelos (d. 1318), concluded as follows: ". . . but, O spectator, stay mourning here, and ask from God that this despot may find henceforth another dignity in Heaven."[50] The display and visibility of one's name inside a church was of paramount importance. We find names in inscriptions, dedicatory and otherwise, periodically accompanying portraits, as in the narthex of the church of Asinou in Cyprus (Figure 19.7). That the graffiti and the inscriptions on tombs and in the painted decoration of a church were part of the same culture is beyond doubt. Many of the formulaic prayers used in both are essentially identical.[51] Some graffiti, like tomb inscriptions, requested the help of the reader. One example from the Parthenon in Athens, which was converted into a church sometime between the fifth and seventh centuries, read, "Remember, Lord, . . . your servant Theophanes the deacon, first cantor, and sacristan. May he who wrote this gain health, and may he who reads it gain happiness."[52]

Why was the writing of names so important? The portraits, inscriptions, and graffiti represented their originators eternally. Those writing the graffiti assumed that visitors and congregants reading them, whether aloud or inaudibly, would thus become agents of commemoration, reenacting time and again prayers for good health or eternal repose.[53] The name connected the prayer to the individual who had originally inscribed it. The reasoning behind this was essentially Nicene, but in reverse. Just as in the icon the signifier shared some of the qualities of the signified, so the signified, here the persons whose names and images were found inside churches, shared the benefit of being constantly present in a house of prayer by means of a textual signifier. Liturgical commentaries communicated the same idea in reference to the *prothesis,* the rite of preparation of the Eucharistic gifts. During the prothesis, the priest, while reading the names of people living and dead, placed bread particles on their behalf near the *amnos,* the central part of the Eucharistic bread that was to be consecrated.[54] Symeon, bishop of Thessalonike (d. 1429), commented:

> The offered particles provide great advantage, for they are in place of
> the persons for whom they are offered, and are a sacrifice offered on their
> behalf to God. . . . Because by lying near the divine bread as it is being con-
> secrated and becomes the body of Christ, [the particle] immediately par-
> takes of His holiness. Placed on the chalice, it is united with His blood.
> Thus it passes on the grace to the soul for whom it was offered. Therefore
> spiritual communion takes place. If the person is one of the pious or one
> of those who, having sinned, have now repented, he receives invisibly the

communion of the [Holy] Spirit in the soul, as we said. As we have learned, he often receives physical benefits.[55]

Symeon summarized beautifully the mechanics of what we might call "grace transference"—the bread particle, by virtue of its proximity to the consecrated host, passed the divine grace to the person it stood for and for whom it was offered. Even more tellingly, Nikolaos Kabasilas, a fourteenth-century theologian, claimed that one

FIGURE 19.7. Images of Saint Sozomenos and a praying monk, narthex, church of Panagia Phorbiotissa, Asinou, Cyprus, thirteenth century. Photo by Vasileios Marinis.

needed not be present physically, because the sanctification that took place during the liturgy addressed only the soul:

> What are the reasons for sanctification? Perhaps the fact that one has a body, rushes to the altar, takes the holy gifts in one's hands, receives them in his mouth, eats them, or drinks them? Not at all. Because many who had all of the above and thus approached the mysteries gained nothing— rather they left being responsible for larger evils. But what are the causes of sanctification to those who are sanctified? The cleansing of soul, the love of God, faith, desire for the mystery, eagerness for the receiving of communion, fervent impulse, running with thirst. These are what attract sanctification. . . . But all these do not pertain to the body, but depend solely on the soul. Therefore, nothing impedes the souls of the dead, like those of the living, to achieve these.[56]

The inscribers of the graffiti counted on a similar movement of grace, a "spiritual communion" that sanctified even those who were bodily absent. Consequently, I consider the prayer graffiti not as transgressions of the uneducated but as other expressions of the Byzantine preoccupation with everlasting commemoration and with proximity, literal but by necessity usually metaphorical, to holiness.

If "the honor given to an image is transferred to its prototype," as the iconophiles claimed, some illustrations from the Chludov Psalter offer an ironic application of this notion.[57] The manuscript dates to the second half of the ninth century and was likely produced in Constantinople for a patriarch or someone in his circle. It belongs to the group of the Marginal Psalters, so called from the miniatures that decorate the broad margins on each page.[58] The illustrations are a visual commentary on the text of the psalms. Some include vehement anti-iconoclastic propaganda. Folio 67r contains the text of Psalm 68 ("Save me, O God, for the waters have come up to my neck"). On the border are two connected illustrations (see Figure 19.4). On the right, on top of a truncated hill representing Golgotha, is Christ crucified, fully dressed and with open eyes. Two soldiers are tormenting him. The one to Christ's right has just pierced the Lord's side with a spear. The soldier to his left is lifting toward Christ's mouth a spear topped by a sponge dipped in vinegar (the vessel containing the vinegar is at the foot of the cross). At the bottom of the page, two iconoclasts are whitewashing a medallion image of Christ. On one level, these miniatures, which comment specifically on verse 22 ("They gave me also gall for my food, and made me drink vinegar for my thirst"), represent in visual terms the ancient rhetorical schema of *synkresis,* or comparison: the acts of the iconoclasts, who are whitewashing an image of Christ, are like those of Christ's tormentors during the Crucifixion. Visual clues enhance the comparison: the spear and sponge that the iconoclasts are using are identical to those of the soldier in the crucifixion scene, just as the forms of the vessels that contain the plaster and the vinegar are identical. The Nicene relationship between image and prototype may be applied: the atrocities the iconoclasts perform on the image of Christ are visually, albeit figuratively, inflicted on the prototype, that is, on Christ's body. A detail that has escaped notice is that the face of one of the iconoclasts (the wild hair indicates his demonic personality) has been scratched. This was likely a depiction of John the Grammarian, the iconoclast patriarch of Constantinople between 837 and 843 and the primary villain in this manuscript. The careful scratching-out of the faces of the iconoclasts, far from being the unseemly reaction of an indignant iconophile, was a calculated response intended to complement the message of the miniature.

We find similar interventions on other pages of the Chludov Psalter and in other manuscripts. Middle Byzantine Menologia, such as that of Basil II (Vat.gr. 1613) and one in the Walters Art Museum (W.521), contain miniatures in which the faces of tormentors or executioners of Christian martyrs have been removed (see Figure 19.5).[59] The marks almost invariably indicate the violence of removing the face, but the scratcher took care to preserve the rest of the body. The permanent disfigurement of a face, even in a manuscript, would have resonated deeply with iconophiles. In one of the most infamous episodes of iconoclasm, the ninth-century Emperor Theophilos punished two Palestinian brothers and leaders of the iconophile party, Theodore and Theophanes, by having insulting verses tattooed on their foreheads.[60] Mutilations of the face had been prohibited since the fourth century by Emperor Constantine I.[61] Emperor Leo III reintroduced such punishments with the collection of laws known as the *Ekloge* in 741.[62] The pertinent articles stipulated that facial mutilations were reserved for the worst offenses, such as sacrilege.[63] According to a later adaptation of the laws, they served "as a sign of [the offender's] wickedness."[64] The mutilation was a constant reminder that a very serious crime had been committed and punished.

On another level, the defacement of John the Grammarian echoed the dialectic of the two miniatures: whatever happened to the image also happened to its prototype. The Acts of Nicaea II stated this explicitly: "Who does not know that when an icon is dishonored the insult applies to the person who is depicted on the icon?"[65] The implication here is very clear: veneration, as well as humiliation, was transferred to the prototype. With this secondary intervention, the iconoclasts in the Chludov Psalter were made to bear the signs of their iniquity and shame unto eternity, visible to all who read the manuscript. Because the pages in the Chludov were created of parchment, the materiality of the manuscript intensified this message and made the act even more real. The standard term for parchment, δέρμα—literally, "skin"—could refer to humans as well as animals. Thus the iconophiles inscribed their insults on the skin of the faces of the iconoclasts. In an ironic reversal, iconophiles resorted to partial iconoclasm in order to make their point convincingly. Or, to paraphrase Joseph Leo Koerner, the images in the Chludov Psalter became both icons and examples of iconoclasm.[66]

In this chapter I have examined several instances of intervention in and on completed works of arts. I have argued that they were all based on two fundamental tenets of Byzantine religiosity. The first was that people's negotiations with the spiritual world involved, in addition to vision, a variety of senses, primarily tactile engagement. Hagiographical sources provide abundant evidence of such exchanges, in which people engaged icons and other paraphernalia of a saint's cult in various ways. Second, the notion that an image was intrinsically linked to its prototype offered the theological framework for such interactions. Neither tenet was simply a manifestation of popular piety. The decisions of the Second Council of Nicaea amply prove that the official church espoused them, explicitly or implicitly. The scraping of plaster, the inscription of graffiti, and the defacement of images of heretics were not cases of barbarism but rather conscious and occasionally sophisticated manifestations of a culture that, despite its reputed and professed disdain for the corporeal and earthly, revealed itself to be intensely concerned with the senses.

I conclude with a story that perhaps elucidates the reasons for our own scholarly and other biases on this topic. It is a story about two sensory (and, one might say, religious) cultures: one the culture of the twenty-first-century Western museum and the other that of twenty-first-century Orthodox practitioners. This story reflects, *mutatis mutandis,* the dichotomy between vision and the other senses that I described at the beginning of this chapter. The devout of one culture, the museum, encourage vision and absolutely prohibit touching. For the devout of the other culture, which retains practices I have been describing here, tactility is of absolute importance. From November 2006 to March 2007, the J. Paul Getty Museum organized an exhibit dedicated to icons and other objects from the monastery of Saint Catherine in Sinai. An article in the *New York Times* stated that the curators anticipated some intense viewer participation, with Orthodox visitors crossing themselves and attempting to touch and even kiss the protective glass cases.[67] When asked about this, a Getty spokesman replied, "We're stocking up on Windex." I submit that this was as good a cultural compromise as any for which one might reasonably have hoped.

NOTES

1. The fundamental study of iconoclasm is Leslie Brubaker and John F. Haldon, *Byzantium in the Iconoclast Era, c. 680–850: A History* (Cambridge, UK: Cambridge University Press, 2011). See also Anthony Bryer and Judith Herrin, eds., *Iconoclasm: Papers Given at the Ninth Spring Symposium of Byzantine Studies, University of Birmingham, March 1975* (Birmingham, UK: Centre for Byzantine Studies, 1977); André Grabar, *L'Iconoclasme byzantin: Le dossier archéologique,* 2nd ed. (Paris: Flammarion, 1984); Kenneth Parry, *Depicting the Word: Byzantine Iconophile Thought of the Eighth and Ninth Centuries* (Leiden: Brill, 1996); Leslie Brubaker and

John F. Haldon, *Byzantium in the Iconoclast Era (ca. 680–850): The Sources* (Aldershot and Burlington, UK: Ashgate, 2001); and Charles Barber, *Figure and Likeness: On the Limits of Representation in Byzantine Iconoclasm* (Princeton, NJ: Princeton University Press, 2002).

2. For an insightful discussion of modern attitudes and biases toward the destruction of images, see David Freedberg, *The Power of Images: Studies in the History and Theory of Response* (Chicago: University of Chicago Press, 1989), 407–428.

3. Cyril Mango, *The Art of the Byzantine Empire, 312–1453: Sources and Documents* (Toronto: University of Toronto Press, 1986), 189.

4. T. K. Johansen, *Aristotle on the Sense-Organs* (Cambridge, UK: Cambridge University Press, 1997), and Charles Barber, *Contesting the Logic of Painting: Art and Understanding in Eleventh-Century Byzantium* (Leiden: Brill, 2007), 95–98.

5. See, selectively, C. Mango, "Antique Statuary and the Byzantine Beholder," *Dumbarton Oaks Papers* 17 (1963): 53–75; Leslie Brubaker, "Perception and Conception: Art, Theory, and Culture in Ninth-Century Byzantium," *Word and Image* 5 (1989): 19–32; Robert S. Nelson, "The Discourse of Icons: Then and Now," *Art History* 12, no. 2 (1989): 140–150; Liz James and Ruth Webb, "'To Understand Ultimate Things and Enter Secret Places': Ekphrasis and Art in Byzantium," *Art History* 14 (1991): 1–17; Liz James, "'Pray Not to Fall into Temptation and Be on Your Guard': Pagan Statues in Christian Constantinople," *Gesta* 35, no. 1 (1996): 12–20; Robin Cormack, *Painting the Soul: Icons, Death Masks, and Shrouds* (London: Reaktion, 1997); Nicoletta Isar, "The Vision and Its 'Exceedingly Blessed Beholder': Of Desire and Participation in the Icon," *RES: Anthropology and Aesthetics* 38 (2000): 56–72; Robert S. Nelson, "To Say and to See: Ekphrasis and Vision in Byzantium," in *Visuality before and beyond the Renaissance: Seeing as Others Saw,* ed. Robert S. Nelson (Cambridge, UK, and New York: Cambridge University Press, 2000), 143–168; Glenn Peers, *Sacred Shock: Framing Visual Experience in Byzantium* (University Park: Pennsylvania State University Press, 2004); Liz James, "Senses and Sensibility in Byzantium," in *Art: History: Visual: Culture,* ed. Deborah Cherry (Malden, MA: Blackwell, 2005), 45–59; Barber, *Contesting the Logic of Painting;* and Bissera V. Pentcheva, "The Performative Icon," *Art Bulletin* 88, no. 4 (2006): 631–655. The study of the other senses, despite the best of intentions, most often consists of neo-Orientalist romanticized descriptions of the Byzantine liturgy, which often mention the flickering candlelight, the lingering aroma of incense, the hypnotic psalmody, and so on. Yet the sources, especially those from Constantinople, tell us a different story, that of a less dignified experience. See Robert F. Taft, "The Decline of Communion in Byzantium and the Distancing of the Congregation from the Liturgical Action: Cause, Effect, or Neither?," in *Thresholds of the Sacred: Architectural, Art Historical, Liturgical, and Theological Perspectives on Religious Screens, East and West,* ed. Sharon E. J. Gerstel (Washington, DC: Dumbarton Oaks Research Library and Collection, 2006), 38–39.

6. On the topic of cultic images as art in the Middle Ages, see the fundamental study of Hans Belting, *Likeness and Presence: A History of the Image before the Era of Art* (Chicago: University of Chicago Press, 1994). See also Jean Claude Schmitt, *Le Corps des images: Essais sur la culture visuelle au Moyen Age* (Paris: Gallimard, 2002), esp. 51–54; Erik Thunø and Gerhard Wolf, eds., *The Miraculous Image in the Late Middle Ages and Renaissance* (Rome: "L'Erma" di Bretschneider, 2004); and Caroline Walker Bynum, *Christian Materiality: An Essay on Religion in Late Medieval Europe* (New York: Zone, 2011), esp. 37–123.

7. *Acta sanctorum,* Oct. III (1953), col. 139B. "Τὸ γὰρ αὐτῆς θεῖον κάλλος, οὐ σχήματί τινι καὶ μορφῆς εὐχροίᾳ διαγλαΐζεται, ἀλλ᾽ ἐν ἀφράστῳ μακαριότητι κατὰ ἀρετὴν θεωρεῖται."

8. On this topic see the succinct comments in Henry Maguire and Alexander Kazhdan, "Byzantine Hagiographical Texts as Sources on Art," *Dumbarton Oaks Papers* 45 (1991): 1, 20.

9. "Τὴν γὰρ γυναῖκα ἐν αὐτῇ τῇ ὥρᾳ ὡς ἐν ὁράματι ἐπιστᾶσα ὁμοιοπλάστως τῆς προγεγραμμένης εἰκόνος καὶ ταύτης τὴν ψόαν πατάξασα, ἀνέστησεν εἰρηκυῖα· Ἄπιθι χαίρουσα, γύναι· υἱὸν γὰρ ἔχεις." Marie-France Auzépy, *La Vie d' Étienne le Jeune par Étienne le Diacre* (Aldershot–Brookfield, UK: Variorum, 1997), 92–93, and Alice-Mary Talbot, "The Devotional Life of Laywomen," in *Byzantine Christianity,* ed. Derek Krueger (Minneapolis: Fortress, 2006), 210–211.

10. On this topic see Gilbert Dagron, "Holy Images and Likeness," *Dumbarton Oaks Papers* 45 (1991): 23–33, and Maguire and Kazhdan, "Byzantine Hagiographical Texts," esp. 4–9.

11. See, for example, Gilbert Dagron, "Le Culte des images dans le monde byzantin," in *Histoire vécue du peuple chrétien,* ed. J. Delumeau, vol. 1 (Toulouse: Privat, 1979), 144–149, and Robert Grigg, "Byzantine Credulity as an Impediment to Antiquarianism," *Gesta* 26, no. 1 (1987): 3–9.

12. Nelson, "To Say and to See," 44. See also Bynum, *Christian Materiality,* 280–286.

13. Dagron, "Holy Images and Likeness," 23–24.

14. Johannes B. Aufhauser, ed., *Miracula S. Georgii* (Leipzig: Teubner, 1913), 10–11.

15. François Halkin, ed., *Bibliotheca hagiographic graeca,* 3rd ed. (Brussels: Société des Bollandistes, 1957), 198. For other instances of images defending themselves, see Brubaker and Haldon, *Byzantium in the Iconoclast Era, c. 680–850: A History,* 210–211.

16. Barber, *Contesting the Logic of Painting,* 7.

17. Talbot has calculated that in healing shrines of the ninth and tenth centuries about 85 percent of miracles "involved some kind of contact with or proximity to the saint's relics or substances associated with the relics." See Alice-Mary Talbot, "Pilgrimage to Healing Shrines: The Evidence of Miracle Accounts," *Dumbarton Oaks Papers* 56 (2002): 159. Gregory of Nyssa (d. ca. 395), speaking about the relics of Saint Theodore, wrote that the faithful approach the relics of the martyr "with eyes, lips, ears, bringing all the senses," and offer their pleas. See Jacques-Paul Migne, ed., *Patrologiae cursus completus, series graeca* (Paris, 1857–1866), vol. 46, col. 740B.

18. Denis Sullivan, *The Life of Saint Nikon: Text, Translation, and Commentary* (Brookline, MA: Hellenic College Press, 1987), 174–176.

19. Virgil S. Crisafulli and John W. Nesbitt, eds., *The Miracles of St. Artemios: A Collection of Miracle Stories by an Anonymous Author of Seventh Century Byzantium* (Leiden and New York: Brill, 1997), miracles 21, 33, and 41. See also Leslie Brubaker, "Icons before Iconoclasm?," in *Morfologie sociali e culturali in Europa fra tarda antichità e alto medioevo* (Spoleto: Centro Italiano di Studi Sull'alto Medioevo, 1998), 1234.

20. Nelson, "Discourse," 150–151. See also Anthony Cutler, *The Hand of the Master: Craftsmanship, Ivory, and Society in Byzantium (9th–11th Centuries)* (Princeton, NJ: Princeton University Press, 1994), 22–29.

21. The image of Nikodemos at the feet of Christ has been damaged, probably as a result of humidity.

22. For a succinct introduction to this foundation, see Nano M. Chatzedake, *Hosios Loukas* (Athens: Melissa, 1997).

23. A set of *enkomia* explicitly mentions that the empty tomb exuded fragrant oil. See Georgios P. Kremos, *Φωκικά: Προσκυνητάριον τῆς ἐν τῇ Φωκίδι μονῆς τοῦ Ὁσίου Λουκᾶ τουπίκλην Στειριώτου* (Athens, 1874), following page 130.

24. Mango, *The Art of the Byzantine Empire,* 157–158.

25. Ibid., 139.

26. See note 1.

27. "... ἡ τῆς εἰκόνος τιμὴ ἐπὶ τὸ πρωτότυπον διαβαίνει." Giovanni Domenico Mansi, ed., *Sacrorum conciliorum, nova, et amplissima collectio* (Florence: Expensis Antonii Zatta, 1759), vol. 13, col. 325D. The acts repeat a formulation by the fourth-century Basil, bishop of Caesarea.

28. "Καὶ ἡ εἰκὼν οὐ κατὰ τὴν οὐσίαν τῷ πρωτοτύπῳ ἔοικεν, ἢ μόνον κατὰ τὸ ὄνομα καὶ κατὰ τὴν θέσιν τῶν χαρακτηριζομένων μελῶν. Οὐδὲ γὰρ εἰκόνα τις ἀναζωγραφῶν ἀνθρώπου τινός, ψυχὴ ἐν εἰκόνι ζητεῖ." Mansi, *Sacrorum conciliorum,* vol. 13, col. 244B.

29. Ernst Kitzinger, "The Cult of Images in the Age before Iconoclasm," *Dumbarton Oaks Papers* 8 (1954): 148.

30. Mansi, *Sacrorum conciliorum,* vol. 13, col. 68A–D.

31. "Καὶ ὁ προσκυνῶν τὴν εἰκόνα, προσκυνεῖ ἐν αὐτῇ τοῦ ἐγγραφομένου τὴν ὑπόστασιν." Ibid., vol. 13, col. 377E.

32. "Τὸ πρωτότυπον οὐ κατ᾽ οὐσίαν ἐν τῇ εἰκόνι... ἀλλὰ κατὰ τὴν τῆς ὑποστάσεως ὁμοιότητα." *PG* 99, col. 420D. See also col. 428C for a similar formulation.

33. "Οὕτω καὶ ἐν εἰκόνι εἶναι τὴν θεότητα εἰπών τις οὐκ ἂν ἁμάρτῃ τοῦ δέοντος ... σχετικῇ δὲ μεταλήψει, ὅτι χάριτι καὶ τιμῇ τὰ μετέχοντα." *PG* 99, col. 344B–C.

34. Kenneth Parry, "Theodore Studites and the Patriarch Nicephoros on Image-Making as Christian Imperative," *Byzantion* 59 (1989): 181–182.

35. On this miracle see George Th. Calofonos, "The Magician Vigrinos and His Victim: A Case of Magic from the Life of St. Andrew the Fool," in *Greek Magic: Ancient, Medieval, and Modern,* ed. J.C.B. Petropoulos (London: Routledge, 2008), 64–71.

36. The image of Christ healing the woman with the issue of blood is found on amulets made of hematite, a stone believed to cure menstrual dysfunction. For an example see Ioli Kalavrezou, ed., *Byzantine Women and Their World* (Cambridge, MA: Harvard Art Museums, 2003), 283–284.

37. Sullivan, *Life of Saint Nikon,* 163–165. Such behavior had very early precedents: during the funerals of both Hypatios, abbot of Rufinianai in Constantinople (d. 446), and Daniel the Stylite (d. 493), the crowds attempted to obtain contact relics from the bodies of the saints. Michel Kaplan, "De la depouille à la relique: Formation du culte des saints à Byzance du Ve au XII siècle," in *Les Reliques: Objets, cultes, symboles,* dir. Kaplan (Turnhout: Brepols, 1999), 19–20; Kaplan, "L'ensevelissement des saints: Rituel de création des reliques et sanctification à Byzance à travers les sources hagiographiques (Ve–XIIe siècles)," *Travaux et mémoires* 14 (2002): 319–322.

38. See, for example, Steven Hawkes-Teeples, ed., *St. Symeon of Thessalonika: The Liturgical Commentaries* (Toronto: Pontifical Institute of Mediaeval Studies, 2010), 110–112, 140–146, 222–230.

39. M. Garidis, "Approche 'realiste' dans la representation du melismos," *Jahrbuch der Österreichischen Byzantinistik* 32, no. 5 (1982): 495–502; Catherine Jolivet-Lévy, "Aspects de la relation entre espace liturgique et décor peint à Byzance," in *Art, cérémonial et liturgie au Moyen Âge: Actes du Colloque de 3e Cycle Romand de Lettres, Lausanne-Fribourg, 24–25 mars, 14–15 avril, 12–13 mai 2000* (Rome: Viella, 2002), 71–88; and Chara Konstantinide, *Ο Μελισμός: Οι συλλειτουργούντες ιεράρχες και οι άγγελοι—διάκονοι μπροστά στην αγία τράπεζα με τα τίμια δώρα ή τον ευχαριστιακό Χριστό* (Thessalonika: Kentro Vyzantinon Ereunon, 2008).

40. Michael Gketakos, *Συμβολὴ εἰς τὴν μελέτην καὶ ἑρμηνείαν τῶν ἀκιδογραφημάτων* (Athens, 1956); Michael Gketakos, *Ἀνέκδοτοι ἐπιγραφαὶ καὶ χαράγματα ἐκ Βυζαντινῶν καὶ μεταβυζαντινῶν μνημείων τῆς Ελλάδος* (Athens: Aster, 1957); Otto Meinardus, "Mediaeval Navigation According to Akidographemata in Byzantine Churches and Monasteries," *Δελτίον τῆς Χριστιανικῆς ἀρχαιολογικῆς ἑταιρείας* 4–6 (1970–1972): 29–52; Anastasios K. Orlandos and Leandros I. Vranouses, *Τὰ χαράγματα τοῦ Παρθενῶνος* (Athens, 1973); Nicole Thierry, "Remarques sur la pratique de la foi d'après les peintures des églises de Cappadoce," in *Artistes, artisans, et production artistique au Moyen Age,* ed. X. Barral I. Altet, vol. 3 (Paris: Picard, 1990), 437–461; Catherine Nazloglou, "Quelques exemples d'akidographemata dans les édifices religieux byzantins et leur signification," in *L'Histoire dans ses variantes: Travaux et recherches des enseignants d'histoire* (Paris:

Belles Lettres, 1979), 37–43; Katerina Delouca, "Les graffitis de navires de l'Occident médiéval dans les monuments byzantins: L'exemple du Théseion," in *Utilis est lapis in structura: Mélanges offerts à Léon Pressouyre* (Paris: Comité des Travaux Historiques et Scientifiques, 2000), 373–377; and Catherine Jolivet-Lévy, "Invocations peintes et graffiti dans les églises de Cappadoce (IXe–XIIIe siècle)," in *Des images dans l'histoire* (Saint-Denis: Presses Universitaires de Vincennes, 2008), 163–178. Several graffiti from Cappadocia have been recorded in Guillaume de Jerphanion, *Une nouvelle province de l'art byzantin: Les églises rupestres de Cappadoce,* 2 vols. (Paris: P. Geuthner, 1925–1942), passim. A comprehensive study of graffiti from some southern Italian churches can be found in Linda Safran, "Scoperte Salentine," *Arte medievale* 7, no. 2 (2008): esp. 73–78; Linda Safran, *The Medieval Salento: Art and Identity in Southern Italy* (Philadelphia: University of Pennsylvania Press, 2014).

41. I follow here the definition of textual graffiti offered by Angelos Chaniotis: "Graffiti are images or texts of unofficial character scratched on physical objects, whose primary function was not to serve as bearers of such images and inscriptions. Graffiti have great affinity to painted texts and images that share these characteristics." See Chaniotis, "Graffiti in Aphrodisias: Images—Texts—Contexts," in *Ancient Graffiti in Context,* ed. Jennifer A. Baird and Claire Taylor (New York: Routledge, 2011), 196. For this image of Saint Barbara and the accompanying inscriptions and graffiti, see André Jacob, "La consecration de Santa Maria della Croce à Casaranello et l'ancien diocèse de Gallipoli," *Rivista di studi Bizantini e Neoellenici* 25 (1988): 147–163, and Jacob, "Deux épitaphes byzantines inédites de Terre d'Otrante," in *Studi in onore di Michele D'Elia: Archeologia–arte–restauro e tutela—archivistica,* ed. Clara Gelao (Matera and Spoleto: R&R, 1996), 166–172. I am grateful to Linda Safran for this information.

42. Véronique Plesch, "Memory on the Wall: Graffiti on Religious Wall Paintings," *Journal of Medieval and Early Modern Studies* 32, no. 1 (2002): 167–197, and Plesch, "Body of Evidence: Devotional Graffiti in a Piedmontese Chapel," in *On Verbal/Visual Representation,* Word & Image Interactions 4 (Amsterdam and New York: Rodopi, 2005), 179–191.

43. Jolivet-Lévy, "Invocations peintes."

44. As noticed in ibid., esp. 166–168. However, in her conclusions the author seems reluctant to disengage the graffiti from images of saints.

45. M. Arranz, *L'Eucologio constantinopolitano agli inizi del secolo XI: Hagismatarion & archieratikon (rituale & pontificale) con l'aggiunta del Leitourgikon (Messale)* (Rome: Pontificia Università Gregoriana, 1996), 227–251.

46. Ὅπερ ἐν τῷ καλλίστῳ προτεμνίσματι τῆς πόλεως κείμενον [τὸ τίμιον σῶμα] ἁγιάζει μὲν τὸν τόπον, ἁγιάζει δὲ τοὺς εἰς αὐτὸν συνιόντας." The quote is from Basil's *Homilia in martyrem Julitta, PG* 31, col. 241.

47. "...καὶ τῶν ἐμῶν πατέρων τὰ σώματα τοῖς τῶν στρατιωτῶν παρεθέμην λειψάνοις· ἵνα ἐν τῷ καιρῷ τῆς ἀναστάσεως μετὰ τῶν εὐπαρρησιαστῶν βοηθῶν ἐγερθῶσιν." *PG* 46, col. 784.

48. On this topic see Vasileios Marinis, "Tombs and Burials in the Monastery tou Libos in Constantinople," *Dumbarton Oaks Papers* 63 (2009): 147–166.

49. The Katholikon of the Chora monastery (now Kariye Müzesi) in Istanbul preserves such tombs. See Sarah T. Brooks, "Sculpture and the Late Byzantine Tomb," in *Byzantium: Faith and Power (1261–1557)* (New York: Metropolitan Museum of Art, 2004), 94–103. For the sculptural decoration of these tombs, see Ø. Hjort, "The Sculpture of the Kariye Camii," *Dumbarton Oaks Papers* 33 (1979): 248–264.

50. Sarah T. Brooks, "Poetry and Female Patronage in Late Byzantine Tomb Decoration: Two Epigrams by Manuel Philes," *Dumbarton Oaks Papers* 60 (2006): 228–229.

51. As noticed in Jolivet-Lévy, "Invocations peintes," esp. 163–164. Some of the painted inscriptions in Cappadocia postdated the completion of the decoration.

52. Orlandos and Vranouses, *Τὰ χαράγματα τοῦ Παρθενῶνος,* 32.

53. Robert S. Nelson, "Image and Inscription: Pleas for Salvation in Spaces of Devotion," in *Art and Text in Byzantine Culture,* ed. Liz James (Cambridge, UK, and New York: Cambridge University Press, 2007), 107–116, and Amy Papalexandrou, "Echoes of Orality in the Monumental Inscriptions of Byzantium," in *Art and Text in Byzantine Culture,* ed. Liz James (Cambridge, UK, and New York: Cambridge University Press, 2007), 166–170.

54. Pan. N. Trempelas, *Αἱ τρεῖς λειτουργίαι κατὰ τοὺς ἐν Ἀθήναις κώδικας* (Athens, 1935), 3–4.

55. Hawkes-Teeples, *St. Symeon of Thessalonika,* 158–160.

56. Sévérien Salaville, ed., *Explication de la Divine Liturgie,* 2nd ed. (Paris: Éditions du Cerf, 1967), 242.

57. On the Chludov Psalter (Moscow Historical Museum ms.gr. 129), see, most recently, *Salterio griego Jlúdov (ms. gr. 129, Museo histórico del estado, Moscú): Libro de Estudios* (Moscow: AyN Ediciones, 2007).

58. On the Marginal Psalters, see Kathleen Anne Corrigan, *Visual Polemics in the Ninth-Century Byzantine Psalters* (Cambridge, UK: Cambridge University Press, 1992).

59. On the Menologion of Basil II and related manuscripts, see Nancy Patterson Ševčenko, *Illustrated Manuscripts of the Metaphrastian Menologion* (Chicago: University of Chicago Press, 1990). The late-fifteenth-century sketchbook of Michael Wolgemut, a Nuremberg master, offers an interesting parallel from the West. It contains several scenes in which the tormentors of Christ are defaced. See Joseph Leo Koerner, *The Reformation of the Image* (Chicago: University of Chicago Press, 2004), 109–110.

60. J.-M. Featherstone, "The Praise of Theodore Graptos by Theophanes of Caesarea," *Analecta Bollandiana* 98 (1980): 93–150. See also Charles Barber, "Writing on the Body: Memory, Desire, and the Holy in Iconoclasm," in *Desire and Denial in Byzantium,* ed. Liz James (Aldershot, UK: Ashgate, 1999), 111–120, and Claudia Sode, *Jerusalem, Konstantinopel, Rom. die Viten des Michael Synkellos und der Brüder Theodoros und Theophanes Graptoi* (Stuttgart: Steiner, 2001), 215–236.

61. For an overview of this practice, see C. P. Jones, "Stigma: Tattooing and Branding in Graeco-Roman Antiquity," *Journal of Roman Studies* 77 (January 1, 1987): 139–155.

62. For the text of the *Ekloge,* see Ludwig Burgmann, ed., *Ecloga: Das Gesetzbuch Leons III. und Konstantinos V.* (Frankfurt am Main: Löwenklau-Gesellschaft, 1983). For an insightful analysis of the articles on corporal punishment, see Evelyne Patlagean, "Byzance et le blason pénal du corps," *Sodalitas: Scritti in onore di Antonio Guarino* 6 (1984): 405–426.

63. For a list see ibid., 406.

64. ". . . ὡς ἂν εἴη σημεῖον φέρων τοῦ οἰκείου πονηρεύματος." P. Noailles and A. Dain, *Les novelles de Léon VI, le sage* (Paris: Les Belles Lettres, 1944), 92.

65. "Τίς γὰρ οὐκ οἶδεν, ὅτι τῆς εἰκόνος ἀτιμαζομένης, πάντως οὗτινός ἐστιν ἡ εἰκών, εἰς αὐτὸν προστρίβεται ἡ ἀτιμία." Mansi, *Sacrorum conciliorum,* vol. 13, col. 325D. See also Freedberg, *The Power of Images,* 414–418.

66. Koerner, *The Reformation of the Image,* 11.

67. Jori Finkel, "After 15 Centuries, St. Peter Finally Leaves Home," *New York Times,* November 12, 2006, Arts / Art & Design, http://www.nytimes.com/2006/11/12/arts/design/12fink .html&_r=1&sq=mount%20sinai%20robert%20nelson&st=nyt&scp=1.

20

Paul Gauguin
Sensing the Infinite

JUNE HARGROVE

Here, near my hut, in utmost silence, I dream of violent harmonies in the natural scents which intoxicate me. Delight enhanced by I know not what sacred horror . . . I divine in the infinite. An aroma of long-vanished joy that I breathe in the present. Paul Gauguin, letter to André Fontainas, March 1899, Tahiti

As death stalked Paul Gauguin (1848–1903) in the Marquesas Islands in French Polynesia, he labored to unite the diverse strands of his aesthetic philosophy and spiritual beliefs in a sensory manifesto that equated art with revelation. This ambitious project culminated in *Contes barbares* (Primitive Tales) (Figure 20.1), painted in the last year of his life. Using the language of synesthesia, Gauguin relied on multisensory cues to elicit shifting constellations of meaning.

Symbolist artists and poets understood synesthesia as the phenomenon whereby one sensory experience stimulates another—a sensation, an association, or an idea.[1] At the end of the nineteenth century, scientific investigations of neurobiology and psychology proliferated exponentially, generating a veritable boom in the study of synesthesia.[2] Despite the scrutiny of the medical and scholarly communities, many outside the sciences considered trans-sensory experiences the equivalent of signs, at once sensuous and metaphysical. Especially in creative or esoteric circles, adherents interpreted synesthetic interconnections as correspondences that bridged the earthly and heavenly spheres. Because the theory of correspondences originated in ideas about divinity, "synesthesia, though a phenomenon of the senses, came to be equated with that which transcends the senses."[3] For Symbolists, this transcendent power of sensory experience resolved the apparent paradox of seeking the spiritual in the material.

In his work, the antithesis of Impressionism and its obsession with empirical perceptions, Gauguin endeavored to convey the incorporeal core of human existence. His purview was the soul, in Symbolist thought the locus of an individual's inner emotions and unconscious ideas. The example of Stéphane Mallarmé (1842–1898),

FIGURE 20.1. Paul Gauguin, *Contes barbares,* 1902, oil on canvas, 130 × 89 centimeters. Folkwang Museum, Essen, W625. Used with permission.

whose poetry externalized the state of the soul (*l'état d'âme*) through allusion and nuance, guided Symbolist thinking in this regard.[4] Deeply influenced by Mallarmé, Gauguin believed that art was a "reflection of the soul of the artist."[5] Reversing the Positivist approach, he exploited the sensorium as a conduit for multivalent experiences that intensified the soul's awareness of higher realms—the divine or the infinite.[6] He espoused the popular mystical trend to seek a cosmic unity whereby the soul became one with the universe. He posited synesthesia as the vehicle through which art might reveal this harmony.

Thus, as in the epigraph that opened this chapter, Gauguin's dream evoked hearing (silence, harmonies) and smell (scents, aromas) as well as sight to provoke profound emotional responses (horror, joy) comparable to ecstasy. The physical and affective effects that he described (intoxication, delight) summon the sublime, the infinite. Similarly, in *Contes barbares* he rallied the senses to ignite the synesthesia that shaped his spiritual quest.

When the artist inscribed *Contes barbares* on the canvas, he had virtually stopped naming his paintings. His adjacent signature, "Paul Gauguin / 1902 / Marquises," is unique in his oeuvre in specifying the location. Three figures occupy most of the space of this painting. First, at the left margin, and highest on the canvas, a crouching man with hunched shoulders wears a loose dress of the type imposed on native women by Christian missionaries in tropical climates. The man's features have long been recognized as those of Dutch artist Jacob Meijer de Haan (1852–1895) (Figure 20.2), painted by Gauguin in 1889. To his left and in front of him, the painting's middle figure echoes sculptures of Buddha seen in photographs that the artist possessed of Javanese friezes on the temple at Borobudur (now in Indonesia).[7] The woman resting on her haunches was Tohotaua, a Marquesan beauty that Gauguin had photographed in his studio (Figure 20.3).[8] The poses reflect the artist's perception of the fundamental differences of character among the three figures, moving across the canvas from an awkward squat to meditative repose to an attitude of calm devotion. The figures' limbs, however, intertwine with their visages in an elliptical composition of perpetual motion.

The incongruous trio congregate amid luxuriant foliage in a sensual landscape abundant with aromatic flowers and ripe fruit. The setting is redolent with the earthy scent of a tainted Eden. A shell rests on the edge of a pool of fresh water from which rise stylized lotuses and a phallic lily. Above, pink blossoms dangle over misty clouds that waft like incense from afar, halting abruptly and mysteriously behind the woman's head. Out of the lavender haze, the specter of a face (Figure 20.4) hovers above and behind her left shoulder at the painting's right margin. No other work by Gauguin insists on this degree of saturation in tantalizing sensations.

Scholars agree that the group comprises the three cultures—Christian, Buddhist, and Maori—that shaped Gauguin's unorthodox faith.[9] Because most interpretations

FIGURE 20.2. Paul Gauguin, *Portrait of Jacob Meyer de Haan*, 1889, oil on wood, 31³/₈ × 20³/₈ inches (79.6 × 51.7 cm). Fractional gift of Mr. and Mrs. David Rockefeller. Museum of Modern Art, New York. Digital image © The Museum of Modern Art/Licensed by SCALA/Art Resource, New York.

dwell on the title's "primitive tales," these explanations revolve around who is recounting what to whom.[10] Given that no one appears to speak, other avenues of inquiry might well yield more penetrating insights. Throughout his career, Gauguin expressed his preference for symbolism structured as parable. As early as 1888 he declared, "I prefer color suggestive of forms, and in composition the parable to the painted novel."[11] This chapter explores *Contes barbares* as a visual parable whose very density of sensory stimuli challenges the viewer to account for their profusion.

Gauguin's calculated distortions of de Haan's portrait thirteen years after he painted the original (cf. Figure 20.2 with Figure 20.1), imbued this doppelgänger with a grotesque mien. De Haan incarnates the *varua ino,* a malevolent spirit, the harbinger of death in Tahitian lore.[12] In addition to gnawing on his fingers, a gesture of flavored oral gratification, and having familiar hornlike locks of hair, the satanic antihero unveils sharp blood-red talons from under the skirt of his Mother Hubbard costume. This feminine garb, flagrantly transgressive, betrays the insidious motives of what it purports to conceal: these shapeless frocks, in Gauguin's mind, epitomized the ruth-

FIGURE 20.3. An enhanced modern copy of a photograph by Louis Grelet of "Tohotaua with a Fan," originally published in Hans Secker, "Ein Bild und sein Vorbild bei Gauguin," *Atlantis,* 1932, 445. The original 1902 photograph is unlocated.

less destruction of native customs, especially sexual mores, by Christian authorities. As the artist deplored in his 1903 autobiography, *Before and After:* "The child kept in school, deprived of physical exercise, the body (sake of decency) always clothed, becomes delicate, incapable of surviving the night in the mountains. . . , Thus we witness the sad spectacle of the extinction of the race, consumptive, infertile, their ovaries destroyed by mercury."[13] In this vein, he inscribed the words "Paradise Lost" under a print that he glued inside the cover of this memoir. Over the years, Gauguin had obsessively pursued the subject of the biblical Temptation and Fall. Prophetically, in *Portrait of Meijer de Haan with a Lamp* he placed a volume of John Milton's *Paradise Lost* (1668) on the shelf beside a postlapsarian platter of picked fruit. On one level, *Contes barbares* is a parable of the fate of Oceanic culture. The self-consuming figure on the left, a double for the syphilitic Gauguin, is at once a clairvoyant who foretells the demise of paradise and the Occidental agent who perpetrates its ruin.

The middle figure in *Contes barbares,* seated in a lotus position, has frequently been mistaken for a woman,[14] but his androgynous appearance manifests the fusion of male and female traits common to traditional descriptions of the Buddha. Androgyny fascinated the Symbolists. Gauguin was intrigued by its ambiguity and its evocation of the mystical unity of the sexes. His version of theosophy embraced the complementary nature of the sexes, in accord with Polynesian beliefs, through which the union of

FIGURE 20.4. Detail from Paul Gauguin, *Contes barbares,* 1902, oil on canvas, 130 × 89 centimeters. Folkwang Museum, Essen, W625. Used with permission.

male and female constitutes the universe, "one active, the other passive, or the soul and the body; one spiritual and hidden, the other material and visible."[15]

In contrast to the complementary gender mix of the Buddhalike figure, the cross-dressing totem blurs the boundaries of sexual identity through deception, pitting clothed against unclothed, the artifice of the civilized versus the innocence of Gauguin's primitive. This sartorial charade owes its substance to the artist's reading of Thomas Carlyle's *Sartor Resartus* (1834), the other book depicted in *Portrait of Meijer de Haan.* Carlyle framed his philosophical inquiry into the nature of belief in terms of the symbolism of clothing, which functions metaphorically to conceal and to reveal the divine. His ideas were influenced by the writings of Emanuel Swedenborg (1688–1772), a scientist and mystic whose reputation flourished in the nineteenth century. Swedenborg proposed a divine universe that reveals its godliness through earthly signs intelligible to the elect, known as correspondences, that connect "heaven with all things of the earth."[16] He maintained that "all the delights of heaven are delights of use [that] can be seen by a comparison with the five bodily senses of man. There is given to each sense a delight in accordance with its use; to the sight, the hearing, the smell, the taste, and the touch, each its own delight. . . . These uses which the senses severally perform are known to those who study them, and more fully to those who are acquainted with correspondences."[17] Swedenborg's theories enhanced the religious dimensions of Carlyle's meditations on revelation, prevalent in *Sartor Resartus.*[18]

In 1897, soon after Gauguin read the complete translation of *Sartor Resartus* in the *Mercure de France,* he undertook writing his scathing indictment "The Catholic Church and Modern Times."[19] As he was painting *Contes barbares* in 1902, he was reworking this text into an independent manuscript titled "The Modern Spirit and Catholicism." There he reiterated his vehement opposition to missionary dress, which he saw as tantamount to the ecclesiastical hierarchy of the church itself.[20] On the canvas he employed the sardonic symbolism of couture, central to *Sartor Resartus,* to expose what he saw as the cloaked hypocrisy of Christianity by comparison with the luminous candor of Buddhist and Maori cultures, signified by the silky golden torsos of the two central figures of *Contes barbares.* Carlyle's text galvanized Gauguin's appreciation of the spiritual depth, as well as the sensory breadth, of correspondences. If, as Carlyle concluded, "the universe is one vast symbol of God,"[21] Gauguin envisioned revelation as the calling of art—the synesthetic transcendence of the senses.

The kneeling woman epitomizes the polysemous meanings that endow Gauguin's art with its complexity. A Marquesan Eve, she is the tragic muse of Polynesian culture annihilated by the forces of colonialism implicit in her demonic companion. Succulent mangoes, strewn on the velvety grass, serve as a tropical proxy for the forbidden fruit of the doomed Garden of Eden. This verdant paradise harbors a world after the Fall, when the satanic tempter has introduced the inevitability of death as the counterpart to life. Through the process of birth, women are inherently vessels of regeneration. And fragrant blossoms, holding the promise of rebirth, continue the cycle of life around this Eve. Her ambrosial crown of frangipani denotes sexual availability and fecundity. The pentameric (five-petaled) flowers at the water's edge, the lily, and the lotus are all perfumed symbols of regeneration or reincarnation.[22] Gauguin gave his personal interpretation of metempsychosis in "The Modern Spirit and Catholicism."[23]

This female figure's significance as the agent of renewal is reinforced by the vaporous cloud that descends to her from a distant horizon. It recalls the swirling cloud of the *raigō* by which Amitābha Buddha (Figure 20.5) arrives to welcome the dying devotee to the Western Pure Land, where the individual will eventually achieve rebirth.[24] Elusive faces seem to tumble across the cloud, potential images that evoke his entourage. According to Pure Land doctrine, heavenly music, delectable scents, and cascades of lotus petals accompany Amitābha on his voyage.[25] Rosy petals echo its

FIGURE 20.5. *Raigō* (*Welcoming Descent of Amitābha*), detail from Jean Buhot, *Histoire des arts du Japon I: Des origines à 1350,* vol. 5 of *Annales du Musée Guimet* (Paris: Vanoest, 1949), Figure 232.

path, like musicians and dancers from the Pure Land, heightening the painting's synesthetic effect.

Gauguin's notion of the non-Western was central to his project to free art from the academic canon. He associated synesthesia with the idea of the primitive ("barbare") that he appropriated from Charles Baudelaire (1821–1867). The poet praised "an inevitable, synthetic, childlike barbarity, which often remains visible in a perfect art (Mexican, Egyptian, or Ninevite) and which derives from the need to see things on a grand scale and to consider them primarily in their overall effect," adding that many "have accused of barbarity all the painters whose vision is synthetic and abbreviated."[26] Baudelaire captured the connotations of the primitive that Gauguin embraced, not only in relation to ancient or remote cultures but also to a style that could impart the immutable forces of cosmic origins and primeval truths through a simplified, synthetic unity. The schematic nature of this "primitive" makes it comparable to a (in this case peculiarly Western European) language of signs, like hieroglyphs, whereby one thing represents another. The painter employed the barbare as a system of signs or correspondences analogous to synesthesia.[27]

Gauguin indicated this in his titles when he coupled the word "barbare" with nouns that specifically denote sound, thereby launching auditory associations that signal the synesthetic dimensions of the paintings.[28] The watercolor *Musique barbare* (Figure 20.6) conveys the premise of synesthesia with the utmost directness. A Tahitian spirit of the dead plays on a musical keyboard, alluding to Baudelaire's "keyboard of *correspondences!*"[29] The moon goddess Hina dominates the center of the painting, while the mask of Ta'aroa, the god of creation, counterbalances a cluster of *ti'is,* minor

FIGURE 20.6. Paul Gauguin, *Musique barbare,* 1892, watercolor on silk, 11.4 × 20 centimeters. Kunstmuseum Basel, Kupferstichkabinett (gift of Dr. h.c. Richard Doetsch-Benziger). Photo by Martin P. Bühler, Kunstmuseum Basel. Used with permission.

deities. These elements constitute the Tahitian cycle of life that Gauguin describes in his *Ancien culte mahorie* (1892). They are rendered with a chromatic fluidity whereby color and form melt one into one another, like notes of a musical chord.

Tales are aural, and the title *Contes barbares* entices the viewer to "listen" to the painting, setting in motion the synesthesia that permeates the canvas. The colors saturate the scene, a dreamlike phantasmagoria that engenders a voluptuous array of sensory titillations catalyzing the viewer's subjective responses. The serpentine line of the pink petals and the cloud intersects with the arabesque shaped by the orange-reds that eventually connect the figures to the fruit. Gauguin composed using rich chords of allied hues interspersed with sharp contrasts and unexpected tonic accents. The chromatic interplay of cool greens and blues generates a luscious somber orchestration broken by paler, higher pinks underscored by cascades of deeper reddish-orange hues. The warmer hues simulate an overarching melodic line running across a strong rhythm of measured verticals, most pronounced in the trees.

The abstract vocabulary of form and color provides a conduit to the imagination. As Gauguin wrote in his notebook, "Diverses choses" (1896–1897),

> Color being enigmatic in itself . . . , we cannot use it any other way than enigmatically . . . to give the musical sensations that flow from . . . its . . . internal, mysterious, enigmatic power. By means of skillful harmonies, we create symbols. Color which, like music, is a matter of vibrations, reaches what is most general and therefore most undefinable in nature: its inner

power . . . color as the language of the *eye that listens,* by its power of suggestion aids the flight of the imagination, opening a new door on the infinite and the mystery of things.[30]

The "eye that listens," a phrase derived from Swedenborg, attributes to one sensory organ the faculty of another, the perfect metaphor for synesthesia.[31] In *Contes barbares* the emphasis on the eye and the absence of the ear in the face obscured in the mist, above the regenerative blossoms, may conjure up this eye that listens. The partial features—the piercing eye, the large nose, and the mustache—resemble those in the artist's self-portrait, such as that in the tiny sketch from his satirical Tahitian newspaper *Le Sourire.*[32] Could this phantom evoke the artist—his soul merging with the infinite?

Gauguin inherited Romantic notions about the capacity of color to express thoughts and feelings. In particular, Eugène Delacroix (1798–1863) extolled the virtues of color, freed from the onerous task of description, as a catalyst for emotions. He championed the musicality of art, "the music of the picture" that conveys "the soul of the painter."[33] This musical/visual paradigm stressed that abstract components—line, form, and especially color—convey the emotional core of an artwork. Artists and critics invoked this paradigm to insist on the nonmimetic elements of the painting, and they used musical terms to verbalize the effects that they were seeking. Baudelaire promoted this quality of Delacroix's oeuvre, where "wonderful chords of colour often give one ideas of melody and harmony, and the impression that one takes away from his pictures is often . . . a musical one."[34] Gauguin made this musical paradigm central to his own strategic synesthesia.[35] He copied passages verbatim from Delacroix's journals into "Diverses choses,"[36] but already, a decade earlier in "Notes synthétiques," he had articulated a musical template drawn from Delacroix:

> Painting is the most beautiful of all arts. In it, *all sensations are condensed;* contemplating it, everyone can create a story at the will of his imagination, and—with a single glance—have his soul invaded by the most profound recollections; no effort of memory, everything is summed up in one instant. . . . Like Music, *[painting] acts on the soul through the intermediary of the senses:* harmonious colors correspond to the harmonies of sounds. But in painting a unity is obtained which is not possible in music, where the accords follow one another, so that the judgment experiences a continuous fatigue if it wants to reunite the end with the beginning.[37]

Gauguin formulated his remarks to combat the prevailing view that music was superior to the visual arts, a view advanced by those who insisted that it produces emotions directly without the intervention of intellectual faculties.[38] He argued that, on the contrary, while painting shares this sensory dynamic, it has the advantage of greater immediacy. The unity of the sensations synthesized into a painting reaches into the soul in a single instant. Color became for Gauguin the musical medium that would catapult his art from mundane mimesis to the creative sublime. While Baudelaire's salon criticism disseminated Delacroix's musical paradigm, the former's poem "Correspondences" (1857) became a touchstone for Gauguin and his circle. Albert Aurier (1865–1893) hailed the principle of correspondences as the bedrock of Symbolism in an essay on Gauguin for the *Mercure de France* (1891).[39] He singled out "Correspondences" to indicate how the poetic license of synesthesia, its polyvalence, inspired the form and content of the Symbolist aesthetic. Gauguin primed Aurier to write this important article acclaiming the revelatory powers of his art.[40] The author credited the modern interpretation of correspondences to Swedenborg. The scientist/philosopher/theologian's ideas were propagated in France not only through the work of Carlyle but, importantly, also by Honoré de Balzac (1799–1850), who had a defining impact on Baudelaire.[41] Gauguin's grasp of the mystical-theological fine points was limited—he probably never actually read Swedenborg; most of his generation knew these theories as filtered through Balzac and reconfigured by Baudelaire. A letter to Émile Schuffenecker (1851–1934) documents Gauguin's extrapolation of ideas from Swedenborg as early as the 1880s.[42]

Aurier reiterated Swedenborg's assertion that artists, like poets, were prophets, endowed with the gift of seeing past superficial appearances: "How rare the happy souls whose eyes are open and who can cry with Swedenborg, that gifted visionary: 'This very night, the eyes of my inner person were opened: they were rendered ready to regard in the heavens, in the world of ideas, and in the inferno!'"[43] He elaborated on how the artist translates ideas into "a special language" where objects in nature appear as signs: "They are the letters of an immense alphabet that only the man of genius knows how to spell."[44]

The exalted status of the artist in Swedenborg's writings neatly coincided with the aura of genius that Gauguin ascribed to himself. In *Cahier pour Aline,* a manuscript he wrote in Tahiti (1893), he recapitulated ideas that had been germinating since he first went to Brittany:

> There is a book in the heavens where the laws of harmony and beauty are written. Swedenborg said the men who can read this book are favored by God. He added that the artist is the true elect since only he has the power to write this reading, one should regard him as a divine messenger—
> And Swedenborg was a scholar![45]

Referring explicitly to the philosopher, Gauguin validated his own credentials as a prophet whose art could reveal divine secrets hidden in the universe.

As Gauguin assumed the mantle of privileged seer, he imbued his themes of death and regeneration with a heady appeal to the senses. These multisensory effects elicited metaphysical correspondences that animated his spiritual concerns, from loss, destruction, and extinction to rebirth, reincarnation, and immortality. The interpenetration of sensations and signs depended on the power of suggestion to unleash the imagination, thus activating the "mysterious center of thought."[46] Gauguin intensified the viewer's sensory awareness to elevate the emotional pitch of the painting to a transcendent state.

Contes barbares claims to demonstrate how synesthesia eclipses banal reality through an effervescent symbolism predicated on sensory perceptions. The painting depends on sensations as well as signs. This equivocal character was precious to Gauguin as he orchestrated the flow of feelings and ideas through his art to rouse the spectator's imagination to entertain the infinite. This canvas is a veritable parable on the phenomenon of correspondences, anchoring Gauguin's conviction that art's sensory apparatus brings the soul into harmony with the universe. Privileging the visionary over the mimetic, *Contes barbares* transcends surface reality not only to enable the audience to glimpse the truth behind appearances but, ultimately, to proclaim that this is the very mission of art. Intoxicating the senses with a feast of stimuli, *Contes barbares* exemplifies Gauguin's professed goal of creating "diverse harmonies that correspond to the state of our soul."[47]

NOTES

This chapter includes material from Hargrove, "'L'Oeil qui écoute': Paul Gauguin's *Contes barbares*," *Revue de l'Art* 169, no. 3 (2010): 25–37. I am very grateful to Therese Dolan for her contribution to my understanding of synesthesia.

1. H. R. Rookmaaker, *Synthetist Art Theories, Genesis and Nature of the Ideas on Art of Gauguin and His Circle* (Amsterdam: Swets and Zeitlinger, 1972 [1959]), 30. See the first extensive study of synesthesia in this context, Filiz Eda Burhan, "Vision and Visionaries: Nineteenth Century Psychological Theory; The Occult Sciences and the Formation of the Symbolist Aesthetic in France," Ph.D. dissertation, Princeton University, Princeton, NJ, 1979.

2. Chrétien Van Campen, "Artistic and Psychological Experiments with Synesthesia," *Leonardo* 32, no. 1 (1999): 9–14.

3. Kevin T. Dann, *Bright Colors Falsely Seen: Synaesthesia and the Search for Transcendental Knowledge* (New Haven, CT: Yale University Press, 1998), 42.

4. Lloyd James Austin, "The Presence and Poetry of Stéphane Mallarmé," in *The Symbolist Movement in the Literature of European Languages,* ed. Anna Elizabeth Balakian (Amsterdam and Philadelphia: John Benjamins, 1984), 43–66, esp. 53, n. 45, and Kerstin Thomas, "'Un paysage est un état d'âme,' Landschaft als Stimmung bei Paul Gauguin," in *Vermessen: Landschaft und Ungegenständlichkeit,* ed. Werner Busch and Oliver Jehle (Berlin: Diaphanes, 2007), 167–185.

5. Daniel Guérin, ed., *The Writings of a Savage: Paul Gauguin,* trans. Eleanor Levreux (New York: Da Capo, 1974), 158–159.

6. Victor Merlhès, *Correspondance de Paul Gauguin: Documents, témoignages,* vol. 1 (Paris: Fondation Singer-Polignac, 1984), no. 162, letter to Émile Schuffenecker, August 1888, Pont-Aven, 216.

7. Douglas Druick and Peter Zegers, "Le Kampong et la pagode: Gauguin à l'Exposition universelle de 1889," in *Gauguin: Actes du colloque, Musée d'Orsay* (Paris: École du Louvre, 1991), 101–142.

8. Bengt Danielsson, *Gauguin in the South Seas* (New York: Doubleday, 1966), 256. See also Hargrove, "*Woman with a Fan*: Paul Gauguin's Heavenly Vairaumati—A Parable of Immortality," *Art Bulletin* 88, no. 3 (September 2006), 552–566.

9. Elizabeth Childs, "L'Esprit moderne et le catholicisme: Le Peintre écrivain dans les dernières années," in *Gauguin Tahiti,* exhibition catalog, Grand Palais, Paris, and Museum of Fine Arts, Boston, 2003–2004, 275–289, esp. 285.

10. Eric Zafran agrees that no one speaks. Zafran, "Searching for Nirvana," in *Gauguin's Nirvana: Painters at Le Pouldu, 1889–1890* (Hartford, CT: Wadsworth Atheneum Museum of Art, 2001), 103–127, quote on 123.

11. Merlhès, *Correspondance,* vol. 1, 306, no. 193, letter to Schuffenecker, ca. December 20, 1888.

12. Robert Levy defines *varua* as the "soul" of a living person, who dies when it leaves, and the *varua ino* as a malevolent spirit. Levy, *Tahitians: Mind and Experience in the Society Islands* (Chicago: University of Chicago Press, 1989 [1973]), 162–163.

13. Paul Gauguin, *Avant et après* (Paris: La Table Ronde, 1994), 93.

14. Richard Brettell, for example, assumes that the two figures are women. Brettell, "Contes barbares," no. 280 in *Gauguin,* exhibition catalog, National Gallery of Art, Washington, DC, 1988–1989.

15. Gauguin, *Ancien culte mahorie,* manuscript, Musée d'Orsay, Paris, 1892, 32. Gauguin lifted parts of his text straight from Jacques Antoine Moerenhout, *Voyages aux îles du grand océan,* 2 vols. (Paris: A Maisonneuve, 1959 [1837]), vol. 1, 563, but this concept is common to theosophical literature.

16. Emanuel Swedenborg, *Heaven and Its Wonders and Hell: From Things Heard and Seen* (1758), trans. John Ager, accessed on June 5, 2012, www.gutenberg.org/ebooks/17368, para. 103, XIII.

17. Ibid., 402.

18. See George Trobridge, *Life of Emanuel Swedenborg* (Whitefish, MT: Kessinger, 2004 [1912]), 331.

19. "L'Eglise catholique et les temps modernes," 1897–1898, follows "Diverses choses," 1896–1897, in the Louvre manuscript of Paul Gauguin, "Noa Noa."

20. Gauguin's text as transcribed in Philippe Verdier, "L'Esprit moderne et le catholicisme," *Wallraf-Richartz Jahrbuch* 46–47 (1985–1986): 299–328, esp. 301.

21. Thomas Carlyle, "Des symboles," *Entretiens politiques et littéraires* 1, no. 1 (April 1890): 2, extracts from *Sartor Resartus,* Book III.

22. The traditional lily, associated in Christianity with the Annunciation, signifies purity, whereas the spath lily has phallic/vaginal shapes that suggest procreation. In Asian religions the lotus symbolizes fertility and reincarnation. Pentameric flowers "symbolisait les dogmes de la résurrection et de l'immortalité de l'âme." *Journal de botanique* 16 (1902): n.p.

23. Gauguin in Verdier, "L'Esprit moderne," 303–306.

24. I am grateful to Yui Suzuki, professor of Japanese art history at the University of Maryland, for her help with this idea. This raigō (*Welcoming Descent of Amitābha*) is a detail from the late eleventh-century Mount Koya triptych (color on silk, collection of Jūhakkain, Kongōbuji, Wakayama Prefecture, Japan). Images of Amitābha Buddha were readily available in Paris, including the Guimet Museum. If not before, Gauguin could have known about Mahayana Buddhism from his friend Ky-Dong (Nguyen Van Cam, 1875–1929), exiled to the Marquesas from Tonkin (Vietnam).

25. "Amida Raigō (Descent of Amida)," description of the artwork from Dartmouth Univerisity, accessed June 5, 2012, http://www.dartmouth.edu/~arth17/AmidaRaigo.html.

26. Charles Baudelaire, "Le peintre de la vie modern" (1863), in *Oeuvres complètes* (Paris: Robert Laffont, 2001), 799.

27. Burhan, "Vision and Visionaries," 172–211.

28. Other examples are *Poèmes barbares* and the 1892–1895 *Contes barbares*.

29. Baudelaire, "Exposition universelle de 1855," in *Oeuvres complètes,* 723, italics and exclamation point in original.

30. "Diverses choses," in the Louvre manuscript of Paul Gauguin, "Noa Noa," addendum preceding folio 138 recto, 3–4, with a line quoting Achille Delaroche, italics in original.

31. Gauguin probably knew this phrase from the writings of Friedrich Nietzsche, who was indebted to Swedenborg for the idea.

32. Paul Gauguin, self-portrait from the masthead of *Le Sourire,* August 1899, reproduced in *Le Sourire de Paul Gauguin,* ed. L.-J. Bouge (Paris: Éditions Maisonneuve), 1952.

33. Eugène Delacroix, *Oeuvres littéraires,* 2 vols. (Paris: Bibliothèque Dionysienne, 1923 [1865]), vol. 1, 63.

34. Baudelaire, "L'Oeuvre et la vie d'Eugène Delacroix" (1863), in *Oeuvres complètes,* 827.

35. See Philippe Junod, *Contrepoints: Dialogues entre musique et peinture* (Geneva: Editions Contrechamps, 2006), and Therese Dolan, "Oeuvres d'art de l'avenir: Manet, Baudelaire et Wagner," in *L'Oeil écrit: Études sur les rapports entre texte et image 1800–1940: Volume en l'honneur de Barbara Wright,* ed. Derval Conroy and Johnnie Gratton (Geneva: Slatkin, 2005), 119–140.

36. Gauguin, "Notes de Delacroix," in "Diverses choses," 222–223, 114 verso–115 recto.

37. Paul Gauguin, "Notes synthétiques" (1886–1888), reproduced in facsimile in Paul Gauguin, *Carnet de Bretagne* (Tahiti: Avant et Après, 2002), n.p., italics mine.

38. Anne Leonard, "Picturing Listening in the Late Nineteenth Century," *Art Bulletin* 89, no. 2 (June 2007): 266–286, esp. 276–278.

39. G.-Albert Aurier, "Le Symbolisme en peinture: Paul Gauguin," *Mercure de France* (March 1891): 155–164.

40. Burhan, "Vision and Visionaries," 304.

41. Rookmaaker, *Synthetist Art Theories,* 28–29.

42. Maurice Malingue, ed., *Lettres de Gauguin à sa femme et à ses amis: Recueillies et préfacées* (Paris: B. Grasset, 1946), 44–46, Schuffenecker, January 14, 1885, Copenhagen.

43. Aurier, "Gauguin," 158.

44. Ibid., 160.

45. Paul Gauguin, *"A ma fille Aline, ce cahier est dédié: Notes éparses, sans suite comme les rêves, comme la vie toute fait de morceaux; Journal de jeune fille,* ed. Victor Merlhès, 2 vols., (Bordeaux: William Blake, 1989 [1893]), vol. 2, manuscript facsimile, n.p.

46. "Diverses choses," 263, 136 recto.

47. Merlhès, *Correspondance de Paul Gauguin,* vol. 1, no. 193, Schuffenecker, ca. December 20, 1888, 306.

21

Sensory Devotions

Hair Embroidery and Gendered Corporeal Practice in Chinese Buddhism

YUHANG LI

In 1877, Xuan Ding (1832–1880) published a collection of short tales titled *Yeyu qiudeng lu* (The Record of an Autumn Lantern on Rainy Nights). One of the stories is "Faxiu fo" (Hair-Embroidered Buddha).[1] The story starts by describing the physical appearance of a Ming dynasty (1368–1644) hair-embroidered wall hanging displayed in Luewang Temple in Donghai (today's Dafeng, Jiangsu Province). This piece is two *zhang* and four *chi* (about eight meters) long and eight chi (about two and two-thirds meters) wide. The detailed description of the image indicates its ambiguous iconography, that of a standing Buddhist icon, which is an atypical hybrid form of Buddha and Bodhisattva.[2] An inscription is transcribed as follows: "I, Upasika female disciple Ye Pingxiang created hair embroidery after washing [my] face and hands in a certain year during the era of Jiajing (1522–1566)."[3] The author then moved on to the colophon on the left margin of the embroidery, in which Yin Qiding, the chief state secretary, explains the reason that Ye Pingxiang created this embroidery.

When Ye Pingxiang was fourteen years old, her father, a state official, was wrongly convicted and was sentenced to death. Ye Pingxiang, desperate to rescue her father, prayed to the deity for help, crying day and night. Then she experienced *gan-ying*, meaning that the spirit responded to her prayers by urging her to make an image of the deity using her skill, namely, embroidery. She purchased a large piece of satin in the market and then plucked out strands of her own hair. Using an extremely sharp metal knife, she further split each hair into four strands. She used these split hairs to embroider the image of Buddha and a scripture on the piece of satin. After two years, she finally finished the piece, but she lost her eyesight in the process. In return for her effort and sacrifice, her father was miraculously released.

The enormous size of the embroidery and the ambiguous iconography of the Buddhist image are unlike those of typical surviving embroidered Buddhist hangings dating to the late imperial period; however, this story is highly suggestive of the correlation between hair-embroidered Buddhist icons—the highest form of devotional embroidery in the late imperial period—and miraculous spiritual power. This story epitomizes the hair embroidery of Buddhist images and elicits speculation about the purposes and functions of hair embroidery in general and the techniques of hair embroidery in particular. It also invites us to ponder why practitioners settled on hair embroidery as a medium suited to the expression of women's profound emotional longings and, as in the case of Ye Pingxiang, their filial piety. How did hair embroidery combine women's bodies (their hair) with a womanly skill (embroidery) to form a unique gendered practice in late imperial China?

Scholars outside the field of Chinese textile studies have gradually begun to pay attention to embroidery as a material medium. In the past two decades, literary, cultural, social-economical, and anthropological studies of women's lives in premodern China have discussed embroidery as a skill of women related to their daily lives, their talent, and their virtue. Different practices of embroidery were related to different aspects of womanhood. Most basically, embroidery was a decorative medium used for stitching cloth, shoes, various accessories, and household products. But it also appeared as the female counterpart to writing, especially as exemplified through paintinglike fine embroidery. Embroidery was conceived as an artistic expression of individual creativity in premodern China.[4] Most scholarship to date on the subject of Chinese embroidery has concentrated on secular production. The relationship between embroidery and religious practice has not been adequately addressed. Although there are brief mentions of the connection between embroidery and women's Buddhist belief, there has been little sustained work on embroidery as a religious practice, on its functionality and performativity, its ritual process, the symbolic meanings of needle pricking, and the subject matter of the embroidery.[5]

The making of religious objects is not just an artisan's job but is at times taken by a devotee as part of his or her spiritual cultivation and religious salvation. I would thus like to shift the emphasis from the way in which practices create meaning through the use of objects to the way in which objects are made. In other words, rather than focusing on how people enact meanings by using objects, I emphasize the way in which people produce meanings as they make objects. Such meanings are in some sense socially constructed; however, once such a meaning is produced, it confronts people with a certain objectivity. In the following discussion of devotional objects—typified by embroidered images of Guanyin images, and, in particular, hair-embroidered Guanyins[6]—I show how a devotional object can bear within it a pious person's sincere enactment as well as her wishes to accomplish both worldly and transcendent goals.

In Ye Pingxiang's case, the tale achieves its dramatic effect through the sensory dimensions of making devotional hair embroidery. Ye Pingxiang not only endured the pain of plucking hair from her own head in order to acquire the corporeal medium for making this religious icon; she also sacrificed one of her senses, her eyesight, in order to transform her sincere piety into a material object. In this chapter, by emphasizing human hair–embroidered Buddhist images, I aim to grasp the sensory dimensions of practices associated with ritual performance. The sensory behaviors and objects employed represent a type of residue that cannot be reduced to the practice of ritual; rather they make rituals and performance possible and inflect them in a particular manner. At the same time, the sensory objects and their corporeal raw materials are constantly inscribed and reinscribed in a web of meanings that are reproduced through performance.

Hair Embroidery: The Highest Form of Devotional Embroidery

Hair embroidery, or *faxiu,* is characterized by its use of natural human hair as thread to stitch images on textiles. There are no clear documents indicating when and how hair embroidery began. A noteworthy adaptation of the legend of the eminent meditation teacher Baozhi (418–514) reveals that the idea of implanting the medium of human head hair onto a religious icon circulated at least as late as the fourteenth century.[7] Baozhi is believed to have acquired a supernatural power that enabled him to empower animals and to animate objects. An anecdote indicates that once Emperor Wu of the Liang (464–549) and Master Bozhi were walking along a river and saw an object floating in the water. When Master Baozhi used his staff to point to the object, it altered its direction immediately and approached him. The object turned out to be a block of purple sandalwood. After witnessing this miracle, Emperor Wu asked a craftsman to carve a statue of Master Baozhi out of this sandalwood. The statue came out looking very much like Master Baozhi except that it lacked hair and a beard. The Liangwu emperor then plucked out his own hairs and implanted them onto the two sides of the face of the statue. The hairs then miraculously grew on the statue.

There are two significant features of the statue. First of all, there is the likeness of the statue to Master Baozhi. Master Baozhi is indeed well known for his long and messy hair, so adding human hair certainly contributed to his likeness in the statue. Second, the mythical power of Master Baozhi extended beyond his physical body and could be manifested through his statue. Usually one cannot see spirit, but through the growth of hair on the statue we see spirit in the temporal realm in the form of life. Growth is a temporal concept that implies transformation. The hair of the emperor— a figure associated with a range of miracles—served as a catalyst to realize the spiritual powers of the meditation master in the statue.[8] The status of the hair changed from nonbeing to being, and this movement entailed the power of life and the spiritual abilities of Master Baozhi.

During the Ming and Qing (1644–1911) periods, hair embroidery occupied a categorical space distinct from that of the modern conception of hair embroidery as a technique used to represent a range of different subjects. Ming- and Qing-period hair embroidery constituted a material means by which pious women might demonstrate Buddhist devotional practice. The majority of the extant hair embroideries and textual sources reveal that the general subjects consisted of the Buddhist images of Bodhisattva Guanyin, Buddha, and Bodhidharma, in descending order of popularity.[9]

Past understandings of hair symbolism in the Buddhist context have been generally connected to the head-shaving ceremony. When men or women enter monastic life, they are required to shave their hair, a symbol of their attachment to the mundane world. For the laity, however, the regenerative capacity of hair plays a more important role in its meaning.[10] Although Buddhist canonical texts contain accounts of both male and female devotees spreading their long hair on the ground for the Buddha or monks to walk on, the cutting of hair as a gift seems to have been restricted to female devotees in Buddhist miraculous tales.[11] Hair thus operates as a gendered medium related to a particular type of religious exchange value.

A story about an impoverished woman who sold her long hair in exchange for offerings to Buddha was first included in the sixth-century Buddhist encyclopedia *Jinglü yixiang* (Different Forms of Sutra and Vinaya).[12] Similar plots also appeared in Ming dynasty Buddhist story collections such as *Fahua lingyan zhuan* (Record of Responsive Manifestations of Lotus Sutra).[13] The protagonists of these stories share two distinct attributes. First, these women are extremely poor and have nothing to offer but their hair. Second, after they cut their hair, it miraculously grows back again to the same length it was before cutting, so they can continue to use their hair as a means of exchange for offerings.

To summarize, we can understand the hair in hair-embroidered Buddhist icons from the perspectives of both the meaning of transferring hair onto a religious icon and the use of the hair as a devotional apparatus. Both involve the meaning of *hair* as a metaphor for regeneration. The story of the sandalwood statue of Master Baozhi allows us to conjecture at least one kind of logic behind transplanting human hair to a religious figurine: the magical regenerative power of hair is able to animate an icon, bringing life to that which is dead or inanimate. A hair-embroidered portrait of Guanyin attributed to Guan Daosheng (1262–1319), the first well-known woman painter from the Yuan dynasty (1271–1368), embodies a similar logic. On this embroidery (Figure 21.1), only Guanyin's hair, eyebrows, and eyelashes are represented with hairs, while the rest of the image, such as Guanyin's robe, face, and other parts of her body, are stitched with silk threads. On the hair-embroidered Buddhist images from the Ming and Qing periods, all parts of the icons are stitched with human hair. In either case, Buddhist practitioners vitalized religious icons by the insertion of hair.

FIGURE 21.1. (Opposite) Attributed to Guan Daosheng (1262–1319), *Guanyin,* Yuan dynasty. Human hair and silk floss on silk, embroidery, 105 × 50 centimeters. Nanjing Museum collection.

One can participate in the efficacy of a religious image in many ways, but animation of the image will certainly imply that it has more spiritual power. Second, Buddhist canonical texts reveal that women are privileged in the use of their own hair as religious offerings, even if their hair is not directly used as offerings in Buddhist icons. People focused on the symbolic meaning of regenerating women's natural hair as an everlasting source. Hair embroidery mingled these two significances of hair. When practitioners employed hair as thread, transferring it onto the images of divine figures in visible, tactile, stitches, this hair, as part of their bodies, became the needleworkers' devotional gifts. Buddhist canonical texts, such as *Dazhidu lun* (Commentary on the Great Prajñā-pāramitā Sūtra), divide gifts into internal gifts, the gifts of the body, and external gifts, the gifts of objects.[14] Reiko Ohnuma categorizes both of these forms as material gifts (*wu bushi*) in contrast to the gift of dharma (*fa bushi*).[15] The hair in the hair embroidery is part of the body externalized as an object.

Buddhist tradition cherishes the stories of Bodhisattvas relinquishing their bodies to the Dharma.[16] A passage from the *Flower Ornament Scripture* contains a particularly important scriptural account of sacrificing part of the body and transforming it into a material object: "Since he first vowed to attain Buddhahood, Vairocana Buddha has been extremely diligent in practice and has offered untellable numbers of bodies and life. He has peeled off his skin and used it as paper, broken off his bones and used them as pens, and pricked himself to draw blood for ink. The scriptures he has copied in this manner are piled as high as Mount Sumeru. He did this out of his great reverence for the Dharma."[17] Vairocana Buddha serves as a model for copying scriptures using his body. As Jimmy Yu has correctly observed, "His body parts are not only used to produce the scriptures, but the scriptures are his bodies."[18] The quoted narrative portrays Vairocana Buddha as an exemplar, as one who inflicts pain on his body and uses parts of his body as utensils to transmit Dharma or the scriptures. Though only Vairocana Buddha could make such an extreme sacrifice, historical and present-day lay and monastic practitioners have aimed to follow in his footsteps by copying scriptures in blood, a part of the human body associated, like hair, with regeneration.

The idea of using parts of the body to substitute for less corporeal, more mundane tools such as ink, a pen, and paper might have inspired hair embroidery as well. The two practices had much in common. First, devotees considered both hair and blood to be body parts capable of regeneration. Second, practitioners underwent pain by pricking blood from their own tongues and fingers and plucking their own hair before creating devotional objects. Third, both blood writing of scripture and hair embroidery required certain levels of skill in creation and execution. Fourth, in their respective practices, devotees transplanted blood and hair from their bodies to paper or silk. Bodily "supplies" were used in the creation of sacred calligraphy or images and transformed into devotional objects. These practices thus initiated a subjective transformation. Those who created these objects of devotion externalized parts of their own bodies in the form of religious objects, literally allied themselves to the divine text or image, and thereby transformed themselves through devotion. Blood and hair, used in this fashion, are distinct from unmediated, or less mediated, relics or bodily remains in the Buddhist context. Though blood and hair are parts of the human body, here they become the materials for making other objects. The personal "life" of blood or hair persists in the icon or scripture, with the blood and hair retaining significance as products of particular human bodies but accruing additional meanings as well.

In early Buddhist texts, the ways prescribed for women to dedicate their bodies were probably limited to the natural products of their bodies, such as long hair. From the fifteenth century forward, however, more and more women combined their skill and talent with resources they found in their bodies. They used their hair instead of thread to stitch the images of Buddhist deities as a way to emulate bodily practices such as the blood writing of scripture. Though there are cases of woman practicing blood writing of scripture and of male hair embroiderers making nonreligious objects, in the majority of cases these practices were divided by gender. Blood scripture writing has been chiefly the province of Buddhist priests, and Buddhist laywomen have produced most hair embroidery. These parallel traditions somehow reflect the conventional discourse that men use paper and brushes, while women use needles and thread. This idea is transmitted into religious practice and manifested as men hold brushes to write in blood on paper and women thread needles with their hair to stitch on silk.[19] In other words, the pain itself is not gendered, but it becomes gendered when embedded in specific material practices.

Plucking Hair: A Buddhist Practice of Self-Inflicted Pain

Hair embroidery is a highly ritualized practice: from obtaining the hair to stitching the image, each stage of the process contains certain religious elements. There are two main steps—plucking hair and splitting the hair. In cases in which Chinese traditional hair embroideries were used as offerings, they were usually made of hair taken from the embroiderer herself. The inscription on an image of Guanyin produced in 1480 clearly indicates that Lin Jinlan, a well-known courtesan from the Chenghua period (1465–1487), used *jishen fa,* "hair from her own body," to make the embroidery on the day of Guanyin's birthday, February 19, in order to heal her own eye disease.[20] Inscriptions on hair embroideries from later periods further specify the action of extracting hair from the embroiderer's head. Ni Renji (1607–1685), a renowned poet and artist of the seventeenth century, stitched Buddha's image when she was around forty-three years old.[21] She embroidered her signature in the following manner: "In the fourth month of the year of *jichou* (1649), this pious woman, née Wu, in honor of my parents plucked my own hairs and made this image of the Buddha to be worshiped and handed down from generation to generation in my family."[22]

The precise nature of the process of extracting hairs from the embroiderer's own head remains unclear. We do not know whether women gradually accumulated the hairs during the progress of making their embroideries or if they pulled out all of the hairs before they made the first stitch. Either way, the embroiderers endured pain as they accumulated enough hair strands to produce an image. The amount of hair needed to make an embroidery varied according to the size, the style, the length of each stitch, and the embroiderer's skill. Although it is difficult to speculate on the concrete number of hairs needed for each hair embroidery, it is important to keep in mind that the practitioners of hair embroidery did not aim to deform themselves. They did not pluck themselves bald; rather they accumulated enough hair to make a devotional object.

Plucking hair is one of many forms of extreme ascetic practice in Buddhism. For instance, *Bailun* (One Hundred Treaties [*Sata sastra*]), the Chinese translation of a Madhyamika Buddhist text attributed to Aryadeva, clearly states that along with branding the body, plucking hair is a good method of self-inflicted physical suffering.[23] However, compared to other forms of violence to the self in the Buddhist context, such as burning one's body and self-cremation, plucking hair is not life-threatening.[24]

Self-inflicted physical pain is not unusual in religious practice. In the examination of the role pain has played in religious rituals around the world, Ariel Glucklich provides an explanation of the psychological reaction when devotees experience pain. In his words, "Religious pain produces states of consciousness, and cognitive-emotional changes that affect the identity of the individual subject and her sense of belonging to a larger community or to a more fundamental state of being. More succinctly, pain strengthens the religious person's bond with God and with other persons."[25] Pain, in other words, is understood to increase one's proximity to the deity. In the Chinese context, this transformation of distance from the divine is framed in relation to the idea of sympathetic response, which implies a compassion for the pain of others. When a given subject inflicts pain on herself in a religious context, she tends to transcend her finitude and approach the Buddha or Guanyin, and in this way she obtains the feeling that she is a recipient of divine sympathy. Divine sympathy is usually considered universal, and self-inflicted pain can serve to individuate the practitioner and construct a personal relationship with the divine. Specifically, in the present case the process of voluntarily suffering pain through the plucking of hair is an integral part of the constitution of a visible form of Guanyin or the Buddha out of the very material substance secured through this pain. Hair embroidery is certainly the highest devotional form of embroidery, for in order to demonstrate enough sincerity to stimulate the divine power, devotees not only use their own hands to make the embroidery but endure physical pain and dedicate parts of their bodies to the devotional object. The personal relationship between the divine and the devotee is built on her physical sense of pain, her hair, her skill, and her devotion.

More important, as Glucklich points out, religious pain is not endured in total isolation; through enduring this pain, the devotee identifies herself with a larger community. Jimmy Yu's research of a wide range of bodily practices of self-inflicted violence in sixteenth- and seventeenth-century China merits attention here. As Yu demonstrates, practices such as blood writing, body slicing, and burning part of one's body can all be seen as linked to a larger phenomenon of people who implemented the "instrumentality of their bodies" to accomplish their various goals of filial piety, chastity, loyalty, benevolence, self-cultivation of the way (*dao*), and many others.[26] Yu connects this observable fact to social, political, doctrinal, and personal crises in the late Ming and early Qing period. He argues that people used the practice of self-inflicted violence as a way of "exercising power and affecting the environment." By so doing, they "demonstrate[d] moral values, reinstitute[d] order, forge[d] new social relations, and secure[d] boundaries against the threat of moral ambiguity." Therefore, in his view, in these practices bodies became sites of "contestation and transformation, both for themselves and for others who witnessed or narrated their stories."[27]

The message in the account of Ye Pingxiang, who, in "Hair-Embroidered Buddha," wanted to rescue her father through her plea for help from the Buddha in the form of a work of hair embroidery, concerns filial piety. This fits into the pattern of the legend of Miaoshan, a form of the most prevalent female deity, Guanyin, who relinquished her eyes and hands to her own father.[28] Hair embroideries made for the purpose of fulfilling filial piety, as evidenced in both surviving objects and textual references, were always dedicated to the embroiderers' birth parents, not to their parents-in-law. It is easy to understand this phenomenon in the cases of embroiderers who were unmarried. However, Ni Renji, by the time she made her hair embroidery of the Buddha's image, had already been widowed for more than twenty years and had fulfilled all her duties as a daughter-in-law. After she returned to her natal home to avoid the turmoil caused by the Manchu conquest, she created the piece in the name of her own parents. This phenomenon seems different from that of exemplary women who have been promoted by Confucian ideology, in which a woman should always prioritize her husband's family. Stories of daughters-in-law practicing *gegu* (flesh cutting) in the hope of saving the lives of their parents-in-law are recorded in books such as *Guanshiyin pusa linggan lu* (Record of Bodhisattva Guanshiyin's Efficacious Responses).[29] Hair embroidery, nonetheless and in distinction, seems to take on a particular significance connected to a woman's own ancestors rather than those to whom she has matrimonial links. The deep association of hair with regeneration likely played a key role in this practice. In its associations with vitality itself, regeneration signifies an intimate connection with one's own birth parents rather than with in-laws.

Splitting Hairs: A Difficult Technique Used for Making Devotional Objects

After obtaining hair, preparing it for stitching is the next crucial step in this ritual process. Surviving examples demonstrate at least three different methods of using hair as thread: (1) using multiple strands of hair grouped together as one strand, (2) using a single hair as a single thread, and (3) using a single hair split into multiple finer strands. These different techniques probably reflect the development of hair embroidery over time as well as levels of individual skill.

An example of multiple-strand hair embroidery survives in the aforementioned portrait of Guanyin attributed to Guan Daosheng (see Figure 21.1). The embroidered inscription on Guan's image indicates that it was likely based on one of Guan Daosheng's paintings of Guanyin.[30] Wearing a white robe, Guanyin holds prayer beads in her left hand and stands in the middle of an ambiguous open space. Parts of Guanyin's hair are piled up on the top of her head. The loose hairs on the right side of her face are blowing in the wind, and the loose hairs on her left side rest on her left shoulder. Contrasting with the fine stitches in silk thread on Guanyin's face and robe, the stitches used to render her hair are primarily longer stitches, with three or four strands of hair grouped together as one strand (Figure 21.2) To give the effect of hair dancing in the wind, the hair stitches point in all directions. The needleworker vividly expressed the materiality of hair.

With respect to the second type of embroidery, in which a single hair functions as a single thread, there is only one surviving example. In 1947, a period much later than that of any of the other objects mentioned in this chapter, a certain Miss Diao from Sichuan made a hair-embroidered white-robed Guanyin. An ink outline was first laid out, and brownish hairs were applied on top of the ink line with very meager stitches. Because the stitches do not follow each other closely and are inconsistent in terms of direction and size, the outline of Guanyin is not smoothly rendered. Traces of broken hairs can be easily observed.

The above two examples seem to represent the periods before and after the Ming and Qing dynasties, showing a change from partial hair embroidery to complete hair embroidery in *baimiao,* or outline style. Unlike its precedents and followers, hair embroidery from the late imperial period can be categorized in the third group of embroideries, featuring the splitting of hairs. Wang Yuan was a native of Gaoyou and was active in the early Qing period. The only Qing woman listed in the section of "talented women" in the Gaoyou gazetteer, her biography describes her skill in hair embroidery. Because of her parents' sickness, she promised to make an image of Guanyin. With respect to her technique, the biography reads, "She split one hair into four strands. Its refinement was magical and it was just like painting without any trace of needles. Viewers celebrated this as a unique skill."[31] With respect to skill, the highest goal of fine decorative embroidery is always to reproduce the effect of painting.[32] The

FIGURE 21.2. Detail of Figure 21.1 (attributed to Guan Daosheng [1262–1319], *Guanyin*, Yuan dynasty, human hair and silk floss on silk, embroidery) showing multiple-strand hair embroidery. Nanjing Museum collection.

principle of emulating painting through needle and thread had colored threads functioning as pigments to cover the painted area. Baimiao as a painting style had already developed during the Song period (960–1279), but the imitation of baimiao in embroidery appeared rather late. The style of hair embroidery from the Ming and Qing periods was clearly based on baimiao painting. Although none of Wang Yuan's hair embroidery survives, a hair embroidery of Guanyin by one of Wang Yuan's contemporaries, Li Feng (from around the seventeenth century), provides us with one of the finest examples of this kind. The calligraphy of a poem by Wang Yuan's father, Wang Xinzhan (also seventeenth-century), was stitched with silk threads on this embroidery. The image represents a seated Guanyin in the usual half-*ruyi* (as one wishes) posture on a grass mat (Figure 21.3). Li Feng rendered the whole image in outline stitch. She closely followed baimiao painting's conventions, with different parts of Guanyin's body in three different tones of black, from lightest to darkest.

FIGURE 21.3. Li Feng, *Guanyin,* 1691, Qing dynasty. Hanging scroll, human hair on silk, embroidery, 68 × 35 centimeters. Beijing Palace Museum collection.

Although hair as a corporeal material for stitching is more intimate than thread, hair embroidery followed the same path as silk embroidery in trying to efface its own materiality and appear as painting. The idea of splitting a hair might not have been driven by religious concerns but might rather have been inherited from the practice of splitting a silk thread into several strands. Embroidery with split silk thread was already difficult enough, but embroidery with split hairs required an even more refined technique that also reinforced the symbolic order. In addition, the complex skills required and the difficulty of splitting a hair added significant value to the embroidery as a devotional object. In particular, the concentration required to split one hair into four implies an intense form of sensory experience. Given that each hair is so fine, one needs a number of different senses, including refined touch and sight, each of which mediates the other and is externalized in the finished object.

Shoubofa, or using one's hands to split a hair, is the term that is often used in various short accounts of hair embroidery. For instance, the Pingyuan gazetteer recorded a Madam Zhao's ability to draw baimiao Guanyin and to split hair to make the image of Guanyin.[33] Besides the ambiguous term *shoubofa,* the only direct reference to methods of hair splitting is from the story of "Hair-Embroidered Buddha." The story asserts that Ye Pingxiang "used a metal blade which was as sharp as the tip of the awn of an ear of rice to split hair into four strands."[34] It is difficult to determine whether this description was the product of its author's literary imagination of how a hair was split or whether it actually reflected the technique of splitting a hair. Splitting hairs certainly required special knowledge. Historians in the twenty-first century do not yet have access to the technical specifics of this practice. Microscopic examination of surviving hair embroideries, however, has produced material evidence of this hair-splitting technique.[35]

Technique, Artistic Refinement, and Devotion

An important issue raised in the discourse of making hair embroidery concerns how one combines a complicated skill with the making of a devotional object. Here the matter at hand is the possible contradiction between being skillful and being devotional. Timothy Ingold's discussion of art and technology in nonreligious craft making is useful in theorizing this issue.[36] Often as practitioners learn more deeply the protocols of skillfully creating an object, they become increasingly alienated from the ritualistic and religious dimensions of creation, which inevitably involve experiencing an immediate connection with the deity. From this perspective, skill becomes a type of mediation that covers up a more elemental relationship to the object. This is especially evident in hair embroidery, because someone skilled in the art may succeed in concealing the presence of hair, thus obscuring its religious significance. In less skilled hands the hair might, conversely, remain more easily recognizable.

The achievement of applying a difficult skill itself became part of the devotional practice during the Ming and Qing periods. In a record of an embroidered Buddha by a Mrs. Chen from Dinghai (today's Zhoushan) in the gazetteer of Qixia Temple, the compiler of the gazetteer praised Mrs. Chen's needlework by saying that "looking at the meticulousness of her knife and ruler, we know the extremity of her sincerity."[37] Here "knife and ruler" is a metonym for needlework. The logic behind this appraisal is that the greater the technical refinement the embroidery displays, the deeper the sincerity ascribable to its creator, the embroiderer. This establishes a direct connection between the degree of artistic refinement and the quality of the artist's devotion.

In his introduction to recitation as a devotional use of sutras in the early medieval period in China, Robert Campany insightfully points out that the number of recitations, both the time spent in continuously reciting and "the number of words or the frequency and speed of recital," is often recorded as a measure of the efficacy of the sutra in various miraculous stories.[38] These different ways of accounting for recitation reveal a core issue in devotional practice: the time and movement involved in any religious ritual and ceremonial activity. The duration of time is measured through the number of actions, which, it is implied, is the very meaning of devotion. Similar to this observation but with a focus on the material object is Wu Hung's discussion of early Chinese ritual art. Wu employs the term "costly art" to categorize the material nature of objects produced for ritual purposes. This type of object is mostly "made of precious material and/or requires specialized craftsmanship and an unusual amount of human labor."[39] The three factors defining ritual art—material, craftsmanship, and labor—facilitate our comprehension of devotional objects, especially the hair-embroidered Guanyin image.

The creation of any object, regardless of its material medium, embodies time and action. The trace of the handiwork is usually concealed behind a polished surface. Embroidery, however, vividly displays the amount of human labor expended in its making. Especially with respect to the early embroideries, every stitch appears on the surface of an embroidered object, and each stitch indicates the tactile and manual action of needle pricking. Embroidery is a labor-intensive activity that is based on the progression of one stitch after the other. The nature of the labor that is expended in making a Buddhist image by means of needle is thus often cherished. Especially during the Song period, writings about the embroidery of Buddhist images increased and often appeared in texts influenced by Chan Buddhism. The symbolic meaning of the needle-drawn stitch in making Buddhist embroidery and the connection between the practitioner/embroiderer's mind and her needle when producing a divine image is elaborated by Su Shi (1037–1101) in "A Eulogy for Embroidered Guanyin Done by Madam Xu from Jing-an County." The poem reads,

The descendant of Taiyue, lives in Jing'an.
She studies the Dao and searches for the mind; the wondrous profundity she
    contemplates.
Contemplating Guanshiyin, (Madam Xu's) earnestness never leaves her face.
After three years, the method of the mind-heart of itself perfected.
Listen, think, and meditate on the lord [Guanyin], (she) appears radiant and
    clear as the sun before your eyes.[40]
The mind is conscious of Guanyin's face, but the mouth cannot express it.
Expressed through the six sense organs, delivers (the appearance of Guanyin)
    by any way that she is capable.
From her hand, it reaches the needle, from the needle it reaches the thread.
How many times to prick the needle? Even a person good with almanacs
    cannot calculate this.
If the needle were a Buddha, there should be ten million Buddhas.
If the needle were not a Buddha, for what reason is there such an appearance?
Who can combine these two and reach the dharma gate of nonduality?[41]

The couplet "If the needle were a Buddha, there should be ten million Buddhas" elucidates the symbolic meaning of needle pricking. In ritual contexts, one needle pricking is a Buddha; hence tens of millions of needle prickings will make tens of millions of Buddhas. Therefore, the more needle pricks, the more Buddhas reproduced. This perhaps explains why in the early stage of Chinese Buddhist embroidery the image and the background were fully covered by stitches; because replication is central to Buddhist devotional practice, performing more stitches would not only reproduce more Buddhas but would also accumulate more merit.[42] Moreover, the line of the poem that reads, "From her hand, it reaches the needle, from the needle it reaches the thread" provides a linear connection demonstrating how the woman's contemplation of a Buddhist image is materialized from her mind to her hands, then to needle and thread, to finally take form on silk or cloth as an image of Guanyin. This process suggests a profound sensory and material connection between a woman's mind, hands, needle, and thread.

In addition to time, in the case of hair embroidery the preciousness of the material accrues from the status of the hair as taken from a woman's body and the way that the devotee obtains hair by suffering pain. As for the specialized craftsmanship that Wu includes in his list, making hair embroidery itself is considered a special skill and one that not every embroiderer acquires. The word *neng,* or ability, is underlined in the accounts of women who can create Buddhist images using hair and needles. For instance, Xu Can, a well-known woman poet from the seventeenth century, besides her filial commitment to drawing 5,048 Guanyin images as a way to pray for her mother's longevity, was lauded for her ability to "use hairs to embroider the icon of Great Being."[43]

This skill set includes a number of possible procedures that range from preparing the hair, cleaning it, and softening it to splitting the hair strands and stitching the hair on silk. As for the stage of preparation, first the oils and dirt on the hair need to be washed away with alkaline water; then the hair must be rinsed with clean water, and finally a special treatment is required to soften the hair.[44] Though we do not know whether embroiderers applied similar methods to hair several hundred years ago, through observing the surfaces of surviving objects we can at least infer several things. First, despite the fact that women during the Ming and Qing periods often applied oil to their hair, no oil stains remain on the background silk of the embroidered pieces.[45] This suggests that the hair must have been cleansed. Second, as we can see from the hair-embroidered Guanyin done by Li Feng, her needle stitches are meticulous and tidy, so the hair thread itself needed to be soft enough to be manipulated as easily as a silk thread. Hence some kind of treatment was probably applied to the hair. Third, when we observe the outlines of body parts such as the face, nose, arms, and hands of Li Feng's Guanyin, we see that the hair strands are much thinner and appear to be a lighter black color (Figure 21.4). How was this visual effect created? Were those body parts made of the legendary split hairs? Scientific analysis might one day conclusively resolve this matter. At present we can certainly say that the innovation of this difficult technique represented an endeavor to make religious objects with finer effect. From Guan Daosheng's use of multiple strands of hair to form one stitch to the technique of splitting one hair into several strands, the finer technique represents an increased amount of concentrated time by the practitioner, since it takes the practitioner's time to learn a skill and to perform a skill. But the type of labor externalized in a skill is more intense and produces objects of a different type of aesthetic quality.

The sincerity of the piety expressed and the artistic refinement are not necessarily proportional. A good visual example from the modern period might help us to problematize this issue. According to the inscriptions on the embroidered Guanyin in the Baoguang temple near Chengdu that I have briefly mentioned, Diao from Sanhechang in the county of Chengdu practiced Buddhism for many years and promised to pluck her hair and use a needle to create a Guanyin embroidery. In 1947, before she entered a monastery and changed her secular name to a monastic name, Chengguo, she embroidered the image of Guanyin with her own hair and offered it to the main temple of Guchuan in Shihuixiang. In this image Guanyin holds a willow branch with one hand and is standing on lotus flowers. Her haloed head faces slightly down; compassion shows in her eyes. The humble quality of Diao's hair embroidery, in comparison with Ming- and Qing-period examples, clearly indicates that she did not have sophisticated training in needlework. However, can we conclude that she was less sincere in her devotion than her predecessors while making this Guanyin image? Indeed

FIGURE 21.4. Detail of Figure 21.3 (Li Feng, *Guanyin*, 1691, Qing dynasty, hanging scroll, human hair on silk, embroidery) showing thinner hair thread on Guanyin's face. Beijing Palace Museum collection.

the roughness of her stitches did not erase the materiality of her hair; on the contrary, it brings out the physical qualities and mannerisms of hair. In particular, Diao made this hair embroidery of Guanyin before she became a nun. By using her hair, the symbol of her secular attachment, she proved her determination to leave the secular world. Her skill may have been no more than average, but her sincerity is vividly reflected.

Conclusion

By investigating the techniques and religious connotations of hair embroidery in late imperial China, we can better understand how women creatively used parts of their bodies to link themselves with religious icons, in particular to Guanyin. Woman devotees expressed their wishes through this highly personal and corporeal devotional practice. We have seen how this form of devotion served to bridge the gap between the devotee and the exalted being through the externalization of a bodily part, the extraction of hair, and the meticulous use of that hair in representing deity. But the symbolic function of hair embroidery could also make it an object of a type of spiritual exchange. We have seen that by bringing hair and embroidery together, women fused pain and labor. The extensive labor time required to complete the work of embroidery contributed to its value; practitioners believed that Guanyin recognized this devotional gift because of that labor time. Hair embroidery further intensified the object because of the pain experienced in the process of its production. This intensity, according to devotees, could then be used to channel Guanyin into the secular realm. In other words, the common human experiences of intensity and pain came to signify closeness to the deity.

As we have seen in the cases of Ni Renji, Wang Yuan, and Lin Jinlan, women used hair embroidery not only to become one with Guanyin through sensory practices but also to show filial piety or, in Lin's case, to cure her eye disease. Lin's actions and aims illuminate her belief that the sensory mediation accomplished in hair embroidery had worldly outcomes, too, making her needlework a medium of Guanyin's intervention in the mundane world. Thus the practice of hair embroidery articulated a supersensuous medium that pointed beyond itself. Detachable parts of the body attain a kind of magical agency. The hair embroideries of Guanyin had a number of different significations and functions, all linked to the particular situations of women in late imperial China. In important ways these material objects served to bring women closer to transcendent dimensions. These sensory practices were also intimately connected to their gendered obligations and sometimes to the bitter nature of their conditions in the secular realm.

NOTES

1. Xuan Ding, *Yeyu qiudeng lu, xuji, juan* 2, in *Lidai biji xiaoshuo daguan,* vol. 22, 219.

2. Bodhisattva is the enlightened being who vows not to enter Nirvana until all other *beings* are enlightened.

3. Xuan Ding, *Yeyu qiudeng lu,* 219.

4. Dorothy Ko, *Teachers of the Inner Chambers: Women and Culture in Seventeenth-Century China* (Stanford, CA: Stanford University Press, 1994), 172–176, and Grace Fong, "Female Hands: Embroidery as a Knowledge Field in Women's Everyday Life in Late Imperial and Early Republican China," *Late Imperial China* 25, no.1 (June 2004): 1–58.

5. Susan Mann has touched on the importance of embroidering Guanyin as a symbol of women's piety. See Mann, *Precious Records: Women in China's Long Eighteenth Century* (Stanford, CA: Stanford University Press, 1997), 182–183.

6. Guanyin is the Perceiver of Sounds or Avalokiteśvara, the Bodhisattva of Compassion.

7. See entry "Zhang Jun," in *Fofa jintang bian,* in *Siku weishou shu jikan* (Beijing: Beijing Chubanshe, 2000), *wuji,* no. 13 ce, 686–687.

8. The Liangwu emperor is associated with several miraculous images. See Koichi Shinohara, "Changing Roles for Miraculous Images in Medieval Chinese Buddhism: A Study of the Miracle Image Section in Daoxuan's 'Collected Records,'" in *Images, Miracles, and Authority in Asian Religious Tradition,* ed. Richard H. Davis (Boulder, CO: Westview, 1998), 152–156.

9. Bodhidharma was a Buddhist monk who lived during the fifth and sixth centuries. He is traditionally credited as the transmitter of Chan Buddhism to China.

10. In the discussion of why hair is used as an important signifier in the Asian cultures, Patrick Olivelle draws our attention to the ways different cultures impose their own grammar on the root meaning of hair. Olivelle, "Hair and Society: Social Significance of Hair in South Asian Traditions," in *Hair: Its Power and Meaning in Asian Cultures,* ed. Alf Hilebeitel and Barbara Miller (Albany: State University of New York Press, 1998), 11–49.

11. The best-known story is that when Sakyamuni was a child, he laid his hair on the mud for Dipankara to walk on, which was a sign predicting his Buddhahood. *Foshuo taizi ruiying benqijing, juanshang,* CBETA T03n0185_p0473a26(03)-29(03). For the use of a woman's long hair for the monk to walk on, see *Fayuan zhulin, juan* 98, *dunü bu, disi,* CBETA T53n2122_p1007a05(10)-06(07).

12. "Changfa nüren shefa gongyang fo" (Woman with Long Hair Offering Her Hair to Buddha), in *Jinglü yixiang, juan* 45, CBETA T53n212_p0235a08-21.

13. *Fahua lingyan zhuan,* CBETA, X78n1539_p0013b14(02)-19(00).

14. *Dazhidu lun, juan* 11, CBETA T1509, 143b.

15. Reiko Ohnuma, "The Gift of the Body and the Gift of the Dharma," *History of Religions* 37, no. 4 (1998): 104.

16. Jimmy Yu, "Bodies and Self-Inflicted Violence in Sixteenth- and Seventeenth-Century China," Ph.D. dissertation, Princeton University, Princeton, NJ, 2008, 40–41.

17. *Dafang guangfo huayan jing,* juan 40, CBETA T10n0293_p0845c07(03)-08(03).

18. Yu, "Bodies and Self-Inflicted Violence," 39.

19. This is a very loose and general observation; as Jimmy Yu's research indicates, in the modern time period women followers could sometimes serve as blood providers. See Yu, "Bodies and Self-inflicted Violence," 50, 68 f.

20. Shanghai Museum collection. Though needlework was probably a major cause of women's loss of eyesight, like that of Ye Pingxiang, it is unclear how much needlework a courtesan would do.

21. For an introduction to Ni Renji's life and artistic achievement, see Ko, *Teachers of the Inner Chambers,* 172–173. For a discussion of Ni Renji's hair-embroidery Buddha, see Hong Liang, "Ming nüshiren Ni Renji de cixiu he faxiu," *Wenwu cankao ziliao* 9 (1958): 21–22.

22. Ibid., 22.

23. See *Bailun,* CBETA, T30n1569_p0168b11(05).

24. For a full study of self-immolation in Chinese Buddhist practice, see James Benn, *Burning for the Buddha: Self-immolation in Chinese Buddhism,* a Kuroda Institute Book (Honolulu: University of Hawai'i Press, 2007).

25. Ariel Glucklich, *Sacred Pain: Hurting the Body for the Sake of the Soul* (Oxford, UK: Oxford University Press, 2001), 6.

26. Yu, "Bodies and Self-inflicted Violence," 1.

27. Ibid., 4.

28. Chün-fang Yü, *Kuan-yin: The Chinese Transformation of Avalokiteśvara* (New York: Columbia University Press, 2001), 321–347.

29. Ibid., 343–344.

30. The authenticity of this embroidery needs to be further investigated. The questions lie in both original painting and embroidery. For a detailed discussion of this subject, see Yuhang Li, "Gendered Materialization: An Investigation of Women's Artistic and Literary Reproductions of Guanyin in Late Imperial China," Ph.D. dissertation, University of Chicago, Chicago, 2011, Chap. 2, 116 f.

31. See entry "Wang Yuan," in *Gaoyou zhouzhi* (Gazetteer of Gaoyou), compiled by Yang Yilu, Xia Zhirong et al., revised in 1813 by Feng Xin et al., reedited in 1845 by Fan Fengxie et al., facsimile reprint in *Zhongguo fangzhi congshu,* no. 29, vol. 3 (Taipei: Chengwen Chubanshe, 1970), 1602–1603.

32. Marsha Weidner, "Women in the History of Chinese Painting," in *Views from Jade Terrace: Chinese Women Artists 1300–1912,* ed. Marsha Weidner et al. (New York: Rizzoli, 1988), 21–23.

33. See entry "Zou Tao zhiqi" (Zou Tao's Wife Madam Zhao) in Zhu Qiqian, *Nühongzhuan zhenglue* (Cunsutang, 1931), 20b.

34. Xuan Ding, *Yeyu qiudeng lu,* 219.

35. For the example of split-hair embroidery, see a collection titled "Rank Promotion Hair Embroidery with the Seal of 'Ji Jin Tang.'" This embroidery was also made in the Kangxi period. Shan Guoqiang, ed. *Zhixiu shuhua* (Shanghai: Shanghai Kexue Jishu Chubanshe and Hong Kong: Shangwu Yinshuguan, 2005), 72. And see Piao Wenying, "Cixiu Milefo xiang kao," in *Guxiu guoji xueshu yantaohui lunwenji,* ed. Shanghai Bowuguan (Shanghai: Shanghai Shuhua Chubanshe, 2010), 207–216.

36. Timothy Ingold, "Beyond Art and Technology: The Anthropology of Skill," in *Anthropological Perspectives on Technology,* ed. M. B. Schiffer (Albuquerque: University of New Mexico Press, 2001), 17–18.

37. See entry "Dinghaixian Chen shi," in Zhu Qiqian, *Nühongzhuan zhenglue,* 9a.

38. Robert Campamy, "Notes on the Devotional Uses and Symbolic Functions of Sutra Text as Depicted in Early Chinese Buddhist Miracle Tales and Hagiographies," *Journal of the International Association of Buddhist Studies* 14, no. 1 (1991): 30.

39. Wu Hung, *Monumentality in Early Chinese Art and Architecture* (Stanford, CA: Stanford University Press, 1995), 24.

40. The sun is a common image of profound wisdom.

41. Su Shi, *Dongpo quanji, juan 95,* in *Yingyin wenyuange siku quanshu* (Taipei: Taiwan Shangwu Yinshuguan, 1983–1986), 1108ce, 524.

42. Sheng Yuyun (Angela Sheng), "Fangzhi vishu, jishu yu fojiao jifu" (Textile Art, Technology, and Buddhist Merit Accumulations), in *Fojiao wuzhi wenhua—siyuan caifu yu shisu gongyang,* ed. Hu Suxin (Sarah Fraser) (Shanghai: Shanghai Shuhua Chubanshe, 2003), 71.

43. See entry "Xu Xiangping," in Zhu Qiqian, *Nühongzhuan zhenglue,* 23b. One of the five thousand paintings might have survived and ended up in the Zhejiang Provincial Museum. It was created in 1658, and the inscription indicates that the painting is her prayer for her mother's longevity. See Zhongguo gudai shuhua jianding zu, ed., *Zhongguo gudai shuhua tumu* (Beijing: Wenwu Chubanshe, 1986–1994), plate zhe1–295, vol. 11, 88.

44. Chen Chaozhi, "Faxiu—zhixiu yiyuan zhong de qipa" (Hair embroidery—An exceptional textile art), *Zhongguo fangzhi* 9 (1994): 48.

45. *Wutou shexiangyou* and *Chatou zhuyou* are the two recipes women use to make hair oil by themselves. See *Kunde baojian,* with a preface written by Sun Jingyun, dated to the forty-second year of the *dingyou* of Qianlong (1777), Yuxiutang edition, vol. 4, 24a,b. Harvard-Yenching Library collection.

22

Shock Value

The Jesuit Martyrs of Japan and the Ethics of Sight

MIA M. MOCHIZUKI

Father Georg Schurhammer, S.J., could not have known what he would uncover in the private quarters of the Casa Professa of the Roman Gesù in the years leading up to World War II. In a remarkable twist of fate, he stumbled upon three paintings of the martyrs of Japan—linked by workshop, material, and subject matter (in the order painted, Figures 22.1, 22.2, and 22.3). Looking closely at the earliest painting, amid the faded landscape of rolling hillocks we see bodies burning at the stake, with cloth, flesh, and wood melting into a viscous ooze only to dissipate in a vortex of black ash. The second image, its very vibrancy suspect, appears to take its chromatic saturation as a license to amp up the carnival-like scene unfolding before us, the burnings augmented by decapitations as long swords relieve people of their heads, which are then mounted on short spikes for gruesome display. Archers, bows at the ready, form the third offensive of death cubed. After this bravura performance, the third painting's matter-of-fact lineup seems relatively tame, restrained, until we see the bodies in the foreground swinging, twisting, and turning, inverted and submerged in stinking pits of offal, the infamous torture of *ana-tsurushi,* in a macabre burlesque of the jostling of life itself.[1]

The cries of these killing fields could hardly seem further from a scholar's inner sanctum. Yet the two were entangled for the exceptional Father Schurhammer, a founder of the Jesuit Institute for Historical Studies in Rome (1932). Embedded in a lifetime of Xavieriana, he would casually note that several paintings of the Japanese martyrs were stored in the Gesù.[2] Of course, with the inevitable upheaval of the Second World War, not to mention the span of intervening years, it was far from self-evident whether these paintings were extant or even still in the possession of the Society of Jesus. Happily, the paintings endure, and thanks to a recent restoration (ca. 2001–2007), magnificently so. They have begun to resurface only recently, usually singly, in exhibitions around the world, if still managing to elude in-depth study.[3]

FIGURE 22.1. Niccolò School, *Martyrdom of Brother Leonardo Kimura, S.J., and Four Companions (November 18, 1619)*, seventeenth century (after 1619). Watercolor on paper attached to canvas. Church of the Gesù, Casa Professa, Rome. Photo by Zeno Colantoni. © Zeno Colantoni—Roma.

But, Schurhammer's triumph aside, why do we keep looking at such scenes of slaughter, appalling atrocities in indisputably, ineffably difficult pictures where the representational capacities of the body truly exceeded their limits? Our empathetic reactions—to touch our unbroken skin for reassurance, to listen for the visceral moans, and to sniff the air delicately, tentatively, for the first whiff of dusky smoke—tell us all. Mauled bodies incriminate, indeed shock, our own senses by proxy. These objects present charged, contested grounds of territories and pictorial space where sensation, a full-fledged assault on the faculties of feeling, resonates with people outside the picture plane, anchored in the shared parlance of embodied experience. Through the slippery oscillations of the eye, the full range of senses interrogates the body, becoming palpably, corporeally acquisitive or, put another way, materialized religion attains agency through the implied sensate link between the subjects depicted

FIGURE 22.2. (Top) Niccolò School, *The Great Martyrdom of the Fifty-two Martyrs of Nagasaki (1622)*, seventeenth century (after 1622). Varnished watercolor on paper attached to fabric. Church of the Gesù, Casa Professa, Rome. Photo by Zeno Colantoni. © Zeno Colantoni—Roma.

FIGURE 22.3. (Bottom) Niccolò School, *Saint Francis Xavier, S.J., Founder of the Japanese Mission, and the Jesuit Martyrs in Japan, 1597–1632,* ca. 1632. Watercolor on paper attached to fabric. Rome, Church of the Gesù, Casa Professa. Photo by Zeno Colantoni. © Zeno Colantoni—Roma.

and the viewer encountered in visual engagement. In short, as horrifying as it is to watch the destruction of life, the flagrant outrage to the senses that martyrdom epitomizes, we nevertheless keep looking. We stare, despite recognizing that seeing is undependable, uncontrollable, at best incomplete, and hopelessly entangled in the passions —in pleasure, discomfort, and pain—because we know that the act of looking shapes us, that seeing, in the terms of James Elkins, promises "metamorphosis," even if its delivery is processed in minute gradations of change.[4] In keeping with the vogue for paleo-Christian archaeology in post-Tridentine Rome, I take a layered approach to these martyrdom paintings, sifting through strata of meaning to unearth a composite whole. By placing these images in their three most relevant pictorial contexts—Japanese Christian material culture, European Ignatian martyrdom imagery, and the visual repertoire of biblically informed violence—I negotiate the Achilles' heel of sight, and *over*sight, to consider the aesthetics of violence, or why we continue to make beautiful images of unspeakable acts and still find them compelling.

Displacement

The first displacement locates the basic coordinates of these martyrdom paintings in the extra-European art workshops initiated by early Jesuits around the world. Made of the same unusual combination of media—watercolor on paper, sometimes varnished and later applied to canvas and possibly silk—the three martyrdom paintings reproduced here can be attributed to the workshop of an intrepid Neapolitan Jesuit, Brother Giovanni Niccolò (Cola or Nicolao, 1560–1626). Based in Japan at the end of the sixteenth century, the Niccolò School produced devotional art as well as books, musical instruments, and clocks for all the Jesuit missions in the East, stretching from India to Japan, at its height a community of some six hundred thousand Catholics in a population of twelve million.[5] In his Japanese workshop, Niccolò executed graceful paintings of the Madonna and child and began to train, at its high point, seventeen European and Japanese brothers in Western-style art making. Under Niccolò's guidance, the workshop painted the delicate features of the postcard-sized *Madonna of the Snow,* preserved for centuries in a hollow piece of bamboo (Figure 22.4).[6] Western compositional and perspectival models were joined with Japanese stylistic conventions, like the hook of a brow or the Virgin's inexplicable beauty mark.[7] Highlights of the atelier's preserved oeuvre include other devotional art, such as a *Salvator Mundi* and pictures of the Crucifixion; portraits, such as the Kobe *Portrait of Saint Francis Xavier,* that deftly combine Western pictorial vernacular with a Japanese-character inscription; landscapes, like the Atami paintings of merry companies; and world maps, displaying a vertiginous cartographic ethnography by showing rulers, cityscapes, and peoples of the world, that populate collections in Kobe, Osaka, and Tokyo. Some of the paintings were *kakemono,* or hanging scrolls; others were two-, six-, or even eight-paneled paired paper screens, or

byōbu; and still others were small panels framed in the elaborate tradition of gold, silver, and mother-of-pearl *maki-e* lacquerware to provide portable private oratories.

Where these martyrdom scenes were completed is significant, for it shows how deeply rooted in them was dislocation from their creation. Dependent on the shifting tides of politics and the favor of local lords, the Niccolò School moved around Japan at least eleven times between 1585 and 1614 before being forced to evacuate to the safety of the Jesuit Church and College of Saint Paul in Macao (destroyed by fire in 1835).[8] Since the establishment of the Diocese of Macao in 1576, the island had become the Portuguese expatriate community's base and a secure Jesuit staging point for entry into Japan, mainland China, Vietnam, Cambodia, and Laos.[9] And it was in Macao that the martyrs of Japan images were painted, quite literally, from a perspective that recognized their unique geographical—and, I would argue, theological—position as products of a multisited Jesuit workshop, in motion from Europe to different locations in Japan and finally to Macao.

After all, the paintings of the martyrs of Japan reproduced here recorded three of the major Christian persecutions of early modern Japan, a dispossessed testimony by those who suffered in solidarity close by, bound not to express their support otherwise. The first painting (Figure 22.1), the *Martyrdom of Brother Leonardo Kimura, S.J., and Four Companions,* captures the deaths of these devout men on November 18, 1619, after suffering four years of imprisonment. A now largely illegible inscription dangles from the beak of an outsized dove in the top left corner. Kimura, a Nagasaki "cradle" Catholic whose grandfather had been baptized by Saint Francis Xavier himself in 1550, was one of the leading painting and engraving masters of the Niccolò School.[10] The second image (Figure 22.2) testifies to the "Great Martyrdom" of fifty-two individuals killed in Nagasaki on August 19, 1622, itself a mute witness to the faith of the Greek *mártys,* or μάρτυς. The third scene (Figure 22.3), a composite eulogy, comprises a visual and verbal roll call of two rows of Jesuit martyrs of Japan from 1617 to 1627 under the watchful eyes of the Apostle of the Indies, Saint Francis Xavier, founder of the mission to Japan, and the trifecta of Paul Miki, João Goto, and Diogo Kisai (d. 1597). Side vignettes are filled with those who died on mission, if were not martyred, like Provincial Matheus de Couros, whose mortal remains are laid out beneath a straw-covered shelter at left.[11] The number of canonized and beatified martyrs in Japan would grow to just under 400 names, excluding those lost to history, and Diego Pacheco (Ryōgo Yūki), S.J., has estimated that over 650 Christians and missionaries were eventually put to death on Nagasaki Hill and in its environs after 1597.[12] Knowledge of the Niccolò School and the depiction of historical events permits a fairly precise estimate of the date and function of these paintings. At least the third painting, the *Jesuit Martyrs in Japan,* was produced in time for the investigative proceedings preceding beatification conducted on behalf of the martyrs in Macao and elsewhere ca. 1628–1632.[13] It is thus likely that all three Japanese martyr paintings constituted part of this evidence, visual testimonies *in absentia* when they arrived in Rome, very possibly already by the 1630s.

Disruption

Rome was the center of Ignatian martyrdom iconography, and its representations occupied a critical mass in the early modern Jesuit imaginarium, an essential component of the mental baggage of any European Jesuit abroad.[14] We need only think of the central importance of *Mary as the Queen of Martyrs* ascending in the dome of the Gesù's Chapel of the Martyrdom of Saint Andrew, and early engravings remind us that the novitiate of San Andrea al Quirinale was also packed with martyrdom scenes.[15] Even if only about half the original Ignatian martyrdom imagery is extant, the theme's critical role in the architecture of vocation, from formation to culmination, for global mission in the service of the Holy See remains clear.[16] The oldest preserved painted martyrdom series of the Society of Jesus (1582) is the group of thirty-one frescoes of early Christian martyrdom

FIGURE 22.5. Niccolò Circignani, *Martyrdom of Christians in Africa during the Reign of Huneric, King of the Vandals* (Fresco 29), 1582. Fresco. Santo Stefano Rotondo, Rome. Photo by Zeno Colantoni. © Zeno Colantoni—Roma.

in Santo Stefano Rotondo, whose ambulatory was transformed by Niccolò Circignani into a veritable panopticon of torture.[17] Justifiably famed for the gore of their deaths, saints of the early church were boiled alive, hacked into lengths, and compressed between two great slabs, innards cascading downward, lucky if they were only beheaded. Most haunting are the details, like the framing stacks of dismembered hands and tongues in the foreground, the grisly harvest of blades and tongs, and the telltale trails of blood from the wrists or lips of saints radically desensitized in works such as the *Martyrdom of Christians in Africa during the Reign of Huneric, King of the Vandals* (Figure 22.5).

Circignani's compositional debt to Jerome Nadal's *Annotations and Meditations on the Gospel* has been widely appreciated: each pagelike vignette offers a framed scene above an explanatory box, with alphabetical letters correlating image and text to graphically recreate the experience of martyrdom in a young Jesuit's mind.[18] Nicolas Standaert, S.J., has noted that Nadal's alphabetical order almost never follows direct, linear sequencing in the *compositio loci,* or "composition of place," in the manner of the Ignatian Spiritual Exercises.[19] So in this scene (Figure 22.5), A, B, and C descend in a serpentine line that pops back up to the out-of-order D above strung-up bodies at the upper left before resuming its dramatic fall to E, the mutilated saints in the foreground, stage left and right. Spiritual discernment was thus founded as much on the embodied imagining of place as on the intentional disruption that built revised attention into the process, the same conceptual framework that premised displacement at the heart of the missionary endeavor.

Even later images of the martyrs of Japan, like those found in the Flemish Jesuit Cornelis Hazart's *Church History of the Whole World* (*Kerckelycke Historie van de Gheheele Wereldt,* 1667–1671), worked just as hard to evoke the experience of martyrdom through sensory evocation—flames engulfing crowds of Christians and, still cringe-worthy, spikes inserted under the nails of a Dominican martyr—as the interruption of pictorial illusion, with glaring inaccuracies in the description of places. Neither the Dutch-Indonesian colonial architecture nor the classicizing temples of Rome in the background were representative of the reality of early modern Japan. The point was not mimetic realism per se, for the disruption of the physical environment could be committed with impunity. The importance lay in an empathetic or subjective realism, pictorial disruption with a purpose, that by identifying realism and its discontents led the way to a spiritual verisimilitude. It was a way of recognizing how the horror of pictorial violence extended beyond the realm of mere mimesis, taking to task the inadequacy of appearances alone.

In this tradition, the martyrdom memorials bombarded the viewer with details of local topographies and particularities of the events, knowledge wrought from a sensory pictorial apparatus: differentiated faces, handwritten names, a side show, a cityscape, boats of onlookers, guards lining bamboo fences, back-up archers, and praying crowds. Swords slice the air, bodies nudge and press against one another, uncomfortably close, and we can taste the tang of saltwater in our mouths, whether from the nearby sea or the sudden parching of fear. The paintings have the flavor of eyewitness testimonials despite the implicit contradiction of the artists' self-evident inability to be there at the same time.[20] Further, the Jesuit workshop in Japan sought to negate the illusion of testimonial that they had worked so hard to replicate with a critical intercession. Rejecting literal translation, these painters honored Nadal's schema by underscoring death as the final neutralization of the bodily senses: the melting flesh of touch, the removal of the head's apparatus for sight and sound, and the unbearable stink of rot and decomposition in the pits that predicated an end never swift enough.

An appendix of apostolic artists at work in a guide for a "True Christian," the *Veridicus Christianus* (1601), by another Flemish Jesuit, Jan David, spells it out for us: the imitation of Christ does not necessarily yield an identical copy. In this image from the guide (Figure 22.6) no two of the artists' canvases look alike, and only one

FIGURE 22.6. Theodoor Galle, *Orbita probitatis ad Christi imitationem veridico Christiano subserviens* (Orb of Virtue for the Imitation of Christ by the True Christian). In Jan David, S.J., *Veridicus Christianus* (Antwerp, 1601), 351. Maurits Sabbe Library, Faculty of Theology and Religious Studies, Katholieke Universiteit, Leuven.

canvas, in the center foreground, copies the model's actions. What we see are the limits, or weak links in the chain, of mimetic imitation, where biblical actions, like the Last Supper and the mocking of Christ, trump the identical depiction of Christ carrying the cross. The goal was to capture Christian behavior, mimesis in deed if not in representation. The model for this mimetic disruption is a Jesus of the Passion, perhaps the best-known example of sensory extremes intertwined with sensational death. And there were as many ways to imitate the *life* of Christ as the *death* of Christ, the latter arguably even more apt for missionaries whose mortal bodies were constantly at risk of burning, decapitation, or submersion. The subtitle of the image—*We Turn Our Eyes unto Jesus, the Author and Witness to Our Faith, Hebrews 12* (*Aspicientes in auctorem fidei, Heb. 12*)— recognizes the complicated relationship between sight, witness, and martyrdom. The susceptibility of the eye, fickle and capricious in its ability to apprehend simulation, was mirrored in the disruption of mimetic realism. Images like the *Orbita probitatis* called for a more flexible visual economy, one that used imitation and went beyond it, to achieve a sensory realism that could aspire to both visual and experiential knowledge *in extremis.*

Crucifixion Economy

Preserved remnants of Japanese Christian material culture, then, reveal the models that Niccolò School artists had at their disposal for treating pictorial schism. A distinct pattern emerges from the many crosses and medallions of the crucifixion or of Christ carrying the cross worn on rosaries and *netsuke,* or sword toggles, by the Christian upper classes; a folio engraving, the *Martyrdom of Saint Andrew* (sixteenth century, Osaka, Namban Bunka-kan), reminiscent of the Gesù's Martyrs' Chapel; and broken shards of hand-sized crucifixes. Jesuits brought a rhetoric of cross and crucifixion with them to Japan that implies that the martyrdom paintings were more than simply another case of *imitatio Christi.* Moreover, the trail of crucifixions was adopted and adapted along the way, from Rome to Lisbon, Goa to Macao, and then to Nagasaki, in stylized polychrome ivories, embroidered silk, and hammered bronze abstractions, and many of these objects were made in Jesuit-administered workshops en route. This was not simply a case of before and after, Europe and overseas destination, but rather one of compounded change along the paths traveled, the tangible fermentation of a visual and theological idea. The Niccolò School martyrdom paintings were sited at just this juncture of local and universal Ignatian crucifixion systems.

What we may call a "crucifixion economy," a Madonna paired with a crucifixion, along with the motto "The Society is made complete by adversity" ("De Societeyt wordt volmaeckt door teghenspoet" or "Societas Iesu persecutionibus formatur"), found its way into the *Imago primi saeculi Societatis Iesu* (1640), published one year after progressively hostile edicts effectively closed Japan to Catholic Europe.[21] This alternative pictorial system, an elastic, experiential mode of representation over the established role of incarnational overtones in inculturation, exchanged suffering for comfort, obstacle for flow, realism disrupted and drained for mimesis.[22] It is no accident that a painter deeply concerned with the incarnational *sudarium,* like Francisco de Zubarán, also produced *Crucifixion with a Painter (Saint Luke?)* (ca. 1660, oil on canvas, Madrid, Prado), highlighting its essential role in the theoretical underpinnings of early modern picture making. Martyrdom did not simply partake of the crucifixion economy; it was a pressure point, a systemwide disruption, what Georges Didi-Huberman has called a "rend" in reality.[23] This is how Zubarán presents Saint Luke's insight: with this rupture, the crucifixion pinpoints a tear in reality, a brief break in the curtain, between actuality and vision, certainty and doubt, sensory experience and the excess of violation. Unlike incarnation imagery's proud heritage of realism, the crucifixion or "other" economy, especially when dealing with non-European others, harnessed the sensory pull toward extrapictorial violence to shatter mimesis and the eidetic call of representation once and for all. It was this less discussed other economy of crucifixion that was responsible for the martyrdom paintings and had particular ramifications for overseas, off-site image production in European-organized religious workshops.

Perhaps the most potent kind of crucifixion imagery we find in Japan was developed in tandem with the escalating persecution of Christians, when wooden placards offered rewards for informing on missionaries and those who sheltered them. These were *fumi-e* tablets, bronze reliefs, often framed in wood, made for the performance of apostasy when Christianity was finally explicitly outlawed, a ceremony mandatory from ca. 1629 to 1857 (Figure 22.7).[24] Inquisitors would watch a suspect carefully to de-

FIGURE 22.7. Anonymous, *Crucifixion fumi-e,* seventeenth century. Bronze. National Museum, Tokyo. Photo courtesy TNM Image Archives.

tect the slightest tremor or hesitation when he was asked to step on the fumi-e panel, demonstrating loyalty to local leaders and religions alike by an iconoclasm manqué. By inviting the accused to physically engage with it, to literally tread on the surface and feel the cool, bumpy relief under foot, perhaps even imprint its message on his soul via the sole, the image extended its reign from the figurative, the metaphorical, to actual bodily danger and violence rubbed smooth by the passing of so many feet, the corporeal inversion of a marble Pietà rubbed smooth by the pliant pressure of centuries of devout lips. Certainly there were other subjects for fumi-e—the requirement was only that it be a Christian scene—but it is striking just how many of these fumi-e accent Christian suffering, with images of the crucifixion and ecce homo, the martyrdom of Saint Sebastian, and the Pietà.[25] If there was one genre that was about witness to faith at its very core, it was that of these diminutive tablets used by inquisitors, made in cruel caricature of Niccolò School artistic production, as if they were refutations not only of its content but also of its method of visual argumentation. In the pictorial economy of crucifixion, the rejection of a crucifixion image quickly led to an all too real crucifixion offstage, with Saints Diogo Kisai, Paul Miki, and João Goto now the bearers of the cross. The sensory campaign launched by the pictorial trauma of the martyrdom paintings had become a distinctly social ontology of the senses.

Body Doubles

And yet we continue to look at biblically inflected images of violence, caught in a Medusan wager—looking even if the cost is death—without really considering the social function of martyrdom.[26] Using the sacrifice of Isaac as an example, René Girard reminded us how resolutely entrenched violence is in the sacred, and thus indirectly underscored the civic character of sensory life, the links from one body to another, where religion finds its most characteristic form in ties that bind, "religare."[27] A socially sanctified scapegoat functions as an outlet for the attack required to mend the riven social fabric. If we extend Girard's theory from one society to the encounter of two worlds and then to the visual rhetoric of the story, we see that we need only an acceptable substitution, a doppelgänger who promises order restored, as in Govert Flinck's *Isaac Blessing Jacob* (Figure 22.8), and this is one role that the Jesuit martyrs in Japan could fulfill.[28] When Isaac fell for Jacob's ruse as the "monstrous double" of Esau, it was not simply the inversion of "mimetic desire," an abstraction. It was the all too close-to-the-bone caricature of like, but different, brother, clad now in goatskin and gloves, the costume of touch in what would be a comedy of errors, if it were not so terrifying. Substitution achieved the alterity of familiarity, not the absolutely other, via sensory identification.

Likewise, the dramatis personae of the "Warring States," or *Sengoku* period of Japan, possessed a surfeit of potentially disturbing shape shifters who blurred already ambiguous confessional and political loyalties.[29] Even in the seemingly innocuous as-

FIGURE 22.8. Govert Flinck, *Isaac Blessing Jacob,* 1638. Oil on canvas. Collection Rijksmuseum, Amsterdam.

sumption of a Buddhist monk's robes by Saint Francis Xavier, the real threat, the less discussed anxiety or unintentional complication of acculturation, was the representation or appearance of *non*difference, the monstrous twin, creating a confusion not unlike that the Trinitarian doctrine of shared essence sowed for those encountering it for the first time.[30] For Tokugawa Ieyasu, missionaries, already liminal, societally marginal figures, became the prime candidates for sacrificial victimhood. We recall that the deciding factor for Fabian Fukan—Buddhist *bonze* turned Jesuit priest (*Myotei Mondo*) become Buddhist once again (*Hou Daisu*)—was Christianity's hesitancy to validate the social and political status quo.[31] Lists of religious affiliations, temple certifications, first drawn up in Nagasaki in 1614 and in Edo by 1623, only increased the impression of a growing need for confessional clarity.[32] It is no surprise, then, that the martyrdom of like figures, cassocks lined up one after another in the *Jesuit Martyrs in Japan,* found its societal parallel in *imitatio crucis* (Figure 22.3). What was at stake, what martyrdom as the "monstrous double" of crucifixion made manifest, was the potential danger of revolutionary repetition when one could mutate into many.

Body doubles were undone the same way that they were made: through dissection by sensation. This is the same impulse we saw in the famously terrifying, raw photographs of prisoners from Abu Ghraib (2004), which horrified not only through the degradation of the human person but also in the specific way that they simulated a crucifixion, though different.[33] The body was elevated on a pedestal, arms outstretched, head and body covered with a black potato-sack shape as the new acephalic "face" of senseless terror, a disquieting update of Christian iconography from Christ's body as *imago mundi* (Leonardo da Vinci), indeed, pace W.J.T. Mitchell, as a flawed "man as measure of the world" (Hildegard of Bingen).[34] Or we can look to Kiki Smith's recent substitution of a flayed anatomical model for the extreme humility of the Queen of Heaven, a transposal of Jacques Lacan's body as a "sac de peau" (bag of skin), for her *Virgin Mary* (1993, wax, cheesecloth, and wood, New York, Pace Wildenstein Gallery).[35] As an allegory of "ouch," this everywoman becomes the antithesis of touch: a body-surface abrasion predicated on the removal of the ultimate boundary and largest living sensory organ of the body, its skin, porous and aching in response. But perhaps most haunting is the deformation, in the sense of Valentin Groebner's "ungestalt," of the traditionally beautiful, the counterpoint to Golgotha's skulls and the botanical novelty of colonialism.[36] The creepy, faux-scientific names—*Anthurium nigrum, Cattleya putida, Passiflora sanguinea*—of Juan Manual Echavarría's orchid, dandelion, and pansy in his *Corte de florero* (*Flower Vase Cut*) series (1997) give the lie to spores constructed from human knuckles, stems of femurs and tibias, and clavicle-crafted petals (Figures 22.9A–C).[37] With a bouquet of innocent bystanders' body parts in a Colombian revolutionary-style "flower vase cut" (*corte de florero*)—head decapitated, arms and legs inserted into the neck (Figure 22.9D)—the fresh blooms of new life have been replaced by fetid decomposition and the inexpungible smell of death.[38] The problem the evisceration by the senses brought into stark relief was the enjambment of that which should naturally be distinct.

How can we keep the twin identities of the martyr paintings in balance: the horrible massacre and the beautiful painting, sensory emoting and mental comprehension? We may even think of this double reaction as the twofold monstrous identity of sensate violence, the reveling and the recoiling feeding on one another, the obscene symbiosis of fascination and revulsion, as we wrestle with the paradox that seeing bodies writhing in pain is pleasing. Since Plato's first description of Leontius's mental conflict in *The Republic* (Book IV), this has been at the heart of the visual history of violence at large, whether in T. J. Clark's erotic poetics of mythology in Nicholas Poussin's *Landscape with a Man Being Killed by a Snake* (1648, oil on canvas, London, National Gallery); Susan Sontag's focus on the staged horror of war in Goya's *The Third of May, 1808* (1814, oil on canvas, Madrid, Prado); and Picasso's *Guernica* (1937, oil on canvas, Madrid, Museo Reina Sofia) or in Andy Warhol's fascination with multiples of death in silkscreens like *Atomic Bomb* (1965).[39] The painful destruction of bodies in *Fifty-two Martyrs of Nagasaki* seems positively pleasant amid the placid seas, gently rolling greenswards, craggy coastline, and parsley-sprig trees.

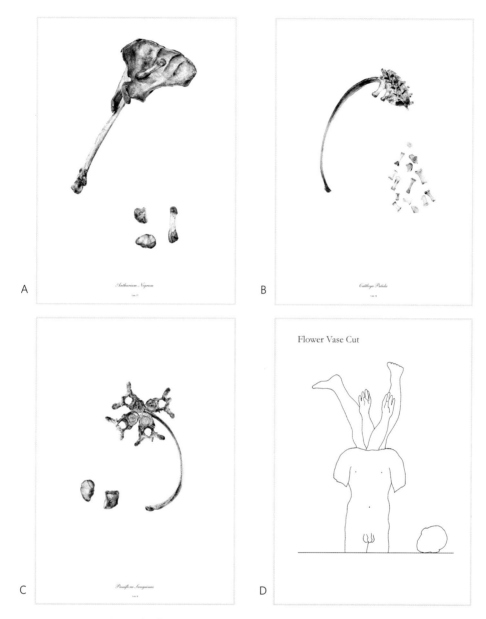

A

B

C

D

FIGURE 22.9. Juan Manuel Echavarría, *Corte de florero* (*Flower Vase Cut*) series, 1997: (A) *Anthurium nigrum,* 57; (B) *Cattleya putida,* 36; (C) *Passiflora sanguinea,* 9; (D) *Corte de florero.* Archival pigment print on paper. From María Victoria Uribe Alarcón, *Matar, rematar, y contramatar: Las masacres de la violencia en el Tolima, 1948–1964* (Bogotá: Centro de Investigación y Educación Popular [CINEP], 1990), [186].

Even the feathery fires and streams of blood bloom like so many red poppies, the eye's novocaine. The florid, floral beauty of Nishizaka Hill's landscape of death at least temporarily obstructs the act, our last hope for reprieve for the identified martyrs and the bodies of the nameless, the voiceless, and the placeless. The South African poet Antjie Krog's frustration with her own profession's contribution to aestheticized societal violence may also be its saving grace: "barely audible / she repeats her arrest / her sentence / melts from her tongue / not in print / not in photographs / not in statistics / everywhere it is damp / rumors of disappearances / torture / and anonymous deaths," concluding that "'aesthetics is the only ethic.'"[40] In the difficulty of looking at this material, we acknowledge the ways that other people become visible (and invisible) to us, that images of suffering "tap into our deepest level of moral motivations by revealing our vulnerability as contingent bodily subjects."[41] The making of an artifact was always a social contract, the material making sentient the external world that would form the basis for ethical content.[42] The power of crucifixion (for Christians) resides in Christ as the body double, the scapegoat, the threshold of the alter ego for every viewer.

Eye/I

One last object, in a brief return to Japanese Christian material culture, post-persecution this time, brings us to the eighteenth-century classical Japanese *Mirror*— idyllic landscape on one side (Figure 22.10A), smooth, reflective surface on the other (Figure 22.10B).[43] Made by Hidden Christians, or *Kakuri Kirishitan, Mirror* tenders a historical eye on the self, the profound depths of what Emmanuel Levinas termed a

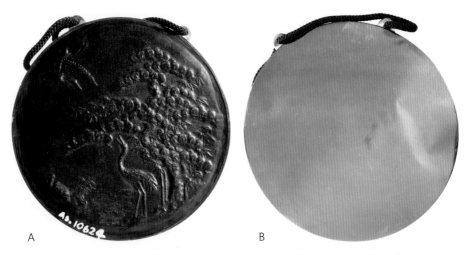

A   B

FIGURE 22.10. Anonymous, *Mirror,* eighteenth century. A and B are the two sides. Glass, metal, bronze. Vatican Ethnological Museums, Vatican City. Photograph © Vatican Museums.

"re-se-voir" to see the self anew. This "epiphany" of sight enabled the face to become an interlocutor for all other senses, the eye that prefaces the emphatic, ever-flawed "I" in sensory redux. As fictions of sentience, the martyrdom paintings go one step further to isolate pure subjectivity for the viewer, their raw subject matter seeming to detach form from the very heart of its production.[44] For pain, the inordinate sensation of burnt flesh, is objectless, unlike smell or touch, desire or fear, which require some *thing* to act upon. Visual depictions of violence, like the martyrdom paintings, raise the specter of "objectless" objects, or images that are all subject.[45] The extreme exteriority of this *Mirror* boomerangs us back to the material technologies of self that connect the senses and sacrifice. Our eyes, our face, our insistent self, and its limits, mortality expansive and uncontained, are why looking at violence, like that in the martyrdom paintings, is so very disturbing.

Mirror also codifies the alterity of reflection. For subjectivity is formed in and through our subjection to the other. The mirrored face eerily echoes the irreducible, ambiguous other, akin but distinct, in a ghostly, haunting, unnamed shell. Levinas has described it as "the encounter with a face that at once gives and conceals the Other . . . in which an event happens to a subject who does not assume it, who is utterly unable in its regard, but where nonetheless in a certain way it is in front of the subject."[46] This is the montage of face/identity and sacrifice we see melting in the martyrs' faces, what Michael Taussig has called "de*face*ment," which functions analogously to Didi-Huberman's disturbance or visual rend, the mystery of the face as the wound to our Doubting Thomas.[47] The face-to-face encounter with the unnamed is what transforms the frontiers of self and other (Psalm 119:19: "I am a stranger in the earth; Do not hide Your commandments from me") into an ethical, intersubjective event, the "touching together" or coming into contact of "*con*" + "*tangere*," a contingent mode of looking that simply happens but can never be produced.[48] Walter Benjamin exactly mirrored this sentiment back to us, in honor of the *fosa común*, in Dani Karavan's monumental *Passages (Homage to Walter Benjamin)*—"It is more arduous to honor the memory of the nameless than that of the renowned. Historical construction is devoted to the memory of the nameless"—with a still life memorial that embalms the lives stilled when crossing the wartime border between France and Spain (Figure 22.11).[49] This is perhaps the "true religion" Robert Orsi tied to boundary crossing and transformative, transgressive encounter, be it of identity or geography, and why looking at violence matters.[50] The very ambiguity and ambivalence of the "body in pain" is soldered to the making and unmaking of the world.[51]

Exterior, reflection, and now projection, *Mirror* has one last secret to reveal. A beam of light directed toward the surface reveals a misty crucifixion scene previously shrouded in darkness, with two figures in prayer below on a wall (Figure 22.12). Like the martyrdom paintings, by itself *Mirror* cannot contain the moral implications of the mass onslaught of human beings that drove and gave sense to these images. All are

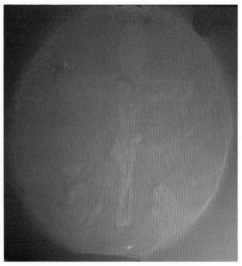

FIGURE 22.11. Dani Karavan, *Passages (Homage to Walter Benjamin)*, 1994. Exile Memorial Museum Consortium, Portbou, Spain. Photo by Jaume Blasi, Barcelona.

FIGURE 22.12. Photograph of Figure 22.10B (anonymous, *Mirror,* eighteenth century) with a beam of light directed toward the surface, revealing a crucifixion scene. Glass, metal, bronze. Vatican Ethnological Museums, Vatican City. Photograph © Vatican Museums.

forced to overcompensate by signifying that which they cannot represent, the first sure step in economic deflation. The reds of the martyrdom paintings perform multiple duties, morphing from blood to fire to fabric in a haze of crimson hues, the arbitrariness of signs clustering around death like so many acquisitive, scavenging vultures, well exceeding the reserve of symbolism proper. To look in growing panic, to look in safety, places the viewer in ethical double jeopardy, with a moral imperative demanding the rewiring of "res" and "signum," fact and allegory, in the wake of crucifixion, when history and cultural context are left silent.[52] Sense precedes cultural signs; meaning resides in the human dimension, indeed the corporate social compact, when the reformatted body of self and other are mapped onto the polemics of beauty and the abject. The oculus, the eye, functions as the "I" that bridges these pairs of competing, disparate realities never joined. The martyrdom paintings reflect or repay the viewer with a fissured self briefly held hostage, the viewer as surety for the captive gaze.[53] The last subject thus becomes the expiation of other subjects, the brief moment when our self colludes with the *counterfeytsel,* in the sixteenth-century sense of portrait, of the utterly ingested painting. Attending to the martyrdom paintings is, among other things, about the preservation of the self through temporary, shifting visual projection and thus our continued communal responsibility to keep watching, keep witnessing.

Conclusion

So the aesthetics of violence leave us with an ethics of the eye. Why do we keep looking, looking even and especially when violence assaults our eyes? The paintings of the Jesuit martyrs of Japan compound access to interrelated, embodied realities—through place and displacement, mimesis and disruption, incarnation and crucifixion, substitution and scapegoat systems, self and other. When the "other" economy of the crucifixion system engaged the many others met on mission, crucifix met *mundus* in the representation of the four elements recast for the peculiarly pictorial dynamics of encounter—in the winds of the caravels, the interminable seas, the bottomless pits of excretion over which martyrs were hung, and the fires—the fires of death at the stake. The sensory experience of place constructed and broke, in a word reoriented, the hold of violence on the body. Displacement comes full circle in the brutal dialectics of early modern conflict, placing a substitution economy in a global context in which sight, sensation, and the other implicate the subject. Looking at violence, in sum, is here a form of social responsibility, an ethics of sight that reminds us why the sensory lives of objects, as one of the prime results of materializing religion, bear a special valence for the global challenges of the world today. But perhaps the final words on the vocation to sight, alterity, and place are best served by Michel de Certeau, S.J., in his comments on Maurice Merleau-Ponty's *Le visible et l'invisible:* "Vision 'captivates' us not only because it is a journey toward external things, but also because it is a *return* to a reality of origin . . . to travel is to see, but seeing is already traveling."[54]

NOTES

Research for this chapter would have been greatly impoverished without the generous on-site aid of Martina Brunori, Bernard Deprez, John Endres, S.J., Nadia Fiussello, Jay Hooks, S.J., Father Nicola Mapelli, Flavia Serena di Lapigio, and Tony Sholander, S.J., and without stimulating conversations with Eduardo Fernández, S.J., and William O'Neill, S.J.

1. Hubert Cieslik, S.J., "The Case of Christovão Ferreira," *Monumenta Nipponica* 29 (Spring 1974): 14–15.

2. Georg Schurhammer, S.J., ed., *Epistolae S. Francisci Xaverii aliaque eius scripta,* 2 vols. (Rome: Institutum Historicum Societatis Iesu, 1944–1945); Schurhammer, *Francis Xavier: His Life, His Times,* 4 vols., trans. M. Joseph Costelloe, S.J. (Rome: Jesuit Historical Institute, 1973–1982); and Schurhammer, *Gesammelte Studien,* vol. 2: *Orientalia* (Rome: Institutum Historicum Societatis Iesu, 1963), 774–775.

3. Gauvin A. Bailey, *Between Renaissance and Baroque: Jesuit Art in Rome, 1565–1610* (Toronto: University of Toronto Press, 2003), 219; *Portugal and the World in the 16th and 17th Centuries,* exhibition catalog, Museu Nacional de Arte Antiga, Lisbon, 2009, 366–367; *Encounter of Cultures: Eight Centuries of Portuguese Mission Work,* exhibition catalog, Vatican Museums, Vati-

can City, 1996, 314; and *Encompassing the Globe: Portugal and the World in the 16th and 17th Centuries,* ed. Jay A. Levenson, exhibition catalog, Smithsonian Institution, Washington DC, 2007, 334–335.

4. James Elkins, *The Object Stares Back: On the Nature of Seeing* (New York: Simon and Schuster, 1996), 11–12 et passim.

5. Gauvin A. Bailey, *Art on the Jesuit Missions in Asia and Latin America, 1542–1775* (Toronto: University of Toronto Press, 1999), 53, 71–72; M. Antoni J. Üçerler, S.J., "The Jesuit Enterprise in Sixteenth- and Seventeenth-Century Japan," in *The Cambridge Companion to the Jesuits,* ed. Thomas Worcester, S.J. (Cambridge, UK: Cambridge University Press, 2008), 153, 164.

6. Mia M. Mochizuki, "Seductress of Site: The Nagasaki *Madonna of the Snow,*" in *Aemulatio: Imitation, Emulation, and Invention in Netherlandish Art, 1500 to 1800, Essays in Honor of Eric Jan Sluijter,* ed. Anton W. A. Boschloo et al. (Zwolle: Waanders, 2011), 76–88.

7. Yoriko Kobayashi-Sato and Mia M. Mochizuki, "Perspective and Its Discontents or St. Lucy's Eyes," in *Seeing across Cultures in the Early Modern Period,* ed. Dana Leibsohn and Jeanette F. Peterson (Farnham, UK: Ashgate, 2012), 21–48.

8. Cieslik, "Christovão Ferreira," 5–11.

9. António Carmo, "The Portuguese Mission in China and Macau," *Encounter of Cultures,* exhibition catalog, Vatican Museum, Vatican City, 1996, 92.

10. *Portugal and the World,* 366; Juan Ruiz de Medina, S.J., *El martirologio del Japón, 1558–1873* (Rome: Institutum Historicum Societatis Iesu, 1999), 215–248, 417–419 and (Figure 1); 440–464 (Figure 2); 287–695 (Figure 3), and Joseph N. Tylenda, S.J., *Jesuit Saints and Martyrs: Short Biographies of the Saints, Blessed, Venerables, and Servants of God of the Society of Jesus,* 2nd ed. (Chicago: Loyola Press, 1998), 38–41, 299–305, 392–394, 466.

11. Diogo de Mesquita, who died on the beach of Nagasaki on November 4, 1614, is included in the lower left corner. Diego Pacheco [Ryōgo Yūki], S.J., "Diogo de Mesquita, S.J., and the Jesuit Mission Press," *Monumenta Nipponica* 26, nos. 3–4 (1971): 439–443.

12. Renzo De Luca, S.J., and Diego Pacheco [Ryōgo Yūki], S.J., "List of Petro Kibe and 187 Companion Martyrs Beatified on November 24, 2008," "Lista de los 205 Beatos Mártires del Japón (Beatificados por Pio IX el 7 de Julio de 1867)," and "The Martyrs' Hill Nagasaki," Twenty-six Martyrs Museum, Nagasaki, accessed September 15, 2010, http://www1.bbiq.jp/martyrs, [26 pp.], and Ruiz de Medina, *Martirologio del Japón,* 847–859.

13. Schurhammer, *Orientalia,* 774–775.

14. Vincent Barletta, *Death in Babylon: Alexander the Great and Iberian Empire in the Muslim Orient* (Chicago: University of Chicago Press, 2010), 145.

15. Bailey, *Between Renaissance and Baroque,* 202–203, 208.

16. Ibid., 21; Leif Holm Monssen, "The Martyrdom Cycle in Santo Stefano Rotundo," *Acta ad archaeologiam et artium historiam pertinentia* 2 (1982): 175–319 and 3 (1983): 11–106; Monssen, "*Rex gloriose martyrum:* A Contribution to Jesuit Iconography," *Art Bulletin* 63 (1981): 130–137; and Kristin Noreen, "*Ecclesiae militantis triumphi:* Jesuit Iconography and the Counter Reformation," *Sixteenth Century Journal* 29 (1998): 689–716.

17. Bailey, *Between Renaissance and Baroque,* 20, 133–148.

18. Jerome Nadal, *Annotations and Meditations on the Gospels,* trans. and ed. Frederick A. Homann, intro. essay by Walter S. Melion, 3 vols. (Philadelphia: Saint Joseph's University Press, 2003–2007).

19. Nicolas Standaert, S.J., "The Composition of Place: Creating Space for an Encounter," *The Way* 46 (2000): 12–17.

20. Cf. Masaharu Anesaki, "Writings on Martyrdom in Kirishitan Literature," *Transactions of the Asiatic Society of Japan,* 2nd ser., 8 (1931): 20–65; Hubert Cieslik, S.J., "The Great Martyr-

dom in Edo, 1623: Its Causes, Course, Consequences," *Monumenta Nipponica* 10 (1954): 27–32; Ruiz de Medina, *Martirologio del Japón;* Dorotheus Schilling, O.F.M., "Zur Geschichte des Martyrerberichtes des P. Luis Frois, S.I.," *Archivum Historicum Societatis Iesu* 6 (1937): 107–113; and Pietro Tacchi Venturi, S.J., "Tre lettere inedite di quattro beati martiri del Giappone," *Archivum Historicum Societatis Iesu* 9 (1940): 40–49.

21. Joannes Bollandus, S.J., Godefridus Henschenius, S.J., Johannes Tollenarius, S.J., Sidronius Hosschius, S.J., and Jacob vande Walle, S.J., *Imago primi saeculi Societatis Iesu, a Provincia Flandro-Belgica eiusdem Societatis repraesentata* (Antwerp, 1640), fol. 571r; Joannes Bollandus, S.J., and Adrien Poirters, S.J., *Af-Beeldinghe van d'eerste eeuwe der Societeyt Iesu voor ooghen ghestelt door de Duyts-Nederlantsche Provincie der selver Societeyt,* trans. Laurent Uwens (Antwerp, 1640), fol. 398r; and Ralph Dekoninck, "La Passion des images: La Traversée des images jésuites entre Ancien et Nouveau Monde," *De zeventiende eeuw* 21, no. 1 (2005): 54–56. By the end of the seventeenth century, the story of the Japanese martyrs had become the single most popular story of Ignatian martyrdom, and the Jesuit martyrs of Japan were mentioned elsewhere in the *Imago.* Bollandus and Poirters, *Af-beeldinghe,* 522; Bollandus et al., *Imago,* 726; Bailey, *Between Renaissance and Baroque,* 65; and Marc van Vaeck, "Encoding the Emblematic Tradition of Love," in *Learned Love: Proceedings of the Emblem Project Utrecht Conference on Dutch Love Emblems and the Internet,* ed. Els Stronks and Peter Boot (The Hague: DANS, 2007), 66–67.

22. François Boespflug, "Le Syncrétisme et les syncrétismes: Périls imaginaires, faits d'histoire, problèmes en cours," *Revue des sciences philosophiques et théologiques* 90 (2006): 273–295; Christoph Markschies, "Synkretismus: V. Kirchengeschichtlich," *Theologische Realenzyklopädie* 32 (2001): 538–552; and Aylward Shorter, *Toward a Theology of Inculturation* (Maryknoll, NY: Orbis, 1999), 3–16.

23. Georges Didi-Huberman, *Confronting Images: Questioning the Ends of a Certain History of Art,* trans. John Goodman (University Park: Pennsylvania State University Press, 2005), 138–228.

24. Yakichi Kataoka, *Fumie: Kinkyō no rekishi* (Tokyo: Nihon Hōsō Shuppan Kyōkai, 1977), 27; Kiichi Matsuda, "Fumi-e," *Kokushi Daijiten* 12 (1991): 322–323; Klaus Koschorke, Frieder Ludwig, and Mariano Delgado, eds., *A History of Christianity in Asia, Africa, and Latin America, 1450–1990: A Documentary Sourcebook* (Grand Rapids, MI: Eerdmans, 2007), 32–33; Akio Okada, "Fumi-e ni tsuite," *Kirishitan kenkyū* 2 (1944): 160–161; and Georg Schurhammer, S.J., "100. Wurden die Holländer in Japan zum 'Bildtreten' gezwungen?" in *Gesammelte Studien,* vol. 4: *Varia* (Rome: Institutum Historicum Societatis Iesu, 1965), 177–178.

25. Thomas DaCosta Kaufmann, "Designed for Desecration: *Fumi-e* and European Art," *Toward a Geography of Art* (Chicago: University of Chicago Press, 2004), 303–340; Mia M. Mochizuki, "Deciphering the Dutch in Deshima," in *Boundaries and Their Meanings in the History of the Netherlands,* ed. Benjamin J. Kaplan et al. (Leiden: Brill, 2009), 63–94; and Takau Shimada and Yuriko Shimada, *Fumie: Gaikokujin ni yoru fumie no kiroku* (Tokyo: Yūshōdō Shuppan, 1994).

26. Cf. Barbara Baert, *Caput Johannis in disco* (Essay on a Man's Head) (Leiden: Brill, 2012), 130–142, and Barbara Baert, "The Johannesschüssel as *Andachtsbild:* The Gaze, the Medium, and the Senses," *Archaeus* 15 (2011): 221–258.

27. René Girard, *The Scapegoat,* trans. Yvonne Freccero (Baltimore: Johns Hopkins University Press, 1989), 154, and Girard, *Violence and the Sacred,* trans. Patrick Gregory (Baltimore: Johns Hopkins University Press, 1977), 8.

28. Girard, *Scapegoat,* 198–212.

29. In the battle for dominance of Japan between three lords—Oda Nobunaga (1534–1582), Toyotomi Hideyoshi (1537–1598), and Tokugawa Ieyasu (1542–1616)—Tokugawa Ieyasu defini-

tively won the Battle of Sekigahara (1600), thereby consolidating his power to become the sho-gun whose dynasty would rule early modern Japan until 1868. Leonard Blussé et al., eds., *Bridging the Divide: 400 Years; The Netherlands and Japan* (Hilversum, Netherlands: Stichting Educatieve Omroep Teleac / NOT, 2000), 13, and Grant K. Goodman, *Japan and the Dutch, 1600–1853* (Richmond, UK: Curzon, 2000), 2.

30. Girard, *Violence and the Sacred,* 64, 161.

31. George Elison, *Deus Destroyed: The Image of Christianity in Early Modern Japan* (Cambridge, MA: Harvard University Press, 1973), 142–184, 257–291, and Monika Schrimpf, "The Pro- and Anti-Christian Writings of Fukan Fabian (1565–1621)," *Japanese Religions* 33 (2008): 50.

32. Cieslik, "Great Martyrdom in Edo," 18, 38.

33. David Ebony, *Botero: Abu Ghraib* (Munich: Prestel, 2006), 6.

34. W.J.T. Mitchell, *Cloning Terror: The War of Images, 9/11 to the Present* (Chicago: University of Chicago Press, 2011), 41–44, 136, quote on 143, 150–159, Plate 4, Figure 35.

35. Rudolf Bernet, "The Encounter with the Stranger: Two Interpretations of the Vulnerability of the Skin," in *The Face of the Other and the Trace of God: Essays on the Philosophy of Emmanual Levinas,* ed. Jeffrey Bloechl (New York: Fordham University Press, 2000), 45–46, and Roberta Panzanelli, ed., *Ephemeral Bodies: Wax Sculpture and the Human Figure* (Los Angeles: Getty Research Institute, 2008), 8–9.

36. Valentin Groebner, *Defaced: The Violence of Visual Culture in the Late Middle Ages,* trans. Pamela Selwyn (New York: Zone, 2004), 150.

37. Michael T. Taussig, *Walter Benjamin's Grave* (Chicago: University of Chicago Press, 2006), 189–218.

38. María Victoria Uribe Alarcón, *Matar, rematar, y contramatar: Las masacres de la violencia en el Tolima, 1948–1964* (Bogotá: Centro de Investigación y Educación Popular [CINEP], 1990), 175, [186].

39. Elizabeth A. Castelli, "The Ambivalent Legacy of Violence and Victimhood: Using Early Christian Martyrs to Think With," *Spiritus: A Journal of Christian Spirituality* 6 (Spring 2006): 1–24; T. J. Clark, *The Sight of Death: An Experiment in Art Writing* (New Haven, CT: Yale University Press, 2006), 236; Plato, *The Republic: Books 1–5,* trans. Paul Shorey (Cambridge, MA: Harvard University Press, 1930), iv, xiv, 398–401; and Susan Sontag, *Regarding the Pain of Others* (New York: Farrar, Straus, and Giroux, 2003), 96–99.

40. Antjie Krog, "*Parool*" (Parole), in Krog, *Down to My Last Skin* (Johannesburg: Random House, 2000), 56–57, and Krog, *Lady Anne* (Cape Town: Human and Rousseau, 1989), 36–37.

41. Giovanna Borradori, "Notes from the Field: Contingency," *Art Bulletin* 94 (September 2012): 346.

42. Elaine Scarry, *The Body in Pain* (Oxford, UK: Oxford University Press, 1985), 175, 281.

43. Emmanuel Levinas, *Humanism of the Other,* trans. Nidra Poller (Urbana: University of Illinois Press, 2003), 31, and Emmanuel Levinas, *Totality and Infinity: An Essay on Exteriority,* trans. Alphonso Lingis (Pittsburgh: Duquesne University Press, 1969), 187.

44. Emmanuel Levinas, *Alterity and Transcendance,* trans. Michael B. Smith (New York: Columbia University Press, 1999), 104, 169; Levinas, *Humanism of the Other,* xxx–xxxi, 32, 44; and Levinas, *Totality and Infinity,* 194.

45. Scarry, *Body in Pain,* 161–162.

46. Levinas, *Alterity and Transcendance,* 103, 171, and Levinas, *Time and the Other,* trans. Richard A. Cohen (Pittsburgh: Duquesne University Press, 1987), 78–79.

47. Barletta, *Death in Babylon,* 29. See also Robert Bernasconi, "The Alterity of the Stranger and the Experience of the Alien," in *Face of the Other,* ed. Bloechl, 63; Emmanuel Levi-

nas, *Otherwise Than Being or Beyond Essence,* trans. Alphonso Lingis (Pittsburgh: Duquesne University Press, 1998), 63, 184; Levinas, *Time and the Other,* 75; and Michael T. Taussig, *Defacement: Public Secrecy and the Labor of the Negative* (Stanford, CA: Stanford University Press, 1999), 3.

48. Mary Ann Doane, "Notes from the Field: Contingency," *Art Bulletin* 94 (September 2012): 349, and Peter Geimer, "Notes from the Field: Contingency," *Art Bulletin* 94 (September 2012): 351.

49. "Schwerer ist es, das Gedächtnis der Namenlosen zu ehren als das der Berühmten: Dem Gedächtnis der Namenlosen ist die historische Konstruktion geweiht." Walter Benjamin, "Über den Begriff der Geschichte," in *Gesammelte Schriften,* ed. Rolf Tiedemann and Hermann Schweppenhäuser (Frankfurt am Main: Suhrkamp, 1991), vol. 1, sec. 3, 1241. See also Ross Birrell and David Harding, dirs., *Portbou: 18 Fragments for Walter Benjamin,* digital film, 2005; Ingrid Scheurman and Walter Scheurman, eds., *Dani Karavan: Hommage an Walter Benjamin; Der Gedenkort "Passagen" in Portbou: Homage to Walter Benjamin; "Passages," Place of Remembrance at Portbou* (Mainz: Philipp von Zabern, 1995); and Taussig, *Walter Benjamin's Grave,* 2–30.

50. Robert A. Orsi, "Snakes Alive: Religious Studies between Heaven and Earth," *Between Heaven and Earth: The Religious Worlds People Make and the Scholars Who Study Them* (Princeton, NJ: Princeton University Press, 2005), 178, 187, 195, 198.

51. Scarry, *Body in Pain,* 23.

52. Levinas, *Humanism of the Other,* 9, 36, 38; Levinas, *Otherwise Than Being,* 63; and Levinas, *Totality and Infinity,* 189–191. For more on silence as an unceasing chain of metamorphoses, see Jozef Fekete, S.J., *Mlčanie, bytie, jazyk: Topológia filzofického mlčania* (Silence, Language, Being: A Topology of Philosophical Silence) (Červený Kostelec: Pavel Mervart, 2012), 273–299.

53. Levinas, *Otherwise Than Being,* 13–14, 184.

54. Michel de Certeau, S.J., "The Madness of Vision," *Enclitic* 7 (Spring 1983): 26. See Luce Giard, "Michel de Certeau's Heterology and the New World," in *New World Encounters,* ed. Stephen Greenblatt (Berkeley: University of California Press, 1993), 317; and Maurice Merleau-Ponty, *Le Visible et l'invisible: Suivi de notes de travail* (Paris: Gallimard, 1964).

Washington, D.C. August 1942. Rev. Vondell Gassaway, Pastor of the St. Martin's Spiritual church standing in a bowl of sacred water banked with roses, each of which he blesses and gives to a member who has been anointed and prayed for by a long line of disciples during the annual Flower bowl demonstration. Photo by Gordon R. Parks. U.S. Dept. Agric. Farm Security Administration. Original neg. LC-USF34-13502-C (missing 1986) Copy negative LC-USZ62-91455

In the facing photograph by Gordon Parks, the Reverend Vondell Verbycke Gassaway, cloaked and vested in liturgical garments and pectoral crucifix, stands in a shallow ritual pool filled with water and ringed by fresh long-stemmed roses. Gassaway faces us, his back toward the preaching lectern in Verbycke Spiritual Church in Washington, D.C., the church he founded in 1928 and led until his death in 1964.[1] Although the church identified as Protestant, it developed its own sensory rituals and practices, drawing on sources in Roman Catholicism, New Thought, Vodou, Spiritualism, and Islam, for example, as well as a range of Protestant denominations. Here Gassaway poses in the pool next to a chalkware statue of a fair-skinned Our Lady of Grace, possibly purchased from a Catholic ecclesiastical supply catalog, a local *botánica,* or a church supply store. A candle burns in front of Our Lady, and she stands on a hand-crocheted doily. At least three devotional bodies confront the viewer of this photograph: those of Gassaway, the corpus on the crucifix he wears, and Mary, the mother of Jesus, represented in the plaster statue. If we also took into account the process by which congregants observed this ritual, the "annual Flower bowl demonstration," we would know that each of the church's members present that day had preceded Gassaway in passing, barefoot, into and out of the pool and its holiness-conferring waters. (Newspapers, seen at lower right, protect the floor from splash damage.) By the time church members emerged from these waters, they would have each received

Gordon Parks, *The Reverend Vondell Verbycke Gassaway Standing in a Ritual Pool of Water Next to a Chalkware Statue of Our Lady of Grace,* Washington, D.C., August 1942. Library of Congress, LC-USF34-013502-C.

a rose that had been blessed by the pastor; each member would also have been anointed and prayed over by a considerable line of fellow churchgoers.

Parks produced a series of photographs, taken around the same time as this one, that provide additional information about the space. We know, for example, that another large statue, this one of Joseph holding the child Jesus (both light-skinned), joins Our Lady of Grace on the lace-covered altar that extends out of the picture space to the viewer's right. A matching candle burns in front of this second painted plaster ensemble. Above Our Lady of Grace, on the wall-mounted bracket visible at the top margin between the head of Mary and the standing floor lamp, is a third chalkware statue of the dark-skinned Saint Martin of Porres, smaller in scale but similarly honored by a lighted candle. The church's educational facility, Saint Martin's Spiritual Center, made this Saint Martin its name-saint. Over Gassaway, hanging from the center of the lintel, a sign lettered "Saint Martin's" lays claim to the space. And "GOD," rendered in capital letters, looks on from above, hovering immediately over Gassaway's shadow/double, authorizing this ministry.

The century beginning around 1850 witnessed the Western proliferation into domestic, ecclesial, and mission fields of devotional objects made of plaster or chalkware. Both Protestants and Catholics made Christian use of this whitest of white media, though Catholic supply houses and manufacturers most frequently produced figural objects, drawing attention to such things as skin color, devotional postures, and bodily comportment. In a Christian culture of conversion that metaphorically and scripturally equated whiteness with purity and salvation, chalkware was not a neutral medium in the material politics of complexion. This common plaster material inexpensively replicated the "color" of marble, alabaster, ivory, and porcelain and further instantiated whiteness as the normative material appearance of Christianity, insistently visualizing, embodying, and categorizing racial difference. As I noted in the introduction to this volume, race, as a nameable category and phenomenon, is fully dependent on the ideological interpretation of *sensed* perceptions of difference. Different media, of course, have different material, sensory, and representational capacities and offer themselves to different uses and possibilities. These are not absolutely constraining, however, and sometimes the point is to make one substance behave like another or to use a medium to subvert its own apparent implications.

Perception is a mutable interface between bodies and the world. It is mutable, in part, because neither bodies nor worlds are impermeable. It is also mutable because it is culturally constructed and inflected. People manage discrepancies between convictions and sensory engagements in different ways at different times and places.

Gassaway's image, in the context of the interior architecture of his church, its signage and decoration, and the sensory rituals engaged there, suggests that subjectivity is simultaneously physical, material, relational, and imaginal.[2] This brief consideration of

Parks's photograph serves here to draw attention to social practice and devotional bodies in ways taken up, in one manner or another, by the authors contributing to this second set of interludes. The photograph demonstrates the involvement of "powerful artifacts," bodies and things, in processes of sacralization or desecration.[3]

SALLY M. PROMEY

NOTES

1. Colleen McDannell, *Picturing Faith: Photography and the Great Depression* (New Haven, CT, and London: Yale University Press), 255–267. I am grateful to McDannell for calling my attention to these additional resources: Gordon Parks, *A Choice of Weapons* (Saint Paul, MN: Minnesota Historical Society Press, 1965, 2010); Hans A. Baer, *The Black Spiritual Movement* (Knoxville: University of Tennessee Press, 2001 [1984]); and Saint Clair Drake and Horace R. Cayton, *Black Metropolis: A Study of Negro Life in a Northern City* (Chicago: University of Chicago Press, 1993 [1945]).

2. Christopher Tilley, *The Materiality of Stone: Explorations in Landscape Phenomenology* (Oxford, UK, and New York: Berg, 2004), 4, in regard to the physicality of subjectivity.

3. Edward Linenthal, "The Instability of Sacred Space: Sacralization and Desecration," *Material Religion* 72 (2011): 279.

23

Acts of Conversion

Sanctification and the Senses of Race in the Art of Sister Gertrude Morgan

ELAINE Y. YAU

I n the prayer room of Sister Gertrude Morgan's Everlasting Gospel Mission, a
hand-painted sign would have summoned visitors to an awareness of Christ as the
"unseen host at every meal [and] the silent listener to every conversation" (Figure
23.1). Placed beneath a portrait of a bearded man assumed to picture the invisible yet
immanent Son of God, Morgan's sign displays her material and sensory piety.[1] For African American Sanctified Christians like Morgan, ritual engagement with the tangible, material world in faith practice might initially seem unusual; here was (and still
is) a liturgical tradition expressed primarily through ecstatic forms of singing, music,
and dance, climaxing at the moment of worshipers' possession by the Holy Spirit.
And so a believer would be transformed from unsaved sinner to righteous saint.[2]
These embodied responses to divine encounter rarely required transcription into enduring, material forms. Yet from 1960 to 1980 in New Orleans, Morgan produced a
body of paintings and drawings in response to her God's command like those adorning her whitewashed prayer room in Owen Murphy's photograph.

By Morgan's own account, her sanctification climaxed at the moment of her
"bridal crowning" in 1957.[3] Doctrinally, *sanctification* described the moment when the
Holy Spirit entered the believer and the lifetime thence devoted to realizing this-
worldly, spiritual perfection through successive invocations of this third member of
the Trinity. In addition to ecstatic worship, manifestations of the Sanctified life have
often included, for example, divine healing and the ability to speak in tongues. Prolif-
erating claims regarding the frequency of these expressions offered proof of spiritual
efficacy among Holiness and Pentecostal sects in the United States throughout the
late nineteenth and early twentieth centuries.[4] If the objective of the Sanctified life
was a perfect life free of sin—and, by extension, being filled with the love of God—
Morgan received a significant boost upon her marriage to Christ, signaling a new era

FIGURE 23.1. Owen Murphy, *Sister Morgan Using a Megaphone and Tapper to Assist in Her Service in the Prayer Room of the Everlasting Gospel Mission,* 1973. Gelatin silver print, 10 × 8 inches. New Orleans Museum of Art (gift of Owen Murphy), 91.65.

of "revelation" in which she was now ever closer to both of these "men." She asserted this reality up until her death in 1980.

The themes of divine calling, holiness and righteousness, and divinely altered identities recounted here are integral to narratives of Protestant sanctification, and yet they are narratives that have not been fully explored in relationship to Morgan's artistic practice. When Morgan received the command to paint around the same time as this pivotal event, what role did visuality play as part of her spiritual experience as the Bride of Christ? What do the sensory engagements of Morgan's spiritual transformation, indubitably coupled with Christ's divine anthropomorphosis, suggest about the artist's embodied racial and gender consciousness?[5] To begin addressing these questions, my chapter approaches her artistic practice as a material performance of Sanctified identity that demonstrates the flexibility of both Sanctified beliefs and racial discourse to recast human identities as divine.[6]

FIGURE 23.2. Sister Gertrude Morgan, *Jesus Christ the Lamb of God and His Little Bride,* ca. 1960s. Mixed media on paper, 9 × 11 inches. Collection of Gordon W. Bailey.

Jesus Christ the Lamb of God and His Little Bride (ca. 1960s), for example, is a rich elaboration of Morgan's divine relationship, with abundant text and striking portrayals of Christ himself. On each side of Morgan's halved compositions, the artist stands in bridal dress—she adopted this color daily in her everyday clothing as well— alongside Jesus, who is tuxedoed, mustachioed, and auburn haired, with peach-colored skin (Figure 23.2). Sweetness and propriety permeate this decidedly noncaricatured, nonsexualized image of a Sanctified embrace. At left, Jesus caresses the petite artist's face and shoulder. Though Morgan's sketchy application of color and wild-eyed expression might signify a gesture of coercion, the surrounding poetic couplets diffuse its force with their intermittent, gentle rhymes. Indeed the curvature of her writing and underdrawing marks suggest that she drew two portrait vignettes in pencil before adding the pen inscriptions and crayon ornamentation that secure the intent of the bluntly outlined forms:

> Jesus Christ the lamb of
> God and his little Bride.
> O is'nt that a lovly couple

he's got her Right By his side
in fact shes in his arms
to. he does his work
through her. You Know
he leads her wh-
ere ever she go.
he uses her
mouth to talk
through. You no its written in
the Bible he's
got some Body
to love him some one
that is Rel-
iable.[7]

Does Christ possess Morgan, or does Morgan possess the spirit of Christ? And what is the nature of this possession? On a narrative level, the poem-drawing suggests that the artist is firmly (and delightedly) ensconced in the embrace of her groom. "O is'nt that a lovly couple," Morgan remarks, pointing the reader to the object to which the demonstrative "that" refers: the "her" that Jesus has "got Right By his side." She further modifies their physical proximity to emphasize the depth of their embrace, for "in fact shes in his arms to." This mounting sense of closeness between Morgan and Christ intensifies with the lines of cursive script that knit them together, and in our process of viewing, the objectifying power of visual representation begins to warm with the movement of the artist's affective thoughts. That is, on another level of sensory and aesthetic perception, picture and writing launch both beings into intimate action and animation: "he does his work through her" and "leads her where ever she go," while her writing-as-action fulfills this work. Like the aqua-blue ground that supports them across the span of the page, Morgan resolutely becomes that "some Body ... Reliable," ready to assume his commission (to be in possession of him) and channel his voice (to be possessed by him).[8] Identities indwell one another here; Morgan's drawing-poem is both a representation *and* a performance of the "drama of embrace" in which self and other merge, cleave, and release in mutual fashion.[9] Sight may be the means by which Morgan awakens us to the implications of embrace ("O is'nt that a lovly couple"), but the mutuality she describes refers to another sensory basis: the "reciprocal motility of touch" occurring at a level of intimacy shared between "the great master and his darling wife."

We wouldn't be off the mark to be startled by the vocabulary of slavery invoked here (the harrowing history of black women sexually victimized by white slave owners does not allow us to overlook it), but we would do well, first, to take seriously her self-designation as "darling wife" and the fealty to Jesus and God the Father that it prompts:

> this is the great master
> and his darling wife.
> they are useing this wife
> for this great Kingdom to
> Brighten up their life. They
> wanted some Body to work
> through and its time for
> them to Be well honored
> and humored and well
> glorified too. I want
> to tell you darling
> dada the world
> is mad and it
> seem like
> they are
> mad with
> I and you. But I'm gone
> stand straight up not part the
> way cause I no you are
> able to carry me through.

Morgan's closing affirmation hinges upon belief in her "darling dada" and his unconditional acceptance and constant devotion to his "darling wife."[10] In these affectionately shared names we receive a "retrospective and recursive insight into the originating terms of the inspiration [of embrace] itself:" a poetics that preserves alterity through bonds of self-giving love sustained over and through the "mad" world that "seem like [it is] mad with I and you."[11] We cannot know the source of this "madness" with certainty, but the point to garner is the intimacy and security of a promise between two speakers that underpins the artwork's textual language.[12] This promise of "connection and intelligibility" inhabits poetic verbal form according to Susan Stewart; thus we sense in Morgan's hybrid lines of rhyme and speech, weighted with irresistibly falling intonations, a firmness in her devotional posture toward God and Christ.[13] We understand "great master," then, as a doxology directed to her intimate and divine interlocutors that declares her devotion.

If, as Stewart writes, "the good faith in intelligibility" accompanies poetic language and is the "means [by] which we recognize each other as speaking persons," the assertive visuality of Morgan's drawing goes beyond soliciting mere recognition.[14] It entreats viewers to recognize its creator as a volitional, sensing, and embodied person. The tension between surface and depth activated by Morgan's formal choices announces her creative presence. One such decision was to complete an interlocking "ground" of writing and picture interspersed with brick-red colored dashes. Words recede if we follow the jaunty turns of crayon marks, only to stretch and rise to the surface as they bend around figures and exert their claim for space and legibility. Morgan's juxtaposition of words and crayon ornamentation forms the bridge upon which perception of the inscribed surface travels from visuality to vitality and back again—between "I see" and "I sense." So the visually garrulous "ground" resounds with Morgan's performative and textual voice, oscillating between graphic notation and linguistic signification. And so it also forms the architecture of Morgan's vital self in which waxy pigment mortars each brick-word. Both rough and prolific, the word-wall divulges her creative agency and spiritual receptivity as she drags crayon across the paper's grain and presses pen's point into its surface.

The perceptual suspension commanded by Morgan's expressionism gains greater power when considered as a destabilizing act upon race's logic that fixes social identities into biological theory. Morgan's racial consciousness would be impossible to deny: not only did she come of age in the Jim Crow South and a black Baptist congregation, but her earlier writing makes reference to "a little black girl like me" and "the Black Man's day."[15] Yet rather than submit to the white taboos and assertions of illegitimacy attached to interracial marriage that permeated twentieth-century American imaginations, Morgan adopted an idea of a light-skinned Christ as her divine partner. Although a broader history of the visual culture of Christianity in New Orleans is necessary to refine my claims for Morgan's artistic intent, the flexibility of Sanctified belief to transcend bodily difference remains the focus of my argument. What Morgan experienced in her sanctification, and what her drawing-poem models as a matter of sensory perception grounded in the social reality of racist segregation, was the *possibility* of reciprocity between dynamically changing identities founded on the irreducible, embodied differences that race defined.[16]

Morgan makes such reciprocity visible in unlike formal symmetries. In the deliberate overlap of Christ's peach hand laid squarely across the brown "skin" of her face, Morgan rivets our gaze with her wide eyes, drawing attention to the tenderness of Christ's hands as he peers downward toward her. He "leads her where ever she go" in this half of the drawing-poem, and Morgan signals this submission of will by framing her visage with two forms of white: the racialized whiteness of Christ's hands and the tonal whiteness of shoe polish that colors his button-down shirt. Coexisting side by side is the symbolic purity coded as an additive color with the originary, transcendental power historically aligned with the "colorlessness" of whiteness. In this interracial coupling, Morgan wields the creative agency of whiteness to picture the incarnate Logos, the primal power that brings forth life, in a move that bends the flexible construct of racialized whiteness to ratify her identity as a black woman while sustaining her converted status as the Bride of Christ.[17] The poem-drawing is both action and reaction, with conviction, emotion, and intelligence suffusing it with—to borrow the rich phrase of Hortense Spillers—the artist-wife's "articulated syntactic particularity."[18]

The vignette at right, an inverse of that at left, completes this image of reciprocity and embodied opposition. The couple's rhyming postures signal the symbolic sameness achieved by the white shoe polish surrounding Morgan's face at left, while the contrasts between skin color and clothing preserve gender and racial difference. Race as a matter of blackness and whiteness stretches to its most fluid across the artwork's halves, its assumed stability loosed from the body. Words for skin and hue slip over and beneath one another in Morgan's belief in mutual spiritual cohabitation, never quite stabilizing into wholly discrete individuals amid the vibrant ground of words. To reaffix any of racism's exclusionary claims within the exposed field of its operations, one would have to struggle within its sensory oscillations. Within these contingencies of her characterizations, Morgan's drawing-poem materializes an aesthetic form that Stewart says "intends toward the future and is never closed by its reception. . . . [It depends on] our sense of the cohesion and ongoingness of persons in general . . . to which we adhere *even when we cannot know its ground.*"[19] Remaining open to knowing another's personhood without knowing the precise conditions of how such knowledge of identities will come—an uncertainty whose other intersubjective guise might be deemed emancipation and social determination—is a remarkable, poetic profession of Morgan's faith because it is an image of devotional relationship that can dispossess race of its biological determinism. We may be tempted to see *Jesus Christ the Lamb of God and His Little Bride* merely in its visual binary terms,[20] but its broader aesthetic manifests the character of poetry itself within its script, mobilizing the "good faith" of language through which we recognize persons as individual voices speaking across time. We, as present and future viewer-beholders, are included in Morgan's audience.

Thus we bear witness to the love between a prophet and her "great master" and to the breadth of her transformation, which now addresses us as a third party. Her signature, "Prophetess Morgan," functions as a sign of affection much like one that closes a love letter, consolidating the emotional response of her missive into her resolve to continue realizing her Sanctified identity as God's mouthpiece. Morgan's signature also enacts her self-possession with a new title defining the power transferred to her from Christ. It is the name from which *Sister* Morgan extends her commitment to the "great Kingdom" as a human voice for the divine. In its totality, the poem-drawing offers the artist's poignant and tangible assertion of interracial relations that cannot remain within the reciprocal relationship between Morgan and God but rushes—as the interpenetration of poetic, sensory engagements demonstrates—into the present of the reader-beholder, who bears the potential of its message.

NOTES

I thank Gordon W. Bailey for generously sharing his time, knowledge, collection, and passion for Sister Gertrude Morgan's artwork discussed here.

1. David Morgan, *Visual Piety: A History and Theory of Popular Religious Images* (Berkeley: University of California Press, 1998), 31.

2. Cheryl Sanders contrasts ecstatic forms with static forms of worship, in which worshipers are "at rest or in equilibrium," storing a potential energy that is released in kinetic, ecstatic forms. See Sanders, *Saints in Exile: The Holiness-Pentecostal Experience in African American Religion and Culture* (New York: Oxford University Press, 1996), esp. Chapter 3, "'In the Beauty of Holiness': Ethics and Aesthetics in the Worship of the Saints."

3. Gertrude Morgan, *A Poem of My Calling,* poem-drawing, Collection of the New Orleans Museum of Art, gift of Maria and Lee Friedlander, 2000.108.

4. Kathryn Lofton, *Oprah: The Gospel of an Icon* (Berkeley: University of California Press, 2011), 132–133.

5. The most comprehensive account of Morgan's life and work is in William A. Fagaly, *Tools of Her Ministry: The Art of Sister Gertrude Morgan* (New York: Rizzoli with the American Folk Art Museum, 2004).

6. Kymberly N. Pinder provides an overview, though brief, of race and gender and Morgan's art in her article "Sister Gertrude Morgan Everlasting," *Outsider* 10, no. 1 (Winter 2005): 16–20.

7. The line breaks, spelling, and language are consistent with the drawing, and "[*sic*]" should be understood throughout when Morgan's text is quoted.

8. Despite injunctions within the African American Baptist church and related Sanctified denominations such as the Church of God in Christ against women preaching, Morgan essentially took on the role of preaching once she settled in New Orleans. See *A Poem of My Calling* (note 3) as one example in which Morgan designates the operations of "preaching" as "teaching."

9. Miroslav Volf, "The Drama of Embrace," in *Exclusion and Embrace: A Theological Exploration of Identity, Otherness, and Reconciliation* (Nashville: Abingdon, 1996), 140–156.

10. Morgan's conception of recognition is quite different from Frantz Fanon's sobering reassessment of Hegel's master–slave dialectic of the exploitative conditions of colonial slavery; Morgan's "big dada," the "great master," seems not to "[scorn] the consciousness of the slave" or display mere "paternalistic curiosity." From her position of black femininity and Sanctified belief, Morgan's art elaborates Fanon's concluding appeal in *Black Skin, White Masks:* "Why not simply try to touch the other, feel the other, discover each other?" Her sensory and religious alternative counterbalances the revolutionary politics of the Martinican psychiatrist. Frantz Fanon, *Black Skin, White Masks,* trans. Richard Philcox (New York: Grove, 2008 [1952]), 195 fn. 10, 196, quote on 206.

11. Susan Stewart, *Poetry and the Fate of the Senses* (Chicago: University of Chicago Press, 2002), 199.

12. Fagaly, *Tools of Her Ministry,* 30, 62–63.

13. Stewart, *Poetry and the Fate of the Senses,* 332. My analysis relies on Stewart's approach to the poetic voice, especially her concern with the production of voiced presence through language's invocation of the senses. Especially helpful in considering Morgan's poetic and written voice is Stewart's discussion of the rhythmic repetition at the core of "invocatory activity" and the rhythmic irregularity associated with the speaking voice. Together these poetic juxtapositions are "animating features that add to the *embodiment* of voice in a poem," the "implicit tie of intelligibility between speaker and listener" (65 and 104, italics in original).

14. Stewart, *Poetry and the Fate of the Senses,* 105.

15. See "Ethiopia," from Morgan's collected papers in the collection of Kurt Gitter and Alice Rae Yelen, New Orleans. A majority of Morgan's papers, except for her letters to art historian Regenia Perry, remain undated. Copies are in the curatorial files at the Smithsonian American Art Museum, Smithsonian Institution, Washington, D.C.

16. Volf, "The Drama of Embrace," 146. He writes, "The equality and reciprocity that are at the heart of embrace can be reached only through self-sacrifice." He continues, writing that such self-sacrifice may "not [be] a positive good, but a necessary *via dolorosa* in a world of enmity and indifference toward the joy of reciprocal embrace. Such self-sacrifice is modeled on Christ's self-sacrifice, which is nothing but the mutuality of Trinitarian self-giving in encounter with the enemy."

17. Elizabeth Abel's argument concerning the construction of race through visible and linguistic signs in photography is central to my argument here: "The language of Jim Crow attempts to recruit the creative power of the originary word to articulate the foundational divisions of the universe out of a primal formlessness. . . . Often less creation than negation, less 'let there be' than 'let there not be,' this language performed a dual function: mapping the social world and exempting white people (the locution of choice) from the implications of that mapping by inflecting Genesis with a tradition of Christian dualism that aligns whiteness with the primacy of the word and the purity of soul that lodges only lightly in an embodied world." Abel, *Signs of the Times: The Visual Politics of Jim Crow* (Berkeley: University of California Press, 2011), 66.

18. Hortense Spillers, "'All the Things You Could Be by Now, If Sigmund Freud's Wife Was Your Mother': Psychoanalysis and Race," in *Female Subjects in Black and White: Race, Psychoanalysis, and Feminism,* ed. Elizabeth Abel (Berkeley: University of California Press, 1997), 145. My analysis builds on Spillers's conception of cultural analysis that interprets African American speech as part of the "substitutive identities" that break toward "new potentialities of becoming."

19. Stewart, *Poetry and the Fate of the Senses,* 331, italics mine. She continues, "This is the prophetic aspect of every poem, regardless of its theme."

20. The history of racialized seeing that would support this inclination is an issue that I intend to develop elsewhere.

24

Spiritual Complexions

On Race and the Body in the Moorish Science Temple of America

JUDITH WEISENFELD

When forty-six-year-old Alec Brown Bey appeared at his local Philadelphia draft board on April 27, 1942, he submitted to the same brief process undergone by an estimated thirteen million other men who were called that weekend in the fourth round of draft registration for World War II.[1] On the first part of the form, Brown Bey provided information about his place of birth, current residence, employment status, and contact person, all of which seemed straightforward (Figure 24.1). However, he found it difficult to feel represented fully and truthfully on the second part of the form, which required the draft registrar to provide a physical description of the registrant, including his height, weight, hair color, eye color, color of complexion, and race. Those people working as registrars no doubt inquired of the men sitting before them their exact height and weight. In this case, registrar George Richman indicated that Brown Bey was six feet two inches tall and weighed 175 pounds. How to characterize the color of a registrant's complexion was partly in the eye of the beholder, but the registrars were also provided with a fixed list of descriptors from which to select—sallow, light, ruddy, dark, freckled, light brown, dark brown, and black. The remaining section of the form called for the registrar to indicate the race of the registrant by checking the appropriate box from a list of options: White, Negro, Oriental, Indian, or Filipino. Brown Bey's conflict in completing the draft registration process stemmed from his feeling that almost none of the racial options listed on this second part of the form conformed to his understanding of himself.

A native of South Carolina, Brown Bey had joined the millions of Southern blacks moving north in the 1920s and 1930s, who, upon arrival, had also met black immigrants from the Caribbean, themselves looking for expanded economic, political, and social opportunities in the urban North of the United States.[2] Although migrants did not generally set out for the North, or immigrants for the United States, with the

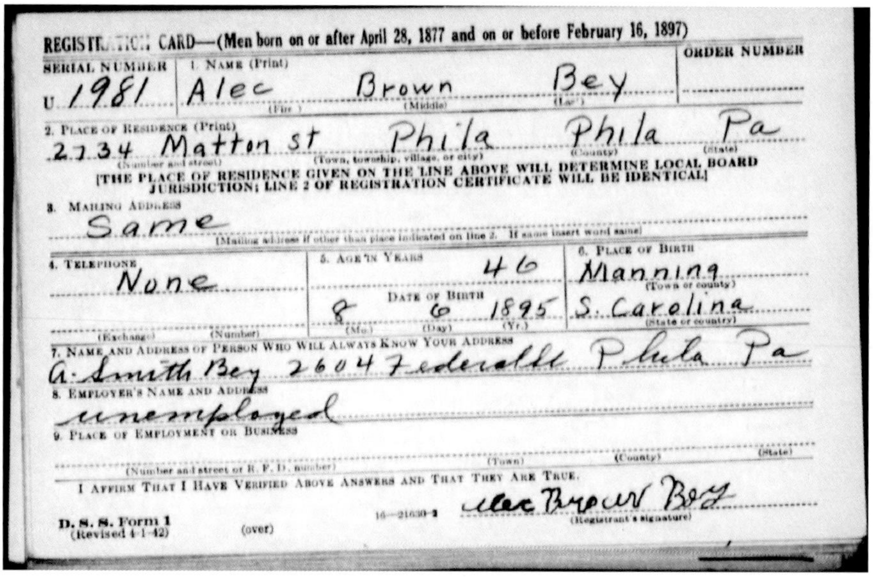

FIGURE 24.1. The first page of Alec Brown Bey's World War II draft registration card. U.S. World War II Draft Registration Cards, Serial Number U1981, Local Board No. 51, Philadelphia, Pennsylvania, April 27, 1942. National Archives and Records Administration, National Personnel Records Center, Saint Louis, Missouri.

express purpose of seeking new religious options, they nevertheless encountered, and many contributed to, a diversifying urban religious culture. To be sure, in terms of numbers of people involved, the most significant religious transformations among African Americans during this period known as the Great Migration took place within Christianity with the rise in participation in black Protestant churches in Northern cities, the increasing importance among these churches of Holiness and Pentecostal churches, and the development of the storefront church.[3] But the religious changes that immigration and migration spurred were not limited to varieties of African American Christianity. In this period and in these urban contexts, people of African descent began, in noticeable numbers, to establish and participate in movements outside of Protestantism, and many turned for spiritual sustenance to theologies that provided new ways of thinking about racial identity and the religious body, sacred history and geography, ritual life, communal structures, and corporate sacred destiny.

These groups were sensational and often controversial additions to the religious landscape of the urban North, with their challenges to established religious orthodoxy, their common focus on a charismatic leader with claims to divinity or prophetic powers, and their members' unusual ideas about their racial identities. Indeed many a Protestant minister declared a "holy war" on the leaders of the new movements, and cultural commentators criticized their dramatic flair as evidence of fraud and manipulation. Writing about the impact of these new religious options on life in New York, one black journalist declared Harlem "the Mecca of Fakers."[4] But for people like Alec Brown Bey who joined these groups, the appeal lay not in the sensationalism that so many branded fakery as in the combination of a powerful and persuasive narrative of intertwined religious and racial identity with the experience of a changed sense of self in the corporate past, communal present, and sacred future. Members experienced this transformed identity in emotive ways, proclaiming feelings of pride in their newly learned true histories and sacred duties but also in their bodies as religious sites, for these alternative understandings of self and community charted new sensory experiences for them as racialized and religious beings.

It is almost certain that when Alec Brown Bey arrived in Philadelphia in the 1930s, his name was simply Alec Brown and that, at that time, he would not have minded being included in the category "Negro," either in daily life or on an official government document such as a draft registration card. But sometime between settling in Philadelphia and appearing before the draft board in 1942, Brown had become a member of the Moorish Science Temple of America (MSTA). Through his encounter with members of this religious movement, which had been founded in 1925 in Chicago by the prophet Noble Drew Ali, himself a migrant from the South, Brown became convinced that he was not a Negro and that to think of and refer to himself as such violated a divine command.[5] To signal his acceptance of the truth of the MSTA's theology, Brown took back what Drew Ali taught was his "true tribal name" of Bey and followed his prophet's call to return to his original religion of Islam.[6] In accord with his beliefs about his religious and racial identity, he asked draft registrar George Richman to amend the preprinted government form so that he could be represented properly. He was *not a Negro*, he told Richman, but a *Moorish American*, a literal descendant of Moroccans although born in America, and, racially, Asiatic.

The surviving draft registration document reveals the depth of Brown Bey's commitment to this religiously derived racial identity and hints at what must have been a tense bureaucratic transaction as he tried to persuade Richman to contravene the accepted American racial categories printed on the card. In this case, Richman crossed out "Filipino" to write in and then check "Moorish American." In many instances, the registrars encountering members of the MSTA who asked that they be represented as Moors or Moorish American made the amendment in relation to the preprinted category "Negro." In others cases, the registrars inserted "Moorish" or "Moorish American" in relation to the racial category "Oriental" that was preprinted on the form, no doubt in response to the Moors' assertion of their Asiatic racial identity.[7] Alec Brown Bey was among the many men who were successful in convincing the registrar to amend the government form and characterize him as Moorish American. However, registrar Richman inserted his own perspective, noting in the section of the form that required him to affirm the truth of the information presented, "Believe he is a negro" (Figure 24.2).[8]

Members of other religious movements that emerged in the black "cities within cities" of the urban North asserted racial identities that differed from the conventional racial taxonomy in force in the United States at the time, and we see evidence of these commitments on their draft registration cards, which have been altered in ways similar to those of members of the MSTA.[9] Joseph Nathaniel Beckles, who was born in Barbados, British West Indies, and immigrated to New York City in 1911, had himself declared an Ethiopian Hebrew on his draft card, as did Walter Workman Walcott, who also came to New York from Barbados.[10] At some point between his arrival in the United States and his participation in the draft registration decades later, Walcott had come to consider himself an Ethiopian Hebrew and had joined Rabbi Wentworth Matthew's Commandment Keepers Congregation in New York. When he registered for the draft during World War II Walcott, now a naturalized citizen of the United States, insisted that his correct racial name be indicated on the form. He asked draft registrar Miriam Levy to cross out "Negro," next to which she had already placed a

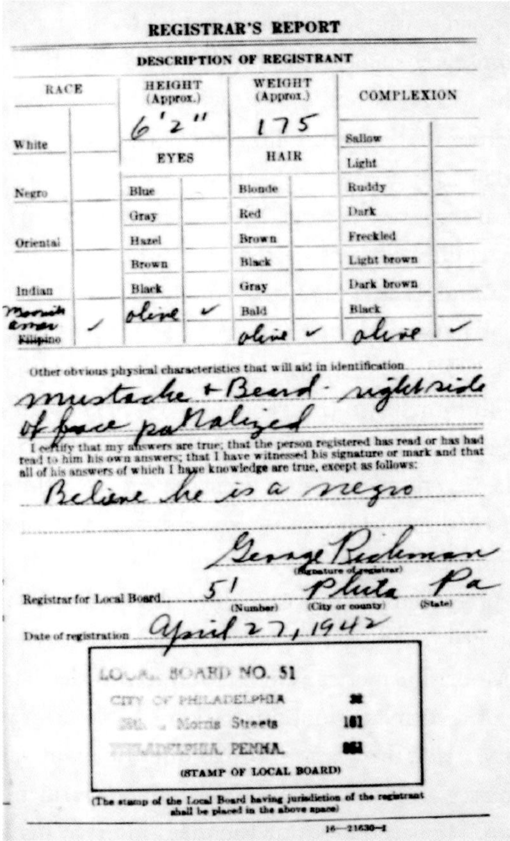

REGISTRAR'S REPORT

DESCRIPTION OF REGISTRANT

RACE		HEIGHT (Approx.)		WEIGHT (Approx.)		COMPLEXION	
White		6'2"		175		Sallow	
		EYES		HAIR		Light	
Negro		Blue		Blonde		Ruddy	
		Gray		Red		Dark	
Oriental		Hazel		Brown		Freckled	
		Brown		Black		Light brown	
Indian		Black		Gray		Dark brown	
Moorish American	✓	olive	✓	Bald		Black	
Filipino				olive	✓	olive	✓

Other obvious physical characteristics that will aid in identification

mustache + Beard · right side of face paralized

I certify that my answers are true; that the person registered has read or has had read to him his own answers; that I have witnessed his signature or mark and that all of his answers of which I have knowledge are true, except as follows:

Believe he is a negro

George Bickman
(Signature of registrar)

Registrar for Local Board 51 (Number) Phila (City or county) Pa (State)

Date of registration April 27, 1942

LOCAL BOARD NO. 51
CITY OF PHILADELPHIA
... Morris Streets
PHILADELPHIA, PENNA.
(STAMP OF LOCAL BOARD)

(The stamp of the Local Board having jurisdiction of the registrant shall be placed in the above space)

16—21630—1

FIGURE 24.2. The second page of Alec Brown Bey's World War II draft registration card showing his desire to be represented racially as a Moorish American and his hair color, eye color, and complexion listed as "olive." U.S. World War II Draft Registration Cards, Serial Number U1981, Local Board No. 51, Philadelphia, Pennsylvania, April 27, 1942. National Archives and Records Administration, National Personnel Records Center, Saint Louis, Missouri.

check mark, and write in "Ethiopian Hebrew," which she did.[11] He was, by this time, a committed member of Matthew's congregation and would soon graduate from the Ethiopian Hebrew Rabbinical School in Harlem and be "elevated to the office of the First Order of the Levitical Priesthood."[12] Also graduating from the rabbinical school that day was Esther Balfour, a West Indian immigrant who had arrived in New York in 1917. Trained in Jamaica as a teacher, Balfour was working as a finisher in a clothing factory but, as a result of her religious education, was able to serve as an advanced Hebrew teacher at the rabbinical school. Balfour's and Walcott's stories stand out because their degree of commitment led them to seek extensive religious education, but they were not alone in having reformulated their religioracial identity in this way.

Perfect Endurance, a member of Father Divine's Peace Mission Movement who had migrated from Georgia, sat before a draft registrar in New York that same April weekend that Alec Brown Bey did in Philadelphia and also made a religious assertion about race.[13] In this case, Perfect Endurance, who had changed his name to reflect his new spiritual state, acted on Father Divine's preaching that "thoughts are things" and that race is a negative product of the mind. Because he had set aside his old self and now understood himself in *nonracial* terms, he asked that the draft registrar indicate his true race, which he considered "Human." The registrar complied, inserting "Human" in the box in which "Negro" had been printed. When Faithful Solomon (Figure 24.3), an immigrant from Barbados and also a member of the Peace Mission Movement in New York, followed the movement's theological imperative to reject racial categories in favor of common humanity, the draft registrar refused to write in what he had requested. Their exchange gives us a sense of the sorts of conflict such a seemingly innocuous assertion could generate. Instead of doing as Solomon had asked, she wrote at the bottom of the form, "Says he is of the human race, but is obviously Negro," as if the two were mutually exclusive (Figure 24.4).[14] Father Divine himself might actually have agreed that one could not be a Negro and human given his teaching that racial categories come not from God but from "the other fellow."[15] In his view, to accept Negro identity (or any racial identity) cut people off from connection to God's divine being. In declaring themselves human beings during the draft registration process, Perfect Endurance, Faithful Solomon, and other members of the Peace Mission Movement were engaging in a practice that enabled them to remain spiritually connected to God.

Registration for the draft was one among many arenas of public contestation for members of groups such as the MSTA, various congregations of Ethiopian Hebrews, the Nation of Islam, and Father Divine's Peace Mission Movement, all of which promoted new ways of thinking about black identity in early twentieth-century America. Members of these groups struggled to be identified and recognized in ways they felt were true to a divine command when serving in the military, voting, applying for drivers' licenses, providing information to census enumerators, and registering their chil-

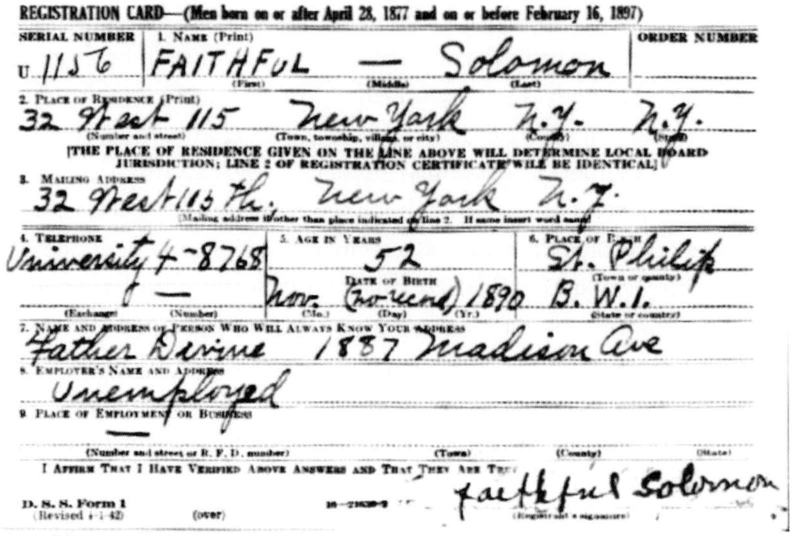

FIGURE 24.3. The first page of the World War II draft registration card of Faithful Solomon, a member of Father Divine's Peace Mission Movement in New York. U.S. World War II Draft Registration Cards, Serial Number U1156, Local Board No. 48, New York, New York, April 26, 1942. National Archives and Records Administration, National Personnel Records Center, Saint Louis, Missouri.

FIGURE 24.4. The second page of Faithful Solomon's World War II draft registration card. Registrar Elizabeth Alexander refused to characterize his race as "human," as he requested, although it appears that she erased a check mark she had placed next to "Negro," a term members of Father Divine's movement rejected, along with all other racial terms. U.S. World War II Draft Registration Cards, Serial Number U1156, Local Board No. 48, New York, New York, April 26, 1942. National Archives and Records Administration, National Personnel Records Center, Saint Louis, Missouri.

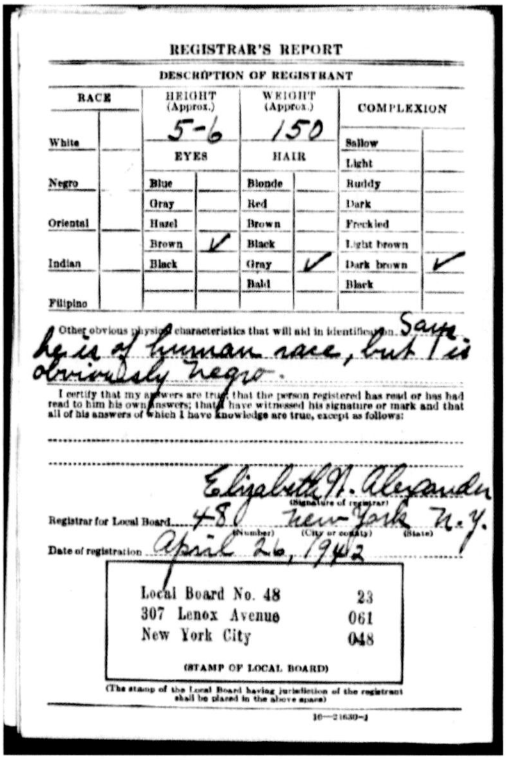

dren in public schools. The assertions by people like Alec Brown Bey of alternative religioracial identities were not isolated acts of whimsy but instances of numerous individuals challenging the power of the state to define them and privileging, instead, divinely given knowledge of what they understood to be their true identities. Central to their transformed senses of self was a commitment to religious and racial identity as interconnected and co-constituting. Indeed, we cannot begin to understand the racial identities of such men and women without exploring their religious identities, and we cannot take full account of how they understood themselves religiously without taking seriously their racial self-understandings and representations.

Much of the scholarship on these groups seeks to evaluate their *religious authenticity,* asking questions about the degree to which they might be considered "really" Muslim or Jewish, for example. And indeed, much recent work has sought to take seriously the religious strivings of the leaders and members of these groups and to do so in a way that makes them legible according to recognizable theological rubrics. Their *racial* claims—that they were Moorish, Asiatic, Ethiopian Hebrew, or even raceless, for example—have not fared as well, with scholars often interpreting such racial reformulations through religious means as the denial of a real, obvious, and fixed racial location in favor of an imagined identity (that is, taking up a position not unlike that of the draft registrar who responded to what had been written on Brown Bey's card by adding, "Believe he is a Negro"). However, the founders, leaders, and members of these groups believed that their racial and religious identities were co-constituted, and, as a result, scholars cannot simply bracket the racial claims that members of the groups made in an attempt to make their movements legible in terms familiar in religious studies.

The draft registration process reveals the importance of the use of correct terminology to members of the MSTA like Alec Brown Bey to represent their understandings of their divinely given identities, including their true individual and group names. But they did more than make verbal assertions, because they understood their bodies as integral to experiencing and projecting those identities. It was one thing to believe that one is and has always been an Asiatic Moor, for example, but for members of these groups, living as such required more than an intellectual commitment. The adoption of a style of dress that Noble Drew Ali prescribed as appropriate for Moors was the most public embodied approach that members took to expressing their belief in their Moorish American and Muslim identity. Everyday Moorish garb consisted, for men, of a red fez and plain suit, and for women, a turban and plain dress. On special occasions, such as the January 8 celebration of the prophet's birthday, members adopted more elaborate costumes that drew on both the sartorial style of Freemasonry and the popular Orientalism of 1920s American culture (Figure 24.5).[16] Moorish Americans sometimes paraded in their garb to solidify their own commitments and project their identity to those outside the group. This form of public,

FIGURE 24.5. Members of the Moorish Science Temple of America posing before the meeting place during their annual meeting, October 1928, with founder and prophet Noble Drew Ali standing in the first row, fifth from left, and flanked by other leaders of the movement dressed in Moorish garb. Photographs and Prints Division, Schomburg Center for Research in Black Culture, The New York Public Library, Astor, Lenox, and Tilden Foundations.

embodied religious expression—the act of clothing the body in dress that matched one's divinely given religioracial identity—was vitally important to members.[17] Dress was not the only embodied way that members of groups promoting alternative religioracial knowledge, including the MSTA, expressed and experienced what they took to be their essential and true identities. The adoption of new names, reformed food practices, and distinctive approaches to health and healing were among the important means that individuals employed to inhabit their connection to the new religious narratives of racial identity that these groups promoted. In addition to helping to locate individuals firmly and fully in the sensory world of their religioracial identities, these varied performances served as significant ways of creating community among those who accepted the groups' claims.

Such embodied performances of religioracial identity undoubtedly engaged the contemporary politics of the black body, speaking to the myriad ways that white

Americans' ideas about race and the body helped to shape the landscape of possibility for black participation in American public, political, and social life. However, in addition to acknowledging the political ramifications of such practices, it is critical to understand them as religious acts and as reflecting members' apprehension of their bodies as significant sites of interface between the divine and divine knowledge, on the one hand, and sacred communities, on the other. Thus choosing to dress as a "Moorish American" was not simply a matter of expressing a political opposition to commonplace or legal definitions of race in the United States but also served important religious functions by making the body into one that was both religiously and racially accessible to the sacred in a form the individual understood to be its true nature. MSTA member Sister Whitehead El underscored the religious significance of knowledge of self, writing, "Allah sent us a prophet and sent him in time with a Holy message which is Divine. He came to let the Asiatics of America know that they are of the ancient family of the Moors. . . . In 1925 the Prophet said, 'I have mended the broken wires and have connected them with the Higher powers.'"[18] Thus clothing oneself as a Moorish American Muslim, for example, restored the true self and renewed a connection to the divine that opened up new religiously grounded sensory experiences.

Although there was much in common in the various groups' approaches to race, religion, and the body, there were striking elements of the MSTA's theology that led to unique understandings of the power of the body as a sensory conduit to the divine. Like the Nation of Islam, various Ethiopian Hebrew congregations, and Father Divine's Peace Mission Movement, the MSTA rejected the term *Negro,* the utility of which as a racial category was the subject of heated debate in broader black culture in this period.[19] Those broader discussions often focused on finding a term that would command respect in American society and aid blacks in the struggle for civil rights. Although such concerns had an impact on members of the MSTA, their impetus for adopting what they believed to be the correct racial name was a desire to submit to the divine order of creation. For them, a race name did more than position groups politically; it shaped the individual self and made it possible to achieve a common sacred destiny. As one member from Philadelphia declared, "Take off the slavery name 'Negro' and give us our God-given name, Moorish-American, and let us be men among men."[20] Knowledge of one's true ancestry restored a connection to the divine, and members of the MSTA embodied and enacted that knowledge through adopting a new (true) name and the correct style of dress. Central to such embodied expression was a commitment to disrupting the expected relationship in the context of America's racial taxonomy between the surface of the body and racial identity. Dark skin and Negro racial identity were not absolute correspondences, members of these groups insisted. Although such embodied practices were important for the movement's public presentation to nonmembers, they were just as powerfully an integral part of daily religious expression. As we have seen, members of the group commonly used the terms

Moorish American, Moorish, and *Asiatic* to describe their conjoined religioracial identity, and many, like Alec Brown Bey, insisted in public contexts that these were the only appropriate racial designations.

In addition to providing a new narrative of racial history that led members to the conclusion that they were Moorish Americans and that Islam was their true religion, Noble Drew Ali provided them with a theology of skin color that became a powerful tool for reorienting their religioracial identities and recalibrating their sensory realities. Accounting for members' use of the term *olive* to describe their complexions as well as other aspects of their physical appearance is central to understanding the religious meaning they made of skin color. Recall that on his draft registration card Alec Brown Bey had himself characterized racially as a Moorish American and that the registrar provided his own sense that this was *not,* in fact, Brown Bey's true racial identity. Brown Bey asked for additional changes to the draft card that reflected the MSTA's theology of skin color, persuading the registrar to describe his eyes, hair, and complexion as "olive," which required inserting an additional category on the preprinted form for each. In his assertion during the draft registration process that his complexion was olive, Brown Bey was not necessarily insisting on an accurate correspondence between the terminology on the registration card and his own visual apprehension of his skin color. Rather, he was making a theological statement, and draft registrar Richman was unlikely to have known that he was engaged in a conflict over Brown Bey's body as a religious site rather than simply struggling to make the description match what was before his eyes.

Brown Bey's understanding of his skin color as a theological principle comes into particularly sharp focus because he declared that every part of his body for which a color description was required should be understood as olive. He was not alone in making such an assertion, and in most other cases, the draft card reveals the difference between the registrar's opinion about the registrant's skin color and the man's own sense of his identity. For example, Albert Malone Bey, a migrant from Georgia to Chicago, persuaded the draft registrar to characterize his complexion as olive even though she had already placed a check mark next to "Black" on the card. In the end, she crossed out the preprinted description and wrote in "olive." In Philadelphia, draft registrar Hazel W. Anderson complied with James Dean El's request to be represented as an olive-skinned Moorish American. However, she added, "Insisted they are Moorish American descent. I would classify race as Negro, complexion as dark brown."[21]

Members of the MSTA's understanding of their skin color as olive derived from a cluster of theological commitments promoted by Noble Drew Ali. It was part of a daily enactment of Drew Ali's teaching that their "Divine name" was "Asiatic" and that they were the literal descendants of Moroccans although born in America.[22] Drew Ali argued that Moors had been "marked" by Europeans with the false names of "Negro, Black, Colored, and Ethiopia" [sic] and that these "nick names" kept the truth of their identity hidden.[23] European renaming or misnaming was simply that, Drew Ali contended, and did nothing to change the essential nature of the descendants of the inhabitants of Africa. "What your ancient fathers were, you are today without doubt or contradiction," he declared in the *Holy Koran of the Moorish Science Temple*. "There is no one who is able to change man from the descendant nature of his forefathers; unless his power extends beyond the great universal Creator Allah Himself."[24] That the use of special language to describe skin color would follow from the argument for Moorish descent was not assured. For Drew Ali and his followers, understanding the truth of their Asiatic identity involved both mind and body. Declarations of olive complexion spoke of ancestry and divine chosenness but also of a special, embodied connection to the divine. Drew Ali preached that the angels who "guard the Holy City of MECCA today to keep the unbelievers away" are also now called Asiatics and that Moorish Americans have "the same father and mother" as these angels, who have "olive" skin.[25]

MSTA members' belief that they were olive-skinned Asiatics who were part of an angelic lineage enjoined them, regardless of what beholders thought they saw, to declare that their color was olive. Such assertions frequently brought Moorish Americans into conflict when they enacted their theology of skin color in daily life. For example, Oscar Smith-Bey, Mary Smith-Bey, and their seven children were living in Philadelphia when census enumerator John McCartney visited them. At the bottom of their census sheet he wrote, "These two families," referring to the Smith-Beys and their neighbors down the street (also Beys), "refused to give information when I refused to mark their color Olive." He then noted that he had gone to the Census Bureau to find out what to do, and someone there had supplied him with information to complete the form. In the column on the census sheet in which the enumerator was required to indicate each individual's "color or race," one can see the traces of the thirteen times McCartney had, in fact, entered "olive." But the Bureau of the Census required that the sheets be submitted with only one of the state-recognized racial categories indicated. Moreover, in 1930 census enumerators were instructed to record all people with African lineage as "Negro," regardless of their self-perception or family history. In the end, McCartney or his supervisors erased "olive" and replaced it with "Negro."[26] Ten years later, census enumerator Mollie Horowitz was collecting information in the Brooklyn neighborhood of Brownsville when she encountered twenty-four members of the MSTA living in two adjacent buildings on Livonia Avenue. Although it is impossible to reconstruct what transpired as she visited these households of people named Bey and El, the census sheet makes clear that they persuaded her to write "olive" in the column that asked for "color or race."[27] Official records contain evidence of many similar instances in which MSTA members deployed their theological understanding of their skin color as olive as the primary way of understanding their racial identity.[28]

To engage fully the religious conviction of someone like Alec Brown Bey that his skin color, eyes, and hair were olive and to do so in the face of all countervailing evidence is to take a step toward entering the sensory and embodied experience of members of black religious movements that promoted alternative religioracial identities. In the case of the MSTA, members refashioned the black body, which they saw as having been mischaracterized as Negro, not only through changes in names and clothing—both of which were essential to suture individuals to their new/true history, religion, and community identity—but also through reinterpreting the very surface and substance of the skin. The MSTA's theology of skin color and members' enactment of their commitment to it provides powerful evidence of alternative ways of racializing religion in the American context. It is important to remember that racial construction has taken place not only through discursive means and *ideas* about bodies and difference but also through the *senses*, and consequently has shaped embodied experience. Contestation with nonmembers over race names and descriptors of complexion in such bureaucratic transactions as draft registration and census enumeration reveals how members rejected the notion that there was a discrepancy between their spiritual understanding and sensory experience of their identities and others' visual apprehension.

NOTES

1. I am interested neither in the draft registration process as such nor in military service in particular, but focus here on the archive of draft registration cards as an unexpected window into how members of the Moorish Science Temple and other black religious movements of the early twentieth century formulated and projected ideas about race, religion, the body, and sensory experiences of racialized embodiment. Alec Brown Bey, U.S. World War II Draft Registration Card (US-WWII-DR), Serial Number U1981, Local Board No. 51, Philadelphia, Pennsylvania, April 27, 1942. On the number of men registering in this round, see *New York Times*, April 28, 1942. All World War II draft registration card and census citations are drawn from the Ancestry.com database.

2. Brown Bey appears in the 1940 census in Philadelphia as living at 273 Manton Street with his wife, Georgia, and three stepsons. Judging by their names, at least three families in adjacent houses also contained members of the Moorish Science Temple. 1940 U.S. Federal Census, Philadelphia County, Pennsylvania, Philadelphia City, Enumeration District 51-1348, Household 57; 1930 U.S. Federal Census, Philadelphia County, Pennsylvania, Philadelphia City, Enumeration District 51-123, Dwelling 12.

3. See, for example, Wallace D. Best, *Passionately Human, No Less Divine: Religion and Culture in Black Chicago, 1915–1952* (Princeton, NJ: Princeton University Press, 2005), and Milton C. Sernett, *Bound for the Promised Land: African American Religion and the Great Migration* (Durham, NC: Duke University Press, 1997).

4. Edgar M. Grey, "Harlem—the Mecca of Fakers," *New York Amsterdam News*, March 30, 1927. See also Ira De A. Reid, "Let Us Prey," *Opportunity* (September 1926): 274–278. On ministers' campaigns against these newer religious movements, see, for example, "Detroit Clergy Wars on Cults after Sacrifice," *Baltimore Afro-American*, December 3, 1932, 19, and "Jersey Pastor Wars on Cults," *Chicago Defender*, October 28, 1933, 4.

5. Drew Ali told his followers that he had been born Timothy Drew in North Carolina on January 8, 1886, and that he had obtained knowledge of the Moors' true history, identity, and religion when he was initiated into ancient mysteries in Egypt. He began his public ministry in Newark, New Jersey, in the first decade of the twentieth century and in the early 1920s moved to Chicago, where he founded the MSTA. Drew Ali died in 1929, and the movement split into a number of factions. See Michael A. Gomez, *Black Crescent: The Experience and Legacy of African Muslims in the Americas* (Cambridge, UK: Cambridge University Press, 2005); Edward E. Curtis IV, *Islam in Black America: Identity, Liberation, and Difference in African-American Islamic Thought* (Albany: State University of New York Press, 2002); and Peter Lamborn Wilson, *Sacred Drift: Essays on the Margins of Islam* (San Francisco: City Lights Books, 1993).

6. Members of the MSTA also adopted the name El as a "true tribal name" and considered Ali an original surname of the Moors. Drew Ali taught, "With us all members must proclaim their nationality and we are teaching our people that they may know they are a part . . . of this said government and know that they are not Negroes, Colored Folks, Black People, or Ethiopians, because these names were given to slaves by slave holders in 1779 and lasted until 1865 during the time of slavery, but this is a new era of time now, and all men must proclaim their free national name to be recognized by the government in which they live and the nations of the earth. [T]his is the reason why Allah the Great God of the universe ordained Noble Drew Ali the prophet to redeem his people from their sinful ways. The Moorish Americans are descendants of the ancient Moabites whom [*sic*] inhabited the North Western and South Western shores of Africa." "Moorish Holy Temple of Science, The Divine Constitution and By-Laws," n.d. [between 1926 and 1928], Moorish Science Temple of America Collection, Schomburg Center for Research in Black Culture, New York Public Library.

7. For example, on the draft cards of Conley El, a migrant from South Carolina to Brooklyn, and Solomon Lovett Bey, a migrant from Georgia to Chicago, among others, registrars wrote the words "Moorish American" next to "Negro." John Knight El, a migrant from South Carolina to Trenton, New Jersey, asked to be characterized racially as a Moorish American, and the registrar wrote this in next to the preprinted category "Oriental." Conley El, US-WWII-DR, Serial Number U2200, Local Board No. 205, Brooklyn, New York, April 27, 1942; Solomon Lovett Bey, US-WWII-DR, Serial Number U1953, Local Board No. 64, Chicago, Illinois, April 27, 1942; and John Knight El, US-WWII-DR, Serial Number U1583, Local Board No. 3, Trenton, New Jersey, April 25, 1942.

8. There are similar cases of draft registrars complying with a registrant's request to be represented racially as Moorish or Moorish American but inserting their own belief that the man "is a Negro." See, for example, Alphonso Bentley Bey, US-WWII-DR, Serial Number U2153, Local Board No. 13, Philadelphia, Pennsylvania, April 27, 1942, and S. J. Horsey Bey, US-WWII-DR, Serial Number U1776, Local Board No. 13, Philadelphia, Pennsylvania, April 27, 1942.

9. For discussions of some of these groups, see Edward E. Curtis IV and Danielle Brune Sigler, eds., *The New Black Gods: Arthur Huff Fauset and the Study of African American Religions* (Bloomington: Indiana University Press, 2009), and Arthur Huff Fauset, *Black Gods of the Metropolis: Negro Religious Cults of the Urban North* (Philadelphia: University of Pennsylvania Press, 2001 [1944]).

10. Joseph Nathaniel Beckles, US-WWII-DR, Serial Number U1274, Local Board No. 79, Brooklyn, New York, April 25, 1942. See also William Lile Braithwaite, US-WWII-DR, Serial Number U366, Local Board No. 54, New York, New York, April 27, 1942, and Elder Isaac Roberson, US-WWII-DR, Serial Number U1339, Local Board No. 64, New York, New York, April 26, 1942. On the history of black Jews in the United States, see Jacob S. Dorman, *Chosen People: The Rise of American Black Israelite Religion* (New York: Oxford University Press, 2012), and James E.

Landing, *Black Judaism: Story of an American Movement* (Durham, NC: Carolina Academic Press, 2002).

11. Walter Walcott, US-WWII-DR, Serial Number U1225, Local Board No. 63, New York, New York, April 27, 1942. Walcott arrived in the United States in 1919 and was naturalized in 1933. He died in Brooklyn in June of 1972. U.S. Petition for Citizenship No. 198034, January 5, 1933, and Social Security Death Index No. 101-16-4197.

12. *New York Amsterdam News,* June 8, 1944.

13. Father Divine founded this group, which by the mid-1930s was called the Peace Mission Movement, around the core principle that he was God in a body. Probably born in Maryland as George Baker, Divine also joined the African American migration to the urban North and would gather many followers from among the new urbanites as well as from among West Indian immigrants and white Americans. In the tradition of the New Thought movements, Divine preached that he had come to free people from the material consequences of negative attitudes of the mind—"thoughts are things," he taught—and he promised health and eternal life in this world to true believers who set aside their old selves. Those of his followers who committed themselves to him fully also devoted themselves to living communally in sex-segregated, celibate communities called Kingdoms. *Spoken Word,* January 4, 1936. For biographical information on Father Divine, see Jill Watts, *God, Harlem U.S.A.: The Father Divine Story* (Berkeley: University of California Press, 1992).

14. Perfect Endurance, US-WWII-DR, Serial Number U548, Local Board No. 48, New York, New York, April 27, 1942, and Faithful Solomon, US-WWII-DR, Serial Number U1156, Local Board No. 48, New York, New York, April 26, 1942.

15. *Spoken Word,* September 8, 1936, 20.

16. See Susan Nance, "Respectability and Representation: The Moorish Science Temple, Morocco, and Black Public Culture in 1920s Chicago," *American Quarterly* 54, no. 4 (December 2002): 623–659.

17. The MSTA was not alone in employing dress to project an alternative religioracial identity in public. For example, members of Arnold Josiah Ford's Congregation Beth B'nai Abraham used dress to experience and express their identity as Ethiopian Hebrews.

18. *Moorish Guide* 1, no. 3 (September 13, 1928).

19. See, for example, the lively random-draw contest conducted in 1932 by the *Baltimore Afro-American* to "settle this business once and for all as to the best race designation." Over the course of five weeks, readers sent telegrams to cast votes for their preferred racial descriptor in the hopes that they would win a cash prize should the statement they submitted explaining their position be selected in a random draw. In the end, the paper received more than six thousand votes, and while "'Negro' garnered the majority of votes, the debate was lively with the term Colored coming in second and readers offering other options including Moorish American, American, Polynationals, Omnationals, and Black." *Baltimore Afro-American,* February 27, 1932. See also *Baltimore Afro-American,* February 6 and 13; March 5, 12, 19, and 26; and April 2, 1932.

20. *Baltimore Afro-American,* March 26, 1932, 21.

21. Albert Malone Bey, US-WWII-DR, Serial Number U1976, Local Board No. 61, Chicago, Illinois, April 27, 1942; James Dean El, US-WWII-DR, Serial Number U378, Local Board No. 19, Philadelphia, Pennsylvania, April 27, 1942.

22. "Koran Questions for Moorish Americans," n.d., Moorish Science Temple of America Collection, 1. This material was first published in a column called "The Voice of the Prophet" in *Moorish Guide* 1, no. 3 (September 14, 1928). Drew Ali included a broader group of peoples than Moroccans under the heading "Asiatic." In a section of the *Holy Koran of the Moorish Science Tem-*

ple of America headed "The Divine Origin of the Asiatic Nations," he wrote, "The key of civilization was and is in the hands of the Asiatic nations. The Moorish, who were the ancient Moabites, and the founders of the Holy City of Mecca. The Egyptians, who were the Hamitites, and of a direct descendant of Mizraim, the Arabians, the seed of Hagar, Japanese and Chinese. The Hindoos of India, the descendants of the ancient Canaanites, Hittites and Moabites from the land of Canaan. The Asiatic nations and countries in North, South and Central America; the Moorish Americans and Mexicans in North America, Brazilians, Argentineans and Chileans in South America. Columbians, Nicaraguans and natives of San Salvador in Central America, etc. All of these are Moslems. The Turks are the true descendants of Hagar, who are the chief protectors of the Islamic Creed of Mecca; beginning from Mohammed the First, the founder of the uniting of Islam, by the command of the Great Universal God—Allah." *Holy Koran of the Moorish Science Temple of America* 45:2–7.

23. "Koran Questions," 5.

24. *Holy Koran of the Moorish Science Temple of America* 47:10–11. The majority of the MSTA's *Holy Koran* is drawn from two texts: Levi [Dowling], *The Aquarian Gospel of Jesus the Christ: The Philosophic and Practical Basis of the Religion of the Aquarian Age of the World and of the Church Universal* (London: L. N. Fowler, 1911), and *Unto Thee I Grant* (San Francisco: Oriental Literature Syndicate, 1925). Drew Ali is likely to have written the introductory material and chapters 45–48. See, for example, Peter Lamborn Wilson, *Sacred Drift: Essays on the Margins of Islam* (San Francisco: City Lights, 1993), 18–25; Edward E. Curtis IV, *Islam in Black America: Identity, Liberation, and Difference in African-American Islamic Thought* (Albany: State University of New York Press, 2002), 56–62; and Susan Nance, "Mystery of the Moorish Science Temple: Southern Blacks and Alternative Spirituality in 1920s Chicago," *Religion and American Culture* 12, no. 2 (Summer 2002): 131–135.

25. "Koran Questions," 4. In MSTA teaching, "an Angel is a thought of ALLAH manifested in human flesh" and used "to carry messages to the four corners of the world, to all nations." "Koran Questions," 3.

26. 1930 U.S. Federal Census, Philadelphia City, Philadelphia County, Pennsylvania, Enumeration District 142, Dwellings 1308 and 1336. The recognized racial categories for 1930 were White, Negro, Indian, Chinese, Japanese, Filipino, Hindu, Korean, Mexican, and Other. On racial categories in the census, see Jennifer L. Hochschild and Brenna Marea Powell, "Racial Reorganization and the United States Census, 1850–1930: Mulattoes, Half-Breeds, Mixed Parentage, Hindoos, and the Mexican Race," *Studies in American Political Development* 22 (Spring 2008): 59–96. The requirement in 1930 that all people of African descent be designated "Negro" effectively eliminated the category "Mulatto," which had been used on earlier census forms, and made impossible the use of any other color or racial descriptor.

27. 1940 U.S. Federal Census, Brooklyn, Kings County, New York, Enumeration District 24-2169, Households 254–258, 261. The racial categories used on the 1940 census were White, Negro, Indian, Chinese, Japanese, Filipino, Hindu, Korean, and Other.

28. The case of Albert Smith Bey, whom Alec Brown Bey had listed as his contact person on his World War II draft registration card, is interesting. In 1930 Smith Bey, a North Carolina native and widower, lived with his brother, his sister, and his children in Darby Township, Pennsylvania, and when census enumerator Dewitt Brown visited them, they persuaded him to list their color or race as "olive." Before he submitted the form, Brown crossed this out and substituted "white." Obviously still concerned that the information he had conveyed about the Smith Beys was incorrect, Brown returned and filed an addendum, listing the entire family once again. This time they convinced him to characterize them racially as Moors. Finally, a supervisor crossed

out "Moor" and declared them "Negro." In 1940 Smith Bey was married and living in Philadelphia with his wife, son, and two lodgers who were also members of the MSTA. The enumerator listed them as Moorish Americans. 1930 U.S. Federal Census, Darby Township, Delaware County, Pennsylvania, Enumeration District 23-60, Dwelling 412; addendum, sheet no. 28B; 1940 U.S. Federal Census, Philadelphia County, Philadelphia City, Pennsylvania, Enumeration District 51-1330, Household 104.

25

Sensing Exclusions
Disability and the Protestant Worship Environment

ERINN STALEY

This chapter brings to bear the perspective of sensory culture studies on mainline worship as an intervention into a contemporary social conflict, the marginalization within and exclusion from churches of people with intellectual and developmental disabilities, including those with autism spectrum disorders. Mainline Protestant churches are sites for practices of religion that seem familiar to many, whether from firsthand experiences or from stock depictions of American Christianity in the popular media. Here the term *mainline* serves as shorthand for those Protestant churches in the United States that are not fundamentalist or Pentecostal, including the Christian Church (Disciples of Christ), Episcopal Church, Evangelical Lutheran Church in America, Presbyterian Church (U.S.A.), United Church of Christ, and United Methodist Church. Members of such churches might contend, quite defensibly, that major differences in belief and practice distinguish mainline denominations and constituent congregations from one another. Even so, it is fair to characterize mainline churches as sharing a sensory culture of worship, meaning that worship generally looks, sounds, and feels a certain way. It smells and tastes a certain way, too, which is mainly to say that it involves taste and smell in very small doses. This mode of worship limits taste to bits of bread and sips of grape juice or wine and avoids smells, save trace odors of candles and flowers (and incense in a minority of mainline churches). Moreover, mainline churches share norms of appropriate conduct. Worshipers are expected to stand and sit on cue; to speak and sing in unison; to direct their gazes at leaders and bow their heads reverently; to hold hymnals, Bibles, and paper bulletins; and to refrain from most other forms of moving, noisemaking, or touching objects that indicate they are not paying attention or that might distract others from listening to the sermon, prayers, or scripture readings. An important limitation of this description is that it better captures the code of conduct that operates in congregations in which the majority of people are white than in churches where this is not the case.[1]

The sensory culture of mainline churches has theological and cultural roots that cannot be disentangled neatly. One theological rationale for the sensory culture of mainline worship, which I argue is dominated by the auditory and makes sensory experiences subject to cognition rather than meaningful on their own terms, is captured by the view of the church that Avery Dulles calls "the church as herald." Dulles writes, "For theologians of this school, language has an assembling function. Christian proclamation is therefore to be understood as a linguistic event in which the body of Christ is constituted and assembled. The Church as an assembly takes place in the very activity of proclamation."[2] A church that understands itself to be tasked with proclamation is inclined to emphasize the sense of hearing and to promote conditions it associates with facilitating "good" hearing (for example, being quiet). Culturally, the expectation of bodily control—that a person can and ought to sit silently and without moving during a twenty-minute sermon—has analogs in the behavior expected at public lectures and classical music performances, among other sites, and it builds on the deep and wide, if not universal, theological and philosophical expectation that a human body is subject to the control of a rational mind. In any case, mainline worship does not perform a self-contained set of beliefs and material practices that is outlined plainly in the Bible or that exists apart from cultural influences and practical determinations.

Accounts of church discrimination against people with intellectual disabilities are found throughout the literature of disability theology, as well in popular media such as blogs by parents of disabled children. Of this experience Brett Webb-Mitchell writes, "People with disabilities and their families tell countless stories of being politely asked to leave worship, or in some cases of being *told* not to come to church, with comments such as, 'I don't think this is a church where you and your family would feel comfortable.'"[3] I am not suggesting that people with intellectual disabilities experience only discrimination in the context of mainline churches or that mainline churches are the only religious sites in which they encounter discrimination. Rather, this chapter considers how a particular mode of religious practice relates to one frequent instantiation of discrimination. In short, the chapter argues that the norms of mainline worship create expectations of appropriate behavior that operate in an exclusionary fashion in the context of a community that makes claims to being inclusionary.

Disability is an experience of limitation that results from the interaction between an impairment of biological structure or function and society. It is a complex category that has many forms, which commonly are divided into physical and intellectual in scholarly literature as well as in popular discourse.[4] An individual may experience only physical disability, only intellectual disability, or both. Whereas physical disability relates to differences or impairments in bodily form, mobility, and sensory function, among other things, intellectual disability relates to less than typical cognitive function (according to IQ tests) and adaptive behavior, such as self-care and communication. The above definition of disability shows reliance on a fundamental theory within disability studies, which is that disability is not purely or principally a biological phenomenon but results from the social construction of some impaired bodies as disabled. Resisting the hegemony of a medicalized view of disability as a problem to be diagnosed, treated, and overcome, the social theory acknowledges the fact of *impairments* and contends that social barriers render them *disabilities*.[5] Accordingly, my subsequent references to disability have in view not impairments alone but social and material interactions with impairments. Continuing to use the language of disability is a way of speaking about the real effects of those social and material relations on people with certain impairments.[6]

Attention to sensory and material studies suggests that the spaces and norms of mainline worship are produced and contingent; they could be otherwise. Likewise, attention to disability studies underscores that the bodies of worshipers are among the "stuff" that is constructed in and by practices of worship. Not only do norms operate in churches—as outside of them—regarding the permissible ways of interacting with the material environment and objects, but they also operate to construct some kinds of bodies as normal and others as deviant, some as welcome and others as intrusive; this, too, could be otherwise. It may be plain to the reader that the material space of worship, including church architecture and the arrangement of objects such as pews and pulpits, can be disabling of people who have physical or sensory disabilities. For example, the presence of stairs and the absence of accessible ramps or elevators restricts the participation of wheelchair users, and the lack of Braille worship bulletins, hymns, and Bible readings diminishes the participation of blind people. It may be less apparent that the sensory culture is unwelcoming of people with intellectual disabilities, so it is to that subject that I now turn. Though this chapter diagnoses a problem, it is not meant to suggest that the impact of mainline churches on intellectually disabled people is always negative. The sensory culture of worship, uses of scripture, and theology can be disabling or empowering in relation to impairments.[7]

The culture of mainline worship presumes that bodies are equipped in particular ways, namely that they are subject to the control of rational minds. Appropriate bodily performance of worship requires following written instructions and social cues, chiefly to sit silently and without moving for significant periods of time, most importantly during a sermon. This posture is meant to signal an inner devotion, to be a sign of spiritual contemplation and belief, and to create the conditions for that piety.

That is, mainline worship both shows the kind of believers such Christians understand themselves to be—modern, intellectual, respectable—and forms them into that kind of believers by avoiding unhelpful or even idolatrous displays of emotion or investment in objects.

In this way, mainline worship is consistent with this form of Christianity's self-understanding and commitment to a logic of modernity.[8] It could be the case, then, that the marginalization within and exclusion from churches of people with intellectual disabilities is in keeping with the identity and work of the church. Indeed, a series of surveys shows that people who are disabled participate in faith communities (not just mainline churches) at lower rates than nondisabled people.[9] The "participation gap" between adults without disabilities and those with severe disabilities attending a place of worship at least once a month was 13 percentage points in 2004 and 20 percentage points in 2000.[10] As Erik Carter reports, research into children's participation shows similar results, such as that "fewer than one-half of children and youth with autism, deaf-blindness, intellectual disabilities, or multiple disabilities participated in religious group activities *at any point* during the previous year."[11] Although some people with intellectual disabilities may not want to attend a mainline church or other place of worship, others may desire to do so but be discouraged by subtle disincentives to attend (for example, people staring or no one speaking to them before or after worship) or by explicit requests that they not return.

Though the sensory culture of mainline worship befits one of that tradition's logics, mainline churches' discrimination against people with intellectual disabilities is inconsistent with another of those churches' logics, that of welcome and hospitality. Mainline churches aspire to be and announce that they are places anyone can attend, hence the ubiquitous "All are welcome" signs, the presence of greeters who identify newcomers, offers of pastoral visits to those considering membership, and so on. Despite these declarations of welcome, these churches have constructed worship as an environment in which all are not, in fact, welcome, such as people with intellectual disabilities or those who are otherwise not capacitated to conform to the norms of the worship culture.[12]

Bringing both sensory and disability studies to bear on practices of mainline worship suggests that expectations of restrained sensory engagement conspire with broader cultural biases against people with intellectual disabilities (that is, that they are lesser humans or less than human) to characterize certain people as disrupters of worship rather than meaningful participants in it. In my view, the logic of hospitality—in a distinctly theological key—is more central to the identity and work of the church than is the logic of respectability and order.[13] To more fully embody their commitment to hospitality, at least in relation to people with intellectual disabilities, mainline churches may seek to reconcile the tension discussed in this chapter by exploring modifications to their sensory and material practices.

NOTES

1. The Pew Forum on Religion and Public Life reports that 91 percent of members of mainline Protestant churches are white (non-Hispanic). "U.S. Religious Landscape Survey: Portrait of Mainline Churches—Demographics," 2008, accessed August 2, 2012, http://religions.pewforum.org/portraits. Mainline churches in which the majority of people are African American or Asian, for example, might differ from my general description in significant ways, including having relatively higher levels of movement and expression. An outsider to such a worship culture might suppose that it is an environment in which a worshiper may move or vocalize freely, when in fact it has its own rules or expectations for appropriate conduct. For example, accepting or encouraging more vocalization than described above does not amount to tolerating any and all expression. These distinct norms of conduct merit consideration but fall outside the scope of this chapter.

2. Avery Dulles, *Models of the Church* (Garden City, New York: Doubleday, 1974), 76.

3. Brett Webb-Mitchell, *Dancing with Disabilities: Opening the Church to All God's Children* (Cleveland: United Church Press, 1994), 4, italics in original.

4. The terms *intellectual disability, developmental disability,* and *cognitive disability* are often used to refer to the same set of conditions. In their specific reference to cognitive function and adaptive behavior, these terms are distinct from *mental disability* (often called mental illness). However, an individual might experience both intellectual disability and mental disability. Additionally, autism spectrum disorders (ASD) are developmental disabilities that relate to communication, social interaction, and behavior; a person with ASD may have low, average, or high intelligence.

5. For a critical introduction to some theories of disability, including social models, see Brendan Gleeson, *Geographies of Disability* (New York: Routledge, 1998), 19–22.

6. Relationships between impairments and environments, broadly construed, are not equally disabling. For instance, most visual impairments in the United States today are not disabilities, given a range of factors, including accessible technologies such as glasses, and cultural acceptance of using those technologies as normal.

7. For more on the relation of scripture and theology to physical disability, see Nancy L. Eiesland, *The Disabled God: Toward a Liberatory Theology of Disability* (Nashville: Abingdon, 1994). For more on the relation of theology to intellectual disability, see Hans S. Reinders, *Receiving the Gift of Friendship: Profound Disability, Theological Anthropology, and Ethics* (Grand Rapids, MI: Eerdmans, 2008), and Erinn Staley, "Intellectual Disability and Mystical Unknowing: Contemporary Insights from Medieval Texts," *Modern Theology* 28, no. 3 (July 2012): 385–401.

8. For a thorough discussion of the dynamics of narratives of modernity, religion, secularization, and aesthetics, see Sally Promey's introduction to this volume.

9. Erik W. Carter, *Including People with Disabilities in Faith Communities: A Guide for Service Providers, Families, and Congregations* (Baltimore: Paul H. Brookes, 2007), 6.

10. Ibid.

11. Ibid., 6, italics in original. See Mary Wagner, Tom W. Cadwallader, and Camille Marder, *Life Outside the Classroom for Youth with Disabilities: A Report from the National Longitudinal Transition Study–2* (NLTS2) (Menlo Park, CA: SRI International, 2003), and Wagner, Cadwallader, and Marder, *The Other 80% of Their Time: The Experiences of Elementary and Middle School Students with Disabilities in Their Nonschool Hours* (Menlo Park, CA: SRI International, 2002).

12. Other groups of people, such as sexual minorities, also feel unwelcome in some mainline churches, whether because of firsthand experiences of discrimination or a sense from popular culture that people "like them"—whatever marginalized class they are part of—are not welcome in churches or other social spaces.

13. Erinn Staley, "Many Minds, One Body: Intellectual Disability, Humanity, and the Church," Ph.D. dissertation, Yale University, 2013.

26

The Divine Touchability of Dreams

ANGIE HEO

What if the activities of awareness and self-awareness were forms not of cognition but rather, as Aristotle maintained, of sensation? What if consciousness, in short, were a variety of tact and contact in the literal sense, "an inner touch," as the Stoics are reported to have said of the "common sense," "by which we perceive ourselves"? Daniel Heller-Roazen, *The Inner Touch: Archaeology of a Sensation* (2007)

In Port Said, a city between Egypt's Suez Canal and the Mediterranean, an icon of the Virgin Mary exudes holy oil (Figure 26.1).[1] Since 1990, year after year the image has attracted thousands of Coptic Christian pilgrims to the Church of Saint Bishoi, where it is housed.[2] Unlike other surrounding icons in the sanctuary, painted and consecrated by priestly hands, this one is an "autoconsecrating" poster replica. It produces and reproduces holy oil by itself. This oil leaves behind worn paper traces in its liquid trail as it travels from the Virgin's outstretched hands to a plastic canopy that captures the oil beneath her feet. From there, the priests of the church collect and distribute the oil as a form of remembrance (*al-dhikra*).

A Dream Turned "Inside Out"

Devotees understand the origins of the icon's miraculous activity to reside in the drama of one woman's dream. On the evening of February 20, 1990, the Virgin Mary (by way of saintly visitation) healed Samia Youssef Basilious of breast cancer. Samia dreamed that the Virgin, assisted by three other saints, performed surgery on her. Within the space of the dream, Samia lay down on a white table as the saints held her hands. Then the Virgin touched her cancerous breast. Startled by a burning jolt of sensation that rushed through her body, Samia pulled her right hand away. The Virgin grabbed it back and held her hand. When Samia awoke, she discovered that she had been healed.

Is dreaming one medium of what the Stoics, and Daniel Heller-Roazen (quoted above in this chapter's epigraph) after them, have called "common sense"? If so, how is

the "common" aspect of the dream experience communicated? And what implications does this hold for the bodily, sensational character of dreams? On their face, dreams signify the innermost secrets of the private self, hidden from public exposure unless made known through symptom or speech. For many, over time the de-divinized realm of dreams introduces traces of the past that arise from the "residuary movements": a kind of phantasm.[3] According to Freud, the "incapacity of dreams" to express logical connections requires verbal translation: words are the primary medium of interpretation.[4] In the case of Samia's miraculous healing, however, the saintly drama unfolded through the tactile interaction of bodily surfaces through the push and pull of holy hands, witnessed from within the dream. The dream enabled the capacity to touch, to partake in the heat of divine healing. Samia's healing also introduced a particular form of material sensation that served as the reproducible template for the production and engagement anew of certain images.

Artifacts of Marian healing constituted remnants of Samia's dream. These included bodily residues and images of surgery that served as a type of evidence and as relics of blessing. In a glass case, the Church of Saint Bishoi displays photos of these remainders found on top of Samia's body—among them, shots of the gauze bandages that had been wrapped tightly around her chest as well as the clotted mass of tumors, preserved in a jar of formaldehyde (Figure 26.2). Here the act of exteriorized eye-witnessing rather than redreaming thus became the preeminent mode of visual testimony. As imprints of sensational healing, these images manifest material extensions

FIGURE 26.2. Display case featuring artifacts from the dream-healing of Samia Youssef Basilious, Port Said, February 20, 2007. Photo by Angie Heo.

of the dream. As veritable contact relics, they represent parts of Samia's discarded flesh and traces of Marian presence. These photos are the material media of testimony and the public witness of a bodily interaction, as intensely tactile as they are visual. Samia had dreamed the dream, but its indexical afterlives were for everyone to see. This reproductive publicity of Samia's body invites the imagining of the originary drama of healing. As pilgrims watch, they witness, in effect, a dream turned "inside out."

From Samia's dream of the Marian hand's touch to the oil-emitting representation of the Virgin in the poster icon, the fleeting interiority of momentary touch became more durably realized in the ritual activity of the icon.[5] In the instructive words of one priest before a crowd of pilgrims, "Her hand exudes oil because that is where the Virgin touched Samia." In this signifying structure of tactile remembrance, the transfer of mimetic capacities from dream image to print image renders holy power perceptible and communicable. By witnessing the icon's capacity to produce oil, pilgrims partake visually in the haptic structure of miraculous healing. The saintly presence is experienced at the level of the superficial and the lateral: pilgrims are touched from within by the bodily surface of an envisioned dream, touched from without at the "skin of the icon."

Through the dissemination of oil, the tactile quality of dreaming is reintroduced into the matter of memory once again. At the entrance of the church, witnesses collect plastic vials of oil taken from the canopy beneath the poster. As another type of relic, the oils of the miracle icon propagate memory beyond the confines of the shrine, into homes and onto other bodies. Oils and their circulability offer the publicly tactile substance of Samia's dream.

Bodying Forth Dreams

The oil is not the only medium that constructed the reenacted possibility of Marian contact. Each time I have visited the icon of the Virgin in Port Said, without fail I have discovered a group of spectators snapping photos with their cameras and mobile phones (Figure 26.3). In addition, on special occasions the Church of Saint Bishoi televises live images of the icon from a monitor situated in the courtyard displaying the detailed passage of oil. Following Charles Peirce's notion of "virtuality," the virtual relation between the icon and these various forms of mass media is one of displacement, of an "external embodiment" that stands for something else.[6] The poster image inaugurates bodily circuits of virtual reproduction, with the interfaces of photography, film, and mobile phone offering emergent spaces of interaction. Such visual technologies render various sensations of the icon externalizable and replicable.

The industry of mass reproducibility also results in new kinds of "touchability" in the introduction of novel bodily capacities to touch and be touched. If the memory of the poster's hand had already begun to fade in the minds of viewers, the icon's bodily mechanicity offered alternative forms of sensational encounter. I first heard of the Marian icon of Port Said in 2006, when Nivin, a young Coptic woman, took me to the popular windmill shrine of the late Pope Kirollis VI located near old Coptic Cairo. What Nivin shared was a form of public memory, dreamed and cinematically so. She elaborated:

> I'll also tell you something that happened. One time I was watching a film
> and there was a [woman in the film] who had breast cancer. So the Lady
> Virgin went and did surgery on her, and took out the tumor from her
> breast. And afterwards, the woman grabbed the hand of the Virgin. So,
> I insisted that I would grab the hand of the Virgin Mother. At that time,
> I was about twenty years old. I said: "I will not sleep, I want to see. And
> afterwards, to take her hand." I insisted, I didn't hesitate. I continued to
> sit on the bed until very late at night. And in the end, I felt . . . have you
> ever gone inside the surgery room before? Have you ever taken anesthesia?
> I have gone many times. I had my tonsils taken out, and my appendix, a
> cyst near one of my ovaries removed also. Anyways, so afterwards, I felt
> that, in that very moment when I was sitting on the bed, I felt as if I had
> taken anesthesia. And I found the Virgin standing next to the bed. She

FIGURE 26.3. Pilgrims snap photos of the icon of the Virgin Mary in the Church of Saint Bishoi in Port Said and capture in videos its oil-exuding activity, December 28, 2010. Photo by Angie Heo.

took my hand and pushed me, sitting me down on the bed. In the same moment, I woke up and I couldn't find her anymore.[7]

At the time I heard this, I knew nothing of Samia's miracle healing or of the icon in Port Said. Only later, when I visited the miracle icon with another friend, did the possibility dawn on me that there was, somewhere out there, an account of Samia's dream mass-mediated through video. Nivin's testimony of its bodily effects combined willful desire with the mimesis of touch. Rather than engaging the oils produced at the bodily surface of the icon, Nivin "tactilely" engaged the visual structure of the miracle.

In interpreting the distinctive nature of her visual experience, Nivin was forthright about the numerous surgical procedures she had undergone herself. She began by describing anesthesia, the cessation of sensation at the liminal border between wakefulness and sleep. In his famous essay "The Work of Art in the Age of Mechanical Reproduction," Walter Benjamin draws an analogy between the cameraman and the surgeon, in distinction to the painter as a magician. In his words, "The magician heals a sick person by the laying on of hands, the surgeon cuts into the patient's body."[8] Like the surgeon at the table, the cameraman operates by way of permeation, from inside the viewer's faculties of perception. Like a kind of "anesthetic," in Nivin's characterization, the dream displaced one sensation for a virtual other. Within the reorganized experience of dreaming, Nivin fulfilled her desire to grab the Virgin's hand by sight, a desire to see and feel as Samia had seen and felt. In this way, Nivin's dream image did not so much express the mimesis of desire as enact it.

Nivin's dream, a redreaming of Samia's dream, bodily incorporated the Virgin's shove, the suspension of sensation, even the memory of organs removed. Samia's tactile and visual encounter with the Virgin, transferred from the icon through the cinematic aura of film, was imitable, and mechanically so. So much so that Nivin's body might testify to this experience even though she had no other knowledge of Samia or of the Virgin's oil-exuding hand. Indeed the mimetic relation between Samia and Nivin was one mediated not by the viscosity of oil but by the filmy quality of dreams. The entire result of Nivin's testimony is that Nivin is seeing a bit differently now. Not knowing other material outcomes of Samia's dream, Nivin participated in the manual reproduction of Samia's experience through other mechanically modern means. She, too, insisted on touching the Virgin by way of a dream.

This testimony presents the imagining of touch as a mimetic practice to be not only held but also ritually remembered and repeated. Through a newfound ability to "see," Nivin and other viewers have engaged the technical capacity to touch through exteriorized images and contact imagined within. Such a perceptual structure of dreams confounds the boundary between inner and outer, soul and body, and asks that we consider sensation itself as a form of "common sense." Here the inwardness of dreams renders a practical offering of divine touch, less embodied perhaps but more "bodied forth."

NOTES

1. This image of the Virgin Mary is widely known as Our Lady of the Miraculous Medal, particularly among Roman Catholics. Among Coptic Christians, this form is known as *al-manzar at-tagalli* or "the transfigurational pose." This is the iconic form of twentieth-century Marian apparitions in Egypt, what one priest explained as the "language in which we understand her." In my fieldwork I have found that Copts do not make the historical connection between this image and the original, from nineteenth-century Catholic France. Rather, I have heard some Copts claim that this is the image of Saint Luke's painting of the Virgin.

2. Egypt's Coptic Christians compose roughly 6–12 percent of a Muslim-majority national population. Of these, more than 90 percent of Copts identify themselves as Coptic Orthodox.

3. Aristotle, "On Divination in Sleep," in *The Complete Works of Aristotle,* vol. 1, ed. J. Barnes (Princeton, NJ: Princeton University Press, 1984), 738.

4. Sigmund Freud, *The Interpretation of Dreams,* trans. James Strachey (New York: Avon, 1965), 347.

5. Samia's dream and the miracle icon eventually resulted in the intervention of police and priests. For the purposes of this chapter's focus on the material structure of "touch" and "touchability," these events and the questions they raise are not engaged here. For more detail, see my essay "The Bodily Threat of Miracles: Security, Sacramentality and the Egyptian Politics of Public Order," *American Ethnologist* 40, no. 1 (2013).

6. Charles Sanders Peirce, "Some Consequences of Four Incapacities," in *Peirce on Signs: Writings on Semiotic,* ed. James Hoopes (Chapel Hill: University of North Carolina Press, 1991).

7. Interview with author, September 14, 2006.

8. Walter Benjamin, "The Work of Art in the Age of Mechanical Reproduction," in *Illuminations* (New York: Schocken, 2008), 233.

27

When the World Is Alive, Spirit Is Not Dismembered

Philosophical Reflections on the Good Mind

LAUREL C. SCHNEIDER

For the past several decades, scholars in religious studies have struggled to overcome the conceptual limitations that—for want of a better shorthand—Cartesian dualisms of body/spirit and profane/sacred have built into the bones of almost every scholarly approach to the study of religion. The prosaic idea that "the spiritual" is something other than "the material" stems from this conceptual bias. The turn to materiality and sensation in contemporary religious studies, theology, and philosophy constitutes an important corrective. If spiritual matters can be fully engaged and, even better, understood *in* and *through* bodily practices, perhaps what counts as spiritual cannot be conceptually divided from what counts as material. And once this corrective is in place, our capacity to apprehend spiritual matters, especially in those religious traditions that have been most misunderstood by the dualistic constructs of academic religious studies, may be blown wide open.

For example, sensuality or the category of the material over against the spiritual is simply not an issue in numerous North American indigenous traditions, especially in conceptualizations and practices of engagement with other-than-human realities. What religious scholars laboring under the spirit/body dualism call the material (or the body or sensation) is a taken-for-granted, a priori element of most traditional Native North American engagement with other-than-human persons. This is so not only because it is in and through the material and sensory practices that such engagement occurs but also because across many of the indigenous cultures of the North American continent, especially those of the eastern and southeastern woodlands, the world's conceptual divisions do not dismember bodies that way. The general point is not that eastern Native North American religious traditions tend to eschew the ethereal practices of contemplation, imagination, and conceptualization in favor of more material practices and ideas (a distinction that already gets us into trouble). Quite the contrary. Dreams, visions, and the hermeneutical practices that accompany them, for example, hold particular sway in the reality structure of religious understanding across many eastern and southeastern North American cultures. Dreams and visions, however, are not fictional, nor are they separable from the bodies and places in which they occur. These practices are often understood to be of the same material realm as the bodies that undergo them. Spirit, whatever it may be (and the languages differ so much that we are often on shaky ground with such words), cannot be cordoned off in understanding from the realm of bodies, food, animals, plants, and the stuff of living. The prosaic and often romanticized lack of a split between spirit and, to put it another way, the prosaic and usually romanticized aliveness and agency of matter in many Native North American cultural traditions makes the rediscovery of the senses in contemporary academic theological discourse long overdue and amusing, to say the least.

Although many books are yet to be written on the complexity of sensation and contemplation across the vast diversity of Native North American cultural and religious traditions, I want to touch on only one aspect of it in both traditional theory and practice shared across a number of tribes traditionally located in the eastern and southeastern, mostly wooded, half of the continent. Let me be clear; I am generalizing across a wide region of the very different and sovereign cultures of the eastern continent, most of which have kept their traditions alive against overwhelming odds of genocide and cultural erasure. But in their vibrant practices of survival, many of these nations share a few aspects of what we might call religious sensibilities that can be summarized together and can be critically illuminating of academic presuppositions and proclivities when it comes to talking about materiality in religion and religious practice.[1] It is always risky to make generalizations about any religious tradition, so my own attempt to think about the difference that materiality makes in some Native American traditions should be taken with a grain of scholarly salt. This is a reflection based on long-term study of the work that Native scholars have produced for public understanding and on personal communication through the years with friends and elders of a few eastern and southeastern Native traditions. I have come to the conclusion that there are differences that have a significant effect here relating to questions of materiality and spirit in religious studies, but this is a conclusion that assumes the validity of taking some general cautionary lessons from the growing body of Native American scholarship.

So the specific material sensibility that I seek to lift up here for reflection, which seems to recur in various ways across a number of Native eastern and southeastern nations, could fall under the rubric of what the Muscogee (Creek) elder Philip Deer called "the Good Mind." The Good Mind is both a status and an objective, and it encompasses the whole range of personal and communal relations with human and other-than-human persons. It is much more than an attitude (which is a common misunderstanding when non-Native persons encounter the term) and cannot be achieved by individuals alone.

The aspect of the Good Mind that relates specifically to the question of materiality and sensation I shall call, for now, bodily attentiveness. By this I mean an active presupposition that the animating powers of life—and so the specific other-than-human persons who inhabit the world and whose activities and attitudes directly affect the life of the community—are available to the body's many senses because they inhabit the physical world in specific and complex ways, much as individual human persons inhabit this world in specific and complex ways. These other-than-human persons (often, traditionally, masters of particular animal or plant communities) may not all be present at the same moment, just as every human friend of mine is not present at the same moment in the same room. The point is that they *could* be present if schedules and travel allowed. The material dimensions of space and presence include the "spirits" in all of their bodily complexity and shifty abilities.

Here is another way to think about this, according to Arnie Neptune, an elder in the Penobscot Nation: "How would you know if your friends were here?" he once asked me, and then answered his own question. "You'd see them. Or you'd know that they could be present. You wouldn't normally say, 'My friends are invisible' or 'They can't communicate.'" Gesturing out the window, he said, "That's how it is for everyone who belongs to the River." By "everyone," Neptune did not mean just the human beings who live on Indian Island in the middle of the Penobscot River. He was referring to a specific and complex reality—the possibility of one's friends showing up wherever one is—but it is an utterly prosaic and unromantic possibility at the same time. Would your friends come if called? Probably. It depends. They are busy; the roads are crowded. You are important to them, but they might be delayed or unable to afford the ticket. But if you were in trouble, and felt they could help, you'd certainly hope that they would come. This is the world we live in. "What's the big deal?" Neptune asked me with a smile.

The point here is that the other-than-human people with whom many eastern Native American religious practices deal—from cultures as divergent as the Mississippean heritage of the Muscogee to the Abenaki heritage of the Penobscot—also inhabit the world in specific and complex ways. They are seldom identical to human people—just as oak people or eagle people are not the same as human people—and so cannot be expected to behave in the same ways or to obey the same conventions, though they can be expected to have agency of their own and to behave unpredictably, as do human people. The critical question for the community is how to deal, religiously, with the unpredictability, agency, and autonomy of powerful other-than-human persons. In the face of unpredictability and power, relationship is everything —if we are related to someone (so the reasoning goes), we can expect more from them—or at the very least know more what to expect, and that is all to the good in an ecology of power. Religious practice is therefore always a negotiation among free agents, which means that there is a large dose of what Anishinaabe literary critic and novelist Gerald Vizenor calls chanciness in every encounter.[2]

The world is heavily populated with other-than-human persons, and it is easy to miss them right in our midst. Attention to the senses, to chance encounters with persons of all species and morphologies, is essential. Religious practice is therefore imbued with a concern for bodily attention, which plays out as a concern for right and courteous practice toward all persons who might turn into friends (or who might harm if offended), and it is this concern for right attention that undergirds the Muskogean notion of the Good Mind. How to be in the world is, for many Native traditionalists, a practice in embodied attention to community building that far exceeds the narrow limits of the human.

Some—but by no means all—of the ritual ways that the Good Mind is taught and practiced among Muscogee traditionalists are through sound (drums, rattles, song) and movement in, for example, the Stomp Dances. In addition to the sensory intensity and relationship with other than human persons that these practices involve, they are aspects of a larger narrative understanding of reality; most songs and dances invoke important stories, and important stories construct the relational world in which human beings live. Variations on this understanding also occur among the culturally distinct tribes of the Wabanaki Federation, the Anishinaabe, and the Haudenasaune Confederacy (among others). It is impossible in such a brief reflection to do justice to the complexity of narrative in even one eastern North American nation, let alone all of them, so suffice it to say here that an emphasis in many of them is on the world-creating dimension of narrative. As Native scholars have pointed out for years, some powerful stories literally matter—bring into being—worlds. This is a fact that Western observers have few tools to comprehend, and missing this point can easily result in a summative mistake that Native epistemologies are only analogically constructed. Traditional Native communities, under this assumption, use stories simply to orient themselves in an objectively independent world. This narrow view of narrative completely misses the common Native fact that the stories create the world as well (hence the caution ritual elders often issue to others to tell stories carefully and in the right seasons). Vizenor, along with a growing number of Native American writers and poets, points out that the issue for the Native person is how to handle the ontic—and very chancy—productivity that stories inevitably carry.[3] Furthermore, the challenge in Native American philosophies is not ontology's totalizing tendencies, as it is in European thought. Rather the challenge in this mode of reasoning is ontology's slipperiness—the porous and promiscuous material excesses that narrative produces beyond the tissue of grammar.

One example of such ontic slipperiness occurs in the scams that the trickster pulls—the cons that this ancestor often unselfconsciously and sometimes without malice masterminds. These scams and misdemeanors do actually help to create the world that human and other animals inhabit. People lose or gain speech, appendages, skills, and any number of relations due to the trickster's mistakes. Mountains become animate heroes, and trees become rivers in response to his or her indecent creativity. It is not necessary to assume a narrow realism here to glimpse possibilities inherent in these accounts, although it reasonable to borrow D. A. Grinde's observation, referring in this case westward to the trickster of the Plains traditions, that "when Jesus Christ walks on water this is treated as 'religious' but when Coyote steals fire . . . it is invariably characterized by the dominant society's discourse as 'legend.'"[4]

The trickster narratives illuminate a deeper logic in Native North American ontological appraisals of the way things are and ought to be. That logic resides in the vatic quality of humor that any serious accounting of physical and sensory experience requires. Vizenor's argument allows for honesty about chance and error even long after the fact and recognizes its material effects in the world that is created, for better or worse, as a result of relational engagement in the world with all of the chancy persons who inhabit it. Here humor, in other words, is not without horror, and it is more than a mere coping strategy. It is an element of a mode of reasoning that recognizes long-term consequences in actions, words, and bodies, even when those consequences can be sketched only in caricature and put metaphorically into stories of possibility. Some things are so serious, in other words, that only humor can touch them.

One could say that trickster deceit and greed undergirds the misanthropic economic structures and the physical spaces of Euro-American religious modernity that is also a globalized colonial modernity, all the while creating a new material reality in which matter and spirit must despair of each other or find each other in new ways. In other words, stories of conquest have created the (modern) world we live in. This view is integral to the philosophy that runs through much contemporary transnational Native writing and teaching. Thomas King has worked with this idea in *The Truth about Stories* and *Green Grass, Running Water,* as have Louise Erdrich in her various novels on Native subjects and Joy Harjo, especially in her later poetry.[5] This tragicomedic approach to philosophy (this "sense" of thinking) follows Vizenor in that it recognizes a fundamental liveliness in creation *and* in narrative, a constitutive trickiness and subterfuge to living and to understanding that cannot be contained or colonized in systems of thought that are too comprehensive, settled, or confident. As a philosophical "sense" of humor, furthermore, Vizenor understands such Native reasoning—and ironic wisdom—to be a force of life. This grants to humor a deceptively heavy weight in which it is possible for attention to the chanciness of religious practices in relation to other-than-human inhabitants of *this world* to "remind Native Americans and non-Native [peoples] alike that 'there is no final, ultimate answer, no infallibility that we can blindly accept and follow. Power, like life, is in motion.'"[6]

Materiality and religious sensibility in Native North American reasoning and practice mean, therefore, that the world itself, its stony bones and vast green and blue skins, is a process of relations, a product and a condition of those relations. The Muscogee notion of the Good Mind means, at least in part, attending *wholly* to these relations, to their bodily reality and to the obligations that such reality engenders. Other-than-human persons are capable of flesh; they coexist with human persons and demand relational courtesies in much the same way that human persons do of one another. But, though persons with all of the meaning, obligation, and legal weight of the term, other-than-human persons are not always human. The world itself is alive and messy with relationships between persons of all sorts. This embodied sacred world is not, at least for some traditionalist Native North Americans, a projection of human imaginative exercises. But the embodied, sacred world is not independent of imaginative embellishments, either. That is the challenge that the particular sense and sensibility I am discussing here poses to Western philosophy and religious studies. The very terms for the structure of physical reality disavow the dualisms that dog "materiality," "sensation," and "spirit" in the West, constituting a real alternative to Western thought about these "matters," and very easy misunderstanding, too. Which brings us back, at least in Muscogee thinking (and that of some of their traditional regional neighbors), to the embodied corrective of what they call the Good Mind.

NOTES

1. It is important to note that geographic designations like eastern and southeastern are politically volatile in relation to many Native American tribes. The Muscogee (Creek) nation, for example, is governmentally located in what is now Oklahoma, but prior to the infamous "trail of tears" was (and its descendants still are) spread across regions of what are now Alabama, Georgia, Florida, and South Carolina. In this chapter I refer to a few cultural associations that are shared across a wide pre-Columbian geographic range in the eastern North American continent. These generalizations should not confuse other significant cultural and historical distinctions between those sovereign nations, cultures, and histories.

2. Gerald Vizenor, "A Postmodern Introduction," in *Narrative Chance: Postmodern Discourse on Native American Literatures,* ed. Gerald Vizenor (Norman: University of Oklahoma Press, 1989), 3–17.

3. In addition to Vizenor's edited volume *Narrative Chance,* see "Literary Animals" in his *Fugitive Poses: Native American Indian Scenes of Absence and Presence* (Lincoln: University of Nebraska Press, 1998), 119–145. See also Joy Harjo, *How We Became Human: New and Selected Poems, 1975–2001* (New York: Norton, 2004), and Thomas King, *Green Grass, Running Water* (New York: Bantam, 1994).

4. D. A. Grinde Jr., quoted by E. Gruber in *Humor in Contemporary Native North American Literature: Reimagining Nativeness* (Rochester, NY: Camden House, 2008), 158.

5. King, *Green Grass,* and *The Truth about Stories: A Native Narrative* (Minneapolis: University of Minnesota Press, 2008). See also Joy Harjo, "The Woman Who Fell from the Sky," in *The Woman Who Fell from the Sky: Poems,* by Harjo (New York: Norton, 1996), 20; and Gerald Vizenor, ed., *Survivance: Narratives of Native Presence* (Lincoln: University of Nebraska Press, 2008).

6. K. Blaeser, quoted by M. A. Bowers in "'Ethnic Glue': Humor in Native American Literatures," in *Cheeky Fictions: Laughter and the Postcolonial,* ed. S. Reichl and M. Stein (Amsterdam: Rodopi, 2005), 253.

28

The Shroud of Bologna
Lighting Up Pier Paolo Pasolini's Sensational Corpus

ARA H. MERJIAN

The light of the body is the eye: if therefore thine eye be single, thy whole body shall be full of light.   Matthew 6:22

His face obscured by shadow, torso gleaming white in a button-down shirt, Pier Paolo Pasolini offers up his body for the projection of his own film, *The Gospel According to St. Matthew,* released eleven years earlier and now cast onto his seated figure in a darkly lit room (Figures 28.1 and 28.2). Staged by the artist Fabio Mauri on May 31, 1975, and titled *Intellettuale* (Intellectual), the performance took place in front of a small audience at Bologna's modern art museum—one of several inaugural events marking the institution's founding in one of the country's more countercultural cities. The roiling 1970s in Italy witnessed not only dueling terrorist activity between extreme left and right factions—the "Years of Lead"—but also, just months after this event, the untimely demise of Pasolini himself. The murder of the country's most prominent cultural figure—slain by a male hustler on a dusty soccer field near the seaside town of Ostia, in still unresolved circumstances—thrust him even more forcefully into the national spotlight. Because Pasolini had been the subject and object of more than thirty trials (for everything from corrupting minors to violations of public sensibility), his body, isolated for public display, was no oddity by 1975.[1] It had come to form part of Italy's permanent cultural furniture.

Like so many phenomena in Pasolini's orbit, Mauri's piece now seems an uncanny prolepsis of the director's fatality. The still unresolved nature of his murder—sexual tryst gone wrong or calculated neofascist assassination?—contributes to the larger entwining of art, life, and death that marked Pasolini's body of work from the start. For his part, Mauri professed discomfort after watching the Bologna performance—an event, he remarked, that seemed quaint on paper but which, in practice, produced the unsettling effect of "an X-ray of the spirit."[2] Just how much of Mauri's discomfort emerged retroactively, in the wake of Pasolini's subsequent murder, is dif-

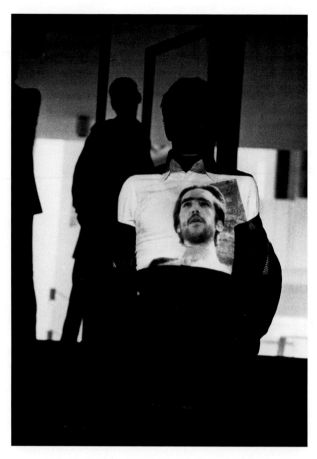

ficult to tease out. But it is an entanglement actively courted in the latter's entire oeuvre. "I see," Pasolini writes in his last books of poems, "with the eye of an image / lynching officials / watching my own extermination / with a still scientific heart."[3] From a string of seemingly coded lyricisms issued on the eve of his death back to professed childhood fantasies of being the crucified Jesus, the trope of martyrdom threads the vagaries of Pasolini's sprawling corpus. It is that thread that his close friend, the painter Giuseppe Zigaina, has subsequently come to stitch into an argument of its own. In a series of polemical texts, Zigaina has proposed that Pasolini not only anticipated his violent end but invited it—the final act of a lifelong performance of embodied self-sacrifice.[4]

In the wake of such theories, we might see the metaphorical martyrdom of Mauri's piece less as a chilling coincidence than as a voluntary corollary. Even Pasolini's more straightforward acts, Zigaina argues—through a close (if often strained) reading of words and deeds—bear upon a larger performative project. The hypothesis will never be proven in any empirical, much less forensic, sense. Yet *Intellettuale* undoubtedly lends it uncanny substance, at once flesh and specter. The apparition of Christ's

FIGURE 28.2. Fabio Mauri, *Intellettuale (Il Vangelo secondo Matteo di / su Pier Paolo Pasolini)*, May 1975. Performance, Galleria Communale d'Arte Moderna, Bologna. Photo by Antonio Masotti.

defiant visage on Pasolini's chest confuses several times over the semantics of creator and creation, progenitor and issue, imputing upon his very person the Passion that he had invoked so many times onscreen and on the page. Like the Shroud of Turin or the Veil of Veronica placed back onto Christ's face, the piece returns the light of Pasolini's cinematic traces to his own form. Further intensifying an autobiographical subtext is the sight of the director's mother, Susanna, who appears in the *Gospel* as none other than the mourning Mary, weeping at the foot of Golgotha. The vision of Susanna/ Mary's woeful visage projected onto her son's abdomen brings home a circularity of art and life, birth and death, the womb and the Pietà. The prepositional ambivalence of the piece's subtitle—*Il Vangelo secondo Matteo di / su Pier Paolo Pasolini* (*The Gospel According to Saint Matthew by / on Pier Paolo Pasolini*)—further underscores such vacillations. The return of Pasolini's film to his own body conjures up, too, an aesthetic "inversion" redolent of the open secret that was his sexuality. He bears, in Mauri's piece, the more metaphysical cross of that passion and its scandalous perversions.

In short, the erotic, oedipal, thaumaturgical, and soteriological inflections of the body in Pasolini's aesthetics seem bound, at every turn, to autobiographical allusion. For all its undeniable narcissism, however, his work resists mere navel gazing. Pasolini's interventions into Italian culture remain some of the most incisive of the century, not only in cinema but in poetry, theater, novels, journalism, and endless polemics. Prominent among these was his interrogation of religion's relevance among a largely nonpracticing Catholic populace (he once deemed Catholicism a "superficial crust" laid over Italian society).[5] Even—or especially—as an atheist, he turned to religion as a source of mystical, irrational energy, a metaphysical force without which, he claimed, ideological practicality would wither. Commenting in 1966 on his attraction to Matthew's gospel as a subject, Pasolini famously remarked that he was himself "an unbeliever who has a nostalgia for a belief."[6] Perhaps what most disturbed Mauri in retrospect—even if he could not articulate it at the time—was the extent to which his piece literally embodied the dialectical tensions intrinsic to Pasolini's work: materialism and mysticism, eroticism and morbidity, sacrality and sacrilege. As a communist who celebrated the rituals of Catholicism, a revolutionary who refused to square his beliefs with the basic creed of 1968, a homosexual who disavowed any whiff of nascent identity politics, and an iconoclast who clung tightly to the icon, Pasolini held up a mirror to Italy's own scandalous heterodoxies. *Intellettuale* lent them a single form on which a further series of images could flicker. As much as conjuring a spiritual X-ray, Mauri's piece conferred on Pasolini a certain opacity. He became a screen for projection in every sense.

We cannot interpret the resulting reflections in strictly formal terms any more than we can Pasolini's aesthetics themselves. Of a piece with Bologna's artistic experimentation was its status as the "Red Center" of Italy, a moniker indebted as much to its politics as to the tiles of its roofs. The victory of Alcide De Gasperi's Christian Democratic Party in 1948 had secured a centrist hegemony that lasted for decades. Bologna occupied a vital position in Italy's political landscape as a site of socialist and communist resistance against both Catholic orthodoxy and the encroachment of postwar consumer culture—the inexorable *omologazione* against which Pasolini railed with increasing intensity (the term is translated in English as everything from "uniformity" to "conformity," "homogenization" to "globalization"). From the extraparliamentary interventions of the leftist Potere Operaio or the free Radio Alice that broadcast poetry, political commentary, and yoga lessons beginning in 1976, Bologna hosted various oppositional activities confluent with its leftist eminence.[7]

The city was not only the place of Pasolini's actual birth (on the Via Zamboni on March 5, 1922) but also his intellectual and political cradle. Mauri and Pasolini first met, in fact, as students there in the 1930s, when the latter studied under the country's most distinguished critic and art historian, Roberto Longhi. Pasolini's affinity for medieval, Renaissance, and Mannerist iconographies—figuring into films from *La Ricotta* and *Mamma Roma* to *Teorema* and the so-called *Trilogy of Life*—stem in great part from his study under Longhi, an apprenticeship that Pasolini once deemed "ontological."[8] Whether playing a student of Giotto in his own version of *The Decameron* or musing on the use of light by Caravaggio in an essay from 1974, Pasolini drew unabashedly on the history of painting.[9] Those uses transcend any facile citation (a bone of great contention between the director and various critics), contributing instead to the "ontology" of his cinematic language at large. The symmetrical spacing, obsessive framing, and "solemn fixity" he practiced with his camera derive in great part from the hieraticism of painterly consecration.

The kind of sacrality his cinema evinced, however, was anything but conventional. For all the relentless centering of the Pasolinian shot, it was Italy's spatial and social margins from which his subjects emerged. Urban and ideological interstices formed the crux of his work after the mid-1950s: Rome's subproletariat shantytowns, the haunts of a "prebourgeois" community left behind by the country's vigorous (if belated) induction into postwar prosperity. Indeed, the "Romanesque" frontality of figures in *Accattone* appeared expressly at odds with those characters' grubby mugs and tattered morality—just as the intermittent overlay of Bach's sublime *Saint Matthew Passion* chafes against the scenes of bathetic violence it accompanies in the same film.[10] In Pasolini's version of Matthew's gospel, the origins of Christian humility are traced to landscapes as unrefined as the gestures of the film's nonprofessional actors. Having been sentenced to prison (though subsequently acquitted) for his interpretation of the Crucifixion in *La Ricotta*—a film that crossed invocations of Pontormo and Rosso Fiorentino with the vulgarity of the Roman *borgata*—Pasolini seemed resigned to courting outrage (Figure 28.3). At the screening of *Mamma Roma* during

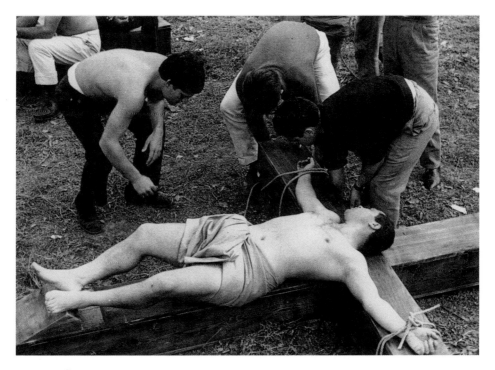

FIGURE 28.3. The set of *La Ricotta*, dir. Pier Paolo Pasolini, 1962. Cineteca di Bologna.

the Venice festival in 1962, a neofascist group denounced the film's characters as "The Apostles of Mud"[11]—testament to the centrality of prostitutes, pimps, and thugs to his narratives of redemption.

Pasolini's communist militancy was no less heretical, however. He had been kicked out of the party in 1947 following accusations of corrupting minors—a scandal that hastened his arrival in Rome in 1950 from his family home in Friuli. If his anti-clerical exposition of the Bible offended state religion, it is equally vital to note the abiding hostility to metaphysics professed by a Lukácsian left in postwar Italy. "Pasolini," Maria-Antonietta Macciocchi wrote not long after his murder, "was the first heretic of the Marxist religion."[12] As much as he clashed with papal doctrine, his faith in a kind of irrational spirituality—a materialism that drew overtly on the mysteries of religious piety—rattled party hacks. Pasolini's iconoclasm was, in short, inextricable from his iconophilia. That paradox curdled on the surface of his art. However, ironically, it increasingly separated his aesthetic and poetic practice from the most innovative contemporary practices. By 1975 Pasolini had come to form a kind of holy relic in his own right—an artifact of aesthetic strategies since rejected by the neo-avant-garde.[13]

In Italy as abroad, the late 1960s and 1970s witnessed the widespread use of the body as a new vector for artistic practice in real time: a practice that sought to circumvent the institutional mediation of aesthetics and its reception. Liberated from the baffle of language, the confines of the frame, or even gallery walls, artists' bodies formed a new material, raw and readymade. Performances by Chris Burden saw him stage violence to his own person, whether by gunfire (*Shoot,* 1971) or by crucifixion on the back of a Volkswagen Beetle (*Trans-fixed,* 1974). Closer to home, artists such as Giovanni Anselmo and Giuseppe Penone invoked the body as sites of phenomenological inquiry, whether in terms of potential physical threat (Anselmo's torsion works) or probing self-scrutiny (Penone's *Developing One's Own Skin,* 1971). To be sure, many works still clung to a certain authorial authenticity, whether in order to ironize it more absolutely (Piero Manzoni's *Living Sculptures,* from 1961) or to reinscribe its methods, however tongue in cheek (Luigi Ontani's dandyish *tableaux vivants,* from the 1970s). This quick sketch, of course, flattens a range of practices—those of Adrian Piper or Vito Acconci, Herman Nitsch or Gina Pane—to a rather reductive plane. My point is that the body in Pasolini's work stands less as a cipher of spontaneous expression than as a plastic element freighted with representational import. It is less an object than a sign.

The artist himself equivocated on this matter. He claimed, on various occasions, to find the cinema free of the semiotic remove to which painting and literature are beholden. Here was reality, unshaped and unalloyed. Yet he also professed to "hate naturalness . . . [to] reconstruct everything."[14] Pasolini's affinity for parable and allegory proceeded in the same vein. In the oracular alembic of Matthew's aphorisms, the director's cinematic evangelism found a fitting linguistic equivalent. Even more apposite models lay, however, in the institution of painting. It was that affinity that perhaps most irrevocably separated his work from contemporary artistic practices of the late 1960s and 1970s, particularly in the dematerializing imperatives of the latter. Shifting from gritty novels penned in dialect to the early directorial efforts of *Accattone* and *Mamma Roma,* Pasolini developed what he termed the "theory of the sacred shot."[15] His cinema applied neorealism's legacies to works more coarse in their humanism—lacking, in fact, any ethical or political teleology other than a resistance to neocapitalist homogenization.

The visual strategies of these works—shot-reverse-shots, dissolves, and cross-fades—renounce the homespun simplicity of neorealism. Even leaving aside the hieraticism of Pasolini's cinema in particular, film reduces real bodies to phantasmatic doubles, flattens and etherealizes flesh and bone into two-dimensional specters. For all of its plunge into the stuff of reality, the celluloid image is inevitably, consummately, metaphysical. It distances and dematerializes the bodies it depicts. Whatever Pasolini's occasional claims to the contrary, that remove remained vital to his work. One critic noted of his *Gospel:* "In front of this admirable film, one is eventually unable to resist thinking of Caravaggio. He too dramatized the holy story through the mere force of his glance and then staged it through an interplay of light."[16] Mauri's performance redoubled the dramatization intrinsic to Pasolini's camera. The chiaroscuro of *Intellettuale* suggests, however, an atmosphere less sensual than stark. Its half-light conjures not merely the mystical, spiritual doubt of Caravaggio's *Saint Thomas* but also the clinical empiricism of Rembrandt's *Dr. Tulp.*

The title of Mauri's piece suggests a cold detachment—as if this "intellectual" were a juridical specimen, displayed under spotlight for examination or interrogation. The subject sits stripped of his name, but bears the standard of an entire cultural caste. The professorial spectacles discernible in Pasolini's wiry silhouette seem to confirm that pedantry. His chest appears as prominently exposed as his head is obscured, rendering his body a makeshift monitor. Still, the performance's dehumanizing elements would have been undermined by an emphatic corporeality. The mesmerizing photographs snapped by Antonio Masotti of the performance fix its duration into an almost sculptural immobility. Yet the rise and fall of Pasolini's torso with each breath, the occasional shift in his seat (inevitable over the film's two-hour course) would have rendered conspicuous his embodiment, even in its self-effacement. The artist, in short, was present.

Just five months later, Pasolini would be rendered irrevocably absent, his visage more literally effaced. Beaten with a plank and run over with his own car in the early hours of a cold November morning, Pasolini's body was offered up one last time to the Italian public (Figure 28.4). In police and newspaper photographs it appeared unrecognizable, a spectacle not of scandalous vitality but of the death so central to his oeuvre—now in practice as much as in theory. Just as cinematic narrative gains sense

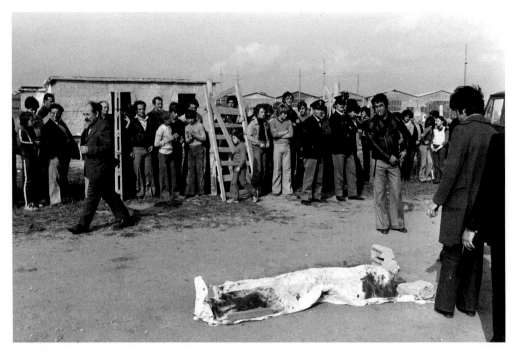

FIGURE 28.4. Crime scene of Pasolini's murder, November 2, 1975, Ostia, Italy. © Corbis.

through the cuts of montage—as Pasolini argues in one of his more adventurous theoretical texts from the late 1960s—so life acquires meaning only through the ultimate interruption of death.[17] In light of his murder, *Intellettuale* gained new meaning, too. Mauri continued to stage the piece for decades after, in venues from Brussels to Boston, Edinburgh to Turin, projecting the *Gospel* onto Pasolini's empty white shirt. Evacuated of flesh and breath, the garment became—and remains—an effigy, in absentia, of a body disappeared for its inconvenience.

NOTES

1. See Laura Betti, ed., *Pasolini: Cronaca giudiziaria, persecuzione, morte* (Milan: Garzanti, 1977). For an incisive reading of Pasolini's chronic indictments (and their attendant cultural elaborations) as a parallel dimension of his nominal art practice, see Barbara Castaldo, "Imputato Pasolini: Una rilettura dei processi tra diritto e letteratura," Ph.D. thesis, New York University, 2007.

2. Fabio Mauri, "Il Vangelo secondo Matteo di / su Pier Paolo Pasolini," in *Scritti in mostra: L'Avanguardia come zona, 1958–2008,* ed. Francesca Alfano Miglietti (Milan: Il Saggiatore, 2008), 205. For a brief summary of *Intellettuale* in the context of Mauri's larger oeuvre, see Barbara Casavecchia, "Body Politics," *frieze* 147 (May 2012): 180–185; Carolyn Christov-Bakargiev and Marcella Cossu, eds., *Fabio Mauri: Opere e aznioni, 1954–1994* (Milan: Carte Segrete, 1994), 164–165; and Miglietti, *Scritti in mostra,* 204–207.

3. I have taken this English translation from Maria-Antonietta Macciocchi, "Pasolini: Murder of a Dissident," *October* 13 (Summer 1980): 11.

4. See Giuseppe Zigaina, *Pasolini e la morte: Mito, alchimia e semantica del nulla lucente* (Venice: Marsilio, 1987); Zigaina, *Pasolini between Enigma and Prophecy,* trans. Jennifer Russell (Toronto: Exile Editions, 1991 [1989]); and Zigaina, *Pasolini e l'abiura: Il segno vivente e il poeta morto* (Venice: Marsilio, 1993).

5. Carlo Hayman-Chaffey, dir., *Pier Paolo Pasolini: A Filmmaker's Life,* 1971, 29 minutes, black and white.

6. When asked at a 1966 press conference why, as an atheist, he had made a film about the life of Christ, Pasolini replied: "If you know that I am an unbeliever, then you know me better than I do myself. I may be an unbeliever, but I am an unbeliever who has a nostalgia for a belief." Quoted in *Ancient Worlds in Film and Television: Gender and Politics,* ed. Almut-Barbara Renger and Jon Solomon (Leiden: Koninklijke Brill, 2013), 222.

7. Even these, for Pasolini, formed only a fainthearted rejoinder to the inexorable advance of consumerism, one set into even more ironic relief in this proudly communist city. See his "Bologna, città consumista e comunista," May 8, 1975, reprinted in Pasolini, *Lettere luterane* (Milan: Garzanti, 2009 [1976]), 61–64.

8. Pier Paolo Pasolini, review of Roberto Longhi, *Da Cimabue a Morandi* (1973), *Il Tempo* 18 (January 1974); reprinted in Pasolini, *Saggi sulla letterature e sull'arte,* vol. 2 (Milan: Mondadori, 1999), 1977.

9. On Pasolini's relationship to painting, see Alberto Marchesini, *Citazioni pittoriche nel cinema di Pasolini da Accatone al Decameron* (Florence: Nuova Italia Editrice, 1994); Franceso Galluzzi, *Pasolini e la pittura* (Roma: Bulzoni, 1994); and, more recently, Matthias Balbi, *Pasolini: Sade e la pittura* (Alessandria: Falsopiano, 2012).

10. See Pier Paolo Pasolini et al., "Pier Paolo Pasolini: An Epical-Religious View of the World," *Film Quarterly* 18, no. 4 (Summer 1965): 32.

11. See Per Piero Spila, *Pier Paolo Pasolini* (Rome: Gremese Editore, 1999), 34.

12. Macciocchi, "Pasolini," 15.

13. For an excellent discussion of Pasolini's relationship to contemporary artistic practice in cold war Italy—marked especially by diffidence though shot through with some notable points of intersection—see Luca Caminati, *Il Cinema come happening* (Milan: Postmedia, 2010). See also Ara H. Merjian, "Pier Paolo Pasolini between Neorealism and Neo-avantgarde," *GAM Magazine* (Galleria d'Arte Moderna, Turin) 4 (Summer 2011); and Ara H. Merjian, "Mascots and Muses: On Pasolini and Warhol," *frieze* 155 (May 2013).

14. Cited in Michael Chanan, "Pasolini and Warhol: The Calculating and the Nonchalant," *Art International* 14 (April 20, 1970): 25.

15. See Pier Paolo Pasolini, "The 'Cinema of Poetry,'" in Pasolini, *Heretical Empiricism,* trans. Ben Lawton and Louise K. Barnett (Bloomington and Indianapolis: Indiana University Press, 1988), 167–186.

16. Jean-Louis Bory, cited in Mira Liehm, *Passion and Defiance: Film in Italy from 1942 to the Present* (Berkeley: University of California Press, 1996), 242.

17. Pier Paolo Pasolini, "Observations on the Long Shot (1967)," in Pasolini, *Heretical Empiricism,* 237.

PART THREE ✳ TRANSFORMATIONS

Tara Murphy (pictured on the facing page) identifies as her personal "guardian angel" the large tattoo inked on her back. Extrapolating from the orientation of the wings, we see that Murphy's angel is indelibly fused, seamlessly interpolated, with her own body. She is embraced by the angel, who, according to the disposition of the wings on Murphy's back, merges with her body and resides within her own skin. She and the angel are one, sharing the same posture and protective stance toward one another.

Transformation is part and parcel of the human condition. The authors in this part of *Sensational Religion* address sensory transformations, including those that might be described as metaphorical, spiritual, material, and spatial.

The construction and reiteration of human subjectivities and affective registers take place in intimate sensory interaction with material objects, the engagement of which is fundamental to this process.[1] Analogical elaboration of materials, with its suggestion that one thing is like another, contributes to the work of imagining transformation, as significance shifts from one substance to another, in an apparently endless loop or even vibration. In content and practice this metamorphic motion suggests the possibility of similar transformations for persons. The power of the idea of transformation lies, in part, in its predication on movement, on motion, from one place or state to another. As Jane Bennett likewise insists, there is an attractive suggestion of "magic" in this mobility.[2] Several chapters in this part of the book elaborate on such somatic and kinesthetic experience: in touristic "pilgrimage" in the American West, where Mormonism forges a new religious modernity, in part by fully investing in the

Tara Murphy, February 23, 2012. Olympic Spa, Koreatown, Los Angeles. Photo by Sally M. Promey.

457

challenges of its own sensory and sensational configuration; in early Muslim bodily ingestion of substances understood to enhance not simply mimesis but also transformation or becoming; and in the embodied performance of contortions necessary to view certain ritual objects in ancient Peru.

The material, it turns out, is part and parcel of the equation: The material encodes, signifies, shapes, and constrains the construction of subjectivities and the processes of their becoming. In a Western cultural system that has tended to produce and replicate binary patterns of thought, dematerialization always implies its opposite. Constant oscillation between the terms of paired sets renders many apparent contradictions functionally irrelevant. This conceptual motion pulls linear developments, appearing to "progress" in a single direction from one term toward another, backward into cyclical rhythms and forms, asserting sensing material bodies as the ineluctable medium of the human condition and signaling a fundamental reticence to let them go.

Transformations, as we surely know, are just as often malignant as benign. One chapter tracks the descent of angels falling into materiality and sensation at the ragged edges of sixteenth-century Christian orthodoxies in Italy. Several authors in this section consider how various forms of trauma (extirpation, execution, "natural" death) get articulated into material and sensory history. In one colonial Latin American circumstance, for example, sensuous experience was precisely the locus for renegotiating religious observance. The through-story here concerns the ways that sensory culture refracts and reforms, often in the midst of violent transformations, including mortal harm to people and objects, in the contexts around it.

SALLY M. PROMEY

NOTES

1. This paragraph owes much to thinking laid out first in Sally M. Promey, "Hearts and Stones: Material Transformations and the Stuff of Christian Practice in the United States," in *American Christianities,* ed. Catherine Brekus and W. Clark Gilpin (Chapel Hill: University of North Carolina Press, 2011), 183–213.

2. Jane Bennett, in *The Enchantment of Modern Life* (Princeton, NJ: Princeton University Press, 2001), 17–18, explores a similar line of thinking: "Morphing transits" of various sorts "enact the very possibility of change. . . . To live among or as a crossing is to have motion called to mind, and this reminding is also a somatic event."

29

Bodies and Becoming

Mimesis, Mediation, and the Ingestion of the Sacred in Christianity and Islam

FINBARR BARRY FLOOD

> *In the eating encounter, all bodies are shown to be but temporary congealments of a materiality that is a process of becoming, is hustle and flow punctuated by sedimentation and substance.* Jane Bennett, *Vibrant Matter: A Political Ecology of Things*

In 2010 it was announced that a special deluxe version of Indian cricket star Sachin Tendulkar's autobiography would be produced in an edition of ten. Costing $75,000 (with the proceeds going to charity), the signature feature of each of these 852-page luxury texts would be a page produced by mixing the cricketer's blood into the paper pulp, accompanied on a separate double-page spread by Tendulkar's DNA profile, developed from his saliva. Like the relics venerated in many religious traditions (also, in theory at least, limited editions), the sanctified codex was intended to facilitate access not simply to an aura generally assumed to be lost in mass (re)production but also to the very essence and stuff of the godlike hero. The comparison may seem anachronistic or facetious, but it is worth considering the publisher's rationale for producing a "blood edition" of the *Tendulkar Opus:* "It's not everyone's cup of tea, it's not to everyone's taste and some may think it's a bit weird. But the key thing is that Sachin Tendulkar to millions of people is a religious icon. And we thought how, in a publishing form, can you get as close to your god as possible."[1]

Reworked for the era of hypercapitalism, in which the media-enhanced image of a sporting hero can assume the status of icon, even the specifics of this canny marketing exercise provide an uncanny echo of earlier devotional practices. Materialized not just *on* the page but *in* it, blood mediates presence, literalizing a homology between bodies and books, blood and ink, that will be familiar to Byzantinists, Islamicists, and Western medievalists, who could cite antecedents from the bloodstained Qur'an of the assassinated caliph Uthman (d. 656) (written with his own hand, according to some versions) through the painted blood that streaks a folio of the ninth-century Khludov Psalter.[2]

Bloodstained codices are the tip of an iceberg insofar as they avail of a material support to mediate access to valorized models, whether caliphs, saints, or sportsmen. One obvious distinction between media icons and spiritual exemplars lies, however, in the appeal to a transcendental signified. When it comes to mediating presence, the bodies and paraphernalia of spiritual exemplars are, like the materials with which they come in contact, understood as being imbued with an aura of sacrality that is both a mark of personal sanctity and a sign of divine grace whose ultimate source lies beyond the sanctified body. Moreover, if the molding of the self in relation to such models highlights the importance of mimetic identification in shaping spiritual identity, the role of transvalued (or even transubstantiated) matter in devotional practices raises more ambiguous questions regarding the boundaries between practices of identification and the nature of personal identity, between modes of imitating and means of becoming. Offering a perspective on mediation, materiality, and mimesis often at variance with the orthodoxies of post-Enlightenment modernity, devotional practices centered around animated matter call into question epistemological and ontological models of subject–object relations that have been deeply internalized and naturalized in Euro-America as a legacy of both the Reformation and the Enlightenment.[3] However arcane these issues seem, they lie at the heart of the disenchantments of modernity, a condition characterized by Jane Bennett as "an inconsistent and paradoxical combination of claims about nature and culture," which "passes itself off as the clean, enlightened alternative to a messy, primitivistic cosmology that confuses the natural with the cultural, mixes the animal with the human, mistakes the inanimate for the animate, and contaminates the moral with the prudential."[4] The endeavor, according to Bruno Latour, is dependent on practices of stratification that operate at various levels. These range from the contingent and conventional relations assumed by Saussurean linguistics through the dematerialization, idealization, and ontological disaggregation essential to the operation of the sign in modern semiotics to the common distinction between the exteriorities of material embodiment and the interiorities of immaterial piety.[5]

Past decades have been marked by increased skepticism about the transcultural and/or transhistorical relevance of such binaries, foundational as they are to culturally and historically specific epistemologies and ontologies universalized as transcendental truths. Writing recently in the wake of the global controversy over caricatures of the Prophet Muhammad (d. 632), for example, the anthropologist Saba Mahmood has argued that traditional concepts of mimesis as imitation or reiteration fail to do justice to the aspirational nature of devotional practice. Rather than a relation of mimesis, Mahmood argues, the relationship between the Prophet Muhammad and the pious should instead be characterized as one of schesis, a "living relation" characterized by an identification that not only collapses temporospatial distance but affects the very stuff of personal identity. Realization of the Prophet's behavior entails embodied habitation, a goal facilitated by the hadith (traditions of the Prophet), which "are lived not as commandments but as virtues; one wants to ingest, as it were, the Prophet's persona."[6] The desire to which Mahmood draws attention is literalized in Islam through the practice of *tabarruk,* the seeking of *baraka,* the immaterial blessing that radiates from the bodies of prophets or saints in life or death or from objects associated with them. Typically, baraka is absorbed through kissing, touching, or rubbing.[7] This haptic and somatic aspect of Islamic devotional practices is invoked in a remarkable preamble to a discussion of Indian religions written around 1030 CE in which the Persian scholar Abu Rayhan al-Biruni presents the investment in devotional images as a matter of class and education rather than of religious difference. Al-Biruni notes the affective power of certain types of depictions and hypothesizes about their impact on uneducated believers, including Muslims:

> These words of mine would at once receive a sufficient illustration if, for example, a picture of the Prophet (*ṣūrat al-nabī*) were made, or of Mecca and the Ka'ba, and were shown to an uneducated man or woman. Their joy in looking at the thing would bring them to kiss the picture, to rub their cheeks against it, and to roll themselves in the dust before it, as if they were seeing not the picture, but the original, and were in this way, as if they were present in the holy places, performing the rites of pilgrimage, the greater (*ḥajj*) and the lesser (*'umra*).[8]

This passage is an important one, raising significant questions about mimesis, surrogacy, and the sacred. In the present context, however, it serves to draw attention to sensory aspects of devotion otherwise documented by inscriptions inviting contact, and by patterns of wear attesting to it, on some of the Christian and Islamic devotional images that are considered here, few of which were in fact produced for the illiterate or the uneducated.

Devotional practices involving bodily engagement with the sacred range from seeing or touching to the consumption of liquids infused with the charisma of primary or secondary relics for apotropaic, prophylactic, and therapeutic purposes. Imbibing or ingesting sacred matter is by no means acceptable to all Muslims or characteristic of Islamic devotional rituals alone but is common to many religious traditions. Incorporating the charisma of the sanctified other into the very essence of the self, they amplify an underlying ambiguity between imitating and becoming that is perhaps central to all devotional practice. In doing so, they also highlight a capacity of materiality to mediate sacrality that operates both transculturally and tranhistorically, however diverse the specific forms and meanings it assumes in particular times and places. Despite this, and although they have attracted the occasional interest of anthropologists and sociologists, practices of ingestion have largely been ignored by historians of art or material culture more broadly. The reasons for this neglect are not hard to discern, even in an era saturated by histories of reception; not only do the objects of such practices (and often the paraphernalia associated with them) fall foul of the "high/low" distinction essential to the canonization of the objects of art history but their ingestion also falls well outside the range of practices sanctioned in modernity as appropriate responses to texts and images. Yet the transubstantiated eucharist of Catholic Christianity is not the only case of devotional ingestion that survives in modernity. On the contrary, practices of ingesting sacred texts and images for prophylactic or therapeutic purposes already satisfied by mass production long before modernity not only continue to flourish but also in some cases have even been adapted for an era of mechanical reproduction. In addition to the consumption of printed images and texts (see below), the advent of photography expanded the possibilities for ingesting the sacred. Long-established practices of reciting efficacious formulas over water for ingestion find modern correlates, for example, in the consumption of water or other liquid media infused through contact with the blessings emanating from photographs of sanctified figures.[9] The ingestion of water infused with the blessing imparted by contact with an image or by the proximate recitation of an efficacious text finds numerous earlier analogies, but the alleged indexical nature of the photograph makes it especially appropriate to such therapeutic functions.

That such practices have been adapted to the technologies of modernity is perhaps not surprising given their longevity. In the eastern Mediterranean, for example, the ingestion of both images and words is attested by a wide range of artifacts and texts relating to both devotional and magical practices well before the advent of Christianity. In Egypt, several pharaonic temples, including those at Luxor and Philae, show evidence of reliefs and hieroglyphs having been scraped in order to remove powder to ingest for amuletic or prophylactic purposes already before the Roman period, leaving gashes up to 40 centimeters long on the surface of the stone. At Edfu, Philae, and many other sites, these practices continued into the Christian era, when the crosses and other Christian signs engraved alongside defaced polytheistic images became the focus of similar devotional activities. Analogous activities have been noted at medieval Christian sites in both Italy and Germany into the modern period.[10]

In Egypt and elsewhere, such practices existed on the margins of more canonical practices of ingesting sacred matter that flourished before and after the Christianization (and later Islamicization) of the eastern Mediterranean. These proliferated as part of what Patricia Cox Miller has dubbed the "material turn" in fourth-century Christianity, a development that signaled "a new subject–object relation, a relation of the human subject to the sanctifying potential of human physicality as locus and mediator of spiritual presence and power."[11] In the centuries before the advent of Islam, access to both presence and power was generally provided by images, relics, and visitation of sacred sites. The ritualized itineraries and peregrinations of pilgrims gave them access to the sacred mimetically in the very places in which sanctified exemplars had walked.[12] Material relics extended this engagement with the sacred, diminishing the gap between matter and spirit by permitting sanctified bodies to be accessed sensually even in places and times far distant from their sites of origin.[13] If, however, mimesis as dynamic reenactment offered one means of embodying pious exemplars, the kissing, licking, or even ingestion of fragments of the sacralized bodies, or of materials transvalued by contact with them, are less easily accommodated under the rubric of mimesis, at least in its commonplace sense of re-presentation or re-staging. On the contrary, such practices point to a desire to collapse a distinction between emulator and emulated that is central to the operation of mimesis as re-presentation. In this sense, as Gary Vikan has noted, the relation of desire that unites pilgrim and sanctified model bears comparison to the ontological indeterminacy exploited in sympathetic magic, in which the relation between model and referent had less to do with imitating than with becoming.[14]

Ingestion was integral to this process of becoming. If the circulation of *eulogiae* (blessings) was intended to bring the efficacious sacrality of these blessings home to the believer in his or her own circumstances, the ingestion of sacred matter took the process to its logical conclusion, taking it into the very substance of the self. Tangible eulogiae brought by early medieval pilgrims from Christian shrines in Palestine and the eastern Mediterranean from the fifth century onward included not only cloth infused by contact and cords or strips of cloth cut to the exact measure of sacred sites, and their component rocks but also edible or ingestible substances such as bread, dew, dust, earth, hair, manna, oil, water, and frequently fruit.[15] Even mass-produced tokens composed of the dust or earth of sacred sites could facilitate the ingestion of the sacred. In the production of such tokens, images of a saint were stamped on tablets of earth from his shrine, the fusion of word, image, and sacred matter blurring the distinction between icon and relic. Their production reflects beliefs in the capacity of sanctity to be both transmitted and, perhaps more significantly, to be mediated materially, thanks to an indexical chain of contact with the saint's body that imbued even mundane or profane materials with a sacrality capable of further transmission, in effect transforming them into part of the saint's "distributed personhood."[16] Typical of such eulogiae are those produced at the shrine of the stylite saint Symeon the Younger in northern Syria in the sixth and seventh centuries (Figure 29.1); fashioned from matter taken from the sacred site (itself sanctified by contact with the saint's body), these were formed into a tablet stamped with the image of the saint, identified in an accompanying inscription.[17] Just as the oil poured over relics to infuse it with sanctity or taken as eulogiae from many other Christian pilgrimage sites in Palestine and Syria could be applied to the body, hagiographic tales describe the external application of such clay tokens. The saint's *vita* also invokes the ingestion of these tokens, however, for it describes how a monk from Symeon's Miraculous Mountain advised a

FIGURE 29.1. Pilgrim token from the shrine of Saint Symeon Stylites the Younger (d. 592), northern Syria. Clay, diameter 3.8 centimeters. The Walters Art Museum, Baltimore, 48.1939.

praetorian prefect suffering from intestinal problems to take some of the saint's hair and the dust of his eulogia, dissolve the mixture, and both drink and wash with the water.[18] The role of the saint's hair in this hagiographical tale anticipates the reported use of similar exuviae in Islam a century or so later, when the Prophet Muhammad's hair, footprints, and even nail parings and saliva were sometimes consumed by taking them into the devotee's body, a topic to which I will return below.

The ability of the crafted image to both instantiate and mediate presence would be hotly contested in Byzantium during the eighth and ninth centuries, but there are strong indications of an increasing blurring of the ontological boundaries between bodies, images, and relics in the preceding centuries. A well-known sixth- or seventh-century hagiographical tale discussed by Vasileios Marinis in Chapter 19 of this volume describes how a devotee of the popular Arabian saints Cosmas and Damian painted their images on the wall of her house to satisfy her desire to see them. On being stricken by illness, the devotee scraped the surface of the painted plaster with her fingernails and ingested the painted fragments dissolved in water, thereby finding an immediate cure from pain effected by the presence of the saints.[19] Such practices were sufficiently widespread to eventually attract the opprobrium of iconoclasts concerned with the dissolution of the ontological divide between image and prototype. A letter written by the iconoclast emperor Michael II in 824 warns the Carolingian emperor about the dangerous practices associated with the veneration of images, including their treatment as if they were living beings, denouncing priests and clerics who "scraped paint from images and mixed it with the offerings and wine [of the eucharist] and after the celebration of the Mass gave it to those wishing to partake."[20] The antecedents of such catholic practices of ingesting the sacred are perhaps to be sought in devotional rituals associated with relics, such as that observed in the fourth century by Lucilla of Carthage, who was in the habit of kissing the bone from a martyr in her possession prior to ingesting the eucharist.[21] Within the polemics of iconoclasm, the eucharist offered a true image of the divine, a foil of real presentation for the falsity of material representation; it was the equivalence implied by their mingling that occasioned scandal.[22]

In these cases, the principle of transubstantiation enjoyed a de facto extension from the eucharistic gifts to painted images of those pious mortals charged with mediating a relationship to the divine. The material colors scraped from the paintings were just that—material pigments. What is implied by their role in the narrative is that they were transvalued if not transubstantiated by their use to delineate the material images of the saints' bodies. In this sense, they acted as flesh—color and enfleshment often being coincident in the painted body—fragments of the saints imbued with the sacrality of body fragments that otherwise served as relics.[23]

The ability of a painted icon to facilitate inherence or immanence in numerous hagiographic and miracle tales finds a chiastic reflection in tales of static living saints, figures who fashioned themselves as images through practices of pious emulation, appearing as neither fully animate nor entirely inanimate.[24] Patricia Cox Miller has argued that the tension between animation and inanimacy or stasis inherent in such presentations of the sacred represents a Christian variant on "an ancient Mediterranean culture-pattern," a reworking of a long-exploited indeterminacy in which eulogiae, icons, and relics are characterized by what Cox Miller (citing Bill Brown) sees as an "ontological instability, an oscillation between animate and inanimate, subject and object, human and thing."[25] The series might be extended to the relationship between the devotee and the focus of devotion, to the tension between mimesis as identification or identity, a relation of superficial emulation versus the ontological ambiguities of participation.[26] These ambiguities are thrown into high relief by mimetic practices that entail not only emulation but ingestion; this much is clear from Exodus 32:20, where the idolatrous Israelites are forced to ingest the golden calf they have made, ground to powder and suspended in a liquid medium, literalizing a biblical trope according to which idolaters become like the inanimate idols that they worship. By contrast, in pre-Reformation and Catholic Christianity, the complex chiasmus of *Imitatio Christi,* of man who is made in God's image aspiring to reproduce the habitus of God made man, is intensified by the ingestion of the eucharistic gifts, through the digestion of which the worshipper not only incorporates the sacred but "is absorbed into the body of Christ and is subsumed within it."[27] The point may well be to achieve "a mutual in-one-anotherness," but to describe this as a mimetic relation seems to stretch the boundaries of mimesis well beyond the generally understood meaning of emulation, imitation, or representation.[28]

As Saba Mahmood's comments on devotion to the Prophet Muhammad suggest, similar ambiguities are operative in the negotiation of the relationship between personal identity and devotional identifications in Islam, even outside the parameters of an incarnational economy. No less than icons and stamped clay tokens, late antique and early medieval hagiographic texts could function as eulogiae, "designed to circulate, a source of blessing for readers as well as for the author."[29] Similarly, the hadith, the textualized records of the deeds and words of the Prophet Muhammad, are characterized as *āthār,* traces or vestiges that permit the faithful access to the Prophet as a mimetic model, whose practices of comportment, dress, and even dental hygiene one can internalize and make one's own.[30] The mimetic potential of prophetic biography represents a specifically Islamic take on the established tradition of affective hagiography that renders the devotional landscape of early Islam perfectly comprehensible from the perspective of late antiquity. More material continuities into the early Islamic period are apparent in the continued collection, circulation, and consumption of eulogiae, which were adopted among the practices of early Islam. The evidence for this takes the form of glass pilgrim flasks produced for Muslims, similar to those known to have contained sanctified earth, oil, and water gathered from pilgrimage sites by Christian and Jewish pilgrims in the sixth and seventh centuries but with a distinctive iconography.[31] There is no evidence for the manner in which the matter contained in such flasks was consumed by early Muslims, but in light of well-documented Christian practices and the viscosity of many of the materials used to mediate sacrality, it is likely that they were applied both externally and internally.

In addition, more profane practices of ingestion similar to those well documented in Egypt even before the Christian era survived in the medieval Islamic world, where they were also employed for therapeutic or prophylactic purposes. Some existed on the margins of canonical devotional practices; among them were rituals associated with a stone bearing the image of a man with a scorpion's tail, which was visible at the entrance to the Great Mosque of Hims in northern Syria in the tenth century (Figure 29.2).[32] This was among a wide array of antique figural *spolia* whose investment with apotropaic or talismanic properties underlay their deployment at the entrances to medieval Islamic cities, mosques, and palaces from North Africa to Iran.[33] The specific form and location of the Hims relief recall the scorpion-men of ancient Mesopotamian art and literature,

FIGURE 29.2. *'Ajā'ib al-makhlūqāt wa gharā'ib al-mawjūdāt* (The Wonders of Creation and the Rarities of Existence), an imaginative depiction of the scorpion-man talisman in the mosque of Hims, Muhammad ibn Mahmud ibn Ahmad al-Tusi, Iraq, 1388. Bibliothèque nationale de France, suppl. pers. 332, fol. 95b.

hybrid creatures that guarded the entrances to magical landscapes; it may well have been intended to protect the mosque against scorpions, a source not only of poisonous irritation but of potential spiritual pollution, since they were among the chthonic forms that jinn were believed to assume.[34] In terms of continuity with earlier practices, what is particularly noteworthy about the scorpion-man of Hims is that clay impressed with the image was believed to protect the house against scorpions and reptiles; dissolved in water and consumed, it was thought to cure the sting of the beast.[35]

According to several hadith, scorpions and poisonous reptiles are among the threats against which charms can be legitimately employed.[36] The deployment of sympathetic means to this end is well documented in the *Picatrix,* the tenth- or eleventh-century Latin translation of the Arabic *Ghāyat al-Ḥakīm,* and in later European texts derived from Arabic sources. These describe the therapeutic consumption of an aqueous solution of incense stamped with the image of a scorpion engraved on a bezoar stone under the rising sign of Scorpio, whose ascendancy also determined the moment when the seal should be impressed on the material of the incense.[37] Considering the relationship between image, signet or seal matrix, and the medium of impression, it is worth noting that the Arabic term *khātam* served to denote both the stamp and the clay or other medium that bore its impression; to the present day, the same term is used to denote the protective or prophylactic formulas inscribed on wooden boards, then washed with water intended for ingestion.[38] With the sympathetic conjunction of image, medium, and zodiacal alignment ensuring its efficacy, the Hims relief appears like a large-scale manifestation of the small-scale amulets and talismans produced across the early Islamic world, many bearing images of snakes, scorpions, and birds intended to both cure and repel.[39]

The tokens impressed with the talismanic image from Hims belong to the universe of popular magic and medicine, but they also have counterparts in early Islamic pilgrimage practices. By the tenth century, and probably much earlier, Shi'i pilgrims were both consuming and taking home tablets comprising earth from the Shi'ite shrines at Kerbala and Najaf in Iraq.[40] Although it is not clear when the practice started, similar tablets composed of the soil of Medina were also produced for pilgrims, stamped with a hadith recalling the Prophet's assertion that the soil of Medina and his own saliva were possessed of curative powers.[41] The same hadith was frequently invoked in *al-ṭibb al-nabawī*, prophetic medicine, a genre of medicinal text produced from the ninth century onward.[42]

Combining sacred image and matter, these clay tokens not only facilitated the mobility of sacred topography but were, like their Christian counterparts, also said to have both prophylactic and therapeutic properties.[43] In both Christianity and Islam, the production of clay tablets comprised of sacred dust points to the importance of multiplicity and replication in disseminating sacrality in times and places far removed from the events of prophetic or saintly biography. Whereas the corporeal relics favored in late antique and medieval Christianity were in theory finite, albeit capable of generating secondary relics, clay tablets had the advantage of potentially infinite production. Body-part relics are extremely rare in the Islamic world due to an Islamic reticence about fragmentation of the sanctified body, general concerns about the ritual pollution that accrues from contact with dead bodies, the premium placed on the integrity of the body, and proscriptions relating to its mutilation. As a consequence, the possibility of proliferation is necessarily intrinsic to the relic in Islam, even that deriving from the sanctified body. In the case of relics of the Prophet Muhammad, the ascription of reliquary value generally derives from one of three circumstances.[44] First, the source of such value might be a direct relationship to the body of the Prophet through derivation from it, most obviously as exuviae; hairs and nail clippings are the most common examples, sheddings whose ability to provide access to their living source was one reason that believers were urged to dispose carefully of their own lest they be abused for magical purposes.[45] Second, a relic might bear a direct relationship to the body of the Prophet as a trace, *athar,* what in Peircean semiotics would be termed an index, a sign that is causally related to its referent. This contact might or might not leave a visible mark; at one end of the spectrum are Prophetic footprints, at the other the hadith themselves. Third, manufactured objects might be sanctified by virtue of a contingent relationship to the body of the Prophet: robes, sandals, and standards are the typical examples, although, depending on where and when one looks, the series could be extended to include shirts and even twigs used for cleaning the teeth. By the nineteenth century, the most extraordinary collection of such relics was housed in the treasury of Topkapi Palace in Istanbul, in which was amassed hairs, sandals, footprints, teeth, and accoutrements of the Prophet as well of those of early caliphs, saints, and prophets.[46] These were gathered from different regions of the Ottoman Empire, especially from the eighteenth century onward, perhaps part of a concerted pietistic response to the twin threats of European expansionism and the rise of militant Wahhabi Sunnism (which rejected the principle of *tawassul,* or intercession, and the veneration of saints and prophets) in the Arabian Peninsula.[47] During this period, images of the Prophet's relics, including those newly arrived in Istanbul, were integrated into devotional prayer books, thus circulating their baraka outside the palace walls in ways that will be considered further below.

Although the first two categories of relic derive directly from the Prophet's body, the third consists of mundane artifacts singularized by infusion with Prophetic baraka. These kinds of relic represent a point of congruence, if not continuity, between Christian and Islamic traditions, an overlap apparent to those jurists who raised occasional objections to the veneration of material objects or to the idea of mediation that they embodied based on concerns about authenticity or the transculturation of Islamic practice. All three classes of relic—exuviae, traces, and contact relics—were the focus of devotional, prophylactic, and therapeutic practices similar to those found in Eastern Christianity in the centuries before the advent of Islam, including practices of ingestion.

According to a hadith, the Prophet applied his spittle mixed with dust as medicine to those afflicted by ulcers or wounds.[48] After his death, the hair, footprints, and even nail parings, sweat, and saliva of the Prophet were kept as relics, sometimes consumed by taking them into the devotee's body.[49] The Prophet himself is said to have distributed the hairs cut from his head as part of the ritual observed during his final pilgrimage to Mecca; dipped in water, the resulting liquid had both apotropaic and therapeutic properties that were efficacious against both illness and the evil eye.[50] As a result, such relics were often favored in funerary contexts, where they would protect the deceased and attest to his or her piety. As he was dying, the first Umayyad caliph Mu'awiya (d. 680) is said to have requested that he be buried in a shirt given to him by the Prophet, whose nail parings the caliph had preserved in a bottle; these were to be ground to a powder and placed in his eyes and mouth, along with the Prophet's hair, according to some accounts. More than one Companion of Muhammad is said to have been buried with a hair of the Prophet on his tongue and each of his eyes, a practice also said to have been followed in the funerary rites of several later rulers, including Nur al-Din ibn Zangi (d. 1174), leader of the counter-Crusade.[51]

Similarly, those seeking the baraka of the Prophet's footprints, robe, or sandals might touch them to their eyes or mouths. The indexical chain central to the production of such secondary relics could even be extended by replication. One of the most common relics, the sandal or *na'l* of the Prophet, circulated in the form of schematic drawings traced from the original and repeatedly copied in their turn. In this way, the most famous example of the sandal relic, that housed in a purpose-built shrine in Damascus, traveled across the Islamic world as a schematic likeness (*mithāl*), which was often incorporated into illustrated eulogies of the Prophet, his tomb, and relics that reached the devout in places as distant as the Maghrib and the Atlantic coast of the *dār al-Islām*.[52] This ability of the copy to circulate the baraka of the original was predicated on an indexical relationship between tracing, relic, and, ultimately, the body of the historical Prophet. Collapsing space and time, the image of the relic assumed the efficacy of the relic, traveling forth to meet the pious in situations far removed from those that the original could attain, to paraphrase Walter Benjamin's well-known comments on technological reproduction.[53]

Echoing the scenario imagined by al-Biruni in the text cited above, images of the sandal and other relics were often inscribed with the injunction to kiss the image or to touch it to one's eyes and face or rub it over them in order to honor its owner and avail oneself of its baraka. Both are enjoined in the texts inscribed around and within the image of the sandal shown here (Figure 29.3), which appears at the end of a two-meter-long painted scroll commemorating the Arabian pilgrimage of a female

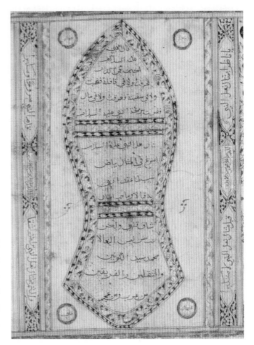

FIGURE 29.3. An image of the Prophet Muhammad's sandal (*na'l*) with texts eulogizing its virtues and those of the Prophet, from a scroll commemorating a pilgrimage to Mecca and Medina in 1432–1433 (British Library, Add 27566, detail).

pilgrim, Maymuna, in 1432–1433; the text invokes the mediating role of the image, asserting (somewhat defensively) that these gestures honor neither the image nor the sandal but its owner.[54] Like the long-venerated Christian icons and manuscript images discussed by Vasileios Marinis in Chapter 19 of this volume, some of the images of the Prophet's sandals found in early modern manuscripts show clear signs of wear from kissing or touching.[55] In Christian and Islamic practice, the application of both relics and their depictions to eyes and mouths and the exchange of saliva inherent in the act of osculation point to a desire to ingest the baraka of the relic, which in other cases was facilitated by the mediation of viscous liquids—milk, oil, water, or unguents—that might be absorbed into the body. Just as the ink from certain inscribed passages of the Qur'an might be dissolved and ingested for its curative or protective properties (see below), the baraka that inhered in the hairs of the Prophet was sometimes ingested by dipping them in water that was then drunk. The most famous and best documented of such ritualized ingestions of baraka was elaborated at the Ottoman court. Beginning in the reign of Selim I (r. 1512–1520), once a year, on the fifteenth day of Ramadan, the *khirka* or *burda* (robe) of the Prophet was subject to a ceremonial washing (more in the nature of a symbolic dipping than a general scrub). As part of the ceremony, the robe was infused with water from the sacred Zamzam well at Mecca that was afterward gathered in bottles and distributed among the Ottoman elite as a relic in its own right, to be consumed as needed, generally drop by drop in an aqueous dilution (Figure 29.4).[56]

In what is the only reference to a footprint of the Prophet in Mecca that is known to me, the Ottoman traveler Evliya Çelebi (d. 1682) describes an analogous practice in which pilgrims filled the depression of the print with rose-water, which they then rubbed on their faces and eyes.[57] It is possible that Çelebi was in fact reporting on the Maqam Ibrahim, the stone that was widely identified as bearing the footprints of Abraham. The confusion may have arisen from the tradition that the feet of the Prophet Muhammad were identical to the size of the prints left by Ibrahim. As early as the 'Abbasid period, it is reported that water from the sacred well of Zamzam was poured on the stone with Ibrahim's prints, then drunk by the pious or stored in bottles and jugs for later consumption.[58] Zamzam water was widely believed to have curative properties; infused with the baraka derived from the Prophet's footprint or robe, its use concatenated a potent sacrality that derived from the condition of contact with both person and place.[59]

Although rejected by some jurists, analogous practices are documented even in relation to the body of the austere Syrian jurist Ibn Taymiyya (d. 1328), during whose lifetime devotees sought to drink the water with which he performed his ritual ablutions and after whose death mourners vied with each other to gather the water in which his body had been washed.[60] The practice was presumably sanctioned by the reported value attributed to the water with which the Prophet Muhammad had per-

FIGURE 29.4. Ottoman vessels containing Zamzam water used to wash the Prophet's robe. Topkapı Sarayı Müzesi (Topkapi Palace Museum), Istanbul, Inv. TSMK 21/763.

formed his ritual ablutions by his Companions, who sought baraka from it. In the nineteenth century, water used to wash the Prophet's tomb in Medina thrice yearly, and even the brooms used in the process, were preserved as relics.[61] Analogous practices still exist in various parts of the Islamic world today, often as parts of the devotional rituals associated with shrines, which Ibn Taymiyya and his successors have consistently tried to regulate. These practices are perhaps best documented in relation to the sufi shrines (*dargah*s) of South Asia, where the ingestion of flower petals or earth surrounding the graves, or of water used to wash the graves, forms part of a redistributional economy that circulates the blessedness that emanates from the bodies of the saints even after death. In a manner comparable to the *prasād* offered to Hindu deities at their shrines, edible substances that absorb some of the sanctity of the deities who partake of them before they are redistributed for ingestion by the pious, such instances of "sensuous media" enchain presence across space and time, linking the proven piety of the dead, or the sacred substance of deities, with the devotional aspirations of the living.[62] Although traditions of prasād are common to both Hindus and

Muslims, this very commonality can also inspire attempts to establish the limits of commensuration when it comes to practices of ingesting the sacred. Until today, Christian insistence upon the unique ontological status of the eucharist explains the presence of signs in the cathedral of Panaji, the capital of Goa, that warn visitors: "Holy Communion is not a prasad. Non-Christians are not allowed to receive Holy Communion."

In the Islamic world, the most fascinating instance of relic ingestion involved a metarelic, a text about a relic, for which no indexical relation to the Prophet is self-evident. This was the celebrated *Qaṣīdat al-Burda* of the Egyptian sufi al-Busiri (d. ca. 1296), a poem in praise of the Prophet's robe written in Mamluk Egypt that enjoyed enormous popularity across North Africa into the early modern period. According to its preface, al-Busiri's poem was written when the poet was stricken by paralysis. On completing the poem, the poet slept and the Prophet appeared to him in a dream, whereupon he recited his poem to the Prophet; by way of reward, the Prophet placed his cloak (*burda*) around the poet's shoulder. When he awoke, he found himself cured.[63]

While the relic of the Prophet's robe (which existed in multiple incarnations) was consistently associated with curative or other miracle-working properties, what is remarkable about al-Busiri's poem is that it acquired some of the curative and talismanic properties associated with the baraka of the original; in this it followed a trend set by at least one earlier eulogy of the Prophet Muhammad.[64] In the preface to his own poem, al-Busiri describes how a blind man was visited by the Prophet in a dream and told to seek healing from the robe; unable to find the original, he successfully availed himself of a copy of al-Busiri's poem, which he applied to his eyes. The words of the ode could be inscribed on signet rings by moonlight (a usage that recalls talismanic practices) and then used to serve a range of apotropaic or therapeutic purposes similar to those associated with the image of the Prophet's sandal—aiding memory or relieving labor pains, for example. The text could be recited over water that was then ingested to absorb the baraka of the robe or dissolved in rose-water and saffron for ingestion.[65] Echoing the contemporary practice of ingesting lemon juice infused with the pulverized stones of Mamluk funerary monuments, the most famous commentary on the burda, that of Muhammad al-Bajuri (d. 1860), commends the curative properties of certain verses of al-Busiri's poem, which he says should be inscribed on a pottery shard, then washed with licorice juice ingested on an empty stomach.[66]

Such practices find a counterpart in the ingestion at the Ottoman court of water infused with the robe itself, but the ability of a textual eulogy to circulate the baraka of the relic had the advantage of making its mediating power accessible to a much wider spectrum of the faithful than the Ottoman elite. In this sense, it might be compared to the way in which tracings of the Prophet's sandal, copied, recopied, and circulated in manuscripts and single folios (see Figure 29.3), rendered its baraka accessible to those living far from Damascus, where the most famous of the sandal relics was kept. Although tracings of the sandal were related to the original by an indexical chain of copying, this was not the case with al-Busiri's text, at least not at first glance. As in the case of the paint ingested from early medieval Byzantine icons, there is no obvious historical relationship to the Prophet that would permit the material text of al-Busiri's poem to take on some of the reliquary value of the cloak that inspired it, or at least its dream image. Instead the investment of al-Busiri's poem points to the status of the dream vision as an instance of real presence, giving direct access to the reality of the Prophet and his healing robe. A well-known hadith insists that, "Whoever has seen me in a dream has indeed seen me."[67] In some cases, the Prophet is said to have appeared to sufi saints in dreams in order to bestow some of his healing saliva on them; in others, the dream vision of the Prophet instantiated a presence sufficient to forge an indexical link with mosques built centuries after his death.[68] In this sense, al-Busiri's words in praise of the robe assumed the status of a secondary relic, bolstered by an indexical chain from the dream presence of the Prophet to his robe to the poetic (re)presentation of that robe, invested with the thaumaturgic properties of the original.

The ontological fluidity inherent in this scenario is common to both Christian and Islamic traditions, in which the prophetic or saintly figure of a dream apparition is not merely an ephemeral chimera but an experience of real presence, transcending time and space in a manner sufficient to forge an originary link in a chain of materially mediated blessing linking the body of the prophet or saint with that of the believer, petitioner, or pilgrim. In the vita of Saint Artemius (d. 363), for example, we hear of a cure effected through drinking a wax seal impressed with the image of the saint following a prescription offered by the saint himself, along with the seal, in a dream.[69] The phenomenon is comparable to the ability of pigment to "jump the species barrier," as it were, in an ontological transformation into de facto saintly flesh. In Christianity, the same eventuality finds numerous counterparts in tales of icons coming to life—bleeding, lactating, or even reaching from their frames to admonish, punish, or avenge themselves—but also in accounts of dreams in which the image of a saint acts as him- or herself. In other words, in both Christianity and Islam, modes of devotional experience regarded as immaterial within the epistemologies and ontologies of modernity were, under the right conditions, considered instances of real presence, fully capable of material effects, including "relic-effects."

The osculation of the Prophet's sandal commanded by the texts inscribed on its image (see Figure 29.3) and the ingestion of his robe's baraka through the medium of the ink used to describe and eulogize it also point to the complex imbrications of oral narratives, textual artifacts, and material relics in fostering both the dispersal of and access to the sacred. In the case of al-Busiri's text, the material words of the poem convey an immaterial blessing that derives from the robe only by virtue of its contact with the body of the Prophet. However, the ingestion of water infused with the text and its displaced blessings followed a precedent long established in relation to the text of the Qur'an, which describes itself (7:82) as a healing and a mercy. Ingestion of the Revelation's blessings by means of its material support (usually parchment or paper and ink) and other mediating substances (most obviously water) in order to absorb and avail oneself of its baraka are well documented both ethnographically and textually in many regions of the Islamic world. Often described as drinking the Qur'an, in fact such practices exploit a distinction between the verbal revelation of the Qur'an and its materialization as written text, distinguished by the Arabic term *muṣḥaf* (plural *maṣāḥif*).

Although the materialization of divine scripture facilitated its ingestion and digestion, we should bear in mind the primacy afforded in many parts of the Islamic world to oral recitation, a mode of accessing scripture in which it also entered the body of the reciter. Here we might recall the biblical account of Ezekiel being commanded to ingest the scrolls containing the divine message that he was to convey to the Israelites by his preaching, his reiteration of divine speech preceded by its literal incorporation; the scrolls are said to have tasted as sweet as honey, prefiguring accounts of ingesting the eucharistic host in Christian tradition.[70] Adding to the dialectic between oral recitation and textualization as modes of investing the body with traces of the divine, premodern practices of reading constituted "a physical act, as the movement of lips, the sounding of words, the tracing of fingers and hands were integral to digesting the text and understanding its meaning."[71]

Setting a precedent later extended to relics of the Prophet and their depictions, the material codex was honored by being kissed, perfumed, and protected from pollution by the touch of those in a state of ritual impurity. In addition, practices of logophagy seem to have been well developed in relation to the material Qur'an in early and medieval Islam, for they are discussed in a number of juridical texts that are informed by a tension between the transcendental nature of the logos and the profane (and potentially polluting) nature of the human body. As a consequence, these discussions are characterized by divergent opinions regarding the religious acceptability of ingestion and its legality, a controversy that has continued to the present day.[72] Early practices of ingesting the Qur'an often made use of ephemeral materials, including Qur'anic verses written in ink on paper, then dissolved in water and drunk for curative or prophylactic purposes—against the evil eye or illness or to ensure an easy childbirth, for example. In addition to appearing in juridical texts, reference to such practices is made in the genre of *al-ṭibb al-nabawī*, prophetic medicine.[73] Efficacious texts, including verses of the Qur'an, could also be inked on the interior of a bowl, dissolved in water, and then ingested, a tradition documented in Egypt well into the modern period.[74] Occasionally, some of the mediating materials infused the sacred draught with additional sources of baraka; citing a recipe attributed to the Prophet, Ibn al-Khashshab (d. ca. 1252) describes how specific Qur'anic verses should be inscribed with saffron on a bowl and then dissolved with water, ideally drawn from the sacred well of Zamzam in Mecca, whose baraka was, as we have seen, also central to the ingestion of prophetic relics.[75] The commonality points once again to overlaps between devotional and therapeutic practices centered on the Prophet and on the Qur'an. The well-known Syrian Shafi'i jurist Abu Zakaria Yahya Ibn Sharaf al-Nawawi (d. 1278) considers the permissibility of someone in a state of ritual impurity touching a variety of objects, including pastries or bread inscribed with the words of the Qur'an.[76] Once again, the production of such unlikely confections finds analogies in devotional practices focused on the Prophet Muhammad. It is reported, for example, that those in debt petitioned the Prophet for help by leaving quantities of wheat at his tomb in Medina (Figure 29.5). Once a year, on the seventeenth of *Dhū'l-qada,* the wheat was gathered and made into bread for public distribution, presumably with the idea of ingesting the baraka that it had accumulated through proximity to the Prophet's body.[77] In addition, many of the textual amulets inscribed with Qur'anic verses intended for ingestion specified their ability to foster prosperity and protect against magic, the evil eye, illness, insects, robbery, and so forth, the same range of protective functions inscribed on the talismanic images of the Prophet's sandals that circulated widely in the premodern and early modern Islamic world.

For jurists who ruled on the legality of ingesting the Qur'an, its permissibility was generally determined in relation to intention. For example, al-Nawawi distinguishes between the ingestion of the words of the Qur'an written on something edible, which

FIGURE 29.5. Ottoman dish containing wheat from the Prophet's tomb in Medina. Topkapı Sarayı Müzesi (Topkapi Palace Museum), Istanbul, Inv. TSMK 21/501.

he sees as acceptable, and the burning of a wooden artifact on which the Qur'an is inscribed, which is prohibited. Both result in the disappearance of the material Qur'an, but ingestion is to be distinguished from destruction, a distinction rooted not in the physical processes of material alteration but in the intention underlying the transformative process.[78] Jurists such as al-Nawawi accept an eventuality attested equally by some of the surface abrasions on medieval Christian icons (see Chapter 19) and on medieval Islamic pilgrimage scrolls (see Figure 29.3), acknowledging that identical material changes may result either from a deliberate act of desecration or from practices of use, veneration, and wear that necessitate the eventual ritualized disposal of well-worn codices.[79] In both cases, the ethical implications of material alteration are determined contextually in relation to intention, with practices of ingestion, kissing, or devotional touching distinguished from those of deliberate defacement and desecration.

By the twelfth century, if not earlier, ephemeral practices of inking the Qur'an on the interiors of ceramic bowls to facilitate ingestion were rendered permanent by the production in Egypt and Syria (and later in Iran and India) of brass or bronze bowls inscribed with Qur'anic formulas, later combined with knots, letters, and magic squares intended to exploit the science of letters (*'ilm al-ḥurūf*). Unlike in the case of the inked ceramic bowls that continued to be produced to order, in metal magic-medicinal bowls incised texts and images were rendered permanent and could therefore benefit multiple users.[80] In the use of such inscribed metal magic-medicinal bowls, the medium of inscription does not actively dissolve in mediating liquids such as milk, oil, or water in the same dramatic way as ink, even if the ingestion of the metal medium on which the text is inscribed is assumed. Instead the combination of text and image infuses the liquid medium with its curative powers in a manner analogous to practices in which efficacious words of the Qur'an or a text such as al-Busiri's *Burda* are placed or recited over water that is then ingested.[81] In one case, multiple mediations—from the ink of inscription and its paper, parchment, or pottery support to the liquids in which it dissolves—facilitate the ingestion of the very words of efficacious text. In the other, contact (even the reverberations of words spoken on the surface of the liquid) infuses the liquid with a potency of sufficient efficacy that its blessings may even be transmitted by a proxy (referred to by the Arabic term *rasūl*, agent or envoy) nominated to drink from the bowl, albeit with some delay in the transmission of the cure to the ultimate beneficiary.[82] The role of such proxies or surrogates raises further interesting questions about relationships of identification and identity and about the relationship between emulating and becoming.[83]

Some of the earliest magic-medicinal bowls contain images and texts reflecting their use for both prophylactic and therapeutic purposes—for example, against colic and cold, to ease the pain of childbirth, or against the poison of biting reptiles and insects or arachnids such as scorpions, sorcery or the evil eye, sore eyes, flatulence, hemorrhaging, or the bites of mad dogs. The linkage between the evil eye and the bite of poisonous insects and reptiles is reflected in several hadith that sanction the use of protective measures against both.[84] The association is manifest in numerous amulets and apotropaic mosaics produced in the eastern Mediterranean in the pre-Islamic and early Islamic period, which, in a classic case of *similia similibus curantur*, depict the evil eye being pierced by fierce animals, poisonous reptiles, and sharp weapons.[85] Both amulets and bowls address the danger of poison penetrating the body, in one case by means of teeth or fangs, in the other by means of an optical exchange invested with haptic qualities according to a theory of vision that evidently favored extramission as the default mode of the gaze.[86]

Combining text and image, the magic-medicinal bowls stand at the intersection between different realms of efficacious practice, one a textual tradition focused on the Qur'an that was sufficiently canonical to be the subject of discussion among early Islamic jurists, the other related to more theologically ambiguous traditions of amuletic, apotropaic, astrological, and talismanic images and texts with a long history in the eastern Mediterranean and the Middle East.[87] They also stand at the intersection between long-established practices of iconophagy and practices of logophagy promoted by the sacrality and potency of scripture in Islam as the revealed word of God.[88] This is further underlined by the fact that some of the earliest magic bowls bearing apotropaic images of poisonous reptiles or birthing women combine Qur'anic inscriptions with a record of their being engraved under particular zodiacal signs. That shown here (Figure 29.6) bears an exterior inscription attesting that it was inscribed while the moon was in the house of Leo, just as the seals mentioned in the *Picatrix* were engraved under the sign of Scorpio to ensure their efficacy when imprinted on matter to be ingested.[89] The overlap between the therapeutic ingestion of clay impressed with images found on seals, talismans, and even stone reliefs such as that in Hims (see Figure 29.2) and practices of drinking the Qur'an to similar effect remind us that juridically sanctioned practices of ingesting sacred texts and relics coexisted and intersected with more popular practices of consuming images and texts for prophylactic or therapeutic purposes.

The strikingly transhistorical and intersectarian character of such practices only underlines the point; many of the same lists of dangers addressed in Islamic magic-medicinal bowls are addressed in Coptic magical texts produced before and after the Muslim conquest, while protection against the related dangers of snakes, scorpions, and the evil eye by means of amulets combining words and images of these dangers has been sought in many parts of the Islamic world into the present day.[90] Moreover, pharaonic-era papyri outlining cures for scorpion bite involving licking images of deities drawn on the hand afflicted by a bite stand at the head of a long line of iconophagic and logophagic cures for scorpion bite that continued well into modernity.[91] Cures for the same malady employed in North Africa in the early twentieth century,

FIGURE 29.6. Inscribed copper-alloy magic-medicinal bowl with interior anthropomorphic and zoomorphic images (now worn), Syria, 1169–1170. (A) Side view; (B) bottom view. Nasser D. Khalili Collection of Islamic Art, MTW 1443.

for example, involved ingesting pious formulas written on paper, dissolved in water, and consumed along with honey and oil.[92] Such ephemeral practices represent a facet of the Islamicized magic-medicinal practices to which the inscribed bowls also belong. Generic antecedents to such practices might be sought in pharaonic stelae of Horus, god of protection, who is depicted trampling crocodiles while holding serpents, scorpions, and other malevolent creatures; inscribed with efficacious texts, such stelae were mounted in a basin for gathering water poured over them, which was then collected for prophylactic and therapeutic use.[93] Equally relevant are the magic bowls produced for different religious communities in southern Iraq between the fifth and eighth centuries and inscribed with texts in Aramaic, Syriac, Mandaic, Middle Persian, and Arabic designed to avert the evil eye or specific demonic forces.[94] There is, however, little indication of direct continuity with pre-Islamic practices. Instead we appear to be dealing with a "family" of practices that were particularly well articulated in relation to the healing powers of sacred text. The ingestion of the Qur'an as a cure for the bites of chthonic creatures recalls, for example, not only accounts of pious Christians ingesting pigments scraped from icons but also the report by Bede (d. 735) that scrapings from the leaves of books (probably insular Gospels) from Ireland, a region known for the absence of snakes, were dissolved in water and given to victims of snakebite in order to expel the poison and ease the pain.[95]

Sometimes the particulars of such ritual ingestions suggest more specific relationships. The washing away of incantations inscribed on wooden boards, presumably for ingestion, is a practice mentioned in Coptic grimoires produced even after the Muslim conquest of Egypt, which recommend inscribing words on a wooden board, then rubbing them with lemon and washing them away with water. In the cases of other Coptic spells, the text was written in honey on an alabaster table, then dissolved in white wine.[96] Analogous practices of ingesting inked texts, including the Qur'an, dissolved in water still flourish in various areas of the Islamic world and are particularly well documented in the Islamicate regions of Sub-Saharan Africa, although they were clearly once more widespread. These practices involve the inscription of repeated Qur'anic formulas (whose content is often seen as related to the required function) by a *mallam* (practitioner) on a wooden board, along with the names of God and other efficacious formulas, sometimes including magical signs, many preserved in manuscripts or printed compendia of apotropaic or talismanic magic imported from Arabic-speaking North Africa and the Middle East.[97] Once the text has been written on the wooden board, a common writing medium in north and sub-Saharan Africa, the ink is then erased from its surface and the liquid by means of which the erasure is affected is collected in vessels for consumption or external application. Liquidized text is administered in doses extending over a specified time period while the patient refrains from polluting or immoral activity. In cases of extreme need (epidemics, pests, fires, etc.), the complete Qur'an can even be written, erased, and distributed to an entire community for ingestion. Like their earlier Egyptian counterparts, the resulting draughts can be used for both medicinal purposes and as charms to protect against the evil eye or magic, to ensure success in love, or to ensure protection and success in specific circumstances, such as initiating a business or undertaking a journey.[98]

Directed toward profane ends, these rituals point to intersections between practices of empowerment for prophylactic, therapeutic, or more nefarious purposes, an overlap that not only blurs the boundaries between devotional and magical practices but that also transcends sectarian affiliation. Versions of such practices of ingestion also enjoyed a remarkable longevity. The preparation of Coptic texts for ingestion by means of infused lemon juice recalls practices documented ethnographically as late as the nineteenth century, when a ferruginous stone in the tomb of the Mamluk sultan al-Mansur Sayf al-Din Qalawun (d. 1290) was rubbed with a lemon and then scraped with a pebble in order to produce a liquid given as a drink to children who were late in starting to speak in order to "untie their tongues."[99] As this suggests, practices of ingesting Qur'anic texts and other efficacious matter are attested both among elite communities and in more popular milieus; the production of metal magic bowls that immortalize bowls produced in more ephemeral media is evidence enough of this. Moreover, unlike relics, access to which was necessarily limited, texts and images were not only more easily manipulated but more convenient to generate. This is reflected in their association with more humble media in therapeutic practices documented in nineteenth- and early twentieth-century North Africa, which entailed the ingestion of curative or protective formulas inscribed on paper, grains of wheat, onion skins, or the shells of eggs, which were then cooked and eaten, or written on plates, which were then wiped cleaned and eaten from. Other practices involved ingesting water that had come into contact with an efficacious image or over which efficacious words had been recited (a practice that recalls the recitation of al-Busiri's poem about the Prophet's cloak over water intended for ingestion) and the inhalation of the smoke of a charm that had been burnt.[100] Such vernacular practices find counterparts in contemporary royal ceremonials: on the occasion of New Year (Nauruz), the Qajar ruler of Iran, Nasir-al-Din Shah (r. 1848–1896) drank from a cup in the interior of which an Islamic scholar had inscribed auspicious verses from the Qur'an, dissolved in liquid, before offering the cup to the closest members of his entourage.[101]

In their use of animated matter, ingestion, and inhalation to draw the object of desire and its efficacious energy into the body, practices of iconophagy and logophagy not only highlight a significant overlap between the material forms and modes of consuming efficacious matter in sacred and profane contexts but also find rarely noted analogies with profane erotic strategies. One such analogy lies in the poetic phenomenon of prosopopoeia, a rhetorical device used to animate material objects through the presence of texts written in the first-person "voice" of the artifact. The phenomenon was known in late antiquity and was quite common in the medieval Islamic world, with a particular concentration of examples in the architecture and arts of the western Mediterranean between the tenth and fourteenth centuries.[102] Yet what is seldom noted is that the earliest recorded instances of prosopopoeia, those found in the milieu of the 'Abbasid court in Baghdad, often occurred in contexts in which the "speaking" artifact mediated between the bodies of lovers. The earliest references to such artifacts are preserved in the tenth-century *Kitāb al-Muwashshā* (The Ornamented Book) by the Iraqi belle-lettrist Muhammad al-Washsha' (d. 936). Among the many inscribed objects that al-Washsha' mentions are those bearing Arabic verses written in the first person so that the literate viewer gave voice to the object when he or she vocalized its associated text. Two classes of such objects are of particular interest. The first are *mandīl*s, or handkerchiefs that were valued as highly personal items and thus passed between lovers as tokens of affection. On one, the author noted the following inscription:

> I am the handkerchief of a lover
> who wipes his tears on me
> Then offers me to his beloved
> who wipes on me some wine.[103]

The context makes clear that the exchange of bodily fluids mediated by the textile —the tears of one lover being wiped against the wine-stained mouth of another— was central to the meaning of a gesture in which the textile mediated the mingling of bodily fluids in an effective displacement of consummation onto the space of the handkerchief. The mediating textile enabled the ingestion of the bodily fluids of one by the other in a manner eulogized, if not encouraged, by a first-person text that itself invited the reader to elide the distinction between artifactual voice, poetic voice, and personal voice, between being, text, and thing. The role of saliva in this ontological collapse finds analogies in more formalized rituals of incorporation; it is not by chance, for example, that in the medieval Islamic world the dissemination of the ruler's baraka or rituals of incorporation into the body politic often operated by the sharing of food from the plate of the ruler, effectively ingesting his saliva.[104]

A more intimate and literal take on the same theme is associated with a genre of talking object consisting of apples inscribed with romantic verses written in golden ink (or even ambergris) through which the apples "speak," invoking their mediating role in passing secrets between lovers. Many of these verses refer to eating and drinking, some making explicit the fact that the "talking" apple passed from the hands of one lover will eventually be eaten by the other.[105] At once the reification of desire and its realization in displacement, the talking apple passed between lovers permits one to take the other into his or her body, effecting a unity in which identities are merged in a manner that enacts a displaced version of sexual congress.

The phenomenon of prosopopoeia has recently attracted some attention for its ability to destabilize the subject–object binary central to Enlightenment and post-Enlightenment epistemology and ontology. In an omission that reflects the hard boundaries drawn between the realms of profane and sacred in modern scholarship, however, its structural (and possible genealogical) relation to the erotics of piety have so far escaped attention. And yet the use of animated matter to mediate (and even consummate) a relation of desire is no less relevant to the practices of ingesting sacred matter that I have discussed here. Whether the object of desire is the baraka emanating from prophet, saint, or logos, the ingestion of the sacred has as its ultimate end not a mimetic imitation of the sacred but a merging of the self with it. Exploiting the process of digestion in which certain substances are incorporated into one's physical being and others discarded, ingestion is especially well suited to this end, for reasons explained in another context by Marsilio Ficino (d. 1499) in his *Three Books on Life* (*De vita libri tres*), a work heavily indebted to Arabic works on alchemy and talismans. Contrasting the efficacy of images designed to harness the powers of heaven for therapeutic ends with that of medicines prepared by those skilled in astrology for the same ends, Ficino insists on the greater potency of medicinal powders, liquids, and unguents compared to images since the former allow for a greater combinatory power, absorbing celestial influences more rapidly than the hard materials of which images are formed. Moreover, applied externally or "taken internally and converted into our very selves (*in nos convertuntur*)," such viscous medicines are absorbed and incorporated into the substance of the body; the celestial draught "flows into the veins and marrow."[106]

A more cynical, but perhaps ultimately more revealing, take on the ability of ingestion to incorporate the mediated object of desire is the parody of both religious practice and scientific humanism encountered in Jonathan Swift's *Gulliver's Travels* (1726). On his travels the narrator visits the Academy of Lagado, where he is introduced to a method of incorporating mathematical knowledge. This entails swallowing thin wafers on which mathematical formulas have been written with an ink composed of an herbal tincture designed to relieve disorders of the head, a kind of forerunner to modern psychoactive drugs.[107] As the wafer dissolves through digestion, the concoction with which the mathematical proposition has been written is released and rises to the brain, bearing its textual content (and thus mathematical knowledge) with it. Ultimately ineffective, this ingenious attempt to incorporate textual content by the mediation of substances that bind to the brain is an obvious parody not only of the eucharist but perhaps also of contemporary practices of ingesting sacred texts and images for prophylactic or therapeutic purposes. Among them, one might mention

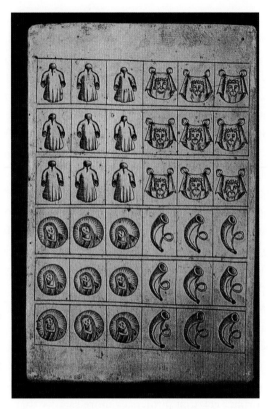

FIGURE 29.7. Sheet with copper-plate engravings of *Schluckbildchen* (images for ingestion) of relics including the tunic of Christ, the *sudarium* of Veronica, a miraculous icon of the Virgin, and the hunting horn of Charlemagne. Germany, seventeenth century, 10.4 × 6.8 centimeters. Plattensammlung Nr. 36, Ursulinen Kloster, Landshut.

the *Schluckbildchen,* tiny printed images (some as small as 2–20 millimeters) of icons of the Virgin or of relics mass-produced as multiples for Germanophone Catholics during the seventeenth and eighteenth centuries (Figure 29.7). Imbued with apotropaic or therapeutic powers, these printed sheets of multiples functioned as "holy pills" that were cut and consumed as needed, typically dissolved in water but also baked in bread or incorporated into other foodstuffs to be fed to humans or livestock to cure fevers or other ailments.[108]

Swift's parody invokes the workings of a material economy in mediating the consumption of immaterial objects of desire, whether baraka or knowledge, in ways that alter the substance of the self; the prescribed manner of ingesting knowledge—swallowing the wafer while fasting, then subsisting on a pure diet of bread and water for three days following—implicitly raises interlinked questions of contamination, efficacy, and ritual that are often made explicit in juridical or scholastic discussions of the need for fasting when ingesting the sacred.[109] The endeavors of the academicians of Lagado also highlight once again the inadequacy of a concept of mimesis as imitation or re-presentation as an explanatory model for what is at stake in these practices of ingestion. Similarly, semiotic models that treat material forms and practices as wrappings for immaterial concepts and ideas that stand at an ontological remove from the medium of their transmission fail to do justice to the ways in which matter mediates and is animated by the sacred and, consequently, to the ontological ambiguities and complexities inherent in practices of ingestion.[110] In the ingestion of the Qur'an, for example, it is not the semantic content of the text that is consumed but the efficacious potency of the word made manifest. Similarly, practices of icon ingestion seek to incorporate not an immaterial concept of the saint accessed through depiction but his or her very essence embodied in the stuff of imaging. As the manifestations of a corporeal desire for the consumption of the sacred, such practices seek to collapse an ontological distinction essential to the operation of mimesis as re-presentation. Insofar as they can be described as mimetic, they are closer to the notion of mimesis as participation, a mode of "sensuous similarity" that is opposed in the writings of Walter Benjamin to "non-sensuous similarity," which is typified by the semiotic conception of words (and, by extension, other representations) as having only a conventional relationship to their referents.[111] In Benjamin's sense, the mimetic has a somatic quality that distinguishes it from the semiotic while adumbrating a distinction between identification as participation and as imitation that is relevant to the devotional practices parodied by Swift.

If Swift's parody exploits the capacity of ingestion to satisfy a literal desire for incorporation, it also highlights a fundamental practical and theoretical distinction between the implications of imbibing knowledge on the one hand and sacrality on the other. Knowledge incorporated through processes of digestion can be transmitted further, whether through didactic means or the production of additional edible inscriptions by one previously enlightened through their consumption. By contrast, those who ingest the sacred are rarely said to undergo a sufficient transubstantiation to become sources of sanctity in their own right, at least not through ingesting sacred matter alone. This stands in striking contrast to the ability of banal artifacts and materials to both absorb and transmit sacrality emanating from relics with which they are in contact or to the widespread notion that pollution is catching, that sacred matter, relics, and texts can be contaminated by a ritually unclean touch.[112] The contrast suggests that systems of sacrality that operate corporeally have a built-in obsolescence, a "shelf life," that mitigates any claims of further transmission on the part of those who ingest sacred matter. The merits of circumscribing sacrality are self-evident both in precluding a fast track to personal sanctity through ingestion and in addressing more prosaic questions of mutilation and pollution during an internal trajectory from ingestion to mastication through digestion to excretion. Necessarily, therefore, it is through this temporal and teleological progression through the body that a charge of sacred energy instantiated materially through proximity to or participation in the sacred is finally discharged.

NOTES

1. Alison Flood, "Sachin Tendulkar's Blood Used to Prepare Special Edition of His Memoirs," *Guardian,* July 19, 2010.

2. Glenn Peers, *Sacred Shock: Framing Visual Experience in Byzantium* (University Park, PA: Pennsylvania State University Press, 2005), 53–54, and Travis Zadeh, "From Drops of Blood: Charisma and Political Legitimacy in the *Translatio* of the ʿUthmānic codex of al-Andalus," *Journal of Arabic Literature* 39, no. 3 (2008): 321–346. For an overview of the homology in the context of a Christian salvific economy, see Jeffrey F. Hamburger, "Body vs. Book: The Trope of Visibility in Images of Christian-Jewish Polemic," in *Ästhetik des Unsichtbaren: Bildtheorie und Bildgebrauch in der Vormoderne,* ed. David Ganz and Thomas Lentes (Berlin: Reimer, 2004), 113–145.

3. In addition to the works cited below, see Caroline Bynum Walker, *Christian Materiality: An Essay on Religion in Late Medieval Europe* (Brooklyn: Zone, 2011). Studies on the early history of the materiality of devotional practices in Islam are few; those of Travis Zadeh (see notes 2 and 72) are exemplary.

4. Jane Bennett, *The Enchantment of Modern Life: Attachments, Crossings, and Ethics* (Princeton, NJ: Princeton University Press, 2001), 97–98.

5. Bruno Latour, *We Have Never Been Modern* (Cambridge, MA: Harvard University Press, 1993), and Webb Keane, *Christian Moderns: Freedom and Fetish in the Mission Encounter* (Berkeley: University of California Press, 2007).

6. Saba Mahmood, "Religious Reason and Secular Affect: An Incommensurable Divide?," *Critical Inquiry* 35 (2009): 847.

7. J. Chelhod, "La *Baraka* chez les Arabes ou l'influence bienfaisante du sacré," *Revue de l'histoire des religions* 148 (1955): 68–88; Josef W. Meri, "Aspects of *Baraka* (Blessings) and Ritual Devotion among Medieval Muslims and Jews," *Medieval Encounters* 5, no. 1 (1999): 46–69; and Meri, *The Cult of Saints among Muslims and Jews in Medieval Syria* (Oxford, UK: Oxford University Press, 2002), 100–119.

8. Edward C. Sachau, *Al-Beruni's India,* 2 vols. (Delhi: Low Price Publications, 1989 [1910]), vol. 1, 111, after the Arabic of Abu Rayhan Muhammad ibn Ahmad al-Biruni, *Kitāb fī taḥqīq-i-ma liʾl-Hind* (Hyderabad: Majlis Dāʾirat al-Maʿārif al-ʿUthmāniya, 1958), 84.

9. For modern Christian practices of ingesting water in which photographs of contemporary saintly figures, deceased or living, have been submerged or with which they have come in contact, see Catherine Mayeur-Jaouen, "La Fonction sacrale de l'image dans l'Égypte contemporaine: De l'imagerie traditionnelle a la revolution photographique," in *La Multiplication des images en pays de l'Islam: De l'estampe à la télévision (17e–21e siècle),* ed. Bernard Heyberger and Silvia Naef (Würzburg: Ergon, 2003), 67, Figure 3; and Heike Behrend, "Photo Magic: Photographs in Practices of Healing and Harming in East Africa," *Religion and the Media* 33, no. 2 (2003): 129–145.

10. Max Junghändel, "Rillen an aegyptischen Tempeln," *Zeitschrift für Ethnologie* 23 (1891): 861–863; Pierre Nautin, "La Conversion du temple du Philae en église chrétienne," *Cahiers archéologiques* 17 (1967): 33; and Claude Traunecker, "Une pratique de magie populaire dans les temples de Karnak," in *La Magia in Egitto ai tempi del Faraoni,* ed. Alessandro Roccati and Alberto Siliotti (Modera: Panini, 1987), 221–242.

11. Patricia Cox Miller, *The Corporeal Imagination: Signifying the Holy in Late Ancient Christianity* (Philadelphia: University of Pennsylvania Press, 2009), 2–3, 5.

12. See, for example, Gary Vikan, "Pilgrims in Magi's Clothing: The Impact of Mimesis on Early Byzantine Pilgrimage Art," in *The Blessings of Pilgrimage,* ed. Robert Ousterhout (Urbana: University of Illinois Press, 1990), 97–107.

13. Martina Bagnoli, Holger A. Klein, C. Griffith Mann, and James Robinson, eds., *Treasures of Heaven: Saints, Relics, and Devotion in Medieval Europe* (New Haven, CT, and London: Yale University Press, 2011).

14. Gary Vikan, *Early Byzantine Pilgrimage Art,* rev. ed. (Washington, DC: Dumbarton Oaks, 2010), 27–29.

15. Daniel Caner, "Towards a Miraculous Economy: Christian Gifts and Material 'Blessings' in Late Antiquity," *Journal of Early Christian Studies* 14, no. 3 (2006): 334–335, 341, 345, 356, 359, and Blake Leyerle, "Pilgrim Eulogiae and Domestic Rituals," *Archiv für Religionsgeschichte* 10 (2008): 222, 231. For an overview of the eulogiae sought by pilgrims and their material containers, see Cynthia Hahn, "Loca Sancta Souvenirs: Sealing the Pilgrim's Experience," in *The Blessings of Pilgrimage,* ed. Robert Ousterhout (Urbana: University of Illinois Press, 1990), 85–96.

16. Alfred Gell, *Art and Agency: An Anthropological Theory* (Oxford, UK: Oxford University Press, 1998), 96–154.

17. Gary Vikan, "Ruminations on Edible Icons: Originals and Copies in the Art of Byzantium," in *Retaining the Original: Multiple Originals, Copies, and Reproductions, Studies in the History of Art,* vol. 20 (1989): 47–59, and Vikan, "Art, Medicine, and Magic in Early Byzantium," *Dumbarton Oaks Papers* 38 (1984): 67–70. For an illuminating and suggestive discussion of the Symeon tokens and their relationship to both amulets and the eucharistic bread, see Bissera V. Pentcheva, *The Sensual Icon: Space, Ritual, and the Senses in Byzantium* (University Park, PA: Pennsylvania State University Press, 2010), 28–36.

18. Paul van den Ven, *La Vie ancienne de S. Syméon Stylite le Jeune, 521–592,* 2 vols. (Brussels: Société des Bollandistes, 1962–1970), no. 124, and Vikan, "Ruminations on Edible Icons," 56.

19. Ernst Kitzinger, "The Cult of Images in the Age before Iconoclasm," *Dumbarton Oaks Papers* 8 (1954): 107, 148, and Cyril Mango, *The Art of the Byzantine Empire, 312–1453* (Toronto: University of Toronto Press, 1986), 139. For a detailed discussion, see Glenn Peers, "Object Relations," in *Oxford Handbook of Late Antiquity,* ed. Scott F. Johnson (Oxford, UK: Oxford University Press, 2012). I am grateful to Glenn Peers for sharing his essay with me before publication.

20. Cited in Ann Freeman, "Carolingian Orthodoxy and the Fate of the Libri Carolingi," *Viator* 16 (1985): 100, and Charles Barber, "From Transformation to Desire: Art and Worship after Byzantine Iconoclasm," *Art Bulletin* 75, no. 1 (1993): 8.

21. Patricia Cox Miller, "'Differential Networks': Relics and Other Fragments in Late Antiquity," *Journal of Early Christian Studies* 6, no. 1 (1998): 122–123. For an extended discussion of the relationship between relics and the eucharist, see G.J.C. Snoek, *Medieval Piety from Relics to the Eucharist: A Process of Mutual Interaction* (Leiden: Brill, 1995).

22. On this point, see Charles Barber, *Figure and Likeness: On the Limits of Representation in Byzantine Iconoclasm* (Princeton, NJ: Princeton University Press, 2002).

23. Liz James, "Color and Meaning in Byzantium," *Journal of Early Christian Studies* 11, no. 2 (2008): 223–233.

24. As James A. Francis notes, "The rise of the holy man, the icon, and biography are deeply connected." Francis, "Living Icons: Tracing a Motif in Verbal and Visual Representation from the Second to Fourth Centuries CE," *American Journal of Philology* 124 (2003): 591.

25. Cox Miller, *Corporeal Imagination,* 120, 145. For the original text, see Bill Brown, "Reification, Reanimation, and the American Uncanny," *Critical Inquiry* 32 (2006): 199.

26. Peter Brown, "The Saint as Exemplar in Late Antiquity," *Representations* 2 (1983): 1–25, and Cox Miller, *Corporeal Imagination,* 60, 140.

27. Francis, "Living Icons," 594.

28. Ann W. Astell, *Eating Beauty: The Eucharist and the Spiritual Arts of the Middle Ages* (Ithaca, NY: Cornell University Press, 2006), 11.

29. Leyerle, "Pilgrim Eulogiae," 228, and Cox Miller, *Corporeal Imagination,* 133.

30. Gordon D. Newby, "Imitating Muhammad in Two Genres: Mimesis and Problems of Genre in Sīrah and Sunnah," *Medieval Encounters* 3, no. 3 (1997): 266–283.

31. Julian Raby, "In Vitro Veritas: Glass Pilgrim Vessels from 7th-Century Jerusalem," in *Bayt al-Maqdis: Jerusalem and Early Islam,* ed. J. Johns, Oxford Studies in Islamic Art, vol. 9, part 2 (Oxford, UK: Oxford University Press, 1999), 113–190, and Helen C. Evans and Brandie Ratliff, eds., *Byzantium and Islam Age of Transition, 7th–9th Century* (New York: Metropolitan Museum of Art, 2012), no. 186.

32. Muhammad ibn Ahmad al-Muqaddasi, *Kitāb aḥsan al-taqāsīm fī maʿrifat al-aqālīm,* ed. M. J. de Goeje, Bibliotheca Geographorum Arabicorum, vol. 3 (Leiden: Brill, 1967), 186; André Miquel, *Aḥsan at-taqāsīm fī maʿrifat al-aqālīm (Le Meilleure repartition pour la connaissance des provinces)* (Damascus: Institut français de Damas, 1963), 231–232; Abū Bakr Ahmad ibn Muhammad Ibn al-Faqih al-Hamadhani, *Kitāb al-Buldān,* ed. M. J. de Goeje, Bibliotheca Geographorum Arabicorum, vol. 5 (Leiden: Brill, 1967), 112; and Henri Massé, *Abrégé du livre des pays* (Damascus: Institut français de Damas, 1973), 136.

33. Finbarr B. Flood, "Image against Nature: *Spolia* as Apotropaia in Byzantium and the Dar al-Islam," *Medieval History Journal* 9, no. 1 (2006): 143–166, and Julia Gonella, "Magic *Spolia* in Medieval Islamic Architecture of Northern Syria," *Muqarnas* 27 (2010): 103–120.

34. Erica Reiner, "Magic Figurines, Amulets, and Talismans," in *Monsters and Demons in the Ancient and Medieval Worlds,* ed. Ann E. Farkas (Mainz: P. von Zabern, 1987), 28–29.

35. Flood, "Image against Nature," 150–151.

36. Muslim ibn al-Hajjaj, *Le Sommaire du Sahih Mouslim,* bilingual (Arabic-French) ed., trans. Fawzi Chaaban (Beirut: Dār al-Fikr, 1992), vol. 2, 402–403, nos. 1136–1137.

37. *The Latin Picatrix,* Books I and II, trans. John Michael Greer and Christopher Warnock (Lexington, KY: Lulu, 2009), 34.

38. In other cases, however, the impression is referred to as the design or engraving (*naqsh*) of the seal (*khātam*). Venetia Porter, "Islamic Seals: Magical or Practical?," in *Magic and Divination in Early Islam,* ed. Emilie Savage-Smith (Aldershot, UK: Ashgate, 2004), 179–180, 182. For prophylactic logophagy, see notes 95–98 below.

39. Porter, "Islamic Seals," and Flood, "Image against Nature," 153.

40. Clifford Edmund Bosworth, *The Mediaeval Islamic Underworld: The Banū Sāsān in Arabic Life and Lore,* 2 vols. (Leiden: Brill, 1976), vol. 1, 86, 88; vol. 2, 199; Helga Venzlaff, "Mohr-e Namāz: Das schiitische Gebetssiegel," *Die Welt des Islams* 35, no. 2 (1995): 250–275; and Meri, "Aspects of *Baraka* (Blessings)," 51–52.

41. Hilmi Aydın, *The Sacred Trusts: Pavilion of the Sacred Relics, Topkapi Palace Museum, Istanbul* (Istanbul: Tughra Books, 2009), 191–192. On the curative properties of the Prophet's saliva and the soil of Medina, see Ibn Qayyim al-Jawziyya, *Medicine of the Prophet,* trans. Penelope Johnson (Cambridge, UK: Islamic Texts Society, 1998), 139–140.

42. Qayyim al-Jawziyya, *Medicine of the Prophet;* Emilie Savage-Smith, "Ṭibb," *The Encyclopaedia of Islam,* new ed., vol. 10 (Leiden: Brill, 2000), 453.

43. Kitzinger, "Cult of Images," 147–148, and Vikan, *Early Byzantine Pilgrimage Art,* 23–24, 31–33.

44. The most comprehensive existing historical study of the Prophet's relics, a generally underresearched topic, is that of Ahmad Taymur, *Al-Āthār al-nabawiyya* (The Prophetic Relics) (Cairo: ʿĪsā al-Bābī al-Ḥalabī, 1971). See also Brannon Wheeler, *Mecca and Eden: Ritual, Relics, and Territory in Islam* (Chicago and London: University of Chicago Press, 2006), 71–98, and Josef W. Meri, "Relics of Piety and Power in Medieval Islam," *Past and Present* (2010), suppl. 5, 97–120. For a useful overview of the veneration of the Prophet's body, see Denis Gril, "Le Corps

du Prophète," in *Le Corps et le sacré en Orient musulman,* ed. Catherine Mayeur-Jaouen and Bernard Heyberger (Aix-en-Provence: Édisud, 2006), 37–58.

45. Cyril Elgood, "Tibb-ul-Nabbi or Medicine of the Prophet," *Osiris* 14 (1962): 175.

46. Süleyman Beyoğlu, "The Ottomans and the Islamic Sacred Relics," in *Great Ottoman-Turkish Civilisation,* vol. 4: *Culture and Arts* (Ankara: Yeni Türkiye, 2000), 36–44; and Aydın, *Sacred Trusts.*

47. Christiane Gruber, "A Pious Cure-All: The Ottoman Illustrated Prayer Manual in the Lilly Library," in *The Islamic Manuscript Tradition: Ten Centuries of Book Arts in Indiana University Collections,* ed. Christiane Gruber (Bloomington and Indianapolis: Indiana University Press, 2010), 120–123, and Alexandra Bain, "The Late Ottoman *En ʿam-ı şerif:* Sacred Text and Images in an Islamic Prayer Book," D.Phil. dissertation, University of Victoria, Saanich and Oak Bay, Victoria, Canada, 1999, esp. 18–33.

48. Ibn Qayyim al-Jawziyya, *Medicine of the Prophet,* 139–140.

49. Ignace Goldziher, "The Cult of Saints in Islam," *Moslem World* 1 (1911): 302–312, and Samuel M. Zwemer, "Hairs of the Prophet," in *Ignace Goldziher Memorial Volume,* ed. Samuel Löwinger and Joseph Somogyi, Part 1 (Budapest: Globus u.a., 1948), 48–54.

50. Meri, "Relics of Piety and Power," 105.

51. Brannon Wheeler, "Relics in Islam," *Islamica* 11 (Summer 2004): 107–108, and Wheeler, *Mecca and Eden,* 72–75.

52. Meri, *Cult of Saints,* 109–111; Meri, "Relics of Piety and Power," 106–112; and Ahmad ibn Muḥammad al-Maqqari, *Fatḥ al-mutaʾāl fī madḥ al-niʿāl,* ed. Ahmad Farid al-Miziyadi (Beirut: Dār al-Kutub al-ʿIlmīya, 2006).

53. Walter Benjamin, "The Work of Art in the Age of Its Technological Reproducibility," in *The Work of Art in the Age of Its Technological Reproducibility, and Other Writings on Media,* ed. Michael W. Jennings, Brigid Doherty, and Thomas Y. Levin (Cambridge, MA: Belknap Press of Harvard University Press, 2008), 21.

54. M. Renaud, *Monuments arabes, persans et turcs du cabinet de M. le duc de Blacas,* vol. 2 (Paris: : L'Imprimerie Royale, 1828), 311–324, and Venetia Porter, ed., *Hajj: Journey to the Heart of Islam* (London: British Museum Press, 2012), 60, Figure 34. For other, later, tile and manuscript images of the sandals bearing similar invitations to kiss and touch them, see Sophie Makariou, ed., *Chefs d'oeuvre islamiques de l'Aga Khan Museum* (Paris: Musée du Louvre, 2007), no. 72, and Bain, "The Late Ottoman *En ʿam-ı şerif,*" 109–110. For later examples of images that evoke the Prophet and his qualities inscribed with invitations to kiss, rub, and touch them, see Gruber, "A Pious Cure-All," 132, 140–141.

55. Meri, "Relics of Piety and Power," 110, n. 52.

56. On the burda, see David S. Margoliouth, "The Relics of the Prophet Mohammed," *Moslem World* 27, no. 1 (1937): 20–27. For a description of the ritual ingestion of this water at the Ottoman court in the early eighteenth century, see Alexandru Dutu and Paul Cernovodeanu, eds., *Dimitrie Cantemir, Historian of South East European and Oriental Civilizations* (Bucharest: Association Internationale d'Études du Sud-ouest Européen, 1973), 142. From the late eighteenth or early nineteenth century, the ritual changed slightly so that the Ottoman elite kissed the robe, with their traces wiped with a kerchief presented to each. Nurhan Atasoy, "Khirḳa-yi Sherīf," *Encyclopaedia of Islam,* new ed., vol. 5 (Leiden: Brill, 1986), 18–10; Aydın, *Sacred Trusts,* 34–40, 197; and Gruber, "Pious Cure-All," 134.

57. Aydın, *Sacred Trusts,* 115.

58. M. J. Kister, "Maqām Ibrāhīm, a Stone with an Inscription," *Muséon* 84 (1971): 483–485. Against this, however, one should note a tradition of depicting the Kaʿba set within the outline of

the Prophet's footprint, documented in illustrated pilgrimage texts as early as the sixteenth century. See Barbara Schmitz, *Islamic Manuscripts in the New York Public Library* (Oxford, UK: Oxford University Press, 1992), 45.

59. On the properties of Zamzam water, see Jacqueline Chabbi, "Zamzam," *Encyclopaedia of Islam*, new ed., vol. 11 (Leiden: E. J. Brill, 2002), 442, and Elgood, "Tibb-ul-Nabbi," 140.

60. Meri, *Cult of Saints*, 105.

61. Aydın, *Sacred Trusts*, 191.

62. Richard Kurin, "The Structure of Blessedness at a Muslim Shrine in Pakistan," *Middle Eastern Studies* 19, no. 3 (1983): 316–318.

63. Suzanne Pinckney Stetkevych, "Al-Būsīrī's *Qasīdat al-Burdah* (*Mantle Ode*) and the Supplicatory Ode," *Journal of Arabic Literature* 37, no. 2 (2006): 145–189; Stetkevych, *The Mantle Odes: Arabic Praise Poems to the Prophet Muhammad* (Bloomington: Indiana University Press, 2010); and Mohiuddin Qadri, *Qasidat al-Burdah: The Poem of the Mantle* (Lahore: Lulu, 2008). On al-Busiri and his historical context, see Victor Danner, "Al-Būsīrī: His Times and Prophetology," in *Islamic and Middle Eastern Societies: A Festschrift in Honor of Wadie Jwaideh*, ed. Robert Olson and Salman al-Ani (Brattleboro, VT: Amana Books, 1987), 41–61.

64. The *Shifā bi-ta'rīf ḥuqūq al-Muṣṭafā* (Healing by Recognition of the Rights of the Chosen One), written by the Maghribi scholar Iyad ibn Musa (d. 1149 CE), trans. Aisha Bewley as *Ash-Shifa of Qadi Iyad* (Inverness, UK: Madinah Press, 2006).

65. Stetkevych, "Al-Būsīrī's *Qasīdat al-Burdah*," 146–147, 150.

66. Rose Aslan, "Understanding the Poem of the Burdah in Sufi Commentaries," M.A. thesis, American University in Cairo, 2008, 82. I am grateful to Iman Abdulfattah for drawing my attention to this thesis. For the related practices in Mamluk funerary monuments, see note 99 below.

67. *Ṣaḥīḥ al-Bukhārī*, Book 87: *On the Interpretation of Dreams*, hadith nos. 122–123; and Muhammad Muhsein Khan, ed., *The Translation of the Meanings of Sahih al-Bukhari* (Chicago: Kazi Publications, 1979) (Arabic–English), vol. 9, 104.

68. Meri, *Cult of Saints*, 111. For accounts of dream appearances of the Prophet in Mamluk Egypt and Syria, sometimes in the context of curing infirmity, see Yehoshua Frenkel, "Dream Accounts in the Chronicles of the Mamluk Period," in *Dreaming across Boundaries: The Interpretation of Dreams in Islamic Lands*, ed. Louise Marlow (Cambridge, MA, and London: Harvard University Press, 2008), 202–220. The hagiography of the eleventh-century sufi sheikh Abu Ishaq of Kazarun explains how he had a dream in which the Prophet Muhammad drew with charcoal the plan of a mosque, which the sheikh then built. Denise Aigle, "Sainteté et miracles en islam médiéval: L'Exemple de deux saints fondateurs iraniens," in *Miracles, prodiges et merveilles au Moyen Age* (Paris: Publications de la Sorbonne, 1995), 64.

69. Vikan, "Art, Medicine, and Magic," 73, n. 45.

70. Ezekiel 2:9–10, 3:1–3. The event is echoed in biographies of the mid-sixth-century Byzantine poet Romanos the Melode, who is said to have been commanded by the Virgin to eat a scroll in a dream, after which he awoke and composed the first of his celebrated hymns. Joseph Yahalom, "*Piyyut* in Byzantium: A Few Remarks," in *Jews in Byzantium: Dialectics of Minority and Majority Cultures*, ed. Robert Bonfil et al. (Leiden: Brill, 2012), 325.

71. Peers, *Sacred Shock*, 52.

72. For an excellent overview, see Travis Zadeh, "Touching and Ingesting: Early Debates over the Material Qur'an," *Journal of the American Oriental Society* 129, no. 3 (2009): 443–466.

73. Ibn Qayyim al-Jawziyya, *Medicine of the Prophet*, 128.

74. Edward William Lane, *An Account of the Manners and Customs of the Modern Egyptians* (London: John Murray, 1895), 263–264.

75. The use of saffron as a medium of inscription appears to have a long history in the context of Egyptian medicinal-magic practices. See, for example, John G. Gager, *Curse Tablets and Binding Spells from the Ancient World* (Oxford, UK: Oxford University Press, 1999), no. 33.

76. Abu Zakariyya Yahya al-Nawawi, *Etiquette with the Quran: Al-Tibyān fī Ādāb Ḥamalat al-Qurʾān* (Burr Ridge, IL: Starlatch Press, 2003), 112, 115, and Zadeh, "Touching and Ingesting," 464.

77. Aydın, *Sacred Trusts,* 196.

78. Al-Nawawi, *Etiquette with the Quran,* 112.

79. J. Sadan, "Geniza and Genizah-like Practices in Islamic and Jewish Tradition," *Bibliotheca Orientalis* 43, nos. 1–2 (1986): 36–58.

80. H. Henry Spoer, "Arabic Magical Medicinal Bowls," *Journal of the American Oriental Society* 55, no. 3 (1935): 256; Emilie Savage-Smith, "Magic-Medicinal Bowls," *Science, Tools, and Magic,* Part 1: *Body and Spirit* (London: Nur Foundation in Association with Azimuth Editions and Oxford University Press, 1997), 72–78; and Almut v. Gladiss, "Medizinische Schalen: Ein islamisches Heilverfahren und seine mittelalterlichen Hilfsmittel," *Damaszener Mitteilungen* 11 (1999): 147–161.

81. See, for example, Elgood, "Tibb-ul-Nabbi," 155–156.

82. Spoer, "Arabic Magical Medicinal Bowls," 255–256, and Savage-Smith, "Magic-Medicinal Bowls," 72.

83. In a future essay I hope to address similar questions of surrogacy and mimesis that arise in medieval Islamic devotional practices and pilgrimage rituals.

84. Muslim, *Le Sommaire du Sahih Mouslim,* vol. 2, 402–403, nos. 1136–1137, and Elgood, "Tibb-ul-Nabbi," 152–154.

85. Katherine M. D. Dunbabin and M. W. Dickie, "*Invida rumpantur pectora*: The Iconography of Phthonos-Invidia in Graeco-Roman Art," *Jahrbuch für Antike und Christentum* 26 (1983): 7–37. Such imagery was known in pre-Islamic Arabia, for a spectacular image of the eye under attack is found on a wall painting datable to the first through the third centuries CE from Qaryat al-Faw in central Arabia, misidentified in recent scholarship as a zodiacal image. 'Ali Ibrahim al-Ghabban, *Roads of Arabia: Archaeology and History of the Kingdom of Saudi Arabia* (Paris: Somogy Art Publishers, 2010), 340, no. 163.

86. On extramission in Islamic thought, see David C. Lindberg, *Theories of Vision from Al-Kindi to Kepler* (Chicago and London: University of Chicago Press, 1976), 18–32; Lindberg, "The Intromission–Extramission Controversy in Islamic Visual Theory: Alkindi versus Avicenna," in *Studies in Perception: Interrelations in the History of Philosophy and Science,* ed. Pieter K. Machamer and Robert G. Turnbull (Columbus: Ohio State University Press, 1978), 137–159.

87. Emilie Savage-Smith, "Amulets and Related Talismanic Objects," and Porter, "Islamic Seals," in *Magic and Divination in Early Islam,* ed. Savage-Smith (Aldershot, UK: Ashgate, 2004), 179–200.

88. Although images of scorpions and other beasts are found along with Qur'anic quotations on Iranian amulets from the ninth century, it us worth noting that the appearance of magic squares seems to be a phenomenon of the Islamic period: Porter, "Islamic Seals," 187.

89. Savage-Smith, "Magic-Medicinal Bowls," 82, no. 25. See also no. 26, inscribed while the moon was in Scorpio.

90. Peter W. Schienerl, "Zur magischen Wirkungsweise rezenter ägyptischer Skorpionamulette," *Archiv für Völkerkunde* 36 (1982): 147–159; Giovanni Canova, "Serpenti e scorpioni nelle tradizioni Arabo-Islamiche," *Quaderni di studi Arabi* 8 (1990–1991): 191–207, and 9: 219–244; Regine Schulz, "Schlangen, Skorpione und feindliche Mächte," *Biblische Notizen* 93 (1998): 89–104; and Jürgen Wasim Frembgen, "The Scorpion in Muslim Folklore," *Asian Folklore Studies*

63 (2004): 112–117. For the antecedents of such practices in Egypt, see Marvin Meyer and Richard Smith, *Ancient Christian Magic: Coptic Texts of Ritual Power* (Princeton, NJ: Princeton University Press, 1994), 18–19.

91. The relevant text recommends reciting over images of the gods Atum-Horus-Heknu, Isis, and Horus prescribed words, which are then to be drawn on the hand of one afflicted by a scorpion bite and licked off by him or drawn on a piece of linen and applied to the throat of the afflicted; alternatively, a herb known as scorpion's herb can be ground and dissolved in beer and wine and ingested by the one suffering a scorpion's sting. J. Borghouts, *Ancient Egyptian Magical Texts* (Leiden: Brill, 1978), no. 84, 55. For the broader context of curative licking and swallowing, see Robert Kriech Ritner, *The Mechanics of Ancient Egyptian Magical Practice* (Chicago: Oriental Institute of the University of Chicago, 1997), 95–96.

92. Edmond Doutté, *Magie et religion dans l'Afrique du Nord* (Algiers: Adolphe Jourdan, 1909), 237.

93. P. Lacau, "Les Statues guérisseuses dans l'ancienne Égypte," *Monuments et mémoires: Fondation Eugène Piot* 25 (1921–1922): 189–209, and Byron E. Shafer, John Baines, Leonard H. Lesko, and David P. Silverman, eds., *Religion in Ancient Egypt: Gods, Myths, and Personal Practice* (Ithaca, NY: Cornell University Press, 1991), 169.

94. Michael G. Morony, "Magic and Society in Late Sasanian Iraq," in *Prayer, Magic, and the Stars in the Ancient and Late Antique World,* ed. Scott Noegel, Joel Walker, and Brannon Wheeler (University Park, PA: Pennsylvania State University Press, 2003), 84–107.

95. William J. Diebold, *Word and Image: An Introduction to Early Medieval Art* (Boulder, CO: Westview Press, 2000), 28.

96. Michael Green, "A Late Coptic Magical Text from the Collection of the Rijksmuseum van Oudheden, Leiden," *Oudheidkundige Mededelingen* 67 (1987): 35, 38.

97. Jack Goody, "Restricted Literacy in Northern Ghana," in *Literacy in Traditional Societies,* ed. Jack Goody (Cambridge, UK: Cambridge University Press, 1968), 235.

98. Goody, "Restricted Literacy," 226–241; Abdullahi Osman El-Tom, "Drinking the Koran: The Meaning of Koranic Verses in Berti Erasure," in *Popular Islam South of the Sahara,* ed. J.D.Y. Peel and C. C. Stewart (Manchester, UK: Manchester University Press, 1985), 414–413; Salah El Mohammed Hassan, "Lore of the Traditional Malam: Material Culture of Literacy and Ethnography of Writing among the Hausa of Northern Nigeria," Ph.D. dissertation, University of Pennsylvania, Philadelphia, 1988, 198–228; and Raymond A. Silverman, "Drinking the Word of God," in *Inscribing Meaning: Writing and Graphic Systems in African Art,* ed. Christine Mullen Kreamer, Mary Nooter Roberts, Elizabeth Harney, and Allyson Purpura (Washington, DC: Smithsonian, 2007), 117–123.

99. Junghändel, "Rillen," 862–863.

100. Doutté, *Magie et religion,* 109–110.

101. Hamid Algar, *Religion and State in Iran, 1785–1906* (Berkeley and Los Angeles: University of California Press, 1969), 156–157.

102. For such inscriptions on artifacts (as opposed to architecture, which has a more extensive bibliography), see Hana Taragan, "The 'Speaking' Inkwell from Khurasan: Object as 'World' in Iranian Medieval Metalwork," *Muqarnas* 22 (2005): 29–44; Avinoam Shalem, "The Otherness in the Focus of Interest: Or, If Only the Other Could Speak," in *Islamic Artefacts in the Mediterranean World: Trade, Gift Exchange and Artistic Transfer,* ed. Catarina Schmidt Arcangeli and Gerhard Wolf (Venice: Marsilio, 2010), 29–44, and Shalem, "If Objects Could Speak," in *The Aura of the Alif,* ed. Jürgen Wassim Frembgen (Munich: Prestel, 2010), 127–147.

103. Al-Washshā', *Le Livre de brocart (al-kitāb al-muwashshā) par al-Washshā ',* trans. Siham Bouhlal (Paris: Gallimard, 2004), 230, and Muhammad ibn Ahmad al-Washsha', *Al-Muwashshā,*

aw al-zarf waʾl-zurufāʾ (Beirut: Dār Sadir, 1965), 264. See also Franz Rosenthal, *Four Essays on Art and Literature in Islam* (Leiden: Brill, 1971), 93–95.

104. Paula Sanders, *Ritual, Politics, and the City in Fatimid Cairo* (Albany: State University of New York Press, 1994), 28–29, and Finbarr Barry Flood, *Objects of Translation: Material Culture and Medieval "Hindu-Muslim" Encounter* (Princeton, NJ: Princeton University Press, 2009), 85.

105. Al-Washshaʾ, *Le livre de brocart*, 219–220, and al-Washshaʾ, *Al-Muwashshā*, 250–251. The invocation of apples and wine in this context invokes a homology between wine and apples found in contemporary ʿAbbasid poetry, in which wine is often described as a liquefied apple, itself solidified wine, while the apple also often functions as a metaphor for the breasts or cheeks of the beloved. M. C. Lyons, *Identification and Identity in Classical Arabic Poetry* (London: Gibb Memorial Trust, 1999), 301.

106. Marsilio Ficino, *Three Books on Life,* ed. and trans. Carol V. Kaske and John R. Clark (Tempe, AZ: Medieval and Renaissance Texts and Studies, 2002), 305–306, 352–353.

107. Jonathan Swift, *Gulliver's Travels,* ed. Robert Demaria Jr. (London: Penguin, 2003), 174. In fact, one of the noted properties of al-Busiri's ode on the Prophet's cloak is the poem's ability to improve the capacity for knowledge when dissolved in water and taken orally.

108. Christian Schneegass, "Schluckbildchen: Ein Beispiel der 'Populärgraphik zur aktiven Aneignung,'" *Volkskunst* 6 (1983): 27–32; Christoph Kürzeder, "Geweyhte Sachen und anberührte Bildlein," in *Maria Allerorten: Die Muttergottes mit dem geneigten Haupt, 1699–1999—Das Gnadenbild der Ursulinen zu Landshut—Altbayerische Marienfrömmigkeit im 18. Jahrhundert* (Landshut: Museen der Stadt Landshut, 1999), 281–283, Figure 3 and catalog nos. I/48g, I/50g, I/56a, and I/56b.

109. Zadeh, "Touching and Ingesting," 464. The issue is frequently discussed in relation to the Christian eucharist. See, for example, Marilyn McCord Adams, *Some Later Medieval Theories of the Eucharist: Thomas Aquinas, Gilles of Rome, Duns Scotus, and William Ockham* (Oxford, UK: Oxford University Press, 2010), 261–275, and Gary Macy, *Treasures from the Storeroom: Medieval Religion and the Eucharist* (Collegeville, MN: Liturgical Press, 1999), esp. 20–35, 68–69. I am grateful to Aden Kumler for these references.

110. Webb Keane, "Subjects and Objects," in *The Handbook of Material Culture,* ed. Chris Tilley (London: Sage Publications, 2006), 198–199; Keane, *Christian Moderns;* Birgit Meyer, *Religious Sensations: Why Media, Aesthetics and Power Matter in the Study of Contemporary Religion* (Amsterdam: Vrije Universiteit, 2006); and Hent de Vries, ed., *Religion: Beyond a Concept* (New York: Fordham University Press, 2008), 647–772.

111. Walter Benjamin, "Doctrine of the Similar" (1933), trans. Knut Tarrowski, *New German Critique* 17 (1979): 65–69, and Michael Taussig, *Mimesis and Alterity: A Particular History of the Senses* (New York and London: Routledge, 1993).

112. In addition to the images of the Prophet Muhammad's sandal discussed above, examples include the sacrality acquired by the gate of Edessa through its function as the locus at which the letter written by Christ to Abgar was displayed and read every time the city was menaced by an adversary. Leyerle, "Pilgrim Eulogiae," 35.

30

Criminal and Martyr
The Case of James Legg's Anatomical Crucifixion

MEREDITH GAMER

A man on a cross. A nail through each palm and another through joined feet, he hangs with arms splayed upward, stretched thin by the weight of his body beneath.

Any reader with a passing knowledge of Christian iconography would assume that this is a description of the crucified Christ, but it is not. Rather, it refers to a life-size plaster cast now in the collection of the Royal Academy of Arts in London (Figure 30.1). Known by its modern name, the *Anatomical Crucifixion,* it is the result of an experiment conceived and executed in 1801 by the sculptor Thomas Banks in collaboration with the painters Richard Cosway and Benjamin West. According to Joseph Constantine Carpue, the surgeon whom the artists enlisted to assist them, who provides us with our only firsthand account of the cast's making, the project originated as follows:

> Some time in the year 1800, three of the greatest men of their time, namely, Mr. West, President of the Royal Academy, Mr. Banks, and Mr. Cosway, . . . having agreed amongst themselves that the representation of the crucifixion did not appear natural, though it had been painted by the greatest artist of his age, wished to put this to a test. They, therefore, requested me to nail a subject on a cross, saying, that the tale told of Michael Angelo and others was not true of their having stabbed a man tied to a cross, and then making a drawing of the effect.[1]

Convinced that an earlier representation of the Crucifixion "did not appear natural," Banks, Cosway, and West decided to "put this to a test."[2] But unlike Michelangelo, who allegedly committed murder for the sake of his art, the men relied instead

FIGURE 30.1. Thomas Banks, R.A., *Anatomical Crucifixion (James Legg),* 1801. Plaster cast, 231.5 × 141 × 34 centimeters. Photograph © The Royal Academy of Arts, London; photo by Paul Highnam.

on a "subject." Specifically, they relied on the body of James Legg, an eighty-year-old Chelsea pensioner who was publicly hanged on Monday, November 2, 1801, for the murder of William Lamb.[3] Having secured prior legal access to Legg's cadaver, Banks, Cosway, and Carpue (West appears not to have been present) gathered that day to watch as Legg was "launched into eternity" at the Newgate "drop."[4] As soon as he was dead, the men nailed his corpse to a wooden cross and allowed it to set. Banks then cast Legg's "crucified" corpse twice: once whole and once after Carpue had flayed it to remove the skin to expose the superficial muscles beneath. The *Anatomical Crucifixion* at the Royal Academy is the second of Banks's two casts and the only one to survive today.[5]

From a scientific point of view, the artists' method was obviously problematic in that it recorded the physical effects of crucifixion on a dead, as opposed to a live, body. However, in its own time the experiment appears to have been deemed a success. An account of it published some decades later in the *Art-Union* (based on information from Carpue) states that the casts "confirmed, to the satisfaction of the gentlemen present, the prevalent opinion that the painters, their predecessors, had generally made their studies from dead models, a method which had imparted to the subject of 'The Crucifixion' the general stiffness so obvious and untrue." By contrast, because Legg's body had "been attached to the cross before the rigidity of death had set in," Banks's casts were thought to "[show] precisely the appearance that the muscles would assume in the transition from life to death upon the cross."[6]

After exhibiting his cast of Legg's unflayed corpse for a time in his private studio on Newman Street, Banks offered both it and the *Anatomical Crucifixion* to the Royal Academy, of which he was a long-standing member, for use as anatomical models.[7] In a letter of July 22, 1802, to the Academy Council, Banks expressed his hope that his "figures on the Crosses . . . might be useful to the Students of the Royal Academy & also to the professor of Anatomy at the time of giving his lectures."[8] His proposal was unanimously accepted, and, with the exception of a brief period in the nineteenth century, the casts never left the academy's possession.[9] Indeed, the *Anatomical Crucifixion,* which currently resides in the Life Room amid myriad other classical and anatomical casts, continues to serve Banks's expressed purpose to this day.

Perhaps because it was so evidently conceived as a source of art-historical and anatomical information and not as a work of high art, the *Anatomical Crucifixion* has remained at the very margins of British art history. On the few occasions when it has been the focus of scholarly discussion, it has been valued primarily for the light it sheds on artistic and institutional practices in Britain at the time of its creation. Thus Julius Bryant has interpreted it as evidence of widespread anatomical interest among Banks and his peers, and Martin Postle has related it to debates within the Royal Academy around the moral status and the relative importance of anatomical instruction.[10] In this chapter, by contrast, I want to address Banks's surviving cast not as an aid to or by-product of artistic creation (though it was certainly both of these things) but instead as a historical, aesthetic, and material object worthy of analysis in its own right.

What is the *Anatomical Crucifixion*? What does it show? One way of answering these questions would be to say that it conjures an image of public execution (by crucifixion) on the body of a man who was himself publicly executed (by hanging).[11] In other words, it is both an iconographic and an indexical representation of a publicly executed body. At first glance, as we have already observed, the iconographic features of the *Anatomical Crucifixion* would seem to overwrite, perhaps even to obliterate, the indexical ones. What we see when we look at Banks's cast is not a hanged criminal but—seemingly, at least—a crucified man, or even Christ himself. Yet I would argue that to the original viewers of Banks's cast, Legg's prior execution was just as present and just as significant as his posthumous crucifixion. Indeed, as we will see, evidence of Legg's criminal status abounds in the cast itself and in the visual and textual archive that surrounds it. Thus the *Anatomical Crucifixion* bodies forth three discrete yet interconnected episodes of spectacular violence: not only Legg's "crucifixion," of which it is an actual, physical record, but also Christ's torment on the cross, which it is meant to simulate, and, equally, Legg's own torment outside Newgate Prison, without which it could not have been made. In doing so, it binds together and calls attention to two key but overlooked features of eighteenth- and early nineteenth-century British sensory culture: the public execution and the religious image.

Although the public execution has long been a central site of inquiry for scholars of British history and literature, it has received virtually no mention from historians of British art.[12] Of great interest instead has been the public *exhibition,* which emerged in London in the 1760s with the founding of Britain's first exhibiting societies, the Society of Artists of Great Britain and the Royal Academy of Arts. Like their Parisian counterpart, the Salon, the annual exhibitions hosted by the Society and the Academy have come to be understood as loci for the development of the modern public sphere and the modern art world alike.[13] The public execution, which has often been framed, most influentially by Michel Foucault, as a backward-looking and fundamentally premodern cultural phenomenon, has had little place in such a narrative.[14] Nor has religious painting, which appeared with relative infrequency on the walls of the Great Rooms at Spring Gardens and Somerset House and which, when it did appear, was forced to compete for space and attention among a dizzying array of other less elevated but more saleable image types—landscapes, genre scenes, and, most of all, portraits.[15]

Banks's *Anatomical Crucifixion* thus provides a striking counterpoint to existing accounts of eighteenth- and early nineteenth-century British art and visuality. An object made from the body of a hanged murderer by three members of the Royal Academy, including its president, it establishes a direct link between two seemingly unrelated spaces—the "modern" Academy and the "premodern" scaffold. In doing so, it invites us to turn our attention from the public exhibition to the public execution as both a site of sensory experience and a source of visual imagery, particularly of religious imagery. Indeed, as I hope to show, the *Anatomical Crucifixion* demands that we redefine our very notion of what was, or could be, a religious image at this moment in time.

"A Clever Agony"

Let us begin by returning to the dubious piece of art-historical lore that set Banks, Cosway, and West's experiment in motion. As Carpue recounts, this held that Michelangelo tied a model to a cross and then stabbed him to death in order to approximate the effects of crucifixion. Though its precise origins are unclear, the tale was evidently well known in the early nineteenth century, for it appears again in a note published in *The Morning Chronicle.* Alluding to Banks's radical sympathies, the journal reported, "The *sculptor* who is said to have meditated the assassination of BONAPARTE, appears to have imitated a painter of old, who designing a crucifixion piece, stabbed a man in order to get a *clever agony!*"[16] Even as they emulated Michelangelo's example, however, Banks and his collaborators also surpassed it in both moral and technological terms. For although Michelangelo was alleged to have induced a genuine "agony" in the body of his unfortunate model, Banks, Cosway, and West merely simulated one in theirs (though the *Morning Chronicle* leaves this point deliciously ambiguous). And whereas Michelangelo could capture these fleeting effects only by translating them into a drawing, Banks was able to record precisely the form of Legg's crucified corpse.

If Banks's method of doing so seems unorthodox to us today, it was not at the time. On the contrary, it built directly on a mode of anatomical model making established several decades earlier by the prominent London surgeon William Hunter. The technique is one that Hunter originally employed for his own magnum opus, the obstetrical atlas *The Anatomy of the Human Gravid Uterus* (1774), whose detailed and highly naturalistic plates set a new standard for anatomical illustration in Britain and beyond. In order to ensure the greatest possible degree of visual accuracy, Hunter cast each of his dissected specimens in plaster for his draftsman, Jan van Rymsdyck, to work from. As Hunter would later explain in the first of his *Two Introductory Lectures* (1784), the aim of such casts was "to preserve a very perfect likeness of such subjects as we but seldom can meet with, or cannot well preserve in a natural state."[17]

When he was named professor of anatomy to the Royal Academy on its foundation in 1768, Hunter applied the same practices to the making of artists' models. Over the next decade, he supervised the production of at least three anatomical figures for use by the Academy's members and students, two of which remain in that institution's collection today (Figures 30.2 and 30.3).[18] Formally and iconographically, Hunter's

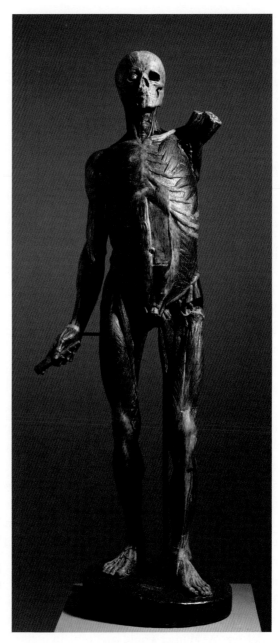

FIGURE 30.2. Unidentified maker (production supervised by William Hunter), *Écorché figure,* cast ca. 1771. Plaster cast, 171.5 × 61 × 47.5 centimeters. Photograph © The Royal Academy of Arts, London; photo by Paul Highnam.

models conform to long-standing conventions of early modern anatomical illustration. Both are shown stripped of skin in order to highlight the body's muscle structure, a mode best known by the French term *écorché* (literally meaning "flayed"), and both quote well-known visual sources: Jean-Antoine Houdon's *Standing Écorché* (1767) and the celebrated Roman marble *The Dying Gaul* (220–230 BCE), respectively. However, in contrast to their continental precedents, which were invariably

FIGURE 30.3. William Pink (production supervised by Agostino Carlini, R.A.), *Smugglerius*, ca. 1834 (original cast ca. 1775). Plaster cast, 75.5 × 148.6 centimeters. Photograph © The Royal Academy of Arts, London; photo by Paul Highnam.

drawn or sculpted by hand, Hunter's models were cast in plaster from actual human corpses, which he dissected and posed before rigor mortis set in.[19]

As would later be the case with Legg, the men whose corpses Hunter cast were last seen alive at London's public execution grounds. Although there was nothing new about anatomists and artists availing themselves of criminal bodies for their studies, the British context is notable for the degree to which this practice was openly and consistently facilitated by the contemporary justice system.[20] In eighteenth-century Britain, the death penalty was meted out for a vast array of offenses, from forgery to poaching to petty theft. At its height, the English penal code (known to later generations as the "Bloody code") counted over two hundred capital offences.[21] In order to distinguish those executed for murder from those executed for more minor offences, in 1752 Parliament passed "An Act for better preventing the horrid Crime of Murder." Under the so-called Murder Act, murder convicts were sentenced not only to death by hanging but also, as a "further Terror and peculiar Mark of Infamy," to dissection. In the vast majority of cases, this meant that immediately after execution their bodies were transported to "the Hall of the Surgeons Company" to be anatomized and exposed to public view.[22] In some cases, however, exceptions were made, as when Hunter, and Carpue after him, requested them instead "in the cause of Art."[23]

In practical and conceptual terms, Banks's *Anatomical Crucifixion* and its lost counterpart were heirs to Hunter's anatomical models. Not only were they made in the same way; they were made with the same aim in mind, namely, to exceed the limits of imitative representation by fusing anatomical truth with the language of art.

Like Hunter's models, Banks's casts of Legg's body rendered the perishable permanent, providing "in every respect a most perfect reproduction of the body as it finally settled."[24] As in the case of that most classically indexical of images—the photograph —their visual rhetoric was one of transparency, transcription, and objectivity. It was also one of anonymity. In the course of being cast, Legg and his predecessors would seem to have undergone a dramatic transformation. Named, once-living individuals, they were quite literally "recast" as generic human specimens, their former identities overwritten by the practical and formal imperatives of the anatomical image.

This process is verbalized with particular clarity in Carpue's account, in which the surgeon abruptly ceases referring to Legg by name as soon as he turns from his crime and trial to his "crucifixion." Referring to Banks, Cosway, and West's appeal to him for assistance, Carpue writes:

> Shortly after this application, a circumstance occurred at the college of Chelsea, which enabled me to comply with their request. A man by the name of Legg, one of the captains at the hospital, having had a dispute with a man named Lamb, a fellow pensioner, entered his bed-room with two loaded pistols . . . and shot Lamb through the thorax. He immediately expired. . . . As Legg was in his perfect senses, there could be no doubt but that he would be found guilty of murder, and executed. Mr. Keate, surgeon general and surgeon of the hospital, was master to the College of Surgeons; to him I applied for the body when executed. . . . He promised to give the sheriff an order that the subject might be given for the purpose provided. A building was erected near the place of execution; a cross provided; the subject was nailed on the cross; the cross suspended; when the body, being warm, fell into the position that a dead body must fall into, let the cause of death be what it may.[25]

Having initially figured in Carpue's narrative as a specific, active presence—a retired army captain, a violent pensioner, and, finally, a convicted murderer—Legg suddenly reappears as a nameless "subject," a representative "body" whose sole value lies in the fact that, when nailed to a cross, it behaves precisely as any other body would.

Yet far from being the purely anonymous image that Carpue's rhetoric might lead us to expect, the *Anatomical Crucifixion* is in fact deeply, even unsettlingly, particular. On the one hand, this particularity is critical to its status as an empirical image. Indeed it is difficult to imagine a more powerful example of the transcriptive capacity of wet plaster than this record of Legg's wasted body, with its seeming infinitude of depressions, projections, fissures, and creases. On the other hand, however, the particularity of Banks's cast inevitably draws attention to Legg as *individual* as well as "subject." Perhaps the clearest instance of this is in Legg's face, with its distinctive and patently nonideal features—low forehead, bulbous eyes (no doubt made more so by flaying), broad nose, weak chin. Even accounting for the elongation that his crucifixion would have caused, we can tell that Legg was a tall man with a wiry, lean physique, formed, we might imagine, by his years of military service. Still more striking than the visual particularity of Legg's body is its very palpability as a body. Chest heaved outward, rib cage exposed, he looks, more than anything, like a human carcass. Doubly lengthened by the pull of gravity and the effects of dissection, his arms seem impossibly thin, as if they might give out at any moment. Signs of physical decay and imperfection abound—in Legg's gut, which sags gently to the right; in his knobbly, asymmetrical legs; and, most dramatically, in the heavy folds of loose muscle that hang down where chest and arm meet, as if his corpse were in the process of detaching from itself, disintegrating. And then there is the vacant space where Legg's genitals once were, as clear a reminder as any that this is a carnal, a fundamentally *un*godly, body.

The specificity and carnality of the *Anatomical Crucifixion* is thrown into even greater relief when we consider it alongside one of its few visual precedents, a woodcut illustration from Jacopo Berengario's *Commentaria* of 1521 (Figure 30.4). Although it seems unlikely that Banks or his collaborators would have been familiar with Berengario's text, the comparison is nonetheless instructive.[26] Berengario is a significant figure in the history of anatomy for the priority he assigned to empirical observation;

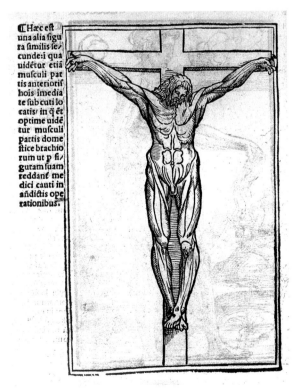

FIGURE 30.4. Jacopo Berengario da Carpi, Crucified male with musculature delineated, in *Commentaria cum amplissimis additionibus super anatomia mundini*, 1521, folio 519 verso. Woodcut, 10.3 × 13.4 centimeters. Wellcome Library, London.

indeed, he was an important model for Vesalius in this respect. Yet his illustration more closely resembles a cinquecento *Crucifixion* stripped bare than a representation of an actually crucified body. In contrast to Legg's strained, sinking form, Berengario's Christ seems weightless; he might as well be levitating as hanging from a cross. And whereas Legg's features have been ravaged by the scalpel's blade, exposing sunken eye sockets, hollow cheeks, and corrugated facial muscles, the gently drooping head of Berengario's écorché remains impossibly whole, graced with perfectly regular features and a lush mane of hair.

Legg is present in the *Anatomical Crucifixion* not only as a physical body but also as a moral—or immoral—body as well. Whether or not they knew his name or the exact nature of his crime, contemporary viewers of Banks's cast would have surely known, or at least surmised, that here was the corpse of an executed murderer. The provisions of the Murder Act were widely known and constituted the only legal source of bodies for anatomical study at the time.[27] Indeed, as Carpue indicates in his account, it was precisely because Legg was so sure to be convicted of murder, and thus sentenced to both death and dissection, that he deemed him a likely candidate for experimentation. Conversely, from a legal perspective at least, Legg's dissection by Carpue, as well as his prior "crucifixion" by Banks and Cosway, was not solely experimental; it was punitive, too. By instructing the sheriff of London to give Legg's body to Carpue instead of transferring it to Surgeons' Hall as usual, the master of the College of Surgeons did not fundamentally alter Legg's sentence; he merely shifted its location.

Saved Souls and Speaking Corpses

As we have seen, Banks and his collaborators were not the first to use a murderer's corpse in this way. In this they had been preceded by Hunter three decades before. But whereas Hunter's casts made reference to anatomical and classical iconographies that effectively distanced their criminal models from the moralized space of the execution ground, the *Anatomical Crucifixion* did nothing of the kind. Instead it appropriated the most iconic of Christian types, and one that resonated in a singular way with Legg's own ignominious end, for what was Christ's crucifixion if not also a public execution? In doing so, the *Anatomical Crucifixion* invited—and still invites—direct, sustained comparison between Legg the murderer and Christ the martyr, between the former's "crucifixion" and *the* Crucifixion, and finally, between the modern and ancient rituals of execution that each underwent.

It is difficult to imagine that the interconnections, at once parallel and dichotomous, between Legg and Christ and the fates they suffered would have been lost on Banks and his collaborators, or that they would have taken them lightly. Whatever it may have been, the *Anatomical Crucifixion* was not a work of blasphemy. Banks himself was a Dissenter, reputed for his grave and sober disposition; Cosway was a spiritual eccentric, with interests ranging from faith healing and animal magnetism to magic and the occult, and an avid collector of Christian historical and devotional texts; and West, a practicing Anglican, was by this time the leading painter of biblical subjects in Britain.[28] Indeed, in addition to the art-historical motivations that Carpue describes, West's own artistic practice, and Cosway's as well, was surely key to the *Anatomical Crucifixion*'s conception. At the time of its making, both men were at work on Crucifixion subjects of their own, West for the monumental west window of Saint George's chapel at Windsor Castle and Cosway for a series of highly finished drawings of scenes from the life of Christ.[29]

Viewed in this light, the *Anatomical Crucifixion* becomes, along with the many things we have already seen it to be, an image of restitution and, at least potentially, of redemption. It is an image of restitution insofar as it takes the body of a murderer— one who committed the ultimate crime against society—and puts it into the service of that society. In addition to "forwarding inquiry," as Carpue writes, "in regard to subjects of painting, sculpture, &c.," by shedding light on the art of the past, Banks's cast forwarded the project of art itself, and the highest form thereof.[30] It contributed to the making of two modern representations of Christ on the cross, representations that held up His suffering as a spur to empathy, emulation, and, finally, revelation. In brief, it took a body that had been set forth as a negative moral example and made it into the source of a positive one.

The full complexity and import of such a transposition becomes clear only when we turn to the space of the public execution itself. According to the broadside published the day of his hanging, Legg's performance here was brief but exemplary. At eight o'clock that morning, he appeared at Debtor's Door of Newgate Prison along with Richard Stark, a second murder convict slated to hang that day. Before an audience of hundreds if not thousands, the men "ascended the fatal platform, attended by the Ordinary and the usual officers. They appeared very penitent, and met their fate in a becoming manner." Within the space of an hour, both were dead. "As soon as the executioner had fixed the ropes, the clergyman took his leave; the fatal signal was then given, and they were launched into eternity, and, we hope, everlasting happiness."[31] This fleeting scene is given crude but potent visual expression in the woodblock print that appeared above the broadside's double-column text (Figure 30.5). A picture within a picture, it is dominated by the perpendicular form of the scaffold, inside which two figures hang against an empty white ground, hands bound, heads covered. The composition is bordered on one side by the stolid brick facade of Newgate Prison and below by two banks of viewers, all of whom attend to the action above with the exception of a single figure, who turns with pointing finger to meet our gaze.

As the broadside text and image suggest, the turn-of-the-century execution unfolded within an age-old twofold framework of penitence and deterrence. As a form of penal justice, it was intended to induce the repentance and thus enable the salva-

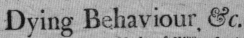

FIGURE 30.5. Unidentified maker, *Dying Behaviour, &c. of James Legg, for the Murder of William Lamb; and Richard Stark, for the Murder of His Wife*, from a broadside of their executions printed by Davenport, George's Court, Clerkenwell, London, 1801. Woodcut. Bodleian Library, University of Oxford, John Johnson Collection, Harding B 9/1 (21).

tion of those who transgressed the law and, at the same time, to discourage those who might harbor similarly criminal inclinations. Tellingly euphemized as the "sheriff's picture frame," the scaffold simultaneously mimicked and inverted the functions of what was then the most common and quintessential of British visual art forms: the portrait.[32] On the one hand, like the portrait, it transformed its "subjects" from private individuals into public figures, fixing and quite literally framing them before a mass audience, as the broadside print shows. On the other hand, and quite unlike the portrait, the scaffold singled out these men and women not for praise or commemoration but for punishment and, ultimately, obliteration. Far from doing honor to those it featured within its three beams, the scaffold held them up as images of ignominy, as sources of terror and warning.[33]

In the case of murderers like Legg and Stark, the admonitory meanings projected onto them in the course of their hangings were amplified by the second half of their sentence. The degree to which punitive dissection at Surgeons' Hall was intended to operate as both an extension and an intensification of the public execution ritual is made ferociously clear in the preambles to two public lectures read in October 1759 over the body of Richard Lamb. The aim of such an event, as the presiding surgeon reminded his viewers, was to "strike a greater terror into the minds of mankind" than even hanging could provide:

> I think few who now look upon that miserable, mangled object before us, can ever forget it. It is for this purpose our doors are opened to the publick, that all may see the exemplary punishment of a murderer, and that it may be impressed on their minds, and be a warning to others to avoid his fate. . . . Happy would it be . . . if this publick occasion, this sight of death, may prove a monitor to every individual here. . . . Let therefore the Anatomical Table in the Surgeons Theatre be a preacher to all this audience: and should their passions run high, and the voice of reason and religion be forgotten, may this dread table present itself to their view, and restrain the arm raised to deprive a fellow creature of life, and, not that only, but raised to destroy themselves.[34]

Whereas the execution ground was metaphorized in predominantly visual terms— with the scaffold as a picture frame and the hanged criminal as its subject—here the encounter with the criminal body is conceived as a full-blown and fully integrated sensory experience. By turns, the lecturer evokes the visual horror of the "miserable mangled object before us," the forgotten "voice of reason and religion," and even the virtual touch of "this dread table," which, by reasserting itself in the mind's eye of the would-be murderer, is called upon to "restrain the arm raised to deprive a fellow creature of life." The surgeon's table is likened to a pulpit from which the inert yet "speaking" body of the dissected murderer "preaches."

The *Anatomical Crucifixion* not only rendered this "preaching" body of the dissected murderer in permanent, plaster form, it reconfigured that body in the image of Christ. Paradoxically, and with at least a hint of dark irony, it likened Legg to the very figure of his salvation. Indeed, in moral and narrative terms, if Legg conformed to any Christian type at all, it was not to Christ but to the penitent thief who was crucified beside Him. In the "condemned sermons" preached in the chapel at Newgate on Sundays prior to executions, this parallel was often made explicit. Although the sermon given before Legg and Stark's executions went unpublished, we can gain some sense of what might have been said from others that were.[35] For example, in 1788 the Reverend Edward Barry implored his listeners "to believe fervently in your hearts, that Christ, the Son of God, came down from heaven, and suffered on the cross, for the sins of a *rebellious world*,—and, 'that *by* his stripes you *are* healed.' . . . See the loving saviour longing to embrace his long lost children!—Behold his flowing tears!—hearken to his expiring groans—'twas all for you!" It was Christ's will, Barry continued, that "that poor convicted criminal, and even,—that thief, shall this day, be with me in Paradise!"[36] If the *Anatomical Crucifixion* is undoubtedly an image of a sinner, it may also be an image of a redeemed sinner, one whose penitence and redemption were effected precisely by and through his execution. In this context, and in those outlined above, Banks's cast emerges as a wholly, if unexpectedly, positive image: the result of a morally licit and technologically progressive experiment, a model of and source for the making of religious art, and a testament even to the spectacular and redemptory power of the British penal system.

Certainly some if not all of these meanings must have been available to those viewers who assembled at Banks's private studio on Newman Street to view the *Anatomical Crucifixion*'s now-lost counterpart. At the very least, we can be sure that his display met with considerable success. According to the *Art-Union*, "This cast excited at the time of its execution much interest among all classes of members of the art," and Banks's studio "for a length of time was resorted to by crowds of persons for the purpose of examining it."[37] But the response of one viewer suggests that, even if the casts themselves were judged in positive terms, they were also recognized—as we might recognize them now—as documents of human cruelty. Here again is the *Art-Union:*

> When the celebrated Dr. Gall saw it, he stood in contemplation before it during several hours,—fully concurred in the opinions of the gentlemen who had instituted the experiment, and, in the spirit of the humanity and philosophy by which he was characterized, observed that, when he considered the cruel mode of death which was inflicted by crucifixion, and which was suggested to him by this figure, it added to the many proofs he had

accumulated, which established to him the fact that man was the most cruel and merciless of all animals.[38]

A man of "humanity and philosophy," Gall (almost certainly Franz Joseph Gall, the renowned physician and inventor of phrenology) objected not to Banks's cast but to the punishment that it simulated. It was the historical practice of crucifixion—not the hanged and posthumously crucified body before him—that confirmed for him the mercilessness of humankind. The implicit distinction that Gall made between ancient and modern modes of execution was consistent with even progressive thought on punishment in Britain at this time. In *Principles of Penal Law* (1771), penal reformer William Eden observes, "It is impossible to read the histories of executive justice in different governments without shuddering at the very idea of those miseries, which men, with unrelenting ingenuity, have devised for each other." Among these "miseries," Eden counts crucifixion. But he is far from condemning capital punishment entirely. On the contrary, he supports death by hanging for murderers and the dissection of criminals as long as they are carried out with as little suffering and as much solemnity as possible.[39]

For Gall it would seem that the only punishment and the only suffering made visible by Banks's cast were those of crucifixion. Crucially, however, he gained access to both through prolonged and careful study of a body that itself underwent punishment, that itself suffered—not on the cross but on the gallows. To quote the *Art-Union* again, it was from "[standing] in contemplation before it during several hours" and "[considering] the cruel mode of death . . . which was suggested to him by this figure" that Gall drew the conclusions he did. However Gall might have parsed the two in his own mind, in point of fact the violence that Legg suffered at Newgate and the violence that his corpse suffered thereafter are inseparably and indistinguishably fused in the *Anatomical Crucifixion*. What are we to make, for example, of the fact that Legg's neck appears "less than ordinarily tense?"[40] Is this a product of his hanging, his crucifixion, or perhaps both? And what of his swollen chest and distended gut; were these features already present by the time his corpse was nailed to its cross, or did they develop only afterward? These are things that Gall could not have known as he looked upon Banks's singular creation. They are things that we still cannot know as we look upon it today.

The *Anatomical Crucifixion* is thus an object with multiple subjects, meanings, and resonances. It is at once a portrait of a murderous body, one whose violent, retributive death is implied but not shown, and an empirical record of fictional pain, an image of a body that has been made to mimic but not to suffer Christ's torment on the cross. And it is an object that could provide Gall with a window onto the misery of Christ's crucifixion without apparently eliciting a shade of sympathy for the hanged, desecrated, and dissected man before him. The paradoxically simultaneous contrasts and syntheses that the *Anatomical Crucifixion* sets up—between cruel and "humane" modes of death, between punitive and salvific suffering, and between pain that is deserving of sympathy and pain that is not—are key to its strangeness and significance as a historical object.

Perhaps most fundamentally, this is a work that speaks to the contingency and changeability of cruelty and empathy alike, based not only on time and place but also on what side of the law (and whose law) we finds ourselves on. In the specific context of eighteenth- and early nineteenth-century London, it further invites us to consider how the forms of visual, sensory, and moral experience generated at the city's scaffolds and in its dissection theaters intersected with and inevitably inflected those generated elsewhere—in the artist's studio, in the Royal Academy's schools, and even before the work of art. For, as we have seen, before becoming a source of religious imagery, James Legg became a religious image himself. He did so not when his corpse was crucified and cast by Banks, Cosway, and Carpue but in the hour or so before, when he stepped out through Debtor's Door and into the "sheriff's picture frame."

NOTES

1. "Obituary: Joseph Constantine Carpue, FRS," *Lancet* 47, no. 1171 (February 1846): 167. The obituary quotes Carpue's account from "an unpublished MS. in his own handwriting." Carpue's original manuscript is currently unlocated.

2. Carpue does not specify which image the men had in mind. However, a likely candidate is *The Three Crosses* by Peter Paul Rubens of 1620 (Museum Boijmans Van Beuningen, Rotterdam), which Cosway owned and displayed in the main drawing room of his residence at 20 Stratford Place. Stephen Lloyd, "The Cosway Inventory of 1820: Listing Unpaid Commissions and the Contents of 20 Stratford Place, Oxford Street, London," *Walpole Society* 66 (2004): 168, 188, Figure 87. Banks, who was good a friend of Cosway, would have been well aware of the picture, too; according to his daughter, the sculptor "was in the habit of passing his evenings frequently with the Cosways, and enjoying with him the inspection of his valuable portfolios of ancient drawings." Charles Francis Bell, ed., *Annals of Thomas Banks, Sculptor, Royal Academician* (Cambridge, UK: The University Press, 1938), 25. On Cosway's art collection, see Lloyd, "Richard Cosway: Collector, Connoisseur, and Virtuoso," in Lloyd, *Richard and Maria Cosway: Regency Artists of Taste and Fashion* (Edinburgh: Scottish National Portrait Gallery, 1995), 73–88.

3. "Trial of James Legg" (t18011028-39), October 1801, *Old Bailey Proceedings Online*, www.oldbaileyonline.org, version 7.0, October 3, 2012. An account of Legg's trial and sentence appeared in *Bell's Weekly Messenger*, no. 290, November 1, 1801.

4. The phrase is from the broadside on Legg's execution and that of another man, Richard Stark. See *Dying Behaviour, &c. of James Legg, for the Murder of William Lamb; and Richard Stark, for the Murder of His Wife. Who Were Executed this Morning, Opposite the Debtor's Door, Newgate,* printed by Davenport, George's Court, Clerkenwell, London, 1801, Bodleian Library, University of Oxford, John Johnson Collection, Harding B 9/1 (21). In his correspondence with the Royal Academy Council, Banks indicates that Legg's "body was given . . . to Mr. Cosway, who with my self attended the Operations of Moulding casting & dissecting it, which dissecting was carefully & intelligently done by Mr. Carpue Surgeon and Anatomist of Leicesterfields." He makes no mention of West having been present or involved in the casts' production. Thomas

Banks to the President and Council of the Royal Academy, July 22, 1802, Royal Academy of Arts Archive, RAA/SEC/2/5/7, Royal Academy, London.

5. Both Julius Bryant and Martin Postle have suggested that the first of Banks's casts may have been destroyed in the course of World War I. Julius Bryant, "Anatomical Crucifixion," in *The Artist's Model: Its Role in British Art from Lely to Etty,* ed. Ilaria Bignamini and Martin Postle (Nottingham, UK: Nottingham University Art Gallery, 1991), 97, and Martin Postle, "Flayed for Art: The Écorché Figure in the English Art Academy," *British Art Journal* 5, no.1 (Spring–Summer 2004): 62, 63 n. 63.

6. "Experimental Cast: The Cast Taken from the Body of James Legg, Chelsea Pensioner, Executed in the Year 1801," *Art-Union* (January 1845): 14.

7. Ibid.

8. Thomas Banks, letter to the President and Council of the Royal Academy, July 22, 1802.

9. Council Minutes, August 7, 1802, Royal Academy of Arts Archive, Royal Academy, London.

10. Julius Bryant, "Thomas Banks's Anatomical Crucifixion: A Tale of Death and Dissection," *Apollo* (June 1991): 409–411, and Postle, "Flayed for Art," 55–63.

11. On the Crucifixion as a scene of public execution, see Mitchell Merback, *The Thief, the Cross, and the Wheel: Pain and the Spectacle of Punishment in Medieval and Renaissance Europe* (Chicago: University of Chicago Press, 1998), 15–18.

12. In the field of social history, see Douglas Hay et al., *Albion's Fatal Tree: Crime and Society in Eighteenth-Century England* (New York: Pantheon, 1975); V.A.C. Gatrell, *The Hanging Tree: Execution and the English People, 1770–1868* (Oxford, UK: Oxford University Press, 1994); and Peter Linebaugh, *The London Hanged: Crime and Civil Society in the Eighteenth Century* (London: Verso, 2003). In literary studies, see John Bender, *Imagining the Penitentiary: Fiction and the Architecture of the Mind in Eighteenth-Century England* (Chicago: University of Chicago Press, 1987), and Lennard Davis, *Factual Fictions: The Origins of the English Novel* (Philadelphia: University of Pennsylvania Press, 1996).

13. Thomas Crow, *Painters and Public Life in Eighteenth-Century Paris* (New Haven, CT: Yale University Press, 1985), 3; David Solkin, ed., *Art on the Line: The Royal Academy Exhibitions at Somerset House, 1780–1836* (New Haven, CT: Yale University Press, 2001); and John Bonehill, "Art History: Re-viewing Recent Studies," *Journal for Eighteenth-Century Studies* 34, no. 4 (2011): 461–470. On the Society of Artists of Great Britain, see Matthew Hargraves, *"Candidates for Fame": The Society of Artists of Great Britain, 1760–1791* (New Haven, CT: Yale University Press), 2005.

14. Michel Foucault, *Discipline and Punish: The Birth of the Prison,* trans. Alan Sheridan (New York: Pantheon, 1977).

15. Notable exceptions to the general neglect of religion in the scholarship on eighteenth-century British art include Marcia Pointon, "Quakerism and Visual Culture, 1650–1800," *Art History* 20, no. 3 (September 1997): 397–431; Jeremy Gregory, "Anglicanism and the Arts: Religion, Culture and Politics in the Eighteenth Century," in *Culture, Politics and Society in Britain, 1660–1800,* ed. Jeremy Black and Jeremy Gregory (Manchester, UK: Manchester University Press, 1991), 82–109; Clare Haynes, *Pictures and Popery: Art and Religion in England, 1660–1760* (Aldershot, UK: Ashgate, 2006); and Matthew Craske, *The Silent Rhetoric of the Body: A History of the Monument and Commemorative Art in England, 1720–1770* (New Haven, CT: Yale University Press, 2007). On the predominance of portraiture at the Royal Academy's exhibitions, see Pointon, "Portrait! Portrait!! Portrait!!!," in *Art on the Line: The Royal Academy Exhibitions at Somerset House, 1780–1836,* ed. David Solkin (New Haven, CT: Yale University Press, 2001), 93–109.

16. *The Morning Chronicle,* no. 9806, October 25, 1800.

17. William Hunter, *Two Introductory Lectures Delivered by Dr. William Hunter, to His Last Course of Anatomical Lectures, at His Theatre in Windmill-Street* (London, 1784), 56. On the relationship between Hunter's casts and the plates of his *Gravid Uterus,* see N. A. McCulloch, D. Russell, and S.W. McDonald, "William Hunter's Casts of the Gravid Uterus at the University of Glasgow," *Clinical Anatomy* 14, no. 3 (May 2001): 210–217.

18. In fact, Hunter had already made one such anatomical model for the Academy's predecessor institution, the Saint Martin Lane's Academy, in 1751. See Postle, "Flayed for Art," 57–58, and Peter Black, ed., *"My Highest Pleasures": William Hunter's Art Collection* (London: University of Glasgow in association with Paul Holberton Publishing, 2007), 27–28. The third anatomical model that Hunter produced for the Royal Academy exists only by implication in a "Bill of expences" for "the getting of the Body from Surgeons' Hall," which Hunter submitted to the Academy's secretary, Francis Milner Newton. Among the items that Hunter lists—a coach hire, tips paid to the men who assisted him, and the body itself—is 16 shillings and 4½ pence for "Extra Expenses included the Night it [i.e., the body] was Moulded." Royal Academy of Arts Archive, RAA/SEC/1/56 recto, Royal Academy, London. On Hunter's involvement with the Royal Academy, see Martin Kemp, ed., *Dr. William Hunter at the Royal Academy of Arts* (Glasgow: University of Glasgow Press, 1975).

19. With the possible exception of the London-based French sculptor Louis-Francois Roubiliac, Hunter appears to have been the first to employ this technique for the making of artists' models. Postle, "Flayed for Art," 56–57, and Martin Kemp and Marina Wallace, *Spectacular Bodies: The Art and Science of the Human Body from Leonardo to Now* (London: Hayward Gallery, 2000), 83–87.

20. See, for example, Katharine Park, "The Criminal and the Saintly Body: Autopsy and Dissection in Renaissance Italy," *Renaissance Quarterly* 47, no. 1 (Spring 1994): 1–33; Andrea Carlino, *Books of the Body: Anatomical Ritual and Renaissance Learning,* trans. John Tedeschi and Anne C. Tedeschi (Chicago: University of Chicago Press, 1999), 92–98; and Andrew Cunningham, *The Anatomist Anatomis'd: An Experimental Discipline in Enlightenment Europe* (Farnham, UK: Ashgate, 2010), 221–231.

21. Norma Landau, "Introduction," in *Law, Crime, and English Society, 1660–1803,* ed. Landau (Cambridge, UK: Cambridge University Press, 2002), 4.

22. 25 Geo. II, c 37. John Cay, *The Statutes at Large from Magna Charta, to the Thirtieth Year of King George the Second, Inclusive* (London, 1758), 111–112. As an alternative to dissection, the act also declared, "That it shall be in the Power of any such Judge or Justice to appoint the Body of any such Criminal to be hung in Chains."

23. The expression is from "Experimental Cast," 14.

24. Ibid.

25. "Obituary," 167.

26. Jacopo Berengario da Carpi, *Commentaria cum amplissimis additionibus super anatomia mundini* (Bologna, 1521), folio 519 verso, Wellcome Library, London. The only other visual precedent that I have so far been able to identify for the *Anatomical Crucifixion* appears in Jacques Gamelin's *Nouveau recueil d'ostéologie et de myologie* (Toulouse, 1779). Neither text was in the Royal Academy library or in Cosway's private book collection at this time. *A Catalogue of the Library of the Royal Academy* (London, 1802), 19–20, and *A Catalogue of the Very Curious, Extensive, and Valuable Library of Richard Cosway, Esq, R.A.* (London, 1821).

27. Cunningham, *Anatomist Anatomis'd,* 224, 230.

28. On Banks, see Bell, *Annals,* 6–7; on Cosway, see Lloyd, "Collector, Connoisseur, and Virtuoso," 77–81; on West, see John Dillenberger, *Benjamin West: The Context of His Life's Work* (San Antonio: Trinity University Press, 1977), 1–8.

29. Helmut von Erffa and Allen Staley, *The Paintings of Benjamin West* (New Haven, CT: Yale University Press, 1986), 361–362, cat. no. 356. On West's commission for Saint George's Chapel, see Jerry D. Meyer, "Benjamin West's Window Designs for Saint George's Chapel, Windsor," *American Art Journal* 11, no. 3 (July 1979): 53–65. On Cosway's late drawings, see Lloyd, *Richard and Maria Cosway*, 80–81.

30. "Obituary," 167.

31. "Dying Behaviour, &c."

32. The phrase first appears in Francis Grose, *A Classical Dictionary of the Vulgar Tongue* (London, 1785).

33. With what success the public execution achieved its goals is another question, one that remains open to historical interpretation. See Thomas Laqueur, "Crowds, Carnival and the State in English Executions, 1604–1868," in *The First Modern Society: Essays in English History in Honour of Lawrence Stone*, ed. A. L. Beier, David Cannadine, and James M. Rosenheim (Cambridge, UK: Cambridge University Press, 1989), 305–355; Gatrell, *The Hanging Tree*, 56–105; and Simon Devereaux, "Recasting the Theatre of Execution: The Abolition of the Tyburn Ritual," *Past and Present* 202, no. 1 (February 2009): 154–156.

34. "Ordinary of Newgate's Account" (OA17591003), October 1759, *Old Bailey Proceedings Online*, www.oldbaileyonline.org, version 7.0, October 3, 2012).

35. Legg and Stark's broadside states, "Yesterday they attended in the chapel, Newgate, to hear the condemned sermon." "Dying Behaviour, &c."

36. Edward Barry, *Sermon Preached to the Convicts under Sentence of Death in Newgate, on Sunday Morning, the 20th April, 1778* (London, 1788), 15–16. In the quote I have corrected several evidently misspelled terms ("world," "children," "thief," and "Paradise") for the sake of clarity. On the religious dimensions of the public execution in this period, see Randall McGowen, "'He Beareth Not the Sword in Vain': Religion and the Criminal Law in Eighteenth-Century England," *Eighteenth-Century Studies* 21, no. 2 (Winter 1987–1988): 192–211, and Andrea McKenzie, *Tyburn's Martyrs: Execution in England, 1675–1775* (London: Hambledon Continuum, 2007).

37. "Experimental Cast," 14.

38. Ibid.

39. William Eden, 1st Baron Auckland, *Principles of Penal Law* (London, 1771), 21–22, 25, 80–81, 244. On the crime of murder, Eden writes, "The proper judgement against deliberate murder, is death; and in the rigid infliction of this judgement both the safety and morality of mankind are greatly interested. It is the voice of nature, confirmed by the law of God, that 'Whoso sheddeth man's blood, by man shall his blood be shed'; and therefore, saith the Mosaical law, 'Ye shall take no satisfaction for the life of a murderer, which is guilty of death; but he shall surely be put to death, so ye shall not pollute the land wherein ye are.'" Ibid., 244.

40. "Experimental Cast," 14.

31

Extirpation of Idolatry and Sensory Experience in Sixteenth-Century Mexico

BARBARA E. MUNDY

S oon after the Spanish conquistador Hernán Cortés entered the Aztec capital of Tenochtitlan in 1519 and took its monarch, Moteuczoma, captive, he sent his men to enter the shrines at the top of the city's most important pyramids and cast out the idols: "The most important of these idols, the ones in whom they have most faith, I have taken from their places and thrown down the steps; and I had those chapels where they were cleaned for they were full of the blood of sacrifices; and I had images of Our Lady and the other saints put there."[1] In this action we glimpse one early moment of what would become a sweeping transformation of the religious practice of the New World's some twenty-five million people in the wake of military conquest. Throughout the sixteenth century, a host of New World religions were banned, legions of indigenous priests executed or stripped of status, and tens of thousands of works of sacred architecture destroyed, along with countless holy objects deemed idolatrous. In sites where sacred rituals had once taken place, their inversions occurred: Instead of seeing the ritual sacrifice of the war captive, gathered peoples saw their politically powerful lords humbled and executed; instead of hearing the chanting of the native hymns, they heard the condemning words of the extirpator's sentence; instead of smelling the fragrance of the tree-sap incense, they breathed air filled with the sear of castigated flesh.

These campaigns to extirpate idolatry have been extensively documented and analyzed by historians over the past century. Their attraction is understandable: extirpation campaigns were by their very nature attempts to set "pagan" beliefs in stark contrast to "orthodox" ones, and therefore can illuminate both. For New Spain, as the northern territory of Spain's American holdings would be known, an area largely coincident with modern Mexico and Central America, scholars of the early twentieth

515

century focused on extirpation from the point of view of the extirpators, using sources written in European languages, sometimes unwittingly revealing how porous the boundaries of orthodox Catholicism could be in the American context. In the past several decades, historians have been more attentive to the responses by indigenous peoples, attempting to answer a question recently posed by David Tavárez: "Can we understand how native defendants [in idolatry trials] thought about their ritual practices and about orthodox Christianity?"[2]

But ritual practice is *felt* more than it is ever *thought*. It is felt in the register of experiences received by the body, like the smell of burning copal incense or the sight of elaborately garbed ritual specialists. Or it is felt in enacted ones, as in moving through the steps of a dance learned though kinesthetic apprenticeship or singing a song so long remembered that it is deeply intertwined with one's sense of self. And if ritual practice is first and foremost a sensory experience, its extirpation must also operate in the realm of the senses. Thus the trauma that results from conquest and extirpation is also most keenly felt on the sensuous register. In this chapter I recenter the question of extirpation campaigns to ask not what its targets thought but how the campaigns *felt*—that is, how their effects registered as bodily, sensuous practices. To do so I draw on a particularly notorious episode of extirpation from my own field of study, sixteenth-century New Spain.

But any exploration of sensuous practice of the past is necessarily dependent on and shaped by the sources available. With time, accounts of these violent events that marked both the initial encounter between Europeans and indigenous peoples and subsequent extirpation campaigns would be expressed in texts created by members of both groups. Images were rarer; the work titled *Bonfire of the Clothes, Books, and Attire of the Priests,* the focal point of this chapter, represents a singular instance (Figure 31.1). During extirpation campaigns that spanned two hemispheres and three centuries, only once did a native artist take up pen and ink to document the destruction of sacred objects from the now idolatrous past. Despite the indigenous pedigree of *Bonfire,* it nonetheless presents the experience of the extirpation in highly mediated form, set within the pages of a book, protected by hard cover. While I am well aware of the role of mediation in shaping representation, in this chapter I set aside that question to offer an exploration of sensuous experience and its continuities in sixteenth-century New Spain. I begin with the historical context that led to the creation of *Bonfire* to describe a singular and singularly brutal moment of the evangelization campaign that unfolded in New Spain, then use it as a window onto the sensuous experience of religious ritual among the Nahua, the dominant indigenous group of central Mexico. But in interpreting this work against other texts of the day, I underscore the continuities in the sensuous experience of religion for the Nahua, so much so that *Bonfire* can be seen as an image of both rupture and continuity.

FIGURE 31.1. Unknown artist, *Bonfire of the Clothes, Books, and Attire of the Priests*, ca. 1575–1582, from Diego Muñoz Camargo, *Descripción de la ciudad y provincia de Tlaxcala*, Ms. Hunter 242, fol. 242r. © Glasgow University Library, Scotland/Bridgeman Art Library International, New York.

Extirpation Campaigns in New Spain

Cortés's act of extirpation in Tenochtitlan was preceded by the acts of Christopher Columbus in the Caribbean and would be followed by actions carried out by the waves of later conquistadors who would eventually bring much of the Americas under the rule of Spain. The calculated rhetoric of extirpation looms large in the accounts of conquistadors who knew that the responsibility to evangelize rather than to exploit material goods won Spain the papal donation of the right to the lands of the New World and the fruits of its people west of the Line of Demarcation. Acts of extirpation were thus offered as justification for military conquest. After a small group of Franciscans (three) made their way to the New World, a second, larger group called "The Twelve" was given papal license to evangelize New Spain, arriving in 1524, with Dominicans and Augustinians soon following, and the responsibility for both extirpation and evangelization shifted to these mendicants.[3] It is thenceforth in their histories that we find most of the records of extirpation, the smashing of idols, the tearing down of shrines, and, less frequently, the mortal castigation of idolaters. In Mexico the scope of the destruction was enormous, even if we take into account any exaggeration on the part of the extirpators. The Franciscan bishop Juan de Zumárraga reported to Spain in 1531 that "more that 500 temples of the idols have been destroyed, as well as more than 20,000 statues of demons, which they worshipped, and are now smashed and burned."[4] Farther to the south, in the Yucatán, the Franciscan Diego de Landa recounted, "We found a great number of books in their [the Mayas'] letters, and since they contained nothing but superstitions and falsehoods of the devil we burned them all"; some scholars estimate that in one auto-da-fé, Landa destroyed at least five thousand "idols" and twenty-seven Maya hieroglyphic rolls, more than double the total number of pre-Hispanic manuscripts that survive today from all the New World.[5]

But nowhere were the very earliest campaigns of extirpation felt more strongly than in Tlaxcala.[6] A fiercely independent Nahua city-state that had resisted conquest by the Mexica of Tenochtitlan (often known as the Aztecs and, like the Tlaxcalans, Nahuatl speakers and thus members of the larger Nahua cultural group), the Tlaxcalans formed a military alliance with Cortés as he passed through the region en route to Tenochtitlan in 1519, and it was in Tlaxcala that Cortés regrouped before his final and destructive assault on the city in 1521. One of Cortés's conditions for continuing this fruitful alliance was that the Tlaxcalans renounce their "idolatry" and accept Christianity. Once the Franciscans arrived, they saw their allies the Tlaxcalans as the most likely converts and targeted them for their first evangelization efforts. Franciscans quickly set up a provisional monastery within the palace of the Tlaxcalan ruler, Maxixcatzin. For three years after their arrival in 1524, the region lived in a "pax indiana" during which the friars, ignorant of native languages, were unable to do much more than pantomime the tenets of the Christian faith to puzzled crowds in the marketplace. Meanwhile, indigenous priests carried out sacrifices both human and animal that were central to religious ritual at the same time that they added Christian feast days to their crowded religious calendar.[7] But in 1527 the head of the Franciscan order in New Spain, Martín de Valencia (ca. 1474–1534), was named guardian of the monastery, signaling Tlaxcala's centrality to the Franciscan enterprise of evangelization. Valencia made a startling break with the status quo that had held in the city by launching an extirpation campaign of heretofore unprecedented violence. As we shall see in greater detail below, in a campaign that lasted about three years, Franciscans cast out the old "idols," or sacred deity images, from temples and destroyed books and paraphernalia, and they also executed native lords deemed idolaters on a scale unparalleled elsewhere. The great historian of Central Mexico, Charles Gibson, usually restrained in his judgments, wrote of these events, "No other non-military occurrence in the whole sixteenth century history of Tlaxcala can compare with [the extirpation campaign] in violence or severity. Its effect upon the religious life of the province must have been extreme. In the history of Tlaxcala conversion it appears as an isolated and extraordinary measure, unprecedented and never repeated."[8]

The extraordinary Tlaxcala campaign of extirpation can perhaps best be thought of as a frontier campaign. The Franciscans who spearheaded it were not the Church's professional inquisitors—this was the role of the Dominicans—instead being called into the breech before the establishment of more formal inquisition processes. Valencia himself seems to have been a man of exceptional piety and zeal who clearly felt empowered to act as necessary in establishing the faith. Insulated from criticism by the still considerable political power of Cortés, who supported the Franciscan mission wholeheartedly, Valencia was free to experiment. It was perhaps more crucial that Cortés also maintained a strong military presence in Tlaxcala, so Valencia was also free from the threat of native backlash or, worse, the specter of indigenous revolt that haunted the Franciscans in the great imperial capital of Tenochtitlan.

Much later, when the wars of conquest were the memories of generations, Tlaxcala would pride itself as the place of the first indigenous baptisms in New Spain. But nothing is easy in the moment, and so it was in Tlaxcala. Despite the triumphant pitch of later histories, Valencia's extirpation campaign among the Tlaxcalans was one of the most brutal and wrenching in all of Central Mexico, tearing at the social fabric to a degree unparalleled in other parts of central New Spain. These campaigns were registered in the *Descripción de la ciudad y provincia de Tlaxcala,* an account of Tlaxcala written by Diego Muñoz Camargo (ca. 1529–1599).[9] The mestizo author of the text (whose mother was an indigenous noblewoman, well connected to the ruling family of Tlaxcala, his father a Spanish conquistador) drew up his manuscript in the mid-1580s in response to a questionnaire about local economy, geography, and history in the New World sent out by the Spanish government in 1577. Rather than mailing his book-length response, Muñoz Camargo went to Spain with his manuscript to deliver it to Philip II in person as part of an attempt to defend the prerogatives the Tlaxcalans enjoyed as early allies of the Spanish.[10]

The first 234 folios of the manuscript are Muñoz Camargo's handwritten responses to the questionnaire, with long sections devoted to Tlaxcala history. But he also attached to his textual manuscript another separately authored work, a pictorial chronicle of events and exploits of the Tlaxcalans between 1519 and 1540 that offered an independent (yet sometimes parallel) narrative to his text. The pictorial chronicle—

a set of 156 pictures that I refer to as the Pictorial History to distinguish it from its textual companion, the *Descripción*—was drawn up by indigenous artists (a number of different hands are discernible) on commission from Muñoz Camargo. They did not invent the Pictorial History of whole cloth, instead patching it together from diverse indigenous sources, most of them paintings that were on display in public buildings belonging to the indigenous government in the center of Tlaxcala. The diverse sources are reflected in the Pictorial History itself, which falls into five component (although unmarked within the text) sections: (1) portraits of the indigenous rulers of Tlaxcala (4 pages), (2) evangelization and extirpation campaigns in Tlaxcala (11 pages), (3) architecture of Tlaxcala (3 pages), (4) allegories of the conquest (7 pages), and (5) Tlaxcalan–Spanish alliances and campaigns of conquest (130 pages).[11] Most of the Pictorial History occupies section 5, where the narrative fans out across Mexico to document the success of the Tlaxcalan partnership with the Spaniards in the battles of conquest (1519–ca. 1542), and these pages are the most frequently reproduced.

The pictures at the beginning, however, which are the focus of this work, start very close to home, with eleven pictures (fols. 238r–243r) that I call the "Extirpation" section documenting the entrance of Franciscan friars into Tlaxcala to evangelize and the extirpations they performed there. Although other parts of the Pictorial History have direct antecedents and copies, this one does not. The only known correspondence is between one of the images (Figure 31.2) and a painting of ca. 1570 in the cloister of the Franciscan monastery of San Miguel, Huejotzingo, a site within thirty kilometers of Tlaxcala. The imagery on these pages of the "Extirpation" section is, as far as we know at present, singular. The emphasis on violence in this section suggests that its artists viewed this history as a defining one in Tlaxcala at the same time that they wrestled with its consequences.

Sensory Ritual in Tlaxcala

The Franciscans who arrived in Tlaxcala quickly realized that the "idolatrous" religion they encountered was deeply felt and widely practiced, even though the categories they had developed to help them understand pagan practice were often badly suited to the New World. In New Spain they saw among the Nahua a pantheistic religion, with innumerable deities worshiped both formally in temple complexes and less formally at home. Scholars now interpret the evidence to suggest deity "clusters" related to three basic cult themes (celestial creativity–divine paternalism; rain–moisture–agricultural fertility; and war–sacrifice–sanguinary nourishment of the sun and the earth), with the deities embodiments of natural forces and phenomena.[12] Most participants encountered this theological constellation in the many public celebrations that were regularly held in honor of the deities; each twenty-day month had a patron who was celebrated with a feast, and other deities had their own special feast days as well.

FIGURE 31.2. Unknown artist, *The Arrival of the Franciscans and Erection of the First Cross,* ca. 1575–1582, from Diego Muñoz Camargo, *Descripción de la ciudad y provincia de Tlaxcala,* Ms. Hunter 242, fol. 239v. © Glasgow University Library, Scotland / Bridgeman Art Library International, New York.

The centerpiece of these feasts was frequently the figure of a specially costumed person known as a *teixiptla* who was believed to be the literal embodiment of the deity, a transubstantiated being whom later Catholic evangelizers saw as a particularly devious form of demonic mischief.

A passage about one of these feasts, Tecuilhuitontli, devoted to the deity of salt, appears in the Franciscan Bernardino de Sahagún's *Florentine Codex,* a book written by Sahagún and Nahua intellectuals in the 1570s. The volume's descriptions of native ritual offer revealing insights about some of the sensuous experiences of indigenous practice, as well as the centrality of human sacrifice to ritual efficacy:

> On the eve of this feast, all the old women sang and danced, as well as the young women and girls. They went held by some short cords which they carried in their hands, one [taking] one end, another the other [end]. These cords they named *xochimecatl* ["flower ropes"]. They all wore garlands of wormwood [flowers] of this land, which are called *iztauhiatl.* A number of the old men led them and ordered the singing. Among them went the woman who was the likeness of this goddess [the teixiptla] and who was to die arrayed in rich ornaments.
>
> On the night before the feast, the women, with the same one who was to die, kept vigil; and they sang and danced all night long. At the break of day, all the priests arrayed themselves and performed a very solemn dance. And all those who were present at the dance held in their hands those flowers which are called *cempohualxochitl* [marigolds, still sacred flowers today]. Thus dancing, they took many captives to the pyramid of Tlaloc [the rain deity], and, with them, the woman who was to die, who was the likeness of the goddess Huixtocihuatl. There they slew first the captives and then her.
>
> Many other ceremonies were performed during this feast; and also [there was] great drunkenness.[13]

Participants danced and sang, ate and drank, garnished themselves with pungent flowers, or fought mock battles in the streets, year in and year out, their actions both affirming and enabling the order of the larger cosmos. Davíd Carrasco has broadly described pre-Hispanic religion in this area as comprising "three major elements . . . the ceremonial center [itself a model of the ideal universe] and celestial event (worldmaking), human creativity and sacrifice in the hands of an elite (worldcentering) and the commitment to rejuvenation (worldrenewing),"[14] and in the description of the public ceremonies above we see all three elements, along with the embedded role of sensory practices in play.

But all these rites and their attendant sensuous experiences would be dramatically disrupted as Valencia swung into action in 1527. The Pictorial History narrates this and the preceding years in chronological order, devoting two pages to the first incursion of friars into Tlaxcala in 1522, immediately following the conquest, an arrival marked by an attentiveness of the Tlaxcalan elite, both men and women, to their cause. But when we turn the page, we arrive at 1523 or so, the period of the "pax indiana" when the three Franciscans had moved on to Mexico City and Tlaxcalans took up their old ways and the human sacrifices continued (Figure 31.3).

FIGURE 31.3. Unknown artist, *Sacrifices among the Tlaxcalans,* ca. 1575–1582, from Diego Muñoz Camargo, *Descripción de la ciudad y provincia de Tlaxcala,* Ms. Hunter 242, fol. 239r. © Glasgow University Library, Scotland / Bridgeman Art Library International, New York.

The center of the picture in Figure 31.3 is dominated by the facade of a stepped pyramid, its wide central staircase leading to the *adoratorio,* or temple, at the top. Appearing as if suspended in midair in this space is Camaxtli, the Tlaxcalan tutelary deity, pictured as a bundle wearing the deity's mask and a flower-patterned cloak knotted over his bundle-body. Below Camaxtli, four indigenous priests hold the arms and legs of a sacrificial victim; the priest at upper left drives an obsidian blade into the victim's chest to extract his heart. Below, on the same vertical axis as Camaxtli and the victim, is yet another victim, whose lifeless body has been pitched from the temple, seen as from above, a smear of red ink standing for the pooling blood from his empty chest, a rare use of color in the manuscript. At the bottom of the picture, two groups of observers witness this scene. On the left are two Spanish men, one of whom holds an owl, and a severed quail head lies at the feet of the other. To the right are the Tlaxcalan nobility, distinguished by their elegant embroidered cloaks. Their leader holds an incense burner aloft in one hand and a soon-to-be-sacrificed quail in the other. Notably, while the native priests perform human sacrifice, the Tlaxcalan elite offer only incense and birds, setting themselves at a certain distance from the human sacrifice; a text written in Nahuatl, set like a title at the top of the page, makes no mention of their presence or participation. Nor does it explain the inclusion of Spaniards; they may represent the many conquistadors who countenanced human sacrifice as long as it did not interfere with their own worldly gain.[15]

The page following, representing the year 1524, is fully given over to the arrival of the twelve Franciscans. The composition is anchored by a central cross, and the ordered and regular figures of the kneeling friars contrast strongly with the crazy swooping of the ten devils above (see Figure 31.2). Once in Tlaxcala, the friars baptized acquiescent Tlaxcalan elites in front of a temple.[16] One page of the Pictorial History is devoted to this pacific conversion, and then we are plunged into the horrific events beginning in 1527 as violence erupts on the five following pages. On the first of these, Franciscans, helped by their Tlaxcalan child converts, set fire to two native temples, and the devils, rendered as they would be in European manuscripts, flee for good.[17] On the next page, the Franciscans are absent, and the child converts take over the campaign. At the top of the page, drawn in the same spare style as the images on the other pages, a player of the parchesi-like game *patolli* is hanged from a gallows set up at the upper center of the page, and beneath him his game board has been thrown into a fire lit for the purpose. A group of Tlaxcalan elites at the upper left witness the punishment meted out to a gambler on this game. In other areas of the image, three child converts discipline two men and a woman by cutting off their hair. On the next page, a Franciscan emerges as agent in the extirpation, spying an elite man preparing sacrifices in a cave. On the same page, the idolater's punishment by hanging is pictured, once again at the upper center of the page and once again with the Tlaxcalan elite as witnesses. On the following page, the Franciscans, aided by the child converts, burn the accouterments of the native priests (see Figure 31.1).

On the last page dealing directly with the extirpations, the Tlaxcalan elite are absent; instead, it is the Franciscans and a Spaniard who oversee the deaths by hanging of five Tlaxcalan men and a woman found guilty of idolatry, their limp figures arrayed in the upper part of the page (Figure 31.4). Below we witness the beginning of the immolation of two men, their still-living, open-eyed figures gazing out as the flames begin to consume their bodies. Only on the final page of the "Extirpation" section do we encounter a pacific scene, with Franciscans removing the indigenous-style cloaks of their child converts and dressing them in Spanish-style tunics, this act of re-dressing echoing that of a Franciscan novice taking his distinctive brown habit from his superior as part of the rite of ordination.

FIGURE 31.4. Unknown artist, *The Castigation of the Tlaxcalan Idolators,* ca. 1575–1582, from Diego Muñoz Camargo, *Descripción de la ciudad y provincia de Tlaxcala,* Ms. Hunter 242, fol. 242v. © Glasgow University Library, Scotland/Bridgeman Art Library International, New York.

In Tlaxcala, as elsewhere, this violent extirpation campaign was intended to eradicate all three elements of pre-Hispanic religion as defined by Carrasco: by destroying temples and deity images, the friars severed connections to a model universe; by stripping an elite class of their ability to carry out rituals and sacrifices, they denied indigenous peoples the means to center themselves in the larger cosmic order; and by interrupting the ritual calendar, they deprived them of the ability to renew their world. But most keenly felt would have been the loss of the practices and experiences that these peoples experienced through the senses—the tastes of the special foods prepared for the monthly feasts, the heavy smells of the garlands of flowers, and the elevated states achieved by all-night dancing and song that allowed connection to the divine.[18]

The sacred world of the Nahua offered linked sensory phenomena; indeed, a certain special charge was felt by means of such linkages. Sacred images often called on other senses, particularly touch and taste, as well as smell. Teixiptla were not only living beings but also images made of amaranth seed, and they were slowly eaten in the months following the feasts: the divine made present through taste.[19] Before the conquest, one of the most valued art forms among the Nahua, particularly in Tenochtitlan, was feather mosaics, images created out of tens of thousands of tiny feathers pasted onto paper supports. The flickering, light/dark qualities of feathers made them carriers of *tonalli*—a Nahuatl word that means something like "life force," a force also released in the sacrifice of a chosen and prepared victim.[20] Tonalli was conceived of as both light and heat, offering a synesthetic sight–touch experience. The bodies of the dead, having lost their tonalli, were cold to the touch. Iridescent feathers were particularly important carriers of tonalli, and their physical properties help us understand why. The shifting hues created by iridescent surfaces can also make it seem as if these surfaces are generating their own light, a glow that is like that of the sun, not just light but also heat. Other such divine forces manifested themselves to a range of senses. For instance, *teotl,* a word meaning the animating force of the divine, was perceived through other senses as much as it was through sight. The deity Ehecatl was felt in gusts of wind; Tlaloc was embodied in the fall of cool rain, the underworld deity Mictlantecuhtli through the gassy stench of decomposition, Itztlacoliuhqui through the sharp cold of frosts that threatened the newly planted maize.

Thus the violent extirpation campaigns, like the one unleashed in Tlaxcala by Martín de Valencia, entailed the cessation of a carefully calibrated ritual life as well as the execution or banishment of an entire caste of native intellectuals who were priests. For conquest-era Tlaxcalans, the severing of the sensory experiences that connected them to the world of the sacred would have been traumatic. They had, of course, been spared the scorched-earth warfare waged against the Mexica in Tenochtitlan, where tens of thousands died. Their world was largely business as usual until 1527. Indeed, the well-documented and robust resilience of Tlaxcala's political class through the sixteenth century and beyond can be traced to their (relatively) happy conquest-era fortunes overall. But we can meter some of the reasons extirpation in general was traumatic through the responses of other indigenous peoples in Mexico. When Cortés destroyed the sculptures of the Templo Mayor in Tenochtitlan, the main temple of the Mexica, he records that "they asked me not to do it . . . for they believed that those idols gave them all their worldly goods, and that if they were allowed to be ill treated, they would become angry and give them nothing and take the fruit from the earth leaving the people to die of hunger."[21] Bishop Landa would recall that his destruction of the books of the Maya "they took most grievously, and [it] gave them great pain."[22]

Two other factors added to the particular Tlaxcalan trauma of 1527–1530: the status of the victims and the role of children. The Pictorial History shows the victims as lords (*tlatoque*), that is, high-ranking members of the nobility. The public exposure and humiliation of people of this rank would have been unthinkable before the conquest, even before 1527, when Valencia took charge (see Figure 31.4). Gibson has reconstructed the identities of four of the executed lords shown in the Pictorial History and named in another indigenous source. They were not fringe players in Tlaxcalan history; among their number were stalwart warriors who fought alongside the Spanish in the conquest (ironically, it is their acts of bravery that are recorded in section 5 of the Pictorial History, the pages that follow). The most notorious of those executed, don Cristóbal Acxotecatl, was an early and fervent convert to Christianity. Thus, to the eyes of the Tlaxcalan public, it was not the socially marginal being executed on the main plaza of Tlaxcala, a city with tens of thousands of residents at the time, but the high nobility who supported the Spanish cause. The damage to the Tlaxcalan social fabric did not stop there: the undoing of don Cristóbal Acxotecatl had come at the hands of his own son; indeed, the Franciscans made it their policy to set children against their parents.

Probably even before Valencia's rise, the Franciscans demanded that the elite send their children to the monastery to be evangelized and educated. Empowered by their Franciscan teachers, the children reported back on the idolatrous acts of their parents and others. Outside of the monastery, these youths carried out vigilante justice. A roaming band of them targeted a native priest in the marketplace and stoned him to death: the social order upended for all to witness. When the Franciscan-trained son of don Cristóbal Acxotecatl accused his father of idolatry, his father had him killed. The murder revealed, don Cristóbal was executed.[23] Thus the traditional social order, according to which elders were respected by their children and each group was loyal to the other, was turned upside down.

Compensation

When it comes to idolatry, the multisensory practices of religion are perhaps the most challenging to the extirpator. Our bodies are like AM radios, and we pick up signals only along the wavelengths allowed by our eyes, ears, mouths, noses, and skin. We have a limited bandwidth, and if the experience of dancing in honor of a pagan goddess is the same as dancing in honor of the Virgin, what separates idolatry from orthodoxy? The question was often asked by critics who were hostile to the mendicant friars in charge of evangelization; indeed, it troubled the friars, including Bartolomé de las Casas, as well. But the solution was mapped out early on by Toribio de Benavente, known by his Nahuatl moniker Motolinía, an influential Franciscan. In his writings he emphasized the physical form of the "idols" as the loci of idolatry rather than the practices that brought worshippers closer to them: "They had idols of stone and wood, and of pottery, and they also make them of maize dough, and of seeds wrapped in maize dough, and they had some large ones, and others even larger, and medium sized ones, and small ones. Some are shaped like bishops, with their miters and staffs, some of which are gilded, and other of turquoise worked in different ways. Other have the shape of men, and have on their heads a mortar instead of a miter."[24] Emphasizing, and targeting for destruction, the visible forms of these idols—that is, hearing the signals coming across on a single station—allowed the wider range of sensuous practices to continue undisturbed; indeed, what is notable about this "spiritual conquest" of New Spain is how little disruption there was to native practices by newly introduced Catholic ones.

The Franciscans, in particular, working in the wake of the extirpation campaigns like the one documented in the Pictorial History, nurtured multisensory practices as part of newly established Catholic rituals. A generation after Motolinía wrote about the threat embodied by physical idols, his fellow Franciscan Gerónimo de Mendieta would write about the marvelous events he witnessed as his native charges celebrated the new faith. For the main Catholic feasts, they created great arches covered with garlands of heavily scented flowers, and after Mass was said, "a dance of well-dressed children left [the church] to the songs of devout couplets or motets, where the choir was joined by master-singers," while elsewhere in the church complex, "there were other dances that caused rejoicing."[25] Although the content of such dances—supplied by new songs in honor of Mary, Jesus, and the saints composed by Franciscans and their acolytes—was entirely orthodox, their form followed those of the pre-Hispanic period. Dancing with slow, decorous steps, the participants moved to the beat of toned wooden drums, the *huehuetl* and the *teponaztli*. They often danced through the night, reminiscent of the night dancing that is frequently a feature of descriptions of indigenous dances, perhaps because the shutting off of the visual would heighten a self-centered focus on the movements of the body and allow one to feel, although not necessarily see, one's connection to the movements of the larger body of dancers.

By the light of day, statues of saints and images were held aloft, the former made of maize paste, the latter out of petals of flowers and feathers, many of the same materials used in the manufacture of the teixiptla. Probably meant to be held in such a now wholly orthodox procession was an icon of Christ as Salvador Mundi made entirely of feathers on a cloth support, in which Christ holds the orb of the world in one hand, raising his other in blessing (Figure 31.5).[26] The source was likely a print imported by the friars into New Spain, but it was interpreted by indigenous artists, probably working in one of the leading feather workshops in Mexico City. The Salvador Mundi is boldly made, with starkly contrastive plumage that could easily be seen from afar:

FIGURE 31.5. Unknown artist, *Christ as Salvador Mundi,* mid-sixteenth century. Feathers on cloth support, 70 × 85 centimeters. Museo Nacional del Virreinato, Tepotzotlán, Mexico. CONACULTA-INAH-MEX. Used with the permission of the Instituto Nacional de Antropología e Historia, Mexico City.

dark hair against skin of alabaster feathers, purple cloak against crimson robe, turquoise background against gold border. Touch is also implicated by the brilliant tropical plumage that creates the surface. Then and now, its silky texture calls out to be stroked, and viewers in Europe sometimes did touch these miraculous feather paintings to prove the reality of their seemingly miraculous facture.[27] But for the indigenous viewer touch seems to have been unnecessary to "see" the object's heat. Aaron Hyman has pointed out that feather workers never touched their material, instead using bone awls and obsidian blades.[28] And by their clever setting of the iridescent surfaces of their medium, feather workers could achieve the effect of moiré silk, the colors changing as the viewer moved, the work shimmering with the heat of tonalli.

Sensory Reengagement

As suggested above, many experiences offered within the precincts of newly constructed Catholic missionary churches evoked, and perhaps directly replicated, those of traditional indigenous practice. Returning to the image with which this chapter began, the *Bonfire of the Clothes, Books, and Attire of the Priests* (see Figure 31.1), we now see the tantalizing connection that lies within and beyond the iconography: through its sensuous expression, the trauma of extirpation is made parallel to religious ritual itself. The image was created by intellectuals who were deeply absorbed in the questions of religious practice and belief and conscious of their role in shaping a history for this emergent entity known as New Spain. The degree to which their images insist on the multisensory nature of this historical trauma is striking. In creating an image that both documents and interprets destruction, the artist offered one that opens up into other registers of the sensuous world. By evoking experiences already familiar on our own sensory registers, it calls us anew to its moment: the orange tongues of fire crackle at the iridescent blue-green quetzal feathers streaming from the crown of Tlaloc, the pre-Hispanic rain deity pictured within. The pitch-stained paper lets off dense smoke, while the wind carries the sweet smell of burning resin. The swirling smoke chokes and blinds viewers. Thus the visible is somewhat ironic here, because sight would have been the one sense most closed off during the actual event of extirpation, particularly to the friars themselves, who nonetheless are pictured as staring upward into the conflagration. Just as the mass of dancers in the dark had a heightened sense of awareness of a reality not necessarily accessible by vision, here the artist records an event whose smoky circumstances would not allow us to perceive it but insists on its presence nonetheless.[29]

In the *Bonfire* the senses are engaged, and the same sensory nodes would have been activated in these "replacement" orthodox Catholic rituals staged within Tlaxcala's Franciscan church compound. We see the silky iridescent plumes of feathers, carriers of tonalli, prominent among the burning headdresses and staffs. A feathered staff marks the central axis and topmost point of the image; to the right is another, peeking out of the flames, although its prominence is compromised by the flames that were added by a later hand in iron-gall ink. Such feathers decorated the altar and processional cross of Tlaxcala's Franciscan church in the 1550s, and feathers were used in the costumes of the dancers of the religious *mitotes,* or sacred dances.[30] As carriers of sacred "heat," feathers were important vehicles to give the weight of ancient sacred practices to newly adopted Catholic ritual across New Spain. In the *Bonfire* image, the feathers beckon, untouched by the damaging flames.

The fire is unmistakable, although it lies behind the salient features of the image. And while fire had generally negative connotations in Christian thought—as in the burning hell fires of eternal punishment—the sort of controlled burn that we witness in the image also played a crucial role in the Mass, as purifying incense was burned to create a sacralized space around the altar, a space perceived through smell alone. Thus we gain some purchase on the question of how all this felt: the continuity of sensuous experiences (the smell of flowers, the sounds of fervent songs, the movement of decorous dances) filled the void that extirpation left in its wake at the same time that these experiences pointed back to the initial rupture, indelible memory traces carried in the body.

But the image of destruction is actually one of preservation. In the bonfire we see eleven precisely delineated masks of deities of the pre-Hispanic pantheon, known best from the host of sources on Nahua religion.[31] One way the human mind makes sense of unparalleled events is, of course, through analogy, and this analogical process was no different for the artists of mid-sixteenth-century Tlaxcala. Considering this image in relation to pictorial analogies at hand in the sixteenth-century source material, both indigenous and European, we will find that what appears, on its surface, to be an image of destruction transforms into one of creation, of new beginning. In central Mexican cosmology, burning was crucial to world renewal as a new age was ushered in.[32] Indeed, central Mexicans seem to have identified another quality that made burning an important part of some sacrificial rituals: the burnt object released unseen energies and visible substances, like smoke and steam, held within. Inga Clendinnen has argued that this need to burn the offering, be it paper or the body of a sacrificial victim, and witness the transformation that occurred, allowed understanding of otherwise unseen connections in the natural world; burning, she points out, led to "parallel transformations in substances perceptually different [which] hinted at hidden resemblance, and so to connection."[33] In short, for the Nahua, evidently destructive rituals, like burning, had as their aim the release of stored energies to renew the world. They also functioned as revelation, making present the once-hidden connections between superficially and visibly different things.

In this context, the burning of ritual paraphernalia depicted in the Pictorial History may not be simply an image of destruction—and in fact, we see nothing actually destroyed. The artist is careful to place the tongues of flame in the background so that we can clearly see the objects in the conflagration. The image shows these sacred objects in the burning orb not destroyed but transformed, like sacrificial victims thrown onto burning pyres, their inner energies released and put to new purpose. In the Pictorial History, the sacred objects that belong to the pagan past but are present as image fragments in the present age release their energies and rise, like a sun, freshly sprung from the horizon, given added hoist by the friars' torches.

Because the Tlaxcalan intellectual who shaped these images in the Pictorial History was likely both Christian and Franciscan-educated, for him to make a visual equation between earlier ritual practice and the extirpation campaigns was a way of setting this historical trauma into a larger frame, mapping recent events of evangelical history onto older frameworks. The images preserved the violence and destruction of the extirpation campaigns at the same time that they seem to have interpreted those same events as a new beginning—the dawn, for better or worse, of a new sun.[34] *Bonfire* brings the indigenous pattern of destruction as creation and Christian world beginnings into alignment.

In Tlaxcala, the violent extirpation campaigns waged by Martín de Valencia from 1527 to 1530 brought physical destruction of sacred spaces and objects, as well as accusations and executions that tore at the larger social fabric. The Franciscans conceived of physical things, temples and idols, as containers of "pagan" religion that allowed them to introduce a set of replacement rituals that drew on the sensory experiences once offered by indigenous practice. At the same time, one of the images produced for the *Descripción, Bonfire,* was particularly insistent about the sensory aspects of extirpation. In positing parallels among earlier ritual traditions, the extirpations of 1527–1530, and the orthodox practices of the moment when the artists created this work, we understand analogic processes at work and the multiple registers by which we make sense of the past from the standpoint of the present.

NOTES

This chapter was developed as part of the first project cycle of the Initiative for the Study of Visual and Material Cultures of Religion, supported by the Henry Luce Foundation, the Yale Institute of Sacred Music, and Yale University. I thank Sally Promey, Richard Meyer, and Mia Mochizuki for their guidance; portions were read at the Columbia University Seminar for the Arts of Americas, Africa, and Oceania; I thank Francesco Pellezzi, Allesandro Russo, and Diana Fane for their helpful comments. Sara Ryu and Aaron Hyman have also been crucial for thinking about the European image in New Spain; Dana Leibsohn read and commented on a draft. I am grateful to all.

1. Hernán Cortés, *Letters from Mexico,* trans. Anthony Pagden (New Haven, CT: Yale University Press, 1986), 106.

2. David Eduardo Tavárez, *The Invisible War: Indigenous Devotions, Discipline, and Dissent in Colonial Mexico* (Stanford, CA: Stanford University Press, 2011), 3. His book provides an extensive bibliography on the idolatry campaigns in New Spain.

3. The basic history of the early evangelization of New Spain is to be found in Robert Ricard, *The Spiritual Conquest of Mexico: An Essay on the Apostolate and the Evangelizing Methods of*

the Mendicant Orders in New Spain, 1523–1572, trans. Lesley Byrd Simpson (Berkeley: University of California Press, 1974). Histories of the early Inquisition in Mexico include Tavárez, *The Invisible War;* Martin Austin Nesvig, *Ideology and Inquisition: The World of the Censors in Early Mexico* (New Haven, CT: Yale University Press, 2009); María Teresa Sepúlveda y Herrera, *Procesos por idolatría al cacique, gobernadores y sacerdotes de Yanhuitlán, 1544–1546,* 1st ed., Serie Etnohistoria (Mexico City: Instituto Nacional de Antropología e Historia, 1999); Jorge Traslosheros, "El tribunal eclesiástico y los indios en el Arzobispado de México, hasta 1630," *Historia Mexicana* 51, no. 3: 485–516; Richard E. Greenleaf, *Zumárraga and the Mexican Inquisition, 1536–1543,* Academy of American Franciscan History Monograph Series (Washington, DC: Academy of American Franciscan History, 1961); and Richard E. Greenleaf, *The Mexican Inquisition of the Sixteenth Century* (Albuquerque: University of New Mexico Press, 1969).

4. Joaquín García Icazbalceta, *Don Fray Juan de Zumárraga, primer obispo y arzobispo de México, estudio biográfico y bibliográfico* (Mexico City: Andrade y Morales, 1881), Appendix 1, 60, translation mine.

5. Diego de Landa, *Yucatan before and after the Conquest* (New York: Dover, 1978), 82; Spanish edition, Landa, *Relación de las cosas de Yucatán,* Crónicas de América, ed. Miguel Rivera Dorado (Madrid: Historia 16, 1985). These are oft-repeated figures; Tozzer's edition of Landa subjects them to some scrutiny. Diego de Landa, *Landa's Relación de las Cosas de Yucatan, a Translation,* ed. and trans. Alfred M. Tozzer, Peabody Museum of American Archaeology and Ethnology Papers (Cambridge, MA: Peabody Museum, 1941), 78.

6. No exact figures for the city's conquest-era population are available. In summarizing colonial sources, Gerhard gives the figure of 120,000 indigenous tributaries in 1519 and suggests that this figure can be multiplied by 2.8 for a total population figure. Peter Gerhard, *A Guide to the Historical Geography of New Spain,* Cambridge Latin American Studies 14 (Cambridge, UK: Cambridge University Press, 1972). This figure is for the entire Tlaxcalan region, not just the urban core. Mendieta gives the total residents for Tlaxcala in 1524 as "more than 200,000." Gerónimo de Mendieta, *Historia eclesiástica indiana,* 2nd ed., ed. Joaquín García Icazbalceta (Mexico City: Editorial Porrúa, 1993), Chapter 15, 217.

7. Motolinía documents the failure of his order to do much toward evangelization in the mid-1520s. Motolinía, or Toribio de Benavente, *Historia de los indios de la Nueva España,* ed. Edmundo O'Gorman (Mexico City: Porrúa, 1969), tratado 1, Chapter 4, 24–28. Andrea Martínez Baracs draws on a wider range of documents to make the same point in *Un gobierno de indios: Tlaxcala, 1519–1750,* 1st ed., Sección de Obras de Historia (Mexico City and Tlaxcala: Fondo de Cultura Economica, Fideicomiso Colegio de Historia de Tlaxcala, Centro de Investigaciones y Estudios Superiores en Antropología Social, 2008), 109–121.

8. Charles Gibson, *Tlaxcala in the Sixteenth Century* (Stanford, CA: Stanford University Press, 1967), 35.

9. The work was written in response to a questionnaire issued by the royal government; in responding, its author created not a short account but a book-length history. The text and images have been reproduced in René Acuña, *Relaciones geográficas del siglo XVI: Tlaxcala,* vol. 4, Part 1, Serie Antropológica 53 (Coyoacán, Mexico: Universidad Nacional Autónoma de México, Instituto de Instituto de Investigaciones Antropológicas, 1982). A facsimile edition of the *Descripción,* a manuscript housed at the Hunterian Museum Library in Glasgow, Scotland, is Diego Muñoz Camargo, *Descripción de la ciudad y provincia de Tlaxcala de las Indias y del Mar Océano para el buen gobierno y ennoblecimiento dellas,* ed. René Acuña (Mexico City: Instituto de Investigaciones Filológicas, Universidad Nacional Autónoma de México, 1981).

10. Gibson, in *Tlaxcala in the Sixteenth Century,* 247–253, discusses the complex versions of Muñoz Camargo's history, as well as the Tlaxcalan motives shaping this and other histories.

11. The best-known source is that of sections 1 and 5, a multiscene pictorial history called the Lienzo de Tlaxcala. The Lienzo once hung in the *ayuntamiento* (indigenous town hall) building of Tlaxcala but is now lost and is known only through later copies. The earliest fragment of the Lienzo de Tlaxcala dates to the sixteenth century and is now in the collection of the University of Texas in Austin. The fullest copy is a lithographic version published in 1892, Junta Colombina, *Homenaje á Cristóbal Colón,* ed. Alfredo Chavero (Mexico City: Oficina Tipográfica de la Secretaría de Fomento, 1892). The relationship between many of the copies was first unraveled by Gibson in *Tlaxcala in the Sixteenth Century,* 247–253, and has more recently been discussed in an essay, Carlos Martínez Marín, "Historia del Lienzo de Tlaxcala / History of the Lienzo de Tlaxcala," in *El Lienzo de Tlaxcala,* ed. Josefina García Quintana, Carlos Martínez Marín, and Mario de la Torre (Mexico City: Cartón y Papel de México, 1983), 35–54, and in Travis Barton Kranz, "Visual Persuasion: Sixteenth-Century Tlaxcalan Pictorials in Response to the Conquest of Mexico," in *The Conquest All Over Again: Nahuas and Zapotecs, Thinking, Writing, and Painting Spanish Colonialism,* ed. Susan Schroeder (Eastbourne, UK, and Portland, OR: Sussex Academic Press, 2010), 41–73. As known copies of the Lienzo de Tlaxcala contain versions of sections 1 and 5 and lack sections 2, 3, and 4, these were likely derived from other sources; thus we find overlapping chronology between sections 2 and 5, with both the former and the latter containing scenes showing the initial baptisms of the Tlaxcalan elite. Muñoz Camargo describes a set of allegorical images that correspond to section 4 as paintings that hung on the walls of the Casa Real, where the *cabildo* (native town council) met (47–48). In addition, Pablo Escalante has suggested correspondences between scenes in section 4 and the Túmulo, or catafalque, erected to mark the death of Charles V in Mexico City. Pablo Escalante Gonzalbo, "Humanismo y arte," in *El arte cristiano-indígena del siglo XVI novohispano y sus modelos europeos,* ed. Pablo Escalante Gonzalbo, Colección de Arte Prehispánico y Colonial / Seminario de Historia del Arte (Cuernavaca, Mexico: Centro de Investigación y Docencia en Humanidades del Estado de Morelos, 2008), 17–18.

12. From Henry B. Nicholson, "Religion in Pre-Hispanic Central Mexico," in *Handbook of Middle American Indians* 10, ed. R. Wauchope, G. F. Eckholm, and I. Bernal (Austin: University of Texas Press, 1971), 395–446.

13. Bernardino de Sahagún, *Florentine Codex: General History of the Things of New Spain,* 12 vols., trans. Arthur J. O. Anderson and Charles E. Dibble (Santa Fe, NM: School of American Research and University of Utah, 1950–1963), Book 2, Chapter 7, 13. For brevity I have used the Spanish summary in the book rather than the longer Nahuatl account, and I have regularized the spelling of Nahuatl words.

14. Davíd Carrasco, *Religions of Mesoamerica: Cosmovision and Ceremonial Centers,* 1st ed., Religious Traditions of the World (San Francisco: Harper and Row, 1990), 23.

15. Motolinía, *Historia de los indios de la Nueva España,* tratado 3, Chapter 1, 22.

16. The Franciscans established four seats upon their arrival in 1524, in Mexico City, in Texcoco, in Tlaxcala, and in Huejotzingo.

17. See Fernando Cervantes, *The Devil in the New World: The Impact of Diabolism in New Spain* (New Haven, CT: Yale University Press, 1994); see also Sabine MacCormack, *Religion in the Andes: Vision and Imagination in Early Colonial Peru* (Princeton, NJ: Princeton University Press, 1991).

18. See, for instance, Louise M. Burkhart, *The Slippery Earth: Nahua–Christian Moral Dialogue in Sixteenth-Century Mexico* (Tucson: University of Arizona Press, 1989); Burkhart, *Holy Wednesday: A Nahua Drama from Early Colonial Mexico,* New Cultural Studies (Philadelphia: University of Pennsylvania Press, 1996); and Barry D. Sell, Louise M. Burkhart, and Gregory Spira, *Nahuatl Theater* (Norman: University of Oklahoma Press, 2004).

19. Sahagún, *Florentine Codex,* Book 2, Chapter 32, 123.

20. Alessandra Russo, "Plumes of Sacrifice: Transformations in Sixteenth-Century Mexican Feather Art," *RES: Anthropology and Aesthetics* 42 (Autumn 2002). On tonalli and the human body, see Jill Leslie McKeever Furst, *The Natural History of the Soul in Ancient Mexico* (New Haven, CT, and London: Yale University Press, 1995), and Alfredo López Austin, *The Human Body and Ideology: Concepts of the Ancient Nahuas,* trans. Thelma Ortiz de Montellano and Bernard Ortiz de Montellano (Salt Lake City: University of Utah Press, 1988).

21. Cortés, *Letters from Mexico,* 106.

22. Landa, *Yucatan before and after the Conquest,* 82.

23. The story of don Cristóbal Acxotecatl is recounted by Mendieta in *Historia eclesiástica,* 236–241, and in the *Descripción;* Gibson, in *Tlaxcala in the Sixteenth Century,* 30–35, gives a somewhat more nuanced reading of the events.

24. Motolinía, or Toribio de Benavente, *Historia de los indios de la Nueva España,* tratado 1, Chapter 4, 27, translation mine.

25. Mendieta, *Historia eclesiástica,* Book 4, Chapter 19, 430, translation mine.

26. See the discussion in Dana Leibsohn and Barbara E. Mundy, *Vistas: Visual Culture in Spanish America, 1520–1820 / Vistas: Cultura Visual De Hispanoamérica, 1520–1820,* DVD (Austin: University of Texas, 2010). See also Russo, "Plumes of Sacrifice."

27. Alessandra Russo, "Feather Wounds: The Incredulity of Pope Sixtus V; or, a Colonial Saint Francis in Rome," paper presented at The First Triennial Conference of the Association for Latin American Art, New York, October 27, 2007.

28. Aaron Hyman, personal communication, 2011.

29. The lack of color, which would enlarge the images' synesthetic potential, has two possible explanations. First is that the pages are meant to evoke a printed book, a point also made by Eleanor Wake in "Codex Tlaxcala: New Insights and New Questions," *Estudios de cultura náhuatl* 33 (2002): 116. Second is that color pigments were expensive and may not have been available to the copyists. Gerhard Wolf et al., *Colors between Two Worlds: The Florentine Codex of Bernardino de Sahagún* (Florence: Villa I Tatti, 2012).

30. James Lockhart, Frances Berdan, and Arthur J. O. Anderson, *The Tlaxcalan Actas* (Salt Lake City: University of Utah Press, 1986).

31. The iconography of this page is explored by Gordon Brotherston and Ana Gallegos, "El Lienzo de Tlaxcala y el manuscrito de Glasgow (Hunter 242)," *Estudios de cultura náhuatl* 20 (1990): 117–140, esp. 120 and 133.

32. In the well-documented New Fire ceremony of the Mexica of the Valley of Mexico, the end of a fifty-two-year cycle was marked by the breakage of ceramics and the kindling of a new fire in the chest of a sacrificial victim. Jill L. Furst argues for a pan-American practice of renewal through new fire in "The Aztec New Fire Ritual: A World Renewal Rite," *Journal of Latin American Lore* 18, nos. 1–2 (1992): 29–36. Byron Ellsworth Hamann focuses on the meaning of breakage in "Chronological Pollution: Potsherds, Mosques, and Broken Gods before and after the Conquest of Mexico," *Current Anthropology* 49, no. 5 (2008): 803–836.

33. Inga Clendinnen, *Aztecs: An Interpretation* (Cambridge, UK, and New York: Cambridge University Press, 1991), 246.

34. Apocalyptic beliefs in pre-Hispanic Central Mexico are cogently discussed in Miguel León-Portilla, *Aztec Thought and Culture,* trans. Jack Emory Davis (Norman: University of Oklahoma Press, 1963), 25–61. A discussion of primary sources on Nahua ideas of five cosmological eras, or suns, is found in Roberto Moreno de los Arcos, "Los cinco soles cosmogónicos," *Estudios de cultura náhuatl* 7 (1967): 183–210.

32

Seeing, Falling, Feeling
The Sense of Angels

MEREDITH J. GILL

I n the early decades of the sixteenth century, the Carmelite friars of the Sienese convent of San Niccolò al Carmine commissioned a large panel. It was to be "of Saint Michael subduing Lucifer," according to Giorgio Vasari, the opinionated chronicler of the arts, writing midcentury. This subject is relatively rare in Italy, though it has a long Byzantine tradition.[1] "Being a man of ideas," as Vasari observed of the artist, the local painter Domenico Beccafumi,

> he [Beccafumi] thought of a new treatment of this theme to prove his ability. Thus he began a shower of nude figures, representing Lucifer and his followers driven out of heaven, though they were rather confused owing to the labour he bestowed on them [Figure 32.1]. The picture remained unfinished, and after Domenico's death it was taken to a room near the high altar at the top of the stairs in the great hospital [Santa Maria della Scala], where it may still be seen. It is remarkable for some nude figures finely foreshortened. In the Carmine, where it was to have gone, another [also by Beccafumi] was placed representing God upon the clouds, surrounded by angels [Figure 32.2]. In the middle is Saint Michael in armour, pointing as he flies to Lucifer, who is driven to the centre of the earth amid burning walls, falling rocks and a flaming lake, with angels in various postures and nude figures swimming about and suffering torment, the whole done with such style and grace that the place seems illuminated by the fire.[2]

Vasari seems right in many respects. Beccafumi's first attempt does register at first as confusing: three attenuated, nude figures dominate the lower regions, while other, more

FIGURE 32.1. Domenico Beccafumi, *Fall of the Rebel Angels,* ca. 1524, oil on wood, 136⅝ × 89⅜ inches. Pinacoteca Nazionale di Siena. Photo credit: Alfredo Dagli Orti / The Art Archive at Art Resource, New York.

FIGURE 32.2. Domenico Beccafumi, *Fall of the Rebel Angels,* ca. 1528, oil on wood, 136 5/8 × 88 19/32 inches. San Niccolò al Carmine, Siena. Photo credit: Scala / Art Resource, New York.

abbreviated bodies lurk in the shadows beside an impenetrable tangle of animal forms. In the upper part of the panel, Saint Michael is dominant, raising his sword over the vanquished rebels. Dressed in a fantasy of antique armor, he looks upward to a small, cloudy vision of God, represented in adept foreshortening. In Beccafumi's second version, however, a different order prevails. A full, red-mantled figure of God effects his judgment with a confident arm. He is flanked by angels who are arrayed more stably above caverns and sulfurous fires at ground level. We sense here sharper, more tactile edges of forms and clearer recession, as well as a pronounced colorism: from red in God's mantle to gilded yellow in Michael's garment and wings, with slashes of blue and pale pink here and there. Lucifer below is all gaping mouth and open claw, unmistakable and monstrous abbreviations for the torments of hell.

In his panels—both of which are over eleven feet high—Beccafumi offers us meditations on a sensational theme and on stylistic self-consciousness. He does this by way of the angels, who are at once the most ubiquitous yet problematic of beings. Across multiple belief systems, they are, strictly speaking, bodiless intelligences. This makes them, then, the most delicate of registers for testing ideas of embodiment, sensory apprehension, materiality, and transformation. Instead of seeing in Beccafumi's second, accepted altarpiece only a deft accommodation of the friars' requirements, as most commentators do, and beyond an artistically inventive yet theologically orthodox diagram of divine retribution, I see Beccafumi wrestling mightily here with bodies and angels, endeavoring to resolve a problem of identity—moral, as well as physical —by way of artful effect and visual quotation. When his angels fall to earth, they become codes for an anxious humanity, and these by way of the very stuff of his materials, his paint. These angels become both present and absent, truth and allegory at one and the same time.

The fall of the angels is a controversial theme from the perspective of orthodox Christian doctrine. Beccafumi also articulates this theme in a transgressive fashion, for his angels are more than figures of mediation. In applying his brush, the artist confronted the corporality of angels alongside the capacity of his art to evoke sensory experience such as sight and touch. He implicitly calls into question the very boundaries of the human senses for which the angels are a confounding measure: whether, for example, the senses are internal to the body or external to it; whether they are discrete or integrated; whether they are located singly in the body or inhabit the cosmos and the surrounding air.[3] For angels have long been identified with air and condensations of it, as no less an authority than Thomas Aquinas (1225–1274) once taught.[4] As bodiless intelligences, in fact, angels may elect to assume any corporeal form. Medieval visionaries believed that they could be present simply as a sensory abundance, constituting cosmologies of color, light, sound, and fragrance that are synonymous with their own pure essence.[5] With their fall, as writers from late antique times onward tell us, angels attained not only humanlike bodies—and these by reason of their flawed choice—

but also those bodies' capacities for metamorphosis, disequilibrium, sensory degradation, and pain.

Vasari tells us that Beccafumi abandoned his first panel because the figures of Lucifer and his followers "were rather confused owing to the labour he bestowed on them"; that is, as most interpreters have deduced, despite being "a man of ideas," the artist did not succeed in this first "new treatment" of the subject "to prove his ability," to exhibit his aesthetic prowess. Directed by his patrons, if we believe Vasari, to the passage from biblical Revelation (20:1–3) in which a vision of an angel overthrows Satan, as a dragon, and imprisons him in a bottomless pit, the artist failed in his first attempt to adequately and decorously adhere to the text—in the "confusion" of his design and possibly also in the excess of nudity among his figures.[6] In the fifteenth century, none other than the Dominican Girolamo Savonarola had decried the apparent indecency of religious art; thus, as modern critics have concluded, for similar reasons of decorum, Beccafumi partially covered every angel in his second panel and more clearly demarcated the composition's architecture, notably the boundaries of heaven and hell. He radically revised and synchronized the positions and actions of God and his agent, Michael, so that where, before, there were vacuums below a wispy God, now a robust, full-figured God dominates the upper third of the panel. In doing this, the artist called on some of his most adept technical abilities—Vasari's "style and grace"—including a kind of prismatic lighting effect and otherworldly color.[7] Perhaps, as has been proposed, the friars needed not only a more legible organization but also a God fully "in control."[8]

There was a Sienese tradition of rendering the fall of the rebel angels as a vertical, hierarchically ordered composition, as in a small panel from the 1340s by the Master of the Rebel Angels (Figure 32.3).[9] Northern European artists, such as the Limbourg brothers, produced early depictions of the angels' vertiginous descent (Figure 32.4). In an illumination of their *Très Riches Heures,* God is seated outside the manuscript page, surrounded by red seraphim and blue cherubim and flanked by choir stalls that reveal the truancy of some of their occupants. These rebel angels are tilting downward, prodded by a small battalion of archangels like coals in a fire as they cascade to earth. When they hit the ground beside Lucifer, their leader, they explode into flames.[10] By Beccafumi's day, the book arts and prints must have lent artists inspiration, particularly given Siena's long-standing role as a trading gateway between the peninsula and northern Europe. Best known, perhaps, of the Michael and Lucifer type is Albrecht Dürer's woodcut of 1498 of Saint Michael and the dragon (Figure 32.5), illustrating another text from Revelation (12:7–9) that treats the defeat of Satan, as a dragon, and his being "thrown down" with his angels, but with no mention of details such as the "bottomless pit."[11] By the sixteenth century, artists commonly elided the two parts of Revelation dealing with the fall of the angels. Beccafumi also condenses his pictorial framework along the same lines as Hieronymus Bosch and Pieter

FIGURE 32.3. Master of the Rebel Angels, *Fall of the Rebel Angels*, 1340s, canvas (originally panel), 25 9/32 × 11 27/65 inches. Louvre, Paris. Photo credit: Erich Lessing / Art Resource, New York.

Bruegel the Elder. In Bruegel's *Fall of the Rebel Angels* of 1562 (Figure 32.6), Michael, at the center, and nine of his colleagues battle the fallen angels, who are already demons, issuing in a squirming torrent from a high, radiant sphere.[12] Here we can just make out several crowned heads of the apocalyptic dragon beast underneath Michael, who is on the same axis as a bloated toad below him, a signifier of the devil and believed to be at the root of pestilence.[13]

Bosch, who understood more than any other early modern artist the moral resonance of sin and the contested theological implications of human fleshliness, took the fall of the rebel angels still further, for he adumbrated not only scripture but also the weight of its exegesis; the Bible is, in the end, quite laconic not only about the creation of angels but also about their fall.[14] On the side panels of the dismembered triptych sometimes called *The World before the Flood,* he portrayed the *Apocalypse by Fire or Fall of the Rebel Angels* (Figure 32.7) and *Noah's Ark after the Flood.*[15] When, according to

FIGURE 32.4. Limbourg Brothers, *Fall of the Rebel Angels,* from *Très Riches Heures,* ca. 1416, illumination on vellum, 11 $^{27}/_{64}$ × 8 $^{9}/_{32}$ inches. Musée Condé, Chantilly, MS. 65, fol. 64v. Photo credit: Réunion des Musées Nationaux–Grand Palais / Art Resource, New York. Photo by René-Gabriel Ojéda.

FIGURE 32.5. Albrecht Dürer, *The Revelation of Saint John, 11: St. Michael Fighting the Dragon,* 1498, woodcut, 15 7/16 × 11 5/32 inches. Bibliothèque Nationale de France, Paris. Photo credit: Bridgeman-Giraudon / Art Resource, New York.

FIGURE 32.6. Pieter Bruegel the Elder, *Fall of the Rebel Angels,* 1562, oil on oak, 46 5/64 × 63 25/32 inches. Musée d'Art Ancien, Musées Royauxe des Beaux-Arts, Brussels. Photo credit: Scala / Art Resource, New York.

FIGURE 32.7. Hieronymus Bosch, *Apocalypse by Fire or Fall of the Rebel Angels,* 1500–1504, oil on panel, 27 ¹¹/₆₄ × 13 ²⁵/₃₂ inches. Museum Boijmans Van Beuningen, Rotterdam.

the Church Father Augustine (345–430), "God created the heavens," he also created spiritual beings, such that "let there be light and there was light" (Genesis 1:3) refers to the creation of angels simultaneously with the creation of light.[16] As first in the hierarchy of created things, the angels are "spiritual" or "intellectual" creatures signified by the "light" (*lux*) in "Fiat lux," a phrase on which Augustine and many later writers dwell in penetrating detail. It was at the moment of light's creation that the rebel angels chose to turn away, to plummet, then, into the dark: "The two different societies of angels," Augustine said, are "not unfitly termed light and darkness" (*City of God* 11, 33).[17] The angels' theophany as light or its absence was an extension of their ancestry among the invisible spirits of the ancient world. Patristic authors, such as Augustine, and medieval commentators, including Dante (1265–1321), elaborated on this genealogy within systems of light metaphysics that could be both metaphorical and scientific. In any case, they privileged sight within the sensory kingdom of divine creation. The angels' fall to earth constituted a radical denial of their ineffable, light-filled existence. They materialized to experience all the multisensory violence of nature; this included changing into hybrid forms and experiencing immoral desires and excruciating physical travail.

Bruegel and Bosch understood the import of this light–dark opposition. Bosch also understood, as Augustine and others did, that the Devil did not sin when he was first made, but that it was pride that caused his sinning.[18] The Devil foreknew before he fell that other angels would follow and that, "without the light of truth, they would abide in the darkness of pride" (*City of God* 11, 19 and 32). Indeed medieval mystics believed that the most miserable of eternal punishments imaginable was to be deprived of the sight of God. With his fall, too, the Devil became the "mockery" of God's angels and the butt of jokes (*City of God* 15, 11 and 12). In Bosch's *Apocalypse by Fire,* the skies burn above a smoldering earth, and, unopposed, demonic forms descend to the ground. The partnering wing shows Noah's ark after the flood. This juxtaposition has its origins in the Second Letter of Peter, in relation to false prophets who destroy themselves:

> For if God did not spare the angels who sinned, but cast *them* down to hell and delivered them into chains of darkness, to be reserved for judgment; And did not spare the ancient world, but saved Noah, *one* of eight people, a preacher of righteousness, bringing in the flood on the world of the ungodly. . . . *Then* the Lord knows how to deliver the godly out of temptations and to reserve the unjust under punishment for the day of judgment, And especially those who walk according to the flesh in uncleanness and despise authority. (2 Peter 2:4–10, italics mine)

Peter singles out lust and defiance—the sins of Adam and Eve. Eating from the tree of the knowledge of good and evil and committing the great sin, like Lucifer, of first knowing something of the ways of goodness and then turning from them, the first couple had to endure the fires of the last days.

Twice Bosch shows the fall of the rebel angels more explicitly above the Garden of Eden; thus the degraded world of later generations is foretold, for one fall—the angels'—leads to another—that of humankind.[19] In a panel for his *Haywain* triptych, God sits within a light rimmed by seraphim and cherubim who take arms against their fallen brothers; these morph into frogs and insects as they fall. In his *Last Judgment* triptych (Figure 32.8), the fight is truly on, and above Eden a black-and-white mêlée ensues, with the lighter angels bearing cross-shaped lances or staffs and swords as the rebels form black wings, as if before our eyes. In both paintings, an angel on earth with a fiery sword lunges after Adam and Eve, as if to affirm the consequences of the tumbling disaster above.

Beccafumi likewise brought together the two passages in Revelation. More importantly, however, he seized on the very question of angels' carnate/incarnate selves in relation to human frailty and error. His angels, languishing anxiously in hell, are unmistakably and unsettlingly human—all the more so for the fact that some, particularly in the middle regions of the first panel, have bat wings and claws. Our viewpoint is at eye level; we are in the company of these damned forms, literally forced up to their chests and flailing arms. We must crane our necks upward, like the fallen angels, and, in the words of the medieval hagiographer Jacobus de Voragine, look up to "see the glory they [we] have lost."[20] But why do we have two panels, and why does Beccafumi shift from full, naked nudes to partially covered half-forms?

Siena's deeply unsettled civic climate in the 1520s surely had its part to play in Beccafumi's prevarications. At the Battle of Camollia in 1526, the Sienese ousted the Medici and their allies, and, with the Sack of Rome in 1527, the city's political regime faced new challenges.[21] The Sienese viewed their military victory as miraculous, and their triumph appeared to be confirmed the following year by the expulsion of Pope Clement VII de' Medici from Rome by the forces of Emperor Charles V. In the summer of 1527, the city's populace staged their own rebellion, sacking the residences of members of the ruling Noveschi and forming a reconfigured and conservative coalition government.[22] At the same time, within the international context of the debate about Catholic reform leading to the Council of Trent, churchmen undertook to reevaluate notions of hierarchy in an inclusive sense, not least the authenticity and authority of the saints relative to God and the communion of the faithful. These currents must have inflected the friars' unusual decision—if theirs it was—to install the commanding form of God the Father where he conventionally did not so conspicuously appear.[23]

Beccafumi's stylistic experimentation had its part to play, as well, in this period of his artistic maturity, and it informs both panels. His debt to works he had seen in Rome, and to Raphael and Michelangelo in particular, is evident in his bold colorism

FIGURE 32.8. Hieronymus Bosch, *Fall of the Rebel Angels,* detail from *Garden of Eden,* left shutter of *Last Judgment* altarpiece, 1505–1508, oil on panel, 64 $^{37}/_{64}$ × 23 $^{5}/_{8}$ inches. Gemäldegalerie der Akademie der bildenden Künste, Vienna. Photo credit: Gemäldegalerie der Akademie der bildenden Künste, Vienna, Austria / Bridgeman Art Library International, New York.

and in his choice of figural language. Saint Michael, as a long-standing and fearsome defender of Christian orthodoxy, enjoyed a revival in the second decade of the sixteenth century as Martin Luther and his northern colleagues mounted their critique of the Catholic Church and Rome. He was a combatant on both sides of the Catholic and Protestant divide. Raphael's second *Saint Michael,* painted at the behest of Lorenzo de' Medici and Pope Leo X and sent as a gift to the French King Francis I in 1518, has long been regarded as a *plaidoyer* for solidarity against Protestantism.[24]

The answer to the question of Beccafumi's rejected panel must also lie, however, with doctrinal propositions attending the character of the fall of the angels itself, as well as its ancient and variant traditions in Judaism and Christianity. The fall touches, further, not only on a definition of evil but also on the long shadow of dualism: that is, within a Judeo-Christian context, on heretical themes pertaining to a self-created evil principle in combat with a benevolent one. In both cases, the rebel angels' actions have always been bound up with the idea of will, beginning with the Jewish Book of Enoch of the early third century BCE, which first fully elaborated on their kind. Related to this, and in the later Hebrew Bible, we read of the contrast between the "sons of God" and the daughters of men, and also of the Nephilim, possibly supernatural beings or their descendents, who consorted with mortal women. Of Enoch himself Genesis tells us only that he was the son of Jared and the father of Methuselah and that he lived before the flood and "walked with God" (5:18–24). In contrast to this circumspect biography, and from as early as the Second Temple Period (536 BCE–70 CE), Enoch possessed a reputation as a visionary and a heavenly traveler who interceded for the wicked angels and authored books of teachings for future generations. His first and most influential work, the *Book of the Watchers* (Fallen Angels), known as 1 Enoch, had a mixed reception after early success. It was rejected by the Rabbinic movement, then accepted by early Christians. Church leaders subsequently repressed the work, after which it was thought to be lost in the West. This loss, though, endowed Enoch with an aura of mystique into early modern times: the mystique of "lost books and secret scrolls, wisdom suppressed and writings forgotten."[25]

Although we cannot link Beccafumi's paintings directly to Enoch, the writer's reputation and traces of the contents of the *Book of the Watchers* available to the Renaissance offer tantalizing correspondences with the ways in which the artist imagined his angels, as well as with motifs in the lower regions of his terrestrial hell. Among Italian intellectual circles, Enoch certainly had his admirers. The renowned Italian philosopher Pico della Mirandola (1463–1494) claimed to have bought a book by Enoch for a handsome sum, though his humanist friend Johannes Reuchlin chuckled.[26] Pico and Christian Kabbalists, in general, were aware that early Christian and Jewish mystical texts such as the *Zohar* referred to Enoch's books.[27] And although scholars in the sixteenth and seventeenth centuries did not accept that this "book of Enoch" dated to antediluvian times, they did recognize it as the source of the dispersed references to Enoch's prophecies about the fallen angels in the New Testament, as well as in early Christian writings such as Augustine's. Until 1773, however, with the Western rediscovery of the *Book of the Watchers* and other early Enochic pseudepigrapha when James Bruce brought three manuscripts to Europe, there were essentially only rumors about the existence of these works in Ethiopia and about their preservation.[28]

Chapter 6 of 1 Enoch tells how the angels desired the daughters of men and, in the days of Jared, two hundred of their number, including the angel Azazel, descended to earth, where they took wives. From their union a race of giants was born.[29] The angels disseminated useful knowledge to humankind, for they instructed women in charms, magic, and botanical lore and men on the manufacture of weapons and other useful arts. From this intermingling came anarchy and violence, and as men lay dying, they uttered cries that were heard in heaven. The four major archangels, Michael, Uriel, Raphael, and Gabriel, channeled those cries to God, alerting him to the deeds of their angelic brethren below. God dispatched Uriel, who warned Noah of the approaching flood and told him how to survive it. God also told Raphael to bind Azazel and cast him out into a dark place in the desert, covering him with rocks. Michael bound Azazel's companions in the same way. There Azazel was to stay until the day of judgment, when he would be cast into the fire. In their earthly prison in the valleys, the angels would abide for seventy generations, waiting until "the judgment that is for ever and ever is consummated." Then they would be hurled into the abyss of fire and remain there in eternity. Michael eradicated the rebels' spirits as well as the offspring of the Watchers because they had both wronged humankind. The giants had given birth to evil spirits "who dwell on the earth." These issued from the giants' bodies "because they are born from men, and from the holy Watchers." Although the fallen angels are punished before as well as during the last judgment, these demons are not punished until that time, so they freely pursue their ways against humankind "because they have proceeded from them."[30]

By the later fifteenth century, the associations brought to mind by mention of the rebel angels and Enoch's name were not limited to Pico's learned circle or to his censors. These associations had by this time accrued an aura of their own, just as an angel himself may potentially possess a host of meanings. As a species of "resonant image," in fact, an angel's evocation in any medium engages "perception, memory, and materiality."[31] Pico's case is instructive. Roman censors banned his nine hundred theses, or *Conclusiones,* in 1487, a year after they were published, and they later condemned his *Heptaplus* (1488–1489), in which he had sought to outline an exegesis of creation in Genesis according to mystical Jewish tradition and the sibylline prophecies.[32] In his work on the Kabbalah, Pico mentions the angel Azazel, whose name occurs in only one biblical passage, in Leviticus (16:7–28), when the Lord gives Moses instructions for the Day of Atonement. Aaron must "cast lots upon two goats, one lot for the Lord and the other lot for Aza'zel." Azazel's goat is intended for atonement.[33] In the Book of Enoch, Azazel has a major role, as we have seen, as the leader of the rebel angels. Further, in the foundational Kabbalistic text, the *Zohar,* two additional rebellious angels, Uzza and Azazel, are expelled from heaven by the Almighty for querying the very creation of humankind. They take on bodies, have sex with women, and teach "magic, witchcraft, and sorcery."[34]

In one of his famous outlawed *Conclusions,* Pico noted that, should a Kabbalist make a mistake in his work, the demon spirit Azazel might devour him. Pico, in an Origenist vein, believed that a human person who dies to the sensible world might be reborn in the intelligible one as an angel; this is in line with the Kabbalists' saying that Enoch was changed into "Metatron, an angel of divinity."[35] In Pico's tenth Kabbalistic *Conclusion,* Metatron assumes a dizzying array of identities: "Pallas by Orpheus, Paternal Mind by Zaroaster, Son of God by Mercury, Wisdom by Pythagoras, Intelligible Sphere by Parmenides." He is chief of angels and a foe of Samael, or Satan, as well as of his commander-in-chief, Azazel.[36] Pico, then, in drawing on both the Bible and the Kabbalah, devised a set of themes that advanced the portrayal of the rebel angels as ancient, potent, and vengeful beings, capable not only of ontological transformation and sensory as well as sensual experience but also of wielding powerful magic.

Pico and his readers would likely have known more popular vehicles for propagating the angelic intersections of Judaism and Christianity in the visual culture of their times. One of these was the *Sefer Raziel,* a guidebook to angel magic that had been available in Latin since the thirteenth century. The *Sefer Raziel* included a well-known childbirth talisman. In their combinations of number, word, and geometry, such powerful forms invoked protective action on behalf of humankind, including action from the angels.[37] The talisman reminds us of the wider presence of the angels, as well as of the inclusion among their number of Enoch's terrifying cast and their colleagues in the Kabbalah.

In the fall of the rebel angels, both angelology and demonology are inextricably bound in the teachings of Jewish apocryphal and apocalyptic literature, and it is essentially here, in these teachings, that the fall has its fullest exposition.[38] These angel narratives evoke an inclusive and arresting sensorium, even an intersensoriality. As we have seen, the fallen angels' heavenly kin displayed their sovereign command of sound, channeling human cries to God after the havoc wreaked by the fall. Meanwhile, the subversive instigators on earth below suffered human—that is, sensory—agonies in places devoid of light, ultimately to be consumed in eternal fire. For their part, the words alone of the Kabbalistic *Sefer Raziel* talisman, including Psalms 91:11–12, were likely read aloud, an aural articulation of the singular and potent presence of the angels as guardians at the painful and dangerous threshold of life itself.

This history is incomplete, however, without taking into account another important set of heterodox teachings. Long after Enoch, around the beginning of the third century CE, the brilliant Christian theologian Origen would advance the idea that human souls originated among the angels, specifically among those of the heavenly hierarchy who made a fateful choice at the moment of Lucifer's dissent. Exercising their will, these angels chose neither to join Lucifer nor to remain with God. Rather, they were disobedient and adopted a neutral stance, eventually coming to earth, where, again as a result of choice, they earned the opportunity through good behavior to ascend to heaven as redeemed souls.[39] There they would find their permanent seats in the celestial bleachers, occupying the empty seats left by the forever-departed rebel angels.

We know that Beccafumi was thinking, in particular, of this contentious subject, and not simply of the battle between Lucifer and Michael, from one overlooked detail that appears only in his first panel, namely the very faint but unmistakable outline of the rows of those heavenly bleachers behind the angels to the right of Michael (Figure 32.9). In fact, these resemble the angels' stalls in another Tuscan context: the imagery accompanying Dante's *Commedia* (Figure 32.10). In the most important set of illustrations after Sandro Botticelli's, the prints for Alessandro Vellutello's commentary on the *Commedia,* the artist depicts the Empyrean as comprising the mazelike rings of stalls of the Celestial Rose and, spinning above these, an

FIGURE 32.9. Detail, Domenico Beccafumi, *Fall of the Rebel Angels,* ca. 1524, oil on wood, 136 5/8 × 89 3/8 inches. Pinacoteca Nazionale di Siena. Photo credit: Su concessione del Ministero per I Beni e le attività culturali. Foto Soprintendenza BSAE di Siena e Grosseto. Photo by Meredith J. Gill.

FIGURE 32.10. Giovanni Britto (attrib.), *Paradiso* 31, 4, 12⁷/₃₂ inches (height of page), in *Dante / Con tauole, argomenti, & allegorie, & riformato, riueduto, & ridotto alla sua uera lettura, per Francesco Sansovino fiorentino* (PQ4302 1564), Albert and Shirley Small Special Collections Library, University of Virginia Library, Charlottesville.

angel-disk, like a lid fixed in the ether, composed of the interlocking heads and wings of the angels.[40]

Origen's perceived sedition lay in the radical idea of the intimate intermingling of substances—human, soul, and angel. His teaching that the soul preexisted in angels before joining the human body and that the angels possessed autonomous wills so that they, like human persons, could make moral choices, had far-reaching and deeply unsettling implications. The Church deemed Origen's teachings heretical in the fifth century, and they were condemned as late as 1439 by the Council of Florence, signaling at once, of course, their enduring vitality as well as their controversy.[41] For, in reality, Origen, in his own day and also among Tuscan literary circles in the fifteenth century, enjoyed something of an equivocal reputation, including sympathetic readers and certain revival. He had had his late antique admirers as well. None other than the Church Father Jerome (ca. 347–420) praised him, to whom he himself was indebted, even though the great philologist was compelled to attack the author in a skirmish with Origen's translator, Rufinus, resulting in a famous broken friendship.[42] Hailed as an exegete by Jerome, yet excoriated in history as a heretic, Origen's reception in late antiquity came to be mirrored in the fifteenth century in that of none other than the Florentine humanist Matteo Palmieri. Palmieri's poem the *Città di vita* (1455–1464), which he modeled on Dante's *Divine Comedy,* dwelt in part on the so-called neutral angels and their journey from heaven to earth and back again.[43] Palmieri was more lenient than Dante, who had discovered the neutral angels in the outermost circle of his *Inferno,* at the gates reserved for cowards; there these shamefully undecided creatures mingled with humanity.[44] Palmieri followed Origen to such a degree that his reputation was likewise forever tarnished by posthumous accusations of heresy and rumors of book burning—a parallel to the burning of Origen's books in the Byzantine era—as well as interdict and censorship.

Dante's neutral angels were "lukewarm" and, as such, in John Freccero's words, they were, for Dante, "more contemptible than the worst of sinners."[45] In their vestibule of hell, they consorted with the souls of the cowardly. For Dante these were "wretches, who had never truly lived" (*Inferno,* Canto 3, 64–69). These miserable beings of the *Inferno,* who are stung to the point of bleeding by wasps and hornets, "never were alive," as Freccero puts it, "since they failed to make the commitment which is the beginning of moral life. The single moment of angelic choice—by implication here . . . as it related to the Fall—recapitulates the whole of man's moral existence." Thus, he continues, angelology was the "control laboratory" for the "analysis of human action."[46]

When Vasari, then, with some ingenuousness, speaks of the "style and grace" of Beccafumi's second panel, the panel that made its way into the church, he was likely responding not just to the clarity of the second design and to the virtuosic language of its technique. In both works he would have seen, as well—and responded to—quotations from the artist's sixteenth-century peers, quotations consciously drawn from scenes of righteous retribution, such as Raphael's *Saint Michael* and Michelangelo's *Punishment of Haman* (1511) from the Sistine Chapel ceiling.[47] These tributes Vasari likely appreciated, along with the richer color scheme of the second panel, which draws attention more actively to the artifice and imitation of the artist.

But the excessive "labor" of Beccafumi that led to the "confusion" in the first panel was an indelible mark of the ambiguous status of those fallen angels themselves, angels who bear the marks of mortal terror and bodily extremis. In the first version, it is not clear who is descending and who is ascending—in fact, who is doing what. An intriguing exchange at the lower center indicates perhaps the artist's ambivalence as to the identity of the angel Lucifer himself and his uncertainty as to Lucifer's relation to Satan. For, by the medieval period, Lucifer was often considered to have become Satan on impact with the earth. In the panel, a standing male figure, older and clothed, bends over an angel with dark wings and attempts to lift him. The exchange here is tender, as of father to son or as lover to lover. Yet Satan as a monster is also here in the painting, for above these two is a squirming hybrid octopus-scorpion-bat creature as opposed to the more traditional winged dragon-type creature of the second panel.

The naked figures, especially those in the foreground, have not exploded into fire, as in earlier depictions of the angels' fall, so much as into materiality itself.[48] Though these figures seem to struggle in their contortions against the limits of their mortal being, and though they look mournfully upward at from whence they came, we are in no doubt of either their suffering or their humanity. To fall is, after all, to become, and to become sensate and vulnerable to feeling. In this the trauma of the angels' fall leads not to an end but to a kind of beginning, to an iconography of creation in which our perception of bodily travail leads to an interrogation of the powers of the body itself. And though the Carmelites would ultimately install another panel in their Sienese church, their own distinctive culture of contemplation might perhaps have been better answered in this unfinished first panel of the fall, in which they would have been directed forever to gaze upon the unresolved, shivering boundaries of persons and angels, of grace and choice, flesh and not flesh.

NOTES

1. Smiljka Gabelic, "The Fall of Satan in Byzantine and Post-Byzantine Art," *Zograf* 23 (1993): 64–74.

2. Giorgio Vasari, *Le vite de' più eccellenti pittori, scultori e architettori nelle redazioni del 1550 e 1568,* ed. R. Bettarini and P. Barrocchi, vol. 5 (Florence: Studio per Edizioni Scelte,1984), 167–168; English translation, *Lives of the Painters, Sculptors and Architects,* ed. W. Gaunt, trans. A. B. Hinds, vol. 3 (London: Dent; New York: Dutton, 1963), 142–143.

3. I take as a point of departure François Quiviger, *The Sensory World of Italian Renaissance Art* (London: Reaktion, 2010), esp. "Sensation and Space," 102–104.

4. "Reply to Objection 3: Although air as long as it is in a state of rarefaction has neither shape nor color, yet when condensed it can both be shaped and colored as appears in the clouds. Even so the angels assume bodies of air, condensing it by the Divine power in so far as is needful for forming the assumed body." Thomas Aquinas, *Summa theologica,* First Part, "Treatise on the Angels," Questions 50–64, Question 51, Article 2: "Whether angels assume bodies," in *Christian Classics Ethereal Library,* accessed August 19, 2009, http://www.ccel.org/ccel/aquinas/summa .FP_Q50_A2.html.

5. See Constance Classen, *The Color of Angels: Cosmology, Gender and the Aesthetic Imagination* (London and New York: Routledge, 1998), 4, 11–60. On medieval angelology and the visual arts, see my *Angels and the Order of Heaven in Medieval and Renaissance Italy* (Cambridge, UK, and New York: Cambridge University Press, 2014).

6. "Then I saw an angel coming down from heaven, holding in his hand the key of the bottomless pit and a great chain. And he seized the dragon, that ancient serpent, who is the Devil and Satan, and bound him for a thousand years, and threw him into the pit, and shut it and sealed it over him, that he should deceive the nations no more, till the thousand years were ended. After that he must be loosed for a little while." Revelation 20:1–3, RSV (New York and Glasgow, UK: Collins, 1971), 240. Diana Norman, for example, surmises that Beccafumi might have been censured by the Carmelites for both his nudes and his "unstructured composition." Norman, *Painting in Late Medieval and Renaissance Siena (1260–1555)* (New Haven, CT, and London: Yale University Press, 2003), 279.

7. Girolamo Savonarola, "Sermons on Amos" (1496), trans. C. E. Gilbert, in Gilbert, *Italian Art 1400–1500: Sources and Documents* (Englewood Cliffs, NJ, 1908), 157–158. As Norman points out (279), an analogy may be drawn with Carlo Ridolfi's account (in *Le maraviglie dell'arte,* 1648) of the critique Titian received from the Franciscan prior of Santa Maria Gloriosa dei Frari for making the apostles in his altarpiece too large, so that they loomed over the Virgin.

8. Gustav Medicus, "Some Observations on Domenico Beccafumi's Two 'Fall of the Rebel

Angels' Panels," *Artibus et Historiae* 24, no. 47 (2003): 209. In their sensitive account of the works, Frederick Hartt and David G. Wilkins allow that the "problem may have been the representation of God the Father" and that the artist may have "misunderstood the requirements of the commission." Hartt and Wilkins, *History of Italian Renaissance Art: Painting, Sculpture, Architecture,* 7th ed. (Upper Saddle River, NJ: Prentice Hall, 2001–2007), 568–570. See also Giovanni Previtali, "Maestro degli Angeli ribelli," in *Il Gotico a Siena: Miniature pitture oreficerie oggetti d'arte,* ed. Previtali, exhibition catalog, Siena, 1982 (Florence: Centro Di, 1982), 215–218. Vasari also mentions a predella for the second panel, comprising five scenes in tempera "con bella e giudiziosa maniera." See Alessandro Bagnoli et al., eds., *Domenico Beccafumi e il suo tempo* (Milan: Electa, 1990), no. 26, 172–173. Two of these may be the scenes from the legend of Saint Michael now in the Carnegie Museum of Art, Pittsburgh: *The Appearance of Saint Michael on the Castel Sant'Angelo* (9 × 14¼ inches) and *The Miracle of Saint Michael on Mount Gargano* (8¾ × 14¼ inches), reproduced in Hartt and Wilkins, *History of Italian Renaissance Art,* Figures 18.35 and 18.36. The second panel acquired a marble frame in 1688, at which time the predella was dismantled. Beccafumi had been to Rome, and he may have been influenced by the fifteenth-century frescoes in the Chapel of Saint Michael in Saints Apostoli commissioned by the Greek Cardinal Bessarion. Both share a common source in Jacobus de Voragine's account of the miracles of Saint Michael. See note 23 ("For when Lucifer wanted to be equal to God . . . ").

9. See Medicus, "Some Observations," 212. The author notes that the "earliest consistent pictorial tradition for the rare full-scale depiction of the Fall of the Rebel Angels theme" is a type favored by Franciscans, as in Cimabue's fresco in the choir of the upper basilica of San Francesco, Assisi. This was followed by subjects such as Jacopo del Casentino's *Fall* (1340) in the Velluti Chapel, Santa Croce, Florence; Spinello Aretino's fresco in San Francesco, Arezzo; and Neri di Bicci's predella panel (ca. 1475) at the Museum Boijmans Van Beuningen, Rotterdam. On the problematic identification of the Master of the Rebel Angels, see Giulietta Dini et al., *Pittura senese* (Milan: Federico Motta Editore, 1997–2002), 109–111.

10. See Larry Silver, "Jheronimus Bosch and the Issue of Origins," *Journal of Historians of Netherlandish Art* 1, no. 1 (2009), http://www.jhna.org/.

11. Albrecht Dürer, *The Revelation of Saint John: 11. Saint Michael Fighting the Dragon,* 1498, woodcut, 154¼ × 111½ inches, Bibliothèque Nationale, Paris. "Now war arose in heaven, Michael and his angels fighting against the dragon; and the dragon and his angels fought, and they were defeated and there was no longer any place for them in heaven. And the great dragon was thrown down, that ancient serpent, who is called the Devil and Satan, the deceiver of the whole world—he was thrown down to the earth, and his angels were thrown down with him." Revelation 12:7–9, RSV, 234.

12. See Ross Hamilton, "Bruegel's Falling Figures," *Viator* 38, no. 1 (2007): 385–404.

13. Silver, citing Renilde Vervoort, "The Pestilent Toad: The Significance of the Toad in the Works of Bosch," in *Hieronymus Bosch: New Insights into His Life and Work,* ed. Jos Koldeweij and Bernard Vermet (Rotterdam: Museum Boijmans Van Beuningen, 2001), 145–151.

14. Bosch deployed the toad as an emblem of lust in his scenes of hell, linking it to nakedness in his *Haywain* triptych (on genitals) and *Garden of Earthly Delights* (on the female breast). In fact, the building at the center of hell on the right wing of the *Last Judgment* triptych opens through an arch framed by toads. Silver records that Vervoort ("Pestilent Toad," 146 n. 17) notes that a similar toad appears in the *Fall of the Rebel Angels* in the Mayer van den Bergh Breviary, attributed to Simon Bening (ca. 1510, fol. 552v).

15. Hieronymus Bosch, *Noah's Ark after the Flood,* 1500–1504, obverse right, oil on panel, 27¼ × 15 inches, Museum Boijmans Van Beuningen, Rotterdam, inv. no. st. 28.

16. Although Augustine thought that angels may even have been created before the heavens and light, he notes that they are not coeternal with God: "It is clear that this *heaven's heaven* which you made in the beginning is some kind of intellectual creation [angels]. Participating in your eternity, though in no sense coeternal with you, O Trinity, this intellectual creation largely transcends its mutability through the intense bliss it enjoys in contemplation of you, and by holding fast to you with a constancy from which it has never fallen since its first creation, it is independent of the spinning changes of time." Augustine, *Confessions* 12, 9, in Gill, *Augustine in the Italian Renaissance,* 186–187, italics in original.

17. "Thus the angels, illuminated by that light by which they were created, themselves became light, and are called 'day,' by participation in the changeless light and day, which is the Word of God, through whom they themselves and all other things were made. This is 'the true light, which illuminates every man as he comes into this world'; and this light illuminates every pure angel, so that he is not light in himself, but in God. If an angel turns away from God he becomes impure: and such are all those who are called 'impure spirits.' They are no longer 'light in the Lord'; they have become in themselves darkness, deprived of participation in the eternal light. For evil is not a positive substance: the loss of good has been given the name of 'evil'" (*City of God* 11, 9). Augustine, *City of God,* trans. Henry Bettenson (New York: Penguin Classics, 1984), 440. See also 11, 19 and 11, 33: "The two different companies of angels, appropriately called 'Light' and 'Darkness'" (in ibid., 468–469).

18. Silver, citing *City of God* 11, 15. As Silver further notes, Bosch was also likely influenced by the popular fourteenth-century *Mirror of Human Salvation.*

19. Hieronymus Bosch, *Fall of the Rebel Angels,* 1500–1502, detail from *Garden of Eden,* left shutter, *Haywain* triptych, oil on panel, 57¾ × 17¾ inches, Museo del Prado, Madrid, inv. no. P02052, and Bosch, *Fall of the Rebel Angels,* detail from *Garden of Eden,* left shutter, *Last Judgment* altarpiece, oil on panel, 64½ × 23½ inches, Gemäldegalerie der Akademie der bildenden Künste, Vienna, inv. nos. 579–581.

20. "For when Lucifer wanted to be equal to God, the archangel Michael, standard-bearer of the celestial host, marched up and expelled Lucifer and his followers out of heaven, and shut them up in this dark air until the day of judgment. They are not allowed to live in heaven, or in the upper part of the air, because that is a bright and pleasant place, nor on earth with us, lest they do us too much harm. They are in the air between heaven and earth, so that when they look up and see the glory they have lost, they grieve for it, and when they look down and see men ascending to the place from which they fell, they are often tormented with envy. However, by God's design they come down upon us to test us, and, as has been shown to some holy men, they fly around us like flies. They are innumerable, and, like flies, they fill the whole air. . . . Still, innumerable as they are, Origen is of the opinion that their numbers lessen when we conquer them." Jacobus de Voragine, "Saint Michael, Archangel," in *The Golden Legend: Readings on the Saints,* vol. 2, ed. William Granger Ryan (Princeton, NJ: Princeton University Press, 1993), 205.

21. In 1524 the Sienese expelled the ruling Petrucci family, and in 1526 they also successfully repelled the intervention of papal and Florentine forces attempting to restore them in the Battle of Camollia. Medicus, "Some Observations," 212–214.

22. Medicus, "Some Observations," 213–214.

23. Hartt and Wilkins, *History of Italian Renaissance Art,* 569.

24. Raphael, *Saint Michael,* oil transferred from wood to canvas, 105½ × 63 inches, the Louvre; see text below; and Dini et al., *Pittura senese,* 362–393, esp. 371–374.

25. Annette Yoshiko Reed, *Fallen Angels and the History of Judaism and Christianity: The Reception of Enochic Literature* (Cambridge, UK, and New York: Cambridge University Press), 2.

26. Ibid., 2.

27. Extracts from the *Book of the Watchers* survived in Syriac Christianity and Byzantium, such that when, in 1606, Joseph Scaliger published sections of a ninth-century text by the Byzantine churchman George Syncellus, readers noted that George quoted "from the first book of Enoch concerning the Watchers." Reed, *Fallen Angels,* 2.

28. Reed, *Fallen Angels,* 2–3, which I follow closely. Bruce's three manuscripts contained the *Mashafa Henok Nabiy.* It was then published and translated and known as Ethiopic Enoch or 1 Enoch to distinguish it from another Enochic pseudepigraphon in Slavonic, 2 Enoch. On this and the subsequent discovery of a Greek manuscript and then Aramaic fragments of 1 Enoch in the Dead Sea Scrolls in the twentieth century, see Reed, *Fallen Angels.*

29. *1 (Ethiopic Apocalypse of)* ENOCH (second century BCE–first century CE), trans. E. Isaac, in *The Old Testament Pseudepigrapha,* vol. 1: *Apocalyptic Literature and Testaments,* ed. James H. Charlesworth (New York: Doubleday, 1983), hereafter "The Book of Enoch," and Edward Langton, *Essentials of Demonology: A Study of Jewish and Christian Doctrine, Its Origin and Development* (London: Epworth, 1949), 107–109.

30. Another ancient Jewish work, the *Book of Jubilees,* referred to the fall of the rebel angels in the days of Jared. The angels' intentions are to teach righteous ways to humankind, for they were dispatched by God. They also consort with women, leading to the birth of the Naphidim. Demons seduce Noah's sons and their children, who complain of the demons. Noah prays for release. See Langton, *Essentials of Demonology,* 111–145, for further variants of these traditions, including the identities of satans and Satan through the second century BCE.

31. "A resonant image would be one that has meaning across a variety of sensory modalities (instead of registering exclusively in the eye's mind) and at the same time makes sense of the symbolic equivalency [between kulaing, warring, courting, and peacemaking]." David Howes, *Sensual Relations: Engaging the Senses in Culture and Social Theory* (Ann Arbor: University of Michigan Press, 2006), 105. Writing of the work of Nadia Seremetakis, Howes notes (45) that she is to be "credited with theorizing how an anthropology of the senses may be extended to material culture by linking perception, memory, and materiality in order to explore how we remember and relive our personal and shared histories through our sensuous experience of the material world."

32. See my entry on Pico in *After Augustine: The Oxford Guide to the Historical Reception of Augustine,* ed. Karla Pollmann (Saint Andrews, UK: University of Saint Andrews; Oxford, UK: Oxford University Press), http://www.st-andrews.ac.uk/classics/after-augustine/.

33. Brian P. Copenhaver, "Number, Shape, and Meaning in Pico's Christian Cabala: The Upright *Tsade,* the Closed *Mem,* and the Gaping Jaws of Azazel," in *Natural Particulars: Nature and the Disciplines in Renaissance Europe,* ed. Anthony Grafton and Nancy Siraisi, Dibner Institute Studies in the History of Science and Technology (Cambridge, MA, and London, UK: MIT Press, 1999), 46–61, esp. 46–47, and Langton, *Essentials of Demonology,* 43–46: "IV. Azazel (The Scapegoat)," 130–132.

34. Copenhaver, "Number, Shape, and Meaning," 46–47.

35. Ibid., 49. Metatron was a "boy" who served God, identified with the "Agent Intellect," understood by Maimonides as the channel through which God sends prophecy to chosen mortals.

36. In Copenhaver, "Number, Shape, and Meaning," 49.

37. Reproduced in Copenhaver, "Number, Shape, and Meaning," Figure 1.11, 48. Between the two bands of circles surrounding the triangles is the text of Psalm 91:11. Pico seems to have organized the number of his *Conclusions* to conform to the mystical numerology of the Kabbalah so that even his writings were intended to operate as an angelic talisman, repelling Azazel and summoning his worthy opponent, Metatron, the angel of ecstatic death. Ibid., 51.

38. ". . . for some of the chiefs of fallen angels [such as Azazel and Satan] are later regarded as the princes of evil spirits; and the union of angels with women is said to give rise to a race of giants who, in turn, become the parents of evil spirits or demons. It was thus, according to one strand of Jewish teaching, that demons originated." Langton, *Essentials of Demonology*, 105–145, quote on 105.

39. Medicus (214–216) was the first to discuss the human form of Beccafumi's angels in light of unorthodox doctrine, including Origin's teachings and their reception by Dante and Palmieri. The classic account for the Renaissance is Edgar Wind, "The Revival of Origen," in *Studies in Art and Literature for Belle da Costa Greene*, ed. Dorothy E. Miner (Princeton, NJ: Princeton University Press, 1954), 412–424. See also Chapter 2 of my *Angels and the Order of Heaven in Medieval and Renaissance Italy* (Cambridge, UK: Cambridge University Press, 2014) on Origen, Matteo Palmieri, and Botticini's *Assumption of the Virgin* (National Gallery, London).

40. Giovanni Britto (attrib.), *Paradiso* 31, 4, in *Dante / Con tauole, argomenti, & allegorie, & riformato, riueduto, & ridotto alla sua uera lettura, per Francesco Sansovino fiorentino (con l'espositione di Christoforo Landino, et di Alessandro Vellutello)* (Venice: Marchio Sessa, 1544–1564). Antonfrancesco Doni noted, in his *Libraria* (1550), that Vellutello "strained his mind, expenses and expended time" in seeing to the engraving of the eighty-seven plates. They may have been the work of Giovanni Britto, who worked as an engraver for Francesco Marcolini in Venice, and they are exceptionally integrated, in terms of their iconography, with Vellutello's commentary. See Deborah Parker, "Gallery," in *The World of Dante*, accessed August 9, 2012, www.worldof dante.org/gallery_vellutello.html.

41. Bruno Cumbo, *La città di vita di Matteo Palmieri: Ipotesi su una fonte quattrocentesca per gli affreschi di Michelangelo nella Volta Sistina* (Palermo: Duepunti, 2006), 32. In 400 the Council of Alexandria condemned Origen as a heretic, and he was condemned again in 553 by the Fifth Council at Constantinople. Pope Gelasius also proscribed him in 494; Origen figures in the apocryphal *Decretum de libris recipiendis et non recipiendis*: "Origenis nonnulla opuscula quae vir beatissimus Hieronymus non repudiat, legenda suscipimus. Reliqua autem omnia cum auctore suo dicimus esse renuenda." D. P. Walker, "Origène en France au début du XVIe siècle," in *Courants religieux et humanisme à la fin du XVe et au début du XVIe siècle* (Paris: Presses Universitaires de France, 1959), 103.

42. Walker, "Origène en France," 103–104, and Elizabeth A. Clark, *The Origenist Controversy: The Cultural Construction of an Early Christian Debate* (Princeton, NJ: Princeton University Press, 1992).

43. Margaret Rooke, ed., *Libro del poema chiamato "Città di Vita" composto da Matteo Palmieri Florentino*, Smith College Studies in Modern Languages 1–2 (October 1926–January 1927) and 1–2 (October 1927–June 1928), and G. Boffito, "L'eresia di Matteo Palmieri, 'Cittadino Fiorentino,'" *Giornale storico della letteratura italiana* (1901): 1–69.

44. Dante, *Inferno*, Canto 3, 31–42:

> And I, in the midst of all this circling horror,
> began, "Teacher, what are these sounds I hear?
> What souls are these so overwhelmed by grief?"
> And he to me: "This wretched state of being is the fate of those sad souls who lived a life
> but lived it with no blame and with no praise.
> They are mixed with that repulsive choir [*quel cattivo coro*] of angels
> neither faithful nor unfaithful [*ribelli*] to their God,
> who undecided stood but for themselves [*Nè fur fedeli a Dio, ma per sè fuoro*].

Heaven, to keep its beauty, cast them out,
but even Hell itself would not receive them,
for fear the damned might glory over them."

The Divine Comedy, vol. 1: *Inferno,* trans. Mark Musa (New York: Penguin, 1971–1984), 90.

    45. John Freccero, "Dante and the Neutral Angels," *Romanic Review* 51 (1960): 5.

    46. Ibid.

    47. See Bagnoli et al., *Domenico Beccafumi e il suo tempo,* nos. 21 and 25, 152–153, 168–171, 48–49. Beccafumi, who had visited Rome before this commission, also quoted from the Hellenistic marble group, the Laocoön, as Nicole Dacos suggests (in *Domenico Beccafumi e il suo tempo,* 46). Most commentators, like her, see the artist making more overt references to Roman paradigms in the second panel.

    48. I owe this apt and resonant encapsulation to Richard Meyer and Sally M. Promey.

33

The Faltering Brush
Material, Sensory Trace, and Nonduality in Chan/Zen Buddhist Death Verse Calligraphies

GREGORY P. A. LEVINE

Death is always only an image.   Michael Camille, *Master of Death*

eath and poetry share a fertile bond.[1] Laments and elegies are composed for the deceased. Innumerable poems contemplate death. There are also poetries of imminent demise, often referred to as death or departing verses. Death verses make up a literary genre that lives in the leave-taking words of the dying. Such verses depend on a death distinguished by the availability of time as well as the cognitive and sensory capacity in which poetry, separate from nonverbal outcry, remains possible. Sudden death without warning—from a stroke that obliterates mental activity, a car that runs a red light and crushes life, and other such causes—yields little in the way of departing verse, be it spoken or materialized in written form.

We find instructions for how to die correctly in many cultures and periods, including the tenth-century *Ōjōyōshū* (Collection on Essentials for Birth in the Pure Land) from the Japanese Buddhist tradition and the fifteenth-century Latin *Ars moriendi* (The Art of Dying).[2] Death poems too have a long history. We may also experience firsthand a dying family member or friend who pushes through pain, fear, or diminishing capacity to speak of what matters most before the arrival of death. We may find ourselves pulled into this moment of last words, listening as never before and stunned thereafter by the echoes. If written down, these final words may assume particular force as lasting material and auratic traces of the deceased writer.

For the dying, the composition of departing verse may be the most time-sensitive of poetic acts—the last chance for words that commune as poetry. In this sense, the verse represents a liminal moment in between the recognition of death's approach and death itself. As readers of a death verse written in the past, we may find ourselves imagining the place and circumstances of the author's approaching demise, perhaps years if not centuries before our time. We follow the words that were followed by their author's death. A death verse may also have a long afterlife—preserved, copied, disseminated, and emulated—when it is believed to embody the teachings of the learned and saintly or to capture the essence of self, humanity, or the absolute. These are words, from among an individual's many speech acts across a lifetime, that may lead us beyond words.

Poets, we might venture, would seem especially inclined, if not required, to leave this world through parting verse, and death verses (Chinese *yijie;* Japanese *yuige;* "the *gāthā* [Sanskrit] left behind") have also been an ancient and enduring part of the premortem protocol and collected memory of Buddhist dying processes (for Chinese and Japanese terms, please see the Concordance).[3] To offer a recent example, we might note the poem composed by the Chan Master Sheng Yen (b. 1930) prior to his death of renal failure on February 3, 2009: "Busy with nothing, growing old. Within emptiness, weeping, laughing. Intrinsically, there is no 'I.' Life and death, thus cast aside."[4]

Not all Buddhist monks and nuns prepare such verses, and indeed many are said to have "returned to the source" (C. *huanyuan;* J. *kangen*) without fanfare, utterance, or trace. This may have been the doctrinal ideal, but Buddhist chronicles frequently tell us that upon a master's death strange fragrances filled the air, mysterious lights appeared, flocks of cranes suddenly took wing, and other unusual multisensory events signaled that a "special death" had occurred.[5] Premodern Chan/Zen Buddhist hagiographic texts such as *The Jingde Era Transmission of the Lamp* (C. *Jingde chuandeng lu;* 1004) are full of such stories.[6] We read in them also that the master generally foretold the time of death, engaged his or her disciples in discourse, abandoned possessions, prepared body and costume, recited and/or wrote a final poem, and passed away in equanimity.[7] Prior to the instant of extinction, therefore, the master established an "angle of repose" through actions, dialogs, objects, and miracles that seem, in hindsight, calibrated to self and community, local history and transhistorical dharma, and what we now call the "politics of death."[8] That a Chan/Zen master would compose poetry and participate in the culture of calligraphy should not surprise us, for the literary and visual arts were and remain fellow travelers of Chan/Zen masters within their teachings on emptiness (Skt. *śūnya;* C. *kong;* J. *kū*).[9]

That said, the preparation of death verses and their calligraphies is neither ubiquitous nor undifferentiated in the Chan/Zen tradition. Certain masters remained silent as death neared. Others admonished, when asked for a departing poem, that everything they had previously said and done constituted their death verse.[10] Some engaged in final dialogs with disciples from which a death verse was harvested posthumously. The Song dynasty master Dahui Zhonggao (1089–1163), meanwhile, informed his disciples, "Without a verse, I couldn't die" and then, employing a time-honored Chan didactic strategy, wrote a death verse to caution against attaching to a master's death verse: "Birth is thus, death is thus. Verse or no verse, what's the fuss?"[11]

That death verses are recorded in the Chan/Zen literature in such great number suggests that, as John Jorgensen puts it, "Language that has soteriological functions is

... 'alive,' [in contrast] to 'dead' language or words."[12] Monastic codes, meanwhile, stipulate display of the death verse beside the master's coffin.[13] When the verse was compiled in a master's collected sayings (C. *yulu;* J. *goroku*) or chronicle (C. *xing-zhuang;* J. *gyōjō*), it spoke well beyond its moments of composition and inscription. The death verse of the Song dynasty master Wuzhun Shifan (1178–1249) was even engraved on wood shortly after his death and circulated thereafter to Japan in the form of rubbings—subsequent representations distinguished by particular materials and sensory-rich processes of carving and printing.[14] In short, the departing poem and its calligraphic presence were important parts of the Chan/Zen "cult of the dying" and, thereafter, its "cult of the dead."

What do such verses convey? Like the Buddha's departing teachings (J. *ihō*) contained in the *Mahāparinirvāṇa Sūtra,* a Chan/Zen master's departing verse might be thought of as a final "ritual enactment and expression of awakened awareness" and a compassionate "teaching act" (J. *seppō*).[15] In this sense, the master's death verse is a prayer for the living that urges their realization of nonduality while revealing the master's particular inflection ("house style," J. *kafū*) of the dharma.[16] Some masters wrote of death as a journey back to the original abode of emptiness; others urged disciples neither to resist what comes nor to cling to what was; some addressed the dispersal of the four great elements by wind and fire; for others there was no past, present, or future, and thus no farewell, only liberation—they were "footloose and fancy-free," as one nun put it[17]—and there was no reason to grieve. Some verses urge us to grasp that both life and death are illusion (J. *genshō genmetsu*). As Huineng (638–713) put it to his disciples: "Just recognize your own fundamental minds and see your own fundamental natures, [which are] neither moving nor still, neither generated nor extinguished, neither going nor coming, neither correct nor false, neither abiding nor going."[18]

Modern commentaries on Chan/Zen death verses often suggest that a verse is the unique, unmediated "expression in poetic form of the Zen master's mental state just before death" that enables us to "imagine the Zen master's final assertion of power over the conflicted final moments of life."[19] Focusing more on social performance than on psychological state, the historian Imaizumi Yoshio suggests that a death verse constitutes the words that are left behind *and* the trace of the ritual of leaving those words.[20] For Bernard Faure, meanwhile, the departing verse was "not simply intended to testify to the master's enlightenment; it was *producing* it and contained, in the literal sense, its 'essence.'"[21]

Death verses are therefore consequential verbal, social, and soteriological performances in Chan/Zen, and they are also significant visual and material presences as calligraphy, conveying the calligrapher's touch, bodily movement, and vision as well as sensibility for the expressive practices of writing. In the weeks, days, or moments before death, a master might inscribe the final verse using a traditional writing brush and ink or, later in the tradition, a modern pen.

In modern commentary we repeatedly read that a master's death verse was writ-ten "immediately prior to death" (J. *shi no chokuzen*). Some verses were brushed prior to the day of death and maintain calligraphic norms as well as recognizable personal inflections found in an individual's prior writings. The master does not appear to "die on the page," as it were, in these examples. Thus there may have been different tempo-ralities in which a master brushed a death verse and different graphic dispositions, even if a death verse by definition is written in reference to the singular approaching event of extinction and often expresses a state beyond presence and absence and be-yond past, present, and future.

Not every master left behind such terminal calligraphies, however, and the ma-jority of medieval death verses that were brushed have been lost over the centuries. Those that survive in monasteries and temples in Japan are often mounted as hanging scrolls, venerated as patriarchal relics, and displayed in proximity to the master's por-trait in annual memorial rituals and other observances.[22]

What Do Death Verse Calligraphies Reveal?

Death verse calligraphies are categorized in Japanese as *bokuseki,* "ink traces," along with many other types of Chan/Zen writings.[23] Because of its association with a mas-ter's death, however, the death verse calligraphy tends to be set apart from other texts written over a lifetime. In addition to its funerary and ongoing memorial ritual instal-lation as a form of contact or trace relic, the death verse may be particularly auratic as writing that concludes the master's multisensory practice of writing: the hand hold-ing the brush, the ink-saturated brush hairs touching the paper with varying pressure, and the arm moving the brush to the inkstone and across the writing surface from top to bottom, right to left.

Many modern viewers distinguish Chan/Zen death verse calligraphies by their calligraphic faltering if not failure: collapsing or incorrect characters, columnar disor-der, and an absence of aesthetic expression (Figure 33.1).[24] These features suggest to some the master's final marshaling of physical, cognitive, and spiritual power in the face of decline to write because a good death depended on it.[25] Not all death verse cal-ligraphies display such graphic turmoil or failure; many bear few signs suggesting collapse and were brushed some time before death. But in looking at death verse cal-ligraphies we might consider the sensory-/bodily-rich acts, materiality, and enliven-ment of the dying master. If brushed just prior to death, might the death verse embody not only the master's teachings and the visuality of calligraphy but also a particular sort of (possibly deteriorating) physiological/neurological sensation? Did the brushed death verse enact the master's graphical vanishing? Were such calligraphies, to borrow Yukio Lippit's characterization of Chan/Zen portraits, "self-annulling icons" through which Chan/Zen masters wrote to unwrite writing?[26]

FIGURE 33.1. Chikotsu Daie (1229–1312), *Death Verse*, Kamakura period, 1312.11.22. Ink on paper, 39.3 × 56.7 centimeters. Ganjōji, Kyoto, Japan. Important Cultural Property. Photo by Gregory P. A. Levine.

We might first note that descriptions of a master's death and a record of a death verse preserved in the Chan/Zen *Lamp* literature or a master's biography inform us in retrospect (and often with embellishment, if not fabrication) how that saintly life resolved in words and actions. The death verse calligraphy, in contrast, not only records the master's poem but also purports to show us here and now, in a sequence of brush-strokes, the master and particular teachings as he or she neared death. The calligraphy visually embodies not death but near extinction or preparation for death, and its strokes leave a residue of touch and movement and perhaps of the individual's diminishing life force—moving toward the obliteration of the senses while materializing transcendence. A death verse calligraphy therefore suggests that we might *see* and (especially if knowledgeable about calligraphy itself) *feel* through the graphic trace the master's approaching death and response to nearing demise, not merely *read* his or her final statement of the dharma after death. But how might the master's brushstrokes reveal looming extinction, a particular response to calligraphy at life's end, and the teaching of nonduality?

We might begin to answer these questions by turning back to Chan/Zen hagiographic texts, which are often precise in their specification of the day and time of death and the master's age at death. Yunmen died, we read, "at the hour of the rat on the tenth day of the fourth moon of the forty-sixth year (949)."[27] Correct posture was imperative; death required a final disciplining of the body while the senses were still active.[28] As the monk Mujū Ichien (1226–1312) put it in his *Sand and Pebbles Anthology* (J. *Shasekishū*; 1283), "Stories of our predecessors in various sects have come down to us from ancient times. Outstanding in wisdom, practice and virtue, they all died as though entering into meditation."[29] The legs were therefore crossed into proper position, the body remained upright, and death arrived. A master's terminal writing was to be produced, according to this protocol, in the fundamental posture of awakening, which itself became part of death verse practice and rhetoric. The master Yangshan Huiji (807–883), we read, recited the verse "Completing seventy-seven years, today it ends. When the orb of the sun is just at noon, the two hands fold the legs."[30]

To the extent that infirmity preceded death, meditation posture might have proved difficult to achieve. One of the more famous cases of adherence to orthodox posture in the dying process is that of the Japanese master Daitō Kokushi (Shūhō Myōchō, 1282–1337). According to Daitō's *Chronicle*, "By noon of the twenty-second [day of the twelfth month], the Master was close to death. He wished to die sitting erect in the posture of meditation. Long troubled by an affliction in one leg, he had been unable to sit in the full-lotus position. He wrenched his leg into place with both hands, breaking it at the left knee. Blood flowed from the wound, staining his robe. The Master then composed his death verse."[31] Daitō's renunciation of bodily infirmity is usually taken as a sign of his indomitable spiritual power, but it also has genealogical and ideological potency, expressed in the tradition that the Daitō was the "reincarnation" (J. *sairai*) of the Chinese master Yunmen, who forced his own injured leg into meditation posture at death.[32] Some acts at death may therefore have reperformed the earlier deaths of patriarchal figures, just as certain death verses and calligraphies allude to earlier authors and writing styles.

The traditional records are rather less exact about the sensory and material dimensions of how masters brushed their death verses. Most state merely that the master left behind a departing verse. Some refer laconically to the place and manner of inscription. In the case of the Japanese master Enni Ben'en (1202–1280), founder of the Kyoto monastery Tōfukuji, we read in one account, "On the fifteenth day of the tenth month, he announced that he would go up to the Dharma Hall to lecture and then to pass away; but his disciples would not permit it. Then on the seventeenth day he told his attendants to call the monks together and to beat the drum in the Dharma Hall to announce his death. Seated in a chair, he wrote his verse of departure from the world and expired."[33] Enni may or may not have actually written his verse while seated in an abbot's chair in the Dharma Hall, but this position would have been fully consonant with the "enthronement" of a master as abbot and living Buddha within the monastery.[34] In some instances, however, the attempt to brush a verse failed. The chronicle of the seventeenth-century Chan nun Yigong, for instance, recounts that "Yigong . . . wrote a few characters, but then laid the brush down and said with a sigh, 'Lifting this pen is like lifting a huge pole.' [The next day], after the first sutra recital, she turned to her attendant and said: 'Yesterday, I composed a gatha but today I will recite it so that you can write it down for me.'"[35] Chan/Zen masters often employed scribes to write official documents, but the reliance upon a disciple for the final verse suggests an especially intimate moment and dharma relationship converging around the graphic embodiment of the master's final teaching.

Rarely are calligraphies themselves described in biographical sources. We find only brief glances, such as the comment that Dahui composed his verse in large script.[36] Quite striking, however, are records that state that the process was completed when the master "threw down the brush and transformed." In these accounts, the final brushstroke of the death verse and the brush cast aside from the hand were the master's last gestures before death.

The Death Verse Calligraphy of Chikotsu Daie

Modern writers sometimes employ the phrase "terminal writing" (J. *makki no sho*) to specify the temporal location of a calligraphy written at life's extremity. Often this is aligned with an effort to distinguish the death verse as a form of writing that transcends calligraphy and art.[37] In these terms, the autographic death verse is not "calligraphic" because—in the face of death—the writer failed to fulfill, or eschewed, calligraphy's venerable logographic requirements and aesthetic inflections. The writing is characterized by slippage rather than control, mismeasure rather than fluidly gauged placement, stutter rather than momentum, and collapse rather than graceful strength or sustained energy. Thus the master's final traces of the brush are about death, not art.[38]

There is something to this, and when commentators discuss death verses in this vein, they often have in mind startling calligraphies that suggest a direct link between graphic and dying processes. Arguably the most astonishing and disquieting example is the calligraphy of the Japanese master Chikotsu Daie (1229–1312), a four-character quatrain (see Figure 33.1):

Surpassing skillful means	高超方便
Self-illuminated and self-so	自證自然
Responding to things as they are	爲物應世
For eighty-four years	八十四年
Chikotsu (cipher)	大慧 (花押)
22nd day, 11th month,	正和元年十一月廿二日
first year of the Shōwa era (1312).[39]	

Chikotsu was a master in the dharma lineage of Enni Ben'en and served as the ninth abbot of Tōfukuji. He also founded smaller temples in Ise Province and the Tōfukuji subtemple Daijian. His death verse calligraphy was originally a treasure of Daijian but later became the property of the Tōfukuji subtemple Ganjōji following Daijian's closure during the late Edo period (1615–1868).[40]

Chikotsu's verse expresses his realization of original nature and equanimity in response to the world's myriad phenomena. It is conventional in its reference to the years of the author's life and allusion to prior death verses, notably that of his teacher Enni, which itself refers to the death verse of Enni's own teacher Wuzhun Shifan (1177–1249).[41] For a viewer familiar with calligraphic conventions, however, the visual disorder of Chikotsu's writing, implying sensory, physical decline, may nearly overcome the poem's verbal content. Helmut Brinker's description of the calligraphy is fitting, if somewhat Romantic: "It is precisely this waning of the master's command over his handwriting that shows dramatically the extreme situation of the dying man. With a heroic effort, he tries to mobilize his last forces. Thus, this work must not be judged according to the usual criteria and aesthetic requirements of calligraphy; rather, it must be seen as a moving human and religious document of a master who was extremely vigorous and energetic during his lifetime."[42]

It is difficult not to find Chikotsu's writing deeply affecting, and in Brinker's description the calligraphy's impact derives not from the elegant artistry we associate with calligraphy but from the master's immense determination as manifested in his profoundly compromised writing, which nevertheless seems to push back against his body's cognitive, physical, and sensory collapse. This perception of unyielding effort in the face of decline is hard to ignore, even if it is, as I suspect, conditioned partly by a perhaps overly literal response to the master's famous portrait statue and its startlingly physical and illusionistic carving (Figure 33.2); a master portrayed in this way would, it seems, create only a death verse calligraphy characterized by heroic effort.

In any case, once Chikotsu's calligraphy is understood to be a "death verse," it is quite difficult to see his "wounded" or "afflicted" writing as anything other than an un-

FIGURE 33.2. *Portrait of Chikotsu Daie,* probably shortly after 1312. Wood, polychrome, 78.3 centimeters tall. Hōkokuji, Ehime Prefecture, Japan. Important Cultural Property. Photograph from Helmut Brinker and Hiroshi Kanazawa, *Zen: Masters of Meditation in Images and Writings* (Zurich: Artibus Asiae Publications, 1996), 82. Photo by Julie Wolf.

mediated graphic embodiment of a momentary triumph over looming death.[43] But before we accept this conclusion, fully or in part, let us look more closely at the calligraphy itself, paying attention to its materials and ink application, the morphology of its Chinese characters, and its textual organization—looking for what they might suggest about the temporal, bodily, and sensory process of calligraphy in this instance.

The paper on which Chikotsu wrote, measuring today approximately 15½ inches in height and 22¼ inches in width, reveals a material condition that may hint at the circumstances of the calligraphy's production.[44] Scattered across the surface are areas of insect damage and some cracks and patches, features of material decay and repair not unusual for a work of this age. Less immediately visible to the eye today are vertical creases or fold marks (J. *orime*). Chikotsu's calligraphy runs across these creases in several places, and the monk's brush wavered at and stuttered slightly over the uneven surface. The paper brought to Chikotsu therefore appears to have been folded loosely, perhaps for storage, and, I would speculate, may have been rushed into use rather than readied pristinely for the moment of final writing. If the paper perhaps implies the sudden, impending death of the writer, the relatively light tonality of the ink may suggest something similar: ink prepared without time to grind the ink stick sufficiently to produce darker brushstrokes indicating a greater density of carbon particles.

Chikotsu's four-character quatrain moves from top to bottom and right to left across the paper. But this is a poem, written on the day of his death, whose columnar structure teeters and collides and whose characters spin off a unified axis and suffer ideographic erosion. The initial four-character phrase begins with three characters in the first column on the right and straggles to its fourth at the top of the second column. What might appear to be the cursive extension of the fourth character, *hō* (方), at the bottom of the first column, may have resulted from the master's failure to lift the brush off the paper. Alternately, Chikotsu may have begun to write the final character of the first phrase, *ben* (便), which should appear at the end of the first line, only to realize that he had left insufficient room and was thus forced to add this character to the top of the next column. The poem's second phrase is, in turn, compressed into the second column below the character left from the first phrase, *ben,* while the third and fourth phrases occupy their own columns. Chikotsu's signature and cipher follow the fourth line but partially overrun each other and are then overwritten by the line of characters specifying the date. This is writing that does not hold to a consistent temporal and spatial graphism, even though its content adheres rather firmly to Chan/Zen rhetoric.

The axes of many characters, moreover, diverge from vertical orientation, especially in the initial column and, dramatically, in the character *ben.* If we imagine Chikotsu seated before the paper with brush in hand, it would seem that he was unable to begin the poem with a firm (perpendicular) physical relationship to the surface; the first character of the first line leans perilously toward the right. As for the character *ben,* perhaps the master's head tilted rightward and his body crumpled clockwise, in turn throwing the character wildly off axis. Equally startling is the disintegration of individual characters, which are sometimes reduced to simplified forms that have none of the controlled energy of cursive writing or even "wild cursive" script (C. *kuangcao*).[45] Characters fly apart or clot; a character's strokes may begin with control but then compress and sag. The same character, or analogous dyads or triads of strokes, may not merely vary but suggest a hand whose grip on the brush, wrist strength, and bodily anchor have suddenly weakened.

The impact of seeing this graphic collapse registers forcefully, it seems to me, not merely because of what we see happening to the calligraphy but, more profoundly, because of what we might sense was happening to Chikotsu the calligrapher. Absent a contemporary description of Chikotsu's act of writing, we might still surmise that physical weakness and failing faculties offer some degree of explanation for such compromised writing. But there is a more specific story that accompanies the calligraphy, namely that Chikotsu, unable to rise from his sickbed to a seated position, was able only to raise his arm upward from his body to write on a sheet of paper held above him by a disciple.[46] To imagine Chikotsu writing in this manner is to readjust our sense of the writer's body and the way a brush meets the surface of the paper, in this scenario a surface held above the writer rather than placed on the floor before him. Without a resisting support behind the paper to push back against the action of the arm and the brush's pressure, the brush might have moved unreliably away from the writer with a loss of friction between brush tip and paper. Surely this would have altered Chikotsu's characters in a material and kinesthetic sense accompanying his cognitive and physiological state. This scenario might also imply that ink ran down the handle of the brush onto Chikotsu's hand and perhaps even his face.

As striking as this account may be, the calligraphy itself may tell a different story, one that suggests that Chikotsu wrote with the paper in front of his body and below his brush. One must surmise that the small dots of ink that appear around certain characters fell with gravity from Chikotsu's brush toward the paper, something that would have been unlikely if the paper had been held above the master. The particular splay of the brush's hairs on the surface of the paper as the ink dried may also suggest that there was a supporting surface behind it. Be that as it may, both accounts prompt us to imagine that the act of writing in the moments before Chikotsu's death might have been compromised and collaborative, with a disciple holding paper above the master or supporting the master in a seated position and possibly preparing ink for him, even bringing the brush to his hand.

The death verses of a handful of other masters likewise manifest slippage and disorientation, including that of the Tōfukuji master Daidō Ichii (1292–1370):

A single song of nonbirth	無生一曲
Harmoniously fills the void	調満虚空
Sunny spring and white snow	陽春白雪
Green clouds and pure wind.	碧雲清風
Daidō Ichii (cipher)	大道一以（花押）
[wrote this] on the twenty-sixth day of the second month, third year of the Ōan era (1370).[47]	応安三年二月廿六日

Daidō's death verse calligraphy elicits the following description from Brinker: "There is no order and stability to the lines any more and the characters are structureless to the degree of illegibility. Most of them tumble loosely around tilting toward the left, as if they were blown down by a thunderous storm. The writer's hand seems totally exhausted so that the uncontrolled movements of the brush are only able to produce scratchy and shaky flourishes that can hardly be identified as characters. These last messy 'ink traces' of Daidō Ichi'i unmistakenly convey the agony of death."[48]

To dismiss this description would be ungenerous, for the writing is indeed startling in its opposition to the poise and elegant imagery of Daidō's poem as well as earlier examples of his calligraphy. The postulation that Daidō's exhausted writing "conveys the agony of death," meanwhile, goes to the heart of the matter. It is perhaps not strictly a question of whether Daidō was actually in agony as he wrote but rather of whether his death was agonizing and in what sense or senses. Was it not expected of a master to die, as Robert H. Sharf puts it, with a "studied disregard for the physical body and utter dispassion in the face of death"?[49] Indeed, one biography of Chikotsu simply states that the master "wrote his *gāthā,* composed himself, and died," without reference to struggle or physical ailment.[50] Or were the pain and failure of the body revealed or openly acknowledged in the inscriptional act? If certainty surrounded the doctrinal idea of the master's transcendence beyond life and death, health and illness, might death prove less certain and more visible in a master's death verse calligraphy? Do we see the dharma and the mind-body parting on the paper in important and affecting ways simultaneous to a verse's literary enactment of awakened status? Or might the apparent sentiment of Daidō's poem—of harmoniously filling the void— perhaps have been what Daidō experienced in his final moments (rather than agony), even with the "agonizing" brushwork?

We cannot know what Daidō or Chikotsu felt, what their precise physical and cognitive conditions were during the moments of their final inscriptions, and this returns us to the age-old debate about whether we can recover what an author or artist thought in the process of creation.[51] It is worth noting, however, that such calligraphies seem to force us to alter the nature of description itself to account for writing that is compromised rather than stylistically magisterial, elegant, or radical.[52]

So what do such writings show and require of us, distant as we are from the moments of their inscription? First, they demand, I think, attention to the materials of calligraphy. To paraphrase James Elkins, we should consider the meanings that happen in the paper and ink before leaping to characterize the state of the maker's mind.[53] We might think, too, of the evaporation of moisture as the ink dried, a material manifestation of time—time, of course, being the critical "deep structure" of a death verse calligraphy. An idealist, meanwhile, might see in Chikotsu's writing an "aesthetic of death" rendered by "death's hand." This interpretation might be anchored in the fact that Chikotsu brushed the verse on the day of his death, with the calligraphy thereby serving as a material and visual metric of his approaching demise. One need not reject this entirely, but it is also valid to see the death verse as an affirmation of living rather than merely as a testament to dying; it is evidence of an individual's own life presence, *still there and still writing.* Perhaps, too, the failing body and mind find their own prominence and lingering presence, even if the master is emphatic that life and death, strength and weakness, writing or no writing are beside the point in awakened non-duality. Moreover, Chikotsu *endeavored* to follow the rules of ink application, character stroke order and structure, and poetic and signature format. He may also have gestured toward a visual community of prior calligraphers and calligraphies, even or especially at this point of disintegration. By no means is this an iconoclastic rejection of calligraphy or language, even if there was reason, as Dahui Zonggao cautioned, to not get "caught up in the snares of writing, and keeping pen and inkstone."[54]

At the same time, Chikotsu's writing does not suggest the free play within the conventions of personal inflection or stylistic disequilibrium that had become routine in East Asian calligraphy from the Northern Song dynasty onward.[55] Instead we find what may be a sensory, corporeal struggle to write in the first place. As barely legible or precipitously off-center graphs, the master's writing may suggest life tilting out of balance and with it an inversion of the traditional metaphorical relationship between calligraphy and the body. Namely, if "'Flesh,' 'bone,' 'sinew,' 'blood,' and 'veins' are all part of the critical vocabulary evaluating the health of one's writing," as John Hay tells us, Chikotsu's calligraphy—under what may have been neurological, cognitive duress—seems to manifest the weakening and ill health of the inscribing body.[56] A calligrapher's choices are conditioned by his or her life condition, individual intention, and the social-artistic discourses of calligraphy itself, but Chikotsu's decisions about the format, morphology, and even personal style of his death verse appear to have been perilously constrained or thwarted. From modern medicine we know that in the final days and hours of life a person's pulse rate and blood pressure become unstable, digestion and elimination begin to shut down, respiration becomes labored, the body shakes, and vision may close off. Much of this was no doubt known, if in different terms, in Chikotsu's period. The master's death verse seems to fall somewhere in this waning process.

If we are to think of these as Chikotsu's "death strokes," we might sense that they verge toward a state in which, to borrow from Michael Camille, the "visual distorts and erases the words rather than holds them up for analysis."[57] Picturing, to put it differently, is overrunning language. Or perhaps the death verse, as it approaches illegibility, becomes a rebus that "writes" death through its features of dissolution while retaining sufficient signs of calligraphy as such. Or we might see Chikotsu's brushstrokes as residing close to the border between writing and marking—a few steps further and it would leave writing as a landscape of signs—forced there by dissociation between the body's sensory and kinesthetic capacities and the master's mental intentions. Comparison to earlier works of Chikotsu's calligraphy, few of which survive, might reveal the relationship between his death verse and his usual "stylistic signature" and just how close to this border of writing and marking his death verse resides.[58] In any case, Chikotsu's final writing may demand that we reconceptualize "calligraphy" to allow for such critical conditions of body, mind, material, and inscription.

Conclusion

If the Chan/Zen tradition began, at least in its hagiographical account, with Śākyamuni wordlessly holding aloft a flower, the death of many masters ended in words and also in acts of writing.[59] There are, in turn, many ways to study a master's death verse calligraphy, and from a distance we are asking about the relationship of text and image to the completion of life as a Buddhist teacher. As far as the hagiographic literature is concerned, in the dance with death the Chan/Zen master leads.[60] The survival of death verse calligraphies, however, gives us a reason and the means to explore more deeply how dying found compelling visual and material form, all the more so in cases in which the calligraphic traces suggest the collapse of writing. The purposefulness of death verses—with masters writing, in some instances, even when writing may have been nearly impossible—and their long preservation also suggest that they were important social and ritual artifacts as much as windows onto the awakened minds of the inscribers.

There may not have been an a priori Chan/Zen death verse calligraphy style, but those calligraphies that present degrees of collapse have been recognized (and lauded) as embodying a distinctive "system" of representation—a system that, from the standpoint of "orthodox calligraphy," would seem to be a vulnerable nonsystem and therefore in accordance with modern, Romantic characterizations of Chan/Zen as obstreperous and aloof from anything that smacks of regulation, mediation, or culturally or historically located concepts.[61] But part of the affective power of such calligraphies arises, I sense, precisely from the writer's desire or need for form; we see the master's brush falter because we can see how his or her brush sought to fulfill calligraphic obligations.

If images are "ontologically constitutive"—if they have a transformative impact on lived reality for a viewer (rather than simply representing some thing)—what was the ontological effect of a death verse?[62] In the postmortem context of funerary and memorial ritual, the effect may have been that of the posthumous presencing of the charismatic teacher through a calligraphic relic and of his or her final teachings being perceived to be "living" and "active" forces that impact a viewer's world. There is no reason to discount the possibility that seeing a death verse after a master's death may inspire realization of nonduality or have an efficacious or miraculous impact.

What the writer of a medieval death verse thought or felt in brushing and then looking on what his or her hand left behind is lost to us. Nevertheless, the inscriptional circumstances and calligraphic form of a master's "terminal writing" may be valuable if we are to learn not simply that the master heroically marshaled his or her remaining strength to hold the brush and bring it to bear upon the paper to inscribe poetry on nonduality but, in a very human act, left behind *particular* traces of language and of the body's sensory and kinesthetic capacities before moving beyond them to return to the absolute. The collapse of calligraphy itself, meanwhile, may yield an especially telling sense of both writing and dying. The ink may be the literal medium, but closing arteries, decaying cognition, obstructed airflow, intensified or dulled sensations, and so forth might be the indirect media of the death verse calligraphy. Perhaps we need to rethink our understanding of "calligraphy" to account for such particular bodily, sensory, material, and mortal circumstances of writing. To move beyond hagiography and Romantic models of interpretation, we may wish to imagine more fully the writing process in relation to life and death, brush and body, visuality and nonduality.

Concordance of Terms

Akashi Koshū 明石湖洲
bokuseki 墨蹟
Chikotsu Daie 癡兀大慧
Chixiu Baizhang qingui
　　勅修百丈清規
Daitō Kokushi 大燈国師
Dahui Pujue chanshi yulu
　　大慧普覺禪師語録
Dahui Zonggao 大慧宗杲
Daijian 大慈庵
Enni Ben'en 圓爾辨圓
gāthā 偈他 or 伽陀
goroku 語録
gyōjō 行状
genshō genmetsu 幻生幻滅
Hōkokuji 保国寺
huanyuan 還源
Huineng 慧能
ihō 遺法
Jingde chuandeng lu
　　景德傳燈録
jisei no ge 辭世偈
kafū 家風

kangen See *huanyuan*
kong 空
kū See *kong*
kuangcao 狂草
makki no sho 末期の書
Mujū Ichien 無住一圓
Ōjō yōshū 往生要集
seppō 説法
Shasekishū 沙石集
Sheng Yen 聖嚴
Shūhō Myōchō 宗峰妙超
Sodōshū 祖堂集
Sumida Sōki 角田宗亀
Tōfukuji 東福寺
Yangshan Huiji 仰山慧寂
Wuzhun Shifan 無準師範
yuige 遺偈
yijie See *yuige*
Yuanzhou Yangshan Huiji chanshi yulu
　　袁州仰山慧寂禪師語録
yulu See *goroku*
Yunmen 雲門
Zutangji See *Sodōshū*

I offer my deep gratitude to the abbot of Ganjōji, Akashi Kōshū, for his gracious permission to view and reproduce Chikotsu Daie's *Death Verse* and to the abbot of Hokokuji, Sumida Sōki, for granting me permission to reproduce the *Portrait of Chikotsu Daie.* For their assistance in viewing the *Death Verse* at the Kyoto National Museum, I thank Yamakawa Aki, Yamamoto Hideo, and Wakasugi Junji.

1. See Xiaofei Tian's observation, "Death and narration seem to share a darkly close relationship," in Xiaofei, *Tao Yuanming and Manuscript Culture* (Seattle: University of Washington Press, 2005), 132.

2. See James C. Dobbins, "Genshin's Deathbed Nembutsu Ritual in Pure Land Buddhism," in *Religions of Japan in Practice,* ed. George J. Tanabe Jr. (Princeton, NJ: Princeton University Press, 1999), 166–175.

3. Early examples of death verses from Japan include the death poem of Prince Ōtsu (663–686) in the *Manyōshū* collection (ca. 759) and the poet Ki no Tsurayuki's (883–946) death verse in the imperial anthology *Shūishū* (ca. 1006). Premodern Japanese texts employ terms such as *jisei no ge* (verse upon departing this world) and *yuisho* (writing left behind); the phrase *imawa no kotoba* (dying words) appears in the "Kiritsubo" chapter of *The Tale of Genji* (early eleventh century). Verses composed before an unplanned death should perhaps be differentiated from those composed and/or recited by monks who then performed acts of self-immolation, although all may cohere in broader Buddhist understandings of death. See James Benn, *Burning the Buddha: Self-Immolation in Chinese Buddhism* (Honolulu: University of Hawai'i Press, 2007).

4. 無事忙中老, 空裡有哭笑, 本來沒有我, 生死皆可拋, trans. Jimmy Yu, posted to the H-NET Buddhist Scholars Information Network February 3, 2009, also available on the website of Dharma Drum Mountain Monastery, accessed February 22, 2012, http://www.dharmadrum.org/wcbe/content/news/view.aspx?sn=599.

5. See the account of the Sixth Chan Patriarch Huineng's death in John J. Jorgensen, *Inventing Hui-neng, the Sixth Patriarch: Hagiography and Biography in Early Ch'an* (Leiden: Brill, 2005), 135. "Special deaths" alludes to the "special dead" in Peter Brown, *The Cult of the Saints: Its Rise and Function in Medieval Christianity* (Chicago: University of Chicago Press, 1981).

6. *Jingde chuangdeng lu,* in *Taishō shinshū daizōkyō* (hereafter *T.*), ed. Takakusu Junjirō and Watanabe Kaigyoku (Tokyo: Taishō Issaikyō Kankōkai, 1924–1936), 2076.51. See also *The Patriarch's Hall Collection* (C. *Zutangji;* J. *Sodōshū;* 952), in *Sōdōshū,* ed. Yanagida Seizan (Kyoto: Chūbun Shuppansha, 1984), and Mujū Ichie, *Sand and Pebbles Anthology* (J. *Shasekishū;* 1238), in Robert F. Morrell, *Sand and Pebbles (Shasekishū): The Tales of Mujū Ichien, a Voice for Pluralism in Kamakura Buddhism* (Albany: SUNY Press, 1985), 261–265.

7. See Jorgensen, *Inventing Hui-neng,* 180–182. On Chan nuns, see Beata Grant, *Eminent Nuns: Women Chan Masters of Seventeenth-Century China* (Honolulu: University of Hawai'i Press, 2009), 84, 103. On the "social or cultural fictions" of Chan/Zen texts, see Jorgensen, *Inventing Hui-neng,* 9–18.

8. On preparing for death, see Bernard Faure, *The Rhetoric of Immediacy: A Cultural Critique of Chan/Zen Buddhism* (Princeton, NJ: Princeton University Press, 1991), 184–191; Yanagida Seizan, *Zen no yuige* (Tokyo: Chōbunsha, 1973), 30–32; and Robert H. Sharf, "The Idolization of Enlightenment: On the Mummification of Chan Masters in Medieval China," *History of Religions* 32, no. 1 (1992): 1–31. "Angle of repose" is from Wallace Stegner's 1972 eponymous novel. On the "politics of death," see Gary L. Ebersole, *Ritual Poetry and the Politics of Death in Early Japan* (Princeton, NJ: Princeton University Press, 1992), 4.

9. See Natasha Heller, "Illusory Abiding: The Life and Work of Zhongfeng Mingben (1263–1323)," Ph.D. dissertation, Harvard University, Cambridge, MA, 2006, Chapter 7.

10. See, for instance, the Japanese monk Bankei in *The Unborn: The Life and Teachings of Zen Master Bankei, 1622–1693,* trans. Norman Waddell, rev. ed. (New York: Macmillan, 2000), 25.

11. J. C. Cleary, *Swampland Flowers: The Letters and Lectures of Zen Master Ta Hui* (Boston: Shambhala, 2006), xvii, and *Dahui Pujue chanshi yulu,* in *T.* 1998A.47.0863a10–11.

12. Jorgensen, *Inventing Hui-neng,* 13.

13. See "Post the departing verse [of the master] to the left of the shrine" (遺偈貼龕左), in *Imperial Compilation of the Pure Rules of Baizhang* (*Chixiu Baizhang qingui; 1335–1338*), in *T.* 48.2025.1127c01. See *The Baizhang Zen Monastic Regulations (Taishō Volume 48, 2025),* trans. Chimura Shohei (Berkeley: Numata Center for Buddhist Translation and Research, 2006), 118–119, and Yifa, *The Origins of Buddhist Monastic Codes in China: An Annotated Translation and Study of the Chanyuan Qinggui* (Honolulu: University of Hawai'i Press, 2002).

14. See Tayama Hōnan, ed., *Zenrin bokuseki* (Ichikawa: Zenrin Bokuseki Kankai, 1955), vol. 1, 11.

15. See Taigen Dan Leighton, "Zazen as an Enactment Ritual," in *Zen Ritual: Studies on Zen Buddhist Theory in Practice,* ed. Steven Heine and Dale S. Wright (Oxford, UK: Oxford University Press, 2008), 167.

16. One might liken the death verse to a gift that transfers merit from the master to the community. Masters often alluded to the *Vimalikirti Sūtra,* the *Heart Sūtra,* koan compilations, and the death verses of prior teachers and patriarchs, creating a rich literary palimpsest.

17. Grant, *Eminent Nuns,* 182.

18. *The Platform Sūtra of the Sixth Patriarch, Translated from the Chinese of Tsung-pao,* trans. John McRae (Berkeley, CA: Numata Center for Buddhist Translation and Research, 2000), 114. Or, as the Buddha was said to have put it, "Those of you who think of me as entering total extinction are not my disciples; those of you who think of me as not entering total extinction are not my disciples." Yanagida, *Zen no yuige,* 48.

19. Imaeda Aishin, ed., *Shintei zusetsu Bokuseki soshiden* (Tokyo: Hakurinsha, 1970), 8; and Tayama, *Zenrin bokuseki,* vol. 1, 109.

20. Imaizumi Yoshio, *Ikkyū oshō nenpu* (Tokyo: Heibonsha, 1998), vol. 2, 253–254.

21. Faure, *Rhetoric,* 189, italics in original. See also Yanagida, *Zen no yuige,* 75.

22. On the death verse and portrait, see Gregory P. A. Levine, *Daitokuji: The Visual Cultures of a Zen Monastery* (Seattle: University of Washington Press, 2005), 251. See also a modern reproduction of Minchō's famous portrait of Enni Ben'en with a transcription of his death verse above his figure in Shiraishi Kogetsu, ed., *Tōfukuji shi* (Kyoto: Shibunkaku Shuppan, 1979), 145.

23. On *bokuseki,* see Levine, *Daitokuji,* Part 3.

24. We might also note portraits that bear above the figure the master's poetic inscription, which in some instances was brushed close to death and shows calligraphy not unlike what is seen in death verses proper. See Tōkyō Kokuritsu Hakubutsukan, Kyōto Kokuritsu Hakubutsukan, ed., *Nanzenji: Kameyama Tennō 700 onki ki'nen* (Tokyo: Asahi Shinbunsha, 2004), 27.

25. I have heard that monks sometimes wrote a death verse each New Year's Day in preparation for death, which might come at any time.

26. Yukio Lippit, "Negative Verisimilitude: The Zen Portrait in Medieval Japan," in *Asian Art History in the Twenty-first Century,* ed. Vishakha N. Desai (Williamstown, MA: Sterling and Francine Clark Art Institute, 2007), 87.

27. Urs App, *Master Yunmen: From the Record of the Chan Master "Gate of the Clouds"* (New York: Kodansha International, 1994), 28.

28. References to dying in meditation posture appear at least as early as the third century CE. Sharf, "The Idolization of Enlightenment," 7.

29. Morrell, *Sand and Pebbles,* 263.

30. 年滿七十七, 無常在今日, 日輪正當午, 兩手攀屈膝. Translated in Andrew E. Ferguson, *Zen's Chinese Heritage: The Masters and Their Teachings* (Boston: Wisdom, 2000), 171; see *Yuanzhou Yangshan Huiji chanshi yulu,* in T. 47n1990_p0588a14–15.

31. Adapted from the translation in Kenneth Kraft, "Zen Master Daitō," Ph.D dissertation, Princeton University, Princeton, NJ, 1984, 304–305.

32. For Daitō as the "second Yunmen," see Kenneth Kraft, *Eloquent Zen: Daitō and Early Japanese Zen* (Honolulu: University of Hawaiʻi Press, 1992), 39.

33. Morrell, *Sand and Pebbles,* 265.

34. For accounts of Enni's passing, see Sugawara Akihide, "Kamakura jidai no yuige ni tsuite: Enni ni itaru rinju sahō no keifu," in *Kamakura jidai bunka denba no kenkyū,* ed. Ōsumi Kazuo (Tokyo: Yoshikawa Kōbunkan, 1993), 75–116.

35. Grant, *Eminent Nuns,* 85.

36. *Dahui Pujue chanshi yulu,* in T. 1998A.47.0863a09.

37. The modern claim that no work of Chan/Zen calligraphy is "art" in a conventional sense falls flat given the explicit emulation by Chan/Zen masters of the brush styles of eminent Chinese calligraphers such as Wang Xizhi, Zhang Jizhi, Huang Tingjian, and Su Shi. Chan/Zen masters were in close exchange with literati cultures and part of a larger scriptocultural community.

38. Japanese monks with whom I have spoken have suggested that the death verse calligraphy is to be treated as distinct from a master's many other writings, while the aura of death may have generally kept such calligraphies separate from the art market.

39. I thank Robert H. Sharf and Raoul Birnbaum for their assistance with this translation. See Helmut Brinker and Hiroshi Kanazawa, *Zen: Masters of Meditation in Images and Writings* (Zurich: Artibus Asiae, 1996), 275, and Higuchi Tomoyuki, "Ganjōji zō Chikotsu Daie zō kō," *Bijutsu shigaku* 17 (1995): 63.

40. For Chikotsu's biography, see "Daijian Buttsū Zenji gyōjō," in Shiraishi, *Tōfukuji shi,* 227.

41. Higuchi, "Ganjōji zō Chikotsu Daie zō kō," 62–64.

42. Brinker and Kanazawa, *Zen,* 274. See also Helmut Brinker, "Zen Masters in Words and Images," *Orientations* (November 1993): 57–58.

43. Yukio Lippit suggested to me that the problem is similar to that involved in the study of a painter's "late style" (such as Rembrandt's paintings of the 1650s–1660s) and the poignancy or heroism that is often seen in it, albeit in retrospect.

44. The calligraphy is mounted as a hanging scroll with a combination of brocade and plain-weave fabrics. The bands immediately to the top and bottom of the paper (*ichimonji*) are an indigo-colored brocade with a pinecone pattern in supplementary weft gold thread; the surrounding fabric bands (*chū-mawashi*) are damask with a peony pattern in supplementary thread with additional silver weft threads; and the top- and bottommost fabrics are a brown-colored plain-woven silk. Stored in its present box are remnants of prior mounting fabrics and a dowel inscribed in ink with the date Kan'ei 19 (1642).

45. The "wild cursive" calligraphy of Huaisu (fl. ca. 730s–770s), such as that used in his *Autobiography* (National Palace Museum, Taipei), employs formal and compositional disruption and dissonance that suggest particular performances of visual rhetoric that may be quite different from a physiologically encumbered act of writing. Arguably, the faltering calligraphy of death verses should be differentiated from writings composed in states of intoxication or religious trance. In the medieval Japanese calligraphic modes known as *kasanegaki* ("clustered writing")

and *midaregaki* ("disheveled writing"), the purposive dissolution of orthodox writing (as a style) was performed to accentuate a particular reception of the textual content. Adele Schlombs, *Huaisu and the Beginnings of Wild Cursive Script in Chinese Calligraphy* (Stuttgart: Franz Steiner, 1998), and Yukio Lippit, "Form and Facture in the *Genji Scrolls*: Text, Calligraphy, Paper, and Painting," in *Envisioning the Tale of Genji: Media, Gender, and Cultural Production,* ed. Haruo Shirane (New York: Columbia University Press, 2008), 59–60.

46. This story was related to me by the present abbot of Ganjōji and Wakasugi Junji, then curator at the Kyoto National Museum.

47. Translated in Brinker and Kanazawa, *Zen,* 110.

48. Ibid.

49. Sharf, "The Idolization of Enlightenment," 5.

50. "Daijian Buttsū Zenji gyōjō," in Shiraishi, *Tōfukuji shi,* 227.

51. The relationship between creativity and illness is a favorite of studies bridging medicine and art history; diagnosis of what ails the artist is often said to explain the artist's work and style.

52. It is probably far-fetched to imagine that masters as a rule purposively postponed inscription so that the body's weakness would deform their writing and make their final calligraphy more "authentic" to approaching death.

53. See James Elkins, *What Painting Is: How to Think about Oil Painting, Using the Language of Alchemy* (New York: Routledge, 2000).

54. Heller, "Illusory Abiding," 340.

55. As the Northern Song dynasty scholar–official luminary Su Shih (1037–1101) put it, the best calligraphy was characterized by "inconstant form but constant principles." Peter C. Sturman, *Mi Fu: Style and the Art of Calligraphy in Northern Song China* (New Haven, CT: Yale University Press, 1997), 10, 33, 44.

56. See Sturman, *Mi Fu,* 7, drawing from John Hay, "The Human Body as a Microcosmic Source of Macrocosmic Calligraphy," in *Theories of the Arts in China,* ed. Susan Bush and Christian Murck (Princeton, NJ: Princeton University Press, 1981), 74–102. Note, too, Michael Camille's statement: "Images register the activity of a whole body—a body tense, weak, fatigued or frail—visible in the strength of the line, the viscosity of paint. The flux of bodily fluids that fourteenth-century people [in the West] thought controlled their humoral dispositions, the bile that darkened and the blood that brightened, were also constitutive of the fluids that were brushed on to the surface of parchment." Camille, *Master of Death: The Lifeless Art of Pierre Remiet Illuminator* (New Haven, CT: Yale University Press, 1996), 5.

57. Camille, *Master of Death,* 2.

58. See Sturman, *Mi Fu,* 54. One extant calligraphy is Chikotsu's inscription dated 1301 on his portrait preserved at Ganjōji, Kyoto. Reproduced in Tōkyō Kokuritsu Hakubutsukan, ed., *Kyōto Gozan: Zen no bunka* (Tokyo: Tōkyō Kokuritsu Hakubutsukan, 2007), 25.

59. See Albert Welter, "Mahākāśyapa's Smile: Silent Transmission and the Kung-an (Kōan) Tradition," in *The Kōan: Texts and Contexts in Zen Buddhism,* ed. Steven Heine and Dale S. Wright (Oxford, UK: Oxford University Press, 2000), 75–109.

60. On predicting death, see Faure, *Rhetoric,* 184–187.

61. On Zen and Buddhist Romanticism, see David L. McMahan, *The Making of Buddhist Modernism* (Oxford, UK: Oxford University Press, 2008), Chapter 5.

62. See James J. DiCenzo, review of *The Ground of the Image* by Jean-Luc Nancy, trans. Jeff Fort (New York: Fordham University Press, 2005), in *Journal of the American Academy of Religions* 75, no. 3 (2007): 709.

34

Transporting Mormonism

Railroads and Religious Sensation in the American West

DAVID WALKER

Railroads offered media of religious sensation in Utah during the nineteenth century. Railroad productions and promotions framed sites of religious encounter and expectation, and they sourced popular knowledge about Mormon lands and culture. In order to justify the occupation and incorporation of Zion, railroads helped construct "religion" in the West.

This chapter tracks trainside observations of Mormonism and argues that they instantiate generative relationships among modern industry, tourism, and religion. Through analysis of company pamphlets, travel guides, letters, church promotions, and the built environment, I demonstrate that railroads helped to create religion by guiding its imagination and platforming its debate. Railroad agents developed new "senses" of religion—new understandings of the term and new prompts by which to identify it—by molding instances of religious "sensationalism." They plotted new locations of interest with new arguments for on-site empirical potential. And they mobilized religious publics, ritualizing interfaith encounters while circumscribing affective expectations. Such products and processes served multiple ends, but a common effect was to secure the place of religion—and Mormonism—in modernity.

Terms of Embarkation

A note on terms is in order. When I refer to railroad literature and media in general, I mean the types of pamphlets published and distributed along train routes, often by passenger departments, generally to promote side trips and stopovers in Utah. I am interested in the package tours developed by railroad agents and in the things developed to sustain them: attractions, news reports, and so forth. Settlement guides and real estate agents enter into the story, too, and they play an important role in the dynamics of interest. But in general I am treating a literature of short-term imagination and round-trip consideration—and thus of "tourism."

Tourism, as I consider it here, is a complex arrangement supporting observation and imagination between different groups within an ever-differentiating society. Dean MacCannell has written that "sightseeing is a ritual performed to the differentiations of society." I take this to mean that, insofar as changes in demographics, economics, and territory (for instance) effect divisions of rank, labor, or place, sightseeing rituals attend to intercategorical spaces, allowing for their intellectual if not functional reduction. Tourist arrangements enable people to devise new theories of humanity capable of integrating new or newly posited differences. Whereas, then, the American incorporation of far-flung Utahn lands required the special theorizing and sensationalizing of "religion" there, Western industrialists, sightseers, and Mormons worked jointly to that end. This occurred especially in the post–Civil War era, after the transcontinental railroad's completion (1869), around the time when The Church of Jesus Christ of Latter-day Saints officially abandoned polygamy (1890), and during Utah's transition to statehood (1896).[1]

The literature, sites, and technologies of Utahn tourism inhabited the spaces between coarticulated forms of religion and irreligion in America, and they created new spaces in which people could think about the terms of articulation and the extents of their application. Tourism is a process *of* differentiation even as it enacts attention *to* differentiation. It is a ritual act of consciousness paid to, and paid within, processes of social distinction and expansion. And in this case tourism was component to the identification of religion in and around Utah.

Terms of Encounter

Railroads' missionary, religion-identifying efforts were not unique to the Great Basin. Having connected lands and markets throughout the West, railroad agents worked also to delineate the geographies and cultures encountered there and to promote tourism and settlement along train routes, among groups.[2] These efforts were neither selfless nor innocent. In railroad media the historian encounters a type of marketing language, warts and all. What is most interesting, in the present instance, is the effect of this marketing language in shaping popular understandings of Mormonism, Western religions, and religion itself.

Positioning itself somewhere between alarmist exposés of Mormonism and Mormon apologetics, most Utahn railroad literature endeavored to keep alive a rhetoric of curiosity and distinctiveness while taking care not to scare away potential non-Mormon tourists and settlers. Authors and agents found this literature to be a space of sensational promise and imperative. The maximizing of passenger traffic in and through Utah necessitated that its religious curiosities be rendered newly visible and visitable. Religions—at least unusual religions—needed to be made objects of touristic visitation. And tourists needed to be enticed by opportunities to debate and discover the stuff of religion in situ.[3]

Railroad literature served these ends by strategically focusing on the geographical and material cultures of Mormonism and by tethering there the sensory expectations of observers. Meanwhile, railroad agents engaged in a type of domesticating comparison between Mormons and other religious groups. Thus they fashioned themselves "ethnographers" as they fashioned—for themselves and others—"religion." Railroad platforms, by their construction, became sites of religious reflection and definition. And Mormons, for their part, forged around them a terrain of mutual benefit. Rather than eradicating or diminishing religion (in general) or Mormonism (in particular), Western railroads helped to create them—and to create modes of their social incorporation—in the world. They did so by occasioning new means of religious encounter and shaping new media by which to consider encounters as such.[4]

Sally Promey has written about Protestantism and modernity's difficulties in coming to grips with the persistent materiality of religion. In her words, "Part of the narrative and theoretical/theological work of both modernization and the Reformation concerned a process of disenchantment of the material universe in favor of 'spiritual' transformation." The "weight" of secularization theory "settled disproportionately on the material practice of religion," just as Protestantism sought to sink "Catholic" or "fetishistic" iconolatry. Therefore, "if Western modernity's narration left any space for religion, its developmental trajectory had to progress from fetishistic engagement to abstract thought, from material involvements and practices to 'belief.'"[5] But narration is one thing and practice quite another. Continues Promey: "From the start these narratives have been insufficient to contain the ways people *actually*" practice religion, including modern Protestants: materially and persistently. Iconoclasm and secularization theories tried to make certain practices seem more than material while making others appear less than spiritual or less than rational. For through such balancing equations Protestants and modernists sought the enchantments of disenchantment and the material comforts of abstraction.[6]

The present project takes shape between the terms of modernity's equations, exploring further the mobilization of interstitial industries in order to better understand their religious work(s). Railroad tourism is a complicating instance of religion-making from the perspective of Reformed theories or for those maintaining inverse proportionalities between modern industry and religious practice. But it challenges even their critics to explore new loci for the theoretical and material constructions of modern religion. After all, the question that occupied nineteenth-century tourists, capitalists, and Mormons remains germane: what is to be made of an industry that promotes religious observation in the world and that maintains a space for religion—

or for peculiar religion—precisely on the grounds of its manifold materiality and visitability?

One argument would be that this was an instance of anti-type manufacturing in America: that, by presenting Mormonism *in site* and *in stuff,* the tourist industry set up an "other" for many Americans, thus forging an opponent for the type of "us-versus-them" discussion necessary to sustain modernist ruptures from premodern things. Dean MacCannell has argued that tourist sites have the ability to organize positive and negative social sentiments and that they can "establish in [people's] consciousness the definition and boundary of modernity by rendering concrete and immediate that which modernity is not." Like something set in amber or a museum unto itself—the "mountain walled treasury of the Gods" was how one railroad company consistently referred to Utah—Mormonism, by this model, might have been the materialistic antitype against which tourists reconceived their own modernity, progress, and religion.[7]

There is considerable truth to this argument; railroads did mobilize an antiquarian market, with all attendant disgusts and desires. But I want also to stress the messiness of the process on the ground—and the productivity of that messiness. For in the rituals of railroading tourism we see the necessary flip side of a phenomenon described elsewhere by Frits Staal in his studies of Vedic practice. Rather than "meaninglessness" or an absence of semantic content, there was in tourism an overabundance of meaning—an excess of meaning produced through the proliferation of semantic opportunities and the multiplication of possible decisions. Railroad agents "put Mormonism into discourse," to twist a phrase from Foucault, and they did so in new ways: by compiling and distributing data on Mormonism, by highlighting Mormon sites and artifacts, by encouraging ethnographic encounters, and by applauding debates and speculations. Meanings and determinations were neither fixed nor absent in this system; nor were they unidirectional, the net gain of "The Mormon" as discursive object notwithstanding. Tourism literature guided readers' eyes and bodies to the material culture and geography of Mormonism, true, but it struck a less prescriptive pose when asking about Mormon religiousness, inviting tourists to render their own judgment. And dotted parameters proved variously productive places.[8]

As a structure, tourism established spaces and languages through which people debated the wobbling pivots of religion relative to the fixed materials of Mormonism. The conversations were guided, but the determinations were multiple.

Railroad Lenses

To make religion visible in Utah, railroad agents shaped a distinctive line of sight. Distinctive but not unprecedented; train-era travel writers followed the example of certain prerailroad tourists and ethnographers—Sir Richard Francis Burton foremost among them—by repopularizing their tone and extending their imagination to a larger traveling public. New authors framed a similar touristic common ground by focusing on Mormon geography, Mormon comparability, and Mormon materiality.[9]

As for geography, railroad guides spoke of the peculiar beauty of the Salt Lake Valley and the Wasatch Mountains, and they suggested that religious response was a natural, if sometimes also volatile and problematic, reaction to their encounter. Consider one 1870 guidebook's description of Weber Canyon, the gorge through which the railroad entered Utah from the East. It feels like "the portal to some enchanted region," the author wrote. In this respect it was characteristic of a broader Rocky Mountain environment in which "everywhere there is something to arrest the eye, to strike the imagination, and to remind one of the wisdom and infinite power of the Architect who built up the mountain-crests and rent their sides with profoundest chasms."[10] But there was something especially impressive about Utahn valleys and canyons—namely that they embodied, in paradigmatic and provocative form, a combination of awe, sublimity, and "curiosity."[11] Echo and Weber Canyons, in particular, were full of rocks jumbled, cracked, or eroded such that many assumed "a supernatural likeness to something not in the least heavenly." Among "towers and spires, turrets and domes," for example, there were the "Witches' Rocks" (Figure 34.1), which, "weird and wild-looking" as they were, "w[ore] a fanciful resemblance to those dreaded and much-abused 'powers' of a dark age of ignorance and superstition."[12] Utah could be—or could be imagined to be—the natural home to religious sentiments both lofty and low.

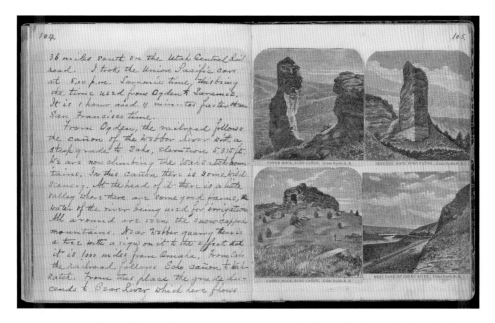

FIGURE 34.1. Clipped Weber Canyon scenes, in [unknown], "Diary of a Voyage" (1874–1875). Yale Collection of Western Americana, Beinecke Rare Book and Manuscript Library, Yale University, New Haven, CT.

With respect to religion and emotional response, guidebooks presented Utahn topographies as predictably affective even if unpredictably effective. Railroads expected that some travelers, by focusing on the sublime, would reflect deeply upon divine wisdom, infinite power, grace, beauty, or the like, even as they imagined that others, by focusing on the curious, might invest rocks with "shallower" or more superstitious attributes. In any case, canyon encounters afforded modern travelers insights into the forms and functions of religious sentiment as guidebooks invited tourists to imagine other people, in times near and far, having had similar reactions in the same places.[13]

Thus primed for better understanding and more active consideration, travelers and readers were reminded of Mormons' 1847 trek through these and the nearby Wasatch canyons. It was only natural that Brigham Young would have paused there to preach to his westward-bound followers, the guidebooks said. In fact, they invented a place for the pause: railroad agents helped to develop the notion that Pulpit Rock (Figure 34.2), so named because of its shape, was the site of an inspirational sermon by Brigham Young. There is no evidence for the claim, but no matter; the resignification of the landform allowed for the better signposting of religion and religious expression in the West. Railroads built an observation deck—quite literally, at the rear of the train—from which tourists could experience religion or conceive of experience. ("Pulpit Rock . . . is on our right hand; we can almost touch it," exclaimed one guidebook.) Moreover, they urged travelers to refocus on Mormonism itself, in anticipation of Salt Lake arrivals, by planting this seed of inquiry: whether Young's words, imaginatively situated atop a fantastic rock amidst otherwise striking scenery, were themselves lofty and divine or curious and superstitious. In Mormonism, did a godly but strange environment effect responses that were more godly than strange or more strange than godly?[14]

If trains taught tourists to safely "play Mormon," guiding them to and along precipices of saintly significance, they also taught them to "play ethnographic," recalling for them the importance of comparison amid pilgrimage and exploration. In particular, at moments and places like these, railroad authors found occasion to cite their travel-writing predecessor Richard F. Burton. Looking down on "the Holy Valley of the West" in 1860, Burton had written that "the pilgrim emigrants, like the hajjis of Mecca and Jerusalem, give vent [there] to the emotions long pent up within their bosoms by sobs and tears, laughter and congratulations, psalms and hysterics. It is indeed no wonder that . . . the ignorant should fondly believe that the 'Spirit of God pervades the very atmosphere,' and that Zion on the tops of the mountains is nearer heaven than other parts of the earth." A few train-era guides reproduced this passage in its entirety, making of it a kind of disciplinary homage. And most retained its topographical sentimentality and notion of taxonomic similarity between Mormonism and Christianity's other "others," Islam and Judaism.[15]

FIGURE 34.2. William Henry Jackson, "No. 104. Pulpit Rock," showing "mouth of Echo Canon where it is said Brigham Young preached his first Sermon in Utah." In Nineteenth-Century Western Stereo-View Collection, 1865–1899, box 1, folder 6, Special Collections and Archives, Merrill-Cazier Library, Utah State University, Logan.

Railroad guides commonly compared the Great Basin and Mormonism to lands of ancient religious significance and to the cultures supposedly rooted there, both ancient and contemporary. They catered to an audience eager to emulate Burton, in part—to an audience excited by the fact that, in the words of one traveler, "the Trans-Continental Railroad has brought within easy reach a land as full of fascination as ever the scenes of Arabian Nights were to our youthful ears." Trains opened worlds ripe with sensory possibilities: of sights and sounds both modern and nostalgic and of opportunities for the physical approximation (if not sensual embrace) of religious others. It was a presumptively robust environment, expectations for which remained high notwithstanding the sometimes subdued, sometimes exuberant, variously ocularcentric or full-bodied articulations of the same travel writers. Railroads carried clients pleased by the notion that modern means had enabled modern people (in the aforecited traveler's words) to "see the curiosities" and observe "freaks of nature" for themselves.[16]

With respect to some questions implicit in such expectations, however, most guidebook authors catered to their audience obliquely and strategically. They did not say whether Mormons were themselves freaks of nature or whether religion was a freakish or natural thing to find in modernity. They did not dwell on Mormon polygamy, either, even though "harems" and "Asiatic sexualities" preoccupied youthful Orientalists and peripatetic comparativists alike. And they did not posit exact genealogical relations between peoples or places. But in all senses they hinted at analytical possibilities yielded through comparison of Utah's arid lands and salty waters to others in the Middle East. Railroads continually (re)moved geography and environment to the forefront of religious consideration, circumscribing sensory expectations while connecting sites of excitement.

Railroads were early and influential promoters of the "America's Dead Sea" motif, for example, and they frequently spoke of the "oriental air" breathed in Salt Lake Valley settlements.[17] Similarly, the Rio Grande Western Railway developed a sketch—a map, rather—to make visual their implications of religious parallelism and the significance of topography and to invite further reflection on the likeness of groups gathered in comparable atmospheres. The "Promised Land" map (Figure 34.3), published in 1891 and reproduced frequently after that, showed geographical similarities between Canaan and "Deseret," or the Mormon Great Basin area.[18]

Maps are never territory, but the visual lie of this particular map—the cartographic similarity created by inverting and exaggerating aspects of Palestinian topography—was a lie in the direction of comparison and material consideration. Here epitomizing the railroad-era trend of evocative cultural geography, the Rio Grande Railway's map stood in for (and replaced) textual assertions of religious heritage, Semitic or otherwise. Its seemingly documentary observations of the "striking comparison" and "compar[able] cut" between "the Holy Land and Utah" enticed readers to explorations and empirical discoveries of their own, on a domestic counterpart to Middle Eastern pilgrimage.[19]

FIGURE 34.3. "The Promised Land!," a map published by the Rio Grande Western Railway. Author's collection.

Travel guides pointed to material factors from which readers might draw their own (mediated) conclusions about religious culture and cultivation in America. Thus reported one Rio Grande guide: "On an eminence overlooking the picturesque valley of the Jordan, the modern metropolis, Salt Lake City, has been built, with its broad streets, its odd shaped Tabernacle, its great Temple . . . and its quaint buildings and edifices." All of this "furnishes profitable speculation in the odd and mysterious," it said, just as (according to a different Rio Grande writer) the "striking similarity in the topography [between] this region and the 'Promised Land of Canaan' . . . furnishes much food for thought." Salt Lake City "has the breath of age, commingled with an atmosphere of comfort and modern amelioration."[20]

There is indeed "food for thought" here: Utah was presented as a site of comfort with a "breath of age" or, alternately, as a site of age with modern updates. It was a place of oddness within similarity, in any case, and of abundant opportunity for "profitable speculation." The speculations that were encouraged by railroad agents were not just of the economic and mineral sort but of the humanistic variety as well. Railroads prompted Americans to become mobile students of culture, with culture—and with religion—located somewhere in the space between Utah's mountains and its "broad streets."[21]

Tabernacles, Temples, Pavilions, and Gutters

Once travelers reached Salt Lake City—once they were ensconced in the ostensibly natural environment of Mormonism—they were guided through Mormonism's built environment as well. Here the search for religion assumed new urgency if not new direction as tourists looked for additional expressions of a religiosity already associated with geography. Motivated by the notion that it could be everywhere or nowhere, visitors looked to find religion in Mormon architecture, infrastructure, and urban planning.

Mormon religious culture might arguably be found in the Salt Lake Tabernacle. The Tabernacle was the site of Sunday services and important church events, and it was an impressive structure in its own right: a massive auditorium capable of seating several thousand people, covered by an apparently unsupported dome, with extraordinary acoustics and featuring one of America's largest organs. Travel guides encouraged its visitation in the interest of architectural curiosity and ethnographic understanding alike. Some authors, though, warned readers that they would likely hear as much there about agriculture and politics as about rituals and theology: "Every possible thing," from crop cultivation to infant baptism, "is discussed from the pulpit which the president thinks necessary for the instruction of the flock," wrote one, noting also that banners celebrating Mormon agricultural and demographic fertility were commonplace. But still they let tourists decide for themselves whether "secular, "mundane" talk and displays constituted, belied, or coexisted with LDS religiosity.[22]

If more fanciful aspects of Mormon religion were to be found inside the Salt Lake Temple, passenger agents, journalists, and tourists generally encountered problems. The Temple was under construction until 1893, so until then they spoke of it in the abstract, the hypothetical, and the future tenses, all the while relying on the imaginations and prospectuses of others, sometimes reprinting sketches provided to them by church representatives. Indeed, both before and after 1893, guidebooks spoke mostly of the Temple's unique outer design, using architectural nouns familiar from preceding Weber Canyon descriptions. (Its "towers and turrets" are "of a very complex order," said one.) But relative to the canyon chapters they left implications of witchcraft off the page here. Guidebooks spoke of Temple matters external and observable, because non-Mormons could not get inside. And their discussions were short (Figure 34.4).[23]

By contrast, railroad agents had much to report about the goings-on at a different church-run facility opened in 1893: Saltair (Figure 34.5). Saltair was a bathing pavilion, water park, retreat center, and dance hall situated on the Great Salt Lake, a short train ride from the Mormon city center. Travel writers had long touted the Salt

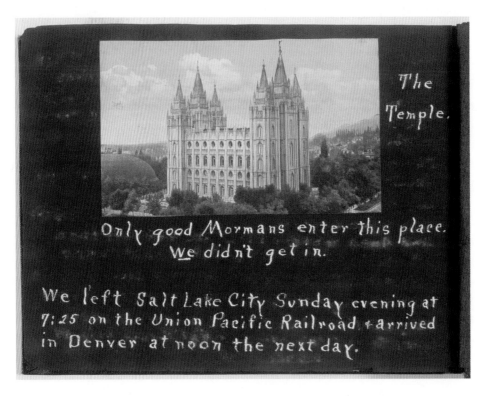

FIGURE 34.4. "The Temple. Only good Mormans [sic] enter this place. *We* didn't get in." Image in 1922 travel diary coverage of the Salt Lake Temple. Autry Library, Autry National Center, Los Angeles; MSA.9.

Lake environs as a great sanitarium of sorts; it had enough fresh air, pleasant weather, hot springs, and mineral baths to rejuvenate the nation's infirm, they said. But among health and pleasure resorts Saltair was uniquely attractive by virtue of its size, appearance, clientele, and Mormon mystique. Like the Temple, it was a fantastic construction: it had towers, "arabesque" minarets, and a central dome, and "when the Pavilion is lighted in the evening with over 1200 electric lights, the whole effect is simply beyond the power of words to portray." There were few better places to consider the curious splendors of Utah than this, a sparkling "Moorish" theme park on "the Dead Sea of America." When tourists could not get into the Temple, they were encouraged to make a day trip to Saltair, where Mormons and non-Mormons could interact and enjoy the healthful climate together (Figure 34.6). Guidebooks invited visitation with eyes open and bathing suits on: "Come and see it for yourself—your verdict must confirm all that has been said, and you will say that the half has not been told."[24]

Railroad writers more actively asserted the religiosity of a different "mundane" fact of Salt Lake life. This was the Mormon waterworks and irrigation system. By guidebooks' accounting, Utahn canals and gutters were special sites of outdoor, extra-ecclesiastical, and thus easily observable correspondence between the natural and built environments of Mormonism. As such they were clear avenues for religious reflection and memory. A Rio Grande Railway guide was typical in the terms and order

FIGURE 34.6. Bathing at Saltair. Yale Collection of Western Americana, Beinecke Rare Book and Manuscript Library, Yale University, New Haven, CT.

of its reporting. It spoke of bathing resorts, pointed tourists to the "turtle-roofed Tabernacle and white granite walls and towers of the Temple," and then ruminated on the grounds around them: "The gutters, or rather, the ditches, carry streams of pure, clear mountain water, which serves to irrigate the gardens, lawns and enclosures, and to these trenches is due the luxuriant growth of trees, flowers, plants and bushes which give Salt Lake City the appearance of one vast park and flower garden. The streets are beautifully clean, especially in the residence portion, and there is an oriental air about the city which carries one back to the banks of the Biblical Jordan, and is unlike that of any other city in the Union."[25] Observations of canals led to appreciations of public decorum, evocations of biblical topography, and reiterations of religious notoriety.

So was Mormon religious culture to be found somewhere in the gutters, streets, and flowers of Salt Lake City? Guidebooks raised the possibility with provocative intent, coupling there the implications of cultural geography with hints of geographical determination in Mormon life. Second to mentions of mountainous beauty and its corresponding awe, then, deterministic links are most apparent in railroad discussions of Mormon agriculturalism and town planning, in which guidebook authors voiced what soon became a common refrain—namely, that the arid lands had required water and that Mormons had effectively invented modern irrigation practices, even as they hybridized older social patterns complementary to the task, such as close-knit villages and communally oriented trade. Mormons were first and foremost an agricultural people, according to this refrain; they were industrious but not industrialized. Thus guidebooks described irrigation as a defining and enabling feature of Utahn settlement, and by their work canals became metonyms for Mormonism itself. Each was a cultural product of a peculiar environment, each sustaining questionably religious and arguably nonindustrial phenomena.[26]

Mormons were *who* they were because of *where* they were. They were contained, or at least containable; and they comported themselves in ways intelligible to the Gilded Age traveler based, if not on agrarian remembrance, on en route readings and alpine encounters. According to these guidebooks, Mormonism occurred within a geography, it imagined a geography, and it could be understood in terms of that geography. It was still a matter of open inquiry "whether Mormonism be a religion or not," one book declared to its readers. But the railroads would tell them where they might find it; they would help them to see it; and they would give them platforms, itincraries, and words with which to get there, play ethnographic, and decide for themselves.[27] Admittedly both Mormonism and religion remained somewhat elusive by this system of instruction, even in their Utahn ubiquity, for neither of them had a single reliable or comprehensive residence. But each was made also—if not predominantly—in the acts and discourses of looking for them (Figure 34.7).

FIGURE 34.7. Places to look for religion, in [unknown], "Diary of a Voyage," 1874–1875. Yale Collection of Western Americana, Beinecke Rare Book and Manuscript Library, Yale University, New Haven, CT.

Mormon Materialities

Tourism not only offered outsiders ways of thinking about Mormonism; it also gave the LDS Church new tools and powers by which to guide conversations in ways befitting its own self-image and institutional longevity. Rather than being a passive object of touristic imagination and literary framing, the LDS Church used and redeployed railroad materials for its own purposes, and it helped shape the terms of their creation in the first place. Indeed church officials negotiated Mormon culture and identity with railroad agents, in time forging a terrain of mutual promotion, benefit, and intelligibility.

Brigham Young and other LDS Church officials made and remade Mormonism itself by, for, and through the railroad age. Young used the occasion of railroad arrival to define an orthodox Mormonism and to institute many of the social programs and postures with which people now associate it. The most obvious example is the ban on coffee and alcohol consumption. Although they dated back to 1830s church dietary codes, the drinking norms gained broad traction and attention only in the late 1860s, when they were advanced as part of an initiative to help new Saints emigrate to Utah over the railroads. Quite simply, Utahn church members were asked to stop drinking coffee and alcohol, to save the money they would have spent on them, and to donate that money to the church so that the church could then buy railway tickets, enticing emigrants and maintaining demographic predominance in Utah.[28]

Less familiar but also consequential for the formation of Mormon orthodoxy was another train-era occurrence: the dispute between Brigham Young and the Mormon "Godbeite" faction regarding church economic priorities and industrial involvements. Young, on the eve of transcontinental railway construction and with an eye to its potentially disruptive effects on territorial trade systems and prices, instituted new mercantile associations among the Saints. William S. Godbe, a Salt Lake City merchant, opposed the measure: he and his compatriots argued for church divestment from "secular" business affairs, and they advocated mining and laissez-faire economics over farming and the regulated, in-group sale of "home manufactures." The debate precipitated the excommunication of the Godbeite party, but it led also to the formalization of recognizably "mainline" LDS priorities respecting "'agrarianism." Their terms are already familiar here. But reintroduction in this context nuances any assumption that railroads' materialistic casts were religiously constraining, at least to Mormon orthodoxy. For, crucially, LDS Church leaders found it occasionally advantageous to embrace and reassert the language of basic Mormon communitarianism, agriculturalism, and nonindustrialization in the railroad era, even as they invested in and incorporated themselves into industry. Such "strategically essentialist" language worked simultaneously against Godbeite ascension and toward touristic attention. By recasting Mormonism's communalist ethos in a more industrial mode, the LDS Church selectively (if paradoxically) offset, managed, and effected American incorporation.[29]

Church leaders took out labor contracts with the major railroad companies, the yields of which were considerable. By keeping such contracts in-house, first of all, the LDS Church limited the numbers of non-Mormon laborers employed to work the lines—thus, again, maintaining demographic predominance. More importantly, though, the proceeds were used to fund internal improvements, cultural initiatives, church branding, and the material upbuilding of Mormondom. Railroad efforts enabled the expansion of Mormon material culture through sites and specifics for which tourists were prepared.[30]

The LDS Church built and operated its own branch railroads to connect with the transcontinentals. The first of these, completed in January 1870, was the Utah Central, which ran between Salt Lake City and Ogden, and soon afterward there were the Utah Southern, extending south from Salt Lake City; the Utah Northern, extending north from Ogden; and others. Brigham Young was president and director of the Utah Central Railroad, his son Joseph was general superintendent, and the LDS Church itself (with Brigham Young as trustee-in-trust) was majority stockholder. Another of Young's sons, John W., presided over the Utah Northern Railroad. With proceeds from this latter enterprise—combined with some $50,000 earned from transcontinental contracts—John W. Young constructed and managed tourist attractions near railroad termini. The Deseret Museum (est. 1869) was one of these, and another was the Salt Lake bathing resort Lake Side (1870).[31]

Saltair was built later, in an 1890s flurry of prestatehood touristic efforts by another group of Mormon businessmen. Like that of John W. Young before them, theirs was a two-pronged project of industry and promotion. The Saltair group constructed the Saltair Railway (later the Salt Lake and Los Angeles Railway) to connect their resort to the city so that they might more easily transport Mormon and Gentile tourists between them. Company board members and LDS officials similarly imagined Saltair to be an "advertising agent" for the territory's "name and fame"; it was to be the "Coney Island of the West," they said, albeit with a more family-centered and wholesome aesthetic. Their promotional language generally stressed familiarity and fun over strangeness, and, in contrast to travel guides, it reserved adjectives of curiosity for conditions of salinity. But architectural decisions belied the distinction with implications of a broader cultural exoticism. Architect Richard K. A. Kletting adorned Saltair with minarets, domes, and arabesque towers, and, in the words of one *Deseret News* reporter, his "semi-Moorish architectural line" evoked "a delightful oriental dream" (Figure 34.8). Although the church's "Coney Island" evinced a larger prestatehood, post-polygamy climate of Mormon accommodation to (and within) American culture, then, accommodation occurred via the deployment of extant touristic modes, means, and motifs: resorts, railroads, Moorish design, and implied

FIGURE 34.8. "Pavilion, Saltair Beach [the 'Coney Island of the West'], Salt Lake, Utah," showing train tracks. Yale Collection of Western Americana, Beinecke Rare Book and Manuscript Library, Yale University, New Haven, CT.

Orientalism.[32] The church thus accepted and incorporated a particular touristic type of Mormon imagination.

Saltair's "architectural line" points in several useful and evocative directions, given its present purposes. The fact that Mormons—their own contentious historical relationship with polygamy notwithstanding—built in a style of "semi-Moorish" exotica then associated with Islam and harems is intelligible in at least two novel respects, given the terms and techniques of tourism. First, though it was long component to anti-Mormon literature and sentiment, Orientalism also offered interpretive possibilities less overtly or unidirectionally anti-Mormon by participating in the development of "less theological conceptualizations of religion" capable of giving Mormonism "a place at the table of American religions."[33] Touristic Orientalism—itself a combination of imperialist exoticization, Enlightenment analysis, and ethnographic imperative—coincided with the retheorizing of materials and geographies in and around religion, and thus with new sensational possibilities. Mormons recognized that fact, and, second, they saw the advantage of embracing Moorish motifs moreover reminiscent of sacred architecture and, indeed, harems. For in publicly displaying them they appropriated also a critique of otherness and aberrant sensuality, sanitizing it in an age, area, and act of transportation. It was no coincidence, after all, that the LDS

Church most actively embraced Moorish architectural themes at the same time that it was reconsidering and phasing out polygamy, that is, during the late 1880s and 1890s. And it was no coincidence that the church did so mainly in areas designed to be tourist attractions—in this case an amusement park and a sanitarium. Thanks in large part to prior acts by Richard F. Burton and his railroading followers, the "open secret" of (past or present) polygamy could be framed there in a way that seemed, if not altogether less dangerous, local and approachable. Saltair's design was a winkingly self-conscious affair; it catered to certain imaginations while also memorializing, historicizing, and replacing them. Attentive to expectations that "modernity" would "liberalize" and "domesticate" Utah, Mormon promoters encouraged intergroup observation and approximation, and they demanded of their visitors speculation in the nature of American religion.

Meanwhile, as some people worked thus along the lake, the Deseret Agricultural and Manufacturing Society—members of which partook in the Godbeite purge— hosted agricultural fairs in the city, applauded its irrigation systems, and praised the (arguably) simple, peaceful, farming orientation of the Mormon people. Society groups and Sunday schools made banners and displays for the Tabernacle, too, and they adorned them with images of mountain valleys, announcements of agricultural yields, memorials of Joseph Smith, and church slogans. "Utah's Best Crop" was Utah's children, declared one of them, in a humorous play on assumptions of Mormon fertility. Collectively the decorations implied that the Great Basin was Mormonism's promised land: that its families had domesticated its wilderness and that its farmers had made its deserts bloom like roses.[34] Utah manifested a golden age in the Gilded Age.

This was the story behind the Tabernacle displays mentioned in some guidebooks' warnings—and some tourists' reviews—of "secular" Sunday presentations. Through them mainline LDS agents argued, to self-justifying and self-congratulatory effect, that proper Mormon settlement had conquered once bleak and barren lands. And through them they also worked, alongside and behind railroad writers, to advance Utah–Holy Land parallels and their industries of observation. This was not the sort of proselytization generally associated with Mormon missionaries; the LDS Church abstained from active evangelization of visitors until 1902, six years after Utah achieved statehood. Nor was it the type of religious practice that some visitors expected. But it was a significant corporate phenomenon nonetheless: such decorations offset stereotypes of Utahn sexual chaos by substituting visions of a differently domestic, arguably urbane, and yet partially rural order, and they demonstrated cultural refinements of a sort informed by geography and effected by industry. In short, they elevated and forefronted signs for which tourists were primed, notwithstanding the occasional disappointment evoked by their encounter.[35]

The church invited non-Mormon ministers to visit on trains and to preach in the Tabernacle, on a pulpit near banners of the sort mentioned above. LDS Church members were encouraged to attend these events, and subsequent Sunday school sessions helped to explain the visitors' words and to compare Mormonism with whatever sects they represented. LDS Church Historian George A. Smith wrote in November 1869 that, since the construction of the transcontinental railroad, "We have had more clergymen of different denominations preach in our Tabernacle than for several years previous, and it has given our people an excellent chance to compare our religion with that of other denominations." Again, in 1871: "We know no better way to show our people the superiority of their faith than by having them see the contrast."[36] The church thus used the tourism industry for self-promotion, using railroads and their literature as levers for strategic religious comparisons of their own. They invited visitors, and they shaped their stays.

The interdependence of Utahn railroads and Utah-based orthodox Mormonism grew over time. It was not long before agents from both sectors joined in the development of package tours in and around Salt Lake City, with railroad agents providing cheap transportation and lodging while church groups led tours of Mormonism's sights. Each used the literature and the infrastructure of the other—"The Promised Land" image, for example, was reprinted widely by the LDS Church press—and both agreed on a baseline for cultural promotion and the objects of religious consideration in terms of material culture and geography. Both agreed tacitly, also, that the enticement to Utahn visitation was foremost among tasks; on-site decisions and promotions were seen as a separate, more open field of possibility.[37]

Railroading Termini

Increasingly through the transition to statehood—and especially after the announcement of polygamy's discontinuance, in 1890—railroad guides encouraged readers to visit Salt Lake City not with a fearful eye for Mormon curiosities but with a hopeful eye for Mormons' contributions to and absorption within a common American culture. They invited visitors not to consider Salt Lake City a distant hothouse of curios but to come to Utah with an eye for architectural and material curiosity nevertheless. In short, they encouraged readers to appreciate the material culture of Mormonism. And perhaps more than that: they encouraged readers—through the alignment of irrigation imagery with Promised Land metaphors, for example—to appreciate the material accomplishments through which Mormons had domesticated and shaped the same topography that (arguably) informed their religiosity. Mormonism retained hints and reminders of a primitive naturism, but it also manifested modes of natural subjugation necessary to modern national growth.

The guidebooks dwelled at length on accomplishments in the realms of architecture and urban planning. The Tabernacle was one of the world's great wonders, and so was (or would be) the Temple. The streets were lined with trees and irrigation ditches, and Brigham Young's houses were worth seeing. These things may have been the sites of theocratic practice in the prerailroad days of geographical isolation but no longer. Now they were relics, of a sort, of an older Mormonism: the Mormonism of Utah's pioneers, a class fading from view. Railroads, by their own accounts, had opened the geography and material culture of Mormonism to widespread enjoyment and visitation, and they invited a kind of retrospective appreciation of Mormon pioneers through their maps and materials.

Thanks to the intervention of the railroads, said their guides, the Mormon Promised Land would persist more as a cartographic and promotional fact than as a political one. Salt Lake City could be safely packaged as a curious but harmless model of alternative social formation, one arguably premodern but now situated within modernity, all the while holding a mirror to look back at its premodern form—one formerly isolated and unknown but now open to transportation and comparison and one inviting the development of shared space and shared American identity. The railroads worked to bring visitors to a land of promised religion and religious promise so that they might think hard about where the "religion" was and what its "promise" would be. And this was an effort in which many Mormons participated. LDS Church members performed harmonious myths of origin and identity, and they designed new material platforms for mutual Mormon–tourist observation.

Thus did the focus on the material culture of Mormonism support a variety of social, political, and definitional moves around the insecure pivot of religion. The structures of tourism were fairly stable, and so were its terms. So what was under debate was the degree to which the materiality of Mormonism constituted or precluded its religiosity. Some clearly intended the "move to material" and the "focus on geography" as a mode of containment. Some intended it as a mode of eulogy or posthumous appreciation. Some used it as a lever to posit multiple Mormonisms. And others used the occasion to retheologize and expand Mormonism's material holdings. The point is that none of it was automatic, immediate, or given. None of it was innocent or neutral, either. What *was* clear was that railroad platforms were platforms of religious definition, of religious theory making, and of religion making. Tourism, then, was an industry of religion.

NOTES

    1. Dean MacCannell, *The Tourist: A New Theory of the Leisure Class* (Berkeley: University of California Press, 1999 [1976]), 13. John Urry, in *The Tourist Gaze: Leisure and Travel in Contemporary Societies* (Thousand Oaks, CA: Sage, 1990), is likewise concerned with the sensory mechanisms of short-term encounters. Studies of religion *and* tourism include the recent Michael Stausberg, *Religion and Tourism: Crossroads, Destinations and Encounters* (New York: Routledge, 2011), with which I agree that "tourism, far from being the other of religion, is a major arena, context and medium for religion in the contemporary global world" (8). Respecting religion and modern industry, I am influenced by the argument of Richard J. Callahan Jr., Kathryn

Lofton, and Chad E. Seales that "religion and industry," being "codependent as institutional bodies, as social organizers, and as moral vantages for national life," work together to "regulate bodies—geological, demographic, and biological—and fit them into the requisite disciplines of modern labor and consumption"; see their "Allegories of Progress: Industrial Religion in the United States," *Journal of the American Academy of Religion* 78, no. 1 (March 2010): 3–4. A final note on terms: I use "Mormon," "LDS," and "Saints" to refer to The Church of Jesus Christ of Latter-day Saints and members thereof. Consistent with both railroading and Mormon usage, I use "Gentile" to refer to non-Mormons.

2. Many such groups—not just Mormons—engaged in projects of cultural reformation or presentation, along with industrialists and travel agents, to religiously constructive ends.

3. J. Spencer Fluhman most fully analyzes the genres of anti-Mormonism (literary, dramatic, scientific, etc.) in *"A Peculiar People": Anti-Mormonism and the Making of Religion in Nineteenth-Century America* (Chapel Hill: University of North Carolina Press, 2012). Toward the end of his study, Fluhman notes the "dramatically" "benign[]" character of references to Mormonism in many railroad pamphlets, given "the [anti-Mormon] protests still raging in other quarters." Railroad boosters accented "familiarly" while still "[p]reserving enough mystery to pique readers' curiosity." Thereby they "suggested a template for Mormon/non-Mormon cooperation at the turn of the century" (145–146). The present chapter develops this theme via emphasis on railroads' multifront participation in religious template building relative to Mormonism.

4. Leonard Arrington's *Great Basin Kingdom: An Economic History of the Latter-day Saints, 1830–1900* (Cambridge, MA: Harvard University Press, 1958) led the way in studies of the Mormon railroading era. My hope is to go one step further: to appreciation of railroads' role in the creation of Mormonism itself, studying the efforts, by churchmen and railroad agents alike, from the 1870s through 1890s, to promote and repackage Mormonism's infrastructure. For my present purposes, *this* was the aspect and era of Mormonism's most significant transportations. The best single source on Salt Lake City tourism in this era is Thomas K. Hafen, "City of Saints, City of Sinners: The Development of Salt Lake City as a Tourist Attraction, 1869–1900," *Western Historical Quarterly* 28, no. 3 (Autumn 1997): 343–377. I see a more univocal and synthetic tourism inhabiting the first thirty years of railroad presence in Utah than Hafen does, and also a different type of religious production, but his periodic analysis will remain an important foundation and counterpoint to my own.

5. Sally M. Promey, "Hearts and Stones: Material Transformations and the Stuff of Christian Practice in the United States," in *American Christianities: A History of Dominance and Diversity,* ed. Catherine A. Brekus and W. Clark Gilpin (Chapel Hill: University of North Carolina Press, 2011), 209, and Sally M. Promey and Shira Brisman, "Sensory Cultures: Material and Visual Religion Reconsidered," in *The Blackwell Companion to Religion in America,* ed. Phillip Goff (Malden, MA: Wiley-Blackwell, 2010), 180–181.

6. Promey, "Hearts and Stones," 209, italics in original.

7. MacCannell, *The Tourist,* 9. See, for example, P. Donan, *Utah: A Peep into a Mountain-Walled Treasury of the Gods* (Buffalo, NY: Matthews Northrup [for the Rio Grande Western Railway], 1891).

8. Frits Staal, "The Meaninglessness of Ritual," *Numen* 26, no. 1 (June 1979): 2–22. Michel Foucault wrote that nineteenth-century society "put into operation an entire machinery for producing true discourses concerning [sex]," that is, that sex was "put into discourse," in *The History of Sexuality: Volume One, An Introduction,* trans. Robert Hurley (New York: Vintage Books, 1990 [1976]), 69, 11. The above argument might usefully be linked to Sally Promey's work again, too. For I am suggesting that, although tourists and railroads jointly deemed Mormonism a discursive object relevant to Americans' religious and (therefore also) secular self-understandings,

they belied implications of singular comprehension with verbose ambivalence, in part by engaging, vocationally, in (what Promey has provocatively called) the "constant oscillation[s]" of significance vis-à-vis religious materials. Promey, "Hearts and Stones," 209.

9. Richard F. Burton had tried earlier in the 1860s to render intelligible distinctive features of Mormon life without making Mormons themselves seem monstrously "other." Burton's account of his 1860 Utahn travels—*The City of the Saints; and Across the Rocky Mountains to California*—was first published in London (1861) and then in the United States (New York: Harper and Brothers, 1862). On *City of the Saints* as a literary mediation between genres of exposé and apology, see also Eric A. Eliason, "Curious Gentiles and Representational Authority in the City of the Saints," *Religion and American Culture* 11, no. 2 (Summer 2001): 155–190.

10. Nelsons' Pictorial Guide Books, *Salt Lake City, with a Sketch of the Route of the Union and Central Pacific Railroad . . .* (New York: T. Nelson and Sons, 1870), 23, 7.

11. I do not mean to imply that this descriptive combination was unique to Utahn literature; it can be found in other travel literature as well, including romances and apocalypses. I am instead pointing to the ways in which railroad guides and agents inhabited such motifs while inhabiting Utah, that is, how they yoked them to industry and deployed them en route to the (re)production of religion in the modern West. On literary and religious descriptions of nineteenth-century American landscapes, especially those deemed tourist attractions, see, for example, John F. Sears, *Sacred Places: American Tourist Attractions in the Nineteenth Century* (New York: Oxford University Press, 1989).

12. [William Henry Rideing], *The Pacific Railroads, Illustrated* (New York: D. Appleton, 1878), 48; *The Pacific Tourist: Adams and Bishop's Illustrated Trans-Continental Guide . . .* (New York: Adams and Bishop, 1881), 119; and Nelsons' Pictorial Guide Books, *Salt Lake City,* 9–10.

13. Henry Ward Beecher similarly reflected on more and less "refined" considerations at Niagara Falls; see his "Niagara Falls, but Not Described," in *Eyes and Ears* (Boston: Ticknor and Fields, 1863), 173–180.

14. The Pulpit Rock myth, in its railroading iteration, dates to ca. 1869, with the descriptive text accompanying William Henry Jackson's stereo-view photograph "No. 104. Pulpit Rock—mouth of Echo Canon where it is said Brigham Young preached his first Sermon in Utah." Jackson was commissioned by the Union Pacific Railroad to document its construction, and variations of this image and text appeared often in Western travel literature. See, for example, *Crofutt's Trans-Continental Tourist's Guide . . . ,* [vol. 3, 2nd rev.] (New York: George A Crofutt, 1871), 91, and *Sights and Scenes in Utah for Tourists . . .* (Chicago: [Union Pacific Railway], 1888), 35. The in-text parenthetical quotation above is from *Sights and Scenes in Utah.*

15. Burton, *City of the Saints,* 193. See, for example, Nelsons' Pictorial Guide Books, *Salt Lake City,* 23; *The Pacific Tourist,* 120; and George Wharton James, *Utah: The Land of Blossoming Valleys* (Boston, MA: Page, 1922), 11.

16. W[illiam] W[ilson] Ross, *10,000 Miles by Land and Sea* (Toronto: James Campbell and Son, 1876), v–vi. Ross's ocularcentric rephrasing arguably tempered the more robust system of encounter presumed by his earlier statements.

17. Milton R. Ochs, *Heart of the Rockies, Illustrated* ([Denver]. Passenger Department, Rio Grande Western Railway, 1890), 134. Cf. Donan, *Utah,* 90. On Orientalism in popular anti-Mormon literature, see Timothy Marr, *The Cultural Roots of American Islamicism* (New York: Cambridge University Press, 2006), 185–218, and Terryl Givens, "Caricature as Containment: Orientalism, Bondage, and the Construction of Mormon Ethnicity in Nineteenth-Century American Popular Fiction," *Nineteenth-Century Contexts* 18, no. 4 (Winter 1995): 385–403.

18. Donan, *Utah,* map at 82. The "Promised Land" map was sometimes subtitled "A Striking Comparison," "Comparative Cut," or "The Holy Land and Utah" over some twenty years of

use, as in, respectively, *A Pointer to Prosperity, a Few Facts about the Climate and Resources of Utah* . . . (Salt Lake City: Passenger Department, Rio Grande Western Railway, 1896); Denver and Rio Grande Railroad, *What May Be Seen Crossing the Rockies en Route between Ogden, Salt Lake City, and Denver* ([Denver?]: S. K. Hooper, 1905); and *Utah, The Promised Land: A Few Specimen Tours* . . . [Denver: Rio Grande Western Railway, 1895]. Thomas K. Hafen rightly describes such comparisons of the Salt Lake Valley with the Holy Land: whereas "early Mormon settlers had noticed the geographic correspondence" without attempting to "use the resemblance to try and attract visitors[,] Easterners involved in western tourism first employed these similarities to entice commercial travelers during the railroad era." Hafen, "City of Saints, City of Sinners," 352. Jared Farmer, too, has recognized that "it was the Union Pacific and the Denver & Rio Grande—not the LDS Church—that most forcefully advanced the Utah–Holy Land comparisons," in *On Zion's Mount: Mormons, Indians, and the American Landscape* (Cambridge, MA: Harvard University Press, 2008), 163.

19. *A Pointer to Prosperity;* Denver and Rio Grande Railroad, *What May Be Seen Crossing the Rockies; Utah, The Promised Land* (see previous note). Cf. William Smythe, "The Progress of Western America," *Irrigation Age* 6, no. 5 (May 1894): 183. The literature on "Holy Land" pilgrimage and the artistic and textual representation of the Middle East is extensive; so, too, is the historiography of Americans' participation therein. See, for example, Bryan F. Le Beau and Menachem Mor, eds., *Pilgrims and Travelers to the Holy Land* (Omaha, NE: Creighton University Press, 1996); Burke O. Long, *Imagining the Holy Land: Maps, Models, and Fantasy Travels* (Bloomington: Indiana University Press, 2003); and John Davis, *The Landscape of Belief: Encountering the Holy Land in Nineteenth-Century American Art and Culture* (Princeton, NJ: Princeton University Press, 1996).

20. *Sight Places and Resorts in the Rockies: A Brief Preachment* . . . , 5th ed. ([Denver: Passenger Department, Denver and Rio Grande and Rio Grande Western Railways], 1903), 52, and *Utah, The Promised Land.*

21. *Sight Places and Resorts,* 52; *Utah, The Promised Land* .

22. *The Pacific Tourist,* 150.

23. "Salt Lake City and Utah Territory," *Crofutt's Western World* 1, no. 1 (January 1872): 4–5, 12. The author continues: The Temple "is to be the glory of Mormon architecture," but, as in the case of the Endowment House, the building in which Temple ordinances were then administered, "The uses . . . we will not state, because we don't know; the profane may not enter therein."

24. *Utah, The Promised Land.* For a general history of Saltair, see Nancy D. McCormick and John S. McCormick, *Saltair* (Salt Lake City: Bonneville Books, University of Utah Press, 1985). Dale L. Morgan, *The Great Salt Lake* (Indianapolis: Bobbs-Merrill, 1947), Chapter 18, gives an overview and history of Salt Lake resorts.

25. Ochs, *Heart of the Rockies,* 134.

26. See, for example, *Pointer to Prosperity,* 15; *Sights and Scenes in Utah for Tourists,* 9; and Donan, *Utah,* 25. See also Union Pacific Railroad, *Irrigation: Its History, Methods, Statistics and Results* (Saint Louis: Woodward and Tiernan, 1894). On perceptions and myths of Mormon irrigation, compare Leonard J. Arrington and Dean May, "'A Different Mode of Life': Irrigation and Society in Nineteenth-Century Utah," *Agricultural History* 49, no. 1 (January 1975): 3–20, and Donald Worster, "The Kingdom, the Power, and the Water," in Thomas G. Alexander, ed., *Great Basin Kingdom Revisited: Contemporary Perspectives* (Logan: Utah State University Press, 1991), 21–38. For the tourist response to suggestions of religious irrigation, see, for example, Fitz Hugh Ludlow, *The Heart of the Continent* (New York: Hurd and Houghton, 1870), 327–328.

27. *The Pacific Tourist,* 152.

28. Arrington, *Great Basin Kingdom,* 250.

29. On the Godbeite schism, see Ronald W. Walker, *Wayward Saints: The Godbeites and Brigham Young* (Urbana: University of Illinois Press, 1998). The term "mainline," used often in reference to mainstream denominations or orthodox norms, was itself a product of the railroad age. On "strategic essentialism," see Gayatri Chakravorty Spivak, "Subaltern Studies: Deconstructing Historiography," in Spivak, *In Other Worlds: Essays in Cultural Politics* (New York: Methuen, 1987), 205.

30. On church contracts with the Union Pacific and Central Pacific, see Arrington, *Great Basin Kingdom,* 258–270.

31. Arrington, *Great Basin Kingdom,* 270–292; Morgan, *Great Salt Lake,* 353; and Joseph L. Barfoot, "Brief History of the Deseret Museum" (Salt Lake City, 1880), P-F 1, Bancroft Library, University of California, Berkeley. The completion of the Utah Central Railroad was an occasion of great celebration for Utah's Mormons. The dedication ceremony mimicked that for the transcontinental railroad in certain respects but with a Mormon bent: the last spike, engraved "Holiness to the Lord," was driven by Brigham Young; the road was dedicated in prayer; and speakers praised the self-reliance and dedication of a people able to build railroads "without outside help."

32. Citations from McCormick and McCormick, *Saltair,* 21, 23.

33. Fluhman, *"A Peculiar People,"* 127.

34. Ross, *10,000 Miles,* 67–68, and *The Pacific Tourist,* 150. The "Utah's Best Crop" image—featuring babies' heads arranged as if blossoming in a field—was designed by Charles R. Savage, Mormon photographer and documenter of the transcontinental railroad's construction. On the Deseret Agricultural and Manufacturing Society, see, for example, Arrington, *Great Basin Kingdom,* 226–228, and Utah State Fair Association, *History of the Utah State Fair Association, Golden Jubilee Exposition, 1856–1928* (Salt Lake City, [1928]). The celebration of Mormon agriculturalism in a different fair setting—at the 1893 World's Columbian Exposition—is discussed by Reid L. Neilson in *Exhibiting Mormonism: The Latter-day Saints and the 1893 Chicago World's Fair* (New York: Oxford University Press, 2011).

35. W. W. Ross described his 1874 Tabernacle visit thus: "I saw two arches, remains of a recent celebration, symbolizing the productions of the soil at two different periods—viz., [18]47, when [Mormons] arrived, and '74, the present. The first was chiefly composed of sage brush and wild sunflower; the second, of branches of the trees adorning the streets, the various grains, including corn and sorghum—all prettily set off by various flowers [etc.]." Ross, *10,000 Miles,* 67, 70. On the postpioneer myth that Utah was a barren, uninhabited wasteland in 1847—a notion advanced in order to tout Mormon accomplishments and liken Utahn pioneers to the biblical patriarchs—see Richard H. Jackson, "The Mormon Experience: The Plains as Sinai, the Great Salt Lake as the Dead Sea, and the Great Basin as Desert-cum-Promised Land," *Journal of Historical Geography* 18, no. 1 (January 1992): 41–58, and Farmer, *On Zion's Mount,* 126–130.

36. George A. Smith, letter to Hon. N. S. Elderkin, November 11, 1869, in Historians Office Letterpress copybooks, 1854–1879 [box 27, item 474], Church History Library, Church of Jesus Christ of Latter-day Saints, Salt Lake City, and George A. Smith, letter to Dr. H. Gould, June 20, 1871, in ibid. [box 28, item 232].

37. For an instance of cooperative touring, see "A Host Enraptured: The City's Guests Entertained in Splendid Style," *Deseret Evening News* (Salt Lake City), April 20, 1894, which documents a visit by members of the International Association of Ticket Agents, who were guided to and through certain of Salt Lake City's tourist attractions and exhibitions (the Tabernacle and Saltair among them) so that they might better represent Salt Lake City.

35

Slippery and Slow

Chavín's Great Stones and Kinaesthetic Perception

MARY WEISMANTEL

For almost a century, scholars in several disciplines have intensively studied the intricate and intimidating carvings on the great stones of Chavín de Huantar, a religious shrine in the highlands of Peru that dates from approximately 1000–300 BCE. As is typical of the Pre-Columbian field, iconographic analysis has dominated these studies. Such an approach, though useful when encountering a recondite style like that of Chavín, also "dissociates the image from the object and space of which it is a part."[1]

In this chapter I want to end that dissociation and to look at the stones in all their rich materiality. This change in focus reveals what iconography cannot: the stones' capacity to engage human viewers in forms of bodily, sensory, and kinaesthetic interaction that are as specific and intentional as any of the signs and symbols found on their surfaces—and as intrinsic to their meaning.

My turn toward materiality and sensory perception arises, in part, from a recent body of work in philosophy referred to as the "new materialism."[2] This intellectual movement, which rejects reigning Enlightenment binaries such as image/word, concrete/abstract, sensation/cognition, body/mind, and emotion/reason, has a particular significance for those of us who study indigenous religious practice in the Americas. As Pre-Columbian scholars, we are all too aware that these conceptual oppositions are not politically neutral: they are the building blocks of an elaborate ideology of difference. As Sally Promey notes in her introduction to this volume, these binaries are also hierarchies that consign non-Western worship—supposedly typified by crudely concrete notions of the sacred and overly emotive forms of worship—to a lower rung on the evolutionary ladder than that of the (Protestant) West.[3] Within this paradigm, non-Western art is denigrated as "primitive," and non-Western religions are mere "fetishisms" or "idolatries."

In response to this pernicious ideology, twentieth-century anthropologists maintained that non-Western systems of knowledge are fully as logical, abstract, and sophisticated as their European counterparts. Lévi-Strauss ardently expressed this argument in the opening pages of *La pensée sauvage,* and he championed a methodology that treats the material cultures of nonliterate peoples as the exact equivalents of written texts.[4] Although not always self-consciously articulated as such, iconographic readings of Pre-Columbian art likewise constitute an attempt to assert the intellectual merit of indigenous systems of belief and an implicit rebuttal of the long history of pernicious racist caricatures of Native South American religious practice beginning with the sixteenth-century depictions of "cannibal feasts" by De Brys.

But as the intellectual and political landscape in Western art history and religious studies has begun to change, that imperative no longer hangs so heavily over the study of a place like Chavín. If, as many of the authors in this volume assert, Western religion operates through material and phenomenological registers as well as abstract and textual ones, perhaps it is finally safe to admit that non-Western religions do the same.

There have been pragmatic as well as ideological reasons for taking an iconographic approach to artifacts like Chavín's stones, which are covered with complex designs and often lack archaeological context. But analysis need not end with iconography: although the stones have been moved, they have not been dematerialized. They continue to exist as unique three-dimensional objects, as well as in the multiple two-dimensional representations that are the usual objects of study, and as such they are amenable to material and phenomenological analysis.

Once we begin to consider the stones as material objects, one odd, obvious fact immediately becomes apparent: the images carved on their surfaces are difficult to see. From Fred Ayres in 1961 to John Rick in 2008, researchers have consistently noted this problem of "poor visibility"[5] and worked to overcome it through artificial lighting, roll-outs, and rubbings (Figure 35.1). The resulting copies are indispensable for iconographic analysis—but in the process of making them, scholars erase an aspect of the artifacts that they set out to study.

What modern writers describe as poor visibility is the physical experience of looking at these monuments with the naked eye, as ancient viewers did. It is not the result of weathering or deterioration; if anything, these objects were more difficult to see in Formative times, before the advent of electric light. Poor visibility is and always has been part of the artifacts themselves, and thus part of what we need to interpret.[6]

This poor visibility has several overlapping components. One is impeded vision: the carvings resist our comprehension through the intricacy of their designs—and also because the manner of their execution impedes rather than assists us in deciphering them. Another is fragmented viewing. The stones force us to interact with them kinetically, moving our bodies, heads, and eyes to take in parts of pictures that cannot

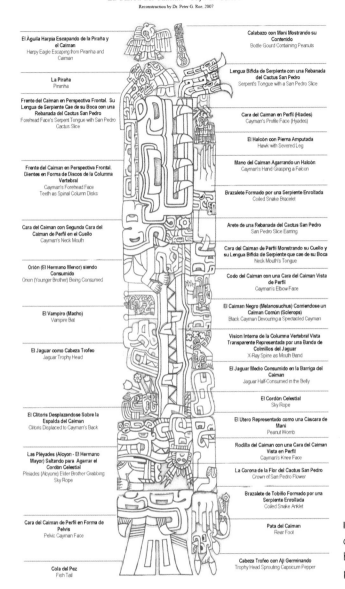

El Dragón Hembra Female Dragon
La Canoa del Caiman Cayman Canoe
Reconstruction by Dr. Peter G. Roe, 2007

El Águila Harpia Escapando de la Piraña y el Caiman
Harpy Eagle Escaping from Piranha and Caiman

La Piraña
Piranha

Frente del Caiman en Perspectiva Frontal. Su Lengua de Serpiente Cae de su Boca con una Rebanada del Cactus San Pedro
Forehead Face's Serpent Tongue with San Pedro Cactus Slice

Frente del Caiman en Perspectiva Frontal. Dientes en Forma de Discos de la Columna Vertebral
Cayman's Forehead Face Teeth as Spinal Column Disks

Cara del Caiman con Segunda Cara del Caiman de Perfil en el Cuello
Cayman's Neck Mouth

Orión (El Hermano Menor) siendo Consumido
Orion (Younger Brother) Being Consumed

El Vampiro (Macho)
Vampire Bat

El Jaguar como Cabeza Trofeo
Jaguar Trophy Head

El Clitoris Desplazandose Sobre la Espalda del Caiman
Clitoris Displaced to Cayman's Back

Las Pléyades (Alcyon - El Hermano Mayor) Saltando para Agarrar el Cordon Celestial
Pleiades (Alcyone) Elder Brother Grabbing Sky Rope

Cara del Caiman de Perfil en Forma de Pelvis
Pelvic Cayman Face

Cola del Pez
Fish Tail

Calabazo con Mani Mostrando su Contenido
Bottle Gourd Containing Peanuts

Lengua Bifida de Serpiente con una Rebanada del Cactus San Pedro
Serpent's Tongue with a San Pedro Slice

Cara del Caiman en Perfil (Hiades)
Cayman's Profile Face (Hyades)

El Halcón con Pierna Amputada
Hawk with Severed Leg

Mano del Caiman Agarrando un Halcón
Cayman's Hand Grasping a Falcon

Brazalete Formado por una Serpiente Enrollada
Coiled Snake Bracelet

Arete de una Rebanada del Cactus San Pedro
San Pedro Slice Earring

Cara del Caiman de Perfil Monstrando su Cuello y su Lengua Bifida de Serpiente que cae de su Boca
Neck Mouth's Tongue

Codo del Caiman con una Cara del Caiman Vista de Perfil
Cayman's Elbow Face

El Caiman Negro (Melanosuchus) Comiendose un Caiman Común (Sclerops)
Black Cayman Devouring a Spectacled Cayman

Vision Interna de la Columna Vertebral Vista Transparente Representada por una Banda de Colmillos del Jaguar
X-Ray Spine as Mouth Band

El Jaguar Medio Consumido en la Barriga del Caiman
Jaguar Half-Consumed in the Belly

El Cordón Celestial
Sky Rope

El Utero Representado como una Cáscara de Mani
Peanut Womb

Rodilla del Caiman con una Cara del Caiman Vista en Perfil
Cayman's Knee Face

La Corona de la Flor del Cactus San Pedro
Crown of San Pedro Flower

Brazalete de Tobilio Formado por una Serpiente Enrollada
Coiled Snake Anklet

Pata del Caiman
Rear Foot

Cabeza Trofeo con Ají Germinando
Trophy Head Sprouting Capsicum Pepper

FIGURE 35.1. Roll-out drawing of the Obelisk Tello by Peter Roe. Used with permission.

be seen all at once; furthermore, the placement of the designs on the stones, and of the stones in the space of the temple, conspires to prevent some images from being seen in their totality.

This impeded, incomplete form of seeing strikes the modern Western viewer as impoverished and inferior. But the inferiority may lie in us: in our inability to grasp the relationship between the bodily phenomenon of visual interaction with an object and the ideational world in which that interaction originally took place. The artifacts we use to convey visual information today—books, maps, laptops, screens—are designed to provide effortless, instant, uniform access delivered to a passive, immobile viewer. The impeded vision of the Chavín stones does something very different: it compels a slow, difficult, thought-provoking viewing process achieved through effortful kinaesthetic interaction with sacred objects. The partial, fragmented vision enforced by the stones may communicate key tenets of Native South American religious thought, just as the forms of visual presentation that we prefer implicitly reinforce the tenets of empiricism.

Impeded Vision

In 1931 a New Yorker named Philip Ainsworth Means wrote a glowing review of a public lecture he had recently attended. The topic of the lecture was a gigantic carved stone from the ancient Peruvian site of Chavín de Huantar that depicted a "dragon-like monster, richly decorated," with a "formidable head armed with fangs" and genitals shaped like a "puma-head."[7] The lecturer was the eloquent and erudite Julio C. Tello, a brilliant young Peruvian archaeologist who had excavated at the site. Tello was a relentless propagandist for the significance of Peru's Pre-Columbian legacy—as well as the first modern scholar to attempt a serious analysis of Chavín art.[8] In the ensuing decades, numerous iconographers have followed in Tello's footsteps by tackling the "dragon-like monster"—today known as the Obelisk Tello—as well as other carved stones from the site: the Lanzón, Raimundi Stela, Black and White Portal, Yauya Stela, and numerous unnamed carvings.

Thanks largely to Tello's efforts, the dragonlike monster has become a canonical image of the ancient Americas, as have other of Chavín's great stones—or, rather, certain drawings of them. One depiction of the Lanzón has frequently adorned Peruvian currency, familiar to millions of Peruvians who handled it daily.[9] Other well-known drawings, used by scholars and students, were commissioned by John Rowe and published by him in 1962. Since its modern inception, the study of "Chavín art" has been a study of copies.

Rowe's drawings are perfectly suited to iconographic analysis, which has long been the preeminent method for analyzing Pre-Columbian art—especially in South America, where the figure of Lévi-Strauss still looms large. Rowe himself, although later known for his vigorous defense of American empiricism against European structuralism, used literary metaphors to describe his approach, calling the distinctive Chavín style a "script" to be "deciphered."[10] In a similar vein, Donald Lathrap described the Obelisk Tello as a visual representation of an origin myth.[11] The giant stones were texts to be read, and the scholar's job was to learn how to read them.

FIGURE 35.2. Roll-out drawing of the relief on the north column of the Black and White Portal. Originally published by John Rowe. Used with permission.

It was no easy feat. Consider, for example, Rowe's rendition of the hybrid human/feline/raptor figures carved on the Black and White Portal (Figure 35.2). Here the visual conventions of Chavín art are fully on display. The interiors of the twin bodies brim with the metaphorical substitutions that Rowe labeled "kennings":[12] orifices are toothed mouths; the joints of the body are replaced by open-mouthed heads, from which the limbs emerge like tongues; spines are represented as long rows of teeth; and snakes take the place of appendages such as hair, feathers, or tassels.[13] The image on another carved stone, the Raimundi Stela, looks like a totem pole: atop a small human body is a stack of endlessly transforming heads with jaguar mouths and serpentine hair.

The imposing twin figures on the Obelisk Tello—Tello's "dragons"—are perhaps the most iconographically complex of all. Most scholars agree with Donald Lathrap, who identified the creatures as caymans, or mythical versions of the *Melanasuchus niger,* the enormous alligator that once dominated the ecosystem of the Amazon River.[14] More recently, Gary Urton has suggested that their hybrid, monstrous qualities are better captured by the Quechua term for a magical serpent, *amaru.*[15]

Smaller animals, plants, mollusks, and other creatures nestle above and around the caymans; curiously, many of them, like the cayman itself, are denizens of the Amazon rainforest—an ecozone far from Chavín's highland valley.[16] The faces, mouths, and limbs of other animals crowd *within* the caymans' bodies in a manner reminiscent of other Native American art styles, such as Nazca, Paracas, Northwest Coast, or Olmec.

This multiplicity of bodies makes it difficult to discern the primary figure. At first, a modern viewer presented with a line drawing of the Obelisk Tello sees only a welter of detail and a confusion of limbs: it is hard to "make out" what is depicted.[17] Much of the appeal of Tello's lectures came from his dramatic and satisfying revelation of the two enormous dragons hidden within the maze.

Tello's lectures began with these main figures and then went on to isolate and identify each of the smaller creatures found on the stone, an approach subsequently followed by Lathrap.[18] But here we must part company with the iconographers and follow Merleau-Ponty:[19] our focus is not the puzzle of what is depicted on the stone but rather the moment of puzzlement itself. What is happening, materially and phenomenologically, at the juncture at which the viewer stands baffled, unable to separate the intertwined creatures or even to discern a central image in the dense network of forms?

If we accept the textual metaphor for Pre-Columbian art uncritically, this bewilderment is a modern problem. If only we had the necessary literacy, the act of "reading" the Obelisk Tello would be easy, its meaning transparent. But the material evidence suggests that the viewer's puzzlement is a reaction not only to the complexity of *what* is depicted on the stone but also to *how* the image is depicted. The difficulty does not lie solely in a lack of familiarity with the Chavín artistic canon, as Rowe suggested: it is literally carved into the stone itself. The ancient carvers who made these images eschewed stylistic strategies that would make our job easier; instead, they created visual forms that I have come to think of as *slippery*.

Slippery Images

Some students of Chavín are disappointed when they finally come face to face with the actual stones: the images are so difficult to see that the experience is less emotionally satisfying than staying home and studying a line drawing. All of the interesting detail, so clearly visible in line drawings, is much less so in real life, where the details vanish and what is most visible is often just a shiny surface. Photographers, too, find the stones frustrating; light reflecting off the Stela Raimundi, for example, makes it difficult to capture the imagery it bears. Like a number of other Chavín monoliths, the stela is less a sculpture than a drawing on stone. Its surface is perfectly flat, highly polished, and covered with narrow, shallowly incised, evenly spaced lines.[20] Figure and ground are differentiated, but otherwise the viewing experience is quite challenging.

The imagery on the Obelisk Tello is easier to see because the carvings are in low bas relief, but it raises another difficulty. The carver(s) who created it refrained from conventional means for emphasizing the central figure, such as making the relief deeper or the lines thicker or heavier. This strategy withholds the information that would allow us to readily differentiate the cayman from the smaller bodies that surround and compose it.[21]

These stylistic choices deliberately slow down the process of seeing, thus calling attention to perception as a physical act that takes place in time. Unlike realist painting or documentary photography, in which the moment of identifying the image is so immediate that we do not even notice its occurrence as a physical or cognitive act, Chavín delays the moment of recognition and makes the viewer work to achieve it.

Whether by means of a highly reflective polish, shallow narrow incised lines, or uniform low relief, Chavín stone carvers created slippery images that prevent the viewer from finding a beginning point for looking. Absent the stylistic conventions that direct the eye, our sight slides over the surfaces of the images like feet on a patch of ice or hands grasping at an object that is oily or wet. A student once reported her panic when studying the images for an exam: she said that looking at the pictures made her feel that "there is nothing to hold on to."

This experience brings the act of seeing into our conscious awareness; once there, our thoughts could move in different directions. Absent the stress of exam taking, viewers who become gradually aware of the giant reptilians on the Obelisk Tello might, for example, fall into an ecological meditation. Their thoughts might rest on actual alligators who float beneath the surface of the waters just as these hide within the design, unseen at first but becoming visible to those who watch and wait.

Don Lathrap's interpretation of the obelisk in "Gifts of the Cayman" offers another possibility.[22] Lathrap suggests that the stone encodes a myth like those recorded by Lévi-Strauss in indigenous societies across the Americas, in which the sacrifice of an originary deity or mother/father figure is the source of useful plants and animals, such as fish, birds, manioc, and chili peppers; these species were created from the cayman's dying body as its children and its gifts to humankind. For someone familiar with this story, looking at the obelisk could gradually reveal the mythic body of the great cayman as a cornucopia of other creatures. This slow sensory/cognitive process might recall and even enact the myth in which the primordial river god(dess) slowly disintegrates into the mundane foodcrops and animals necessary for everyday life.

My point is not to insist on either of these interpretations but simply to observe that the giant caymans are not the only things that signify on the Tello Obelisk; the act of seeing them is also meaningful. By making us work to find the underlying bodies that connect the claws, limbs, eyes, and teeth in the composition, the stone invites multiple, unpredictable discoveries about how bodies connect, as well as about the act of seeing itself—a point I return to below.

In the next section I discuss how scale, three-dimensionality, and placement of the Chavín stones create a kinaesthetic experience that involves the entire body and challenges the mind to feats of memory. These factors do more than slow down the process of discovering and recognizing the images on the stones; they also render it fragmentary and incomplete.

Fragmented Vision

Much of my visit to Chavín and to museums now housing many of its stones involved a surprising degree of bodily interaction: edging around the Lanzón, twisting my body and tilting my head to get different angles on it; running my fingers along the hidden edge of the Black and White Portal and wishing, absurdly, that my head could fit into the tiny gap between the pillar and the wall; or standing on tiptoe trying to bring the upper reaches of the Obelisk Tello into focus. I felt as though the great stones were making strange and uncomfortable physical demands on me—a reaction that reveals the great temporal, cultural, and material divide between modern viewers and the ancient makers. Nonliterate peoples, undisciplined by the tyranny of the written page, which dictates a passive, stationary way of looking, often create works that make these kinds of kinaesthetic demands. We are accustomed to watching moving pictures; at Chavín, the stationary stones move *us*.

This kinetic aspect becomes more apparent if we look at the sculptures in context: the immediate context of a perceiving human body and the larger context of the site of Chavín. The scale of these works, their three-dimensionality, and their placement at the site each engages a perceiving human interlocutor in different forms of motion. To see the images, the viewer must move forward and backward to get them in focus; look up and down or from side to side to compare paired images; and ultimately travel through the site, moving inward and downward toward a hidden chamber (a destination possibly not reached by all pilgrims).

These new demands are made on the mind as well as the body; for example, many of them challenge the short-term memory, requiring that the viewer compare different vistas that cannot be seen all at once. The images that the viewer seeks exist in their totality on the stones, but Chavín repeatedly refuses to grant access to that totality—except in the mind's eye, and perhaps not even then.

Close and Distant Viewing

Few of the great stones of Chavín are in situ today, but certain aspects of the viewing experience are still recoverable simply by comparing the size of the human body to that of the giant stones, and the size of the stones to the scale of the carvings on their surfaces. One thing becomes immediately apparent: their complex, convoluted designs seem ill fitted to their scale. The monoliths are large—on average, one and a half to two times taller than the human body. The details of the designs, executed in fine shallow lines or low bas relief, are very small. It is impossible for a person standing in front of any of the major monoliths to have the entire design in sight and in focus. Stand back far enough to see the whole, and the details disappear; move in close enough to see the details, and we lose the whole.

This peculiarity becomes more apparent if we compare the big stones to smaller objects that bear similar images, such as Cupisnique ceramics, worked gold pieces, or a carved stone cup now at Dumbarton Oaks. On these small hand-held works, scale and design work together. The intimate size of the objects is suited to the human body and gives the viewer full access to the entire image; one can examine it in close focus and trace out the intricate designs by turning the object in one's hand.

A second comparison, to other monumental art from Formative Peru, also highlights the curious interplay of scale and design at Chavín. The clay friezes of Garagay or Moxeke, for example, are big and bold, executed in high relief at a scale that can be seen from afar, immediately and in their entirety;[23] the well-known stone carvings at Cerro Sechín (first excavated by Tello) are also large in scale and extremely simple in design. In contrast, the complex detail and restrained execution of the Chavín stones seem designed for intimacy—and yet their scale makes that intimacy impossible.

If they had been made in a large, bold style, the images would be clearly visible despite their large size; if their scale were small and intimate, the images would be visible in their entirety despite the complexity of the design and the fineness of the execution. As I argue elsewhere, this curious contradiction between style and scale is mirrored in the architecture of the site, which similarly mixes monumentality and intimacy;[24] again, the contrast to the overwhelming scale and bold visibility of coastal sites is instructive. At monumental sites across the Americas, gigantic works of architecture emblazoned with bold imagery overwhelm the visitor, even from a distance. The monumental art of Chavín is less accessible: it requires us to move toward it— and then to back away again.

This kind of seeing-in-motion is how we see more generally as we move about the world: small, even imperceptible, constant movements of our head and eyes allow us to perceive figure and ground, foreground and background, and so to remain oriented and informed. Our vision is constantly oscillating between perspectives, but we are accustomed to processing this information so quickly that we experience it as a single viewing experience. Chavín pulls apart this fusion of perspectives, making us aware of the actual disjuncture between close and distant, here and there.

The three-dimensionality of the sculptures expands this operation still further by wrapping fundamentally two-dimensional images around three-dimensional objects. This requires the viewer to engage in a more complex set of movements: not between getting close and moving away but rather between the image before one's eyes and one that is momentarily absent.

The Stela Raimundi is famously anatropic or reversible: when seen upside down, the features of the primary face resolve themselves into the features of a quite different face. This phenomenon is readily demonstrable in the classroom, where the instructor simply flips the image on the screen—but in real life, neither the enormous stone nor the body of the viewer could be easily reversed. Whether the Raimundi stood horizontally or vertically, the "flip" required to appreciate the image's anatropism requires a vertigo-inducing feat of viewing in which the mind leaves the body's limitations behind.

The Obelisk Tello is still more challenging in this regard. Students and scholars today find the twin figures of the cayman/amaru enigmatic—even when looking at them in their entirety as images on the printed page or projected on a screen. They must have been even more puzzling to prehistoric viewers because, as Urton notes, each of the giant amarus wraps around two of the stone's four sides and cannot be seen all at once.[25] Body parts that could help in identifying the animal are separated: the limbs, feet, and genitalia occupy one narrow plane at a ninety-degree angle from the larger surface that holds the creature's head, torso, and tail. We must move back and forth to see two sides and assemble the entire cayman in our mind's eye.

This mental image is still only half the picture; there is the amaru's twin to consider. The two hybrid creatures are largely alike yet filled with differences that are an iconographer's delight—like the visual puzzles modern children enjoy, which ask the viewer to find minute differences between two apparently identical pictures. Ancient viewers could not do this as we do it today, by placing the two side by side; for them the task would require moving back, forth, and around the stone, holding the images of the two sides in mind the whole time while ferreting out the differences hidden among the similarities.

These characteristics are more remarkable when we remember that Chavín de Huantar was a pilgrimage site for most of its very long history. Thus most viewers of the obelisk saw it only briefly, on a journey seeking enlightenment far from home. It was surely impossible to fully master the complex imagery of the obelisk while playing this kinetic game of present-and-absent, especially given the stone's great height. For example, modern iconographers have discussed the possibility that the two creatures represent the sky and the sea, respectively, because one cayman has a harpy eagle hovering above its head, while above the other is a *Spondylus* oyster. But few viewers of the actual stone would be able to discern these carvings, located high on the obelisk's uppermost part. In the end, many pilgrims must have left the site remembering viewing experiences that were not only slow, slippery, and impeded—but fundamentally incomplete.

The Obelisk Tello stands today in a well-lit room designed to assist, not impede, viewing—yet it still resists easy access in all the ways I have described. These viewing challenges pale, however, compared to those offered by the few stones still in place at the site itself.

In Situ

The temple complex of Chavín comprises a tightly interconnected set of stone-faced buildings, plazas, terraces, staircases, passageways, and underground channels. It is especially known for the networks of dark, stone-lined interior passageways known as *galerías,* at the heart of which lies the monolith known as the Lanzón. A journey through the site from exterior to interior, from the carved blocks on the temple facade to the most sacred sculpture hidden at its very heart, shows that the stone images of Chavín were placed with what seems an almost perverse determination to obscure visibility.

As visitors approached the largest building of the temple complex, they would have seen a facade crowned by rows of finely worked ashlar blocks. (They are now piled up in various locations, their exact original positions no longer known.) Shallow, polished low-relief carvings on the surfaces of these blocks reveal intricate designs of multiple faces, bodies, and eyes, repeating as in a hall of mirrors or a hallucination. Close scrutiny of these works is fascinating, even mesmerizing; yet they were mounted so far above the ground that these designs must have been completely illegible.[26] Even if they were brightly painted, it would have been possible to see that *something* was carved on them but not to know what.

As we approach the exterior of the largest building, the twin pillars of the Black and White Portal (Figure 35.3) come into view. These are at ground height, accessible to sight and even to touch. Nevertheless, they, too, are examples of seeing that is not only slowed and impeded but *prevented.* Students of Pre-Columbian art know these carvings from Rowe's drawings, where they appear as dramatic mirror-image figures on two bold black-and-white squares. In contrast, visitors to Chavín see no such sight. The figures disappear in a web of barely legible lines traced across light-colored stone; like the carvings on the Raimundi Stela, the incisions are shallow and uniform, the surfaces highly polished and reflective. But this is only a minor problem. Because the images are wrapped around cylindrical pillars, they cannot be seen all at once. Even worse, the pillars stand only inches from the framing walls of the doorway so that large portions of the designs are hidden from view. Since they were put in place, no one (except perhaps the gods) has ever seen the two chimeras in their entirety again.

Rodriguez Kembel suggests that the portal may have been moved from its original position during the Formative Period;[27] if so, the pillars might once have been visible in their totality and relocated only after their imagery had become so familiar that no one needed to see the whole piece to know what was there. This is interesting

FIGURE 35.3. Photograph of a column of the Black and White Portal. Note placement of the column in close proximity to adjacent wall, blocking a portion of the relief. Photo by Amy Roe. Used with permission.

but speculative; we know that the other monument still in situ, the Lanzón, has never been moved, and its location, too, offers a peculiarly challenging form of viewing.

Coming to the Lanzón, we arrive at the heart of Chavín, where we find one of the site's most extreme examples of kinetically challenging and fragmented viewing. This granite prism, christened the "Great Lance" by Tello, may have begun life as a naturally occurring stone worshipped long before the rest of Chavín de Huantar was built. In fact, it is hypothesized that the entire temple complex was gradually constructed around this originary holy place, described by some scholars as an *axis mundi*. Early in the site's history, worshipers erected a small stone chamber around the freestanding monolith, in keeping with highland religious tradition. Over the centuries, as the site grew in importance, successive generations continued building until they had completely entombed the stone and its network of surrounding galleries (Figure 35.4), turning the monolith into an underground deity.[28]

The Lanzón (Figure 35.5) lacks the iconographic complexity of later carvings, but it nevertheless has an oddly affecting presence. As John Rowe observes, it possesses "an awe-inspiring quality which can be felt even by a present day unbeliever, but which photographs and drawings fail to communicate."[29] In pictures, the Lanzón is crude and somewhat unimpressive; in life, it is an object of great chthonic power.

This power originates not in the figure carved onto the stone's surface but in its striking architectural setting. The tall splinter of stone stands at the end of a claustro-

FIGURE 35.4. Photograph of one of the "galerías" using modern electric light. Photo by Amy Roe. Used with permission.

FIGURE 35.5. The Lanzón. Photo by Mary Weismantel.

phobically small and windowless passageway within the underground galerías, trapped in a secret room that can barely hold its massive form. As Tom Cummins says, the statue "exceeds the architectural space that envelops it": the relationship between sculpture and architecture "is not based on a sense of visual harmony but of discord."[30] Here, in the setting of the site's most significant stone, the conflict between intimacy and monumentality reaches an even greater extreme.

The scale and form of the room have another effect as well. More than twice as tall as any human being, the narrow granite prism is difficult to see in its entirety; this problem is greatly exacerbated by the chamber's tight quarters and convoluted shape, which force viewers into such close proximity that the statue continually dissolves into fragments. Only incoherent, partial views are possible: one of my photographs shows only a long spine or rope; another is a distorted close-up of the eye and nose seen from below; a third offers a glimpse of the clawed feet, and so forth. And yet, as Cummins points out, photos such as these offer a more accurate impression of what seeing the Lanzón is actually like than do the roll-out drawings, which depict "a visually coherent figure."[31]

That the ultimate vision at this sacred site offered only fragments of images could have had one of several effects. It might have impressed on viewers their own inadequacy as mere mortals compared to the gods, or lesser human beings in comparison to priests and leaders. Or it could have been an invitation to share impressions of the stone with other pilgrims in a collaborative discussion of what they had seen, as contemporary Amazonians do with dreams.[32] And, as I discuss below, it could also relate to one of the most significant epistemological tenets of Native South American thought: perspectivism.[33]

Indigenous Vision

For at least two thousand years, indigenous South Americans traveled great distances to Chavín de Huantar in search of a transformative religious experience. They found what they sought in the great stones of Chavín, which effected that transformation by inducing specific sensory and embodied practices. In their encounters with the stones, pilgrims experienced a slow, slippery, demanding kinaesthetic process that, in the end, provided only fragments of images. What, then, were the underlying ontological principles that this perceptual engagement revealed, expanded, or confirmed for these seekers?

One source of answers is the animist religions found among Native South American communities of Amazonia today,[34] which have often been used as sources of ethnographic analogy to Chavín. The strong supporting evidence of this analogy includes the Amazonian fauna and flora depicted on the Obelisk Tello as well as the frequent visual references to hallucinogens throughout Chavín art, so reminiscent of the twentieth-century Amazonian shamanic practices documented by anthropologists.[35]

Analogies based on twentieth-century religious practice must be used with caution, given the great temporal distance involved. Nevertheless, this animist philosophy appears to be deeply integrated into the very principles that govern pictorial composition at Chavín, just as Western ontologies shape the conventions of naturalistic art. The partial, shifting forms of vision that the great stones impose on their viewers gave kinaesthetic and bodily form to key metaphysical concepts, including the illusory nature of everyday perception, the interconnectedness of all living things, and perspectivism.[36]

Amazonian religiosity holds that the mundane vision of reality is inherently partial and incoherent and that it is only through ritual practices specifically aimed at changing our perception that we may gain access to a more accurate vision of the world. When we see humans, animals, plants, minerals, or bodies of water as separate from one another, we are failing to see the world as it really is. The goal of training in shamanic practice or in art making is to acquire access to a hidden reality otherwise glimpsed only in dreams: an animate world in which all things are interconnected and alive.[37] The complex iconography of the Chavín stones, in which bodies are incorporated within one another, and their stylistic conventions, which make it difficult to differentiate one body from another, embody this religious precept. For believers, the composite bodies carved on the great stones may have taught a more accurate way of seeing, in contrast to the false vision of secular life, in which bodies appear as separate entities.

The partial nature of human vision is also implied by some representational conventions used by Chavín artists to depict the body, which remind us that when we look at one another we see only part of the whole. As in the case of ancient Egyptian and other premodern art, figures are often contorted to show different perspectives at once: for example, a frontal torso but legs and feet in profile. And like Northwest Coast and other Native American art forms, Chavín art at times uses X-ray depiction, split representation, "flayed-pelt convention," and other means to reveal aspects of physiognomy, such as the interior skeleton or organs or the body's entire surface, that could never be visible to a spectator in real life.[38] These conventions appear to us, as modern viewers, to defy reality; but what they actually defy is time. A snapshot—our preferred technology for representing seeing as we understand it—captures instantaneous sight: a glimpse from a single angle. Chavín representations instead deliver the multiple perspectives available only over time and through movement as the bodily relationship changes between seer and seen.

The stones themselves require us to look at the same thing from more than one perspective, whether different sides of the same object, as on the Obelisk Tello; anatropic shifts, as on the Stela Raimundi; or alternating views of the interior and exterior of a body, as in the case of the naked spine and fleshed limbs of the Lanzón. This demand can be related to an essential characteristic of contemporary Native American phenomenology: "perspectivism."[39]

This belief, which is closely associated with shamanic practice, asserts that reality is differently constituted depending on one's perspective. Humans, animals, spirits, the living, and the dead each perceive a completely different—but reciprocally constituted—reality. Shamanic apprenticeship allows practitioners to overcome the limitations of their own perspective and to shift from reality to reality—from seeing as a spirit sees to seeing through the eyes of different animals. It is a dangerous process, for these new forms of vision must be acquired without the students' losing themselves and their own human perspective along the way.

According to this philosophy, to see the world as it really is means to escape one's own limited perspective—but not by achieving a transcendent vision. There is no single overarching reality that trumps the limited vision of individuals and species; there is only the multiplicity of differing points of view. One achieves a more accurate understanding of the world not by abandoning the point of view provided by one's own bodily experience but by gaining access to other reciprocal embodied and sensory paradigms constituted across radical difference: human/animal, living/dead, hunter/prey.[40] In contemporary Amazonian religion, this is what makes powerful shamans powerful: the painstaking and hazardous acquisition of the ability to shift from one embodied perspective to another and the understanding that there is no single, comprehensive, panopticon-like perspective. The multiplicity is all.

Theorists such as Alfred Gell and Maurice Merleau-Ponty conceptualize perception as a historically specific process through which material objects constitute or transform their viewers—a process in which viewers actively participate.[41] The Chavín stones may embody this dialectical, generative relationship even more than do works of art produced elsewhere because it is so closely aligned with the philosophical beliefs held by their carvers.[42] Like modern-day Amazonian animists, the ancient hybrid bodies of Chavín iconography display multiply embodied perspectives visible through constantly shifting, partial, effortful perception. This is the promise that the stones make to their human viewers: that through kinaesthetic looking they may achieve a more intersubjective perspective on the world.

As I discussed in the introduction to this chapter, the iconographic emphasis of Pre-Columbian studies, which eschews attention to the phenomenological aspects of art and religious practice, is partially born from the anxiety of the subaltern: we fear that by paying attention to the bodily aspects of these religions, we might play into the prejudices of those who assume that Native Americans are incapable of higher levels of philosophical thought. But forcing the sacred objects produced by Native Americans to act like the written word may not be the best strategy for rebutting such claims. In fact, new materialist philosophy suggests that by divorcing mind and body, this strategy replays the very prejudices it seeks to overturn. Ironically, the most effective way to recover the subtlety and nuance of ancient South American religion may be to plunge into the minutiae of bodily experience in a place like Chavín de Huantar. The very qualities that make the great stones of Chavín the most unmodern, such as their insistence on slow, slippery, impeded, and fragmented vision, may be those that will ultimately demonstrate most fully their great contribution to human understanding.

NOTES

I am grateful to John Rick, who has been very generous with his time and with information about Chavín; to several colleagues at Northwestern, including Lars Toender and Michelle Molina, who shared my forays into the writings of Merleau-Ponty; and to Sally Promey, who invited me to include Chavín in this volume.

1. Tom Cummins, "Felicitious Legacy of the Lanzón," in *Chavín: Art, Architecture and Culture,* ed. William J. Conklin and Jeffrey Quilter (Los Angeles: Cotsen Institute of Archaeology Press at the University of California, 2008), 280–281. This quote is from an essay about one of the great stones of Chavín, the Lanzón, by art historian Tom Cummins; his essay, with its wide-ranging set of spatial and comparative questions, is a welcome exception to the reign of iconography.

2. Diana Coole and Samantha Frost, eds., *New Materialisms: Ontology, Agency, and Politics* (Durham, NC: Duke University Press, 2010), and Jane Bennett, *Vibrant Matter: A Political Ecology of Things* (Durham, NC: Duke University Press), 2010.

3. See Richard L. Burger, *Chavín and the Origins of the Andean Civilization* (London: Thames and Hudson, 1995); Alana Cordy-Collins, "Chavín Art: Its Shamanic/Hallucinogenic Origins," in *Pre-Columbian Art History: Selected Readings,* ed. A. Cordy-Collins and J. Stern (Trinidad, CO: Peek, 1977); Cummins, "Felicitious Legacy"; John H. Rowe, "Form and Meaning in Chavín Art," in *Peruvian Archaeology: Selected Readings,* ed. John H. Rowe and Dorothy Menzel (Trinidad, CO: Peek, 1977); Donald W. Lathrap, "Gifts of the Cayman: Some Thoughts on the Subsistence Basis of Chavín," in *Dumbarton Oaks Conference on Chavín, October 26–27, 1968,* ed. Elizabeth P. Benson (Washington, DC: Dumbarton Oaks Research Library and Collection, 1973); R. T. Zuidema, "An Andean Model for the Study of Chavín Iconography," *Journal of the Steward Anthropological Society* 20, nos. 1–2 (1992); Peter G. Roe, "How to Build a Raptor: Why the Dumbarton Oaks 'Scaled Cayman' Callango Textile Is Really a Chavín Jaguaroid Harpy Eagle," in *Chavín,* ed. Conklin and Quilter; Gary Urton, "The Body of Meaning in Chavín Art," in *Chavín,* ed. Conklin and Quilter; and Mary Weismantel, "Coming to Our Senses at Chavín de Huantar," in *Making Senses of the Past: Toward a Sensory Archaeology,* ed. Jo Day, Center for Archaeological Investigations Occasional Paper 40 (Carbondale: Southern Illinois University, 2013).

4. Claude Lévi-Strauss, *La Pensée sauvage* (Paris: Plon, 1961).

5. Fred D. Ayres, "Rubbings from Chavín de Huantar, Peru," *American Antiquity* 27, no. 2 (1961): 239–245, and John W. Rick, "Construction and Ritual in the Development of Authority at Chavín de Huantar," in *Chavín,* ed. Conklin and Quilter.

6. Weismantel, "Coming to Our Senses."

7. Philip A. Means, "New Clues to Early American Culture: The Discoveries of an Archaeologist in Peru Suggest a Link between the Civilization of Mayas and Incas," *New York Times Magazine,* May 20, 1934, 12, cited in Suzette Doyon-Bernard, "Jackson Pollock: A Twentieth-Century Shaman," *American Art* 11, no. 3 (1997).

8. Julio C. Tello, *The Life and Writings of Julio C. Tello: America's First Indigenous Archae-ologist,* ed. Richard L. Burger, 1st ed. (Iowa City: University of Iowa Press, 2008), and Richard L. Burger, "The Intellectual Legacy of Julio C. Tello," in *The Life and Writings of Julio C. Tello,* ed. Burger.

9. Cummins, "Felicitious Legacy," 279.

10. Rowe, "Form and Meaning," 72.

11. Lathrap, "Gifts of the Cayman."

12. The comparison to textual analyses of metaphors used in ancient Nordic song is an awkward one; Urton criticizes Rowe on these grounds in his "The Body of Meaning."

13. Rowe, "Form and Meaning," 72.

14. Lathrap, "Gifts of the Cayman," 338.

15. Urton, "The Body of Meaning," 222.

16. Lathrap, "Gifts of the Cayman."

17. Urton, "The Body of Meaning," 217–218.

18. Lathrap, "Gifts of the Cayman."

19. Maurice Merleau-Ponty, "Cezanne's Doubt," in *Sense and Non-Sense,* trans. Hubert L. Dreyfus and Patricia A. Dreyfus (Chicago: Northwestern University Press, 1964), and Merleau-Ponty, *Phenomenology of Perception,* trans. Colin Smith, 2nd ed. (New York: Routledge, 2002).

20. The stones may once have been brightly colored; the incised lines could simply have served to guide the painter, like lines in a coloring book. Large painted cotton cloths such as the Callango Textile offer supporting evidence of this possibility, but these textiles may represent a southern tradition of polychrome art not seen in the north (where Chavín de Huantar is located). Polychrome painting would certainly make the images easier to see, but it would not resolve all of the visual dilemmas posed by the great stones.

21. Mary Weismantel, "Encounters with Dragons: The Stones of Chavín," in *RES: Anthropology and Aesthetics* (forthcoming), and Doyon-Bernard, "Jackson Pollock," 27.

22. Lathrap, "Gifts of the Cayman."

23. On Garagay, see Burger, *Chavín and the Origins,* 64, and Richard L. Burger and Lucy C. Salazar, "The Manchay Culture and the Coastal Inspiration for Highland Chavín Civilization," in *Chavín,* ed. Conklin and Quilter. On Moxeke, see Tello, *The Life and Writings of Julio C. Tello.*

24. Weismantel, "Coming to Our Senses."

25. Urton, "The Body of Meaning," 217–218.

26. The soil surfaces in modern times and contradictory wall dimensions given in different publications prevent me from stating an exact height for these ashlar blocks' original positions. However, John Rick confidently asserts that many of them were cornices at the very tops of exterior temple walls, above the normal human ability to see the carved images on their surfaces. John W. Rick, personal communication, Chavín de Huantar, Peru, 2005. Jerry Moore cites Lumbreras's figure of twelve meters above ground for the height of the Old Temple walls. See Luis Lumbreras, "Excavaciones en el Templo Antiguo de Chavín (sector R): Informe de la sexta campaña," *Ñawpa pacha* 15 (n.d.), cited in Moore, *Architecture and Power in the Ancient Andes: The Archaeology of Public Buildings* (Cambridge, UK: Cambridge University Press, 1996); the walls of the New Temple (Building A) are higher.

27. Silvia Rodriguez Kembel, "The Architecture at the Monumental Center of Chavín de Huantar: Sequence, Transformations, and Chronology," in *Chavín,* ed. Conklin and Quilter, 35–84.

28. Rick, "Construction and Ritual."

29. Rowe, "Form and Meaning," 9.

30. Cummins, "Felicitious Legacy," 287.

31. Ibid., 288.

32. Norman E. Whitten, *Sacha Runa* (Urbana: University of Illinois Press, 1976).

33. Eduardo Vivieros de Castro, *From the Enemy's Point of View: Humanity and Divinity in an Amazonian Society* (Chicago: University of Chicago Press, 1992).

34. It is important to recognize that many modern-day indigenous Amazonians are not animists but practicing Catholics or evangelical Christians; others embrace a mixture of faiths. Furthermore, there has recently been debate among scholars about definitions of the term *animism* as contrasted with *totemism* and *perspectivism*. See Bruno Latour, "Perspectivism: 'Type' or 'Bomb'?," *Anthropology Today* 25, no. 2 (n.d.): 1–2; for the purposes of this chapter, I use *animism* to refer to all of these.

35. I use the term *animist* here rather than *shamanic,* the term of choice of previous Chavín scholars, because of the trenchant critique offered by Klein et al. See Cecelia Klein, Elisa Mandell, and Maya Stanfield-Mazzi, "The Role of Shamanism in Mesoamerican Art: A Reassessment," *Current Anthropology* 43, no. 3 (2002): 383–419. Anthropologists who have documented these practices include Burger, *Chavín and the Origins;* Cordy-Collins, "Chavín Art"; Lathrap, "Gifts of the Cayman"; Roe, "How to Build a Raptor"; Douglas Sharon, *Shamanism and the Sacred Cactus: Ethnoarchaeological Evidence for San Pedro Use in Northern Peru* (San Diego: San Diego Museum of Man, 2000); Constantino Manuel Torres, "Chavín's Psychoactive Pharmacopoeia: The Iconographic Evidence," in *Chavín,* ed. Conklin and Quilter; and Urton, "The Body of Meaning."

36. Eduardo Vivieros de Castro, "Cosmological Deixis and Amerindian Perspectivism," *Journal of the Royal Anthropological Institute* 4, no. 3 (September 1998): 469–488.

37. Michael Brown, *Tsewa's Gift: Magic and Meaning in an Amazonian Society* (Tuscaloosa: University of Alabama Press, 2006); Michael J. Harner, *The Jívaro: People of the Sacred Waterfalls* (Berkeley: University of California Press, 1984); Gerardo Reichel-Dolmatoff, *Amazonian Cosmos: The Sexual and Religious Symbolism of the Tukano Indians* (Chicago: University of Chicago Press, 1971); and Norman E. Whitten, *Sicuanga Runa* (Urbana: University of Illinois Press, 1985).

38. Rowe, "Form and Meaning," and Roe, "How to Build a Raptor."

39. Vivieros de Castro, "Cosmological Deixis."

40. There is an insightful exploration of similar issues in Rebecca Stone-Miller, "Human–Animal Imagery, Shamanic Visions, and Ancient American Aesthetics," *RES: Anthropology and Aesthetics* 45 (2005): 47–68, but note the caveat in note 33 above.

41. Alfred Gell, *Art and Agency: An Anthropological Theory* (Oxford, UK: Clarendon, 1998), and Maurice Merleau-Ponty, "Cezanne's Doubt," and *Phenomenology of Perception.*

42. Weismantel, "Encounters with Dragons."

36

Spiritual Sensations and Material Transformations in Hawai'i Volcanoes National Park

SALLY M. PROMEY

He ola ka pōhaku. There is life in the stone.   Ancient Hawaiian saying

A placard posted near the Wahine-kapu Steam Vents at Hawai'i Volcanoes National Park (HAVO) (Figure 36.1) locates the visitor on a map ("You Are Here") and initially frames the viewing experience in scientific vocabulary.[1] Two paragraphs into this geological discourse, the font and subject shift to declare the landscape embodied spiritual terrain. A boldface subtitle heralds "Pelehonuamea (Pele)" as "Goddess of all things volcanic." The text continues: "The mana (spiritual energy) of Pele is powerful, and her presence surrounds you. She is the lava rock you walk on, the glistening gold strands of volcanic glass in the cracks, and the breath of steam that engulfs you. Please be respectful of this sacred area and what it means to the Hawaiian culture by staying on park trails and by not littering the steam vents." A nearby placard asserts that "a Hawaiian landscape . . . is often a site of great spiritual significance."

On initial viewing from the Western academic perspective that I inhabit by training, HAVO informational signage exhibits certain peculiarities: the signs include multiple registers of experience and content and seem at once to address audiences scientific, scholarly, reverential, and devout. The text moves almost seamlessly from one to the other. The National Park Service (NPS), the format suggests, is simply providing information. Here the information is of an educational, spiritual, and regulatory sort, and the primary audiences are presumably tourists of both natural and cultural phenomena. Native Hawaiians constitute a second presumed audience, and the NPS has consulted in recent years with a formally constituted group of local *kūpuna* (elders) to ensure that the park's interpretation meets the group's standards and has their approval. Here scrutiny of the text by Native Hawaiians is not intended primarily to educate this group but to reflect the consultative process of being educated by them, to address indigenous interests and content, and to build continued

FIGURE 36.1. National Park Service signage, Wahine-kapu Steam Vents, Hawai'i Volcanoes National Park, May 2011. Photo by Sally M. Promey.

collaboration with this second population of visitors to the park, from whose ancestors the land was stolen through illegal annexation by the U.S. government and its interests in the late nineteenth century.[2] There is no getting around the fact that, at HAVO, the NPS occupies a Native Hawaiian sacred site.

A bit farther down the Crater Rim Drive, the NPS Thomas A. Jaggar Museum on volcanology, dedicated on this site in 1987, shares a parking lot with its immediate neighbor, the U.S. Geological Survey's observatory, where scientists study Hawai'i's volcanoes.[3] Easily visible from the Jaggar Museum's outdoor viewing area, steam billows skyward from the fire pit of the active Hale-ma'uma'u Crater in the larger Kī-lau-ea Caldera (Figure 36.2). The NPS informs visitors that beneath their feet moves fiery molten stone, red hot and capable of mortal harm, which has been belching and surfacing now and again, fairly consistently, since the current eruption began on January 3, 1983. Within HAVO, barriers and tourist guides announce the closure of Crater Rim Drive due to toxic gas emissions from the earth.

Informational signage inside and outside the museum names the park's acreage as the "land where the goddess dwells" (present tense) and invites visitors to experience for themselves "the spirit within this awe inspiring wahi kapu" or "sacred land-

FIGURE 36.2. National Park Service signage outside Jaggar Museum overlooking Kī-lau-ea Caldera, Hawai'i Volcanoes National Park, May 2011. Photo by Sally M. Promey.

scape" of volcanic rock. While some signage acknowledges a specific Native Hawaiian cultural source for this interpretation, the signs generally anticipate that contemporary visitors of any ethnicity or heritage will share a common response: "As you enter this wahi kapu, prepare to be inspired, for Native Hawaiians believe this to be the home of Pelehonuamea (Pele), the creator and creative energy that formed these volcanic islands." The texts on these signs juxtapose multiple frames of reference within their own literal frames. Each placard carries the header "National Park Service / U.S. Department of the Interior" in its upper right-hand corner.

It is not the inclusion of information about ancient Hawaiian culture and religion that elicits my attention here but rather the preference for the terms "spiritual" and "sacred"; the integration of the scientific and the spiritual; the NPS promotion of spiritual positioning, sensation, and feeling within the contemporary visitor ("experience for yourself the spirit within"; "prepare to be inspired"; "[Pele's] presence surrounds you"); and the apparent conflation of past and present moments in Hawaiian practice and tradition. Science and spirituality become mutually reinforcing truths. Even in its geological exhibitions, the NPS reiterates Pele's embodied dominance in this scene; among its geological samples are displays labeled "Pele's hair" and "Pele's tears." According to NPS signage, visitors to the park enter an embodied spiritual sensorium, indigenous and natural.[4]

Sensation is always, as Christopher Tilley and others have argued, "emplaced."[5] It occurs in a particular location because it exists within bodies and at their ostensible perimeters, manifesting the interfaces among and involvements of body, object, and world. Kathleen Stewart's description of "ordinary affects" usefully refines Tilley's assertions: "*Something,*" she says, "throws itself together in a moment as an event and a sensation; a something both animated and inhabitable."[6] The senses operate as mediating faculties. At HAVO, as elsewhere, sensation offers and constitutes what Tilley has characterized as a "communion, or coexistence, between body and thing." The human body, he suggests, is "continually improvising its relationship with things precisely because it is not a closed mechanical system but constantly opening out itself to the world as it moves in it."[7]

Emplacement is an especially useful category at HAVO because place and location are so fundamentally important to Hawaiian culture and identity formation. In this context, individuals and groups are inextricably linked to ancestral lands and districts, with connections to specific deities and emplaced practices associated with them.[8] The home of Pele, for example, is Kī-lau-ea, and, most specifically, the fire pit at Hale-maʻumaʻu Crater. The human lineal descendants of this familial deity most effectively, appropriately, and respectfully engage her through practices carried out on and in this land. Here, in specific Hawaiian ritual activities, in various moments of instantiation, the bodies of persons quite literally meet the bodies of gods.

Two important examples concern rituals attending human birth and death. Generations of Hawaiian women, after childbirth, have brought the *piko* or umbilical cord to Puʻu-loa for deposit in ancient petroglyphs (*kiʻi pōhaku*) shaped like dots, cupped marks, and concentric circular indentations in long-hardened stretches and waves of lava rock now located within HAVO's boundaries. This ritual spatial and biological practice is believed to ensure the longevity, spiritual strength, and health of offspring and families. It has continued into the twenty-first century, though with less frequency, and is most common among those with direct ancestral connections to this place. In addition, in Hawaiian traditional culture, human bones (*iwi*) constitute the bodily receptacles for and medium of the person's *mana,* their spiritual energy or life force.[9] A common Native Hawaiian self-designation is Kanaka ʻŌiwi, or People of the Bone.[10] Bones of ancestors (*iwi kūpuna*) and family are treated with the utmost care and special reverence. Considered the most sacred of objects and most cherished of possessions, historically bones have been hidden from human sight in secret burial caves and other well-protected locations. In the past, and in some cases into the twentieth century at least, descendants of Pele have ritually interred ancestral bones, and sometimes entire corpses, in the fire pit at Hale-maʻumaʻu Crater. H. Arlo Nimmo reports that, in the historical literature, the "most commonly described ceremony held at the crater is one that accompanied the disposal of human bones. Various writers report the widespread Hawaiian belief that souls of persons who were related to Pele dwelt with her in the volcano. . . . Such an eternal cohabitation seemed to be ensured if the bones of the deceased were deposited in the volcano crater." Nimmo's sources also describe the conviction that when the dead or their bones were thrown into Hale-ma'uma'u, "they [became] fire and lava . . . and [were] worshipped."[11]

The evocation of emplaced sensations, feelings, and related ideas in landscapes and geographies, in past and present, is far from uncommon, as (for example) voluminous Western literatures on the spiritualities and spiritual affects of nature, in general and in particular, also attest. Spiritualized understandings of nature have informed Western engagement of this Hawaiian geography since the arrival of the first Europeans and Americans, who imported Christian interpretations and imposed habits of Western thought.[12] The language of spirituality in recent HAVO signage, however, appears to be doing something different, now adopting a position of deference to traditional Hawaiian understandings that do not separate the spiritual world from the secular, the sacred from the scientific. Archival evidence supports this conclusion. Prior to the cultural renewal and revitalization of political activism initiated in the Hawaiian Renaissance of the 1970s and 1980s, HAVO signage was almost exclusively scientific (and this despite the inclinations of some of the park's constituencies to personify the volcano goddess for purposes of fund-raising and tourism). Coincident with the Hawaiian Renaissance and with concurrent and subsequent U.S. legislative developments like the American Indian Religious Freedom Act (AIRFA, 1978) and the Native American Graves Protection and Repatriation Act (NAGPRA, 1990), HAVO began increasingly to incorporate cultural information and spiritual language in its signage. Park documentation generally suggests that HAVO leadership in these years sought the most expansive interpretation of the law of the land to grant greater voice and participation to local Native Hawaiians in an attempt to redress past (and current) transgressions on the part of the NPS and the U.S. government. It is important for our purposes here, in a book on sensation and material practice and in a section of the book on transformations, that, alongside other things that it does, park service signage enlivens the experiential register of sensation as a bridge between the scientific and the spiritual, strategically deploying the sensory as evidence for spiritual presence. The signage implies that the NPS at HAVO understands sensation to play an important role in the production and communication of the sacred. This is consistent with the content of advocacy on the part of the Kūpuna Council. In draft minutes of meetings, kūpuna explicitly refer to the steam of the Wahine-kapu vents and the sulfur of the Kukaeopele banks in terms of embodied deity.[13] Other meeting records indicate the interest of park employees in directing visitor attention to multisensory experience at HAVO.[14]

Appeals to physical sensations (produced by heat and steam and sulfur, for example) here invoke spiritual sensations—and spiritual sensations presumably register interfaces and involvements between the visitor's body and an "other" world.[15] The world of HAVO is a world constituted by the body of the goddess, a world in which, the signage claims, "her presence surrounds you." The years of the Hawaiian Renaissance witnessed an upsurge of interest in Pele throughout the islands, with many ceremonies and other activities dedicated to her. Some of these have become annual celebrations. Hula dancers come to Kī-lau-ea each year at the time of the Merrie Monarch Hula Festival, for example, to conduct ceremonies in recognition and honor of Pele.[16]

In its narration of the park's spirituality, the NPS employs the landscape's relative strangeness to park visitors from abroad: its steam vents with their breathy moist, sometimes sulfur-scented and -flavored, mists; its volcanically heated salty ocean waters; the odd sharp, crunching, sliding sounds of lava rock under foot; the slow-moving orange-hot surge and drift of sticky, viscous forms of lava inching toward the sea; its trade winds and sunshine that transform air into a palpable, pleasurable, ever-present, moving substance; the undulating landscape of ancient petroglyphs; the visitor's periodic visual and material encounters with offerings and other accessories of devotional activity. The fact that this literally unstable volcanic place stands in such immediate proximity to the processes of its own creation magnifies its scientific/spiritual hermeneutics. The park is a landscape already fundamentally strange to foreigners. This strangeness accrues, in part, from the island's status as a fairly small land mass containing eleven of the earth's thirteen ecological zones. The park features tropical foliage and waterfalls, pristine beaches, pounding surf, and rainforest as well as snow-capped peaks and barren lava fields and volcanic desert. HAVO, furthermore, inhabits one island in a chain of even smaller islands, all created by volcanic activity on the ocean's floor and sited at many hundreds and thousands of miles removed from main-lands in any direction. These factors all contribute to a touristic experiential backdrop of instability, sensory intensification, and disorientation.

At the Jaggar Museum the integration of science and spirituality is the work of a team of NPS designers in collaboration with Hawaiian artist Herb Kawainui Kāne, whose large-scale paintings of Hawaiian volcano gods, especially Pele, shape the exhibition and signage (Figure 36.3).[17] Kāne was also a canoe builder, a founder of the Polynesian Voyaging Society, and an early contributor to the Hawaiian Renaissance. He began working in various capacities with the NPS in Hawai'i in the 1970s. In 1984, about two years prior to Kāne's selection for the Jaggar project, the Pure Land Buddhist Honpa Hongwanji Mission of Honolulu celebrated him as a "living treasure of Hawai'i." The museum displays Kāne's artwork, woven seamlessly into its educational program, and NPS gift shops sell reproductions of Kāne's paintings as well as his pub-

FIGURE 36.3. Interior display at Jaggar Museum, including one of Herb Kawainui Kāne's paintings of Pele, Hawai'i Volcanoes National Park, May 2011. Photo by Sally M. Promey.

lications, including a book on Pele, a work Kāne said he undertook as a result of the museum design assignment.[18]

Here and elsewhere, especially in the Hawaiian Islands and among Native American populations in the continental United States, the NPS puts spirituality explicitly into formal circulation. In this process, this most porous of religious categories accomplishes substantial work.[19] Eliciting a range of visitor behaviors at Kī-lau-ea's rim and in the caldera, it simultaneously frames, protects, invites, discourages, and facilitates spiritual, sensory, and material practice of various sorts. The spiritualized bodies in this scenario do not belong only to the goddess. Within Western modernity as constructed by secularization theory, and especially in the United States, it is not just "primitives" elsewhere, or primitives past, who figure as religious remnants but also contemporary "indigenous" populations whose cultures, and indeed whose very bodies, become placeholders for a diffuse spirituality. From this perspective, these individuals and groups *locate* the spiritual within modernity or, more accurately, alongside it.[20] As manifested within this Western system of thought, native bodies, representatives of "traditional religions," become repositories of spiritualities, the subjects/

objects of imaginative construction. Native bodies are thus fluid, flexible, shape-shifting around modern expectations and needs but also ossified, bordered, contained by secular ideologies claiming the indigenous sensory past and present as the raw material of (largely fictive) historical and geological narratives. In such renditions, it is not only devotional objects that accessorize, ornament, and authenticate the touristic spiritual experience of HAVO and its performative spaces but also native devotional bodies as well. This reading sits alongside, and parallel with, my earlier suggestion that the park service, whose personnel include Native Hawaiians, strives to inhabit, narrate, and recommend something akin to a native subject position here. It is difficult to completely isolate these various strands in the circumstances of this moment in Hawaiian modernity.

Signage articulates the spirituality of place, and agreement with respect to this assertion is apparently not restricted to practitioners of contemporary Native Hawaiian religion but is shared by Christian park employees, tourists, and other visitors at HAVO. On the day of a recent visit, for example, one park ranger volunteered that he settled in this part of the Islands in part to learn spiritual lessons from Native Hawaiians and that he consequently belongs to a nearby Hawaiian-language Christian church choir. He recommended that I stop to hear self-described "Praise and Worship leader" Rupert Tripp Jr., who was singing that day at the main NPS Kī-lau-ea Visitor Center. Tripp, according to his "Music of the Heart" website, lives in Volcano, Hawai'i, and writes and records music "for the glory of my Lord and Savior Jesus Christ." When I went to listen that afternoon, the musician had gone on lunch break, but the literature he left on his table, including a flyer on NPS letterhead, identified his performance as part of a "series of Hawaiian cultural programs sponsored by Hawai'i Volcanoes National Park and Hawai'i Natural History Association."

At the Jaggar Museum, furthermore, two observant Jehovah's Witnesses, perhaps responding to the ostensible spiritual license of the place, set up their table of pamphlets near the main entrance to the museum and observation deck. No one on-site the day of my visit recommended music of any other sort or offered literatures disconnected from the park's spiritual performances. The NPS's official embrace, even promotion, of the Hawaiian spirituality of this place seemingly, and at least occasionally, elicits the display of other religious freedoms and evangelism protected by the First Amendment to the Constitution of the United States.[21] The volcanic landscape, and the NPS characterization of it in its signage, did not specifically anticipate Rupert Tripp or the Jehovah's Witness literature arrayed on a table in the sun at the Jaggar Museum's entrance gate. The NPS signage did, however, frame the possibility of such performances.[22] In evoking Hawaiian spiritualities rather than Hawaiian religions, in promoting the spiritualized sensory landscape, the NPS and other agencies make public space for the religious within the secular state. Rupert Tripp and the two Jehovah's Witnesses apparently recognized this on the April day of my 2011 visit to HAVO.

If Western secularization theory exiles religion to the individual interior, shaping our understandings of the spiritual in accordance with this presumably inviolable (and politically silenced) interiority, spirituality, native and otherwise, often eludes these boundaries and operates materially as well as immaterially without these constraints.

Spirituality, in its very fluidity, though, can also restrict and regulate. The NPS designation of HAVO as wahi kapu, attended by its translation of the term as "*sacred landscape*," provides attentive tourists with one possible interpretive register for another sort of island signage within and beyond the park's borders. Invariably the first and largest word on these sometimes manufactured, sometimes hand-lettered signs is an uppercase "KAPU" (Figures 36.4 and 36.5). Often the signs identify federal, state, or local government property as well as private, individually owned real estate. They also mark burial sites and similar sites of immediate social, cultural, and historical significance. The term *kapu* can mean "ritually restricted," "prohibited," or "off limits" as well as "sacred," "holy," or "consecrated." *Kapu* here signals the borders—and fixes the boundaries—of contested spaces, contested ethnic and religious "properties." Kapu signs hail beholders at a boundary, arrest their attention and motion, noting the threshold of potential transgression.[23] These spaces, labeled "sacred," erect literal "no trespassing" signs that carry with them a touch of the mortal threat of an ancient Hawaiian religious system. Despite the fact that the Hawaiian monarchy and elites renounced this system before the arrival of Western missionaries, tourist guides repeatedly remind visitors that *kapu* is the same word as *taboo* and that the historical penalty for violation was frequently death.[24]

At HAVO an important chapter in this story concerns just what it is that makes kapu this particular wahi and how this translates elsewhere on the islands. As the official signage maintains: "The mana (spiritual energy) of Pele is powerful, and her presence surrounds you. She is the lava rock you walk on." In this rendition, the very

FIGURE 36.4. Kapu signage, Kai-lua-Kona area off Māmalahoa Highway, Hawai'i Island, August 2013. Photo by Sally M. Promey.

FIGURE 36.5. Kapu signage near the remains of Haukalua Heiau adjacent to Laʻa-loa ("Very Sacred") Beach Park, Kai-lua-Kona, just off Aliʻi Drive, Hawaiʻi Island, May 2011. Photo by Sally M. Promey.

earth, the volcanic rock that forms the island, *is* the goddess Pele: it is simultaneously her body, her creation, her residence, her possession. Living lava, liquid stone, shapes a world in the process of coming into being. Pele's creative (and destructive) activity instantiates this most durable lithic medium in the very course of taking solid form, at the breathy, hissing, steam-saturated point where fire meets air and water, where veins of fluid molten lava meet sky and ocean. The landscape and, by commonly invoked synecdoche, the stones that constitute the landscape, hold the power and memory of creation and its connection to Native Hawaiian divinity. In this scenario, individual stones become tangible, circumscribable pieces of the corporeal spiritualities of the land; and the NPS aims to direct and orchestrate a particular sort of Hawaiian re-enchantment. In doing so, its displays and signage frame spiritual performance and stage public inducements to it. At HAVO, material offerings to Pele authenticate the designations of the landscape, especially the stones, as sacred, or kapu, and as bodily manifestations of this deity.[25]

The most common sort of contemporary offering, the Ti (Kī) bundle (Figure 36.6), is simply composed: a lava rock wrapped in a leaf of the Ti plant. Other plant matter, flowers, or small objects may be tucked into the bundle or set beside it; all that is necessary to this mediation, however, is a lava rock and a single Ti leaf, placed at a spiritually auspicious site, such as near ancient petroglyphs, at a *heiau* (or temple), on a grave site, or at some identifiable threshold of an active caldera, crater, or steam vent.[26] On the well-marked four-mile HAVO Kī-lau-ea Iki Trail, a rough pyramid of lava rocks at precisely the point of entry into the active caldera itself has accumulated many such offerings (Figure 36.7).[27] The varying degrees of desiccation of the Ti-leaf wrappings suggest that petitioners have left the bundles over an extended period and at different times. Beyond the pyramid (a marker of the sort often called a cairn), a largely barren hardened lava rock field stretches out, its jagged vents emitting heat and mildly scented

FIGURE 36.6. Ti bundle, Kī-lau-ea Iki Trail, Hawai'i Volcanoes National Park, May 2011. Photo by Sally M. Promey.

FIGURE 36.7. Lava rock cairn with Ti bundles, Kī-lau-ea Iki Trail, Hawai'i Volcanoes National Park, May 2011. Photo by Sally M. Promey.

rising steam. Across the surface, surreally regular zigzags of ferns periodically punctuate the floor of the caldera, taking hold in seismic crevasses heated by moisture from below.

Polynesian Ti grows plentifully in Hawaiian gardens and in the wild, but not in the caldera itself, to which it must be carried. The plant's leaves support many common uses. These have included rain capes and coverings, shelter thatching, food wrappings, and skirts. Ti is also a preferred ingredient in certain healing practices and in the production of offerings and leis. The plants, with their large, smooth, long leaves, are widely believed to dispel evil and bring good fortune. Pele (among other gods) is said to have considered Ti sacred. Ti plants, because of their long association with divine power, with protection as well as decoration, often grow around the perimeters of Hawaiian homes, Christian churches (Figure 36.8), Buddhist temples, hula platforms, and burial grounds.[28]

Of interest to me here is the fact that HAVO rangers claim authority to separate "authentic" from "inauthentic" Pele offerings and to remove those they deem inauthentic.[29] In the case of the ranger who volunteered this information (which is supported by documentary evidence in HAVO archives), those offerings that require removal are made with soda or alcohol cans and bottles rather than (or in addition to) the "natural" material of lava rock, the substance of Pele's body and the artifact of her creation. Since rangers rarely witness the ritual leaving of offerings by devotées, they cannot effectively monitor which individuals and groups are leaving what sorts of materials. Instead, at HAVO rangers base their assessment of authenticity solely on the appearance and media of the Ti bundle, lei, or other gift. HAVO monitors appear to be efficient: on my visits to the park, I have rarely seen offerings employing these commercial materials, though I have seen many of them at sites outside the park.[30]

NPS measures of devotional authenticity (and the values and judgments they exercise) seem peculiar here in several regards. Despite the fact that these standards have taken shape in consultation with the HAVO Kūpuna Council, it is noteworthy, but hardly surprising (in this matter and many others), that not all Native Hawaiians

FIGURE 36.8. Ti growing along perimeter of He-lani Church, Congregational, Hawai'i Island, March 2012. Photo by Sally M. Promey.

are in agreement. There seems to be no uniform or widely shared position in this regard. Perhaps most important, the park service claims that it is easy to discern authentic offerings because these contain only natural materials. If you see brandy or rum bottles or cigarettes, I've been told repeatedly, you know that you have an inauthentic offering, likely left, rangers assert, by Asians or other tourists who, in the opinion of park personnel, have no clear right to leave offerings in this place. This argument seems to me to be insufficient on at least two counts. First, there is ample evidence that "unnatural" items, like red silk and specifically brandy bottles, were used by nineteenth-century Hawaiians in offerings to Pele on precisely this part of the island.[31] On the single occasion when I have seen, in the park, an offering including an alcohol bottle and cigarettes, someone had carefully arranged its placement on a natural altar ledge formed by volcanic stone jutting up from the floor of the Kī-lau-ea Caldera along the Kī-lau-ea Iki Trail (Figure 36.9). The offering included Ti leaves, lava rock, and, importantly, red ʻōhelo berries, a fruit with a long history of dedication to Pele.[32] Second, given the realities of immigration to the islands as early as the late eighteenth century and of intermarriage across the intervening generations, many Hawaiians have embraced and made their own various Asian religious traditions as well as Christianities and (more recently) New Religious Movements. This makes it extremely difficult to presume to speak for, let alone measure, "pure" Hawaiian religion or

FIGURE 36.9. Offering in the caldera, Kī-lau-ea Iki Trail, Hawaiʻi Volcanoes National Park, August 2013. Photo by Sally M. Promey.

spiritualities in the present. Many Hawaiians who self-identify as indigenous also self-identify as Christian or New Age or Buddhist as well, and certainly many Hawaiians are also Asian. This is part of what Herb Kāne meant when he said, in the course of a formal objects repatriation hearing at which he was called to testify on behalf of Hawaiian tradition, "we are all *part* Hawaiian these days."[33]

Pele and other ancient gods and ancestors sustain contemporary connections to stones and rocks and inform the Hawaiian stories that take the various powers of particular island stones as their subject. Many island sites ground and manifest this interpretive framing. Some of these narratives about *pōhaku kapu* (sacred stones) concern pōhaku as dwelling places of specific spirits or gods, some concern individual persons who have undergone transformation into stone, some mark spiritual thresholds in the land, and some concern other ancient histories and spiritualities.[34] Unofficial signage attached to a tree near Moloka'i's "Very Sacred Rock" (Figure 36.10), for example, calls attention to the prominent phallic stone and its purported powers to enhance fertility among women who bring appropriate offerings and spend a night in the wild within its shelter.

Other "stony" tales concern the miraculous feats of Ka-mehameha I and members of Hawaiian royalty. Here we might list the boulder-sized Naha stone, now located in front of the public library in Hilo, by which Ka-mehameha I demonstrated his

FIGURE 36.10. Signage at Ka-ule-o-Nānāhoa Rock, Pā-lā'au State Park, central Moloka'i, February 2012. Photo by Sally M. Promey.

bodily strength and fulfillment of prophecy; the sacred site of the Kū-kani-loko Birth-stones (Figure 36.11) in Wahi-a-wā, Oʻahu, where royal women in childbirth sought connection to gods, chiefs, and ancestors; or the sea-polished rocks of Puʻu-koholā Heiau, reputedly smoothed by the energies of ocean gods whose activity enhanced the power of these stones taken from the rough surf at the foot of the cliffs of Pololū Valley, and then passed hand to hand by a chain of warriors over the twenty-five-mile distance to the temple site. Finally, some stories about rocks concern current convictions about such lithic objects as Oʻahu's so-called Wizard Stones, Kāhuna Stones, or Stones of Life (Figure 36.12), which were renamed (Nā Pōhaku Ola Kapaemāhū Ā Kapuni) and reinstalled in 1997 on a lava rock platform with a new lava rock altar near the beach at one end of Wai-kīkī by the Department of Parks and Recreation of the City and County of Honolulu.[35] These stones are said to contain still-powerful spiritual energies invested in them centuries ago by four eminent ancient Tahitian kāhuna who were experts in ritual knowledge and specialists in healing. On the day of my August 2013 visit there, someone had left a woven Ti lei offering.

Among the most broadly circulated twentieth- and twenty-first-century articulations of the spiritual power of Hawaiʻi's volcanic stones is the description of Pele's curse. This "tradition" likely originated with a 1940s park ranger and plays off certain Native Hawaiian understandings of the operations of gods and the powers of objects.[36] The curse is now, however, widely discounted and generally deplored by the NPS at HAVO and by the HAVO kūpuna consultants especially.[37] According to Pele's curse, anyone who takes a volcanic stone (a part of the goddess herself, or her creative property) from the islands invites bad luck. The sources of information about this curse are many.[38] Tourist guidebooks are first among the media that prepare travelers to face with some trepidation the potential acquisition of a lava rock souvenir. HAVO receives many packages of lava rocks each year, through the U.S. Postal Service and other mail carriers, returned by worried travelers from abroad, who are hopeful that good fortune will come back to them if they send Pele's body parts home to Hawaiʻi.

Volcano Gallery (no relation to the NPS or its Volcano Art Center but instead a division of a local business concern called Rainbow Moon) has made an enterprise of lava rock return, an activity that might be interpreted as a touristic kind of goddess repatriation. Volcano Gallery's website tells beleaguered travelers how to return volcanic rocks to Rainbow Moon, which promises to perform appropriate rituals on the former tourist's behalf.[39] Specifically, the website elaborates, employees of Rainbow Moon will make each rock an offering to Pele. They will wrap the rock in a Ti leaf for good luck, place the bundle in a respectful location "close to the home of Pele," and add an orchid, a petition for the goddess's "forgiveness." This distinguishes Rainbow Moon, it reports, from HAVO, whose employees will simply toss returned rocks on a pile of similar objects behind the Visitor's Center. Importantly, this turns out not to be the case exactly: when I went looking for the pile of volcanic stones, what I found a

FIGURE 36.11. (Top) The Kū-kani-loko Birthstones (Figure 36.12) in Wahi-a-wā, Oʻahu, August 2013. Photo by Sally M. Promey.

FIGURE 36.12. (Bottom) Nā Pōhaku Ola Kapaemāhū Ā Kapuni, also called Stones of Life, Wai-kīkī, Honolulu, Oʻahu, August 2013. Photo by Sally M. Promey.

FIGURE 36.13. Lava rock return site (detail) near the main Kī-lau-ea Visitor Center, Hawai'i Volcanoes National Park, March 2012. Photo by Sally M. Promey.

very short distance behind the Visitor's Center and a related NPS maintenance facility was actually an elaborate altarlike structure with some evidence of what appeared to be current ritual practice or at least very careful placement of received offerings (Figure 36.13).

Unlike the NPS, Rainbow Moon, for its ritual intervention, welcomes voluntary donations of $15.00. It also invites clients to send testimonies, which have, over time, facilitated the assembly of an e-archive of lava rock stories.[40] This website and the information it disseminates contribute to the Western choreography of spiritual and sensory performance at HAVO and elsewhere on the islands. The testimonies presented by Rainbow Moon and also those accumulated over time by the NPS suggest that it is continental U.S., mostly Christian, tourists who extend and sustain this particular variation on Hawaiian economies of activated objects.[41]

When I began thinking about this chapter, I intended to write a short piece I would title "The Soul of Things" about now-renowned American art critic James Jackson Jarves (who first went to Hawai'i in 1837, well before he became a critic), nineteenth-century English-born Boston geologist and spiritualist William Denton, and their convictions about the spiritual agency of objects, including lava rocks from the

Kī-lau-ea volcano on the Big Island of Hawai'i. For Jarves and Denton, at various points in their lives, objects operated as the tangible receptacles for or sensory media of certain kinds of spirit manifestations. Jarves, some years after his Hawai'i sojourn, maintained that objects absorbed or collected electromagnetic impulses or life force from anyone with whom they had ever come into contact.[42] Denton believed that certain things contained a kind of transferrable object memory, an energy retained and transmitted by the object to a person capable of sensing it.[43] By many measures, stone might seem an unlikely candidate for activation or enlivening, its obdurate materiality and tactility the very opposites of presumably ineffable spirit. Precisely this opposition, however, and its susceptibility to enchanting metaphorical and material transformations, has long rendered stone a fitting repository, in many specific cultural contexts, for spirit habitation and material agency.

Instead of following the nineteenth-century influence of Hawaiian stone on Jarves and Denton, this chapter has pursued a later and different approach to volcanic stones and the various spirits understood to permeate them, lava rocks and the sensory sacred landscapes they constitute. The focus here has concerned the deployment of spiritualities in relation to these devotional bodies, sensations, and places by the NPS and other Hawaiian agencies or agents. The work accomplished in this latter maneuver, especially by the NPS, is multiple and various, situated against the backdrop of immensely complex histories of American imperialisms (political, religious, cultural, and commercial). Here NPS parsing of the spiritual calls into conversation questions about whose gods, whose spirits, whose bodies, whose interests are in this land. In ceding ground to Pele, the NPS (among whose local employees, as I have noted, are Native Hawaiians) overtly and voluntarily acknowledges Hawaiian spiritual ownership of the land. It also appeases possible complainants and wards off litigation in a period of amplified native claims and Hawaiian nationalist activism.[44]

This land *is* sacred, the signage declares—its spirituality is Hawaiian and can be felt on the site. But this NPS signage, marked to signal that the land is the property of the U.S. Department of the Interior, also claims custodial authority of the land and its Native Hawaiian spiritualities for the United States. As custodian, the NPS officially aims to impose an attitude of hushed reverence on tourists and visitors, mandating the appropriate mode of bodily approach to the deities and vitalities of these things and places. The signage requires specific behaviors and warrants a zone of respect with which no reasonable-minded person can quibble. In one strategic maneuver the NPS offers, and professes, connection, accommodation, and atonement—as well as appropriation.

Spiritual ownership is not about material possession or property. While various sensory cues structure the felt experience of grounded presence, from the perspective of the federal government represented by the NPS, spiritual ownership is arguably a "strategically vague," qualified ownership that falls outside a capitalist land economy though it in actuality serves to reify it.[45] Pele's most sacred sites (the steam vents, the fire pit, the petroglyphs) are here also the most populated tourist attractions. For its part, the NPS at HAVO expends careful thought and considerable energy in providing and safeguarding native access for cultural and ritual purposes. Ample evidence suggests that many native practitioners highly value the protections that NPS custodianship offers to sacred places and objects. Native Hawaiians nonetheless also find themselves subject to NPS authority when, for example, they register for permission to gather natural ritual materials on park lands. They must, furthermore, modify the ideal times and places of their ritual observances to preserve the sacrality of the rites and to diminish the likelihood of disturbance by tourist spectators. And they encounter boardwalks, roadways, parking lots, toilet facilities, maintenance structures, and scientific observatories on their most sacred lands. In narrating sensory spiritualities rather than more institutionalized forms of religion, the NPS reiterates implicit packaging of property rights. Spiritual ownership by one party coexists with property ownership by another. The signage navigates this unstable divide, holding disparate definitions together, asserting compatibility. The signs and their irreconcilable assemblies of information teeter on the edge of a "barely suppressed history of conflict."[46] The NPS and the U.S. government it represents here claim Pele's body as their own.

But this is not the only thing the signage does, and this is certainly not a conclusive end to the story. On the part of Native Hawaiians, in the current moment, designation of something as *sacred* is both an internal assessment of value and character *and* a wise legal and political strategy for establishing rights and authority.[47] Subsequent to NAGPRA, use of the word *sacred* has become transformative in new ways, moving the conversation into still insufficiently charted legal terrain where application of this religious category to an object may render it subject to repatriation and native repossession. What this might mean, if anything, is not yet at all clear, but the formal reclamation of the term *sacred* with respect to sites of traditional Hawaiian ritual practice and the related proliferation of signage naming and labeling things and places sacred, or kapu (Figures 36.14 and 36.15), is suggestive in the context of NAGPRA's use of this terminology.[48] At HAVO, visual, material, textual, devotional, and sensory interpretive interventions and alterations name, perform, and demonstrate the place as sacred landscape, as wahi kapu. The official NPS renaming of the steam vents as Wahine-kapu is but one fairly recent example. This return to an earlier Hawaiian place name signals the site's dedication to Pele, one of whose traditional epithets is Wahine-kapu (sacred woman). She is especially present here, HAVO signage indicates, in ways that can be authenticated by its articulation of sensation. The name Wahine-kapu also marks this locale's ritual use in bodily cleansing and spiritual purification among Native Hawaiian women of Pele's familial descent, whose on-site practice secures their lineal identification with this sacred ancestor and place.

Across the islands, kapu signage, in the context of NAGPRA, represents a visible expression of authority and even territorial sovereignty.[49] At HAVO itself, the

FIGURE 36.14. Kapu signage on Route 19 between Honoka'a and Wai-mea, Hawai'i Island, May 2011. Photo by Sally M. Promey.

FIGURE 36.15. Kapu signage near a burial site in Wai-pi'o Valley, Hawai'i Island, May 2011. Photo by Sally M. Promey.

most frequently reiterated request from members of the Kūpuna Council is that these park sites be acknowledged, and publicly signed, as *sacred*. In remarking on this, I do not mean to imply that this request and inclination is in any way disingenuous. I do mean, rather, that whatever else it accomplishes, in post-AIRFA, post-NAGPRA legislative terms it sets in motion the possibility of modified material and spatial native claims on the landscape. It revitalizes spiritual possession in potential relation to

NAGPRA's repatriation procedures and demonstrates that tradition is not only consistent with transformation but also always in the dynamic process of it. Greg Johnson's interest in the study of "how various groups harness the symbolic to the material, the cultural to the natural, and the legal to the religious" is certainly useful here; his work demonstrates other ways and instances in which "repatriation processes have catalyzed a religious explosion in Hawai'i."[50]

In addition to privileging "present-day adherents" (the park's "living cultures"), NAGPRA sets certain categories of things apart for repatriation under law. These include "human remains, funerary objects, sacred objects, or objects of cultural patrimony."[51] These terms raise an interesting set of questions about the current status of sacred places like HAVO. Can a sacred landscape be a *sacred object?* Perhaps it can in a tradition with such fundamental emphasis on lineal connections to specific bounded places. Perhaps it can when place is constituted by the body and creative natural artifacts of the goddess herself.[52] Perhaps it can when lava flowing from Pele's abode is literally commingled with the volcanically incinerated bones of ancestors, when lava rock, and thus the land itself, is infused with native ancestral remains. Perhaps it can in a culture that accommodates understandings of particular pōhaku as familial relations, as relatives.[53] Perhaps it can when current members of a native population, looking for workable analogies, compare the taking of volcanic rocks from HAVO with the desecration of a Christian church, with touristic theft of its architectural members or liturgical furnishings.[54] Perhaps it can where living rock has concrete everyday implications in contemporary practice.

Sensory activity, scripted by multiple, often overlapping, secular and religious histories, is emplaced, enacted, and interpreted in relation to specific material objects and material bodies. At HAVO, the NPS calls to attention the experience of physical sensations, elicited by numerous localized Native Hawaiian and touristic engagements with this rocky, molten, steamy, breathy landscape of fire, water, and stone. In the process it provides concrete evidence for material transformation, a renewed sacralization, a re-enchantment, of this landscape.

In this new context, then, usage of the terminology of the sacred raises the possibility of, and expands the parameters for, competing coexistent national claims on the land, not just of "one nation under God" but of an *other* nation, an ancient nation —at least at Kī-lau-ea, a nation with contemporary authority "under goddess."

NOTES

I am grateful to my colleague Kate Lingley at the University of Hawai'i at Mānoa for her careful reading of and significant contributions to this chapter; to Isaac Weiner at the Ohio State University for similar labors; to Ty P. Kāwika Tengan for invaluable advice about Hawaiian language usage; to Roger Fallot and Kathryn Lofton for Hawaiian travels shared; and to Tracy Laqua and Laura Schuster of the NPS at HAVO for granting me access to archival materials and generously making time to accommodate my visits and my questions. An invitation to write for *freq.uenci.es: a collaborative geneology of spirituality,* curated by Kathryn Lofton and John Lardas Modern (http://freq.uenci.es/), kickstarted my thinking on this subject.

1. HAVO is the official National Park Service abbreviation for Hawai'i Volcanoes National Park. For Hawaiian terms and place names I have relied on *Hawaiian Dictionary,* revised and enlarged edition, by Mary Kawena Pukui and Samuel H. Elbert (Honolulu: University of Hawai'i Press, 1986), and *Place Names of Hawai'i,* revised and expanded edition, by Mary Kawena Pukui, Samuel H. Elbert, and Esther T. Mookini (Honolulu: University of Hawai'i Press, 1974).

Following the example set by Ty P. Kāwika Tengan in *Native Men Remade: Gender and Nation in Contemporary Hawai'i* (Durham and London: Duke University Press, 2008), xiii, I use the terms "Native Hawaiian" and "Hawaiian" "interchangeably to refer to ethnic Hawaiians with any degree of [native] ancestry."

2. The duly constituted and diplomatically recognized independent Kingdom of Hawai'i was overthrown by agents of the United States in 1893; the Hawaiian Islands were formally annexed by the United States in 1898. In 1993, President William J. Clinton issued a formal apology on behalf of the government of the United States for the illegal acts of overthrow in 1893.

3. The Jaggar Museum is named after Thomas Augustus Jaggar, Jr. (1871–1953), a geologist from the Massachusetts Institute of Technology largely responsible for founding Hawai'i Volcanoes Observatory in 1912 and for its direction from 1912 to 1940.

4. Since the beginnings of the park system nationwide, the appropriation of the language of spirituality in NPS promotions of the natural landscape has characterized its publicity and promotions, its rationale for its existence, and its articulation of its relations to native populations. See, for example, Lynn Ross-Bryant, *Pilgrimage to the National Parks: Religion and Nature in the United States* (New York: Routledge, 2013). My chapter suggests, however, that something different is happening in HAVO, a significant variation on NPS history in this regard.

5. Christopher Tilley, *The Materiality of Stone: Explorations in Landscape Phenomenology* (Oxford, UK, and New York: Berg, 2004), 25. Tilley quotes from E. S. Casey, *Senses of Place* (Santa Fe, NM: School of American Research Press, 1996), 18.

6. Kathleen Stewart, *Ordinary Affects* (Durham, NC, and London: Duke University Press, 2007), 1, italics in original.

7. Tilley, *Materiality of Stone,* 10.

8. "Most Hawaiians living in the volcanic areas of Hawai'i, the districts of Ka'ū, Puna, and Kona, at the time of European contact, traced their ancestry to Pele." H. Arlo Nimmo, "The Cult of Pele in Traditional Hawaii," *Bishop Museum Occasional Papers* 30 (June 1990): 43.

9. See, for example, Greg Johnson, *Sacred Claims: Repatriation and Living Tradition* (Richmond: University of Virginia Press, 2007), 6, 33, and 102–103, and Glen Grant, *Obake Files: Ghostly Encounters in Supernatural Hawai'i* (Honolulu: Mutual Publishing, 1996): 25–27.

10. Johnson, *Sacred Claims,* 38.

11. Nimmo, "Cult of Pele," 73–78, quotes on 73–74. Past Pele clan burials in kapu areas of HAVO have been registered in minutes of the Kūpuna Council. See, for example, the minutes from April 11, 2001, p. 12, in HAVO 16337, Box 1, Folder 20, A20, Kūpuna Meetings, HAVO, 2001.

12. Visitors' descriptions of the site, ranging over the nineteenth and twentieth centuries, drew frequently on Christian scriptural understandings of hell, sometimes in tandem with notions of paradise (as Eden and/or heaven). See, for example, excerpts from early Volcano House guest registers collected in Darcy Bevens, ed., *On the Rim of Kī-lau-ea: Excerpts from the Volcano*

House Register, 1865–1955 (Hawaiʻi National Park: Hawaiʻi Natural History Association, 1992), esp. 39, 40, 44, 47, 50, 55, 130–146, and 164.

13. *Kukaeopele* means "Pele's dung" or "Pele's excrement."

14. See, for example, draft minutes of Kūpuna Council Meetings on March 14, 2002, esp. p. 3, and on November 20, 2002, pp. 3–4, in HAVO 16337, Box 1, Folder 2, A18, Kūpuna Council Meetings, 2001–2003.

15. I am not declaring that this is generally the case; I am, rather, remarking on the apparent NPS assumption that it is the case here. The NPS, however, is by no means alone, at HAVO or elsewhere, in energizing the senses, in specific historically locatable ways, as mediators, or bridges, between worlds.

16. Nimmo, "Cult of Pele," 84.

17. See, for example, the entry on Kāne in M. J. Harden, *Voices of Wisdom: Hawaiian Elders Speak* (Kula, HI: Aka Press, 1999), 204–211.

18. Herb Kawainui Kāne, *Pele: Goddess of Hawaiʻi's Volcanoes,* expanded ed. (Captain Cook, HI: Kawainui Press, 1987), acknowledgments page.

19. A number of scholarly works have recently contributed to historicizing the category of "spirituality"; among them the works of Leigh Schmidt, Kathryn Lofton, John Modern, and Courtney Bender are perhaps most notable in this context.

20. I thank Tisa Wenger for substantive contributions to these ideas.

21. I use the word "promotion" with respect to HAVO activities related to Native Hawaiian spiritual practice because the NPS on this site invites native participation in offering blessings and chants (*oli*) at such events as the dedications of buildings, exhibits, and signage. The dedication of the new Jaggar Museum building in 1987, for example, included an oli in Pele's honor, a Hawaiian blessing, and the ritual untying of a lei made from the *maile* plant; see HAVO 16337, Box 8, Folder 36, A87, Dedication of Jaggar Museum, HAVO, 16 January 1987. The remobilization of living native tradition, and with it Hawaiian religion, also provides an interpretive frame for the frequency of blessings, chants, opening and closing prayers, and other ceremonies and ritual practices offered at local, state, and federal functions, especially those in some way concerning Hawaiian culture and its sites and objects. Because many Hawaiians are also Christian or Buddhist or self-describe as New Age practitioners, observances at such official events often include multireligious elements and forms.

22. For an interesting and at least tangentially related argument, see Robin Bernstein, "Dances with Things: Material Culture and the Performance of Race," *Social Text* 27, 4 (2009): 67–94. The protections offered by the First Amendment are unequal protections, privileging certain recognizable forms of religiosity over others. On this subject, see, for example, Winnifred Fallers Sullivan, *The Impossibility of Religious Freedom* (Princeton, NJ: Princeton University Press, 2005).

23. I thank Mary Weismantel for encouraging me to think further in these directions.

24. Hawaiian history abounds in important particularities. Not only did the Hawaiian monarchy and elites renounce their traditional religious system just prior to the uncannily timed arrival of Christian missionaries; Hawaiians also set no racial requirement for citizenship in their kingdom. Furthermore, Native Hawaiians were not organized into tribal units in the manner of Native American populations on the continent. Although Western empires' unjust and unjustifiable possession and redistribution of Hawaiian lands have been very much at issue in the course of immigration and incursion, the reservation system as used to constrain and move native populations in the continental United States was not introduced in Hawaiʻi.

25. And cf. Jane Bennett, *The Enchantment of Modern Life: Attachments, Crossings, and Ethics* (Princeton, NJ: Princeton University Press, 2001), 5.

26. Some evidence suggests that although lava rock and Ti leaves have long been combined to form offerings, and while wrapping is a common Hawaiian activity in a range of registers, earlier traditional offerings involving these two materials located the volcanic rock atop a leaf of sacred Ti, presumably to keep it from blowing away. Whatever its past forms, the Ti bundle, wrapped, clothed, or adorned, with Ti containing the stone and moderating exposure, constitutes this offering's most common current shape. A recent brochure ("Nā Wahi Pana: Respecting Hawaiian Sacred Sites") designed and printed by 'Ahahui Mālama I Ka Lōkahi and the Kailua Hawaiian Civic Club and distributed at some NPS sites, pictures a Ti-wrapped stone and maintains that "wrapping a rock in a ti leaf is not a traditional offering and it alters the integrity of the site when left on heiau walls and platform." Ti-wrapped stones, nonetheless, number among the most frequently encountered offerings at Hawaiian sacred sites.

27. There is some historical evidence that a heiau dedicated to Pele once existed near this place. Nimmo, "Cult of Pele," 70.

28. See, for example, Donald P. Watson and Warren W. J. Yee, *Hawaiian Ti,* Cooperative Extension Service, University of Hawai'i, circular 481, reprinted June 1976, 5.

29. For conversation on this subject in HAVO records, see, for example, HAVO 16337, Box 1, Folder 8, A18, Hawaiian Advisory Group—Offerings, 1995–2000, and HAVO 16337, Box 1, Folder 11, A18, Hawaiian Issues, especially a printed e-mail thread titled "Shrine Offerings" and dated November 9, 2000.

30. At Maui's Hale-a-ka-lā National Park, on the other hand, I was told by an NPS ranger that it is official policy there to remove every offering, because any object that introduces plant material from one ecological zone to another may also introduce insects and diseases. A colleague in Hawai'i, Kate Lingley, recounts that Native Hawaiians periodically contest this policy, asserting their own claims on the sacred space of Hale-a-ka-lā as well as Hawai'i Island's Mauna Kea. From this perspective, the presence of international astronomical observatories on Mauna Kea amounts to desecration.

31. Nimmo, "Cult of Pele," 68-69, 78, 84.

32. Ibid., 66–67.

33. Greg Johnson, in his published research on NAGPRA cases, reflects on the unsettled complexity of what constitutes "native" in Hawaiian terms. See, for example, Greg Johnson, "Ancestors before Us: Manifestations of Tradition in a Hawaiian Dispute," *Journal of the American Academy of Religion* 71, no. 1 (June 2003): 335. Kāne quotation from Johnson, *Sacred Claims,* 95, italics added.

34. See Grant, *Obake Files,* 3, and Van James, *Ancient Sites of Hawai'i: Archaeological Places of Interest on the Big Island* (Honolulu: Mutual Publishing, 1995), 30–31.

35. On these subjects, see Van James, *Ancient Sites of O'ahu: A Guide to Hawaiian Archaeological Places of Interest* (Honolulu: Bishop Museum Press, 2010 [1991]), esp. 27–28, 109–110, and 113–114.

36. Nimmo, "Curse of Pele," 49–50.

37. HAVO 16337, Box 1, Folder 20, A20, Kūpuna Meetings, HAVO, 2001; see especially the draft minutes of the April 11, 2001, meeting, 7–8.

38. Linda Ching and Robin Stephens, *Power Stones: Letters to a Goddess* (Honolulu: Powerstones, 1994), 10 and 90–95.

39. See http://www.volcanogallery.com/lavarock.htm; and http://www.volcanogallery.com/. I last visited these pages of the site on September 16, 2012; it had been most recently edited or updated on August 8, 2012.

40. It is likely that Rainbow Moon invites these testimonies because it knows that the NPS has, for years, received many similar letters of testimony.

41. Lest we mistake these notions of activated objects among Protestant Christians as singular aberrations, on February 28, 2013, televangelist Pat Robertson of the Christian Broadcasting Network asserted on the air, in a *700 Club* segment, that "demonic spirits attach themselves to inanimate objects" such that it pays to "rebuke any spirits" inhabiting used clothing purchased from secondhand stores. Viewed on April 13, 2013, http://www.youtube.com/watch?v=4xvRjfuu3BU.

42. Charles Colbert, "A Critical Medium: James Jackson Jarves's Vision of Art History," *American Art* 16 (Spring 2002): 18–35. Jarves's understanding of the ability of objects to accumulate power is not so different from contemporaneous Native Hawaiian understandings, especially concerning stone. I am currently pursuing this research, aiming to understand whether and how Jarves's years in Hawai'i might have contributed to the shape of his later engagement with spiritual sensations in material practice.

43. I am grateful to Michelle Morgan for reacquainting me with Denton and his book titled *The Soul of Things; or, Psychometric Researches and Discoveries* (Boston: Walker, Wise, and Co., 1863). See Morgan's work on Denton in Chapter 3 of this book.

44. See Johnson, *Sacred Claims.* An active sovereignty movement includes numerous groups with varying specific agendas and goals. Among them, some advocate for the return of the Hawaiian Islands to the "monarchy-in-exile." Posters, placards, bumper stickers, and billboards, made by hand and by machine, assert these claims on the visible and visitable landscape.

45. In another context, Wendy Cadge notes the "strategically vague" framing of spirituality in the contemporary moment. Cadge, *Paging God in the Halls of Medicine* (Chicago: University of Chicago Press, 2013), 193.

46. Mary Weismantel, remarks in response to my paper at the Vibrant Materiality conference, Northwestern University, April 27, 2012.

47. On similar subjects, see Johnson, *Sacred Claims,* and Tisa Wenger, *We Have a Religion: The 1920s Pueblo Indian Dance Controversy and American Religious Freedom* (Chapel Hill: University of North Carolina Press, 2009).

48. This naming as "kapu" has a commercial side, too: the terminology and its symbols have gained ground on the properties of Western resort chains in Hawai'i, which now profit from their public assertions of respect for native traditions.

49. Of course the signs are posted to protect the sites, to keep unauthorized people away, and to prevent misbehavior, vandalism, and sacrilege. In this current legal landscape, however, they also potentially carry new freight.

50. Johnson, *Sacred Claims,* 3 and 13.

51. Claims of "present-day" kinship or cultural affiliation must be established by a "preponderance of evidence," which can include "geographical, kinship, biological, archaeological, anthropological, linguistic, folklore, oral tradition, historical, or other relevant information or expert opinion." Claimants, furthermore, "do not have to establish cultural affiliation with scientific certainty." See the NAGPRA legislation as quoted in Johnson, *Sacred Claims,* 76. The NPS occupies multiple subject positions. It would be inaccurate to suggest that there is opposition between the NPS and NAGPRA here. The NPS is, in fact, charged with NAGPRA's implementation. HAVO NPS employees have collaborated actively in building documentary evidence for native claims on sacred objects, grave goods, and human remains.

52. A favored HAVO name for Pele is Pelehonuamea, which means "Pele the sacred earth person" or "Pele of the sacred land." For a list of Pele's epithets with translations, see Nimmo, "Cult of Pele," 44.

53. HAVO 16337, Box 1, Folder 2, A18, Kūpuna Council Meetings, 2001-2003, draft minutes of the meeting of November 19, 2003, 2–3.

54. HAVO 16337, Box 1, Folder 20, A20, Kūpuna Meetings, HAVO, 2001; see the draft minutes of the meeting of April 11, 2001, 7

37

Religion, Sensation, and Materiality
A Conclusion

SALLY M. PROMEY

Investigating religion by way of the senses and materiality offers a set of possibilities for reexamining relations among practices, habits, beliefs, volition, affect, sensations, and stuff. This is not to emphasize practice rather than belief, affect instead of volition, or body over brain but rather to underline the intimate, messy relations among them.

In a very real sense, the successful conclusion to a volume of this sort might best circle back to its introduction, without simple repetition but with the advantage of having traversed the intervening pages. Our work here represents a journey just begun.

Multisensory scholarship promises more robust histories materially, spatially, organically, psychologically, interpersonally, and communally. Intersection with religion is key because assumptions about religion in modernity, and especially about presumed incompatibilities between "modern" religion and material sensation, have so decisively intervened in these narratives to date. One outcome of habituation to particular ways of "enlightened" knowing has been the apparent desensitization of artifacts and objects.

But time and again we encounter evidence that secular modernity in the West has not been what it has made itself out to be. It has, in fact, been shaped through a process of purging, purifying, and neutralizing, from within itself, those things most dear to it, those things most fearful: casting them out into other vessels in contrast to which it has then come to understand itself. These might well be described, in the words of religious studies scholar Nancy Levene, offered in another context, as "things expelled but not relinquished."[1]

By this new account, aestheticization, with all its apparent neutralizations, actually often respiritualizes both secular and religious objects, articulating them back into new domains of animation and understanding. Interiorization is not, after all, necessarily desensitization. Neither does what is interiorized necessarily remain there. Attending to materiality and sensation demonstrates that the demarcation between interior and exterior, between belief and practice, is much more arbitrary than we have often otherwise presumed. From the perspective of human subjectivity, intersubjectivity, and subject–object relations, what is "outside" occupies space "inside"; what is already "inside," that which has already located itself there in some prior process of incorporation, integrates, aggregates, and remanifests itself vis-à-vis what is "outside." At the interfaces, the senses operate in both directions.

We have been left with many central episodes for which the academy cannot adequately account, with discrepancies between the story on the ground and the academy's narration of itself. In this volume, one final example (and there are many other differently shaped but similarly invested stories) concerns the active content of the founding years of the School of Fine Arts at Yale University. John Ferguson Weir, that institution's first dean of fine arts, was a liberal Episcopalian. He and his wife, Mary, were also avid spiritualists, participants in séances, believers in sensory communication with other worlds. Weir served Yale's fine arts program for forty-four years, during which time he wrote and lectured widely on subjects concerning religion, aesthetics, and art objects.[2] This part of Weir's history at Yale has never been told and only recently even remarked.[3] When, in 1879, Weir sought a suitable candidate for the university's first professor of art history, he hired Congregationalist clergyman James Mason Hoppin, an eighteen-year veteran Yale professor of homiletics (1861–1879) who also held a law degree from Harvard. Hoppin taught in this fine arts capacity for twenty years, bringing (along with Weir) a liberal Protestant believer's perspective to bear on the process of shaping visual and material arts education at this elite academic institution. Here, in particular, the spiritual indeed "haunt[ed] projects of secular classification," as Finbarr Curtis has more generally suggested.[4]

In some ways this entire volume has been about inhabitations, transgressions, and transformations: where we locate ourselves, the obstacles and barriers we encounter, and the possibility of metamorphosis. Perhaps the ultimate transformation addressed throughout concerns modernity's ideological obsession with disenchantment, a disenchantment swept forward by strong currents of alienation that have bifurcated and dichotomized religion and modernity.[5] As authors assembled here, we endorse careful reevaluation of historical evidence concerning sensory and material cultures of religion. Our aim is nothing less than to yield a different, less socially alienating, more accurate, multidimensional, "enchanted," and enchanting modernity.[6]

NOTES

1. Nancy Levene, "Kant and the Worlds of Religion and Reason," lecture delivered at Yale University, October 22, 2012.

2. It is worth considering in far more detail the impact of liberal Protestant aesthetic the-

ologies in the shaping of arts institutions in the United States. I am indebted to Marian Wardle, curator of American art at Brigham Young University Museum of Art, and Danielle Hurd, who was at the time an M.A. student in history of art at Brigham Young University, for drawing to my attention Weir's commitments in this regard.

3. Sally M. Promey, "Visible Liberalism: Liberal Protestant Taste Evangelism, 1850 and 1950," in *American Religious Liberalism,* ed. Leigh Eric Schmidt and Sally M. Promey (Indianapolis: Indiana University Press, 2012), 76–96; see also Marian Wardle, ed., *The Weir Family, 1820–1920,* exhibition catalog, Brigham Young University Museum of Art (New Lebanon, NH: University Press of New England, 2011).

4. Finbarr Curtis, panelist, "A Fabulous Rumor: Critical Interpretations of John Lardas Modern's *Secularism in Antebellum America* (University of Chicago Press, 2011)," in the Cultural History of the Study of Religion Group and the Religion, Media, and Culture Group at the Annual Meeting of the American Academy of Religion in Chicago, November 2012; see also John Lardas Modern, *Secularism in Antebellum America* (Chicago: University of Chicago Press, 2011), xxix.

5. Gil Anidjar concurs: "Christianity, then, actively disenchanted its own world by dividing itself into public and private, politics and economics, indeed, religious and secular." Anidjar, "Secularism," *Critical Inquiry* 33, no. 1 (Autumn 2006): 59; see also 62.

6. A growing number of scholars, including Bruno Latour, Jane Bennett, Modern, and Curtis agree: "Disenchantment is one of the most significant enchantments of the secular age"; Curtis, "A Fabulous Rumor." One premise for Jane Bennett's *The Enchantment of Modern Life: Attachments, Crossings, and Ethics* (Princeton, NJ: Princeton University Press, 2001) is the "telling of an alter-tale" of enchanted modernity (4). I am grateful to Kati Curts, editorial associate for this volume, for urging me to think boldly about outcomes of this collaborative work in relation to themes of modern individuation and social alienation.

CONTRIBUTORS

BETTY LIVINGSTON ADAMS is adjunct professor at Rutgers University, New Brunswick, New Jersey, and an associate minister (Baptist). Her scholarship explores nineteenth- and twentieth-century African American / American religious and social history through the lenses of gender, race, and class. Her current book project is titled *"Work and Serve the Hour": The Politics of African American Women's Christian Activism in a Northern "Ideal Suburb," 1898–1945* (New York University Press, forthcoming).

HORACE D. BALLARD JR. is a doctoral candidate in American Studies at Brown University. His academic interests include the visual cultures of religion, the history of romanticism, the influence of eighteenth- and nineteenth-century European aesthetics on American art, and the Beat Generation. He teaches in the Education Department at the Museum of the Rhode Island School of Design.

MARY CAMPBELL is assistant professor of American art history at the University of Tennessee, Knoxville. She is currently working on a book for the University of Chicago Press that explores the intersections of pornography, stereography, and early Mormon theology. Before becoming an art historian, she received a J.D. from Yale Law School; she continues to publish on intellectual property and art law.

JAMES CLIFTON is director of the Sarah Campbell Blaffer Foundation and curator in Renaissance and Baroque Painting at the Museum of Fine Arts, Houston (MFAH). The author of essays on early modern European art, Clifton was chief writer for the documentary films *The Face: Jesus in Art* (2001) and *Picturing Mary* (2006) and has curated several exhibitions, including *The Body of Christ in the Art of Europe and New Spain, 1150–1800* (MFAH, 1997) and (with Walter S. Melion) *Scripture for the Eyes: Bible Illustration in Netherlandish Prints of the Sixteenth Century* (Museum of Biblical Art, New York, and Michael C. Carlos Museum, Emory University, Atlanta, 2009).

KATI CURTS is a doctoral candidate in American religious history in the Religious Studies Department at Yale University. Her research interests include critical theories of religion, performance, and mediation; identity formation and religious, popular, and consumer cultures in nineteenth- and twentieth-century America; and methods and practices of classification and collection in the study of religion. She is editorial associate for *Sensational Religion.*

FINBARR BARRY FLOOD is William R. Kenan Jr. Professor of Humanities at the Institute of Fine Arts and Department of Art History, New York University. Research interests include the art and architecture of the Islamic world, cross-cultural dimensions of Islamic material culture, theories and practices of image making, and technologies of representation. *Objects of Translation: Material Culture and Medieval "Hindu-Muslim" Encounter* (Princeton University Press, 2009) and *Islam and Image: Polemics, Theology and Modernity* (Reaktion Books, 2014) number among his recent books.

MEREDITH GAMER is a doctoral candidate in the Department of the History of Art at Yale University. Her research has been supported by fellowships and grants from the Center for Advanced Study in the Visual Arts, the Huntington Library, and the Paul Mellon Center for Studies in British Art. She is currently completing her dissertation with the support of a Charlotte W. Newcombe Doctoral Dissertation Fellowship from the Woodrow Wilson Foundation. That project, titled "Criminal and Martyr: Art and Religion in Britain's Early Modern Eighteenth Century," explores the visual culture of capital punishment in this period.

MEREDITH J. GILL is professor and chair in the Department of Art History and Archaeology at the University of Maryland, College Park. She is an historian of Italian art and architecture from the late medieval era through the sixteenth century. She is the author of *Augustine in the Italian Renaissance: Art and Philosophy from Petrarch to Michelangelo* (Cambridge University Press, 2006). Her book *Angels and the Order of Heaven in Medieval and Renaissance Italy* appears in 2014, also from Cambridge University Press.

PERIN GUREL is assistant professor of American studies at the University of Notre Dame. Her first book manuscript, "Wild Westernization: Gender, Sexuality, and the United States in Turkey," is currently under review. It explores how conflicts over the concept of Westernization in Turkey have historically influenced and continue to influence U.S.–Turkish relations, cultural production, and sexual politics.

JUNE HARGROVE, professor of art history at the University of Maryland, has written many articles in preparation of her book on Paul Gauguin in the Marquesas Islands. She is also the curator of *Carrier-Belleuse: The Master of Rodin,* an exhibition for the Palace of Compiègne. Hargrove's work focuses on European art, particularly French, from the eighteenth century to the early twentieth. Her scholarship investigates the historical context of art, with an emphasis on the impact of global transformations on style and content in painting and sculpture.

ANGIE HEO is a research fellow at the Max Planck Institute for the Study of Religious and Ethnic Diversity in Göttingen, Germany. She is currently working on an ethnographic study of images, media technology, and Coptic Christianity in contemporary Egypt.

PAUL CHRISTOPHER JOHNSON is professor of history and Afroamerican and African studies and director of the doctoral program in anthropology and history at the University of Michigan, Ann Arbor. Johnson's interests include the history and ethnography of the religions of the African diaspora in Brazil and the Caribbean, religion and race, religion and migration, the modern history of Brazil, theories of religion, and the history of the study of religion. His current book project investigates the genealogy of the idea of the possessed body in relation to questions of governance, slavery, and civil risk.

DANA E. KATZ is Joshua C. Taylor Associate Professor of Art History and Humanities at Reed College. She is the author of *The Jew in the Art of the Italian Renaissance* (University of Pennsylvania Press, 2008) as well as several articles and essays on the representational Jew in Renaissance Italy. Whereas her first book examines the dialogical relationship between violence and tolerance in Renaissance art, her current book project explores the urban form of the Jewish ghetto in Venice from the sixteenth century to the eighteenth as a discourse on space, surveillance, and ethnic enclosure.

CHRISTOPHER KRAMARIC is a doctoral student in American studies at Yale University. His research interests include critical theories of materiality, affect, and performance; the spatial politics and political economy of twentieth- and twenty-first-century U.S. capitalism; new suburban histories of poverty and economic insecurity since the 1970s; and ethnographic methods. He curates the Initiative for the Study of Material and Visual Cultures of Religion's *Material Objects Archive,* an online gallery and collaborative workspace, and is editorial associate for *Sensational Religion.*

GREGORY P. A. LEVINE is associate professor of the art and architecture of Japan and Buddhist visual cultures in the Department of the History of Art, University of California, Berkeley. He has written on the art and architecture of the Japanese Zen Buddhist monastery Daitokuji, the modern construct of "Zen art," cultures of exhibition and viewing in premodern and modern Japan, calligraphy connoisseurship and forgery, and the modern collecting and study of "Buddhist art." His current research focuses on fragments of Buddhist images within devotional and modern contexts in Asia and the West.

YUHANG LI received her Ph.D. in East Asian languages and civilizations from the University of Chicago in 2011 and is teaching Chinese art history at the University of Wisconsin, Madison. Her primary research interest is gender and material practice in relation to Buddhism in Ming and Qing China.

KATHRYN LOFTON is professor of American studies and religious studies at Yale University. Her research investigates the inseparability of religion and its cultural constructions and, likewise, the extent to which culture itself is embedded in religious histories. Her first book, *Oprah: The Gospel of an Icon* (University of California Press, 2011) used the example of Oprah Winfrey to explore the formation of religion in modern America. She is currently working on a study of sexuality and religion, an analysis of parenting practices in twentieth-century America, and a religious history of Bob Dylan.

VASILEIOS MARINIS is assistant professor of Christian art and architecture at the Institute of Sacred Music and the Divinity School, Yale University. He has published on a variety of topics ranging from early Christian tunics decorated with New Testament scenes to medieval tombs and Byzantine transvestite nuns. A monograph on the interchange of architecture and ritual in the medieval churches of Constantinople is forthcoming in 2014 from Cambridge University Press.

ARA H. MERJIAN is assistant professor of Italian studies and art history at New York University. He is the author of *Giorgio de Chirico and the Metaphysical City* (Yale University Press, 2013) and is currently researching a book on Pier Paolo Pasolini and the history of art.

RICHARD MEYER is Robert and Ruth Halperin Professor in Art History at Stanford University. *Outlaw Representation: Censorship and Homosexuality in Twentieth-Century American Art* numbers among his early publications. In 2009 he curated *Warhol's Jews: Ten Portraits Reconsidered* for the Jewish Museum in New York and the Contemporary Jewish Museum in San Francisco. Recent books include *What Was Contemporary Art?* (MIT Press, 2013) and a volume co-authored with Catherine Lord and titled *Art and Queer Culture* (Phaidon, 2013).

MINOO MOALLEM is professor of gender and women's studies at the University of California, Berkeley. She is the author of *Between Warrior Brother and Veiled Sister: Islamic Fundamentalism and the Cultural Politics of Patriarchy in Iran* (University of California Press, 2005). She is currently working on a book on the commodification of the nation through consumptive production and circulation of such commodities as the Persian carpet; a research project on gender, media, and religion; and another project on Iran–Iraq war movies and masculinity.

MIA M. MOCHIZUKI is Thomas E. Bertelsen Jr. Associate Professor of Art History and Religion at the Jesuit School of Theology, Santa Clara University; the Graduate Theological Union, Berkeley; and the Department of the History of Art, University of California, Berkeley. Her interdisciplinary research addresses problems in early modern religious art, especially Reformation (Catholic and Protestant), Netherlandish, and global Baroque art, particularly the Portuguese and Dutch networks. She is author of *The Netherlandish Image after Iconoclasm, 1566–1672* (Ashgate, 2008) and is currently completing a book titled "The Jesuits and the Earliest European Art in Japan, 1549–1639."

HAROON MOGHUL is a doctoral candidate at Columbia University researching Muhammad Iqbal and Islamic reformism in late colonial South Asia. He is a fellow at New America Foundation, author of *The Order of Light* (Penguin, 2006), and a public speaker.

MICHELLE MORGAN is a Ph.D. candidate in the American Studies program at Yale University. Her dissertation examines race and empire in the antebellum period, looking at the physical landscape, labor practices, and material culture of natural resources and extraction technologies such as gold, coal, and ivory.

BARBARA E. MUNDY is associate professor of art history at Fordham University. She is author of *The Mapping of New Spain* (University of Chicago Press, 1996); co-author with Dana Leibsohn of a website/DVD, *Vistas: Visual Culture in Spanish America, 1520–1820* (University of Texas Press, 2010); and co-editor with Mary Miller of *Painting a Map of Sixteenth-Century Mexico City: Land, Writing, and Native Rule* (Yale University Press / Beinecke Library, 2012). Her research interests center on indigenous art created in the Spanish colonies, especially in New Spain; cartography in the early modern period; and the role of collections in pre-Columbian art history.

MARGARET OLIN is senior research scholar in the Yale Divinity School, Yale University. Among her publications are *Touching Photographs* (University of Chicago Press, 2012); *The Nation without Art: Examining Modern Discourses in Jewish Art* (University of Nebraska Press, 2001); and *Monuments and Memory, Made and Unmade,* co-edited with Robert S. Nelson (University of Chicago Press, 2003). With Steven Fine and Vivian Mann, she co-edits the journal *Images: A Journal of Jewish Art and Visual Culture.*

SALLY M. PROMEY is professor of American studies and professor of religion and visual culture at Yale University, where she is founding director of the Initiative for the Study of Material and Visual Cultures of Religion (mavcor.yale.edu) and deputy director of the Yale Institute of Sacred Music. Her publications include two award-winning books, *Painting Religion in Public: John Singer Sargent's* Triumph of Religion *at the Boston Public Library* (Princeton University Press, 1999) and *Spiritual Spectacles:*

Vision and Image in Mid-Nineteenth-Century Shakerism (Indiana University Press, 1993). Most recently, she is co-editor (with Leigh Eric Schmidt) of *American Religious Liberalism* (Indiana University Press, 2012). Her research explores sensory, material, and spatial practices of American religion. Studies of the public display of religion, the material manifestations of scriptural metaphor, and the co-constitutive histories of Western religious and artistic modernities number among her current projects.

KATHRYN REKLIS is assistant professor of modern Protestant theology at Fordham University in New York City and co-director of the Institute for Art, Religion, and Social Justice, which she co-founded with AA Bronson in 2009. Her work concerns the field of early modern and modern Protestant theology and focuses on questions of aesthetics and embodiment in the Reformed tradition.

LAUREL C. SCHNEIDER is professor of religious studies at Vanderbilt University, where she teaches Native American religious traditions, contemporary and postmodern Christian thought, and gender studies. She is the author of *Re-imagining the Divine* (Pilgrim, 1999) and *Beyond Monotheism: A Theology of Multiplicity* (Routledge, 2007) and editor (with Catherine Keller) of *Polydoxy: Theologies of Multiplicity and Relation* (Routledge, 2010).

ERINN STALEY completed her doctoral degree in the Department of Religious Studies and the Program in Women's, Gender, and Sexuality Studies at Yale University in 2013. Her current work evaluates concepts central to modern Christian thought in light of intellectual disability and disability theory. Staley is visiting lecturer at Wellesley College.

YUI SUZUKI is associate professor of art history at the University of Maryland. She is a specialist in Japanese Buddhist art. Her recent book, *Medicine Master Buddha: The Iconic Worship of Yakushi in Heian Japan* (Brill, 2012), explores the primacy of icons in disseminating the devotional cult of the Medicine Buddha. Her current research, "Possessions and the Possessed: The Multi-sensoriality of Spirits, Bodies, and Objects in Heian Japan," reconsiders the roles of ritual objects and human bodies as mediators between the material and spiritual worlds.

DAVID WALKER is assistant professor of religious studies at the University of California, Santa Barbara. His research focuses on intersections of religion, settlement policy, industry, and tourism in the nineteenth-century American West. He has also published on spiritualism and ritual studies.

ISAAC WEINER is assistant professor in the Department of Comparative Studies at the Ohio State University. He is the author of *Religion Out Loud: Religious Sound, Public Space, and American Pluralism* (New York University Press, 2014). Areas of research interest include religious pluralism, critical theories of religion, and religion in public space.

JUDITH WEISENFELD is professor of religion and associate faculty in the Center for African American Studies at Princeton University. She is the author most recently of *Hollywood Be Thy Name: African American Religion in American Film, 1929–1949* (University of California Press, 2007) and is currently at work on a project titled "Apostles of Race: Religion and Black Racial Identity in the Urban North, 1920–1950."

MARY WEISMANTEL is professor of anthropology and director of gender studies at Northwestern University. She is the author of two books and numerous articles about gender, sex, race, food, adoption, and other topics based on her ethnographic research in the Andean region of Peru, Bolivia, and Ecuador and, more recently, on museum and field research on Pre-Columbian art. Her theoretical interests center on materiality, material culture, and new materialist theory and on multiple forms of inequality and engagement across difference, including gender, sexuality, animal–human relations, and class.

ELAINE Y. YAU is a doctoral student in the History of Art Department at the University of California, Berkeley, and Wyeth fellow in American art at the Center for Advanced Study in the Visual Arts in Washington, D.C. Her dissertation explores Sister Gertrude Morgan's painting and performance practice in New Orleans and nationally from 1960 through 1983.

INDEX

Page numbers for entries occurring in figures are followed by an *f* and those for entries in notes, by an *n*.

Afghanistan, Bamiyan Buddhas in, 6–7

Africa, ingestion of Qur'an in, 480

African American(s): aestheticization of, 276, 289; at fine art exhibitions, 281; Great Migration by, 413–15; in Harlem Renaissance, 279, 280; in Interracial Conference Movement (*See* Interracial Conference Movement); making visible corporeal presence of, 276, 279, 281, 288; religious identity of, transformations in, 414–24. *See also* Moorish Americans

African American art: Church Women's Committee's use of (*See* Interracial Conference Movement); Harmon Foundation exhibitions of, 279–86, 280f, 283–85f, 288; by professionals vs. amateurs, 282

African art, in Interracial Conference Movement, 275, 279, 281, 288

Afro-Brazilian religions: contemporary, significance of photographs in, 37, 45n49; policing of, 45n44; popularity of, 28; Rosa (Juca) in, 26, 32–40; vs. Spiritism, 28; spirit possession in, 26, 28, 29, 32–40

agency: as limited to humans, 8; of objects, 4, 8–9, 206, 642–43; of photographs, 26

Aghasi, Hussein Gullar, 303

Aghili, Javad, 305–14, 307f, 310f, 311f, 314f; *Ashura*, 310–13, 311f; career of, 306; *Me'râj*, 306–8, 307f; on process of coffeehouse painting, 304, 308; *Siavash*, 309–10, 310f, 312; themes of paintings of, 298, 305–14; *Woman Playing Daf*, 313, 314f

agriculture, Mormon, 592–93, 594, 597

AIRFA. *See* American Indian Religious Freedom Act

airplanes, Muslim prayers in, 251–53

airports: Muslim prayers in, 251–53; profiling in security screenings at, 251–52

ajari, 67, 75–76, 83n1

Alberti, Leon Battista, *De re aedificatoria*, 170

alcohol consumption, Mormon ban on, 594

alcohol containers, in offerings to Pele, 637–38, 638f

Alexander, Elizabeth, 418f

allegory: etymology of term, 129n3; Johnson's (Charles Ellis) self-portrait as, 263, 264, 269; study of religion via, 115, 129n3

Altona (Germany), eruv in, 195

amaru, 609, 614

Amazonians, perspectivism of, 618–20

American exceptionalism, food art in, 240

American Indian Religious Freedom Act of 1978 (AIRFA), 629

American Russian Institute, 223n9

Amherst College, 121

Amitābha Buddha, 347–48, 348f, 353n24

amulets, against djinns, 92

analogy, material transformation through, 14. *See also* allegory

Anatomical Crucifixion (James Legg) (Banks), 495–510, 496f; Hunter's anatomical models as antecedent of, 499–502; loss of first cast, 497, 508, 511n5; origins of project, 495–97, 499; particularity of, 502–3; public execution in, 497, 498, 504–10; scholarship on, lack of, 497–98; source of body for, 497, 505–7, 510n4; visual precedents for, 503–4, 512n26

anatomical models: *Anatomical Crucifixion* (Banks) as, 497; by Hunter, 499–502, 500f, 501f, 504, 512nn18–19

Anatomy of the Human Gravid Uterus, The (Hunter), 499

Ancien culte mahorie (Gauguin), 349

Anderson, Benedict, 191

Anderson, Hazel W., 422

Anderson Cooper 360° (television show), 239, 241

androgyny, in *Contes barbares* (Gauguin), 345–46

angels: bodies of, 540–41; as bodiless intelligences, 540; creation of, 542, 546; guardian, 456f, 457; in Moorish Science Temple of America, 423, 427n25; neutral, 552, 553–54; in origin of human souls, 552, 553

angels, depictions of fall of rebel, 537–55; by Beccafumi, 537–41, 538f, 539f, 547–49, 552, 552f, 554–55; by Bosch, 541–47, 545f, 548f; by Bruegel, 541–46, 544f; by Dürer, 541, 544f; by Limbourg brothers, 541, 543f; by Master of the Rebel Angels, 541, 542f

Anidjar, Gil, 653n5

animals, depictions of, on Chavín de Huantar stones, 608–10, 611, 614

animism: among contemporary Amazonians, 618–20, 623n34; use of term, 623nn34–35

Anishinaabe, 444

Annotations and Meditations on the Gospel (Nadal), 382

Anselmo, Giovanni, 452

Anthropological Exposition (1882), 29, 42n22

anthropology: criminal, 43n26; photography and, 29, 43n26; spirit possession in, 30–31

anthropomorphism, of planchettes, 55–58

Anton, Charles, 272n7

Antoni, Janine, 241

AO. *See* Action Office

Apocalypse by Fire or Fall of the Rebel Angels (Bosch), 542, 545f, 546–47

Appadurai, Arjun, 206, 212n10

Apple, 154

apples, 482–83, 493n105

Arabic language, in Iran, 298, 312, 319n52

Arabs, eruvin in Jewish relations with, 196–98

architecture: habit and, 159; modernism in, 138–39; Mormon, 589–90, 595–97, 598–99; public, arts projects in, 6; suburban, 138–39; Taylorism in, 142; visual and tactile reception of, 159–60, 177

Arcimboldo, Giuseppe, 131n6

Aretino, Spinello, 556n9

Aristotle, 10, 321

Arnold, Thomas, 318n43, 319n48

Arrington, Leonard, 600n4

Arrival of the Franciscans and Erection of the First Cross, The (unknown artist), 520, 521f

art: Gauguin on meaning of, 341, 343, 347, 350–51; as replacement for religion, 5–6; in secularization theory, 2, 5–7. *See also specific kinds*

Art Center (New York), 280, 284–85

art criticism, on New Negro Art Movement, 281, 282–83, 284–85

Artemios (saint), 325, 474

Arthur, Chris, 206

artistic refinement, in hair embroidery, 367–71

artists: bodies of, as artistic medium, 452; illness and creativity of, 579n51; as prophets, 351–52

Art Journal, 216–17

Arts, The (journal), "Russian Icons" (Barr) in, 216–22, 217f, 221f, 222f

Art-Union, 497, 508–9

artworks: Catholic objections to, 258; in relation to time, 215. *See also specific kinds and works*

Asabashō (Shōchō), 74

Asad, Talal, 2, 5, 8, 12, 115, 254n6

Asbury Park (New Jersey), Hotel Berkeley-Carteret in, 275, 276f, 288, 292n1

asceticism, Buddhist, hair plucking in, 362

ASD. *See* autism spectrum disorders

Ashura (Aghili and Blookifar), 310–13, 311f

Asia, hair symbolism in, 372n10. *See also specific countries*

Asiatic racial identity, of Moorish Americans, 415, 422–23, 426n22

assimilation, of former slaves in Brazil, 26, 31–32

Atatürk, Mustafa Kemal, 94

atheism, of Pasolini, 450, 455n6

Athens (Greece), Parthenon in, 331

athletes, Muslim, 255n16

Atlantic Monthly (magazine), 264–65

Atlas Shrugs blog (Geller), 250

Atomic Bomb (Warhol), 388

audience, of Hawai'i Volcanoes National Park signage, 625–26

auditory religious practices: adhan as, 225–28; church bells as, 227, 228; in Hindu bathing ritual, 233–34, 237; in mainline Protestantism, 429–30, 433n1

Augustine (saint), on angels, 546, 550, 557nn16–17

Augustinians, in New Spain, 518

Aurier, Albert, 351

Authentic Account of Three Generations in Japan, 70

authenticity: Catholic reform as reevaluation of, 547; concern about, in Islamic practice, 469; of offerings to Pele, 637–39; religious, scholarship questioning, 419; in representations of djinns, 90, 91, 95, 108

autism spectrum disorders (ASD), 429, 433n4

avant-garde, 6

"Avant-garde and Kitsch" (Greenberg), 6

Avogadori di Comun, 173

Ayat Al-Kursi, 92

Azadmehr, Javad, 300

Azazel (angel), 550–51, 558n37

Azevedo, Militão Augusto de, *Portrait with Spirit*, 28–29

Aztec. *See* Mexico

Bailun, 362

baimiao, 364–65, 367

Bajuri, Muhammad al-, 473

bodily attentiveness: definition of, 443; and Good Mind, 443, 444

body(ies): anatomy of (*See* anatomical models); of angels, 540–41; of artists, as medium, 452; on Chavín de Huantar stones, 619–20; and cities, reciprocal relationship between, 175; control of, in mainline church services, 430, 431–32; of the dead (*See* dead, the); disabled, social construction of, 431; experience of, in stereography, 262–65, 267, 272n5; gifts of the, in Buddhism, 360; of God, in Mormonism, 268; of Moorish Americans, 419–24; of Mormon men, 268–72; nude (*See* nudity); in Pasolini's works, 447–54; in religioracial identity, 419–21; of women, measurements of, 121

body doubles, and Japanese martyrdom paintings, 386–90

body–mind dualism, Descartes on, 8

Body of Christ in the Art of Europe and New Spain, The (exhibition), 205

body–spirit dualism, in Native American religious practices, lack of, 441–42

Bologna (Italy): communism in, 450; consumerism in, 450, 455n7; *Intellettuale* (Mauri) in, 447; Pasolini's life in, 450; as "Red Center" of Italy, 450

bones, human, in Hawaiian culture, 628–29, 647n11

Bonfire of the Clothes, Books, and Attire of the Priests (unknown artist), 516, 517f, 530–31

Book of Mormon, 265–67, 267f, 272n7, 272n11

Book of Touch, The (Classen), 49

books: and blood, 459; burning of, in New Spain, 518, 519, 527

Bosch, Hieronymus, 541–47; *Apocalypse by Fire or Fall of the Rebel Angels,* 542, 545f, 546–47; *Garden of Earthly Delights,* 556n14; *Haywain* triptych, 547, 556n14; *Last Judgment* triptych, 547, 548f, 556n14; understanding of sin, 542, 546, 557n18

Boston (Massachusetts): Museum of Fine Arts in, 216, 218; Public Library of, 18n24

Boston Journal of Chemistry, 54

bowls: holy water in, 235; Qur'an written on, 477–80, 479f

Braude, Anne, 62nn8–9

Brazil: abolition of slavery in, 26, 31; assimilation and nationalization of former slaves in, 26, 31–32; gradual process of emancipation in, 32; Spiritism in, 28, 41n15, 42n20. *See also* Afro-Brazilian religions

Brazil, photography in, 25–40; defining the nation through, 29, 42n21; indigenous subjects of, 29, 42nn21–22; Juca Rosa photo, 26, 32–40, 34f; objectivity in, 27, 29; rise of, 26–28; spirit possession linked with, 26, 29–31

Breck, Joseph, 219

Brennan, Thomas J., 226

Brettell, Richard, 353n14

bricolage, eruvin compared to, 187, 200n17

Brinker, Helmut, 568, 572

Britain: public executions in, 498–99, 501, 505–7, 509–10; public exhibitions in, 498–99; touching of religious objects in, 213n21. *See also* London

British Museum (London): *Hajj* exhibition at, 211, 213n24; *Treasures of Heaven* exhibition at, 209–11, 212n17, 213n23

Britto, Giovanni, 553f, 559n40

Bronson, AA, 231, 233–34, 236

Brooks, Caroline Shawk, *Dreaming Iolanthe,* 245n3

Brown, Candy Gunther, 62n9

Brown, Capability, 146

Brown, Dewitt, 427n28

Brown Bey, Alec, 413–24; draft registration by, 413, 414f, 415–16, 416f, 422; migration of, 413–15, 424n2; racial and religious identity of, 413–14, 415, 422, 424

Bruce, James, 550, 558n28

Bruegel, Pieter, the Elder, 541–46; *Fall of the Rebel Angels,* 542, 544f

Bryant, Julius, 497, 511n5

Buddha, embroidered images of, 355, 358; by Mrs. Chen, 368; by Ni Renji, 361–62, 363; by Ye Pingxiang, 355–57

Buddha, on death, 577n18

Buddhism: blood writing of scriptures in, 360–61; in *Contes barbares* (Gauguin), 343–44, 345–46, 347–48; Esoteric, 67, 73, 74, 77–78; goma (fire rite) in, 67–69; and hair embroidery (*See* hair embroidery); head-shaving ceremony in, 358; Heian-period (*See* Heian Japan); portraits of masters in, 564–65, 577n24; Tendai, 67, 83n1

Buddhist death verses, 561–75; aesthetics of, 572–73; of Chikotsu Daie, 564, 565f, 567–74, 578n44; display of, 563, 564; faltering calligraphy in, 564, 567–75, 578n45, 579n52; hagiographic texts on, 562, 564–67, 574; history of, 561–63, 576n3; impact of, 561–62, 574; lost vs. extant, 564; modern scholarship on, 563–65; vs. other writings of masters, 564, 578n38; prevalence of, 562–63; teachings contained in, 563; timing of composition of, 562, 563–65, 577n25, 579n52

Buddhist monasticism: death verses in (*See* Buddhist death verses); head-shaving ceremony in, 358

Buguet, Édouard, 26, 42n19

Bühler-Rose, Michael, 231; *I'll Worship You, You'll Worship Me*, 233–34, 233f, 237

Bulletin of the Museum of Fine Arts, 216

Buondelmonti, Cristoforo, *Map of Candia*, 169f

Buraq: in *Me'râj* (Aghili), 306–7, 307f; in popular art, 318n43

Burden, Chris, 452

Bürolandschaft, 146

Burton, Richard F., 584, 586, 587, 597, 601n9

business life, scholarship on intersection of religion and, 137–38

Busiri, al-, *Qaṣīdat al-Burda*, 473–75, 493n107

Butler, Nelly, 61n7

Byzantine sacred art, 321–35; erasure of faces on, 321, 326, 334–35; functions of, 321–22; graffiti on, 321, 323f, 330–35; interactions with, 322–29, 335, 464–65; as "lifelike," 323–24; motivations for defacement of, 321, 326–27; scraping of paint from, 321, 326–28, 464–65

Byzantium: hierarchy of senses in, 321, 336n5; iconoclasm in, 328, 333–34, 465; materiality in religion of, 321, 329–30

cabinet photographs, 27, 41n10

Cadge, Wendy, 650n45

Cahier pour Aline (Gauguin), 351

Callahan, Richard J., Jr., 599n1

Calle, Sophie, *L'erouv de Jerusalem,* 196

calligraphy, Buddhist: as art, 567, 578n37; death verse (*See* Buddhist death verses)

call to prayer. *See* adhan

Calo, Mary Ann, 281, 295n44

Camaxtli (deity), 523, 523f

Camille, Michael, 561, 573, 579n56

Camollia, Battle of (1526), 547, 557n21

Campany, Robert, 368

Campbell, Mary: biographical highlights, 655; chapter by, 261–72

Candia (Crete), Jewish quarter of, 168–70, 169f, 180n27

Candlin, Fiona, 210

Candomblé: possession shots in, 37, 38f, 46n51; significance of photographs in, 37, 45n49

canon law, on interfaith physical contact, 172–73

Cantarina, Rachel Hebrea, 176

Caravaggio, 450, 453; *Saint Thomas,* 453

Carlyle, Thomas, *Sartor Resartus,* 346, 347, 351

Carpue, Joseph Constantine, in *Anatomical Crucifixion* (Banks), 495, 497, 499, 502, 504, 505, 510n2, 510n4

Carrasco, Davíd, 522, 525

Carrington, Hereward, 65n50

Carroll, Michael, 301

carte de visite photographs, 27–28, 33–34, 41n10

Carter, Erik, 432

Casarano (Italy), Santa Maria della Croce in, 323f, 330

Casas, Bartolomé de las, 527

Casentino, Jacopo del, *Fall,* 556n9

Castelli, Elizabeth, 298–99

Castigation of the Tlaxcalan Idolators, The (unknown artist), 524, 525f

Castillo, Lisa Earl, 45n49

Castro Albuquerque, Fillipe Jansen de, Jr., 44n36

Castronovo, Russ, 62n9

"Catholic Church and Modern Times, The" (Gauguin), 347

Catholicism: art of, destruction in revolutions, 216; art of, repurposed in Protestantism, 10; bowl of holy water in, 235; devotional objects of, in Protestant churches, 399–400; iconoclasm in, 258; in Italy, Pasolini's critique of, 450; liturgical calendar of, in Venice, 161–62; in New Spain, 518; papal infallibility in, 42n21; plaster or chalkware devotional objects in, 400; reform in, as reevaluation of authenticity, 547; split with Protestantism, materiality in, 2; "theft" of, by Juca Rosa, 33, 44n36

Church of Jesus Christ of Latter-day Saints (LDS). *See* Mormonism

Church of Saint Bishoi (Port Said), icon of Virgin Mary in, 435–40, 436f, 439f, 440n1

Church of the Gesù (Rome), 380

Church Women's Committee (CWC) of the Commission on Race Relations, 275–92; antidiscrimination resolution of, 287; antilynching resolution of, 294n39; decline of, 289–91; funding for, 289; goal of, 276–77, 291–92; membership restrictions of, 292n3; in Race Relations Sunday, 289–91, 290f, 295n48; theology of, 277, 292n4. *See also* Interracial Conference Movement

Cidor, Peggy, 201n39

cigarettes, in offerings to Pele, 638

Cimabue, 556n9

cinema. *See* movies

Circignani, Niccolò, 381–82; *Martyrdom of Christians in Africa during the Reign of Huneric,* 381, 381f

Circumcision (Signorelli), 208

circumcision, nocturnal rituals associated with, 166

cities: Iranian, coffeehouses in, 302–3; reciprocal relationship between bodies and, 175; walls of, role of, 168, 170

citizenship: Iranian, coffeehouse painting in, 298–99, 303, 305, 309; in Kingdom of Hawai'i , 648n24

Città di vita (Palmieri), 553–54

civility/civilization, 4, 94, 115, 120, 154, 203–4, 218, 247–48, 289, 318n36, 346

Clark, T. J., 388

Classen, Constance, 11, 207, 210, 213n20; *The Book of Touch,* 49

Clement VII (pope), 547

Clendinnen, Inga, 531

Clifton, James: biographical highlights, 655; chapter by, 205–11

Clinton, William J., 647n2

clothing: of Ethiopian Hebrews, 426n17; of Jews, 172–73; of Moorish Americans, 419–20, 420f, 421

Coates, James, *Photographing the Invisible,* 63n15

Code of Maimonides, The (Maimonides), 185, 201n30

coffee consumption, Mormon ban on, 594

coffeehouse(s), history of, 300–303

coffeehouse painting: alternative terms for, 297, 316n1; definition of, 297; in Iran (*See* Iranian coffeehouse painting)

cognition–sensation dualism, Descartes on, 8

cognitive disabilities, definition of, 433n4

Cohen, Alan, 191, 192f

collages, as composites, 116

colonialism. *See* New Spain

color(s): on Chavín de Huantar stones, 622n20; in *Contes barbares* (Gauguin), 349–51; in Heian Japan, symbolism of, 75; in Pictorial History of Tlaxcala, lack of, 535n29

color line. *See* racial segregation

Columbus, Christopher, 517

combination prints, 131n6

comedy tropes, djinns as, 94, 109n14

Commandment Keepers Congregation, 416, 417

Commedia (Dante), 552–54, 553f, 559n44

Commentaria (Berengario), 503–4, 503f, 512n26

Commission on Race Relations, of FCC, in Race Relations Sunday, 289–91, 290f, 295n48. *See also* Church Women's Committee

common law, on interfaith physical contact, 172–73

common sense: dreaming as medium of, 435–36; sensation as form of, 435, 440

communalism, Mormon, 594–95

communion, *Sweet Jesus* (Cavallaro) and, 242. *See also* Eucharist

communism, in Italy, 450, 452

compassion (exhibition), 231–37, 232f, 233f, 235f

"Composita" (Stoddard), 113–29, 114f; component sitters' response to, 113, 121–29, 123f; individual portraits used in, 113, 129n1; play based on, 113, 122–27; production of, 113, 116–21, 119f

Composita: A Drama in Three Acts (Ruble), 113, 122–27, 124f, 125f

composite photographs: origins of, 116–17, 131n6; saintliness compared to, 128; Stoddard's production of, 113, 116–21, 117f; technical processes used in, 118–20, 128; "types" in, 116, 117–18, 126, 128. *See also* "Composita"

Compte, Louis, 27

computer games: djinns in, 89–90, 95, 96–101, 97f; lag time in, 98–99

computer-generated imagery (CGI), 103, 105

Comte, Auguste, 27, 41n7

Conceição, João Maria da, 34

Conclusiones (Pico della Mirandola), 550, 551, 558n37

conduct norms, in mainline Protestantism, 429–30, 431–32

Cones, Bryan, 241

Congregational Council, 287

Congress, U.S., on polygamy, 270

Conley El, 425n7

Connecticut. *See* New Haven

Connolly, William, 2, 13, 20n61

Constantine I (Roman emperor), 334

Constantinople, Hagia Sophia in, 321, 324

Constitution, U.S. *See* First Amendment

constructed objects, agency of, 8

consumerism: Iranian, rise of, 308; Italian, Pasolini's critique of, 450, 455n7. *See also* merchandising, religious

contemporary art, historical art as, 215

Contes barbares (Gauguin), 341–52, 342f, 346f; androgyny in, 345–46; Buddhism in, 343–44, 345–46, 347–48; Christianity in, 343–45, 347; color in, 349–51; figures in, 343–48; inscription on, 343; Maori culture in, 343–44, 347; sound in, 349–50; synesthesia in, 341, 343, 347–52; title of, 343, 344, 348–49; as visual parable, 344–52

Coole, Diana, 8, 19n42, 20n61

Cooper, Anderson, 239, 241

copies: of Chavín de Huantar stones, 606, 607f, 608; of Russian icons, 220, 221f

Coptic Christians: icon of Virgin Mary and, 435, 440n1; ingestion of the sacred by, 478, 480, 481; population of, 440n2

corporate culture, of Herman Miller, 141–42, 154–55

corporations, as sects, 154–55

corporeal, 1, 160, 175, 177, 257, 265, 267, 269, 271, 276, 288–89, 306, 314–15, 335, 371, 376, 453, 468, 540, 573, 634–35. *See also* body

Corpus Domini predella (Uccello), 164–65, 165f

correspondences: Swedenborg on, 346–47, 351; in synesthesia, 341, 351–52

"Correspondences" (Baudelaire), 351

Corte de florero series (Echavarría), 388, 389f

Cortés, Hernán, 515, 517, 518, 519, 526–27

Coryat, Thomas, 174

Cosmas (saint), 327–28, 464–65

Cosway, Richard: in *Anatomical Crucifixion* (Banks), 495–97, 499, 505, 510n2, 510n4; religious beliefs of, 504–5

Council of Alexandria (400), 559n41

Council of Constantinople, Fifth (533), 559n41

Council of Florence (1439), 553

Council of Nicaea, Second (787), 328, 334, 335

Council of Ten, 161

counterculture, 152

Couros, Matheus de, 380

courtyards, eruvin and, 184–87

covenant, in Neo-Calvinism, 140

Cox, Robert, 48, 61n5

creativity, illness and, 579n51

Creek (Muscogee) nation, 442, 443, 444, 446, 446n1

Crete, Jewish residential segregation in, 168–70, 169f, 180n27

criminal anthropology, 43n26

criminality, and sin, 124–25, 127, 128

Critique of Judgment (Kant), 10

Cromwell, Oliver, 216

Crow, Thomas, 215

crucifixion: in *Anatomical Crucifixion* (Banks), 495–97, 496f, 504–5; in Japanese martyrdom paintings, 384–88; in Pasolini's *La Ricotta,* 451, 451f; in *The Three Crosses* (Rubens), 510n2

Crucifixion and Iconoclasts, The (Chludov Psalter), 325f, 333

Crucifixion fumi-e (anonymous), 385f

Crucifixion with a Painter (Zubarán), 385

cruelty, of crucifixion, 508–9

Crystal Palace (New York), 245n3

cubicles, 135–55; development of, 135, 144–49; reasons for design of, 135–37; reception and use of, 152–55; religious aspects of, 137; sensorial experience limited by, 136, 137, 153; worker unhappiness with, 135–36. *See also* Action Office

cult of the dead and dying, in Chan/Zen Buddhism, 563
cultural interactivity, in multiplayer online computer games, 99
cultural patrimony: under NAGPRA, 646; Russian icons as, 6, 220
Cummins, Tom, 618, 621n1
Curtis, Finbarr, 652, 653n6
Curtis, Vesta Sarkhosh, 318n40
Curts, Kati: biographical highlights, 656; chapter by, 113–29; comments on, 20n58
CWC. *See* Church Women's Committee
Cyprus, church of Asinou in, 331, 332f

Dacos, Nicole, 560n47
Daguerre, Louis, 27, 41n8
daguerreotypes, 27. *See also* photographs
Dahui Zhonggao, 562, 567, 573
Daidō Ichi'i, 571–72
Daigo (emperor of Japan), 85n30
Daitō Kokushi, 566
Damian (saint), 327–28, 464–65
dancing rituals: Hawaiian, 630; Tlaxcalan, 528
Daniel the Stylite, 338n37
Dannehl, Karin, 212n9
Dante, 546; *Commedia,* 552–54, 553f, 559n44
Darwin, Charles, 117
David, Jan, *Veridicus Christianus,* 383–84, 383f
Dawson, Charles, *The Quadroon Madonna,* 279, 280f
Dazhidu lun, 360
dead, the: bodies of, in Islam, 468; bones of, in Hawaiian culture, 628–29, 647n11; cult of, in Chan/Zen Buddhism, 563; in photographs (*See* spirit photography); photos of, in Brazil, 28, 29; in Spiritualism, 48
Dean El, James, 422
Dearborn (Michigan), adhan in, 226, 227
De architectura (Vitruvius), 175
death, during meditation, 566, 578n28. *See also* dead, the
death penalty. *See* executions
death verses: definition of, 561; history of, 561–62; impact of, 561–62; terms for, 562, 575, 576n3. *See also* Buddhist death verses
Deer, Philip, 442
De Gasperi, Alcide, 450
deities, Mormon men as, 268–72, 273n21. *See also specific deities*

De Iudaeis et aliis infidelibus (Susannis), 172–73
Delacroix, Eugène, 350, 351
Deleuze, Gilles, 312
democracy, of cubicles, 137
Denton, William: experiments of, 49, 50, 58–60, 65n46; *The Soul of Things,* 59; on spiritual agency of objects, 642–43
departing verses. *See* death verses
De Pree, D. J., 140–41, 142, 154
De Pree, Hugh, 141
De Pree, Max, 141
De re aedificatoria (Alberti), 170
Descartes, René, 11, 13; *Discourse on Method,* 8
Descripción de la ciudad y provincia de Tlaxcala (Muñoz Camargo), 519–20, 533n9
Desecration of the Host, The (Uccello), 164–65, 165f
Deseret Agricultural and Manufacturing Society, 597
Deseret Museum (Salt Lake City), 595
Deseret News, 595
desire: in Mormonism, 269, 274n26; in prosopopoeia, 481–83
destruction, vs. transformation, through fire, 531–32
deterrence, as goal of executions, 505–7
developmental disabilities: definition of, 433n4; marginalization of people with, 429–32
Devil, sin of, 546
devotion, genealogy of term, 130n4
devotional objects: Christian, 399–400; "Composita" (Stoddard) as, 121–29
Devotion by Design (exhibition), 207–9, 208f, 209f, 210, 212n15
Dewey, John, 228
dharanis, in spirit pacification, 79
dhikr, 248
Diana (princess of Wales), 210
Diao, Miss, 364, 370–71
Didi-Huberman, Georges, 43n26, 385, 391
dietary codes: Mormon, 594; Muslim, 255n16
differentiation: for comparison (*See specific kinds*); in tourism, 582
Dilbert comic strip (Adams), 153
Dinç, Mevlüt, 96, 99
disabilities: definition of, 430–31; vs. impairments, 431, 433n6; social construction of, 431

disabilities, people with: marginalization in mainline churches, 429–32; participation gap among, 432

disability studies, 431–32

Discourse on Method (Descartes), 8

discrimination, against people with disabilities, 429–32. *See also* racial discrimination

Disdéri, André Adolphe E., 41n10, 43n24

disease transmission, beliefs about Jews and, 173–74

disenchantment, 652, 653nn5–6

displacement, in Japanese martyrdom paintings, 378–80, 393

disruption, in Japanese martyrdom paintings, 380–84

distance, in sight vs. touch, 160

Distomo (Greece). *See* Hosios Loukas monastery

distractions, in cubicles, lack of, 135, 136

"Diverses choses" (Gauguin), 349–50

diversity, religious, in U.S., 225–28

Divine, Father, 417, 426n13

djinns, 89–108; artistic depictions of, 92–93, 93f, 109n9; denial of existence of, 90–91, 101; vs. goblins, representations of, 91, 95, 96–97, 100, 102; hoax image of "real," 100–101, 100f, 101f; in Istanbul Kıyamet Vakti (game), 89–90, 95, 96–101, 97f; in *Musallat* (movie), 89–90, 95, 101–8, 104f; origins of stories about, 91–92; in Ottoman Empire, 92–94, 109n14; in Qur'an, 91–92, 108; in strategic Westernization, 90–91, 93–94, 95, 108; tethering, use of term, 90; twentieth-century stories of, 93–95

Dominicans, in New Spain, 518

Doni, Antonfrancesco, *Libraria,* 559n40

Donis, Alex: *Jesus Christ and Lord Rama,* 256f, 257; *My Cathedral* series, 256f, 257

Donohue, William, 239, 243, 244, 257–58

Douglas, Aaron, 285, 289–91, 290f

Douglass, Frederick, 53, 63n26

Doyle, Arthur Conan, 30, 43n28, 65n46

draft registration for World War II, racial identity in, 413–19, 422

dragon-like monsters, on Chavín de Huantar stones, 608–10

Dreaming Iolanthe (Brooks), 245n3

dreams: in Native American religious practices, 442; of saints and prophets, real presence

in, 474, 490n68; of Virgin Mary, healing through, 435–40

dress. *See* clothing

Drew Ali, Noble, 415, 419, 420f, 422–23, 425nn5–6, 426n22, 427n24

Dr. Tulp (Rembrandt), 453

du'a (prayer), 248

du'a as-safar, 253

dualisms: Cartesian, 8, 441; and fall of rebel angels, 549; in Native American religious practices, 441–42; in religious studies, 254n6, 441; in secularization theory, 7; in U.S., Islam as challenge to, 247–48

Dulles, Avery, 430

Dumbarton Oaks, 325, 327f

Dungeons and Dragons (game), 96

Dürer, Albrecht, *The Revelation of Saint John,* 541, 544f

Dutch Reformed Church, 140, 141

Dying Gaul, The (marble), 500

Eames, Charles, 141

Eames, Ray, 141

Eastman, Mary, 125–26

eating. *See* dietary codes; food; ingestion

Ebreo, Samuel, 166

Ebreo, Vita Almeda, 177

Ebreo, Zacaria da Pesaro, 176–77

Ebreo dal Zante, Abram Treves, 177

Echavarría, Juan Manual, *Corte de florero* series, 388, 389f

Echo Canyon (Utah), 585, 587f

Eclectic Magazine of Foreign Literature, The, 55

Eco, Umberto, 211

écorché, 500

ecstatic forms of worship, 403, 410n2

Eden, William, *Principles of Penal Law,* 509, 513n39

Edessa, gate of, 493n112

education: in Interracial Conference Movement, 277; public, Muslim prayer in, 252; of women, debate over effects of, 120–21, 128

Egan, Edward, 239

Egypt: Coptic Christians in, 440n2; icon of Virgin Mary in, 435–40, 436f, 439f, 440n1; ingestion of the sacred in, 462

Ehecatl (deity), 526

8 Lessons on Emptiness with a Happy End (Abramović), 234, 235f, 236 elephant dung, 258

Elkins, James, 378, 572

Ella Bonner (Mumler), 50f

Elturk, Steve, 225

embroidery: eyesight loss through, 355, 357, 373n20; as female counterpart to male writing, 356, 361; functions of, 356; rise of scholarship on, 356. *See also* hair embroidery

Emerson, Ralph Waldo, "Nature," 273n16

emotion: vs. affect, 20n57; color as medium for, 350; in secularization theory, 5; senses intertwined with, 11

emplacement, 628–29

enchantment, 652, 653n6

Encyclopaedia Iranica, 319n44

Encyclopedia of Occultism and Parapsychology, The (Shepard), 59

Endurance, Perfect, 417

England, touching of religious objects in, 213n21. *See also* Britain; London

Enlightenment: iconoclasm and taste in, 9–10; knowledge as project of, 13, 651; rift between religion and modernity in, 2

Enni Ben'en, 567, 568

Enoch, Book of, 549–50, 551, 558nn27–28

Entombment of Christ and the Marys at the Tomb, The, 322f, 326, 337n21

Erdrich, Louise, 445

ergodicity, 110n26

ergonomics, 152

eroticism, prosopopoeia and, 481–83

erouv de Jerusalem, L' (Calle), 196

eruvin, 183–99; artistic depictions of, 191–92, 192f, 196–98, 198f; cost of, 186, 195, 200n11; food in, 185–86; functions of, 184; invisibility of, 185, 188, 193, 198–99; manuals for, 200n16; maps of, 188, 190f, 191, 192f; materials used in, 187–88, 188–91f; objections to, 185, 195–96, 201n37; objects carried within, 193–94; origins of, 184, 185–86; planning of, 186–87; symbolic transfer of property for, 194–95, 201n30; weekly checking of, 188–91, 193

"Eruw/'Judentore'" (Freimark), 201n32

Escalante Gonzalbo, Pablo, 534n11

Esoteric Buddhism, 67, 73, 74, 77–78

ethics, of sight, 393

Ethiopian Hebrews: clothing of, 426n17; draft registration by, 416–17

ethnography, in railroad tourism, 583, 584, 586

ethnopoetics, of Iranian coffeehouse painting, 304–5

Etymologiae (Isidore of Seville), 168

Eucharist: antecedents of, 465, 473, 475; vs. ingestion of relics, 465; ingestion of the sacred through, 465–66; prothesis in, 331–32; and *Sweet Jesus* (Cavallaro), 242

Euclid, 123–24

eugenics, composite photography in, 117

eulogiae, 463–66

"Eulogy for Embroidered Guanyin, A" (Su Shi), 368–69

Europe: modernism of, popularization in U.S., 138–39; objectivity of photography in, 41n7. *See also* specific countries

Evanston (Illinois), North Shore Hotel in, 289

Eve. *See* Garden of Eden

Evelyn, John, 174

Eve of the Feast of the Redeemer (Bella), 162, 163f

Everlasting Gospel Mission, 403, 404f

Every Saturday (journal), 53–55

evil eye, 477–78, 491n85

exchange, hair as medium of, 358

executions, public: in *Anatomical Crucifixion* (Banks), 497, 498, 504–10; in Britain, 498, 501, 505–7, 509–10; goals of, 505–7, 513n33; of Tlaxcalan idolaters, 524, 525f, 527

exhibitions, vs. executions, in Britain, 498–99. *See also specific exhibitions*

Exodus, book of, 465

eyeglasses, Urim and Thummim as holy, 266

eyes: in composite photographs, 118–19; evil, 477–78, 491n85. *See also* vision

Eyesight Alone (Jones), 157n25

Ezekiel, book of, 475

faces, erasure of, on Byzantine sacred art, 321, 326, 334–35

Fahua lingyan zhuan, 358

Fall (Casentino), 556n9

Fall of the Rebel Angels (Beccafumi, ca. 1524), 537–41, 538f, 547–49, 552, 552f, 554–55, 555n8

Fall of the Rebel Angels (Beccafumi, ca. 1528), 537–41, 539f, 547–49, 554, 555n8

Fall of the Rebel Angels (Bening), 556n14

Fall of the Rebel Angels (Bruegel), 542, 544f

Heidegger, Martin, 31, 43n33

Heintz, Joseph, the Younger, *Procession of the Redentore,* 162, 163f

hell, Hawai'i Volcanoes National Park compared to, 647–48n12

Heller-Roazen, Daniel, 435

hematite, 338n36

Henry VIII (king of England), 216

Heo, Angie: biographical highlights, 657; chapter by, 435–40

Heptaplus (Pico della Mirandola), 550

heretics, in Byzantine sacred art, erasure of, 321

Herman Miller, 135–55; corporate culture of, 141–42, 154–55; early designers at, 140–41; entry into office furnishings, 142–44; establishment of, 140; five principles of, 141; location of headquarters of, 135, 139–40; Neo-Calvinism and, 140–42, 154; in popularization of European modernism in U.S., 138–39; as public company, 152; public image of, 139–40; Taylorism and, 142; on worker unhappiness with cubicles, 135. *See also* Action Office

Herman Miller Research Corporation, 142

Herreros, Juan, 142

Heschel, Abraham Joshua, 183

hierarchy: of binaries, 605; of senses, 11, 177, 321; of workers vs. values, in cubicles, 137

hijab, functions of, 248

Hilchot Talmud Torah (Maimonides), 166

Hinduism: bathing ritual in, 233–34, 237; hands in, 47; ingestion of the sacred in, 472–73

history paintings, of Feast of the Redeemer in Venice, 162, 163f

Hobbes, Thomas, 43n30

Holloway, Thomas H., 45n44

Holly, Michael Ann, 207

Holmes, Oliver Wendell: Smith (Joseph) compared to, 265–67, 269; on stereography, 263, 264–65, 266–67, 272; "The Stereoscope and the Stereograph," 264–65, 266

Holy Koran of the Moorish Science Temple, 423, 426n22, 427n24

Holy Virgin Mary (Ofili), 239, 257–58

holy water, bowl of, 235. *See also* water

home decor, modernism in, 138. *See also* Herman Miller

Home Furnishings Daily, 144

homosexuality, in Iranian coffeehouses, 301–2

hookah, 301

hooks, bell, 244

Hoppin, James Mason, 652

Horowitz, Mollie, 423

horror movies, Turkish, djinns in, 89–90, 94, 95, 101–8, 104f

Horus, stelae of, 480

Hosios Loukas monastery (Distomo): *The Entombment of Christ and the Marys at the Tomb* at, 322f, 326, 337n21; Katholikon in, 324f, 326; pilgrimages to, 326–27; tomb of Luke in, 326, 337n23

hospitality, in mainline churches, 432

Hotel Berkeley-Carteret (Asbury Park), Church Women's Committee at, 275, 276f, 288, 292n1

hotels, racial discrimination by, 286–89, 295n41

Houdon, Jean-Antoine, *Standing Écorché,* 500

Hours at Home (periodical), 54

Howes, David, 558n31

Huaisu, 578n45

Huineng, 563

Hula dancers, 630

human body. *See* body

human hair. *See* hair

human sacrifice, in Tlaxcala, 522–24, 523f

Hume, David, *Natural History of Religion,* 2

humor: and djinns, 94, 109n14; and Native American trickster stories, 445

Hunter, William: anatomical models by, 499–502, 500f, 501f, 504, 512nn18–19; *The Anatomy of the Human Gravid Uterus,* 499; *Two Introductory Lectures,* 499

Hussein (imam), martyrdom of, 309, 310–13, 311f, 317n14

Hyman, Aaron, 530

Hypatios, 338n37

Hyper-Covenantism, 140

IBM, 156–57n24

Ibn al-Khashshab, 475–76

Ibn Taymiyya, 471, 472

Ibrahim (scriptural figure). *See* Abraham

Ichijō (emperor of Japan), 85n28

icon(s): as aesthetic objects, 218; Byzantine, interactions with, 322–27, 335; "Composita" (Stoddard) as, 121–29; genealogy of term, 130n4; vs. prototype, 321, 328–29, 334, 465;

icon(s) (*continued*)
 of Virgin Mary, in Egypt, 435–40, 436f,
 439f, 440n1. *See also* Russian icons
iconoclasm: in Byzantium, 328, 333–34, 465; of
 Catholics, 258; and taste, in Enlightenment,
 9–10
"Iconoclasm during the French Revolution"
 (Itzerda), 19n45
iconography, of Chavín de Huantar stones, 605,
 606, 608–10, 620
identity. *See* gender identity; racial identity;
 religious identity
idol, in secularization theory, 4–5, 8
idolatry extirpation, in New Spain, 515–32; images depicting, 516, 517f; indigenous experience of and responses to, 516; records of, 516,
 518; scope of, 518, 519; start of, 518–19. *See
 also* Tlaxcala
Idzerda, Stanley, 206–7
IKEA, 154
IKV. *See* Istanbul Kıyamet Vakti
Illinois, Interracial Conference Movement in,
 279, 281, 289. *See also* Chicago
illness, and creativity, 579n51
Illustrated Legends of the Kitano Shrine, 73, 74f,
 81
I'll Worship You, You'll Worship Me (Bühler-
 Rose), 233–34, 233f, 237
image(s): agency of, 9; genealogical relation to
 icon, 130n4; photographs as, 25–26; in relation to word, 14; of relics of Muhammad,
 470–71, 470f
imaginative painting, coffeehouse painting as,
 297
Imago primi saeculi Societatis Iesu, 384–85,
 395n21
Imaizumi Yoshio, 563
Imam Ali Conquers Jinn (unknown artist), 92,
 93f
IMDb. *See* Internet Movie Database
imitation, vs. becoming, 460, 461. *See also*
 mimesis
immersion: in computer games, 98, 99, 100;
 in modern experience of djinns, 90, 91; in
 movies, 105–6
immigration, to U.S.: critics of, 119–20; Dutch,
 to Michigan, 140; laws restricting, 132n10; in
 urbanization, 119
impairments, vs. disabilities, 431, 433n6

imperialism, secularization theory and, 8
incarnation, material world in, 14
India, planchettes in, 54–55
indigenous religious practices: new materialism
 and, 605, 621; as "primitive," 605–6; in secularization theory, 631. *See also specific groups*
Indra (deity), 78
Industrial Designers Society of America, 152
industrialization: in popularity of planchettes,
 57–58; in popularity of Spiritualism, 48, 57;
 in U.S., 119, 138, 142
industry, Mormon involvement in, 594–95. *See
 also* furniture industry
ingestion of the sacred, 459–85; in Hinduism,
 472–73; in modernity, 462; vs. prosopopoeia,
 481–83; scholarship on, lack of, 461–62;
 Swift's parody of, 483–85
ingestion of the sacred, in Christianity, 462–66;
 through Eucharist, 465–66, 473; on pilgrimages, 462–63; from relics of saints, 463–65,
 474; through *Schluckbildchen,* 484; from
 scraping of Byzantine art, 327–28, 464–65
ingestion of the sacred, in Islam, 461, 466–81;
 through baraka, 461, 469–76; on pilgrimages, 466, 468, 471; from Qur'an, 471,
 475–81; from relics of Muhammad, 464,
 468–75, 476
Ingold, Timothy, 367
Initiative for the Study of Material and Visual
 Cultures of Religion, 3
ink, 360, 364, 456f, 457, 471, 475, 477, 480,
 482–83, 516, 523, 531, 563, 564, 570–71, 573,
 575
inscriptions: on Buddhist hair embroidery, 361–
 62, 365, 370; on *Contes barbares* (Gauguin),
 343; on Japanese martyrdom paintings, 380;
 on tombs, 331. *See also* writing
insect bites, 477–78
Institute for Art, Religion, and Social Justice:
 compassion (exhibition) at, 231–37, 232f, 233f,
 235f; establishment of, 231
intellectual disabilities: definition of, 430–31,
 433n4; marginalization of people with,
 429–32
Intellettuale (Mauri), 447–50, 448f, 449f, 453,
 454
intention, in ingestion of Qur'an, 477
Interior, U.S. Department of, 627, 643. *See also*
 National Park Service

Park, 625; of Utah as the "promised land," 588, 599

Maqam Ibrahim, 471

Marcolini, Francesco, 559n40

marginalization, of people with disabilities, in mainline churches, 429–32

Marginal Psalters, 333

Marinis, Vasileios: biographical highlights, 658; chapter by, 321–35; comments on, 464, 471

marketing. *See* advertising

Marks, Laura, 308, 316n7

marriage: interracial, in *Jesus Christ the Lamb of God and His Little Bride* (Morgan), 408–9; plural (*See* polygamy)

Martínez Baracs, Andrea, 533n7

Martin of Porres (saint), 400

martyrdom: in Japan (*See* Japanese martyrdom paintings); in Pasolini's works, 448

Martyrdom of Brother Leonardo Kimura, S.J., and Four Companions (Niccolò School), 375, 376f, 380

Martyrdom of Christians in Africa during the Reign of Huneric (Circignani), 381, 381f

Martyrdom of Saint Polyeuktos, The, 326f

Mary. *See* Virgin Mary

masculinity, Iranian, 301–2, 303, 307, 312–13, 318n29

Masotti, Antonio, 448f, 449f, 453

Massachusetts. *See* Boston

Massey, Doreen, 320n64

massively multiplayer online computer games (MMOGs), djinns in, 89–90, 95, 96–101, 97f

Master of the Rebel Angels, *Fall of the Rebel Angels,* 541, 542f

material culture of religion, in secularization theory, 2–3

materialism, new, 8, 19nn42–43, 206, 605, 621

materiality: in Byzantine religion, 321, 329–30; critique of, by religions, 72; of photographs, 25–26; in Protestantism's split from Catholicism, 2; ubiquity of, 4

material practice, use of term, 3

material world: agency of, 4, 8–9, 206; capacity for transformation in, 14

mathematical knowledge, ingestion of, 483–85

Matrix, The (movie), 103

Matthew, Wentworth, 416, 417

matzos, in synagogues, 185, 186, 187f, 200n7, 200n10

Maui, Hale-a-ka-lā National Park in, 649n30

Mauna Kea, 649n30

Mauri, Fabio, *Intellettuale,* 447–50, 448f, 449f, 453, 454

Mauri, Susanna, 449

Maxixcatzin (Tlaxcalan ruler), 518

Maya, burning of books of, 518, 528

Maymuna (pilgrim), 471

McCartney, John, 423

McDannell, Colleen, 273n21

McGarry, Molly, 48, 62nn8–9

Means, Philip Ainsworth, 608

measurements: in composite photographs, 118–20, 128; of women's bodies, 121

Mecca, Zamzam well at, 471, 472f, 476

media coverage: of "Composita" (Stoddard), 113; of Islam in U.S., 247–48; of planchettes, 53–55; after Turkish coup of 1980, 94–95; of Turkish djinns in modern culture, 90–91

mediation: in coffeehouse painting, 298–304, 312–14; and ingestion of the sacred, 459–66, 469–77, 482–85; photography as form of, 25–26, 31, 39; sound in, 227; spirit possession as form of, 31; in Spiritualism, 55–58

medical photography, 29–30, 43n26

Medici, Lorenzo de', 549

Medici family, 547

medicinal use, of Byzantine sacred art, 321, 325, 326–29, 464–65

Medicine Buddha, 70, 74

Medicus, Gustav, 556n9, 559n39

medieval period, secularization theory on, 5

meditation, dying during, 566, 578n28

medium (media of production): agency of, 8–9; representational capacities of, 400. *See also specific media*

mediums: in childbirth in Heian Japan, 76–78, 77f; gender of, in Heian Japan, 76, 86n49; paraffin molds of spirit hands produced by, 58–59; spirits writing on bodies of, 52–53, 63n25

Mehmed Siyah-Kalem, 92

meigen, 80–81, 81f, 86nn60–62

Melanasuchus niger, 609

Melismos, 329

Mello, Henriqueta Maria de, 36

Memleketin Sahipleri (Makal), 94

memory: in photography, 27; in viewing of Chavín de Huantar stones, 612

men, Iranian: in coffeehouse paintings, 313; in coffeehouses, 301–2; as naghals, 297

men, Mormon, as gods, 268–72, 273n21

Mendieta, Gerónimo de, 528, 533n6

mental disability, vs. intellectual disability, 433n4

Me'râj (Aghili), 306–8, 307f

Me'râj, in coffeehouse paintings, 306–8, 307f

merchandising, religious, 209, 209f, 210, 315. *See also* consumerism

Mercure de France (magazine), 347, 351

Merjian, Ara H.: biographical highlights, 658; chapter by, 447–54

Merleau-Ponty, Maurice, 20n61, 610, 620; *Le visible et l'invisible,* 393

Merrie Monarch Hula Festival, 630

Meso-America, chocolate in, history of, 242–43

Mesquita, Diogo de, 392n11

Mestçi, Alper, 102

metal bowls, Qur'an written on, 477–80, 479f

metaphor, material transformation through, 14. *See also* allegory; analogy

metarelics, 473

Metatron, 551, 558n35, 558n37

Metropolitan Museum of Art (New York), Russian icons at, 218–19, 220, 222

Mexica (Aztec): attempt to conquer Tlaxcala, 518; New Fire ceremony of, 535n32; Spanish conquest of, 515, 517, 526–27

Mexico: colonial, extirpation of idolatry in, 515, 518; pre-Hispanic, chocolate in, 242. *See also* Tlaxcala

Meyer, Birgit, 46n60

Meyer, Richard: biographical highlights, 658; chapter by, 215–22; comments on, 6, 259n1

Meyerowitz, Lisa, 293n22

Miaoshan, 363

Michael (archangel), 550

Michael (saint): in *Fall of the Rebel Angels* (Beccafumi), 537, 540, 541, 549; in *Fall of the Rebel Angels* (Bruegel), 542; in *The Revelation of Saint John* (Dürer), 541

Michael II (Byzantine emperor), 327, 465

Michelangelo: anatomical models used by, 495, 499; Beccafumi influenced by, 547–49, 554; *Punishment of Haman,* 554

Michigan: adhan in, 225–28; Dutch immigration to, 140; furniture industry in, 140, 156n13. *See also* Herman Miller

Michigan Star Furniture Company, 140

Mictlantecuhtli (deity), 526

Middle East, Utah compared to, in railroad literature, 586–89, 588f, 591, 598–99, 601n18. *See also specific countries*

migration: African American, 413–14; Mormon, 594

Miki, Paul, 380, 386

Miller, Daniel, 8, 72

Miller, Patricia Cox, 462, 465

Milton, John, *Paradise Lost,* 345

mimesis: and ingestion of the sacred, 461, 463, 465–66, 484–85; in Jesuit martyrdom imagery, 382, 384; and Muhammad, 460–61, 466

mind–body dualism, Descartes on, 8

Ming period (China), hair embroidery in, 357–58, 364–65, 368

miniature painting, Iranian coffeehouse painting compared to, 305, 306, 308

minorities, marginalization of, in mainline churches, 433n12

miracles. *See* healing

Miraj Nameh, 319n44

Mirror (anonymous), 390–92, 390f, 392f

Mirror of Human Salvation, 557n18

miscegenation: in *Jesus Christ the Lamb of God and His Little Bride* (Morgan), 408–9; in Venice, 171–77

missionaries. *See* Christian missionaries

Mitchell, S. Weir, 63n20

Mitchell, W.J.T., 388; *What Do Pictures Want?,* 9

MMOGs. *See* massively multiplayer online computer games

Moallem, Minoo: biographical highlights, 658; chapter by, 297–316

Mochizuki, Mia M.: biographical highlights, 659; chapter by, 375–93

Moddaber, Mohammad, 300, 311–12

Modena, Leon, *The Life of Judah,* 167

Modern, John Lardas, 61n5, 653n6

Modern American Spiritualism (Hardinge Britten), 51–53, 63n18

modern art: construction of, 6; formalism of, 6; Iranian, 297, 299, 316n11; New Negro Art as, 282, 285, 291; Russian icons as sources for, 220–21 modernism, European, popularization in U.S., 138–39

modernity: binaries of, 7; disenchantment in, 652, 653nn5–6; Enlightenment rift between religion and, 2; ingestion of the sacred in, 462; secularization theory of (*See* secularization theory)

"Modern Spirit and Catholicism, The" (Gauguin), 347

modularity, of cubicles, 146–48, 147f

Moerenhout, Jacques Antoine, 353n15

Moghul, Haroon: biographical highlights, 659; chapter by, 247–53

monasticism. *See* Buddhist monasticism

Mondrian, Piet, 138

mono-no-ke (spirit): etymological origins of term, 71; Heian-period beliefs about, 70–71; vs. jaki, 84n12, 84n18; in ninth-century documents, 70–71, 84n9; pacification of, 75–82; possession by, 71

Moore, Jerry, 622n26

Moore, R. Laurence, 47–48, 57

Moorish Americans, 415–24; clothing of, 419–20, 420f, 421; draft registration by, 415–16, 416f, 422, 425nn7–8; origin of category, 415; racial and religious identity of, 415–24

Moorish architecture, Mormon use of, 595–97, 596f

Moorish Science Temple of America (MSTA), 415–24; bodies in, role of, 419–24; establishment of, 415, 425n5; racial and religious identity in, 415–24; tribal names in, 415, 425n6

Morgan, Gertrude, 403–9, 404f; *Jesus Christ the Lamb of God and His Little Bride*, 405–9, 405f; preaching by, 410n8; racial consciousness of, 408–9; sanctification of, 403–4, 409

Morgan, Michelle: biographical highlights, 659; chapter by, 47–61

Mormonism, 261–72; arrival in Utah, 586; *Book of Mormon* in, 265–67, 267f, 272n7, 272n11; dietary codes in, 594; establishment of, 265–66; as God's chosen people, 268, 273n20; grace in, 261, 264, 268–69; Johnson (Charles Ellis) in, 261, 263f, 270–71; men as gods in, 268–72, 273n21; polygamy in (*See* polygamy); Pulpit Rock in history

of, 586, 587f, 601n14; in railroad tourism (*See* railroad literature); salvation in, 261, 268–69, 270; women in, subservience of, 273n21

Mormons, use of term, 600n1

Morning Chronicle, The (newspaper), 499

Moroni (angel), 265

Morse, Samuel, 49

mosaics, feather, 526

mosques: conditions for qualifying as, 254n15; functions of, 248

mosques, U.S.: adhan in, 225–28; growth in demand for, 249; opposition to, 225–28, 249–51, 252, 254n11; Park51, 247, 249–51

Moteuczoma (Aztec ruler), 515

Mother (Kim), 22f, 23

Mother and Daughter (Waring), 284, 285f

Motolinía (Toribio de Benavente), 527–28, 533n7

mourning, Spiritualism and, 48

movies: Iranian, film-e Farsi, 313, 320n61; Turkish, djinns in, 89–90, 94, 95, 101–8, 104f. *See also specific movies*

Moxeke (Peru), 613

MSTA. *See* Moorish Science Temple of America

Mu'awiya (caliph), 469

mug shots, 132n7

Muhammad: djinns and, 92; dreams of, real presence in, 474, 490n68; face of, in Persian painting, 308, 318n44; ingestion of relics of, 464, 468–75, 476; in *Me'râj* (Aghili), 306–8, 307f; and mimesis, 460–61, 466; wheat left at tomb of, 476, 476f

Mujū Ichien, *Sand and Pebbles Anthology*, 566

"Mulatto" category, in census, 427n26

Mumler, William, 26, 50f, 63n18

Mundy, Barbara E.: biographical highlights, 659; chapter by, 515–32

Muñoz Camargo, Diego: *Descripción de la ciudad y provincia de Tlaxcala*, 519–20, 533n9; Pictorial History commissioned by, 517f, 519–20, 521f, 522–24, 523f, 525f, 527, 530–32, 534n11, 535n29

Murasaki Shikibu, 75, 76–77, 79, 85n28, 85n35, 86n60

Murder Act of 1752 (Britain), 501, 504, 512n22

Murer, Domenico Gregorin, 168

Murphy, Owen, *Sister Morgan Using a Megaphone and Tapper to Assist in Her Service in the Prayer Room of the Everlasting Gospel Mission,* 403, 404f

Murphy, Tara, 456f, 457

Musallat (movie), djinns in, 89–90, 95, 101–8, 104f

Muscogee (Creek) nation, 442, 443, 444, 446, 446n1

Museum of Fine Arts (Boston), Russian icons at, 216, 218

Museum of Fine Arts (Houston), *The Body of Christ in the Art of Europe and New Spain* exhibition at, 205

museums: dialog between object and viewer in, 207–8; gift shops of, 209, 209f, 210; physical environment of, 212n10; Russian icons transformed by, 6–7, 216, 218–19, 220, 222; secular, exhibition of religious art in, 203, 205–11; touching prohibited in, 207, 210, 335. *See also specific museums*

Museu Nacional (Rio de Janeiro), *Anthropological Exposition* at, 29, 42n22

music: at Hawai'i Volcanoes National Park, 632; Iranian, coffeehouse painting's influence on, 298; sacred, in secular museums, 208–9, 212n15; vs. visual arts, Gauguin on, 350–51

Musique barbare (Gauguin), 348–49, 349f

Muslims, U.S.: adhan of, 225–28; as challenge to secularism, 247–53; internalization of popular opinions of Islam by, 247–53; media coverage of, 247–48; number of, 247, 249; public performance of prayer by, 249–53. *See also* Moorish Science Temple of America

Mutual Responsibility of the Country (Bar Hama), 198, 199f

My Cathedral series (Donis), 256f, 257

My Sweet Lord (exhibition), 239

Nadal, Jerome, *Annotations and Meditations on the Gospel,* 382

Nagel, Alexander, 211, 213n20, 213n23, 215

naghali: coffeehouse painting linked to, 297, 302–3; definition of, 297, 302

NAGPRA. *See* Native American Graves Protection and Repatriation Act

Naha stone, 639–40

Nahua, pre-Hispanic religious practices of, 516, 520–24. *See also* Tlaxcala

Nahuatl cultural group, 518

Nahuatl language, 518

nail clippings, of Muhammad, 464, 468, 469

Najmabadi, Afsaneh, 307, 318n42

names: early Hawaiian place, return to, 644; in graffiti on Byzantine sacred art, 331; tribal, in Moorish Science Temple of America, 415, 425n6

Napoleon III, 41n10

narrative stories, Native American, 444–45

Nasir-al-Din Shah, 481

National Association of Deans of Women, 286–87

National Conference of Social Work, 287

National Council of Churches, 296n51

National Gallery (London), *Devotion by Design* exhibition at, 207–9, 208f, 209f, 210, 212n15

nationalism: Hawaiian, 643, 650n44; Iranian, 298, 299, 315, 318n36; Turkish, 90, 91, 94

nationalization, of former slaves in Brazil, 26, 31–32

National League of Americans of Russian Origin, 218

National Park Service (NPS), U.S.: Hawaiians in, 632, 643; language of spirituality used by, 631, 647n4. *See also* Hawai'i Volcanoes National Park

National Urban League, 287

Native American(s), geographic designations for, 446n1

Native American Graves Protection and Repatriation Act (NAGPRA), 629, 644–46, 650n51

Native American religious practices, 441–46; Good Mind in, 442–46; perspectivism in, 618–20; spirit/body dualism in, lack of, 441–42; trickster stories in, 444–45. *See also specific groups*

Native Hawaiians. *See* Hawaiians

natural history, in religious studies, 132n7

Natural History of Religion (Hume), 2

"Nature" (Emerson), 273n16

Nawawi, Abu Zakaria Yahya Ibn Sharaf al-, 476–77

"Negro" category: in census, 423, 427n26; debate among African Americans over, 421, 426n19; on draft registration cards, 415–17;

polyvinyl chloride (PVC), as medium, for eruv, 187

pope: evangelization in New Spain required by, 517–18; infallibility of, 42n21. *See also specific popes*

popular culture, in Iranian coffeehouses, 302–3

Portrait of Chikotsu Daie, 568, 569f

Portrait of Jacob Meyer de Haan (Gauguin), 343, 344, 344f, 345, 346

Portrait of Saint Francis Xavier (Niccolò School), 378

portrait photography: in Brazil, of Juca Rosa, 26, 32–40, 34f; in Brazil, popularity of, 27–28; spirits in, 26

portraits: Chan/Zen, 564, 577n24; scaffold compared to, 507

Portrait with Spirit (Azevedo), 28–29

Port Said (Egypt), Virgin Mary icon in Church of Saint Bishoi in, 435–40, 436f, 439f, 440n1

Portuguese Filipino Code, 45n47

positivism, in Brazil, 27, 29, 42n15, 42n20

possession, spirit. *See* spirit possession; property ownership

poster art, Iranian, 303, 305, 315

Postle, Martin, 497, 511n5

posture: meditation, dying in, 566, 578n28; in office design, 143

posture photographs, 121

Poussin, Nicholas, *Landscape with a Man Being Killed by a Snake,* 388

power, in Heian Japan, and spirit possessions, 72

pragmatic aesthetics, 105–6, 108

prasād, 472–73

prayer, in graffiti on Byzantine sacred art, 330–31, 333

prayer, Muslim, 248–53; in air travel, 251–53; call to (adhan), 225–28; kinds of, 248–49; public performance of, 249–53

prayer beads, Buddhist, 78, 80f

praying hands imagery, 60

preaching, by women, injunctions against, 410n8

Pre-Columbian era, new materialism and, 605, 621

premodernity: in secularization theory, 4–5, 8; Western view of Islam as, 203, 247–48

press coverage. *See* media coverage

Price, Mary, 44n34

pride, sin of, 546

primitive, the, and synesthesia, Gauguin on, 348

"primitive" African art, 275, 281

Primitive Culture (Tylor), 31, 43n29

"primitive" peoples: attachment to objects among, 4–5, 8; indigenous people of Americas as, 605–6; in secularization theory, 4–5, 8, 631

Primitive Tales (Gauguin). *See Contes barbares* (Gauguin)

Prince, The (Machiavelli), 177

Principles of Penal Law (Eden), 509, 513n39

Principles of Scientific Management (Taylor), 142

prisoners, photographs of, 29, 117, 132n7

Priuli, Lorenzo, 172, 176, 177

privatization: and cubicles, 135, 153; and disenchantment of Christianity, 653n5; and Iranian coffeehouses, 303; and Japanese martyrdom paintings, 379; Locke (John) on, 254n3; and Muslim prayer, 248–49, 253; of religion, secularization theory on, 5–6; and sound of adhan, 203, 227; and touch, 49; transportation between public and private space (*See* eruvin); in Turkey's strategic Westernization, 94. *See also* interiorization

Procession of the Redentore (Heintz), 162, 163f

profane, the, blurring of line between the sacred and, 211

profiling, in airport security screenings, 251–52

Promey, Sally M.: biographical highlights, 659–60; chapters by, 1–15, 625–46, 651–52; comments on, 583, 600n8, 605; introductions by, 23–24, 203–4, 257–59, 399–401, 457–58

Promised Land, Utah compared to, in railroad literature, 588–89, 588f, 598–99, 601n18

Proof Palpable of Immortality, The (Sargent), 49–51, 63n18, 65n46

property, symbolic transfer of, for eruvin, 194–95, 201n30

property ownership, vs. spiritual ownership, 643–44

prophets, artists as, 351–52

Propst, Robert: development of cubicle design by, 135, 144–49; *The Office,* 150–51, 152, 157n36; on problems facing office design,

142–43, 151, 156n21; on reasoning behind cubicles, 136–37; on reception of cubicles, 153

proselytization, Mormon, 597

prosopopoeia, 481–83

Protestantism: Catholic art repurposed in, 10; Catholic devotional objects in, 399–400; as presumed universal form of religion, 128; sensory practices in, 12; split with Catholicism, materiality in, 2; touching of religious objects in, 213n21

Protestantism, U.S.: devotional objects in, 399–400; people with intellectual and developmental disabilities in, 429–32; race relations as outside purview of, 277; shared sensory culture of worship in, 429–30; women of, role in race relations, 275–78, 282, 289–92

Protestant Reformation, naming of problems and solutions in, 151

prothesis, 331–32

prototype, vs. icon, 321, 328–29, 334, 465

public activism, by religious women, in Interracial Conference Movement, 278

public buildings, arts projects in, 6

public executions. *See* executions, public

public opinion, U.S., on Islam, 247–53

public schools, Muslim prayer in, 252

public space: Muslim prayer in, 248–53; transportation between private space and (*See* eruvin)

Pulpit Rock (Utah), 586, 587f, 601n14

Punishment of Haman (Michelangelo), 554

Puritan stone carving, 7

Putnam's (magazine), 54

qahveh khaneh painting, use of term, 316n1. *See also* coffeehouse painting

Qajar era (Iran), coffeehouse painting in, 297

Qalawun, al-Mansur Sayf al-Din, 481

Qaṣīdat al-Burda (al-Busiri), 473–75, 493n107

Qazwini, Al-, *Kitab 'Ajā'ib al-makhlūqāt wa Gharā'ib al-Mawjūdāt*, 92

qibla markers, in air travel, 253

Qing period (China), hair embroidery in, 357–58, 364–65, 368

Quadroon Madonna, The (Dawson), 279, 280f

Quickborner Team, 146

Qur'an: in air travel, 253; djinns in, 91–92, 108; ingestion of, 471, 475–81. *See also* scripture

race, construction of, 5, 400, 411n17

race relations, as religious issue, Church Women's Committee on, 275–78. *See also* Interracial Conference Movement

Race Relations Sunday, 289–91, 290f, 295n48

racial consciousness: and Interracial Conference Movement, 277; in *Jesus Christ the Lamb of God and His Little Bride* (Morgan), 408–9

racial discrimination: Church Women's Committee resolution against, 287; and composite photography, 117, 127; by hotels, 286–89, 295n41

racial identity: in draft registration for World War II, 413–19, 422; of Moorish Americans, 415–24; religious identity tied to, 414–24; and skin color, 421–24

racializing of senses, 19n33, 400

racial segregation, and Interracial Conference Movement, 277–78, 286–89

racial violence, in U.S., after World War I, 277

Radcliffe-Brown, Alfred, 43n29

raigō, 347–48, 348f, 353n24

railroad(s), in creation of Mormonism, 583, 594, 600n4

railroad literature and media of Utah, 581–99; comparisons with Middle East in, 586–89, 588f, 591, 598–99, 601n18; curiosity about Mormonism in, 582–83; definition of, 581–82; ethnography in, 583, 584, 586; geography in, 585–86, 593, 599; marketing language of, 582; Mormon involvement in, 594–99; in new understandings of religion, 581, 583, 584; package tours in, 598, 603n37; popular understandings of Mormonism shaped by, 581, 582–83; on Salt Lake City, 589–93, 590–93f, 598–99

Raimundi Stela (Chavín), 609, 610, 614, 615, 620

Rainbow Moon, 640–42, 649n40

Ramadan, fasting in, 255n16

Ramos, Antonio de Paula, 33

Rancière, Jacques, 316n6

Raphael (archangel), 550

Raphael (artist): Beccafumi influenced by, 547–49, 554; *Saint Michael*, 549, 554; *Sistine Madonna*, 10

Rappaport, Jason, 187f

Rashi, 200n10

Rohde, Gilbert, 140

Roman Catholicism. *See* Catholicism

Romanos the Melode, 490n70

Rome (Italy): Church of the Gesù, 380; sack of (1527), 547

Rosa, José Sebastião. *See* Rosa, Juca

Rosa, Juca: followers of, 33, 35–36, 44n38; photograph of, 26, 32–40, 34f; police investigation of, 35–36, 45n47; trial of, 32–33, 44n36

rosaries, multiple uses of, 209

Rose Mandala Mirror (Stathacos), 232f

Rosemary's Baby (movie), 103

Rosenzweig, Franz, 183

Ross, W. W., 601n16, 603n35

Roubiliac, Louis-Francois, 512n19

Round Table (periodical), 54

Rowe, John, 608–9, 609f, 610, 615, 616

rowzeh khani, 300

Royal Academy of Arts (London): *Anatomical Crucifixion* (Banks) at, 495, 497; establishment of, 498; Hunter's anatomical models at, 499, 512n18

Rubens, Peter Paul, *The Three Crosses,* 510n2

Ruble, Zulema A., *Composita: A Drama in Three Acts,* 113, 122–27, 124f, 125f

Rufinus, 553

Rumi, 318n35

Russian Americans, on U.S. exhibitions of Russian icons, 218

Russian icons: aestheticization of, 6–7, 216–22; conservation of, 219–20; copies of, 220, 221f; in Russian Revolution, 216–18; transformation into secular art, 6–7, 216–22, 223n19; U.S. exhibitions of, 216, 218–19, 220

"Russian Icons" (Barr), 216–22, 217f, 221f, 222f, 223n9

Russian Revolution (1917), religious art in, 216–18

Rustam (mythic hero), 318n40

Rutherford County (Tennessee), opposition to mosques in, 252, 254n11

Rymsdyck, Jan van, 499

Sabbath boundary. *See* eruvin

sacred, the: blurring of line between the profane and, 211; ingestion of (*See* ingestion);

meaning of, in Native American Graves Protection and Repatriation Act, 644

sacred art. *See* religious art

sacred music, in secular museums, 208–9, 212n15

sacred stones: agency of, 642–43; in Hawai'i, 639–42, 639f, 641f, 642f

Sacrifices among the Tlaxcalans (unknown artist), 522–24, 523f

Safavid era (Iran): coffeehouses in, 301; depiction of Muhammad's face in, 319n44; lion as symbol in, 307

saffron, 476, 491n75

Sahagún, Bernardino de, *Florentine Codex,* 521–22

Saint Barbara, 323f, 330

Saint Francis Xavier, S.J., Founder of the Japanese Mission, and the Jesuit Martyrs in Japan (Niccolò School), 375, 377f, 380, 387

saintliness, compared to composite photographs, 128

Saint Martin Lane's Academy, 512n18

Saint Michael (Raphael), 549, 554

saints: Byzantine interactions with depictions of, 324–29, 337n17, 464–65; dreams of, real presence in, 474; material cults of, in Paris, 18n20; relics of (*See* relics). *See also specific saints*

Saint Thomas (Caravaggio), 453

Sakyamuni, 372n11, 574

salat, 248–53; definition of, 248–49; gender neutrality of, 249; public performance of, 249–53, 254n15

salat al-jumu'ah, 249

saliva, of Muhammad, 464, 469, 474

Salpêtrière Hospital (Paris), 29–30

Saltair (Utah), 590–91, 591f, 592f, 595–97, 596f

Saltair Railway, 595

Salt Lake City (Utah): Deseret Museum in, 595; irrigation system of, 591–93, 597; railroad literature on, 589–93, 590–93f, 598–99; Tabernacle in, 589–90, 590f, 597–98, 602n23, 603n35

salvation, in Mormonism, 261, 268–69, 270

Salvator Mundi (Niccolò School), 378

Sampaio, Gabriela dos Reis, 32, 34–35, 36

Samuel, Geoffrey, 78

sanctification: definition of, 403; manifestations of, 403; of Morgan (Gertrude), 403–4, 409; in Morgan's *Jesus Christ the Lamb of God and His Little Bride,* 405–9

sandals, of Muhammad, 469–71, 470f, 473–74, 476

Sand and Pebbles Anthology (Mujū Ichien), 566

Sanders, Cheryl, 410n2

San Francisco Daily Morning Chronicle, 54

sanmai, 81–82

Sans personne à qui parler (Bauer), 196–98, 198f

Santa Maria della Croce (Casarano), 323f, 330

Santería, spirit possession in, 39

Sanudo, Marin, 171

Saqqakhaneh painting, 316n11

Sargent, Epes: *Planchette,* 53, 56–57, 63n18; *The Proof Palpable of Immortality,* 49–51, 63n18, 65n46

Sartor Resartus (Carlyle), 346, 347, 351

Satan, relation to Lucifer, 554. *See also* Lucifer

Satmar Hasidim, on eruvin, 195–96

Savage, Charles R., 603n34

Savonarola, Girolamo, 541

scaffolding, in executions, 505–7

Scaliger, Joseph, 558n27

Scarry, Elaine, 58

Schachter, Ben, *Five Towns Eruv,* 191, 192f

Schluckbildchen, 484, 484f

Schmidt, Leigh Eric, 16n1

Schneider, Laurel C.: biographical highlights, 660; chapter by, 441–46

schools, public, Muslim prayer in, 252

Schreiber, David, 194

Schuffenecker, Émile, 351

Schultz, Richard, 141

Schurhammer, Georg, 375

Schwartz, Joseph N., 142, 144, 145, 150

science: in composite photography, 116–17, 120–21, 128–29, 131n6; dramatized personification of, 123–25; in Hawai'i Volcanoes National Park signage, 625–32; of letters, 477; and liberal religion, 278, 281; parody of, in *Gulliver's Travels,* 483; photography and positivism, influence on, 27, 29–30; photography as enactment of, 29, 32; physical, in new materialism, 8; relationship to Spiritualism and animal magnetism, 47, 53–54, 56–57, 60, 61n2; of religion, discursive construction of, 132n7; social, in Interracial Conference Movement, 276–78; and study of sensory cultures of religion, 3; in synesthesia, nineteenth-century study of, 341; and Taylorism, 142; vision as sense of, 11, 117

Science (journal), 113, 118–19, 119f

Scientific American (magazine), 54, 54f

scientific management, 142

scopophilia, 243

scorpion-man talisman, 466–68, 467f

scorpions, 466–68, 477–78, 491n88, 492n91

scraping: of Byzantine sacred art, 321, 326–28, 464–65; of Egyptian sacred art, 462

scribes, Buddhist death verses written by, 567

scripture: and disability, 429, 431; embroidery of, 355; hands in, 47; hell in, 647–48n12; as repository of knowledge, 14; and whiteness of Christian devotional objects, 400; writing in blood, 360–61. *See also specific works*

sculpture, food, 240–41, 244n3

Seales, Chad E., 600n1

séances, spirit hands at, 51–53

sects, corporations as, 154–55

secular, the, in relation to religion, 115, 248

secular art, Russian icons transformed into, 6–7, 216–22, 223n19

secularism: definitions of, 248; in U.S., Islam as challenge to, 247–53

secularization theory, 2–9, 12–14; art in, 2, 5–7; binary oppositions in, 7; challenges to, 4, 13–14, 651–52; consequences of dominance of, 13–14; fetish and idol in, 4–5, 8; indigenous practices in, 631; material religion in, 2–3; medieval period in, 5; "primitive" peoples in, 4–5, 8, 631; spirituality vs. religion in, 633; streamlined approach to narrative of, 12–13

Sedgwick, Eve, *Touching Feeling,* 60

seer stones, 266, 269, 272n11, 273n16

Sefer Raziel, 551

segregation. *See* gender segregation; racial segregation; residential segregation

Sei Shōnagon, *The Pillow Book,* 86n49

self-immolation, death verses written before, 576n3

Self-Portrait (Johnson), 282, 283f

self-portraits: by Johnson (Charles Ellis), 261–65, 262f, 269–72, 272n5; by Johnson (William H.), 282, 283f

Smith, Joseph F., 274n29

Smith, Kiki, *Virgin Mary,* 388

Smith, William, 266

Smith Bey, Albert, 427n28

Smith-Bey, Mary, 423

Smith-Bey, Oscar, 423

Smith College: composite photograph of class of 1886 (*See* "Composita"); debate over women's education and, 120–21; establishment of, 129n1

Smugglerius (Pink), 501f

snake bites, 480

social construction: of disabilities, 431; of race, 5, 400, 411n17

social criticism, photography in, 41n7

social science, 32, 276–78

social status, and spirit possession, 71

Société des Études Spiritiques, 28

Society of Artists of Great Britain, 498

Sodré, Domingos, 44n39

Solomon (prophet): djinns and, 92, 93, 108; eruvin and, 185

Solomon, Faithful, 417, 418f

Song Dong, 241

Song dynasty (China): calligraphy in, 573, 579n55; death verses in, 562, 563

Sontag, Susan, 29, 41n7, 43n31, 388

soul: angels in origin of, 552, 553; Symbolist view of, 341–43

Soul of Things, The (Denton), 59

sound: of adhan, 225–28; in *Contes barbares* (Gauguin), 349–50; in hierarchy of senses, 11; in Hindu bathing ritual, 233–34, 237; in history of senses, 10–11; in mainline Protestantism, 429–30, 433n1; in spirit pacification in Buddhism, 78–79; technologies for enhancing, 11; vs. vision, intrusion by, 227–28

Sourire, Le (newspaper), 350, 354n32

Southern Poverty Law Center (SPLC), 254n10

Soviet Central State Restoration Workshops, 219–20

Soviet Trinity, The (enamel box top), 221–22, 222f

Soviet Union, Russian icons in, 6, 216–22, 223n19

Sozomenos (saint), 332f

space, in Judaism, 183–84. *See also* eruvin

Spanish colonies, chocolate in, 242–43. *See also* New Spain

speech, ingestion of, 475

Spence, Lewis, 65n46

Spencer, Herbert, 117

Spencer, Robert, 252

Spillers, Hortense, 409, 411n18

Spinoza, Baruch, 13, 20n61

spirit entities, Heian-period beliefs about, 69–71. *See also specific entities*

Spiritism, in Brazil: French influence on, 28, 41n15; origins and rise of, 28; positivism and, 42n15, 42n20

"Spirit of Christianity and Its Fate, The" (Hegel), 183–84, 199

spirit pacification rites, in Heian Japan, 70–71, 75–83, 84n11

spirit photography: in Brazil, lack of, 28–29; definition of, 26; objectivity of photographs and, 30; spirit hands in, 49–51, 50f, 63n15

spirit possession: in Afro-Brazilian religions, 26, 28, 29, 32–40; in Brazil, photography linked with, 26, 29–31; in Heian Japan, 71–72, 75–83, 84n21; as marginal cultural experience, 71–72, 84n25; origins of, 30; photographs taken during, 36, 37–40, 38f, 45n46, 46n51; vs. tethering of djinns, 90; as universal anthropological category, 30–31; in Western world, 24

Spiritualism: antecedents of, 61n2; in Brazil (Spiritism), 28, 41n15, 42n20; and industrialization, 48, 57; number of followers of, 48, 62n8; origins of, 48, 51, 61n7; philosophy of, 47–48, 60–61; photography in popularization of, 26; reasons for popularity of, 48, 62n9; and Yale University fine arts program, 652

Spiritualism, hands in, 47–61; history of scholarship on, 47–48, 61n5; outward orientation of, 60, 65n51; paraffin molds of, 49–50, 58–60; on planchettes, 49, 53–58; at séances, 51–53; in spirit photographs, 49–51, 50f, 63n15

spirituality: in Interracial Conference Movement, 279; NPS use of language of, 631, 647n4 (*See also* Hawai'i Volcanoes National Park); in relation to religion, 632–33

spiritual journeys, in secular museums, 211

spiritual ownership, of Hawai'i Volcanoes National Park, 643–44

spiritual senses, in history of senses, 11

SPLC. *See* Southern Poverty Law Center

Spratt, George, 131n6

Staal, Frits, 584

Staite, Emma, 241

Staley, Erinn: biographical highlights, 660; chapter by, 429–32

Standaert, Nicolas, 382

Standing Écorché (Houdon), 500

Stark, Richard, 505, 506f, 507, 508, 513n35

Stathacos, Chrysanne, 231; *Rose Mandala Mirror,* 232f

static forms of worship, 410n2

Stausberg, Michael, 599n1

Stephen the Younger (saint), 323

stereography: bodily experience in, 262–65, 267, 272n5; *Book of Mormon* as, 266, 267f, 272n11; and composite photography, 116–17; Holmes (Oliver Wendell) on, 263, 264–65, 266–67, 272; by Johnson (Charles Ellis), 261–65, 269–72; proper viewing of, 262–63; in railroad tourism, 585f, 587f, 593f

"Stereoscope and the Stereograph, The" (Holmes), 264–65, 266

stereoscopes. *See* stereography

Stewart, Kathleen, 628

Stewart, Susan, 407, 409, 410n13, 411n19

Stijl, De, 138

Stocking, George, 43n29

Stoddard, John T.: camera designed by, 116, 117f; career of, 116; composite photographs produced by, 113, 116; *Science* article by, 113, 118–19, 119f; technical processes used by, 118–20, 128. *See also* "Composita"

stone(s): agency of, 642–43; hematite amulets, 338n36; ingestion of, 462, 473, 481; Maqam Ibrahim, 471; Puritan carving of, 7; sacred, in Hawai'i , 639–42, 639f, 641f, 642f; seer, in Mormonism, 266, 269, 272n11, 273n16. *See also* Chavín de Huantar stones; lava rock

Stones of Life, 640, 641f

Stow, Kenneth, 172

strategic Westernization: definition of, 90, 93; in Turkey, 90–91, 93–94, 95, 99, 108

Strong, Josiah, *Our Country,* 120

Student Volunteer Movement, 288

subject, valuation of form over, in aesthetics, 205

subjectivity, in Japanese martyrdom paintings, 390–93

Sub-Saharan Africa, ingestion of Qur'an in, 480

subservience, of Mormon women, 273n21

suburbanization, U.S., European modernism in, 138–39

Suchard Chocolat, 243

Sufism, 313, 318n35

Sunnism, Wahhabi, 469

supernatural, in secularization theory, 4–5, 8

supersessionism, binaries in, 7

superstitions, in secularization theory, 4–5, 8

Susannis, Marquardus de, *De Iudaeis et aliis infidelibus,* 172–73

Su Shi, "A Eulogy for Embroidered Guanyin," 368–69

Su Shih, 579n55

Süt Kardeşler (movie), 94

Suzuki, Yui: biographical highlights, 660; chapter by, 67–83

Swedenborg, Emanuel, 346–47, 350, 351, 354n31

Sweet Jesus (Cavallaro), 239–44, 240f

Swift, Jonathan, *Gulliver's Travels,* 483–85

Swing Low, Sweet Chariot (Johnson), 279, 280f

Symbolists: on androgyny, 345; on the soul, 341–43; on synesthesia, 341, 351

Symeon (bishop of Thessalonike), 331–32

Symeon the Younger (saint), shrine of, 463–64, 464f

synaesthesis: definition of, 69; in Heian Japan, 69, 72–82; vs. synesthesia, 83n4

Synagoga, 174, 176

synagogues, matzos in, 185, 186, 187f, 200n7, 200n10

Syncellus, George, 558n27

synesthesia: definition of, 83n4, 341; Gauguin's use of, 341, 343, 347–52; nineteenth-century study of, 341; racial and spatial juxtaposition as experience of, 288; in stereography, 264–65, 267, 269; vs. synaesthesis, 83n4

Syria: Great Mosque of Hims in, 466–68, 467f, 478; shrine of Symeon the Younger in, 463–64, 464f

tabarruk, 461

taboo, as synonym for kapu, 633

Tagebücher (Kafka), 183, 184, 193–94, 199

Tahiti: loss of native customs in, 345; in *Musique barbare* (Gauguin), 348–49; *varua ino* in, 344, 353n12

Takiguchi, 86n61

Wabanaki Federation, 444

Wahhabi Sunnism, 469

wahi kapu, 626–27, 633, 644

Wahine-kapu Steam Vents, 625, 626f, 644

Walcott, Walter Workman, 416–17, 426n11

Walker, David: biographical highlights, 660; chapter by, 581–99

Wallace, Alfred Russell, *Perspectives in Psychical Research,* 30

Wallace, David Foster, *The Pale King,* 153

Wallinger, Mark, *Zone,* 191–92

walls: of cities, role of, 168, 170; of cubicles, 145, 149; of Venetian ghetto, 167–71, 175

Wal-Mart, 154

Wang Xinzhan, 365

Wang Yuan, 364–65

Warhol, Andy, *Atomic Bomb,* 388

Waring, Laura Wheeler, *Mother and Daughter,* 284, 285f

Warren (Michigan), adhan in, 225, 227

Warring States. *See* Sengoku period

Washburn, Margaret Bryan, 128

washing rituals: Hindu, 233–34, 237; Muslim, 248–50, 254n10

Washington, D.C.: Library of Congress in, 18n24; Verbycke Spiritual Church in, 399–400

Washsha', Muhammad al-, *Kitāb al-Muwashshā,* 482

water: in Hindu bathing rituals, 233–34, 237; holy, bowl of, 235; ingestion of the sacred in, 462, 471–72, 472f, 474–76, 477; in Muslim washing rituals, 248–50, 254n10; in Salt Lake City, 591–93, 591f, 592f, 597

wax molds of spirit hands, 49–50, 58–60

Webb-Mitchell, Brett, 430

Weber Canyon (Utah), 585, 585f, 590

Weekman, Michael, 61n7

Weiner, Isaac: biographical highlights, 660–61; chapter by, 225–28

Weir, John Ferguson, 652

Weir, Mary, 652

Weisenfeld, Judith: biographical highlights, 661; chapter by, 413–24

Weismantel, Mary: biographical highlights, 661; chapter by, 605–21

Weitzmann, Eyal, 200n17

West, Benjamin: in *Anatomical Crucifixion* (Banks), 495–97, 499, 505, 510n4; religious beliefs of, 505

West Bloomfield (Michigan), adhan in, 226

Westernization, strategic. *See* strategic Westernization

Western world: Islam viewed as premodern in, 203, 247–48; sensory cultures of religion in, 11–12; spirit possession in, 24. *See also specific countries and regions*

What Do Pictures Want? (Mitchell), 9

wheat, at tomb of Muhammad, 476, 476f

Whisper Piece (Ono), 234–35, 235f

white (color): frequency in Christian devotional objects, 400; in Heian Japan, 75

White, Harriet M., 126

white Americans, in mainline Protestant churches, 433n1

Whitehead El, 421

whiteness: of "Composita," 120, 127, 128; in *Jesus Christ the Lamb of God and His Little Bride* (Morgan), 408–9

Who Breaks, Pays (Jenkin), 53, 64n29

Wilkins, David G., 556n8

will, in fall of rebel angels, 549, 552, 553

William E. Harmon Foundation. *See* Harmon Foundation

Williams, Raymond, 316n10

Wilson, Stephen, 18n20

Winfield, Pamela, 77

Winthrop, John, 273n20

wire, as medium for eruv, 183, 186–87, 188, 191, 193–94, 196, 198

Wise, Stephen, 293n23

Wittgenstein, Ludwig, 37, 45n50

Wizard Stones, 640

Wolgemut, Michael, 340n59

Woman Playing Daf (Aghili), 313, 314f

women: chocolate consumption by, 243; debate over effects of education of, 120–21, 128; embroidery by, 356; Iranian, as naghals, 297; Iranian, in coffeehouse paintings, 313; Jewish, Christian fears about sexuality of, 174–75; measurements of bodies of, 121; Mormon, subservience of, 273n21; preaching by, injunctions against, 410n8; Protestant, role in race relations, 275–78, 282, 289–92; religious enthusiasm of, 132–33n11; as typological classification, 126

Wood, Christopher, 215

Woodruff, Wilford, 270, 274n29

word, in relation to image, 14

workers: hierarchy of, cubicles and, 137; unhappiness with cubicles, 135–36. *See also*
labor
"Work of Art in the Age of Mechanical Reproduction, The" (Benjamin), 159–60, 177, 439
World of Warcraft (game), 96, 109n19
World's Columbian Exposition (1893), 245n3
World War I, changes in U.S. after, 277
World War II, racial identity in draft registration for, 413–19, 422
worship: ecstatic forms of, 403, 410n2; static
forms of, 410n2
writing: of Buddhist scriptures in blood, 360–
61; embroidery as female counterpart to, 356,
361; from Qur'an, ingestion of, 471, 475–80;
about relics, ingestion of, 473–75; by spirit
hands, 52–58, 63n25
wudu', 248–50, 254n10
Wu Hung, 368, 369
Wu of Liang (emperor of China), 357, 372n8
Wuzhun Shifan, 563, 568

Xuan Ding, *Yeyu qiudeng lu,* 355
Xu Can, 369–70, 374n43

yad (hand; pointer), 47
Yale University: eruv at, 195; School of Fine
Arts at, 652
Yangshan Huiji, 566
Yasuakira (prince), 85n30
Yau, Elaine Y.: biographical highlights, 661;
chapter by, 403–9
"Years of Lead," 447
Yehoshua (rabbi), 195
Ye Pingxiang, 355–57, 363, 367, 373n20

Yeşilçam, 105
Yeyu qiudeng lu (Xuan Ding), 355
Yiddish Policemen's Union, The (Chabon), 193,
196
Yiengpruksawan, Mimi, 72
Yigong, 567
Yin Qiding, 355
Yin-Yang masters, 75, 81, 85n37
yorimashi, 76, 77f, 85n42
Young, Brigham: on God's chosen people,
273n20; Johnson (Charles Ellis) in family of,
261, 270; and railroad tourism, 586, 594, 595,
599, 603n31
Young, John W., 595
Young, Joseph, 595
Yu, Jimmy, 360, 363, 373n19
Yunmen, 566
Yuval, Israel Jacob, 200n10

Zafran, Eric, 353n10
Zamzam well, 471, 472f, 476
Zeeland (Michigan), 139–40. *See also* Herman
Miller
Zen Buddhism: death verses in (*See* Bud-
dhist death verses); portraits of masters in,
564–65, 577n24
Zifir (novel), 95
Zigaina, Giuseppe, 448
Zohar, 549, 551
Zone (Wallinger), 191–92
zoorkhaneh, 301
Zorattini, Pier Cesare Ioly, 176
Zubarán, Francisco de, *Crucifixion with a
Painter,* 385
Zumárraga, Juan de, 518